Better Business

Michael R. Solomon

Mary Anne Poatsy

Kendall Martin

PRENTICE HALL

UPPER SADDLE RIVER, NJ 07458

VP/Publisher: Natalie E. Anderson
AVP/Executive Editor: Jodi McPherson
Director, Product Development: Pamela Hersperger
Editorial Project Manager: Kristen Kaiser, KMK Editorial Services
Development Editor: Shannon LeMay-Finn
Editorial Assistant: Rosalinda Simone
AVP/Executive Editor, Media: Richard Keaveny
Editorial Media Project Manager: Ashley Lulling
Production Media Project Manager: John Cassar
Senior Marketing Manager: Maggie Moylan-Leen
Marketing Assistant: Justin Jacob
Senior Managing Editor: Cynthia Zonneveld
Production Project Manager: Lynne Breitfeller
Manager of Rights & Permissions: Charles Morris
Senior Operations Specialist: Nick Sklitsis

Operations Specialist: Natacha Moore
Design Development Manager: John Christiana
Interior Design: Blair Brown
Cover Design: Blair Brown
Cover Illustration/Photo: Gettyimages/Nick Vedros & Associates
Cover, Visual Research and Permissions: Karen Sanatar
Director, Image Resource Center: Melinda Patelli
Manager, Rights and Permissions: Zina Arabia
Manager: Visual Research: Beth Brenzel
Image Permission Coordinator: Richard Rodrigues
Photo Researcher: Sheila Norman
Composition: GEX Publishing Services
Full-Service Project Management: GEX Publishing Services
Printer/Binder: Quebecor World Color/Versailles
Typeface: 10.5/13 Palatino

Credits and acknowledgments borrowed from other sources and reproduced, with permission, in this textbook appear on appropriate page within text (or on page 537).

Pearson Education Ltd., London
Pearson Education North Asia Ltd., Hong Kong
Pearson Education Singapore, Pte. Ltd
Pearson Educación de Mexico, S.A. de C.V.
Pearson Education, Canada, Inc.

Pearson Education Malaysia, Pte. Ltd.
Pearson Education—Japan
Pearson Education, Upper Saddle River, New Jersey
Pearson Education Australia PTY, Limited

Prentice Hall
is an imprint of

www.pearsonhighered.com

10 9 8 7 6 5 4 3 2
ISBN-13: 978-0-13-225121-1
ISBN-10: 0-13-225121-3

Dedication

To Rose

Michael R. Solomon

For my husband Ted, who unselfishly continues to take on more than his fair share to support me throughout this process; and for my children, Laura, Carolyn, and Teddy, whose encouragement and love have been inspiring.

Mary Anne Poatsy

For all the teachers, mentors, and gurus who have popped in and out of my life.

Kendall Martin

➤ **Brief** Contents

➤ Contents

To read the entire mini chapter, visit
www.mybizlab.com

CHAPTER 13 Product Development and Pricing Strategies 368

CHAPTER 14 Promotion and Distribution 398

➤ **About** the Authors

Michael Solomon

Michael R. Solomon, Ph.D. is Professor of Marketing and Director of the Center for Consumer Research in the Haub School of Business at Saint Joseph's University in Philadelphia. He also is Professor of Consumer Behaviour at the Manchester School of Business, The University of Manchester, U.K. Prof. Solomon's primary research and consulting interests include consumer behavior, branding, and marketing applications of virtual worlds . He has written several textbook and trade books; his *Consumer Behavior* text is the most widely-used in the world. Michael often speaks to business groups about new trends in consumer behavior and marketing strategy.

Mary Anne Poatsy, MBA, CFP

mpoatsy@comcast.net

Mary Anne is a senior faculty member at Montgomery County Community College, teaching various computer application and concepts courses in face-to-face and online environments. She holds a BA in psychology and education from Mount Holyoke College and an MBA in finance from Northwestern University's Kellogg Graduate School of Management.

Mary Anne has more than 11 years of educational experience, ranging from elementary and secondary education to Montgomery County Community College, Muhlenberg College, and Bucks County Community College, as well as training in the professional environment. Before teaching, she was a vice president at Shearson Lehman Hutton in the Municipal Bond Investment Banking Department.

Kendall Martin, PhD

kmartin@mc3.edu

Kendall has been teaching since 1988 at a number of institutions, including Villanova University, DeSales University, Arcadia University, Ursinus College, County College of Morris, and Montgomery County Community College at both the undergraduate and graduate level.

Kendall's education includes a BS in electrical engineering from the University of Rochester and an MS and a PhD in engineering from the University of Pennsylvania. She has industrial experience in research and development environments (AT&T Bell Laboratories) as well as experience with several start-up technology firms.

At Ursinus College, Kendall developed a successful faculty training program for distance education instructors. She makes conference presentations throughout the year.

➤ Acknowledgments

L ike any good business, this project could not have been completed without the dedicated efforts of a talented group of people to whom we are eternally grateful. The authors would like to take this time to thank the many colleagues, friends, and students who have contributed toward our vision of an introductory textbook that excites and challenges students.

From the very conception of *Better Business* to the last page produced, a remarkable board of reviewers at schools across the nation has guided us with wise counsel. Our joy in working with such talented and student-centered faculty is deep. We extend our sincerest gratitude to our reviewers.

The division of Business Publishing at Prentice Hall has been incredible in devoting time and resources to the creation of the *Better Business* learning system. We are indebted to Jodi McPherson, our executive editor, who had the vision for a new introduction to business textbook system that engages and excites students. Without her vision, passion, dedication, and drive, this textbook would not exist. Jodi excels at everything she does, and we are honored to have the opportunity to work with such a brilliant executive editor. Our thanks also extend to our project manager, Kristen Kaiser–KMK Editorial Services, who has diligently kept us on track with only gentle threats when we went astray! Kristen's fine management skills enabled this complex project to be completed on time—a feat not easily accomplished. We are also grateful to Shannon LeMay-Finn, our development editor, for her advice, keen eye, and calming support. Her input ensured that the many components of this project met a high standard of excellence and quality that most products have a hard time matching. Maggie Moylan-Leen, senior marketing manager, has been very instrumental in shaping the message of the book. We are so appreciative of her keen attention to all the marketing details that are so important in a successful new launch. We're also appreciative for the dedication of the media team of Dave Moles, Ashley Lulling, and Sean McGann, who were instrumental in the development of all the multimedia products that comprise my*biz*lab, and their efforts to ensure that it works seamlessly with the textbook. Additionally, we would like to thank Blair Brown and Lynne Breitfeller in their efforts in the design and production of *Better Business*. Lastly, our thanks to Jerome Grant, president of business publishing, and Natalie Anderson, VP/publisher of introductory markets, who had faith in our vision and backed this project with the necessary financial and human resources to make our vision a reality.

This project was also blessed with the contribution of many resources outside Pearson Publishing. Jennifer Auvil and Kristen Intlekofer of Words & Numbers, Inc., were instrumental in the development of *Better Business*, and we are incredibly thankful for their contributions and expertise. Craig Beytien and his team, especially Erin Parker, from Content Connections, LLC, also provided us with many tools and services that have been instrumental in the development and production of *Better Business*.

We would be completely negligent if we did not acknowledge all the incredibly talented and devoted designers, permissions researchers, and others who contributed to the project and to whom we extend our sincerest thanks.

Additionally, we would like to thank the many supplement authors for this edition: Diane Coyle, Kate Demarest, Pam Janson, John Kavouras, Linda Koffel, Martha Laham, LeeAnn Bates, and Carol Moore.

Everything we do is inspired by the experiences we have in the classroom. We want to thank and encourage our students, whose experiences, struggles, victories, and honesty have shaped this project turn by turn. May *Better Business* serve our students as a stepping-stone to meaningful careers and lives.

Last, but not least, close to home, our families have sacrificed much to let us focus on the project. We appreciate their patience and support over the last several years.

Reviewers

Platinum Reviewers

Patricia Bernson, County College of Morris
Chuck Bowles, Pikes Peak Community College
Kate Demarest, Carroll Community College
Karen Edwards, Chemeketa Community College
Carol Gottuso, Metropolitan Community College
Steven Huntley, Florida Community College at Jacksonville

Pam Janson, Stark State College of Technology
Phyllis Shafer, Brookdale Community College
Steven Skaggs, Waubonsee Community College
Dan Wubbena, Western Iowa Technical Community College

Product Development Reviewers

Bob Bennett, Delaware County Community College
Subasree Cidambi, Mount San Antonio College
Kathleen Dominick, Bucks County Community College

William Huisking, Bergen Community College
Kenneth Jones, Ivy Technical Community College
Sally Wells, Columbia College
George Williams, Bergen Community College

Market Reviewers

Wendi Achey, Northampton Community College
Joni Anderson, Buena Vista University
Lydia Anderson, Fresno City College
Natalie Andrews, Sinclair Community College
Sally Andrews, Linn Benton Community College
Roanne Angiello, Bergen Community College
Brenda Anthony, Tallahassee Community College
Maria Aria, Camden County College
Corinne Asher, Henry Ford Community College
Susan Athey, Colorado State University
Michael Aubry, Grossmont College
David Bader, Columbus State Community College
Mazen Badra, Webster University
Michael Baran, South Puget Sound Community College
Ruby Barker, Tarleton State University
William Barrett, University of Wisconsin
Denise Barton, Wake Technical Community College
Dick Barton, El Camino College
Crystal Bass, Trinity Valley Community College
Jeffrey Bauer, University of Cincinnati
Christine Bauer-Ramazani, Saint Michael's College
Leslie Beau, Orange Coast College

Gayona Beckford-Barclay, Community College of Baltimore County
Robert Bennett, Delaware County Community College
George Bernard, Seminole Community College
Rick Bialac, Georgia College and State University
Danielle Blesi, Hudson Valley Community College
Malcolm Bowyer, Montgomery Community College
Steven Bradley, Austin Community College
Charles Braun, Marshall University
Edwin Breazeale, Midlands Technical College
Sharon Breeding, Bluegrass Community Technical College
Richard Brennan, North Virginia Community College
Robert Bricker, Pikes Peak Community College
Lisa Briggs, Columbus State Community College
T.L. Brink, Crafton Hills College
Dennis Brode, Sinclair Community College
Katherine Broneck, Pima Community College
Harvey Bronstein, Oakland Community College
Deborah Brown, North Carolina State University
Sylvia Brown, Midland College
Janet Brown-Sederberg, Massasoit Community College

Lesley Buehler, Ohlone College
Barry Bunn, Valencia Community College
Carroll Burrell, San Jacinto College
Marian Canada, Ivy Technical Community College
Diana Carmel, Golden West College
John Carpenter, Lake Land College
Tiffany Champagne, Houston Community College
Glen Chapuis, St. Charles Community College
Bonnie Chavez, Santa Barbara City College
Sudhir Chawla, Angelo State University
Lisa Cherivtch-Zingaro, Oakton Community College
Desmond Chun, Chabot College
John Cicero, Shasta College
Michael Cicero, Highline Community College
Subasree Cidambi, Mt. San Antonio College
Joseph Cilia, Delaware Technical & Community College
Mark Clark, Collin County Community College
William Clark, Leeward Community College
Paul Coakley, Community College of Baltimore County
Ken Combs, Del Mar College
Jamie Commissaris, Davenport University
Rachna Condos, American River College
Charlie Cook, University of West Alabama
Solveg Cooper, Cuesta College

Douglas Copeland, Johnson County Community College

Julie Couturier, Grand Rapids Community College

Brad Cox, Midlands Technical College

Diane Coyle, Montgomery County Community College

Chad Creevy, Davenport University

Geoff Crosslin, Kalamazoo Valley Community College

H. Perry Curtis, Collin County Community College

Dana D'Angelo, Drexel University

Mark Dannenberg, Shasta College

Jamey Darnell, Durham Tech

Shirley Davenport, Prairie State College

Helen Davis, Jefferson Community Technical College

Peter Dawson, Collin County Community College

David Dearman, University of Arkansas

Sherry Decuba, Indian River Community College

Andrew Delaney, Truckee Meadows Community College

Donna Devault, Fayetteville Tech

Susan Dik, Kapiolani Community College

Gerard Dobson, Waukesha County Technical College

Kathleen Dominick, Bucks County Community College and University of Phoenix Online

Ron Dougherty, Ivy Technical Community College

Francis Douglas, Tuggle Chapman University

Karen Drage, Eastern Illinois University

Nelson Driver, University of Arkansas

Allison Duesing, Northeast Lakeview College

Timothy Durfield, Citrus College

David Dusseau, University of Oregon

Dana Dye, Gulf Coast Community College

C. Russell Edwards, Valencia Community College

Stephen Edwards, University of North Dakota

Stewart Edwards, North Virginia Community College

Susan Ehrfurth, Aims Community College

Patrick Ellsberg, Lower Columbia College

Susan Emens, Kent State University

Karen Emerson, Southeast Community College

Theodore Emmanuel, State University of New York Oswego

Kellie Emrich, Cuyahoga Community College

Steven Ernest, Baton Rouge Community College

Mary Ewanechko, Monroe County Community College

Marie Farber-Lapidus, Oakton Community College

Geralyn Farley, Purdue University

Janice Feldbauer, Schoolcraft College and Austin Community College

Mary Felton-Kolstad, Chippewa Valley Technical College

Louis Ferracane, University of Phoenix

David Fitoussi, University of California

Joseph Flack, Washtenaw Community College

Jacalyn Flom, University of Toledo

Carla Flores, Ball State University

Carol Flowers, Orange Coast College

Jake Flyzik, Lehigh Carbon Community College

Thomas Foley, Kent State University

Craig Fontaine, Northeastern University

Joseph Fox, Asheville-Buncombe Technical Community College

Mark Fox, Indiana University

Victoria Fox, College of DuPage

Charla Fraley, Columbus State Community College

John Frank, Columbus State Community College

Leatrice Freer, Pitt Community College

Paula Freston, Merced College

Fred Fry, Bradley University

Albert Fundaburk, Bloomsburg University

William Furrell, Moorpark College

Michael Gagnon, Kellogg Community College

Wayne Gawlik, Joliet Junior College

George Generas, University of Hartford

Vanessa Germeroth, Ozarks Technical Community College

Gerald GeRue, Rock Valley College

John Geubtner, Tacoma Community College

Katie Ghahramani, Johnson County Community College

David Gilliss, San Jose State University

Eric Glohr, Lansing Community College

Constance Golden, Lakeland Community College

Gayle Goldstone, Santa Rosa Junior College

Alfredo Gomez, Broward Community College

Phillip Gonsher, Johnson County Community College

Robert Googins, Shasta College

Karen Gore, Ivy Technical Community College

Gretchen Graham, Community College of Allegheny

Selina Griswold, University of Toledo

John Guess, Delgado Community College

Kevin Gwinner, Kansas State University

Lawrence Hahn, Palomar College

Semere Haile, Grambling State University

Lynn Halkowicz, Bloomsburg University

Clark Hallpike, Elgin Community College

Paula Hansen, Des Moines Area Community College

Frank Harber, Indian River Community College

LaShon Harley, Durham Tech

Jeri Harper, Western Illinois University

Deborah Haseltine, Southwest Tennessee Community College

Carol Heeter, Ivy Tech Community College

Linda Hefferin, Elgin Community College

Debra Heimberger, Columbus State Community College

Dennis Heiner, College of Southern Idaho

Cheryl Heitz, Lincoln Land Community College

Charlane Held, Onondaga Community College

Heith Hennel, Valencia Community College

Dorothy Hetmer-Hinds, Trinity Valley Community College

Linda Hoffman, Ivy Technical Community College

Merrily Hoffman, San Jacinto College

Gene Holand, Columbia Basin College

Phillip Holleran, Mitchell Community College

Robert Hood, Chattanooga State Technicial Community College

Sheila Hostetler, Orange Coast College

Larry Hottot, North Virginia Community College

William Huisking, Bergen Community College

Lynn Hunsaker, Mission College

Johnny Hurley, Iowa Lakes Community College

Kimberly Hurns, Washtenaw Community College

Holly Hutchins, Central Oregon Community College

Linda Isenhour, Eastern Michigan University

Katie Jackson, Columbus State Community College

Linda Jaeger, Southeast Community College

Dolores James, University of Maryland University College

Larry Jarrell, Louisiana Technical University

Joe Jenkins, Tarrant County College

Brandy Johnson, Columbus State Community College

Dennis Johnson, Delaware County Community College

Floyd Johnson, Davenport University

M. Gwen Johnson, Black Hawk College

Carroll Jones, Tulsa Community College

Kenneth Jones, Ivy Technical Community College

Gayla Jurevich, Fresno City College

Alex Kajstura, Daytona Beach College

Dmitriy Kalyagin, Chabot College

Radhika Kaula, Missouri State University

John Kavouras, Ohio College of Massage Therapy

Dan Keating, Fox Valley Technical College

Albert Keller, Dixie State College of Utah

Ann Kelly, Georgia Southern University

Jeffrey Kennedy, Broward Community College

Jeffrey Kennedy, Palm Beach Atlantic University

Daniel Kipley, Azusa Pacific University

William Kline, Bucks County Community College

Susan Kochenrath, Ivy Technical Community College

Linda Koffel, Houston Community College Central

Todd Korol, Monroe County Community College

Jack Kraettli, Oklahoma City Community College

Jim Kress, Central Oregon Community College

John Kurnik, St. Petersburg College

Paul Laesecke, University of Denver

Martha Laham, Diablo Valley College

Mary LaPann, Adirondack Community College

Deborah Lapointe, Central New Mexico Community College

Rob Leadbeater, Mission College

David Leapard, Eastern Michigan University

Ware Leatha, Waubonsee Community College

Ron Lennon, Barry University

Angela Leverett, Georgia Southern University

Sue Lewis, Tarleton State University

Kathleen Lorencz, Oakland Community College

John Luke, Delaware County Community College

John Mago, Anoka Ramsey Community College

Jan Mangos, Valencia Community College

Christine Marchese, Nassau Community College

James Marco, Wake Technical Community College

Suzanne Markow, Des Moines Area Community College

Gary Marrer, Glendale Community College

Calvin Martin, Davenport University

James Martin, Washburn University

Kathleen Martinez, Red Rocks Community College

Thomas Mason, Brookdale Community College

Marian Matthews, Central New Mexico Community College

Kevin McCarthy, Baker University

Gina McConoughey, Illinois Central College

Lisa McCormick, Community College of Allegheny

Pamela McElligott, Meramec Community College

Edward McGee, Rochester Institute of Technology

Donna McGill-Cameron, Yuba College

Vince McGinnis, Bucks County Community College

Lorraine McKnight, Eastern Michigan University

Bruce McLaren, Indiana State University

Juan Meraz, Missouri State University

Miriam Michael, American River College

Jeanette Milius, Iowa Western Community College

Carol Millard, Scottsdale Community College

John Miller, Pima Community College

Linda Miller, Northeast Community College

Pat Miller, Grossmont College

Morgan Milner, Eastern Michigan University

Diane Minger, Cedar Valley College

Susan Mitchell, Des Moines Area Community College

Theresa Mitchell, Alabama A&M University

Joseph Molina, MiraCosta College

Carol Moore, California State University

Wayne Moore, Indiana University of Pennsylvania

Richard Morris, Northeastern State University

David Murphy, Madisonville Community College

Gary Murray, Rose State College

John Muzzo, Harold Washington College

Mark Nagel, Normandale Community College

Conrad Nankin, Pace University

Kristi Newton, Chemeketa Community College

Steven Nichols, Metropolitan Community College

Simon Nwaigwe, Baltimore City Community College

Mark Nygren, Brigham Young University

Asmelash Ogbasion, Southwest Tennessee Community College

Cynthia L. Olivarez Rooker, Lansing Community College

David Olson, California State University

Anthony O'Malley, Baruch College

Lori Oriatti, College of Lake County

Robert O'Toole, Crafton Hills College

Mary Padula, Borough Manhattan Community College

Esther Page-Wood, Western Michigan University

Lauren Paisley, Genesee Community College

Dyan Pease, Sacramento City College

Jeffrey Pepper, Chippewa Valley Technical College

Clifford Perry, Florida International University

Melinda Phillabaum, Indiana University/ Purdue University

Rose Pollard, Southeast Community College

Jackie (J. Robinson) Porter, Eastfield College

Kathleen Powers, Henry Ford Community College

Dan Powroznik, Chesapeake College

Sally Proffitt, Tarrant County College

Joe Puglisi, Butler County Community College

James Pullins, Columbus State Community College

Kathy Pullins, Columbus State Community College

Bobby Puryear, North Carolina State University

Anthony Racka, Oakland Community College

Robert Reck, Western Michigan University

Philip Regier, Arizona State University

Delores Reha, Fullerton College

David Reiman, Monroe County Community College

Robert Reinke, University of South Dakota

Gloria Rembert, Mitchell Community College

Reina Reynolds, Valencia Community College

John Ribezzo, Community College of Rhode Island

Cheri Rice, Stark State College of Technology

Carla Rich, Pensacola Junior College

Gayle Richardson, Bakersfield College

Dwight Riley, Richland College

Renee Ritts, Cuyahoga Community College

Susan Roach, Georgia Southern University

John Robertson, Amarillo College

Robert Robicheaux, University of Alabama

Tim Rogers, Ozarks Technical Community College

June Roux, Delaware Technical & Community College

Carol Rowey, Community College of Rhode Island

Mark Ryan, Hawkeye Community College

Ray Saenz, Del Mar College

Joanne Salas, Olympic College

Andy Saucedo, New Mexico State University

Jacqueline Scerbinski, Kingsborough Community College

David Schaefer, Sacramento City College

Elisabeth Scherff, Alabama A&M University

Glen M. Schmidt, University of Utah

Tobias Schoenherr, Eastern Michigan University

Marcianne Schusler, Prairie State College

James Scott, Central Michigan University
Carolyn Seefer, Diablo Valley College
Eugene Seeley, Utah Valley State College
Gary Selk, University of Alaska
Pat Setlik, William Rainey Harper College
Dennis Shannon, Southwestern Illinois College
Richard Sherer, Los Angeles Trade Technical College
Lynette Shishido, Santa Monica College
Lance Shoemaker, West Valley College
Carole Shook, University of Arkansas
Dwight Shook, Catawba Valley Community College
Susan Sieloff, Northeastern University
William Silver, University of Denver
Denise Simmons, North Virginia Community College
Lakshmy Sivaratnam, Johnson County Community College
Jacqueline Slifkin, Monroe County Community College
Kimberly Smith, County College of Morris
Fred Sole, Youngstown State University
Sandra Sousa, Bristol Community College
Ed Southeard, Chattanooga State Technical Community Colllege
Ray Sparks, Pima Community College
Rieann Spence-Gale, North Virginia Community College
Cheryl Stansfield, North Hennepin Community College
Keith Starcher, Indiana Wesleyan

Carol Steinhaus, Northern Michigan University
Jim Stemach, College of the Redwoods
John Stern, Davenport University
Richard Stewart, Gulf Coast Community College
Jack Stone, Linn Benton Community College
Connie Strain, Arapahoe Community College
John Striebich, Monroe County Community College
Chelakara Subbaraman, Central Michigan University
Dottie Sutherland, Pima College
Deanna Teel, Houston Community College
Carol Thole, Hartnell College
Michael Thomas, Henry Ford Community College
Alexis Thurman, County College of Morris
Frank Titlow, St. Petersburg College
Kathy Toler, Asheville-Buncombe Technical Community College
Edward Tolle, Ivy Tech Community College
Terry Tolliver, Indiana University/Purdue University
Fran Ucci, College of DuPage
Shafi Ullah, Broward Community College
Dorothy Umans, Montgomery College
Robert Urell, Irvine Valley College
Richard Vaughan, Durham Tech
Sal Veas, Santa Monica College
Kam Vento, Lassen Community College
Victor Villarreal, Austin Community College

Richard Vobroucek, State University of New York-Rockland
Carol Vollmer-Pope, Alverno College
Randall Wade, Rogue Community College
Richard Warner, Lehigh Carbon Community College
Michael Washington, Eastfield College
Louis Watanabe, Bellevue Community College
Bill Waters, Clackamas Community College
Tom Watkins, Solano Community College
Sally Wells, Columbia College
Susan Wheeler, Folsom Lake College
Donald Wilke, Okaloosa-Walton College
Fred Williams, University of Michigan
George Williams, Bergen Community College
H. Brock Williams, Metropolitan Community College
Doug Wilson, University of Oregon
Marcus Wilson, Fullerton College
Mildred Wilson, Georgia Southern University
Colette Wolfson, Ivy Technical Community College
John Womble, Cedar Valley College
Merrill Yancey, Ivy Technical Community College
Sandra Yates, University of District of Columbia
Bernard Zannini, Northern Essex Community College
Charles Zellerbach, Orange Coast College

➤ Letter from the **Authors**

When we set out on this project, we had several goals in mind...and one guiding philosophy. We wanted to have a conversation with our students, not write a book that we hope they read. We wanted to change the expectations we have of students coming to class unprepared. Why can't they come more prepared, and with a desire to know about business? Why can't we have a little fun with the course while teaching them about the lighter side of business? We think we can, and we wanted to give you and your students a better choice.

To that end, we worked tirelessly on being selective in our topics and our resources to help students. We've touched every piece of the system and made selections that get right to the point and have purpose. We set up the entire portfolio in a question–answer format to get students to want to know the answer and see more...not simply because it will be on the test. We paid more attention to the details because that is where it often comes together for students. We push them online and then pull them back into the text for a complete experience.

We think we've made a difference and a choice worth considering. We hope you think so too.

betterbusiness a better**experience**

Better Business offers the content students need for a solid overview of business, but in a *better* way. By presenting the material in a stimulating way, ***Better Business*** encourages students to come to class prepared to have better conversations and a truly engaging classroom experience.

Better Business is tightly integrated with **my*biz*lab**, Pearson's revolutionary new online learning system. **my*biz*lab** gives instructors easy access to a variety of media, homework, and activities to get students interacting with business and not just reading about it.

The end result is a ***better experience***...

for both students and instructors!

better experience a **new take** on the traditional textbook!

▼ Objectives 1-6

1. What are the traits of an effective **entrepreneur**, and how do these characteristics often lead to business success? (p. 133)

Entrepreneurs and the **American Dream** pp. 133-137

➤ **What is an entrepreneur?** We've all heard of Starbucks, Nike, and Microsoft, but you probably don't associate these big-name companies with small business. But at one point, each of these companies started off as small businesses. They were all started by **entrepreneurs**—people who assume the risk of creating, organizing, and operating a business. Entrepreneurs most often start a business to satisfy a need in the market that is not being adequately fulfilled. This area of need is called an **opportunity niche.**

Better Business communicates the fundamental business concepts in a clear and engaging conversation, not dense text. The ***Question & Answer*** format is found throughout the text, offering students an intuitive framework for the material.

Better Business is tightly integrated with **my*biz*lab**, so throughout the chapter students are directed to **my*biz*lab** for immediate review and reinforcement of the material.

▼ You have just read **Objective 1**

Think you got it? Check out the Study Plan section @
www.my*biz*lab.com.

Teasers are placed at the beginning of each objective to pique students' interest in the material so they will read on.

Becoming a successful entrepreneur involves a complex blend of skill, savvy, and luck. Before embarking on such an endeavor, however, you'll need to familiarize yourself with a few concepts. Test your entrepreneurial vocabulary with the following **quiz**.

1. "It's all about fulfilling an opportunity niche!" Liza, a budding entrepreneur, exclaims. Liza is likely referring to
  a. a need in the market.
  b. a storage nook.
  c. a sense of belonging.

2. A system thinker is someone who
  a. contemplates the technological side of a business.
  b. focuses on the entire process of turning an idea into a reality.
  c. designs methods of doing things.

3. Micropreneurs are likely to
  a. be petite.
  b. hire thousands of employees.
  c. enjoy running a small business.

4. When you hear the word *gazelle*, you think
  a. antelope.
  b. fast-growing business.
  c. graceful.

Are you confident in your understanding of entrepreneurial lingo? Or do you need a primer in the use of these terms? Whatever the case, read on for in-depth information on entrepreneur basics, types of entrepreneurs, and what it takes to be an entrepreneur. ➤

better experience   **better conversations**

BizChat boxes explore "hot topics" in business to help students connect the chapter material with what's going on in business today. *BizChat* boxes can be used to spark thoughtful discussion in class or virtual discussion via **my***biz***lab**.

Biz**Chat**

What's in a Name?

Naming a business should be fun, but it can be stressful, especially if you make some of the more common mistakes:

Mistake 1 | Involving friends, family, employees, or clients in the naming decision. You want to make the name communicate the key elements of your business, not the combined efforts of your friends and family.

Mistake 2 | Description + Product = Name. Although it seems catchy at the time, the result of company names that try to marry description with product is forced and often trite. A service franchise named QualiServe or a day spa named TranquiSpa ultimately aren't the right choices.

Mistake 3 | Using generic names. Gone are the days when General Electric or ACME Foods work as corporate names. In such highly competitive times when new products or services are fighting for attention, it's best to choose a more unique name.

Mistake 4 | Making up a name. While using generic names may not be good, be careful to avoid names that are obscure, hard to pronounce, or hard to spell unless there is solid market research behind it.

Mistake 5 | Using geographic names. Unless you plan to stay local, including a specific geographic name may imply that you won't go beyond that regional territory.

TIP: You might need to hire a company to create a name for you. Acura, Flixx, and Compac are all names that were created by experts.

For more information and discussion questions about this topic, check out the BizChat feature on www.my*biz*lab.com.

◉ Off the Mark iSmell

The dot-com era produced many businesses that just couldn't get off the ground. One example was the iSmell, a product that plugged into a computer's USB port and ~~~~~~~ ferent ~~~~~~~ onjure ~~~~~~~ iSmell ~~~~~~~ ut its

◉ On Target Facebook

When Mark Zuckerberg, a Harvard student, came up with the idea for Facebook, he didn't realize that he was spearheading a billion-dollar organization. The idea behind "The Facebook," as it was originally called, was to provide a forum for students on the Harvard campus to network and display pictures of themselves and their friends. The site was launched on February 4, 2004, and within a month, half of the undergraduates on the Harvard campus were users of the site. Expansion came quickly, as Dustin Moskovitz and Chris Hughes joined Zuckerberg to help promote the site. Within two months, the entire Ivy League was included in the Facebook network. In September of 2005, these entrepreneurs decided to allow high schools to join the network. Finally, on September 11, 2006, the general public was allowed to join Facebook, so long as all potential members had a valid e-mail address were at least 13 years old.

Mark Zuckerberg's brainchild has become so successful that he reportedly turned down a $750-million offer to purchase Facebook. Media giants such as Google and Yahoo! have been attempting to outbid each other for ownership of Facebook, but Zuckerberg claims that he is not interested in parting with his creation. And why should he be? The site has over 70 million active users worldwide and is constantly expanding!

These sections illustrate positive (*On Target*) and negative (*Off the Mark*) outcomes to business ventures related to the chapter material. These can fuel dialogue to make the material engaging and memorable.

Mini chapters are five special sections in the book and within **my***biz***lab** that give students additional information on key topics in business, including Special Issues in E-Commerce, Constructing an Effective Business Plan, Business Communications, Finding a Job, and Personal Finance.

Better Business and **mybizlab** offer students multiple ways of reviewing the chapter, including *Q&A Chapter Summaries*, *Self-Tests*, and *Critical Thinking Questions*. Multiple activities are also provided to get students interacting with the material and with each other: *Team Exercises*, *Web Exercises*, *Web Cases*, *Video Cases*, and *Ethics and Corporate Social Responsibility Exercises*.

Chapter Summary
Find your Study Plan and Study Guide @ www.mybizlab.com.

1. **What are the traits of an effective entrepreneur, and how do these characteristics often lead to business success? (pp. 133-137)**

- An **entrepreneur** (p. 133) is someone who assumes the risk of creating, organizing, and operating a business.

- Entrepreneurs are innovative, risk-taking individuals who are motivated to succeed and who are flexible and self-directed. They work w... leadership skills, and are...

2. **What is the role an... business within the... (pp. 138-142)**

- A **small business** (p. 13... ently owned and operate... has fewer than 500 emp... annual revenue.

- Small businesses are im... reasons. They account fo... nomic output; help fo... companies with product... nies do not or cannot su... and services to consume... will not provide; and em... the private workforce.

3. **What... of fra... entre...**

- A **franc... the bus...**

- The reasons new businesses fail include accumulating too much debt, inadequate management, poor planning, and unanticipated personal sacrifices.

5. **How do resources, including the Small Business Administration, mentoring sources, business incubators, and advisory boards provide assistance and guidance to small-business owners? (pp. 152-153)**

Team Time

Starting a Business: Brainstorming

Assemble into groups of four or five.

1. Before meeting as a group, think about what you are passionate about, and whether there is a potential market involving your interests. Develop one or two ideas for potential businesses based on your passions. Do not consider any idea impossible at this stage.

   a. Consider if there is something missing in the current market. For example, are you passionate about locally grown organic vegetables but are frustrated that there isn't a place nearby to purchase these items? If so, you've developed an idea for a local farmers market.

Ethics and Corporate Social Responsibility

Social Responsibility: Forming a Plan of Action

Milton Hershey, founder of Hershey Chocolate Company, dedicated himself to caring about his customers, his employees, and his community at large. Hershey felt that giving back to the community was not only his moral obligation, but also a crucial part of his success.

Step 1. Imagine that you operate a business in your community (choose from a restaurant, a landscaping service, or a beauty salon).

Step 2. As a class or in smaller groups, discuss the ways in which your business can contribute to customers, employees, and the community in socially responsible ways. Write down a list of ideas that your group came up with.

Step 3. Create a social responsibility plan for your company. In the document, describe your business and the ways in which your business can contribute to specific organizations in your community. Be as specific with your plan as possible.

Web Exercises

1. **A Closer Look at Franchising**
Using the Internet, research a franchise that you think would be a viable investment opportunity for you. Put together a brief report that outlines the following information about your chosen franchise: fees (initial and ongoing), location/site assistance, training and ongoing support, marketing assistance, competition (both from other businesses and additional franchises within the organization), and the pros and cons of starting a business with this franchise.

"Are You a Born Entrepreneur?" (www.forbes.com/2005/11/15/entrepreneur-personality-quiz_cx_bn_ 1116quiz.html). After reading the article, complete the entrepreneurial personality quiz. What aspects of your personality make you a good candidate to be an entrepreneur? What is holding you back?

4. **The Cost of Borrowing**
How expensive is it to borrow funds for a new business? Using the Internet, research some of the new business

better **experience** for students **my**_biz_**lab!**

my_biz_**lab** is an innovative, interactive online program that combines assessment, reporting, and personalized study, all in ONE place. Throughout **_Better Business_**, students receive prompts to log in to **my**_biz_**lab** and immediately apply and assess their knowledge of the chapter concepts. With **my**_biz_**lab**, students don't just read about business, they INTERACT with it through business simulations and other engaging exercises.

BizSkills are real-world scenarios that invite students to assume the role of a decision maker at a company to apply the concepts they have just learned. Students are scored on the brief, five-minute simulation and then directed to the eBook, quizzes, outlines, and other learning aids to help reinforce the concepts.

> ALL MEDIA WAS WRITTEN BY THE AUTHORS
> TO ENSURE STUDENTS HAVE A
> SEAMLESS LEARNING EXPERIENCE.

my*biz*lab offers students a pre-test that will generate a personalized **Study Plan** where they see exactly the topics that require additional practice. The **Study Plan** links to multiple learning aids, such as videos, the eBook, and flashcards, for additional help. After students work through the learning aids, they can take a post test to see their improvement and prove their mastery of the topics.

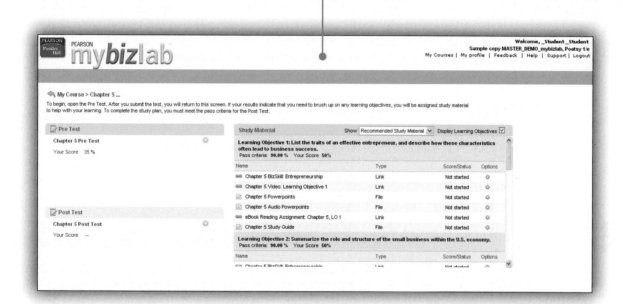

my*biz*lab gives students access to many resources to benefit all learning styles:

They can access the **eBook**, including the complete glossary and index, as well as a complete electronic study guide.

The **Video Library** features a variety of topical business videos, including all of the text-specific videos students will need to watch in order to complete the end-of-chapter Video Case.

Students can download **MP3 files** for on-the-go review of chapter objectives and summaries.

www.**my*biz*lab**.com

Interactive Document Makeovers ask students to analyze and correct business documents such as e-mail messages, letters, memos, blogs, and resumes. Immediate feedback is provided.

A simple, concise **Business Plan Exercise**, written to accompany the Business Plan Mini Chapter, can be assigned at any point during the course.

better **experiences** **my**_biz_**lab** and...

my_biz_**lab** is an innovative media package for instructors! **my**_biz_**lab** matches the organization of the textbook, is pre-loaded with content and resources for every chapter, is fully customizable, and includes a flexible course management system for any type of course, whether traditional lecture-based, hybrid, or fully online! **my**_biz_**lab** is the ONLY Intro to Business online tool that allows students to interact with chapter resources while supplying instructors with robust tools for course management and delivery.

> Authors Mary Anne Poatsy and Kendall Martin present an Orientation Video for instructors explaining the tools needed to effectively incorporate **Better Business** and **my**_biz_**lab** into their course.

The **BizChats** from the text can be brought to life via discussion boards in **my**_biz_**lab**. Suggestions for use of the **discussion board** are provided in the Instructor's Edition.

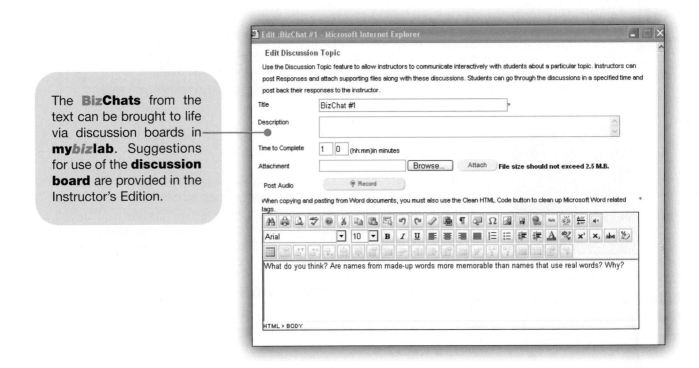

my_biz_**lab** offers instructors multiple **Regional Examples** that they can use to tailor their lectures, home-work, and activities for relevance. Suggestions for using these **Regional Examples** with the **my**_biz_**lab** discussion board are offered in the Instructor's Edition.

The **my**_biz_**lab Video Library** features videos from our ABC collection and business resource library. Each video was customized to directly match the **Better Business** text objectives with a condensed format to allow instructors to show in class or assign for homework right in **my**_biz_**lab**.

superior resources for instructors!

Electronic Gradebook

Assign homework, practice, or quizzes in **my**biz**lab** and the results will be automatically scored so students receive immediate feedback!

The **Electronic Gradebook** automatically records student results on homework, tutorials, quizzes, and tests. Instructors have control over managing and calculating grades, which can be exported to a spreadsheet program such as Microsoft Excel.™

Better Business and **my**biz**lab** give instructors access to a **Test Item File** and **TestGen** test-generating software containing over 4,000 questions in multiple-choice, true/false, short answer, and essay formats. Each question references the corresponding learning objectives, textbook pages, and difficulty level. The **Test Item File** includes coverage for the objectives within the chapter, including questions for the **BizSkills**, **BizChat**, and other highlighted features. With these features, instructors can then test on the topics they discuss in class in addition to the terms and definitions.

Audio PowerPoints are available in **my**biz**lab** for students to reinforce the lecture. Instructor PowerPoints offer *Teaching Tips and Beyond the Book* informational slides, and **Classroom Response System (CRS) PowerPoints** are also provided for instructors who want to use a classroom response system to encourage class participation or facilitate in-class quizzes.

Better Business – Instructor's Edition

Available in **my**biz**lab** and also in print, the Instructor's Edition includes the following:

- **In-Class Activities**, including **Icebreakers** and **Quick Questions**, stimulate class participation and discussion.

- **Teaching Tips**, **Annotations**, and **PowerPoint References** help instructors use the course content to the fullest.

- **BizSkills Summary Sheets** summarize each **BizSkill** and offer instructors tips on how to use the **BizSkills** in suggestions for both traditional and online courses.

- **Guide to Enhancing the Online Course** provides teaching techniques specifically for online courses.

- Suggestions for utilizing assets offered in the **Better Business** package will also be noted on the annotated syllabi.

- **Lecture and Chapter Outlines** as well as audio summary files are also provided for each chapter.

➤ Prologue

Ten Easy Rules **for** Business Success

Rule #1: Don't try to learn everything about business just from a book.

Business is about people. If you want to be a business success, leave your house and find someone who needs help with his or her business—and help them. Find a "master" at business: a person who you think is brilliant in terms of how he or she manages finances, how he or she markets and sells his or her product or service, how he or she treats employees, and the originality of his or her thinking. Then stick close and do whatever you can to help that person. It may start with meaningless errands, but one day you'll be the person standing there when a real opportunity arrives. Until that day, you'll be learning by watching a master business person run a company.

Rule #2: It's all up to you.

You've heard that before, right? You've bought textbooks, read some of the material, but maybe still haven't ended up with the grade you wanted. So the key to success is not just buying the book or just reading it. Instead, your success depends on three skills:

- finding,
- understanding, and
- applying the information within the resources of this textbook.

So how can you guess what your instructor wants from you? It all starts with knowing your own brain.

Rule #3: Know your learning style.

First, determine what kind of learner you are. Knowing your learning style can help you select and use the study strategies that best fit the way you learn. ▼ **Table 1** will help you figure out whether you learn best by seeing (visual), hearing (auditory), or touching/doing (tactile and kinesthetic). Read the word in the left column of the chart and then answer the questions in the successive three columns to see how you respond to each situation. Your answers may fall into all three columns, but one column will likely contain the most answers. The dominant column indicates your primary learning style.

After you've determined your primary learning style, you can best match up the textbook, system, and resources from your instructor to help you get an A. And, if you can figure out how to succeed in this course, you can apply the same study strategies to succeed in other courses.

Note that your instructor also has a specific style of learning and teaching with which he or she is most comfortable. Watching how your instructor works can be a great clue to helping you succeed in the course. For example, does he or she talk without ever drawing

"Simpkins, I'd like to introduce you to the secret of my business success."

▼ **Table 1**

What's Your Learning Style?

When you...	Visual	Auditory	Kinesthetic & Tactile
Spell	Do you try to see the word?	Do you sound out the word or use a phonetic approach?	Do you write the word down to find if it feels right?
Talk	Do you dislike listening for too long, or listen only sparingly? Do you favor words such as *see*, *picture*, and *imagine*?	Do you enjoy listening but are impatient to talk? Do you use words such as *hear*, *tune*, and *think*?	Do you gesture and use expressive movements? Do you use words such as *feel*, *touch*, and *hold*?
Concentrate	Do you become distracted by untidiness or movement?	Do you become distracted by sounds or noises?	Do you become distracted by activity around you?
Meet someone again	Do you forget names but remember faces or remember where you met?	Do you forget faces but remember names or remember what you talked about?	Do you remember best what you did together?
Contact people for class or business	Do you prefer direct, face-to-face, personal meetings?	Do you prefer talking on the phone?	Do you prefer talking with people while walking or participating in an activity?
Read	Do you like descriptive scenes or pause to imagine the actions?	Do you enjoy dialogue and conversation or hearing the characters talk?	Do you prefer action stories or are you not a keen reader?
Do something new at school or work	Do you like to see demonstrations, diagrams, slides, or posters?	Do you prefer verbal instructions or talking about it with someone else?	Do you prefer to jump right in and try it?
Put something together	Do you look at the directions and the pictures?	Do you prefer verbal instructions or talking about it with someone else?	Do you ignore the directions and figure it out as you go along?
Need help with a computer application	Do you seek out pictures or diagrams?	Do you call the help desk, ask a neighbor, or growl at the computer?	Do you keep trying to do it or try it on another computer?

Adapted from Colin Rose (1987). Accelerated Learning. Source: http://www.chaminade.org/inspire/learnstl.htm

a picture? Or does he or she use visuals to illustrate points? Figure out your instructor's learning style and use it to predict what kind of interactions he or she wants in the classroom and on your assignments.

Rule #4: Use the system, not just the textbook.

Most likely, when you shelled out the cash to buy your textbook, you thought you were just getting a book, right? As it turns out, you bought a "system." ▼ **Table 2** walks you through everything that comes with the purchase of this book. Remembering your learning style, consider how each of these resources can help you study and learn!

Rule #5: Connect with people.

Business is all about people. Right now, your business is getting a great grade in this class. As in any business, there are many people available to provide help: instructors, fellow students, and school staff. Look around for these people—and then enlist their help.

▼ Table 2

Better Business Resource Guide		
Resource	**Where is it?**	**When does it help me?**
BizSkills (interactive game-like media that let you try out your skills in many common business situations)	On mybizlab.com	For test prep Concept reinforcement
PowerPoint Presentations	On mybizlab.com	Before the chapter starts For test prep
Study Guide	Printed Study Guide or On mybizlab.com	In study groups For test prep Concept reinforcement
Mybizlab Web site Resources	On mybizlab.com	In study groups For test prep Concept reinforcement
MP3/iPod-Ready Chapter Objectives and Summary Files	On mybizlab.com	When you're on the go For test prep Concept reinforcement
Chapter-Specific Videos and Exercises	On mybizlab.com	When you're on the go Concept reinforcement
End of Chapter Exercises	On mybizlab.com or At the end of each chapter	When you're on the go For test prep Concept reinforcement

Get to Know Your Instructor: Go to Office Hours

Your teachers can be your most helpful contacts on campus. Not only can they become mentors, but as you near graduation, they can write job recommendations or references. They can't do that unless you get to know them beyond the focus of the course. So plan to make a couple of trips to office hours—even if you know everything.

Review the Syllabus

If you have trouble speaking up in class, try this strategy. The syllabus is one of the most important documents in the course. It acts as a binding contract between you and the professor. Read the syllabus in detail as soon as it comes out. Then, in the next class, ask at least one question about it. It will show the professor you're serious about meeting your responsibilities in class—and will get you in the habit of speaking in class.

Create or Join a Study Group

Find study buddies early. In the first few days of class, try to get acquainted with at least two classmates in every course. Watch the people in your class to figure out who seems to know what's going on, who seems dependable, and who you could work well with. Approach those people and ask if they wouldn't mind forming a study group. You don't need to meet all the time—the group can be available on an "as needed" basis. But it's good to have a group of connected students who can help you prep for exams, confirm or clarify points made during class, and exchange notes if you miss a class. (Trust us: it's much better to have a buddy give you the information you missed than to ask the instructor, "Did I miss anything important?")

Use the People Around You

Do you know students who already took this class? Spend some time with them and ask the right questions. What sections of the course will demand more time out of your schedule? What tools in the library helped them out with the projects?

Be sure to look around the class for older students. Many colleges are seeing a large influx of people returning to college after successful careers. These people have that precious thing you may lack: real-world experience. Buy someone a cup of coffee and ask him or her for advice that helps you in the course or in finding a job.

Teaching assistants assigned to the course are another great resource. They're most likely closer to your age, so you may find it easier to reach out to them for help.

Use All the Resources the School Provides

The faculty and staff at your school want you to succeed—we all take pride in our students' accomplishments! So be sure to investigate all the resources available to you at your school. Talk to your advisor about services such as the following:

Writing Support

Many schools provide special clinics that can help you with your writing. Some also provide writing labs where you can get assistance in editing and proofreading your work.

Support Services

Look for support services that offer help with note-taking techniques, strategies to combat stress in test taking, and workshops on helping you organize and manage your time. If you discover that you have a pattern of specific struggles (for example, you always underperform on tests), see if free screening for learning disabilities is offered. You may need specific testing accommodations (like additional time or larger-print exams) or you may be eligible for help with an in-class note-taker. The key is to become your own best advocate. Be informed—know how your mind works and what conditions make you perform your best.

When studying for a test, I've found that it's very helpful to use a partner and a study guide. I like to come up with a study guide full of questions relating to every important topic that I think will be on the test and write the answers directly below them. Then, my partner and I go through the study guide and quiz each other. This way we can read aloud all of the main ideas and begin to remember key concepts. After we have gone through the study guide a couple times, we quiz each other from memory. Once we've memorized small concepts, it's easier to understand the "bigger picture."

—Mallory Hensel, **student**

Rule #6: Behave like an academic all-star.

Take Awesome Notes

Even if you're a strong auditory learner, you'll benefit from taking notes. Awesome notes are the key when you review and prepare for papers and exams. Several note-taking strategies are helpful. Experiment and see which one best meets your needs. One popular strategy is the Cornell System.

Use the Cornell System

When using the Cornell System, you don't need to rewrite or retype your notes. Begin by setting up your 8 ½ by 11 inch notepaper as shown in Figure 1. Draw a vertical line 2 ½ inches from the left side of the page. This is the recall column. You take detailed notes to the right of this margin—and write key words or phrases in the recall column. Next, draw a horizontal line about an inch or so from the bottom of the page for a summary. You can also use a product like Microsoft One Note, which comes preloaded with a Cornell Note System template (see ▼ **Figure 1**).

The key is to follow five simple steps:

1. **Record facts and ideas**
   - Record as many facts and general ideas as you can in the large six-inch column. Don't try to capture everything the instructor says; strive to capture key ideas or main points.
2. **Reduce to key points**
   - As soon as is practical after the lecture, read through your notes and make them more legible if necessary. Fill in any missing ideas.
   - Now, use the small column. Next to each set of lecture points, jot down ideas or key words that will give you the idea of the lecture.

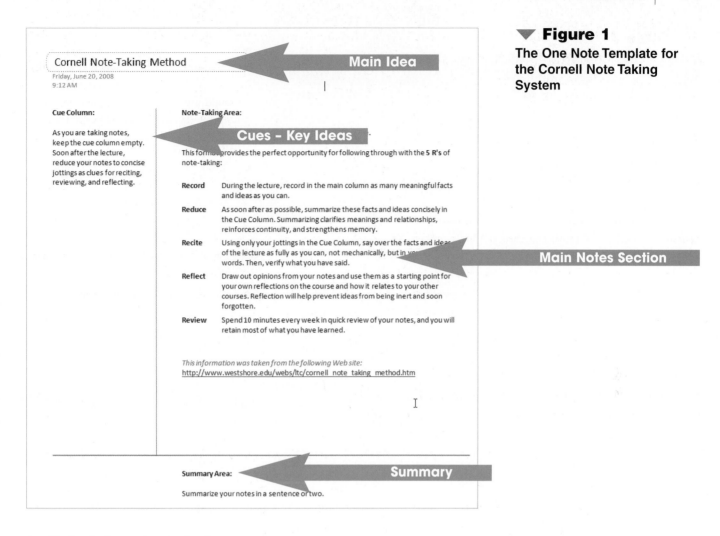

3. **Recite the key points out loud**
   - Cover up the right-hand portion of your notes and recite the general ideas and concepts of the lecture. As dorky as it seems, it's important to vocalize these points. Reciting out loud is an effective way to learn because hearing your thoughts helps you sharpen your thinking process, and stating ideas and facts in your own words challenges you to think about the meaning of the information. When reciting, cover up your notes in the six-inch column while leaving the cue words uncovered and readily accessible.

4. **Reflect**
   - Try to find connections between these ideas and things taught in other lectures and other courses—even in your own life experience.

5. **Review**
   - To review your notes for a test, or to use the ideas in a paper, go through the main ideas in the recall column.
   - To get the general theme of several lectures or of the course in general, overlap your notes to show only recall columns.
   - Summarize the main points of each page or each topic at the bottom of the page.

▼ **Table 3** shows how much material we all forget over time. Over 50 percent of what you learned yesterday is gone today, unless you review! Employing the Cornell System helps you retain the information you received in lecture or from your reading.

Build Mind Maps

A mind map is a graphic representation of the content of a lecture or reading. ▼ **Figure 2** shows one example. Many visual learners find mind-mapping beneficial because it organizes a lecture graphically. Many free online resources, including software and templates, can help

▼ Table 3

Percentage of Material Forgotten Over Time	
Time from First Learning to Relearning	**% of Material Forgotten**
After 20 minutes	47%
After 1 day	62%
After 2 days	69%
After 15 days	75%
After 31 days	79%

Source: http://www.ppslc.com/college_success.php

I use a mind map to arrange the material before writing a paper. It helps me get all of my ideas on paper and makes the information easier to organize logically.

—*Laura Poatsy*, **student**

you begin to use mind maps. One such free product is Free Mind (available at http://sourceforge.net/projects/freemind). Even if you just have paper and pencil, you can build useful mind maps. Here are a few concepts and strategies to get you started.

Use Simple Graphics

- Boxes or circles capture main ideas or key words. The main topic of the lecture should be boxed and placed in the middle of the mind map. Smaller boxes will radiate from this central idea, but might also have subsequent ideas radiating from them as well.

- Arrows are used to connect boxes or circles. They represent transitions from one idea to another.

- Clouds represent important ideas that are off topic. They are generally not connected to boxes and often sit outside the main concepts in the map.

Add colors

As soon as is practical, review your mind map. Redraw or reposition ideas, if necessary, to best capture and reflect connections between key ideas and concepts. Then, add colors to connect ideas or concepts that aren't necessarily connected by arrows but share the same theme (such as those topics that have been pointed out that will be on the test, that were from a PowerPoint presentation, or that should be further explored).

▼ Figure 2
An Example of a Mind Map of this Prologue

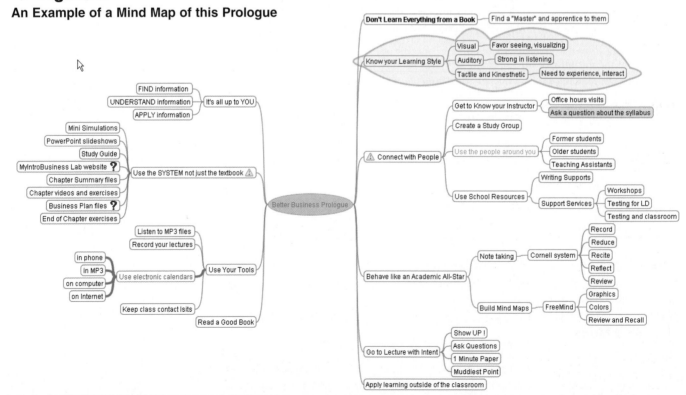

Review and recall

Similar to the smaller column used in the Cornell System, you can use the boxes and colors to help you connect the main ideas of several lectures while preparing for a test or paper. Consider creating a *progressive mind map* (separate from individual lecture mind maps) that will relate how specific topics relate to the course overall.

To show you this idea in practice, we've created a progressive mind map, created with the free product Free Mind, that covers the points of this prologue. The Mind Map is available at www.mybizlab.com. Walk through it on your computer, expanding and collapsing the different links. Reviewing the mind map is a good review of the prologue, underscoring the relationships between ideas.

Rule #7: Go to lecture with intent.

How did today's lecture work for you? One of the most memorable of your life? Or did you think the instructor had slipped into speaking ancient Greek? The attitude and plan you have for using lecture time can change the entire experience for you. Try these quick fixes to get you on track.

> You should know the material so well you can explain it to others so that they understand it – even your mom.
>
> —*Brett Neslen*, **student**

Show Up!

As Woody Allen says, "Eighty percent of success is showing up." It's basic advice, but many students lose sight of how important it is to come to class. You should be punctual, if not early; be attentive; and be noticed. Don't get lost in a crowded lecture hall. Sit near the front and ask good questions so that the professor gets to know your face and name. It's just as important that the professor knows you as it is that you know your professor (see Rule #5).

Ask Questions

If you're confused during class, ask a question right then. Don't think, "I'll look really dumb if I ask this," or "I'll probably understand it after I read the text," or "I'll wait to ask someone else, or go to office hours tomorrow." Asking now will save you time and effort and will probably help other students in the room. You'll learn so much more if you ask questions in class. If you do need to contact your instructor after class to clarify a point, stop by office hours rather than asking the question electronically or over the phone. Keep in mind, face-to-face visits trump e-mail or voicemail. Now, aren't you glad you invested some time earlier to get to know your instructor (Rule #5)? After all, it's easier to ask for help from someone with whom you already feel comfortable.

Write a One-Minute Paper

Immediately at the end of class, take one minute and write all that you can recall from today's lecture. Try to identify what the main take-away points are by highlighting key ideas. Forcing yourself to be quick and brief helps you to capture the main ideas without the smaller details providing distraction.

Write Down Your "Muddiest" Point

When class is finished, also take a quick moment to write down two sentences that describe the most confusing part of today's lecture. Keep this in one specific part of your notebook—it's a great thing to bring along to study group or to office hours. It will work well to create your own personalized study guide for the next exam too.

Rule #8: Use your tools: cell phone/MP3 player/laptop.

Undoubtedly, you come to class armed with at least a cell phone—and may even have a separate MP3 player and a laptop. Here are a few ideas of how you can use these tools to get you to that A.

Listen to the MP3 Files Provided with This Text

This text comes with MP3 files that contain chapter objectives and the summary. Use them for a quick review of the text content and to prep for tests.

Record Audio or Video of the Class

Most MP3 players can be equipped to record audio files, even in stereo. An Apple iPod, for example, can record using a microphone accessory. It could pick up class discussions even if you just sat it by your desk. If your professor is willing to carry yours in her pocket and wear a lapel mike, you can be sure to have the best sound quality.

Any cell phone that has a built-in camera can record video. Although the video may be low resolution, it will still be a useful review of what was said back on Tuesday. By adding a larger memory card (many phones now can use 8GB cards) you can record back-to-back lectures with no storage problems.

Laptops equipped with a camera can do the best job of video recording. Cameras such as the Logitech QuickCam Pro 5000 plug right into a USB port and actually track the voice of the lecturer, moving to keep him or her in focus even if he or she walks around the room while lecturing.

Many instructors are now beginning to create their own audio recordings of lectures and deliver them as podcasts to the class. If your instructor is not, ask for permission to record him or her and explain that you are happy to make the files available to him or her or to post them to the other students.

> Take breaks during a study session—just be sure to come back to the work!
>
> —*Devin Kownurko,* **student**

Use Your Phone's Calendar

Organization is a critical skill for success. Enter assignment deadlines into your cell phone's calendar. You also can use organizational tools such as Microsoft Outlook or Google Calendar to track key due dates and access them from your laptop.

Keep a Class Contact List in Your Phone

Collect the contact information for at least three classmates and for your professor. Be sure to have it all—home phone, cell phone, IM identity, and e-mail address. This way, you'll have the information at your fingertips when you really need it and don't have your notebook with you. This habit will create all kinds of opportunities for you later in the real world. Successful folks call it "networking"!

Rule #9: Read a good book.

What is the best investment you can make in yourself right now? If there were something that could promise you an A in this course and that would help you to succeed in college in general, it would be worth paying for, right? There is: this book, plus your time. Really, all you need to succeed in this course is this book and its resources, plus some investment of your own time. Doing well in this course is a good start at getting As in follow-up business courses you may take. That leads to a great job after graduation, followed by huge wealth, fame, and fortune! (Well, maybe not those last three, but you get the picture.)

➤ Logitech QuickCam Pro 5000 is a useful device that tracks the voice of the lecturer, moving to keep him or her in focus even while he or she is walking around the room.

Extra Tips for the Online Learner

Taking this class online? Here are some additional tips for success:

1. Purchase your textbook and any other course materials before class begins. If you're buying online, allow for delivery time.

2. Check your technology needs. Make sure your computer, software, and Internet connection are sufficient for the requirements of the course before the class starts. Faulty technology is not a good excuse for missing assignments in an online course. Have a backup computer you can use, just in case.

3. Establish a regular study time. Without specific classroom meeting times, it's easy to forget about the class. Time passes quickly and before you know it, your "other life" has taken precedent and you're playing catch-up to meet the requirements of the course. Set a regular study time that works with your schedule when you can log into the class and do whatever work may be required.

4. Be proactive asking questions about assignments. If you have questions on an assignment, remember that sometimes getting answers is not immediate. You should always count on things taking more time than in a classroom.

5. Participate in discussions and ask questions. Your online instructor should provide a way for you to interact with other students and ask questions. Active participation will enable you to grasp the material better—and to know your classmates better.

6. Exchange contact information. Although it's harder to meet and interact with others in an online class, try to get contact information for at least one or two people with whom you can share information and questions.

7. Make sure the instructor knows who you are. Take the time in the first week or so to introduce yourself to the instructor via e-mail or through the class chat room. It's harder for an instructor to get to know you in an online course than in a traditional face-to-face class.

8. Know how to work your class Web site and course management software. Especially know how you can get and submit your assignments, check your grades, and communicate with your instructor, as well as with your classmates.

9. Be organized and don't procrastinate. Especially if the class is self-paced, make sure you know when the big assignments and tests are due. As soon as you get your syllabus, record all assignment due dates on your own personal calendar.

10. Become comfortable expressing your ideas in writing. You'll need to communicate in a professional way about both course content and your professional life.

Rule #10: Apply these rules outside the classroom.

Most of these classroom tips also can apply to your career. For example, Rule #2 suggests you find, understand, and apply the information from this textbook system to meet the demands of your instructor. In your working life, you'll need to find out what your boss or client wants and figure out the best way to meet his or her needs. Likewise, Rule #3 encourages you to understand how you best learn. Revisit Table 1 again—many of the actions apply to a business context as well. Knowing your learning style will help you be successful in business as well as in the classroom.

Because business is all about people, think about how you can apply the strategies in Rule #5 to your job. If you can, get to know your boss or supervisor. They, too, can become your mentors and be instrumental in recommending you for advancement within the company. Bosses don't have office hours, but you can stop by their offices periodically to just say hello or ask to meet them for lunch or coffee every month or so. Get to know the people you work with and develop a contact list. You never know when you may need to contact someone in the office when you're not there, or vise versa. So, get a co-worker's e-mail, home or cell phone numbers, and maybe even his or her IM address. Again, it's much better to have someone in the office to ask, "What did I miss?" or "Can you help me?" than running to your boss (or not having anyone at all) to ask the same questions. Also, don't ignore the other people outside your immediate office. Get to know the cleaning staff, the elevator attendants, and the security guards in your building. They can help you in a pinch and are more willing to do so if they know your face and name.

Do you think you won't ever take notes again once you're out of the classroom? Think again. The workday includes attending lots of meetings, even when they occur over the phone. Use your college career and Rule #6 to perfect note taking so when you get to the business world, you'll have that skill down pat. And although you might occasionally get lucky with an instructor that ignores your absences in the classroom, such luck most likely will not follow you into the office. To get ahead, you must come to work—and you must be there physically and mentally. Don't be afraid to ask questions; good questions indicate that you're thinking about the situation at work and trying to apply it to what you already know. If things don't make sense, or you don't understand something, ask someone for clarification.

We suggested ways you can use your cell phone, MP3 player, and laptop in the classroom in Rule #9. These tools can also be used in the office as well. Again, you need to make sure people know and agree to you taping/recording them, but having good records of meetings and discussions can be helpful to you and to your colleagues. And because many people are afraid of technology, establishing yourself as someone who is comfortable and innovative with technology can also be a good thing.

Finally, don't stop learning and reading! In Rule #9 we encouraged you to read this book. When you find a career you're interested in pursuing, seek out books for advice and insight about that career. There is no end to learning—it's a lifetime activity, so embrace it.

We hope you have found these rules helpful and will be able to apply them to your academic and professional careers. Good luck in whatever endeavors you pursue!

The **Ten Easy** Rules for Business Success

Rule #1: Don't try to learn everything about business just from a book.

Rule #2: It's all up to you.

Rule #3: Know your learning style.

Rule #4: Use the system, not just the textbook.

Rule #5: Connect with people.

Rule #6: Behave like an academic all-star.

Rule #7: Go to lecture with intent.

Rule #8: Use your tools: cell phone/MP3 player/laptop.

Rule #9: Read a good book.

Rule #10: Apply these rules outside the classroom.

chapter 1

Business Basics

▼ Objectives 1-6

1. What are **profits**, and how do **businesses** and **non-profit organizations** compare? (p. 3)

2. What is the difference between a **good** and a **service**, and what are the **factors of production**? (p. 4)

3. How do **competition**, the **social environment**, **globalization**, and technological growth challenge and provide opportunities to business owners? (p. 6)

4. What are four types of businesses? (p. 15)

5. How do **sole proprietorships**, **partnerships**, **corporations**, and **limited liability companies (LLCs)** differ from one another as forms of business? (p. 19)

6. How do life skills translate to the business environment? (p. 22)

For more chapter resources, go to www.my*biz*lab.com.

p. 15
Types of Businesses
▼ **Objective 4**
Wawa convenience stores are located in the mid-Atlantic region of the United States. While the chain has over 500 stores, it is still considered a small, regional business. What would Wawa have to do to expand its business and become a national franchise?

p. 19
Types of Business Ownership
▼ **Objective 5**
Estelle Peterson is the sole proprietor of a private duty nursing business, which she runs out of her home in New York City. She is being harassed by creditors who are trying to seize her personal assets as the result of legal proceedings against her business. Why do creditors have the right to seize Mrs. Peterson's personal possessions? Can this happen to all business owners?

p. 3
The Business Landscape
▼ **Objectives 1 & 2**
The business landscape in the United States is vast and varied. Steve Chen, Chad Hurley, and Jawed Karim launched the video-sharing Web site YouTube. Meanwhile, the Chang family opened a small Chinese restaurant. What do these seemingly unrelated businesses have in common?

p. 6
Common Business Challenges and Opportunities
▼ **Objective 3**
Leroy Washington is the owner of a local deli in Florida. When a Quiznos franchise moved in across the street, Washington had to think creatively to deal with the new competition. How did he manage to keep his small deli in business despite the major franchise across the street?

p. 22
Taking Business Personally
▼ **Objective 6**
Do you run your life like a business? Managing a business requires many of the same financial and personal skills that you use in your daily life. Understanding how you use business concepts and methods in your life may help you understand how they are used in business.

The **Business Landscape** pp. 3-5

➤ Both YouTube and the Changs' Chinese restaurant are **businesses**—entities that offer goods and services to their customers in order to earn a profit. The business models of YouTube and the Changs couldn't be more different. After all, one is a new media portal that hosts hundreds of millions of videos, while the other is a family-run eatery in a small town. However, both organizations represent the varied spectrum of business in the United States. In this chapter, you'll learn about the basic skills it takes to run a successful business.

Benefits of Businesses

What can profits do? A **profit** is earned when a company's **revenue** (the money a business brings in) is greater than its **expenses** (the money a business pays out). More often than not, profit is the driving force behind a business's growth. As more profit is generated, a company is able to reward its employees, increase its productivity, or expand its business into new areas.

In 2005, Steve Chen, Chad Hurley, and Jawed Karim, three twenty-something tech company employees, decided to pool their resources and expertise to launch the video-sharing Web site YouTube.[1] The three hatched the idea at a dinner party in San Francisco, and in less than a year, they developed a Silicon Valley company that became a huge phenomenon. Meanwhile, the Chang family was developing a plan to open a restaurant. Over three decades ago, the Chang family, immigrants from Hong Kong, settled in a small town in Pennsylvania and set out to fulfill their goal of opening a Chinese restaurant. The Changs purchased the restaurant from an ad in the local newspaper. Although opening a restaurant was challenging, the Changs built a reputation for treating people like family and developed a loyal customer base. What do the billion-dollar Web site and a small-town family restaurant have in common? ➤

Nonprofit organizations like the American Diabetes Association operate like a business but do not pursue profits. Instead, they seek to service their community through social, educational, and political means.

The proprietor of a business is not the only one who benefits from earned profits. A successful business benefits society by providing the goods and services we need and want. Businesses also provide employment opportunities for members of the community. Because they offer desired goods and services, provide employment, and generate income and spending in the economy, successful businesses contribute to the quality of life by creating higher standards of living for the entire society.

Do all businesses need to create a profit? Not every organization that generates revenue and pays expenses is necessarily considered a business. They may operate like a business, but **nonprofit organizations**, as their name suggests, do not go into business to pursue profits. Instead, a nonprofit organization seeks to service its community through social, educational, or political means. Organizations such as universities, hospitals, environmental groups, and charities are nonprofit organizations because any excess revenue is used to further their stated mission.[2]

Goods and Services

Do all businesses create a product? Whether a business is for-profit or not, one of its goals is to provide some sort of product to its customer base. A product can be either a good or a service. **Goods** are any physical products offered by a business. A roast beef sandwich at Arby's, a 42-inch LCD television at Best Buy, and a Honda Civic at your local car dealer are all considered goods because they are tangible items. Conveyer belts, pumps, and sundries sold to other businesses are also goods, even though they are not sold directly to consumers. On the other hand, a **service** refers to an intangible product that is bought or sold. Unlike a polo shirt on the rack at Hollister, services cannot be physically handled. Services include products such as haircuts, health care, car insurance, and theatrical productions.

Some companies actually offer products that are both goods *and* services. Take, for example, an establishment like the T.G.I. Friday's franchise of restaurants. When you order a sirloin steak at the restaurant, you're paying for the good (a fire-grilled sirloin) as well as the service of preparing, cooking, and serving the steak. You'll learn more about goods and services in Chapter 13.

The Factors of Production

To fully understand how a business operates, you have to consider the **factors of production**, the resources used to produce goods and services. For years, businesses focused on four traditional factors: labor, natural resources, capital, and entrepreneurial talent. However, in the twenty-first century economy, an additional factor has become increasingly important: technology.

- **Labor.** Obviously businesses need people to gets things produced. **Labor** is the human resource that refers to any physical or intellectual work people contribute to a business's production.

- **Natural resources.** Most workers who provide the labor to produce a good need something tangible to work with. **Natural resources** are the raw materials provided by nature that are used to produce goods and services. Soil used in agricultural production, trees used for lumber to build houses, and coal, oil, and natural gas used to create energy are all examples of natural resources.

- **Capital.** There are two types of capital: *real capital* and *financial capital*. **Real capital** essentially refers to the physical facilities used to produce goods and services. **Financial capital**, on the other hand, is money used to facilitate a business enterprise. Financial capital can be acquired via business loans, from investors, or through other forms of fundraising, or even by tapping into personal savings.

- **Entrepreneurs.** An **entrepreneur** is someone who assumes the risk of creating, organizing, and operating a business and directs all the business resources. Entrepreneurs are a human resource, just like labor, but what sets entrepreneurs apart from labor is not only their willingness to bear risks but also their ability to manage an enterprise effectively. Successful entrepreneurs are rewarded with profits for bearing risks and for their managerial expertise.

- **Technology.** **Technology** refers to items and services such as smartphones, computer software, and digital broadcasting that make businesses more efficient and productive. Successful companies are able to keep pace with technological progresses and harness new knowledge, information, and strategies. Unsuccessful organizations typically fail because they have not kept pace with the latest technology and techniques.

You will learn more about labor (Chapter 9), capital (Chapter 15), entrepreneurs (Chapter 5), and technology (Chapter 10) later on in the text.

Recall the examples of YouTube and the Changs' Chinese restaurant at the beginning of the section. Although the products offered by these businesses vary considerably, the two businesses are similar because they were started by creative entrepreneurs determined to make a profit. For Steve Chen, Chad Hurley, and Jawed Karim, these profits came in the form of billions when YouTube was sold to Google for $1.7 billion in 2006.[3] For the Chang family, the profits are much more modest—they make a solid living, but are far from seeing a ten-figure profit. Nevertheless, the Changs, like the founders of YouTube, have realized a dream by starting a successful business.

▼ You have just read **Objectives 1 & 2**

Think you got it? Check out the Study Plan section @
www.mybizlab.com.

Common Business Challenges and **Opportunities** pp. 6-14

In 1998, Leroy Washington inherited his family's deli. The deli had a loyal clientele with a regular lunch crowd. However, a Quiznos franchise moved into a lot directly across the street. As a national franchise, it had a great deal of name recognition from print ads and commercials. It also had a larger space, more workers and ovens, and a more extensive menu. Leroy found his lunch crowd dwindling as people switched over to the national chain with its faster service and greater variety of sandwiches. In order to compete, Leroy had to get creative. Instead of just offering traditional deli choices, his deli expanded its menu to include Cuban pressed sandwiches and an "early bird special" light fare dinner menu. Leroy hoped that the changes would appeal to the large number of Cuban immigrants and senior citizens populating the area. ➤

➤ Dealing with competition is just one of the many challenges that business owners such as Leroy Washington face in the twenty-first-century economy. However, as Leroy found, confronting these challenges can sometimes lead to opportunities for growth as well. In this section, we'll discuss how competition, the social environment, globalization, and technology manifest themselves as both challenges and opportunities in the business world.

Competition

How does competition influence business? In a market-based economy such as that of the United States, there is an emphasis on individual economic freedom and a limit on governmental intervention. In this type of market, competition is a fundamental force. **Competition** arises when two or more businesses contend with one another to attract customers and gain an advantage. The United States' private enterprise system is predicated on the fact that competition benefits consumers because it motivates businesses to produce a wider variety of better and cheaper goods and services.

A competitive environment is where a free-market economy thrives. Competition forces companies to improve their product offerings, lower their prices, aggressively promote their brands, and focus on customer satisfaction. Having to compete for a finite number of consumers usually weeds out less efficient companies and less desirable products from the marketplace. Because profit is the ultimate goal, it is the job of a successful business to convince customers that its product is either better or less expensive than that of its competitors.

For example, consider the explosion in high-definition television sales over the last few years. Because more manufacturers and retailers have jumped into the HDTV market, prices for sets fell drastically in 2008. In fact, the sales of flat-panel high-definition televisions—once the sole dominion of high-end retailers and manufacturers—is on pace to reach an overall market value of $65 billion in the near future.[4] Since buyers are able to find moderately priced HDTVs at such diverse retailers as Amazon.com, Costco, and Best Buy, prices come down because these stores are able to turn over merchandise quickly and in high volume, which allows them to narrow the margin between the price they pay and the price the customer pays.[5] At the same time, consumer electronics specialty stores such as Tweeter compete by claiming to offer exceptional customer service.

How do competitive challenges affect prospective employees?

In a competitive environment, it is essential for a company to empower workers to feel free to deal with customer needs. This means employers seek workers who have interpersonal, communication, and decision-making skills. Companies today need to be more reactive to customers' needs to retain their competitive advantage. Therefore, more companies are placing greater decision-making responsibilities with employees, rather than having decisions trickle down through layers of management. This also means greater employee satisfaction and more career advancement opportunities.

Biz**Chat**

Apple: Taking a Bite Out of Microsoft?

Apple and Microsoft have a history of bitter rivalry revolving around the desire to dominate the personal computer market. The main point of contention between these companies was the Graphical User Interface (GUI), which is the user interface for the main program that runs personal computers. Apple released the first GUI to include folders and long file names in 1983. When Microsoft released Windows 2.0 in 1988, Apple took Microsoft to court, complaining that the "look and feel" of the Windows interface was stolen from the Apple interface. This suit continued until 1992 when Apple finally lost. Microsoft led the competition in the early 1990s. It became an industry standard to have Windows operating systems pre-installed on most PCs, which were dominating the computer market at the time. The ten-year battle finally ended when Apple announced an official alliance with Microsoft in 1997. Microsoft and Apple agreed to a five-year deal in which Microsoft would continue to develop Office software for Apple computers and Apple agreed to bundle Microsoft's Internet Explorer in all its operating systems.[6] The computer industry went through some tough times around the turn of the century, but Apple and Microsoft remained two of the most successful companies in the world. The element of competition between these companies drove them to succeed and perhaps led to the production of higher-quality operating software than if no one challenged them. As you see, competition helps keep companies on their toes.

For more information and discussion questions about this topic, check out the BizChat feature on www.my*biz*lab.com.

Social Environment

How does the social environment affect businesses? A **social environment** is an interconnected system of different demographic factors such as race, ethnicity, gender, age, income distribution, sexual orientation, and other characteristics. Social, economic, and political movements and trends cause the social environment in the United States to constantly change; an influx of immigrants can change the racial demographic, or an economic slump can change the income distribution demographic. These changes affect where we live, what we buy, and how we choose to spend our money. Businesses must consider the shifts and changes in the social environment when making decisions in order to best serve their employees, customers, and community. Let's discuss three specific issues surrounding the social environment that present potential challenges and opportunities for today's businesses.

An Aging Population

Not only are older Americans living longer, healthier lives, they are also better educated, wealthier, and have achieved a higher standard of living than previous generations. *Baby boomers*, the generation born between 1946 and 1964, represent the majority of the aging population in the United States. Not only do the 78 million baby boomers make up the largest population group in the United States, they are also the wealthiest. Baby boomers, who in 2008 were between the ages of 44 and 62, have an estimated spending power of over $2 trillion a year. This makes baby boomers a large and lucrative target for businesses. Cosmetic company Revlon is eager to make a profit off the aging population by releasing an anti-aging beauty line called Vital Radiance that is aimed at baby boomer women. Revlon is hoping this new line will generate $200 million in new sales.[7]

Although an aging population presents many opportunities for corporations, it also presents challenges for the U.S. economy. In October 2007, Federal Reserve Chairman Ben Bernanke warned that the nation will be faced with difficult choices as baby boomers reach retirement age. Some potential problems include higher taxes, a reduction in government spending on entitlement programs such as Social Security and Medicare benefits, or a higher federal budget deficit.[8] This is primarily because economic forecasters predict a shift in the demographics in the United States, which will greatly affect the labor force. According to the Social Security Administration, by 2010, the number of Americans over age 65 will increase at a faster rate than the number of Americans aged 20 to 64. This trend will continue until 2035. As shown in ▼ **Figure 1.1**, the result of such a trend could be a severe labor shortage for many years.

Despite these challenges, catering to the needs of an older population will ultimately present businesses with opportunities for growth, especially for the health care, pharmaceutical, and travel industries. After all, a bigger population translates to a larger market for these goods and services.

Increasing Diversity

In business there is no one-size-fits-all method to managing employees and appealing to customers because every person is different. As the United States becomes more diverse, it is important for businesses to mirror that diversity in their workforce. A May 2007 census report revealed the U.S. minority population had topped 100 million in 2006, making one in three residents a minority. This means that in some companies, minorities may account for the majority of the workforce. At clothing retailer Men's Wearhouse, minorities represent 54 percent of the company's 11,508 employees.[9]

Change in Workforce and Retired Age Groups

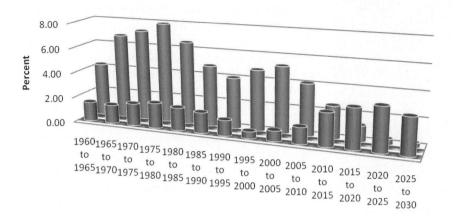

■ 65 and over age group   ■ 20-64 age group

However, in today's business climate, increasing and managing a company's diversity involves more than just employing an ethnically diverse workforce. Companies must develop a diversity initiative that outlines their goals and objectives for managing, retaining, and promoting a diverse workforce. A diversity initiative might include a nondiscrimination policy, minority network, or diversity education. According to Harvard sociology professor Frank Dobbin, "To increase diversity, executives must treat it like any other business goal."[10]

Although the inclusion and advancement of racial minorities in the workplace is an important step in establishing a diverse workforce, it is only part of the process. Today, the term "minority" applies to more than just people of different ethnicities. Some minority groups represent a person's gender, culture, religion, sexual orientation, or disability. Companies must include these minority groups in their diversity initiative to ensure that all minority employees are treated fairly by management and coworkers.

The Green Movement

In a 2007 United Nations study, many of the world's most respected environmental scientists reported that the threat of global warming and climate change is real.[11] As environmental anxieties become prevalent throughout society, it's important for business to get involved in a **green economy**—one that factors ecological concerns into its business decisions. Businesses that manufacture products that contribute to higher emissions of carbon dioxide and consume inordinate amounts of fossil fuels must adapt to this new environmental awareness if they want to be relevant in a green economy. Toyota has seen its sales increase thanks in large part to its Prius hybrids, which run on electricity as well as gasoline. Hybrids have not only become hot sellers; they've become part of our popular culture.[12]

A focus on environmental issues also opens a brand new market that will be increasingly important in the future. The demand for more green products presents new opportunities for entrepreneurs to meet those needs. These "green-collar" jobs can revitalize large swathes of the United States manufacturing economy that have been decimated. Creating wind energy turbines, installing solar panels, and weatherproofing houses and office buildings are going to be necessary businesses of the twenty-first century.

➤ A focus on environmental issues is opening up markets such as wind turbines that will become increasingly important in the future.

The Social Environment and You

As a prospective employee, any one of these social issues will probably affect the company for which you end up working. Since workers are increasingly retiring at later ages, competition for certain jobs and for career advancement might be fiercer than in years past. On the other hand, the culture of business is constantly shifting to meet the ever-evolving needs of U.S. demographics. This means more opportunity for employees who can navigate a diverse environment. In addition, jobs aimed at responding to the needs of the growing green economy will also likely present new opportunities for job seekers. Entrepreneurial possibilities always exist for those who have the vision and desire to succeed and are willing to take risks.

Globalization

How has globalization affected businesses? You're familiar with multinational companies such as Nike, McDonald's, or Coca-Cola. **Multinational enterprises**—companies that have operations in more than one country—are among the leaders of a movement called globalization. **Globalization** is the movement toward a more interconnected and interdependent world economy. This means that economies around the world are merging as technology, goods and services, labor, and capital move back and forth across international borders. For example, FedEx, the world's largest express transportation company, conducts business in more than 220 countries and territories around the world.[13] Although the concept of globalization is essential for corporations such as FedEx, it is still a highly controversial subject for many people. Globalization has sparked fierce debates among politicians, businessmen, and the general public for the past few decades. We'll discuss the controversies surrounding globalization in greater depth in Chapter 4.

The effects of globalization on the business world vary widely, from economic transformation in India to the shutting down of major manufacturing plants in the United States. The Internet and modern technological advances are making it possible for a company of any size from anywhere in the world to compete globally. Lower tariffs and other trade restrictions give U.S. companies the option to export or import goods to and from other countries or to conduct their business overseas. Instead of building their products in plants at home, a growing number of companies are choosing to relocate their production facilities overseas or subcontracting at least some components of their products to foreign companies around the world at low costs. This is called **offshoring**. The low labor costs in countries such as China and India make these countries ideal locations for multinational companies seeking technology services and manufactured products at a low cost.

Globalization presents both benefits and risks to the U.S. economy. For example, lowered production costs allow prices on consumer products to go down, meaning that you as a consumer benefit by purchasing goods at lower prices. Yet concerns remain about the workers in the United States who lose their jobs to workers overseas. Increased competition from international companies, fluctuations in the value of the U.S. dollar, security and patent protection concerns, and unstable political climates in foreign countries are additional risks that globalization has created for U.S. companies.

Benefits and risks aside, one thing is for sure: globalization is here to stay. In order to stay competitive in the global market, companies must work to enhance quality and develop and implement innovative strategies for the long term. The increasingly global nature of business increases the demand for workers who can communicate with international business partners, have up-to-date technological talents, can demonstrate excellent communication and creative problem-solving skills, and possess leadership skills.

Technological Changes

Why does the pace of technological change present challenges to businesses today? Over the past 20 years, advancements in information technology (IT) have been revolutionary. In today's business world, it's a necessity to stay on the cutting edge of technology in order to remain competitive. No matter the business, technology can be used to keep a company flexible, organized, and well connected—either with customers or employees. There is no question that keeping up with the pace of technology is an expensive and time-consuming operation. The rapid pace of technological innovation means that computers are outdated after three years and obsolete after five.[14] Add on to that the cost of applicable software, training, and infrastructure, and it is no wonder that IT is often the single largest expense in many companies.[15] But cost isn't the only challenge to consider. In the same way that robotics completely revolutionized the automotive industry, advancements in computer and telecommunication technology are completely changing the foundation and focus of how many businesses are run.

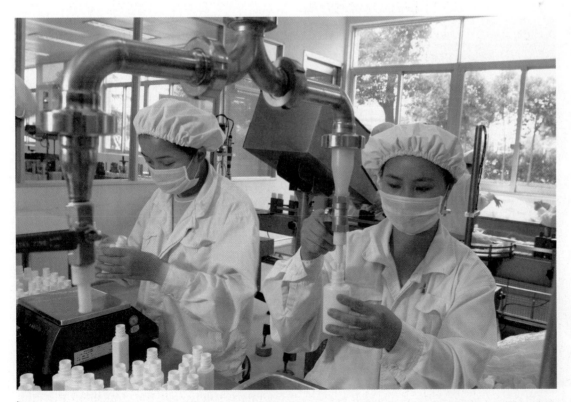

➤ Globalization makes it possible for German company Nivea to manufacture some of its products in Shanghai. These products later turn up on store shelves in the United States and other countries around the world.

" Today's CIOs [chief information officers] are being asked to transform companies through information technology, a transformation that requires breaking old habits, learning new ways to do business and developing an unwavering focus on growing and preserving shareholder value. " [16]

—Jean-Claude Aube, Principal at professional services firm Deloitte

What benefits does technology provide to business?

Technology, when used and implemented effectively, can help streamline businesses, cut costs, and increase productivity, security, transparency, as well as communications with customers. Giving employees what they need to get their work done more efficiently and effectively is the simplest way to increase productivity. If employees can get more work done in a shorter amount of time, productivity goes up. When employees are more productive, they are more valuable. This, in turn, makes the whole company more valuable. But these technological benefits aren't limited to just helping employees work more efficiently and effectively; they help streamline the internal operations of the business so the business can be more effective, efficient, and productive.

➤ Technology makes it possible to work from virtually anywhere. Is that a good thing?

Thirty years ago, businesses were often centrally located with all employees in one building. Today, this is less common. Technology is making it possible for employees to **telecommute**, or work from home or another location away from the office. The "virtual global workforce," or telecommuters who work on a global scale, expands the pool of potential employees, so that the right employee can be found for the job no matter where he or she works.[17] Teleconferencing is keeping CEOs and other corporate representatives from having to travel constantly for meetings. It is also allowing companies to communicate easily, no matter the distance. Both of these advancements are saving money on what used to be necessary expenses. With less travel, there is less money spent on plane tickets, hotel rooms, and food, and with more employees telecommuting, many businesses can operate out of smaller offices, which are cheaper and easier to manage.

What role does the Internet play in technological growth?

If IT is the tool that is changing the function of business, the Internet is the tool that is changing the scope. Although IT by itself would be extremely influential for the business world, the Internet makes it truly revolutionary. In 1995 the Internet was just starting to proliferate. Even though it had been commercially available for years at that point, the Internet had only recently become viable after the advent of the World Wide Web a few years before. Many people were intimidated by this new technology, and there weren't high hopes for companies that operated solely on the Internet. But this changed in 1995 when both eBay.com and

Amazon.com launched. These companies showed that such an endeavor was not only possible, but also potentially lucrative. Their high-profile success paved the way for the general acceptance of public e-commerce.[18] We'll discuss business technology in more detail in Chapter 10.

E-commerce

E-commerce primarily consists of two different kinds of business: *business-to-consumer (B2C)* and *business-to-business (B2B)*. B2C interactions are the ones you're probably most familiar with, such as buying books at Amazon or songs or movies from iTunes. Business-to-business (B2B) involves the sale of goods and services, such as personalized or proprietary software, from one business to another.[19] Although both are fairly similar in many ways, the ways in which they differ are significant. B2B e-commerce often involves large transactions to few customers, customized products and pricing, and numerous managers from both businesses making sure that the transaction is beneficial to both parties. This process is obviously more involved than typical B2C transactions, such as downloading a new ringtone for your cell phone or bidding on an item listed on eBay.

Every year, e-commerce becomes a more significant element of the overall economy. E-commerce has been growing rapidly since the new millennium, forcing many businesses to either adapt or be left in the dust. As ▼ **Figure 1.2** shows, by the end of 2007, online sales accounted for 3.5 percent of total retail sales.[20] This is up from just 0.6 percent of total retail sales at the end of 1999. So far this trend shows no sign of stopping. As it becomes easier for consumers to find even the most obscure items at competitive prices, e-commerce will continue to be a driving force in our economy. In April 2008, retail sales were stagnant or achieving minimal growth for months on end. E-commerce, on the other hand, continued to grow. By the end of 2007, e-commerce sales had grown 18 percent against total retail growth of 4.7 percent.[21]

Although this is an impressive amount of growth over a very short period of time, it is important to note that the commercialization of the Internet has only been around for a little over a decade. The Internet, as a medium for sales, has yet to

▼ **Figure 1.2**
E-Commerce Sales,
1999–2007

Estimated Quarterly U.S. Retail E-Commerce Sales as a Percent of Total Quarterly Retail Sales: 4th Quarter 1999–4th Quarter 2007

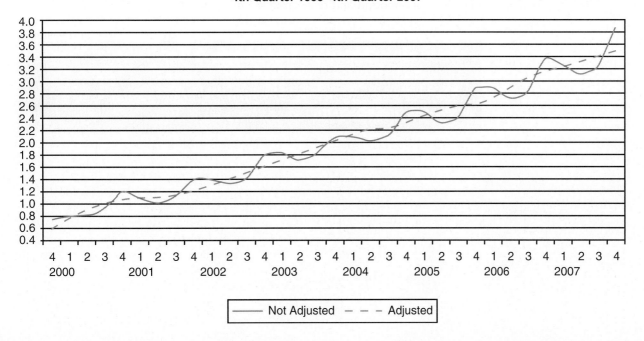

reach its full potential.[22] As the Internet and its influence continue to grow, so will its economic importance and necessity for businesses. This growth will also affect the dangers and concerns that are associated with such prevalence.

Online Security

The widespread access to information that the Internet affords affects business in a variety of ways. Personal information such as Social Security numbers, credit card numbers, addresses, and passwords are all accessible online. This sensitive information, even when it is secured, can be vulnerable to hackers. Since businesses are the ones who often store this and other types of personal information, the responsibility is on them to take measures to protect consumers' online privacy. It's no coincidence that as the number of people and businesses who trade and store personal information online rises, so does the number of people who are victims of identity theft—the illegal gain and use of personal information. A 2005 study estimated that identity theft costs U.S. businesses and their customers up to $56.6 billion annually.[23]

Privacy is another important issue for businesses. E-mails, internal documents, and chat transcripts all contain private information that is not intended for public viewing. Nevertheless, many of these documents can be accessed online, due to the fact that online storage has become a convenient alternative to hard drives. Web e-mail and Web-based documents are also becoming more common. Even gaining access to your desktop at work or at home from a remote location is a simple process that is becoming more popular. And with all of this universal access, it's increasingly difficult to ensure that information remains private. Web-based storage and services offer many benefits to business. Yet privacy and security concerns cannot be overlooked. Over time, technology will continue to introduce challenges.

Review the story about Leroy Washington at the beginning of this section. When competition from a national franchise threatened his business, Leroy confronted the challenge head-on. To capitalize on the diversity of the area—particularly the sizable populations of both Latinos and seniors—Leroy diversified his menu. His strategy was a success. The Cuban pressed sandwiches became a local favorite. Moreover, the deli was soon packed every day from 3:30 to 5:30 PM, when the "early bird special" fare—consisting of sandwiches, soups, and salads at reasonable prices—was offered. As Leroy Washington demonstrated, challenges and opportunities abound and overlap in the business world.

▼ You have just read **Objective 3**

Want a review? Check out the Study Plan section @
www.my*biz*lab.com.

Types of **Businesses** pp. 15-18

➤ What's the difference between a small business and a large corporation? What about everything in between? A small business has different goals and challenges than a large company. Small businesses often provide limited goods or services to a small population, like a local dry cleaner. A large multinational corporation, such as Procter & Gamble, supplies a wide range of goods or services to many countries. A local or regional business will have very different needs and concerns. In this section, we'll look at the different types of businesses and what constitutes each.

In 1964, Grahame Wood opened a convenience store in Folsom, Pennsylvania. The business's focus was on providing fresh dairy products and produce, as well as a full-service delicatessen. This marked the beginning of the Wawa chain of convenience stores, which serve the mid-Atlantic region of the United States. The chain now consists of over 500 stores in five states.[24] Although Wawa is certainly successful, it's still a regional company that does not currently serve a national or international market. Regional businesses such as Wawa face unique challenges that don't affect larger businesses, especially involving access to adequate funding and insurance. Wawa continues to expand in the mid-Atlantic and may one day move into the category of a national business. Is that the best move for this regional chain? ➤

Local and Regional Businesses

What defines local or regional businesses? Take a walk around your town or city, and you'll see a variety of local and regional businesses. Used bookstores, bakeries, shoe repair shops, boutiques, restaurants, and specialty shops are often local businesses. A **local business** is usually one of a kind, and it relies on local consumers to generate business. A company is local if there is only one outlet that serves a limited surrounding area. A local catering company in Baltimore, for example, would have one kitchen and would cater events in Baltimore and the surrounding cities. Local companies generally have a small number of employees and are associated with the town or city in which they are located. **Regional businesses** serve a wider area although, like local companies, they do not serve a national or international market. Wawa is an example of a regional convenience store.

What special challenges do local and regional businesses face?

The most common challenge for local and regional businesses is managing money. Poor financial planning, as well as unfavorable economic conditions, can lead to bankruptcy. **Undercapitalization** occurs when a business owner cannot gain access to adequate funding. The business can no longer afford to produce goods or provide services, and it goes bankrupt. The owner must anticipate the cost of doing business, as well as estimate the revenue that the business will generate. To avoid going into debt, the owner should have enough projected revenue to cover expenses for the first year. So if the owner of a local catering company has $100,000 in expenses and he expects to generate $75,000 in the first year of business, then he should have at least $25,000 to fund the company. Even with adequate funding, there is always a chance that the current economy will not support the business. Many small businesses fail when the economy slows down because consumers are less likely to spend extra money.

Business owners also have to take taxes and insurance costs into consideration, such as a health insurance plan to cover employees. They also need liability insurance, which will protect the company in the event of stolen or damaged property or if an employee is injured on the job. If a local jewelry store is broken into and jewelry is stolen, liability insurance will cover the cost of the broken window and the stolen property. If the jewelry store is not insured, the business could go bankrupt if the owner can't afford to cover the loss and damages.

National Businesses

What defines national businesses in the United States? You could travel from New York to Los Angeles and you'd be able to find an Old Navy anywhere along the way. All Old Navy stores essentially look alike and carry similar merchandise, all within a similar price range. With companies such as this, the customer knows what to expect. A **national business** has several outlets through-out the country, but it does not serve an international market. It provides goods or

▶ Stores like Old Navy are considered national businesses in that they have several businesses throughout the United States but do not serve an international market.

services to virtually all U.S. residents, no matter where in the country they live. A car insurance company such as Allstate is another example of a national business. It has offices in 49 states and serves the entire country. Similarly, CVS Pharmacy has over 6,200 locations and can be found anywhere in the United States. National companies such as these have become standard symbols of U.S. business.

What special challenges do national companies face? Like local and regional companies, national companies also have to worry about their budget and managing their finances. But they have other concerns that local businesses don't have. Since laws vary from state to state, national companies have to be aware of state laws in every state where they do business. For example, each state has its own tax laws. In most states, retail businesses are required to apply for a state sales tax permit in order to collect sales tax from their customers. Every state imposes a corporate income tax, but the rate varies across states. And some states, such as New Jersey and Rhode Island, require businesses to pay for temporary disability insurance.[25] These laws can be difficult to keep up with and prevent companies from having standardized policies for operations.

Another challenge that national companies face is a longer, more complex supply chain. The **supply chain** is the process by which products, information, and money move between supplier and consumer (see ▼ **Figure 1.3**). The product flows from supplier to manufacturer to wholesaler to retailer to consumer. If the product is returned, it flows from the consumer back to the retailer. Information flow includes orders and delivery status, and financial flow includes manufacturing costs, payment, credit terms, and profit.

The bigger a business is, the longer and more complicated the supply chain becomes. Products, information, and finances must flow smoothly to all parts of the country in a timely manner. Products often get backed up in long supply chains, which can result in delayed shipments and late payments. If not managed properly, long supply chains can be inefficient because products and materials have to pass through more warehouses and sustain more shipments. A lack of communication among companies in the chain can cause mix-ups and delays, especially if there is a sudden change in the process. A national company must therefore rely on the cooperation of all representatives in each service area to keep the supply chain running smoothly.

Multinational (International) Businesses

What categorizes a company as multinational (or international)?
Companies such as McDonald's don't exist only in the United States. You can now find a McDonald's in more than 100 countries, all serving distinctly U.S. food. However, not every McDonald's is exactly the same. They have all been adapted to fit the culture of the country in which they're located. This is the nature of the multinational business. As we discussed earlier, multinational businesses make

▼ **Figure 1.3**
The Supply Chain

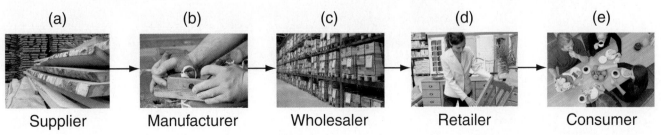

(a)	(b)	(c)	(d)	(e)
Supplier	Manufacturer	Wholesaler	Retailer	Consumer

and/or sell products in several countries. They are businesses that have expanded to provide goods or services to international consumers or serve only one country, but have suppliers or production facilities in other countries.

What special challenges do multinational companies face?

Every country has different corporate laws and business practices, and multinational companies must be familiar with the laws of the countries in which they operate. Laws concerning the import and export of goods vary greatly from one country to another. Things can get particularly complicated if a product is shipped to one country for assembly, then shipped to another for packaging, and then shipped to yet another country for distribution. Often, several countries are involved in the manufacture of one product, in which case the laws and regulations of all of those countries must be adhered to. It might be necessary for a U.S. company to work with the governments of foreign countries if there are strict importing restrictions or a multitude of taxes. Safety regulations, quality control, copyrights, and patent rights are just some of the laws that multinational corporations have to keep in mind when doing business in foreign countries.

Cultural differences have as much impact as legal differences on international business. Some of these issues, which we'll discuss further in Chapter 4, include the following:

- Countries may have different business hours or workweek schedules. For example, in Spain, workers tend to take lunch from 1:30 to 3:30 PM.
- Values and customs relating to business etiquette may vary. For example, timeliness is valued in Germany, but less important in Italy.
- Violating local taboos can be a concern, such as the preference for group harmony in many Asian countries.
- Multinational companies may have difficulty determining wages for foreign workers and pricing for international markets because the standard of living in industrialized nations is so different from that of developing countries.
- The language barrier presents a challenge to businesses that are trying to establish themselves in foreign countries. This is especially a problem for U.S. businesses, as only nine percent of U.S. citizens are fluent in a foreign language.[26]

Multinational companies also have to contend with many important economic differences among countries, such as the different levels of economic development, interest rates, and inflation rates that make international business more complicated than purely domestic business.

The move from being a regional business to a national, or even multinational, business is an exciting one, but it also brings a new set of challenges. While Wawa, profiled at the beginning of this section, currently deals with those issues that impact a regional chain, expanding the brand to a more national presence would bring different problems that would have to be addressed, which is why businesses must proceed carefully when making such decisions.

▼ You have just read **Objective 4**

Want to learn more? Check out the Study Plan section @
www.mybizlab.com.

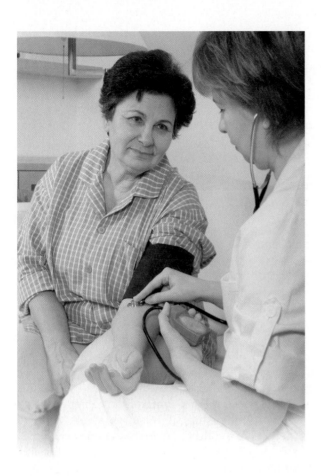

Types of Business Ownership pp. 19-21

Every company, no matter how large or small, begins with an idea. When this idea turns into a business, it can take one of several different ownership structures, each with its own advantages and disadvantages. The most common types are sole proprietorship, partnership, and corporation. Let's take a brief look at these types of business formats as well as limited liability companies (see ▼ **Table 1.1**). We'll review each of them in more detail in Chapter 6.

Estelle Peterson runs a private duty nursing business out of her home. She is the sole proprietor of this business, which gives her a great deal of freedom in deciding how her business should be run. While Estelle has been moderately successful in her business for several years, she has recently experienced a series of setbacks. This is a result of several lawsuits that have been filed against her company, due to the illegal conduct of two of the nurses on her staff. As sole proprietor of the business, Estelle is legally liable for the actions of her employees. She is struggling to pay off her growing legal debts, and creditors are calling her with threats of seizing some of her assets. How could Estelle have avoided these problems? ➤

Sole Proprietorship

A **sole proprietorship** is a business that is owned by one person. A sole proprietorship does not need to register with the state and it is not legally separated from the owner. This means the company's debts are the responsibility of the owner, and the owner pays personal income tax on his or her profits rather than corporate taxes. A sole proprietorship is simpler to operate and is under less government regulation than other businesses, but there is also more risk involved. If the company is sued, the owner is liable. If the company owes a debt that the business can't afford to pay, the creditors can legally collect personal assets, such as funds from the owner's retirement accounts, property, or cars. A sole proprietorship is not protected by *limited liability*, which would require owners to only be responsible for losses up to the amount they invested. Limited liability safeguards personal assets from being seized as payment for debts or claims.

▼ **Table 1.1**

Comparisons of Business Ownership Forms			
	Sole Proprietorship	**Partnership**	**Corporation**	**Limited Liability Company**
Business Documentation	None	Written or oral agreement	Articles of incorporation	Articles of organization
Risk	Unlimited liability	Unlimited liability	Limited liability	Limited liability
Taxes	Taxed as personal income	Taxed as personal income	Separate filing, double taxed	Taxed as personal income (can vary)
Management	Owner manages all business	Partners share management	Managed by owners and shareholders	Managed by members

Partnership

A business owned by two or more people that is not registered with the state as a corporation or a limited liability company (LLC) is a **partnership**. The owners of a partnership pay tax on their portion of the business income instead of paying corporate taxes. Each owner is also responsible for paying off any debts or lawsuits. Therefore, similar to a sole proprietorship, if business assets are not sufficient to meet business debts, debtors can collect personal assets from all business owners. However, unlike a sole proprietorship, in a partnership, profits and liability are shared between two or more people.

There are two types of partnerships: general and limited. A **general partnership** is simpler and less expensive to establish and pools the talent of partners, but it carries more risk for all partners because they are all financially liable and are not protected by limited liability. In a general partnership, every partner participates in the daily management tasks of the business and they all have some degree of control over the decisions that are made. In a **limited partnership**, there is at least one partner who controls business operations and is personally liable. The other partners are limited partners, who don't have much, if any, control over management decisions. They contribute capital to the business and are protected by limited liability.

◎ On Target Nantucket Nectars: Tom and Tom Partnership

Tom First and Tom Scott were college buddies at Brown University who did not want to climb the traditional corporate ladder. After graduation, the friends moved to Nantucket, Massachusetts, and started a floating convenience store called Allserve. Based from Tom and Tom's red boat in Nantucket Harbor, the company provided delivery service of almost any item, from newspapers to laundry, to neighboring boats. While Allserve proved to be a modest success, the pair soon had another idea. They decided to sell their own natural juice blend, and soon Nantucket Nectars was born. Popularity of the juice spread quickly in Nantucket, and Allserve purchased a distribution company to expand the reach of its products. While many national chains are now carrying their products, Tom and Tom maintained their local roots by starting the Juice Guys Juice Bar in Nantucket.[27] This partnership is an example of how a successful business can be started by two eager and driven people. Tom and Tom have come a long way since their days as floating delivery boys in Nantucket Harbor, and they are now running a nationally recognized corporation.

Corporation

A **corporation** is a business that is a legal entity separate from the owner or owners. The business owners have limited liability, so they are not personally responsible for debts incurred by the company. If someone sues Microsoft, for example, the plaintiff can collect money from the corporation but cannot take Bill Gates's car, nor any personal property or money from any shareholders. Since corporations have limited liability, shareholders' personal assets are protected.

Although incorporating a business protects business owners from personal bankruptcy, it can sometimes make running a business more complicated. First, corporations must keep thorough financial records that detail every transaction the business makes. Second, corporations might experience conflict between management and stockholders. Third, corporations must report income generated by the business in separate corporate tax returns. If some of the profits are paid to owners (stockholders), then that income to them is taxed again as personal income. So, corporate profits can be taxed twice. It is up to the business owners to decide whether the advantages of incorporating a business are worth the extra work.

Limited Liability Company

Another business format that is relatively new is called a **limited liability company (LLC)**, which blends characteristics of both corporations and sole proprietorships and/or partnerships. Like corporations, LLCs are companies in which the owners have limited personal liability for the debts and actions of the company. They require articles of organization and are separate legal entities. However, LLCs provide the advantage of avoiding double taxation often associated with corporations and the tax forms are much simpler. LLCs are also simpler to maintain than corporations because they are subject to fewer government regulations and reporting requirements. Owners of an LLC are called *members*. In most states, LLCs may be "single member," or owned by one person. LLCs are a popular choice for many new businesses due to the safety, flexibility, and tax benefits they provide.[28]

The Players in Business Ownership

Who can be affected by a company's type of business ownership? A **stakeholder** is someone who is affected by a company's actions or who has an interest in what the company does. Corporate stakeholders include employees, shareholders, investors, suppliers, and society at large. Sole proprietorships usually have fewer stakeholders than large corporations. Partnerships, LLCs, and corporations may have many stakeholders, some who are only remotely affected by the business. Adidas, for example, is an international corporation whose stakeholders include their employees, customers, and foreign laborers, among others. The ownership and the activities of the Adidas corporation affect all of these people.

Review Estelle's story at the beginning of this section. Because Estelle is the sole proprietor of her nursing business, she is financially and legally responsible for all aspects of the business. This means creditors have a right to seize her personal possessions, and she must pay off her business debts or risk damage to her personal credit. Looking back, Estelle wishes she had chosen an LLC as the format for her business. An LLC would have provided her flexibility in managing her business, as well as ease in tax filing. Yet Estelle would not be personally liable for her business's debts.

▼ You have just read **Objective 5**

Want to test your skills? Check out the Study Plan section @ **www.mybizlab.com.**

Taking Business Personally pp. 22-23

Taylor Evans is a very organized and orderly person. He prides himself on being efficient and meticulous with his school-work, finances, and social life. His friends joke with him about this and tell him that he runs his life like a business. But Taylor doesn't take offense; why shouldn't he run his life like a business? His life is just as complicated and complex. He has revenue, expenses, and assets. He participates in commerce. Taylor even likes to keep up with the latest technology to make sure he runs his life most efficiently. Taylor is always looking for cost-effective ways to operate his life, and any profits (or money he has left over after paying his bills) are set aside for future purchases. In many ways, his life *is* a business. How is your life like a business?

Each of you probably has a different level of familiarity with the basics of business. Some of you may have witnessed the operations of a business first hand while working at a job. For others, your business knowledge may be limited to what you've read or seen on TV. Regardless of your prior work experience, you all have experience running a business, and that business is your life. Similar to a small company, your life requires careful planning, precise record keeping, and openness to change. To help you understand some of the business concepts discussed in this book, let's look at how you run your "business."

Are you a sole proprietorship or a partnership? If you're a single individual, not married, then you work as a sole proprietorship. You're responsible and liable for all of your debts and actions. If you're married, then you work as a partnership. Both you and your partner are responsible for each other's debts and actions.

How do you receive funding? Regardless of whether you have a job, you're receiving money from somewhere. It could be from work, a family member, a student loan, or your own savings. Although these funds are not essential to your existence, they are needed to secure the necessities of life. Similarly, all businesses need funds to operate. Ideally, a business would produce revenue right away; however, some businesses may operate on funds received from a bank loan, investors, or their own capital.

What are your expenses? Rent, clothing, food, tuition—these are expenses whether they are paid for with cash, credit, or a loan. Ultimately, you will want to generate enough revenue, or income, to cover your expenses and have some left over. However, the lives of some students operate a bit like a start-up business; you may have to pay for expenses with loans until you have enough experience to generate a profit.

How does the social environment affect your life? The social environment probably presents similar opportunities and challenges to you as it does to businesses. How do you deal with these opportunities and challenges? Are you open to learn from people who are different from you? Do you embrace diversity?

How do you relate to people from an older generation? What about the green movement? Are you finding ways to make your lifestyle more eco-friendly? It is important to address these issues in order to live a more harmonious life and prepare yourself for the modern work environment.

How does globalization affect your life?
Not only is the world getting smaller for businesses, the world is getting smaller for you. Your favorite music group may be a band from Germany. You might like to chat online about movies with a friend from Japan. Just as businesses now have the opportunity to work with other firms from all over the world, you have the ability to make friends or connections on any continent.

How do you keep up with new technology?
Whether or not you consider yourself to be tech-savvy, chances are you still use some sort of technology to run your life. Perhaps you use online banking, or buy things over the Internet. Similar to a business, if you don't keep up with new technology, you may find yourself in trouble.

➤ Most e-commerce requires credit cards to complete transactions.

What sort of e-commerce do you use?
As we learned in this chapter, e-commerce is becoming a popular form of purchasing goods. What sort of things do you buy online? Many students have found that buying textbooks online is much cheaper than at the school bookstore. Perhaps you even sell things over the Internet. Posting old clothing or other unwanted items on eBay might be your way of making a few extra dollars or more room in your closet.

How do you keep your "business" secure?
While businesses work to keep personal information secure, so should the customer. You can help keep your information secure by changing your online passwords on a regular basis, making sure your wireless connections are secure, switching to paperless mail, or removing personal information such as phone numbers or addresses from your Facebook or MySpace page. Keeping your personal information secure can help you avoid identity theft or other dangerous blows to your financial health.

What types of goals do you have?
The goals of a business typically revolve around reaching financial success. You too might have certain financial goals you would like to achieve in your life. To reach these goals, you'll need to make informed decisions about how you spend and save your money. Mini Chapter 2 can help you manage your personal finances and plan for the future.

So you may see, Taylor isn't so crazy after all. Many of the same concepts and strategies used to run a business can be used to monitor your day-to-day activities. As you learn new business concepts in upcoming chapters, you may find them easier to understand by applying them to your own life. However, not everything is parallel. The business world has its own unique modes and methods that may not always connect to your life, and vice versa. Good luck with the course!

▼ You have just read **Objective 6**

Want to quiz yourself? Check out the Study Plan section @ **www.my*biz*lab.com.**

1. What are profits, and how do businesses and nonprofit organizations compare? (pp. 3-5)

- **Profits** (p. 3) are earned when a company's **revenue** (p. 3) exceeds its **expenses** (p. 3).

- A **business** (p. 3) is an entity that offers goods and services to its customers in order to earn a profit. A **nonprofit organization** (p. 4) is a business that does not pursue profits, but instead seeks to service its community through social, educational, or political means.

2. What is the difference between a good and a service, and what are the factors of production? (pp. 4-5)

- **Goods** (p. 4) are the physical products offered by a business. **Services** (p. 4) are intangible products such as a haircut, health care, or car insurance.

- The **factors of production** (p. 5) are the resources used to create goods and services. These five factors of production include **labor** (p. 5), **natural resources** (p. 5), **capital** (p. 5), **entrepreneurs** (p. 5), and **technology** (p. 5).

3. How do competition, the social environment, globalization, and technological growth challenge and provide opportunities to business owners? (pp. 6-14)

- **Competition** (p. 6) arises when two or more businesses contend to attract customers and gain an advantage over one another. Competition forces companies to improve their product offerings, lower their prices, aggressively promote their brand, and focus on customer satisfaction.

- **Social environment** (p. 8) encompasses demographic factors such as race, ethnicity, gender, age, income distribution, sexual orientation, and other characteristics. An aging population, increasing diversity, and the green movement both challenge and pose opportunities to business owners.

- **Globalization** (p. 10) involves the merging of economies around the world as technology, goods and services, labor, and capital move back and forth across international borders. Although globalization provides profitable opportunities, such as increased markets and offshoring, it also leads to greater competition for U.S. businesses and workers.

- Technology items and services such as smartphones, computer software, and digital broadcasting make businesses more efficient and productive. E-commerce, document management, workflow technologies, and identification management software all provide these opportunities. At the same time, keeping up with the pace of technology is an expensive and time-consuming operation for many businesses.

4. What are four types of businesses? (pp. 15-18)

- A **local business** (p. 16) is usually unique and relies on local consumers to generate business.

- **Regional businesses** (p. 16) are companies that serve a wider area than local businesses, but do not serve national or international markets.

- A **national business** (p. 16) has several outlets throughout the country, but it does not serve an international market. It provides goods or services to all U.S. residents, no matter where in the country they live.

- **Multinational enterprises** (p. 10) (also known as multinational companies or corporations, multinational businesses, or international businesses)—companies that have operations in more than one country—are among the leaders of a movement called globalization.

5. How do sole proprietorships, partnerships, corporations, and limited liability companies (LLCs) differ from one another as forms of business? (pp. 19-21)

- A **sole proprietorship** (p. 19) is a business that is owned by one person; it is not registered with the state, and it is not legally separated from the owner.

- A **partnership** (p. 20) is a business owned by two or more people that is not registered with the state as a corporation or a limited liability company (LLC).

  - In a **general partnership** (p. 20), every partner participates in the daily management tasks of the business and each has some degree of control over the decisions that are made.

  - In a **limited partnership** (p. 20), there is at least one partner who controls business operations and is personally liable.

- A **corporation** (p. 20) is a business that is a legal entity separate from the owner or owners.

- **Limited liability companies (LLCs)** (p. 21) are companies in which the owners have limited personal liability for debts and actions of the company, but also provide owners with tax advantages and management flexibility inherent in sole proprietorship and partnerships.

6. How do life skills translate to the business environment? (pp. 22-23)

- You are either a **sole proprietorship** or a **partnership** (p. 22).

- You have funds, **expenses**, and **profits** (p. 22).

- You are affected by **globalization** and **technology** (p. 23).

- You have concerns with security.

For an audio file of the Objectives and Chapter Summary, see the Student Resources section @ www.my*biz*lab.com.

Key Terms

businesses (p. 3)

competition (p. 6)

corporation (p. 20)

e-commerce (p. 13)

entrepreneur (p. 5)

expenses (p. 3)

factors of production (p. 5)

financial capital (p. 5)

general partnership (p. 20)

globalization (p. 10)

goods (p. 4)

green economy (p. 9)

labor (p. 5)

limited partnership (p. 20)

limited liability company (LLC) (p. 21)

local business (p. 16)

multinational enterprise (p. 10)

national business (p. 16)

natural resources (p. 5)

nonprofit organization (p. 4)

offshoring (p. 10)

partnership (p. 20)

profit (p. 3)

real capital (p. 5)

regional business (p. 16)

revenue (p. 3)

service (p. 4)

social environment (p. 8)

sole proprietorship (p. 19)

stakeholder (p. 21)

supply chain (p. 17)

technology (p. 5)

telecommuting (p. 12)

undercapitalization (p. 16)

Multiple Choice   Correct answers can be found on page 503.

1. **Which of the following are all factors of production?**

   a. Labor, natural resources, capital, entrepreneurs, and technology

   b. Labor, capital, entrepreneurs, and motivation

   c. Natural resources, entrepreneurs, profits, and creativity

   d. Labor, profits, natural resources, technology, and motivation

2. **Competition forces companies to do all of the following, EXCEPT**

   a. improve their products.

   b. lower prices.

   c. earn higher profits.

   d. promote their brand aggressively.

3. **Which of the following is a current sociocultural trend?**

   a. A decrease in the overall U.S. population

   b. An increase in the population of Americans aged 30–45

   c. A decrease in the U.S. minority population

   d. An increase in the population of Americans aged 65 and over

4. **Telecommuting makes it possible for**

   a. companies to better manage their supply chains.

   b. employees to find higher-paying jobs.

   c. companies to keep all information secure.

   d. employees to work from home or another location away from the office.

5. **If a firm decides to shift the production of goods or services to an overseas company, this firm is**

   a. diversifying.

   b. offshoring.

   c. telecommuting.

   d. forming a partnership.

6. **Which of the following is NOT a risk of globalization for U.S. businesses?**

   a. An increase of jobs for those who are well trained and educated

   b. The political climate of foreign countries

   c. The rise and decline of the U.S. dollar

   d. Breaches in security and patent protection

7. **E-commerce**

   a. has struggled since its inception in the early 1990s.

   b. becomes a more significant element of the overall economy every year.

   c. does not affect most consumers.

   d. is dominated by sole proprietorships.

8. **To avoid debt, a new business owner should have enough projected revenue to cover expenses for the first**

   a. six months.

   b. year.

   c. two years.

   d. five years.

9. **Which of the following is NOT a challenge facing national companies?**

   a. Tax laws

   b. A complex supply chain

   c. International employment laws

   d. Worker's compensation

10. **What are the four most common types of business formats?**

    a. Sole proprietorship, partnership, corporation, limited liability company

    b. Limited partnership, stakeholder, shareholder, corporation

    c. Sole proprietorship, general partnership, stakeholder, multinational company

    d. Limited liability company, partnership, corporation, regional company

Self-Test

1. Businesses are entities that offer goods and services in order to earn a profit.
   ☐ **True** or ☐ **False**

2. A profit is earned when a company's revenue is equal to its expenses.
   ☐ **True** or ☐ **False**

3. The supply chain is the process by which products, information, and money move between supplier and consumer.
   ☐ **True** or ☐ **False**

4. Safety regulations, quality control, copyrights, and patent rights are some of the laws that multinational corporations must keep in mind when doing business in foreign countries.
   ☐ **True** or ☐ **False**

5. A corporation is a business that is a legal entity that defines the relationship between two or more business partners.
   ☐ **True** or ☐ **False**

Critical Thinking Questions

1. Consider all of the factors of production: labor, natural resources, capital, entrepreneurs, and technology. Is each of these resources a vital part of the school you attend or the company for which you work? Which factors do you believe are most important to the goods and services provided by your organization?

2. It is not unusual to encounter businesses that have streamlined their activities to accommodate ecological factors. The text uses a change in auto sales as an example of how businesses are directly affected by the green movement. Can you think of other examples of businesses that might be forced to alter their business decisions based on ecological factors? How might these decisions affect their profits?

3. Most business owners agree that keeping up with the pace of technological change is a challenging task. Imagine you are the owner of a new business and must decide what technology would best suit your needs. From what types of technology would this business benefit? Consider the factors of production, organization, and communication in your decision.

4. Considering the rapid increase in e-commerce, it is likely that you have purchased or sold some sort of product online. If you haven't, perhaps you have at least browsed the Web pages of eBay or your favorite clothing store. Can you list a few companies or organizations that do not offer their products or services online? How does their status and growth compare with similar companies who do offer goods and services online?

5. Review the various business formats: sole proprietorship, partnership, corporation, and limited liability company. What do you think are some of the major benefits and challenges of each format? If you were to start a business, what kind of business would it be, and what type of business organization would best suit it and why?

Team Time

The Competitive Edge

You now know that competition arises when two or more businesses contend to attract consumers and gain an advantage over one another. Divide into three groups: Company A, Company B, and Consumers. *Company A and B:* collectively decide what type of business you want to represent; for example, sports apparel companies, beauty salons, or pet care agencies. Then choose a product or service applicable to that type of business. (Both groups should choose the same type of business and product or service.)

Process

Step 1. *Companies A and B:* Decide how you will present your product to your customers. Focus on the following factors:

→ **packaging/presentation**

→ **price/budget**

→ **quality**

Consumers: Compile a list of what is important to you when choosing this product or service.

Step 2. *Companies A and B:* Provide a brief presentation to your competition and consumers. *Consumers:* Provide in-depth feedback to both companies as to how they could improve; consider your initial list.

Step 3. *Companies A and B:* Use the consumer feedback to alter your product or service to gain advantage over your competition. *Consumers:* Discuss how the two companies compared to real-life companies offering similar products or services. Would you consider purchasing from either of these two companies? Why or why not?

Step 4. *Companies A and B:* Present your product again. Explain why your product or service surpasses that of your competition.

Step 5. *Consumers:* Discuss the changes made by both companies and consider how they accommodated your needs. Did each company effectively incorporate your feedback into its revised presentation? Choose one company that you think gained the competitive advantage.

Step 6. *Entire Class:* Openly discuss the factors real companies must face in competition. Were these factors considered in the challenge?

Ethics and Corporate Social Responsibility

Cultural Awareness: An Unwritten Law

There are many challenges facing multinational companies. Complete the following exercise to experience one challenge.

Process

Step 1. Divide into six groups, each representing one of the following countries: China, France, Germany, Japan, Mexico, and the United States. Examine the cultural practices, customs, and values of the country you will represent. This may be done in class if you have Internet access, or as homework.

Step 2. Each group should pair together with a second group as follows: United States with Japan, Mexico with Germany, and China with France.

Step 3. Each group should produce one scenario of a business transaction that would be affected by cultural differences found in your research. Fabricate specific companies, characters, interactions, and resolutions.

Step 4. Answer these questions and discuss with the class:

→ **What were some challenges encountered in your business scenario and how did you overcome them?**

→ **Why is it important for multinational companies to research a foreign country with which they intend to conduct business?**

Web Exercises

1. **Are You Savvy to Society?**
   Imagine you are starting a new business. To what demographic area would you market? Think about the following factors: race, ethnicity, gender, age, income, and sexual orientation.

   Visit www.census.gov to locate reports on the demographic area you are interested in. Do you believe your business can thrive in this area? If not, what area would be conducive to your future customers?

2. **Keep Your Identity!**
   Imagine owning a business and learning that the personal information of your customers has been stolen. What legal trouble would you be in? What could you have done to prevent it? Visit www.idtheft.gov to investigate the answers to these questions.

3. **Ever-Changing E-Trends**
   Did you know there are Web sites dedicated to keeping businesses and consumers up-to-date on the latest e-commerce news and trends? Check out www.ecommercetimes.com and find a recent e-commerce trend, and write a brief summary.

4. **Budget Planning at Your Fingertips**
   What tools are available to help a business budget its finances? Type "business budget plans" into any search engine. Using examples online, write a brief budget plan for a start-up company of your choice.

5. **Comparing Companies**
   Choose two of the ten national companies featured in the Top Ten list on p. 18. Go to www.business.gov to research the laws applicable in the states in which these companies are based. How do the worker's compensation and tax laws differ for each company? Which company do you think was more difficult to establish based on state laws?

Web Case

To access the Chapter 1 Web case and exercise, see the End of Chapter Assignments section @ www.my*biz*lab.com.

Video Case

To access the Chapter 1 Video case and exercise, see the End of Chapter Assignments section @ www.my*biz*lab.

chapter 2

Economics and Banking

p. 42
Degrees of Competition
▼ Objective 3

Once a player owns all the property of the same color in this famous board game, he or she has a monopoly and controls all that happens on that property. While that's the goal of the board game, large monopolies are rarely allowed in the United States. Microsoft was investigated by the U.S. Department of Justice for illegally holding a monopoly. What is a monopoly? Why are there laws against it? And how does it differ from an oligopoly, monopolistic competition, and perfect competition?

p. 31
Economics Basics
▼ Objective 1

Why does water cost less than diamonds? It's a matter of supply and demand—a problem that Bryan Weirmoyer faces as a sales executive for a real estate development company.

p. 45
Economic Indicators
▼ Objective 4

Greg Johnson is managing the lumber inventory of a large lumber company. During years of booming housing development, ordering inventory has been simple because of the large numbers of new housing starts. These days he's not sure about his company's direction. Although new housing starts are still high in his immediate area, he's not sure if such high growth will continue. Are there measurements of the economy that he can use to help him make his decision?

p. 35
Determining Price: Supply and Demand
▼ Objective 2

For many business owners, weathering shifts in supply and demand is like riding a roller coaster. The levels of supply and demand for a given good or service shift constantly, each influenced by a variety of factors. Consider, for example, the effect of a faster oven on a baker's ability to supply bread, or the impact of a low-carb diet craze on the demand for the baker's muffins. From this dynamic economic landscape, a price for goods and services is determined.

p. 50
Government and the Economy
▼ Objectives 5 & 6

Joaquin and Jacinta are looking to buy their first home. What information do they need to make sure they stay within their budget? Can government actions have an impact on what Joaquin and Jacinta do?

Economics Basics pp. 31-34

Bryan's dilemma of diminishing sales is due to the economic concept of supply and demand. Have you ever wondered why water, a basic commodity that is critical to life, is priced so low, and diamonds, which aren't necessities, are expensive? It might seem that utility would have a large impact on price in that the more useful an item is, such as water, the greater its price. Instead, this paradoxical situation illustrates a different relationship, which is the fundamental concept of economics—supply and demand. Supply and demand determine how goods are priced and exchanged. The exchange of products and services between people, companies, and even countries is the very root of economics. In this chapter, we'll take a look at the laws of supply and demand, discuss economic indicators, and look at how the government affects the economy. First, let's examine some economics basics.

It was the third phone call this week, and Bryan Weirmoyer knew it wouldn't be the last. Bryan is the sales executive of a residential and commercial real estate developer in eastern Pennsylvania. As a sales executive, Bryan sells properties to clients for commission. Last year, he enjoyed taking phone calls that generally ended by closing contracts for the construction of new homes. But now, the phone doesn't ring much, and when it does, it's generally a call to cancel contracts Bryan had worked so hard to negotiate. Why were there so many sales last year and so few this year?

Economics Defined

So what is economics? **Economics** is the study of how individuals and businesses make decisions to best satisfy wants, needs, and desires with limited resources. It is about businesses making **goods** (such as books, pizza, or computers) or supplying **services** (such as giving haircuts, painting a house, or installing a home entertainment network) that we want or need to buy.

Because businesses don't have enough tools, money, or products to provide *all* the books, pizza, or haircuts that we want, they must decide what and how much to make. Not everyone will be able to have what he or she wants because of the limited resources (such as money, space, or time) and supplies. Therefore, economists look at how resources are distributed in the marketplace and how equitably and efficiently those resources are disbursed.

There are two basic studies of economics: *microeconomics* and *macroeconomics*.

Microeconomics

Microeconomics is the study of how individual businesses, households, and consumers make decisions to allocate their limited resources in the exchange of goods and services. When Bryan Weirmoyer, the real estate sales executive from our opening story, tries to determine how a change in prices may help generate sales or analyzes the number of existing houses that are already for sale in the local market, he is using the microeconomic principles of supply and demand.

Macroeconomics

Macroeconomics, on the other hand, looks at the bigger picture. Macroeconomics is the study of the behavior of the overall economy. Economy-wide occurrences such as changes in unemployment, interest rates, inflation, and price levels are all part of the study of macroeconomics. Macroeconomists, for example, look at how a change in interest rates affects the demand for housing, or how a change in the housing market affects the overall economy. The government and individuals in a society also affect the manner in which resources are allocated and define the economic system in which goods and services are allocated.

Different Types of Economic Systems

What are the different types of economic systems? Economists have created several economic models to categorize the world's many economic systems. These economic models include:

- traditional economies
- planned (or controlled) economies
- market economies
- mixed economies

Traditional economies were found in earlier agrarian communities, which were primitive in nature and based on a strong social network. Very few traditional economies exist today. Most economies today represent some form of a mixed economic system or a market economic system. ▼ **Table 2.1** summarizes the features of the three most common basic economic models.

▼ **Table 2.1**

World Economic Models			
Type of Economy	**What to Produce**	**How to Produce**	**For Whom to Produce**
Planned (Controlled)	Government or other centralized group determines what to produce.	Government or other centralized group determines and controls the resources and means of production.	Government or other centralized group determines wages and sets prices. Resources and products are distributed to common group.
Market	Individuals and private firms make decisions based on consumer needs and wants.	Individuals and private firms determine the production methods. The focus is on efficiency and profitability.	Individual income ultimately controls purchasing decisions.
Mixed	Individuals determine what to produce with some level of government involvement.	Individuals and government control resources and determine production methods.	Government distributes some goods and services through selected social programs. Individual income determines purchasing decisions for other goods and services.

Planned Economic Systems

In a **planned economic system**, the government plays a greater role in determining the goods and services that are provided and how they are produced and distributed. Both communism and socialism are planned economic systems.

Communism **Communism** is an economic system in which a state's government makes all economic decisions and controls all the social services and many of the major resources required for production of goods and services. Karl Marx, the originator of communist principles in his book *The Communist Manifesto*, envisioned the workers themselves eventually taking over the government's responsibilities to provide the services. No communist country has achieved this level of Marx's vision. Existing communist states, including North Korea and Cuba, are failing economically. This is a result of the problems that have arisen with communist systems, such as shortages of goods and services. In fact, in the later years of the twentieth century, most former Soviet republic states and Eastern European countries turned from a communism-based economy to a market economy to combat these problems.

Socialism **Socialism** provides that the government owns or controls many basic businesses and services so that profits can be distributed evenly among the people. In socialist economic systems, governments traditionally run some of the social services such as education, health care, retirement, and unemployment as well as other necessary businesses such as utility companies (telephone, electric, water, sewer). The government charges high tax rates to pay for the services it provides. For example, compared with the highest marginal income tax rate charged in the United States in 2006 (about 40 percent), Finland, a country in which many social services are administered by the government, had a rate of close to 51 percent. Denmark's and the Netherlands' respective rates for that year were about 60 percent and 52 percent.[1] Although citizens of these countries pay higher tax rates, they benefit from social programs that tax proceeds are used to fund. For example, education at even the best universities in the Netherlands is free, and women receive one year of fully paid maternity leave.[2] And recent studies have indicated that the most satisfied people in the world are from Denmark.[3]

Although many feel government-controlled and -supplied social services provide a fair and equitable distribution of such services, a concern with *true* socialism is a diminishing motivation for workers. In a true socialist system, workers turn over their earnings and profits to the state rather than keep their own earnings, so the incentive to work hard is reduced. Therefore, it's difficult to find purely socialist economies. Many socialist and communist countries are beginning to change their economies into a free market economy through the practice of **privatization**—the conversion of government-owned production and services to privately owned, profit-seeking enterprises.

Market Economies

In a **market economy**, individuals are able to make their own economic decisions. For example, there may be several pizza parlors in your town, and each one may sell slices of pizza at different prices—no one is restricting the number of pizza parlors, nor is anyone controlling what price they can charge. Similarly, you are free to choose any pizza you'd like to buy. This freedom of choice for both the buyer and seller defines a free market economy.

Capitalism is the economic system that allows such freedom of choice and encourages private ownership of the resources required to make and provide the goods and services we enjoy. Capitalism has become a major influence in the Western world's economic system. In a capitalist economy, the production and pricing of goods and services are determined through the operation of a **market**—the mechanism by which buyers and sellers exchange goods and services.

Mixed Economies

Today, most economic systems are a **mixed economy**, which is a blend of market and planned economies. Most Western European countries, for example, operate with a mixed economy of privately owned businesses and government control of selected social programs, such as health care. Although the United States is closest to a capitalist economy, there is still some government intervention. One way to think about the various mixed economies and how they relate to either a market or demand economic system is to place them on a continuum, as shown in ▼ Figure 2.1.

Business and Economics

Why do business managers need to be concerned with economics? It's important for business managers and owners to understand the principles of economics because the very nature of business is to provide items or services for purchase in exchange for something, generally money. Businesses need to know how much of their products to produce or of services to offer, as well as how much to charge for these products and services. This is one dilemma Bryan Weirmoyer faces as the need for new housing begins to dwindle. His decisions affect other areas of the business, such as land acquisitions and staffing.

Additionally, business managers need to be aware of the potential impact that government decisions (such as changing interest rates) and the decisions of collective businesses (the general level of unemployment) can have on their individual business or industry. Bryan watches carefully as the decision to raise or lower interest rates is made, because he knows that the smallest change in interest rate will influence the homebuyer's attitude toward mortgages, affecting Bryan's market directly. So, understanding economics, how prices are determined, the relationship of supply and demand, and the involvement of government is instrumental to operating a successful business.

| Planned Economy | Cuba | Russia | India | United Kingdom | Japan | United States | Market Economy |

▼ **Figure 2.1**

Continuum of Economic Systems: Degree of Government Control[4]

▼ You have just read **Objective 1**

Think you got it? Check out the Study Plan section @ **www.mybizlab.com.**

Determining Price: Supply and Demand pp. 35-41

➤ In the days of bartering, when people traded goods or services without an exchange of money, the "price" of something was determined by the needs of each person in the bartering exchange and what they were willing to trade. For example, if you wanted milk and had no cow, but you did have chickens, you were willing to give up eggs for some milk. You would look for someone who wanted to trade his or her milk for your eggs. At the end of the trade, everyone was happy because you got the milk you needed and the other person got the eggs he or she needed.

However, there were problems with this exchange system. Bartering can be inefficient and inconsistent. What if the person who had the cow didn't need chickens, or what if the cow owner thought his milk was worth a chicken, but you thought it was only worth a dozen eggs? To offset some of the difficulties of bartering, the concept of currency, or money, was developed. **Currency**, a unit of exchange for the transfer of goods and services, provided a consistent standard, the value of which is based on an underlying commodity, such as gold.

In a system using currency, items such as milk, eggs, and chickens were assigned a price, or a value, based on how much the item was worth against the standard. Today, although we do have currency, ultimately the price for a product or service is determined by two fundamental concepts of economics: supply and demand, which we'll discuss in more detail later in the chapter.

Supply and demand is actually a very complicated process because many factors are involved, such as income levels and tastes, as well as the amount of competition in the market. However, if we ignore those factors for the moment (and economists do this all the time—it's called "all else held constant") and just examine the fundamentals, we find that the **market price** for a product or service is the price at which everyone who wants the

Imagine you're a baker and have just realized your dream of opening your own gourmet bakery. Are you ready to ride the roller coaster of supply and demand? Test your supply and demand savvy by taking the following **quiz**.

1. You purchase a turbocharged oven that bakes three times faster than a conventional oven. Your supply of fresh breads and rolls will go:

   a. up
   b. down

2. The price of flour skyrockets. Your supply of cakes and cookies will go:

   a. up
   b. down

3. A highly publicized scientific study claims that low-carb diets help people lose weight faster than any other type of diet. The demand for your jumbo muffins will go:

   a. up
   b. down

4. The construction of luxury condos nearby brings an influx of young, single, wealthy professionals to the area. The demand for your specialty scones will go:

   a. up
   b. down

Answers: 1. A; 2. B; 3. B; 4. A
If you got. . .
0-1 answers correct: Good try. You're not supply and demand savvy yet. Don't worry, because after reading this section, you will be.
2-3 answers correct: Nice effort. You're semi-savvy in the fundamentals of supply and demand. Read this section carefully to build on your knowledge base.
4 answers correct: Congratulations! You're supply and demand savvy. Read this section to learn even more. ➤

> Currency developed as a means to make the exchange of goods and services more consistent and equitable.

item can get it without anyone wanting more or without any of the item being left over. The need for an item is *demand*, and the availability of that item is *supply*.

The closest real-world example of determining a market price that is based on pure supply and demand is the auction process, like that found in eBay. In an auction process, bidders state the price they are willing to pay for a particular item. The price increases depending on the demand: the greater the demand, the higher the price the bidders are willing to pay. Supply also affects price: if similar or identical items are available for auction, the price is kept lower. When a unique item is auctioned, prices tend to be higher because demand is higher and supply is lower. Eventually, the winning bid establishes the market price.

Supply

What is supply? **Supply** refers to how much of a product or service is available for purchase at any given time. Supply is dependent on the resources that are required to produce the product or offer the service, such as land, labor, and capital (buildings and machinery), and the quantity of similar products that can easily be substituted for the product and that are competing for the consumer's attention. However, if all of these factors are ignored or held constant, then supply is directly affected by price.

Supply is derived from a producer's desire to maximize profits. The more money a business can get for its good or service, the more of its product it is willing to supply. In economic terms, the amount supplied will increase as the price increases; also, if the price is lower, less of the product is supplied. This is known as the **law of supply**.

Let's look at an example. If Eddie opens a coffee kiosk in the middle of a college campus, he will want to supply more cups of coffee at the price of $2.00 per cup than at the price of $0.50 per cup. The reason for this is obvious: Eddie has a greater incentive to supply more cups of coffee if he can sell them at $2.00 rather than at $0.50 each. Notice in Table 2.2 that Eddie supplies only 10 cups of coffee at $0.50 per cup. However, if Eddie can charge $1.25, he has a greater incentive to supply more cups of coffee and produces 70 cups. Finally, at the price of $2.00, Eddie wants to supply even more cups of coffee, and his supply increases to 115. We can illustrate this relationship between supply and price in a graph, which economists call a **supply curve**, like the one shown in Figure 2.2. You can see that Eddie's desire to supply, or sell, more cups of coffee is affected by price. The more he can charge, the more he will want to supply. However, as you can imagine, the *demand* for coffee has a very different reaction to price.

▼ Table 2.2

| The Relationship Between Price and Supply ||
Price ($)	Coffee Supplied (cups)
0.50	10
0.75	30
1.00	50
1.25	70
1.50	85
1.75	100
2.00	115

Demand

What is demand? **Demand** refers to how much of a product or a service people want to buy at any given time. People are willing to buy as much as they need, but they have limited resources (money). Therefore, people will buy more of an item at a lower price than at a higher price. In our coffee example, as shown in ▼ **Table 2.3**, students buy 12 cups of coffee when Eddie charges $2.00 a cup, but they buy 120 cups of coffee from Eddie at $0.50 a cup. In other words, as price decreases, demand increases. Again, economists illustrate the relationship between demand and price with a graph that they call a **demand curve**, as shown in ▼ **Figure 2.3**.

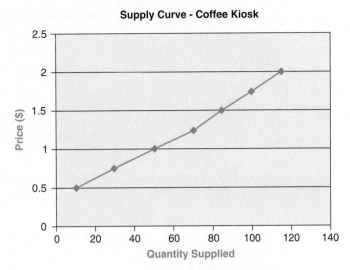

▼ **Figure 2.2**
The Supply Curve
The supply curve illustrates the incentive to supply more of an item as prices increase.

Factors That Determine Price

What factors determine price? As you've seen here with Eddie's coffee kiosk, there is an obvious conflict when setting a price. The higher the price, the more the product is likely to be supplied, but the lower the price, the more customers will likely purchase, or demand. If these two concepts of pricing are at odds with each other, then what determines the final price? Holding all other factors constant, prices are set at a point where supply equals demand. The supply-demand relationship is one of the fundamental concepts of economics. At Eddie's Coffee Kiosk, for example, at some point, supply and demand balance each other out. Although Eddie would love to sell coffee at $2.00 a cup (or even more), he realizes that not too many students are willing to buy coffee at that price. At the price of $2.00 a cup, Eddie would not completely use up his entire supply, and he would end up with a **surplus**.

As Eddie begins to lower his price, he finds that more students are willing to buy his coffee. However, if Eddie lowers his price too much, to $0.50 a cup, for example, then the demand would be so great that Eddie would run out before he was able to satisfy all the students who wanted coffee, creating a **shortage**.

▼ **Table 2.3**

The Relationship Between Price and Demand	
Price ($)	**Coffee Demand (cups)**
0.50	120
0.75	95
1.00	72
1.25	55
1.50	38
1.75	23
2.00	12

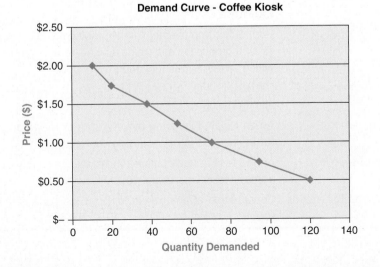

▼ **Figure 2.3**
The Demand Curve
The demand curve illustrates that demand increases as prices decrease.

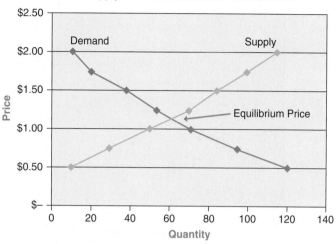

Supply and Demand Curves - Coffee Kiosk

▼ **Figure 2.4**
The Equilibrium Price
The perfect or equilibrium price is determined at that point where supply equals demand.

Ideally, Eddie would strive to determine a price at which he is willing to supply the coffee and at which students are willing to buy (demand) the coffee without anyone wanting more or without any coffee being left over. The price at which supply equals demand is the **equilibrium price**, or market price. The equilibrium price is illustrated in a supply-and-demand curve, as shown in ▼ **Figure 2.4**. In this case, 60 cups of coffee is equally demanded and supplied at a price of $1.15.

Factors That Shift Supply

What makes supply change? Imagine what would happen if you owned a gourmet bakery and the price of flour increased dramatically. What would happen if you bought a new turbocharged oven that could produce more baked goods faster than a conventional oven? Both of these occurrences would affect your supply. There are many factors that can create a change in supply. These factors, known as the **determinants of supply**, are:

- technology changes
- changes in resource prices
- price expectations
- number of suppliers
- the price of substitute goods

Changes in any of these factors that help to create a product or service can affect its supply and shift the supply curve to the left (have a negative impact on supply) or to the right (have a positive impact on supply). ▼ **Table 2.4** summarizes the key determinants of supply. Let's look at each in a bit more detail.

Technology Changes

Improvements in technology enable suppliers to produce their goods or services more efficiently and with fewer costs. A baker who purchases a new turbocharged oven is able to make more fresh breads and rolls in less time.

▼ **Table 2.4**

Examples of Determinants of Supply	
Determinants of Supply	**Example**
Technology changes	Continuing improvements in technology result in lower costs of production and create a higher level of productivity, which increases quantity and lowers price.
Changes in resource prices	Decrease in the cost of lumber increases the number of new homes built.
Price expectations	An anticipated lowering of interest rates may indicate a future increase in new housing contracts.
Number of suppliers	An increase in homebuilders increases the supply of new homes and decreases the cost of new homes.
Price of substitute goods	Construction of apartment buildings is an alternate construction project to building new single-family residences.

Changes in Resource Prices

The price of the resources that are used to produce a good or service affects the cost of production. An increase in resource prices increases the cost of production and reduces profits, thus lowering the incentive to supply a product. An increase in the cost of flour would raise the price of fresh baked goods.

Price Expectations

Price expectations reflect the producer's best guess at the *future* price of a good. Current supply may be increased or decreased depending on expectations of future prices. If prices are expected to increase in the future, the supplier may reduce supply now to supply more later at higher prices. Similarly, if prices are expected to decrease in the future, the supplier may make every attempt to deplete supplies now at the higher price.

Number of Suppliers

The supply of a product or service increases as the number of competitors increases. It makes sense that often the number of suppliers increases in more profitable industries. Think about what Starbucks has done to the coffee bar. Although Starbucks remains the leader in the retail coffee market, there are many companies, such as Dunkin' Donuts and McDonald's, that are marketing to coffee drinkers, thus increasing the supply of coffee. Similarly, as an industry becomes less popular, due to a change in technology, for example, the number of suppliers decreases. When the digital camera became popular, the number of suppliers of film cameras decreased.

Price of Substitute Goods

The price of comparable substitute goods affects the supply of a product also. If there are other equally comparable goods that are available at a lower price, the supply of your goods will be affected. For example, if margarine, a substitute for butter, is priced lower than butter, then the supply of butter may be affected by consumers switching from butter to margarine.

A change in any of these determinants of supply will affect the supply of a product and shift the demand curve. If the change is a positive effect, thereby increasing supply, the supply curve shifts to the right. Negative changes decrease supply and shift the supply curve to the left. Again, we're assuming that everything else is held constant.

Factors That Affect Demand

What factors affect demand? Just as there are factors that affect the supply side, there are also factors that affect a product from the demand side. These factors, known as the **determinants of demand**, are:

- changes in income levels
- population changes
- consumer preferences
- complementary goods
- substitute goods

A positive change in any of these determinants of demand shifts the demand curve to the right, and negative changes shift the demand curve to the left.
▼ **Table 2.5** summarizes the determinants of demand. Let's look at each in a bit more detail.

▼ **Table 2.5**

Determinants of Demand

Determinants of Demand	Example
Changes in income levels	A loss of job will reduce discretionary income and decrease the amount of coffee one buys. A promotion may allow a homeowner to buy a larger house or a house in a better neighborhood.
Population changes	An increase in young, working professionals in a neighborhood may increase the demand for coffee shops and single-family homes.
Consumer preferences	Needs and wants change based on fads and often manipulation by advertisers. A health alert concerning the negative effects of caffeine might reduce the demand for coffee.
Complementary goods	If the construction of new houses is in demand, complementary goods such as appliances and other home goods are also in demand. A reduction in new housing would negatively affect these other industries.
Substitute goods	Products or services that can be used in place of another. In the housing industry, modular housing or trailers can be substituted for building a new home from scratch.

Changes in Income Levels

When income levels rise, people are able to buy more products. Conversely, when income levels go down, most people cut back on spending and buy fewer products. Therefore, as we'll discuss later in this chapter, when the economy enters a recession and people begin to lose their jobs, the demand for some goods and services decreases. An improving economy will bring an increase in spending as more people find jobs and create an increase in demand for some goods and services. Change in income levels is one factor that affects the housing market, for example. With an increase in income, people can afford to buy a home for the first time or can afford to upgrade to a bigger, more expensive home if they already own.

Population Changes

Vacation rentals in resort communities experience demand shifts when populations swing due to seasonal changes. Increases in population create greater demand for utilities (telephone, electric, sewer, and water) and public and consumer services such as banks, drugstores, and grocery stores.

Consumer Preferences

Demand for a product can change based on what is "cool" or "popular" at any given moment. Tickle Me Elmo dolls, X-Box 360 game machines, and the Apple iPhone are all products that had high initial demand. As the demand for these items increases, there is a shift in the demand curve to the right. As demand begins to wane, the demand curve shifts to the left.

Complementary Goods

Products or services that go with each other and are consumed together such as the iPod and iTunes are considered **complementary goods**. The demand for iTunes is great as long as consumers are buying and using iPods. If a new technology renders the iPod obsolete, the demand for iTunes also decreases, shifting the demand curve for iTunes to the left.

Substitute Goods

Goods that can be used in place of other goods, such as Coke for Pepsi or McDonald's Quarter Pounder for Burger King's Whopper, are **substitute goods**. Suppose, for example, someone reported getting violently ill after eating a McDonald's Quarter Pounder. The demand for the Burger King Whopper might increase, shifting the Whopper's demand curve to the right.

So, as the owner of a bakery, how would you determine prices for your goods? You should be able to answer this question by now. It is merely a factor of supply and demand. A higher price provides you with an incentive to supply more baked goods. Conversely, a lower price will increase demand for these goods. The simple solution is to set prices at a point at which supply equals demand. Ideally, you would determine a price at which you are willing to supply various baked goods and at which customers are willing to purchase the goods without creating either a surplus or a shortage.

On Target: Nintendo Wii

In November 2006, Nintendo's release of a new game console system, the Nintendo Wii, was greeted by eager consumers and surging sales. Six months after its launch, Nintendo moved 6 million units worldwide. The systems, priced at $250 each, represented a shift in strategy. With the Wii, Nintendo chose not to focus on high-tech graphics, instead creating a smaller, cheaper, simpler system with a remote controller and built-in motion sensors. The result? In the month of April alone, the Nintendo Wii sold 360,000 units in the United States. In contrast, the Sony PlayStation 3, a $600 Blu-Ray powered system with advanced graphics, sold only 82,000. Demand was so high for the Wii that Nintendo struggled to keep up with production.[5]

Consider the factors that led to the high demand for Nintendo Wii. For example, how might advertising or word of mouth affect consumer preferences? How might the price of the Wii, especially compared with other video game products on the market, have influenced its sales?

▼ You have just read **Objective 2**

Want a review? Check out the Study Plan section @
www.mybizlab.com.

42

Degrees of Competition pp. 42-44

In 1996, Microsoft developed its own Web browser, Internet Explorer, and tried to pressure computer manufacturers and Internet service providers to carry it exclusively. As a result, the U.S. Department of Justice began investigating the corporation for attempting to establish a monopoly over the market. In 1999, a U.S. District Court found Microsoft to be in violation of the Sherman Antitrust Act and ordered the company to break up. In 2001, an appeals court overturned this order but maintained that Microsoft was illegally holding a monopoly.

What exactly is a monopoly? And why doesn't the government allow large monopolies to exist in the United States?

Some products or services have no substitutes, whereas others share the market with many similar products. The amount of substitutes for a certain product or service determines the *level of competition*. Four degrees of competition exist:

- monopoly
- oligopoly
- monopolistic competition
- perfect competition

Keep in mind that these degrees of competition are four points on a scale, not absolute measures. For example, many industries fall somewhere between monopolistic competition and oligopoly.

Monopoly

What is a monopoly? If one Internet company were the sole provider of Internet services and no other companies' Internet services were available to the public, that company would be considered a monopoly. Likewise, if Eddie's Coffee Kiosk is the only place students can buy coffee on campus, then Eddie has a monopoly. A **monopoly** occurs when there is only one provider of a service or product and no substitutes for the product exist. In the United States, as well as in other countries, large monopolies are rarely allowed. In fact, the U.S. Federal Trade Commission must review mergers between large competitors to determine whether the combined firm would result in a monopolistic situation. For example, the Federal Trade Commission was involved when Gillette and Procter & Gamble merged in 2005. Because these companies produced several similar personal hygiene products, Procter & Gamble was required to sell certain products before the merger to avoid creating a near-monopoly by the newly merged company.

In the United States, natural monopolies are an exception. Utility companies, such as those that sell gas or water to consumers, may be permitted to hold monopolies in an effort to conserve natural resources. However, the government regulates the prices for these goods and services.

Oligopoly

Can another company enter a monopoly? In Eddie's situation, let's say that a bookstore on campus opens a café, offering coffee to the students. Students now have a choice to buy coffee either at the bookstore or at Eddie's Coffee Kiosk. The situation has now changed from a monopoly to an oligopoly. An **oligopoly** is a form of competition in which only a few sellers exist. When there are few sellers in a given market, each seller has a fairly large share of the market. Typically, oligopolies occur in industries in which there is a high investment to enter, so oligopolies are often major corporations in certain areas such as the airline, automobile, and tobacco industries.

Because there is little differentiation between products, competition is strong in an oligopoly, and prices differ only slightly, if at all, between the few suppliers. If one company cuts prices, its action is usually matched quickly by the competition. Therefore, competition in an oligopoly is centered on product differentiation (making one product stand out from another) more than on price.

Monopolistic Competition

What happens when there isn't much differentiation between products? Let's assume that the campus cafeteria begins to offer Dunkin' Donuts brand coffee. Assume that the perception among students is that Dunkin' Donuts coffee is superior to Eddie's and the bookstore's. The added choice of a perceived superior product creates monopolistic competition. **Monopolistic competition** occurs when there are many buyers and sellers, little differentiation between the products themselves (coffee vs. coffee), but there is a *perceived* difference among consumers, who thereby favor one product offering over another. Eddie's Coffee Kiosk faces new competition that is perceived to be better than his product, and demand for his coffee decreases, as shown in ▼ **Figure 2.5**.

Monopolistic competition is everywhere. Think of the traditional strip mall or local shopping center in your neighborhood where most likely there is a pizza parlor, dry cleaner, hair or nail salon, bank, and dollar store. These mom and pop

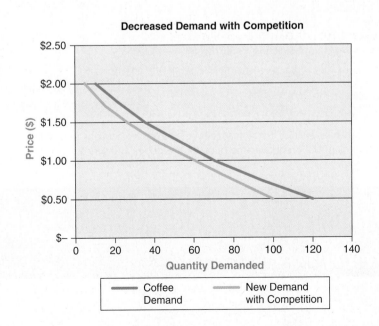

▼ **Figure 2.5**
Demand and Competition
Increased competition negatively changes coffee demand and moves the demand curve to the left.

stores are traditional monopolistic competitive businesses because there are many buyers and sellers and the products are similar, but not identical. Often, the distinction between products is price.

Perfect Competition

What happens when products are almost identical? Perfect competition occurs when there are many buyers and sellers of products that are virtually identical and any seller can easily enter and exit the market. When these conditions exist, no single supplier can influence the price. In reality, there are very few, if any, examples of perfect competition. However, agricultural products such as grains, fruits, and vegetables come close. Many of these products appear to be identical, and, because there are many sellers in the market, no single seller can set the price for these products.

Competition encourages businesses to make creative decisions and gives customers options. Because of this need for competition, U.S. businesses face stiff penalties if they are found holding illegal monopolies. Microsoft was punished in 1999 and continued to face effects of the legal battle years later, with the appeal court's ruling in 2001 and a $611 million fine in 2004 from the European Union.[6] Stiff penalties such as these exist to discourage companies from creating monopolies. By keeping a close watch on monopolies, the U.S. government ensures that no single seller drastically influences the price of a certain service or product.

➤ Utility companies, such as those that sell gas, water, or electricity, may hold monopolies, but the government then regulates the price for the goods and services to protect consumers.

▼ You have just read **Objective 3**

Want to learn more? Check out the Study Plan section @
www.mybizlab.com.

Economic Indicators pp. 45-49

➤ The economy plays a big part in business. In Greg's situation, the economy is affecting new housing starts, which in turn affect Greg's business. Which aspects of the economy should Greg watch to help him make his business decisions? How can we tell how well or how poorly the economy is doing?

In the previous section, you learned about several factors that affect supply and demand. Another factor that affects supply and demand is the overall state of the economy. In a good economy, demand for most consumer goods and business expansion will be high. In a bad economy, the opposite will be the case. The economy is an indicator of how well or poorly businesses are doing in general. Because changes in the economy can affect a business, managers need to be aware of a number of key **economic indicators** and how they relate to business. Economists primarily use the following three economic indicators to determine how well businesses are performing overall:

Greg Johnson needs to decide how much inventory to purchase for his lumber company. He has seen new housing starts decline over the past several months, but knows that if certain conditions change, he could be supplying lumber for another housing boom. Similarly, his staffing needs can change as quickly as his inventory supply. Not knowing whether demand might pick up, how is he to decide how much inventory to hold or what staff to keep or let go? ➤

- the gross domestic product (GDP)
- consumer and producer price indexes
- the unemployment rate

We'll look at these economic indicators as well as productivity in this section.

The Gross Domestic Product

How do we determine the health of an economy? The broadest measure of the health of any country's economy is the **gross domestic product (GDP)**. The GDP measures economic activity—that is, the overall market value of final goods and services produced in a country in a year.

Countries by GDP, 2007

Country	Millions of U.S. dollars
United States	13,860,000
China	7,043,000
Japan	4,417,000
India	2,965,000
Germany	2,833,000
United Kingdom	2,147,000
Russia	2,076,000
France	2,067,000
Brazil	1,838,000
Italy	1,800,000

It is important to note that only those goods that are actually *produced* in the country are counted in the country's GDP. (Hence the term *domestic* in *gross domestic product*.) For example, the Tokyo-based high-tech company Toshiba has a plant in Lebanon, Tennessee, that manufactures color television sets. The value of the TV sets produced in the Tennessee plant is counted in the U.S. GDP, not in Japan's GDP.

What's the difference between GNP and GDP? Most countries outside the United States use GDP to measure their economic health. Until 1991, the United States used the **gross national product (GNP)** as its economic yardstick, but changed to GDP to allow for fairer comparisons between world economies. The GNP attributes earnings to the country where the firm was owned, not where the product was manufactured. Therefore, those Toshiba TV sets made in Tennessee would not be included in the U.S. GNP, whereas the Nike apparel and footwear produced outside the United States would be included. So the GNP measures the U.S. income resulting from production, whereas the GDP measures production in the United States, regardless of country of ownership.

How does the GDP act as an economic indicator? The GDP is the most widely used indicator of economic growth by most countries worldwide. When the GDP goes up, the indication is that the economy is in a positive state. Goods and services are being produced and businesses are doing well. A downward moving GDP indicates problems with the economy because fewer goods are being produced, fewer services are being sold, and businesses are not doing well and may have to lay off employees or shut their doors altogether. Therefore, business owners such as Greg use GDP data to forecast sales and adjust production and investment in inventory.

Consumer and Producer Price Indexes

What else is used to gauge the health of the economy? There are two price indexes used as economic indicators: the consumer price index and the producer price index. You may not hear about these indicators often, but you've probably heard of inflation and deflation. A consistent increase in either indicator indicates inflation. **Inflation** is a rise in the general level of prices over time. A decrease in the rate of inflation is **disinflation**, and a continuous decrease in prices over time is **deflation**. Later in the chapter, we discuss how the government also uses these indicators to make monetary policy decisions to control inflation and deflation.

How are changes in the price of consumer goods measured? The **consumer price index (CPI)** is a benchmark used to track changes in prices over time. The CPI measures price changes by creating a "market basket" of a specified set of goods and services (including taxes) that represent the average buying pattern of urban households. The value of this market basket determined by the combined prices of these goods and services is compared to its value in a prior period (generally a month), and the change is noted. Monthly CPI tracks the changes in prices of goods and services purchased by households.

What goods and services are included in the CPI? The basket of goods and services is evaluated by the U.S. Bureau of Labor Statistics to ensure that it reflects current consumer buying habits. The market basket in use as this book is being written was determined by tracking the spending habits of over 10,000 families during

BizChat

How Much Money Do You Need to Get By?

The cost of living is the average monetary costs of the goods and services required to maintain a particular standard of living. It is closely related to the CPI. In fact, in order to keep up with inflation, the Social Security Administration calculates automatic cost of living adjustments to Social Security benefits based on annual percentage increases in the CPI. As you can imagine, the cost of living varies greatly by state and city. For example, the cost of living in New York City or San Francisco is much higher than in Topeka, Kansas, or Charlotte, North Carolina. Why do you think this is? What factors account for the differences?

For more information and discussion questions about this topic, check out the BizChat feature on www.my*biz*lab.com.

two years, 2001 and 2002. The expenditure items are classified into 200 categories, which are further arranged into eight major groups (see ▼ **Figure 2.6**):

- food and beverages
- housing
- apparel
- transportation
- medical care
- recreation
- education and communication
- other goods and services (such as tobacco and smoking products, haircuts and personal services, and funeral services)

Does the CPI measure changes in all prices? The CPI measures changes in prices of consumer goods only. It does not measure changes in prices of goods used to create the goods, such as capital and resource expenditures. The **producer price index (PPI)** tracks the average change in prices at the wholesale level (that is, from the seller's perspective). Therefore, it tracks prices of goods sellers use to create their products or services, such as raw materials, product components that require further processing, and finished goods sold to retailers. The PPI excludes energy prices and prices for services.

Why are price indexes important? Change in prices is an important economic indicator as it is a measurement of purchasing power and triggers some business decisions. During periods of increasing prices as reflected by the CPI, the purchasing power of a dollar decreases—meaning that less is bought with a dollar today than could have been purchased with the same dollar yesterday. To compensate for such price increases, wages eventually need to be increased. Businesses in turn must eventually increase prices to compensate for the higher cost of labor. Similarly, if the price to produce goods or services increases, businesses will need to pass on those cost increases in the

Official CPI Composition

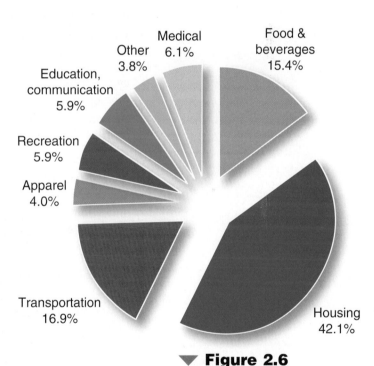

▼ **Figure 2.6**
CPI Components

form of higher prices, again decreasing the consumer's purchasing power. Therefore, business leaders watch the CPI and PPI to determine the rate at which consumer and wholesale prices change, respectively.

The Unemployment Rate

What other indicators are used to measure the economy? The **unemployment rate** measures the number of workers who are at least 16 years old who are not working and who have been trying to find a job within the past four weeks and still haven't found one. Because there are different reasons why people are not working, there are several different measurements of unemployment:

- **Frictional unemployment** measures temporary unemployment in which workers move between jobs, careers, and locations.

- **Structural unemployment** measures permanent unemployment associated when an industry changes in such a way that jobs are terminated completely. Many steel workers and miners lost jobs due to a decline in those industries. More recently, newspaper typesetters have been replaced by computers. These workers can learn new skills or receive additional training in an effort to keep their jobs or find new ones.

- **Cyclical unemployment** measures unemployment caused by lack of demand for those who want to work. This generally follows the economy. Companies must cut back their work force when there is a downturn in the business cycle. Once the demand for goods and services increases, companies begin to hire again.

- **Seasonal unemployment** measures those out of work during the off-season, such as those employed in snow- or beach-related industries, agriculture, and/or holiday activities.

Why is unemployment an important economic measure? Businesses, as well as government policy makers, pay close attention to unemployment rates. High unemployment results in an increase in unemployment benefits and government spending on social programs, such as Social Security, welfare (now called Temporary Assistance for Needy Families, or TANF), and Medicare. High unemployment can also result in increases in mental stresses and physical illnesses and can bring on increases in crime as well. It's costly for

"I'd like you to head up the new team of recently let go."

businesses to lay off workers and then, as the economy improves eventually, hire and train new employees. In a declining economy, businesses prefer to reduce their workforce through retirement and natural attrition, which takes

" Productivity—the goods and services produced from each hour of work—is the magic elixir of economic progress. It's why we live better than our grandparents did, without working longer hours. " [7]

—Alan Greenspan, former Chair of the Federal Reserve Board

planning. Ironically, if the unemployment rate drops too low, the concern is that more workers have increased buying power and spend more, which ultimately causes prices to increase, resulting in a higher inflation rate. Therefore, the challenge is to keep both inflation and unemployment low—a difficult task since they seem to have an inverse relationship to each other.

Productivity

How is productivity of the workforce measured? In its broadest terms, **productivity** measures the quantity of goods and services that human and physical resources can produce in a given time period. There are many factors that go into the productivity measure. For example, comparing output to the amount of labor used is one popular measure.

Why is measuring productivity important to businesses? No matter how it's measured, productivity is an indicator of a business's health. An increase in productivity indicates that workers are producing more goods or services in the same amount of time. Therefore, higher productivity numbers often result in lower costs and lower prices. Increasing productivity means that the existing resources are producing more, which generates more income and more profitability. Companies can reinvest the economic benefits of productivity growth by increasing wages and improving working conditions, by reducing prices for customers, by increasing shareholder value, and increasing tax revenue to the government, thus improving GDP. In aggregate, overall productivity is an important economic indicator of the economy's health.

So, how do all these indicators help Greg and his inventory decision? After ensuring there is inventory to fill current needs, Greg keeps a close eye on all economic indicators, especially the CPI and unemployment rate to help guide his future buying decisions. As explained above, movements in the CPI determine the trend of current prices. Such trends can help Greg determine whether it's better to stock up now at lower prices or wait to buy later if prices are expected to fall.

Equally important is the unemployment rate. Greg's business, like so many others, is tied closely to the new housing industry. Unfortunately, Greg is feeling the pressures of a sagging housing industry and a declining economy. Because there is less for his employees to do, he has already laid off workers. A continued downturn in the housing industry will have a negative effect on the unemployment rate, an indicator for Greg that his inventory might not move quickly. Although none of the indicators can guide Greg's decision precisely, watching the indicators over time allows Greg to get a feel for future expectations and helps him make better business decisions.

▼ **top**
5 Countries by Productivity, 2006

Country	Average wealth produced per worker per year (US dollars)
United States	63,885
Ireland	55,986
Luxembourg	55,641
Belgium	55,235
France	54,609

▼ You have just read **Objective 4**

Want to test your skills? Check out the Study Plan section @ **www.mybizlab.com.**

Government and the **Economy** pp. 50-55

Joaquin and Jacinta Robertson have been saving for years to buy their first house. Over the past several years, the interest rate that banks charge for home loans has been at historically low levels. Recently, however, all Joaquin and Jacinta hear on the news is about the rapid changes in the stock market, reports from the chairman of the Federal Reserve Bank about changes in interest rates, and debates on how the government might change its tax policies to control the economy. They aren't sure what effects all of this will have on their ability to take out a loan and buy a home. Is now the best time to buy a house? ➤

➤ If you or someone you know has tried to buy a house or make any big investment, you may have realized that the state of the economy can have a big impact on your decision. What makes the economy change? How does the government help control the economy? What do you need to be aware of when making decisions on large investments? These are the questions we'll address in this section of the chapter. Let's start by discussing some economic policies.

Economic Policies

Why does the state of the economy change? Between 1979 and 1981, the rate of inflation was at its highest level—reaching nearly 15 percent. Only seven years before and five years after that high inflationary period (1972 and 1986), inflation was hovering around 2 percent.[8] Over time, the economy naturally goes through periodic increases and decreases. Economists refer to these increases and decreases as the **business cycle**.

There are four stages of the business cycle as illustrated in ▼ **Figure 2.7**.

- *Peak:* This occurs when the economy is at its most robust point. The peak occurs when an expansion ends and a recession begins.
- *Recession:* By definition, a **recession** is a decline in the GDP for two or more successive quarters of a year. In recessionary times, corporate profits decline, unemployment increases, and the stock market reacts with large selling sessions that result in decreasing stock prices. A very severe or long recession is a **depression**. Depressions are usually associated with falling prices (deflation). After the onset of the Great Depression of 1929, the government used policies to control the economy to avoid another such depression.
- *Trough:* A *trough* occurs when the recession hits bottom and the economy begins to expand again.

- *Expansion or recovery:* Eventually, after a recession or even a depression, the economy hits a trough and begins to grow again and therefore enters into an expansionary or recovery phase. Eventually, the recovery will hit a peak, and the cycle begins again.

How does the government control the swings in the business cycle? Ideally, the economy could stay near its peak all the time. But left to its own forces and in reaction to external actions on the economic system such as wars and variations of the weather, it is inevitable that the economy cycles through peaks and troughs. To smooth out the swings in the business cycle, the government influences the economy through its **fiscal policy**, in which the government determines the appropriate level of taxes and spending, and through its **monetary policy**, in which the government manages the supply of money.

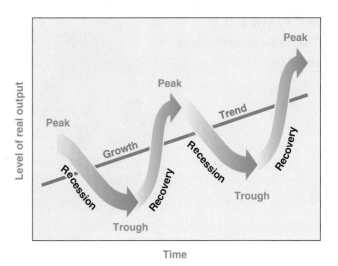

▼ **Figure 2.7**
The Business Cycle

Fiscal Policy

Why does the government increase taxes? Threats of *increasing taxes* are a concern to Joaquin and Jacinta. They feel they pay too much already and need as much of their paychecks as possible to make their anticipated mortgage payments. However, they are told that an increase in taxes is necessary to offset rising inflation. Higher taxes translate into fewer consumers spending money, which in turn slows the growth of businesses and consequently slows down the economy by reducing the amount of money in the system. *Decreasing taxes* does not have quite the opposite effect on the economy as increasing taxes. It would seem that if increasing taxes would slow down an economy, a tax cut would help stimulate the economy. Although that is partially true, the amount of money entering into the system is dependent on how much of the reduction in taxes consumers spend and how much of the tax cut consumers actually save. Money put into savings does not help stimulate the economy immediately. To stimulate the economy faster, the government uses another form of fiscal policy: government spending.

How does government spending help stimulate the economy? Another tactic in fiscal policy that the government uses to help fuel a lagging economy is increasing government spending. The government spends money on a wide variety of projects, such as infrastructure improvements and those that benefit the military, education, and health care. Government spending increases cash flow to the economy faster than decreasing taxes since it's an immediate injection of funds into the system. Often, government spending creates additional jobs, which also helps stimulate the economy. During periods of high economic growth, the government may decrease its spending, potentially affecting interest rates.

Monetary Policy

Besides changes to fiscal policy, what else can be done to control the economy? The **Federal Reserve System (the Fed)** is the central banking system in the United States. Created by Congress to be an independent governmental entity, it includes 12 regional Federal Reserve Banks (see ▼ **Figure 2.8**) and a Board of Governors based in Washington, D.C. The Fed also includes the Federal Open Market Committee (FOMC), which sets the policies of the Fed,

▼ **Figure 2.8**
The 12 Federal Reserve
Districts

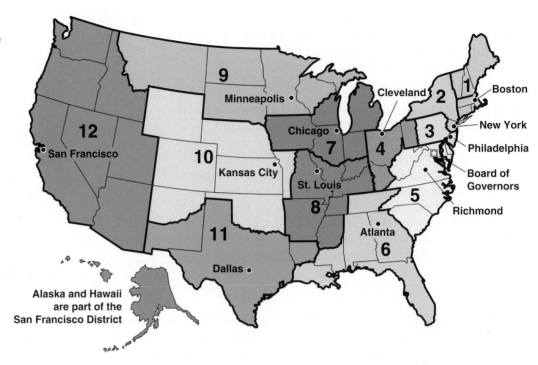

including monetary policies. The Fed manages the country's money supply through its monetary policy to control inflation. It accomplishes this by:

- changing certain interest rates
- buying and selling government securities
- trading in foreign exchange markets

The Federal Reserve Banks carry out most of the activities of the Fed.

What is the money supply? When determining the amount of money in our system, it is natural to think of all the coins and bills held by people, businesses, and banks. However, that would only represent a portion of the money supply. **Money supply** is the combined amount of money available within the economy, but there are different ways to measure money supply (see ▼ **Figure 2.9**):

- **M-1:** Coins, bills, traveler's checks, and checking accounts constitute the narrowest measure of our money supply, which is referred to as **M-1**. M-1 assets are the most liquid in that they are already in the form of cash or are the easiest to change into cash.

- **M-2:** Another part of the money supply is that which is available for banks to lend out, such as savings deposits, money market accounts, and certificates of deposit less than $100,000. (You'll learn more about these items in Chapter 16.) This layer of the money supply, in addition to the M-1 layer, constitutes **M-2**.

- **M-3:** A third layer of the money supply is **M-3**. M-1 and M-2 plus less liquid funds, such as the larger certificates of deposit (greater than $100,000), money market accounts held by large banks and corporations, and deposits of Eurodollars (U. S. dollars deposited in banks outside the United States) comprise M-3.

Why is the money supply important? Money has a direct effect on the economy since the more money we have, the more we tend to spend. When we as consumers spend more, businesses do better. Demands for resources, labor, and capital increase due to the stimulated business activity, and, in general, the economy improves. However, there can be too much of a good thing. When the money supply continues to expand, eventually there may not be enough goods and services to satisfy demand, and, as was previously discussed, when demand is high, prices will rise. (Remember that demand curve? It shifts to the right.) Inflation results from an increase in overall prices. Economists carefully watch the CPI to monitor inflation, especially because they don't want inflation to go too high.

An opposite effect can also happen when the supply of money becomes limited following a decrease in economic activity. When the economy begins to slow down due to decreased spending, either disinflation (reduced inflation) or deflation (falling prices) results. To help manage the economy from being in the extreme economic situations of inflation or deflation, the Federal Reserve uses three tools to affect money supply (see ▼ **Table 2.6**):

- open market operations
- the discount rate
- reserve requirement

Open Market Operations

What are open market operations? The primary tool the Fed uses in its monetary policy is **open market operations**, buying and selling U.S. Treasury and federal agency bonds in the "open market." The Fed does not place transactions with any particular security dealer; rather, the securities dealers compete in an open market. When the Fed buys or sells U.S. securities, it is changing the level of reserves in the banking system. When the Fed buys securities, it adds reserves to the system, money is said to be "easy," and interest rates drop. Lower interest rates help stimulate the economy by decreasing the desire to save and increasing the demand for loans such as home mortgages. Since Joaquin and Jacinta would benefit by getting a mortgage with the lowest interest rate possible, they should watch for reports that would indicate what the Fed intends to do with its open market operations.

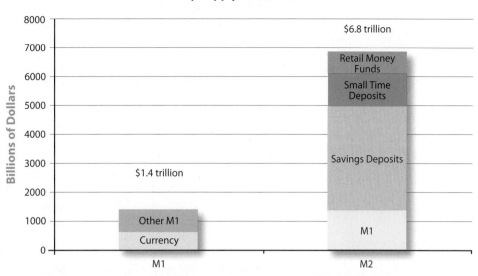

Money Supply Measures, June 2006

▼ **Figure 2.9**
Money Supply Measures for M-1 and M-2
Although we may think of currency as the largest component of money supply, this figure shows that it is only a fraction of total money supply. Note: the Federal Reserve Board of Governors stopped publishing M3 data after March 2006.

▼ **Table 2.6**

Federal Reserve Bank Monetary Policy		
Federal Reserve System Action	**Increase supply of money to stimulate economy and off-set potential deflation/recession**	**Decrease supply of money to "cool" economy and tame concerns of inflation**
Open market operations	Buy securities	Sell securities
Discount rate	Lower discount rate	Increase discount rate
Reserve requirement	Lower reserve requirement	Increase reserve requirement

When the Fed sells government bonds, it decreases the amount of reserves in the system, causing interest rates to increase. Open market operations is probably the most influential tool the Fed can use to alter money supply.

The Discount Rate

What is the discount rate? The Federal Reserve Bank is the bank's banker, or "lender of last resorts."[9] Occasionally, commercial banks have unexpected needs for funds and turn to the Federal Reserve Bank for short-term loans. When these banks borrow money from the Fed, they are charged a lower interest rate, called the **discount rate**. By lowering the discount rate, commercial banks are encouraged to obtain additional reserves by borrowing funds from the Fed. The commercial banks then lend out the reserves to businesses, thereby stimulating the economy by adding funds into the economic system. However, if the economy is too robust, the Fed can increase the discount rate, which discourages banks from borrowing additional reserves. Businesses are then discouraged from borrowing because of the higher interest rates.

Is the discount rate the same as the Federal Funds rate? It's often reported in the news that the Fed intends to change the "Fed Funds rate" in its efforts to stabilize the economy. The Fed Funds rate is not the same as the discount rate. The **Fed Funds rate** is the interest rate that banks charge other banks when they borrow funds overnight from one another. (Banks avoid dipping below their required reserves by borrowing from each other—the Fed requires banks to have so much money on "reserve" depending on the deposits in the bank and the other assets and liabilities held by each bank.) Despite the TV news, the Fed does not control the Fed Funds rate directly. Instead, the Fed Funds rate is the "equilibrium price" created through the Fed's open market operations and the exchange of securities.

The excess reserves that are available to lend between banks come from securities that the Fed buys and sells through its open market operations. If there are many excess reserves on hand, banks have adequate funds to lend to other banks. On the other hand, if excess reserves are not as plentiful, banks lend funds to one another more sparingly. To increase the Federal Funds rate, the Fed sells bonds in the open market. Banks buy the securities, thus reducing their excess reserves available for loans. The decrease supply increases the Fed Funds rate.

The opposite holds as well. To decrease the Federal Funds rate, the Fed will buy bonds in the open market. Buying securities from banks increases the banks' excess reserves, making money supply more available, which decreases the Federal Funds rate and helps stimulate the economy. ▼ **Figure 2.10** shows the trend of Fed Funds rates over the past several decades.

Remember Joaquin and Jacinta? While the Fed Funds rate does not have a direct impact on mortgage rates, it does have an indirect effect since interest rates respond to economic growth and inflation. Reports on the news that the Fed is striving to change the Fed Funds rate will indicate to Joaquin and Jacinta whether it's likely that interest rates will increase or decrease in the near future.

Reserve Requirements

What are reserve requirements? The **reserve requirement**, determined by the Federal Reserve Bank, is the minimum amount of money banks must hold in reserve to cover deposits. Although the Fed rarely uses the reserve requirement as

Trend of Fed Funds Rate (1990-2008)

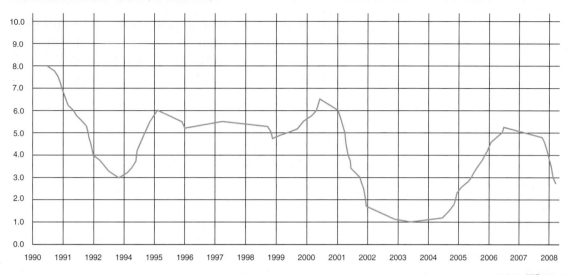

▼ **Figure 2.10**

Trend of Fed Funds Rate (1990-2008)

a means of monetary policy, they can increase or decrease the reserve requirement to ease or tighten the money supply, respectively.

To better understand reserve requirements, you need to know a bit about how banks work. When you deposit money into a bank, the money does not sit in a vault waiting for the time when you want to withdraw it. Instead, banks use your deposited money to make loans to others: people, small businesses, corporations, and other banks. Banks make money by the interest charged on those loans. However, the bank must be able to give you back your money when you demand it. Therefore, the banks do not lend out the entire balance of deposits. Banks retain a reserve that is sufficient to cover any demands by their customers for funds on any given day. This includes trips to the ATM machines, use of debit cards, requests for loans, and payment of checks that you write. If the banks don't have enough funds to cover daily demands, customers might get nervous that the bank may lose their money, and so they will withdraw all their funds. In fact, this concern is what contributed to the bank run in 1929 at the beginning of the Great Depression. At that time, people were so nervous about banks not being able to cover their deposits that the massive withdrawals forced many banks to close.

It's important to be aware of the overall state of the economy when making decisions on large investments. Because the government's actions affect the economy, it's also important to be aware of what these actions are and their effects. For example, in making their decision about whether to buy a home, Joaquin and Jacinta would benefit from paying attention to the Fed's open market operations. If the Fed buys securities, it's likely that interest rates for mortgage loans will decrease. Additionally, Joaquin and Jacinta can look to the Fed Funds rate, which indirectly affects mortgage rates. These two factors can help them determine the best time to buy a home.

▼ You have just read **Objectives 5 & 6**

Want to quiz yourself? Check out the Study Plan section @
www.mybizlab.com.

1. What is economics, and what are the different types of economic systems? (pp. 31-34)

- **Economics** (p. 31) is the study of how individuals and businesses make decisions to best satisfy wants, needs, and desires with limited resources, and how efficiently and equitably resources are allocated.

- There are different types of economic systems.

  - Planned economic systems are types of economics in which the government has more control over what is produced, the resources to produce the goods and services, and the distribution of the goods and services. Communism and socialism are planned economic systems.

  - Market economies, represented by capitalism, give control of economic decisions to the individual and private firms.

  - Most modern economies in the Western world are mixed economies, which are a blend of market and planned economies.

2. What are the principles of supply and demand and the factors that affect each principle? (pp. 35-41)

- **Supply** (p. 36) refers to how much of a product or service is available. The amount supplied will increase as price increases. Supply is affected by:
  - technology changes
  - changes in resource prices
  - price expectations
  - price of substitute goods
  - number of suppliers

- **Demand** (p. 37) refers to how much people want to buy at any given time. The amount demanded increases as price declines. Demand is affected by:
  - changes in income levels
  - consumer preferences
  - changes in population
  - changes in prices of substitute or complementary goods
  - changes in expectations

3. What are the four degrees of competition, and how does competition affect supply? (pp. 42-44)

- There are several degrees of competition, including **monopoly**, **oligopoly**, **monopolistic competition**, and **perfect competition** (pp. 42–44).

- In a monopoly, where only one seller supplies a product or service, supply may be limited. Supplies may increase with an oligopoly, in which a few sellers exist. Monopolistic competition allows for many sellers, increasing the supply and choices for consumers. Similarly, there are many sellers in perfect competition, which also increases the supply of a product or service.

4. How do economic indicators—particularly the gross domestic product (GDP), price indexes, the unemployment rate, and productivity—reflect economic health? (pp. 45-49)

- The **GDP** (p. 45) measures the overall market value of final goods and services produced in a country in a year. When the GDP goes up, the indication is that the economy is moving in a positive direction.

- The **consumer price index (CPI)** and **producer price index (PPI)** (pp. 46–47) are indicators of **inflation** or **deflation** (p. 46).

  - The CPI tracks changes in prices over time by measuring changes in prices of goods and services that represent the average buying pattern of urban households.

  - The PPI tracks the average change in prices of those goods the seller uses to create her products or services such as raw materials, product components that require further processing, and finished goods sold to retailers.

- The **unemployment rate** (p. 48) is watched as an indicator of how productive the workforce is, and an increasing unemployment rate generally has a corresponding increase in government spending on social policies (such as welfare and unemployment payments).

- Increasing **productivity** (p. 49) means that the existing resources are producing more, which generates more income and more profitability. Overall productivity is an important economic indicator of the economy's health.

5. What are the four stages of the business cycle? (pp. 50-51)

- The four stages of the **business cycle** (p. 50) are peak, **recession** (p. 50), trough, and expansion or recovery.

6. How does the government use both fiscal policy and monetary policy to control swings in the business cycle? (pp. 51-55)

- The government's **fiscal policy** (p. 51) determines the appropriate level of taxes and government spending. An increase in taxes translates into lower consumer spending and helps contain an economy that is growing too quickly. Lowering taxes will stimulate spending and help boost a lagging economy.

- The government's **monetary policy** (p. 51) manages the **money supply** (p. 52) to control inflation by changing interest rates, buying and selling government securities, and/or trading in foreign exchange markets.

- The **Federal Reserve System** (p. 51) is responsible for the monetary policy and uses **open market operations** (p. 53), changes in the **discount rate** (p. 54), and manipulations of the **reserve requirements** (p. 54) to help keep the economy from experiencing severe negative or positive swings.

For an audio file of the Objectives and Chapter Summary, see the Student Resources section @ www.my*biz*lab.com.

Key Terms

business cycle   (p. 50)

capitalism   (p. 33)

communism   (p. 33)

complementary goods   (p. 40)

consumer price index (CPI)   (p. 46)

currency   (p. 35)

cyclical unemployment   (p. 48)

deflation   (p. 46)

demand   (p. 37)

demand curve   (p. 37)

depression   (p. 50)

determinants of demand   (p. 39)

determinants of supply   (p. 38)

discount rate   (p. 54)

disinflation   (p. 46)

economics   (p. 31)

economic indicators   (p. 45)

equilibrium price   (p. 38)

Fed Funds rate   (p. 54)

Federal Reserve System (the Fed)   (p. 51)

fiscal policy   (p. 51)

frictional unemployment   (p. 48)

goods   (p. 31)

gross domestic product (GDP)   (p. 45)

gross national product (GNP)   (p. 46)

inflation   (p. 46)

law of supply   (p. 36)

M-1   (p. 52)

M-2   (p. 52)

M-3   (p. 52)

macroeconomics   (p. 32)

market   (p. 33)

market economy   (p. 33)

market price   (p. 35)

microeconomics   (p. 32)

mixed economy   (p. 34)

monetary policy   (p. 51)

money supply   (p. 52)

monopolistic competition   (p. 43)

monopoly   (p. 42)

oligopoly   (p. 43)

open market operations   (p. 53)

perfect competition   (p. 44)

planned economic system   (p. 33)

privatization   (p. 33)

producer price index (PPI)   (p. 47)

productivity   (p. 49)

recession   (p. 50)

reserve requirement   (p. 54)

seasonal unemployment   (p. 48)

services   (p. 31)

shortage   (p. 37)

socialism   (p. 33)

structural unemployment   (p. 48)

substitute goods   (p. 41)

supply   (p. 36)

supply curve   (p. 36)

surplus   (p. 37)

unemployment rate   (p. 48)

Multiple Choice Correct answers can be found on page 503.

1. Economics is the study of
   a. how individuals and businesses satisfy wants and desires.
   b. how resources are allocated.
   c. supply and demand.
   d. All of the above

2. Denmark and the Netherlands have high marginal income tax rates. The income derived from such taxes goes to pay for health care and other social services for all citizens of each country. This arrangement is an illustration of what kind of economic system?
   a. Communism
   b. Socialism
   c. Traditionalism
   d. Market economy

3. When the automotive industry replaced humans with robots in its assembly process, more cars could be produced in less time. This change in technology would shift the supply curve in which direction?
   a. To the right
   b. To the left
   c. No change would occur.
   d. There is a shift along the demand curve only.

4. Which is not considered a determinant of demand?
   a. Income levels
   b. Changes in income levels
   c. Changes in resource prices
   d. Consumer preferences

5. USB cables, CDs, and LCD monitors are
   a. complementary goods for computers.
   b. substitute goods for computers.
   c. relative goods for computers.
   d. None of the above

6. The gross domestic product (GDP) measures
   a. the overall market value of final goods and services produced in a country in a year.
   b. the aggregate amount of money available within the economy denoted by different asset types.
   c. the quantity of goods and services that human and physical resources can produce in a given period of time.
   d. the number of workers who are not working and who have been trying to find a job within the past four weeks and still haven't found one.

7. Inflation is monitored by watching changes in the
   a. PPI.
   b. CPI.
   c. GNP.
   d. GDP.

8. Which of the following is not a stage in the business cycle?
   a. Expansion
   b. Trough
   c. Peak
   d. Repression

9. A form of competition in which only a few sellers exist is
   a. monopoly.
   b. oligopoly.
   c. perfect competition.
   d. monopolistic competition.

10. When the Fed buys or sells securities, it is engaged in which form of monetary policy?
    a. Changing the reserve requirement
    b. Changing the discount rate
    c. Open market operations
    d. None of the above

Self-Test

True/False Correct answers can be found on page 503.

1. Microeconomics is the study of the behavior of the overall economy.
   ☐ **True** or ☐ **False**

2. In a market economy, individuals are able to make their own economic decisions.
   ☐ **True** or ☐ **False**

3. The equilibrium price is determined when supply and demand balance each other out.
   ☐ **True** or ☐ **False**

4. Monopolistic competition is when there is only one supplier for a good or service.
   ☐ **True** or ☐ **False**

5. A lifeguard who is collecting unemployment in October is an example of frictional unemployment.
   ☐ **True** or ☐ **False**

Critical Thinking Questions

1. How have the Internet and the availability of immediate news content affected the supply and demand for newspapers and other printed material (such as textbooks)? Discuss the impact of technology on those industries that produce printed information.

2. The text discusses unemployment rate as a measure of economic performance. Another way to gauge economic performance is to count the number of jobs or number of people employed in the economy. Discuss the differences between these two measurements of job creation. Is either measurement better than the other?

3. Look in the newspaper or on the Internet to find the most current economic indicators, such as the unemployment rate and CPI. What forces are working to improve or worsen the economy?

4. What are the advantages of capitalism? What are the advantages of socialism? What are the disadvantages of these two economic systems? How does this information relate to your everyday life?

5. The text defines the GDP as the measurement of economic activity—the market value of products and services that are produced in a country in a year. Think about other things that may "help" the GDP that are really not good for our society in general, such as the economic activity required to clean up oil spills or increases in consumer debt to buy more goods. In addition, there are other situations that may "hurt" the GDP by limiting expenditures on items, but help the overall good of society such as reusing plastic bags or installing solar water heaters (thus limiting spending on oil/gas/electricity). Does the definition of GDP need to be revised?

Team Time

The Great Debate

Your instructor will divide the class into three groups and assign each group one of the following debate topics. Once in your group, divide the group into two smaller groups to prepare stances on your assigned debate issues.

Debate Topics

1. Wal-Mart is interested in creating an industrial loan bank in Utah. What are the implications of having a retail giant enter the banking industry? Should this be allowed?

2. Minimum wage laws were introduced in the 1930s to protect workers after the Great Depression. In the 2008 presidential election, minimum wage increases were a topic of discussion. What impact does increasing the minimum wage have on unemployment? Does increasing the minimum wage benefit the worker, or does it ultimately result in higher unemployment?

3. Taxation and tax cuts are fodder for volatile debate among political leaders. Many propose that tax cuts help strengthen the economy by freeing money to increase spending. Others propose that past tax cuts have not had a positive effect on the economy and have only caused greater stress on the government budget and reduced the government's ability to spend on important public needs. Do tax cuts benefit the economy?

Process

Step 1. After dividing your group into two debate sides, meet separately to discuss the issues of the debate.

Step 2. Group members should then individually prepare their responses to their side of the debate issue.

Step 3. Gather your smaller groups and go over the responses provided by each group member. Develop a single list of responses.

Step 4. Determine who will be the group's primary spokesperson for the debate.

Step 5. Each group will be given 5 minutes to present its side of the issue. After each group has presented its argument, each team will be given 5 minutes to prepare a rebuttal and then 3 minutes to present the rebuttal.

Step 6. Repeat this process with the other groups.

Ethics and Corporate Social Responsibility

Economic Inequality

Economic inequality refers to the differences of assets and income between groups. It has long been the subject for great discussion and can refer to the inequality between individuals, city/rural areas, countries, or economic structures. As a class or on an individual basis, discuss the following:

1. How do you define economic equality? For example, is economic equality simply making sure everyone has equal income, or is it enough to provide all equal opportunity to earn income?

2. Is economic equality feasible? Would other problems result from economic equality?

3. One method used to measure differences in national income equality around the world is the national Gini coefficient. Research the Gini coefficient. Which countries have the most equality? Which have greater inequality?

4. What other methods could be used to measure economic equality?

Web Exercises

1. **Getting Acquainted with Your Local Federal Reserve Bank**
   What Federal Reserve Bank branch is nearest your home or school? Go to the Web site of your local Federal Reserve Bank and outline its latest policies. What kind of information does the Web site give you?

2. **Buying a Home**
   How much would it cost to buy a home today? You read the story of Joaquin and Jacinta and their questions about buying a new home. Their decision centered on mortgage interest rates. What are the current mortgage interest rates in your area? Find a mortgage calculator online and calculate the monthly mortgage payment for several different scenarios of home cost, interest rate, and length of loan. How do these variables affect the amount you can afford to pay the bank every month?

3. **Learning More About Supply and Demand**
   Go to www.lemonadestandgame.com and play a round or two. Using information you learned from this chapter, write a brief paper about your experience. How much money did you make each time you played the game?

What are the important variables? How does this game illustrate the effects of supply and demand?

4. **Pro Sports and the Economy**
   How do professional sports and the economy interact? Play Peanuts and Crackerjacks (http://www.bos.frb.org/peanuts/indexnosound.htm), and test your knowledge of basic economic principles in the context of professional sports. Write a brief summary of your experience. What did you learn from playing the game?

5. **Monetary Policy: You're in Control**
   How would it feel to be in control of the monetary policy for a country? Play MoPoS (short for: Monetary Policy Simulation Game—http://www.rbnz.govt.nz/education/0116902.html). Once you download this game, you act out the role of a fictitious central bank by implementing monetary policy in a simple virtual economy so you can get a feel for the options and limitations of monetary policy. Write a brief summary of your experience. What did you learn from playing the game?

Web Case

To access the Chapter 2 Web case and exercise, see the End of Chapter Assignments section @ www.mybizlab.com.

Video Case

To access the Chapter 2 Video case and exercise, see the End of Chapter Assignments section @ www.mybizlab.com.

Ethics in Business

p. 67

Personal Ethics Meets Business Ethics
▼ **Objectives 3 & 4**

Randy Marks had a recipe for success with his pottery business, but it flew in the face of his personal beliefs. What do you do if your own ethics conflict with success in business?

p. 71

Corporate Social Responsibility
▼ **Objectives 5 & 6**

Although the primary focus in business often seems to be on making money, many businesses also make meaningful contributions to the social, environmental, and economic development of the world. The question remains, however: Can a corporation be held responsible for its actions the same way people are held accountable for theirs?

p. 78

Dangers of a Weak Ethical Focus
▼ **Objectives 7 & 8**

Sometimes it seems that if you break ethical standards just a bit, you'll come out ahead. But does it really pay in business to ignore ethics? Or do good guys come out ahead?

p. 82

Business Opportunities Created by Ethical Needs
▼ **Objective 9**

By creating new markets based on ethical needs and by going green, many companies reap financial rewards, improve employee morale, and make valuable contributions to the world.

p. 63

Ethics: The Basics
▼ **Objectives 1 & 2**

Ethics and business—many people consider these terms to be nearly opposite in meaning. How can you maintain your own personal integrity while still fulfilling your business responsibilities? Examining your own personal ethical code is the first step in successfully navigating this potentially tricky terrain.

p. 85

How Businesses Develop an Ethical Environment
▼ **Objective 10**

If you want to lead your business to a more ethical future, how do you begin? Developing an ethical environment is a goal that all business managers hope to achieve.

Ethics: The Basics pp. 63-66

> After reading the box on the right, it can be useful to summarize what you've written in a list. Later you'll see that businesses follow a similar plan when creating their own statements of values. Why is this important? It will be easier for you to work with or for a business if you have a well-defined statement of personal values.

Ethics Defined

So what exactly *are* ethics? **Ethics** refers to the study of the general nature of morals and of the specific moral choices a person makes.[1] In effect, ethics are the guidelines you use to make decisions each day. But not all people share the same ethics. Many systems of ethical conduct exist. Some are based on religious systems, some are cultural or national, and some have been passed from generation to generation within a specific ethnic group.

Systems of Ethical Conduct

What are the different systems of ethical conduct? One ethical system is **moral relativism**, a perspective that holds that there is no universal moral truth but instead only people's individual beliefs, perspectives, and values. This means that there is no single view that is more valid than any other; therefore, no single standard exists to assess ethical truth. According to moral relativists, each person has his or her own ideas of right

---

Have you ever examined your own personal ethical code? Although it takes time and effort, if you have a clear idea of what values are most important to you, it may be easier to handle situations in your professional life that require you to make complex ethical decisions. ▼ **Table 3.1** outlines one way to analyze your own ethical system. Let's look at each step in the process:

1. First, write down what kind of person you are—what is your *character*? Would a friend describe you as helpful and kind? Ambitious and greedy? Be honest in your assessment of yourself.

2. Next, make a list of the *beliefs* that influence your decision making. For example, would you feel comfortable working in a lab that tests on animals for medical research purposes? Think about whether your answers are "flexible"—that is, how committed are you to adhering strictly to your ethical positions?

3. Next, consider your *behavior* with regard to the places you work and live and how you relate to the people around you. Would you like to change anything about your behavior? For example, do you ever find yourself gossiping or speaking in a way that creates a more divisive workplace? You may feel justified in the comments you're making, but is your ethical position on gossiping creating the kind of environment you ultimately want?

4. Now that you have your beliefs written down, think about *why* you believe them. Have you accepted these beliefs without investigation, or do they stand up to the test of real-world experiences in your life? Would it be worth making a short-term sacrifice to uphold these values? ➤

▼ **Table 3.1**

	Question	Examples
Base Character	What characteristics would others use to describe you?	Honest, reliable, kind, self-centered, aggressive
Beliefs	What are the most important beliefs you hold and use to make decisions in your life?	"Nice guys finish last." "Hard work always pays off."
Behavior	How do your relationships reflect your character and beliefs?	I have mostly shallow relationships because I tend not to follow through on my commitments. I have many deep, long-lasting friendships because I value friendship and work to retain my friends.
Why	Where did your beliefs and your view of your character come from?	Family, religion, movies, personal experiences, etc.

Determining Your Code of Personal Ethics

and wrong, so who are you to judge anyone else? Imagine trying to organize any group of people—a family, a company, or a country—according to this ethical system.

Another ethical system is **situational ethics**, in which people make decisions based on a specific situation instead of universal laws. Joseph Fletcher, a Harvard Divinity School professor, developed situational ethics because he believed that applying the Golden Rule—treating others as you would like to be treated—was more important in making ethical decisions than applying complex sets of moral rules. Because it challenged the idea that universal rules exist and can be applied to every situation, Fletcher's ethical system was considered very controversial.

Many other ethical systems exist, some of which are defined by religious traditions. For example, **Judeo-Christian ethics** refers to the common set of basic values shared across both Jewish and Christian religious traditions. These include respecting property and relationships, respecting one's parents, and being kind to others.

But don't some people behave without regard for ethics? It is true that sometimes people act in a manner that violates the beliefs they hold or the beliefs of the ethical system they say they follow. **Unethical behavior** can be defined as behavior that does not conform to a set of approved standards of social or professional behavior. This is different from **amoral behavior**, in which a person has no sense of right and wrong and no interest in the moral consequences of his or her actions.

Personal Ethics

What are personal ethics? Every day you have thoughts that lead you to say and do certain things. As you choose your words and actions, you're following a set of **personal ethics**, the principles that guide the decisions you make in your life. Sometimes, people have a very clear, well-defined set of principles that they follow. Other times, a person's ethics are inconsistent or are not applied the same way in every situation. Still other times, people have not taken the time to clarify what they value most.

Sometimes, it seems clear that making an unethical decision will produce an immediate benefit. This is when it is most challenging to adhere to your own ethical system. Consider this example: When applying for her dream job, a college senior exaggerates a bit on her resume about her experiences and responsibilities during an internship to seem more qualified. Is this lying or is it justified behavior?

Now consider how you treat property. Say you bring home a few pads of paper, some pens, and a stack of blank CDs from the supply closet at work. Is this stealing? What if it was just one piece of paper you brought home? Some would say it depends on whether you use the material to do work at home. What if you used some of it on work projects and some on personal projects? And what if it wasn't you who were taking office supplies, but someone else with whom you work? It's often easy to have one view when you're taking the supplies and another when it's the person you like least in the office.

"*Interesting business proposal. We'll have to run it by illegal.*"

How do a person's ethics develop? Life experiences offer all of us opportunities to develop our personal ethics. We also need to decide whether the behavior we see around us makes sense within the ethical systems we have learned from our family, our place of worship, or our first-grade teacher. Sometimes, our experiences lead us to abandon some ethical rules and to adopt others. And for some of us, our ethical rules are modified depending on what is at stake.

How can an ethical life get me ahead? Sometimes, ethics feel like an abstract ideal, ideas that would be nice in a utopian world but that don't have any real impact on your life in the here and now. But there are some clear benefits from living ethically.

First, society has established its own set of rules of conduct as *laws*. It's no surprise that ignoring or being inconsistent in following these principles can have an immediate impact on your life. Whether it is complying with a law about the way you run your business or following laws that affect your personal life, decision-making principles that work within society's legal boundaries can make your life much simpler.

Living ethically may even be good for your health. When your day-to-day decisions are in conflict with the values that you consider most important, you often feel stressed and angry. In situations in which there is constant conflict between what you value and what actions you're forced to take, a variety of types of mental and physical damage may follow.

For example, Renate Schulster was a vice president for the human resources department at a financial services firm.[2] She was asked to investigate an employee's allegation of sexual harassment. Schulster's investigation led her to believe that the chief executive officer (CEO) of the corporation was guilty of the offense. Her personal ethics dictated following through with the employee's claim, which put

Biz**Chat**

Can Living Ethically Make You Happy?

Research suggests that happiness itself is a result of living ethically. Psychology has established this as a new focus with the birth of an area of psychology known as *positive psychology*. Dr. Martin Seligman of the University of Pennsylvania[3] pioneered this field to discover the causes of happiness instead of addressing the treatment of mental dysfunctions. Seligman's research has shown that by identifying your personal strengths and values, as shown in ▼ **Table 3.2**, and aligning your life so you can apply your personal strengths and values every day, you will see an increase in happiness (and a decrease in depression) equivalent to the effects of antidepressant medication and therapy. Finding a way to identify and then apply your ethics and values to your daily life does indeed have an impact on your happiness.

For more information and discussion questions about this topic, check out the BizChat feature on www.my*biz*lab.com.

▼ **Table 3.2**

Virtues and Strengths for Authentic Happiness		
Virtue	**Definition**	**Character Strength**
Wisdom	The acquisition and use of knowledge	Creativity, curiosity, open-mindedness
Courage	The will to accomplish goals in the face of opposition	Authenticity, bravery, persistence, zest
Humanity	Tending to and befriending others	Kindness, love, social intelligence, empathy
Justice	Just behavior or treatment	Fairness, leadership, teamwork
Temperance	Strengths that protect against excess	Forgiveness, modesty, prudence, self-regulation
Transcendence	Forging connections to the larger universe	Gratitude, hope, humor, appreciation of beauty

*Adapted from **American Psychologist** July 2005, Positive Psychology Progress—Empirical Validation of Interventions by Seligman, Park, and Peterson*

her at odds with the company. As the pressure from the conflict between her own values and those of the CEO of the company grew, she sought psychological counseling for the emotional impact of the stress. She was eventually able to recover her medical and legal expenses from the employer and left the position. Renate held on to her integrity; however, the battle was not an easy one.

As you probably found when analyzing your own ethical system at the beginning of the chapter, personal ethics are a large part of how people define themselves, their roles in society, and their business conduct. By investing careful thought into your own personal ethical standards, you can be clearer on what you must do in conflicting work situations. What exactly you will do may be a little more difficult. Nonetheless, a personal analysis like the one you completed earlier will help guide you to rise to the challenge.

▼ You have just read **Objectives 1 & 2**

Think you got it? Check out the Study Plan section @
www.my*biz*lab.com.

Personal Ethics Meets Business Ethics pp. 67-70

▶ We often find ourselves torn between several choices, and finding a path that works for both you and the company you work for can be challenging. In some settings, the line between right and wrong can be difficult to see. Other times, your own personal values just won't align with the company's, and you may wish you had understood more about the company's sense of ethical culture early in your career there, before you invested your time and effort. Let's look at some examples, resources, and techniques to help you navigate ethical conflict in the workplace.

"It was a beautiful glaze," Randy Marks says with a sigh. His small pottery shop, Oak Hills Tile, depends on orders from individuals and small architecture firms who are looking for authentic, custom pieces of tile to adorn their kitchens, floors, or fountains. "I used copper and a special firing method to give the glaze a stunning crimson color," Randy explains. "It was our best-selling item." An architect in New York City quickly signed Oak Hills to produce a much larger number of tiles for his clients. This meant more hours and more employees hired at Oak Hills to handle this boom. However, part of the production process entailed additional copper to be introduced during firing, and a thick black smoke was produced, laced with toxic copper. As orders increased, more often than not, the kiln in the back of the workshop was spewing this smoke into the air, in contrast to the clean white smoke produced by normal glazes.

But Randy had been part of environmental groups in his community for years, so he knew how detrimental to the environment this process was. How could he find a way to stay true to his ethical standards and still be mindful of his responsibilities to his employees and customers? ▶

You as a Person and as an Employee

What role do personal ethics have in a business environment? Our personal ideas of right and wrong influence our actions, words, and thoughts. But how does that carry over into the work environment? After all, at work our employer is purchasing our time and energy. As employees, our responsibility is to follow the ethics that the owner or director has established for the business. However, a business owner has no control over or even input into your conduct outside the office.

But is this true really? Perhaps at one time this model applied to life in the United States, but the modern workplace is more complex. Today, behavior, integrity, and honesty off the job relate to on-the-job performance. For example, in the modern workplace, workers telecommute, working from home using technologies to connect electronically to office documents and meetings. In this newly expanded workplace, an employer may indeed care if an employee drinks at home during the workday or experiments with drugs recreationally after hours. The business environment is a changing landscape, and the lines of privacy laws are becoming blurred. Do employers really have a say over

employees' behavior outside the office if that behavior may affect the company for which he or she works?

Likewise, stockholders (people who own stock in the company) and employees sometimes have a say over the behavior of management outside the office. In 2004, Boeing[4] was recovering from a set of scandals involving how it obtained military contracts. The aerospace leader fired its current CEO and hired a former Boeing employee, Harry C. Stonecipher, to lead the company back to stability. Fifteen months later, Stonecipher, who was married, was discovered having an affair with a female employee. The very same code of conduct Stonecipher had created and pointed to as a sign of the return of ethical conduct at Boeing was used to force his resignation. There were no charges of sexual harassment, and the woman did not work directly for Stonecipher. He never showed her any

> In 2004, Boeing fired its CEO Harry Stonecipher for unethical conduct. Ironically, Stonecipher had been hired to lead Boeing back to stability after a number of scandals had rocked the aerospace company.

favored treatment within Boeing. But there still was a conflict between his personal ethics and his role in the business. It took a great toll on him personally as well as the company he was working to restore.

What if you are asked to do something that is outside of your understanding of ethical behavior? It can be challenging to decide

whose ethics to follow, yours or your company's, and each path has legal and moral consequences. For example, Andrea Malone[5] was ordered by the president of her company to fire an employee who had a brain tumor because the tumor had lowered the employee's productivity. Andrea knew the Americans with Disabilities Act covered such situations and that it was a violation of federal law to fire the employee under these conditions. However, her company insisted she fire the employee and say that it was for other reasons, not the tumor. Andrea chose to leave the company rather than fire the person unfairly, but she has since had difficulty finding other employment. Andrea held to her personal ethics, but was not properly prepared for the short-term consequences.

And what if you find you are taking part in unethical activity without having known that you were doing so? Before Bruce Forest[6] accepted a job offer to be a human resources director, he asked the firm about rumors that they hired undocumented immigrants. He was assured that was no longer the case, but soon after Bruce started to work for the company, reports began arriving that such illegal hiring was a continuing practice. His boss ordered Bruce to stop investigating the situation, saying that the company would prefer the risk of being fined by the INS (now called the U.S. Citizenship and Immigration Services). The fine the company would have to pay was "an acceptable business expense," according to Bruce's boss. So now Bruce was complicit in this activity and had to make some tough decisions. Should he move his family, take a pay cut, and lose his promised bonus, or stay knowing he's now a party to this deception?

To stumble unknowingly into unethical and even illegal activity brings consideration of our own ethics to the forefront. Both inside and outside the office, people can find themselves involved in situations that are difficult for them ethically, but it is especially difficult when your job is on the line. Consider Mark Whitacre,[7] a senior executive with the agricultural giant Archer Daniels Midland (ADM). ADM was involved for years in a multinational price-fixing scheme. **Price fixing** occurs when a group of companies agree among themselves to set the products' prices, independent of market demand or supply. Based on such price fixing, ADM stole millions of dollars from its customers by agreeing with its own competitors to set a product's price. Whitacre was a participant in all illegal activities and was set to rise to the very top of the organization. His wife, however, became increasingly conflicted with what was happening at ADM and with her own ethical values. She finally threatened to divorce Whitacre unless he found a way to end his involvement. Whitacre then went to the FBI and agreed to tape secret meetings at ADM, ultimately recording over 250 hours of incriminating audio and video tape. Although some people decide they will be flexible with their own ethical standards at the workplace, it can often take a toll on their mental state, their relationships, and their physical health.

▶ ADM was at the center of an international price-fixing scandal, meeting with its own competitors to set the price and amount of product it sold. This huge conspiracy was uncovered because ADM employee Marc Whitacre became an FBI informant for two years.

What did Randy Marks, the owner of Oak Hills Tile, decide to do when his personal ethics and business ethics collided with the production of the special pottery glaze? No one was "watching"—there was no censure from any environmental authority, and no laws were being broken. But the conflict for Randy was too much. "I had campaigned against factory emissions of air pollution for years," Randy said. "The ethical conflict was too great; I had to stop making the glaze." Randy's decision led to difficult times for the shop. The New York architect cancelled his order—the glaze had been the winning factor for his business. The workers in the shop were also frustrated. They loved producing such interesting, beautiful pieces, and the new orders meant extra hours and extra earnings. Their shop was so small, they argued, how could a little smoke possibly matter in the big scheme of things? Randy had to be firm, explaining over and over again that his personal ethics had to be consistent with his workplace ethics, and that he was sure that in the long run, Oak Hills Tile would benefit from his decision.

Identifying a Company's Ethics

How do I examine a company's ethics? Some companies may have a written **code of ethics**, or a statement of their commitment to certain ethical practices. Additionally, many companies have a public **mission statement** (sometimes called a *corporate vision*) that defines the core purpose of the organization—why it exists—and often describes its values, goals, and aspirations. Consider the following mission statement of Fetzer Vineyards:

> We are an environmentally and socially conscious grower, producer, and marketer of wines of the highest quality and value. Working in harmony and with respect for the human spirit, we are committed to

sharing information about the enjoyment of food and wine in a lifestyle of moderation and responsibility. We are dedicated to the continuous growth and development of our people and business.[8]

This mission statement has led to 100 percent organic wine production, awards for conservancy of energy, and a company-wide English as a Second Language training program offered as part of its education package to employees. Paul Dolan, president of Fetzer Vineyards, states, "When the first words of your mission statement are *environmentally and socially conscious*, it opens up new perspectives on how to operate the entire business."[9]

Smaller firms, like Randy's Oak Hills Tile, often benefit from the same kind of focus on key principles. Although Oak Hills Tile does not have a formal written mission statement, Randy's behavior and willingness to discuss his decision behind discontinuing the popular glaze let each employee see clearly the priorities Randy holds for the business. Even though the employees did not easily accept his decision, they felt the larger mission of the business was well defined and respected.

How can I find out the best and worst aspects of a company's ethical conduct?

In addition to a company's code of ethics and mission statement, other resources allow you to evaluate the acts of responsibility of and legal violations by any given company. For example, you can check the legal compliance of a corporation by researching actual charges that have been filed or cases that have been judged against the company. Web sites like www.lawcrawler.com help you find relevant case law generated by lawsuits filed by or against many corporations.

There are also organizations like the Boston College Center for Corporate Citizenship (www.bcccc.net), which works with corporations to help them define, plan, and institute their corporate citizenship. The center also highlights companies that act in positive ways by publicizing responsible corporate activities and listing on its Web site reports in the general media of ethical issues in business. By doing so, the center works with companies to "leverage their assets to ensure both the company's success and a more just and sustainable world."[10] We'll discuss other ways you can assess a company's ethics and sense of corporate responsibility in the next section.

▼ You have just read **Objectives 3 & 4**

Want a review? Check out the Study Plan section @ **www.mybizlab.com.**

Corporate Social Responsibility pp. 71-77

➤ Corporate decisions reflect a company's desire to fulfill a sense of corporate social responsibility. Every day, large companies like Gap, Disney, and Shell, as well as medium-sized firms and small local businesses, must make decisions regarding corporate social responsibility. Let's look at what it means, who it affects, and how companies can achieve it.

The Five Pillars of CSR

What is corporate social responsibility? **Corporate social responsibility (CSR)** can be defined as a company's obligation to conduct its activities with the aim of achieving social, environmental, and economic development. All business organizations, regardless of their size, have a corporate responsibility. By being socially responsible, a company makes decisions in five major areas (see Figure 3.1):[14]

1. human rights and employment standards in the workplace

2. ethical sourcing and procurement

3. marketing and consumer issues

4. environmental, health, and safety concerns

5. community and "good neighbor" policies

Let's look at each of these areas.

Read the following examples of recent corporate actions.

- Gap, Inc., a major clothing retailer with factories around the world, launches a program called P.A.C.E.—Personal Advancement, Career Enhancement—in Delhi, India, with plans to expand to Cambodia and Turkey. The program aims to help women in developing countries by providing them with education and leadership training.[11]
- The Walt Disney Company bans cigarettes from its family films.[12]
- Shell Oil works toward reducing emissions of nitrous oxide and sulfur dioxide—both of which contribute to smog and acid rain—from its facilities.[13]

Now, think about what these actions have in common. Why did Gap, Disney, and Shell make these decisions? What do you think was their motivation, or goal? What kind of effects have these decisions likely had? ➤

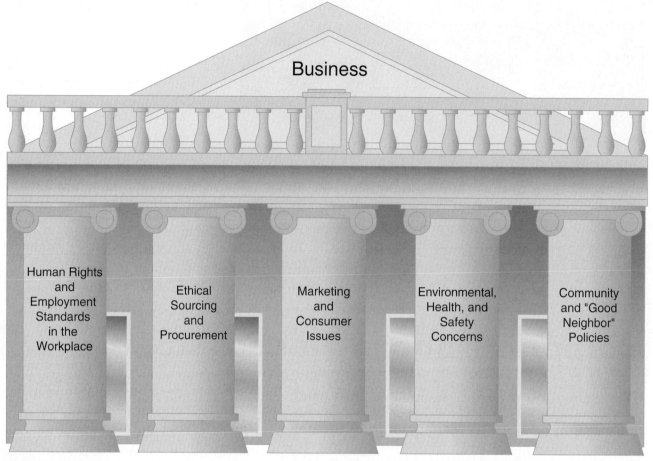

Business

Human Rights and Employment Standards in the Workplace

Ethical Sourcing and Procurement

Marketing and Consumer Issues

Environmental, Health, and Safety Concerns

Community and "Good Neighbor" Policies

▼ **Figure 3.1**
The Five Pillars of CSR
Corporate social responsibility is the collection of policies covering five major areas and can be the foundation of a business.

Human Rights and Employment Standards in the Workplace

CSR concerns affect the world outside the office in both the local and global communities. For example, employment standards—how a company respects and cares for its employees—are reflected locally in the policies a company sets and the impact the company has on the community. As a business interacts more with the global marketplace, the company will have to make decisions about working with companies with different ethical standards on tough issues like child labor, pollution, fair wages, and human rights. The owners of No Sweat, for example, know a great deal about avoiding interaction with companies that have different ethical standards. No Sweat, a United States-based apparel company, decided not to employ manufacturers that use sweatshops to make clothing. Although using sweatshops would allow the company to produce the clothing at lower costs and receive higher profits, No Sweat's owners believe that the use of sweatshops is unethical.[15]

Ethical Sourcing and Procurement

Finding a source for raw materials and making agreements with suppliers is an aspect of many businesses. In today's global marketplace, many companies find themselves working with international suppliers. Once a business has to consider purchasing materials from a supplier in a different country or even a different region of the country, they are tied to environmental and social concerns in that area. Consider a company that has an assembly plant in a different country. That company is now tied to the social conditions there. To keep its supplier operating or to keep an assembly plant running smoothly, the company has a vested interest in the quality of the schools in that area so that the local workforce is educated. The banana supplier Chiquita, for example, has recently begun to improve conditions for its workers by constructing housing and schools for employees' families.[16] It takes a very aware and thorough commitment to CSR for a business to make decisions such as these.

Marketing and Consumer Issues

Marketing can often present ethical challenges. In addition to issues regarding truth in advertising, marketers must consider messages that may be manipulative even if they are not outright lies. For example, advertising of tobacco on television has been prohibited by law in the United States since 2002. Some, however, argue that having an actor smoke a particular brand of cigarette in a blockbuster Hollywood movie is just as influential. These are the types of marketing and consumer issues that companies must consider if they are to behave in a socially responsible way.

Environmental, Health, and Safety Concerns

Many industries, and even small companies, make decisions every day that affect the environment and the safety of their workers or their neighbors. From multinational manufacturing giants to the local auto body shop, any industry involved with processes that produce toxic waste must make decisions that directly affect the environment. Meanwhile, the production of toxic materials is moving at a far faster pace than the growth of proper storage facilities and techniques, so disposal becomes more and more expensive. What are the short- and long-term costs of ignoring these concerns? Companies that have a CSR focus concentrate on ways to make such decisions in a socially sound way.

Community and "Good Neighbor" Policies

Finally, CSR is concerned with how the company affects the community, particularly the surrounding neighborhood. This issue has been a challenge for Wal-Mart for years. In the 2005 documentary *Wal-Mart: The High Cost of Low Price*, film director Robert Greenwald argues that Wal-Mart pays its "associates" so little that the arrival of a Wal-Mart outlet in a community actually costs the community.[17] Because workers are paid poorly and are not offered medical benefits to cover their children, Medicaid expenditures increase. In addition, Greenwald argues that many of the local smaller businesses cannot compete with the giant and are forced to close. Adding insult to injury, often a community has given Wal-Mart subsidies to attract them to the area. Finding a way to be good corporate neighbor is important to avoid the tensions and bad publicity that Wal-Mart has struggled against.

The Conflict of CSR in the Business Environment

Can a corporation really be socially responsible?

Nobel Prize-winning economist Milton Friedman said, "Asking a corporation to be socially responsible makes no more sense than asking a building to be."[18] He argued that an abstract idea, like a corporation, cannot perform human functions, such as meeting responsibilities. There has long been debate around these ideas. A company does have a unique responsibility to its stockholders: They expect a profit at the end of the year. It is difficult to measure whether that responsibility outweighs a long-term responsibility to the community or the planet. There can be a conflict between the company's need to produce profit

► Wal-Mart's impact on a community is debated in the film *Wal-Mart: The High Cost of Low Price*.

for its shareholders and the demands of quality in the product it delivers to its customers. With so many competing interests, companies must carefully analyze the idea of appropriate social and corporate responsibility.

The Benefits of CSR

What are the benefits of CSR? Having a strong and clear ethical policy helps a business in a number of ways.[19]

- The company develops a positive reputation in the marketplace with consumers as well as with its suppliers and vendors.
- The company enjoys strong recruitment and retention of the best available talent.
- Efficiency increases when companies use materials efficiently and minimize waste.
- Sales increase through new product innovations and environmentally and ethically conscious labeling.

Although businesses reap benefits while being socially responsible, management at very high strategic levels needs to have a common vision of how the interests of the business can be supported by an effective CSR policy.

Measuring CSR

Is it possible to measure a company's level of CSR? It may seem impossible to measure something as complex as CSR, but there are reports that present a useful picture of the overall strength of a company's CSR effort.

Social Audits

A **social audit** is a study of how well a company is doing at meeting its social responsibilities. It is an internal systematic examination measuring and monitoring what goals the company has set, what progress it has made, and how resources such as funding and manpower have been applied to the goals of CSR.

Ratings and Rankings

In addition to social audits, companies like Boston College's Center for Corporate Citizenship (mentioned earlier) assess corporate responsibility and publish their findings. And companies like the Calvert Investment Company provide corporate responsibility ratings and reports to consumers. The Calvert Company assigns companies a score between 1 (well below standard) and 5 (superior) in the categories of environment, workplace, business practices, human rights, and community relations. A "Calvert Leader" is defined as a "company with consistently high performance in all issue areas."

In addition to social audits and the Calvert ratings, a number of magazines, such as *Fortune*, publish lists of admired companies each year. Other organizations award businesses for superior CSR. For example, past winners of the Business Ethics Awards, given by *Business Ethics* magazine, have included companies such as Chroma Technology, Corp., which manufactures optical filters. In this global company, employees hold all seats on the board of directors. In addition, no employee makes more than $75,000 or less than $37,500 each year. Another recent winner was Clif Bar, Inc., a manufacturer of organic energy bars. In 1990, Gary Erickson started the company in his kitchen with $1,000. In 2000, he was about to accept an offer of $120 million for the company. At the last minute, he learned that the purchasers were planning to move Clif Bar out of state and let all current employees go. He felt his integrity and vision were at stake, and so he canceled the deal and took over the company again. Clif Bar is known for giving employees extended sabbaticals. The company is also powered entirely by renewable energy.

Self-Reporting

Self-reporting by companies of their own efforts in addressing ethically complex issues and issues of social responsibility is also becoming more prevalent. For example, in June 2006, Time Warner presented a report to its stockholders discussing its advances in corporate citizenship, including its focus on journalistic integrity, socially responsible programming (including such issues as the depiction of smoking in films), content accessibility, consumer privacy, content diversity, and child protection.[20]

Corporate Philanthropy

Many companies participate in **corporate philanthropy**, donating some of their profits or resources to charitable organizations. Often companies view such charitable activity as a marketing investment that builds a stronger relationship with the community and with their own employees. Consider the Target, Corp., store chain. The retailer donates 5 percent of its pretax profits to charity, which comes to about $3 million dollars a week. This is more than twice the average of other American corporations.

Another example is the Bill and Melinda Gates Foundation, started by Microsoft chairman Bill Gates. With an endowment of $33 billion, the Gates Foundation has tackled issues like global infant survival rates, has begun an initiative for a malaria vaccine, and is working to upgrade public access to technology. Even though the foundation is not directly associated with Microsoft, it has had a positive impact on the public perception of Microsoft.

▼ top

10 *Fortune's* **Most Admired Companies, 2008**

1. Apple
2. Berkshire Hathaway
3. GE
4. Google
5. Toyota
6. Starbucks
7. FedEx
8. Procter & Gamble
9. Johnson & Johnson
10. Goldman Sachs

The Challenges of CSR

What challenges does CSR pose? It's clear that the many conflicting demands facing businesses today pose numerous ethical challenges. Consider the dilemma facing companies that produce unique products, like pharmaceutical companies that develop medications to treat AIDS. What is their exact moral and ethical obligation with regard to the AIDS pandemic in sub-Saharan Africa? AIDS killed 1.6 million people in Africa in 2007. Tuberculosis killed approximately 550,000 that same year, and at least 1 million people die from malaria each year, mostly children.[21] Meanwhile, 70 percent of the population exists on less than $2 a day and is unable to pay for the medications at a price point that would reimburse pharmaceutical companies for their research investment. It is a challenge for modern business leaders to balance their need to respond to investors and produce a profit with their desire to alleviate human suffering. There is no fixed training that can prepare business decision makers so that they are equipped to navigate such difficult decisions.

➤ The Bill and Melinda Gates Foundation commits more than $1.5 billion a year in grants to global health and development projects such as funding the search for a vaccine to prevent malaria.

As noted above, some corporations do manage to consistently balance the demands of social responsibility and successful business practices. A company like Intel scores high as an industry leader in the commitment to the practices of strong CSR. Environmentally, it has decreased the emissions from its operations over the past four years, mitigating its impact on global warming. It has shown a strong commitment to its employees by providing benefits for domestic partners as well as carefully monitoring workers for exposure to hazardous chemicals. The company also has human rights policies in place in all of the countries it operates, and it donates computer equipment to many organizations, supports many charitable organizations through monetary donations, and is responsive to community needs.

The Effects of CSR on Society

How does CSR affect society as a whole? Business does not operate separately from society as a whole, so CSR affects us all in many ways.

Environmental Effects

Environmentally, how businesses operate has both local and global effects. For example, people living in the Silicon Valley area around San Francisco rely on groundwater for their main supply of water. This leaves the entire Silicon Valley area dependent on proper industry practices by the many semiconductor manufacturers in the area. If these companies allow chemical contaminants to enter the groundwater system, the entire region suffers.

Businesses raise troubling environmental questions on a global scale as well. Some say that allowing free trade—in which countries produce and sell products anywhere in the world—will produce an "export" of pollution to less developed countries. Would companies move "dirty industries," those that have a high risk of pollution, danger to workers, or toxic damage of the environment, to a country where environmental regulations are lacking? It's increasingly important for industry leaders to have some structured ethical system to make such complex, long-reaching decisions.

Economic Effects

As an individual, CSR affects you as well. Financially, the long-term consequences of businesses implementing a strong CSR plan have an impact on the prices you pay for products, the products that are available, as well as the quality of these products. Both your short-term savings and long-term investments also rely on interest rates that are related to the perception of how stable your business is. Industries that act in ways that jeopardize their own long-term sustainability can create economic ripples that affect your bottom line.

Effects on Employee Morale

Think of your own career. Your potential for advancement, your day-to-day work environment, and your overall sense of purpose and value are affected by the degree to which the company you work for practices sound CSR. The ethical culture of a company and its leadership have an effect on its workers every day. Sometimes, this effect is a positive one. Consider the Kaplan Thaler advertising agency, the fastest-growing advertising firm in the country, started by Linda Kaplan Thaler and Robin Koval.[22] The company, which began as a one-client start-up in 1997 and reached billings of more than $1 billion in 2006, prides itself on creating unique advertisement campaigns—like the Aflac duck campaign—that grab viewers' attention. Yet with all of its success, the core philosophy of the company is that it pays to be nice, described in Thaler and Koval's book, *The Power of*

Nice. After spending years at high-powered, high-pressure firms where "those who eat their young get raises," they founded a firm dedicated to the principles of being empathetic, assuming the people around you are out to help you, and remembering that emotionally well-adjusted people earn higher incomes, live longer, and have more satisfying lives.[23] The company founders' beliefs affect the employees at Kaplan in each part of their workday.

Even from the initial interview, aspects of a company's CSR plan may be apparent. Some companies find that personality testing of job candidates helps them find employees that match their own corporate values. Tools like the Hogan Personality Inventory assess a candidate in areas such as interpersonal sensitivity, stress tolerance, and learning approach. As a job seeker, you'll want to decide whether you value a company for using these tools or if their use violates your sense of appropriate business/personal privacy boundaries.

The Effects of Individuals on CSR

Can I affect how businesses operate ethically? There are many ways that you as an individual can work toward a more ethical world filled with more ethical businesses. In addition to contributing by means of your own personal conduct, both at the workplace and outside it, your choices about where and on what to spend your money greatly influence corporate behavior. Companies survive only because consumers buy their products or use their services. If you don't believe in a company's ethics, you can take your business elsewhere.

Meanwhile, if you choose to invest money in mutual funds and the stock market, you have another opportunity to make a statement about corporate ethics. **Socially responsible investing (SRI)** is investing only in companies that have met a certain standard of corporate social responsibility. This means funds managers look at the social and environmental behavior of companies to decide which companies to include and exclude from the investment fund portfolio. As a shareholder, you can also use your voice to encourage a company to improve or maintain a high standard of ethics.

Finally, when you choose an employer, you're making a clear statement on ethical conduct by offering the company your valuable time and energy. By agreeing to work for a company, you're saying that you agree with its mission and ethics.

Corporate social responsibility is a complex idea that requires companies and consumers to examine the ethical implications of their actions. Review the examples at the beginning of this section. Which of the "five pillars" are Gap, Disney, and Shell addressing with their actions? Do you agree with the ethical implications of their actions? Are they making a real difference? Why or why not?

▼ You have just read **Objectives 5 & 6**

Want to learn more? Check out the Study Plan section @ **www.mybizlab.com.**

Dangers of a **Weak Ethical Focus** pp. 78-81

"To me, it was stealing, and bottom line: stealing is wrong." The software firm that Lana Phillips worked for had finished developing a program to deliver movie content on-demand to home cable subscribers. Before it could break into the market, however, it needed to test its product and make appearances at big electronics trade shows. To test the program, the company needed data—that is, DVD movies. But DVD movies are copyrighted and protected with specific software encoding schemes so they cannot be copied onto a computer hard drive. As the testing phase approached, the word came down from management: Purchase some DVDs, break the encoding scheme, and rip them to hard drives to use as testing. After all, the managers reasoned, the company was not going to make money off violating the DVD copyrights—it was just using it to test its software. And if it worked well, it would then run demos for clients and at trade shows using those DVDs. What was the harm?

The company consulted its attorneys and half felt the use of the DVDs might be illegal and half felt it could be defended. Lana suggested some other solutions: The company could use Hollywood films that were older and not covered by copyright protection, or it could use public domain documentaries, which were freely available for public use. Company managers worried what the impact on business would be. Would a product shown running a 30-year-old movie or an unknown documentary grab the attention of buyers on a busy Vegas tradeshow floor? The danger on the other side was that a successful product launch by the company might not save it from facing legal action years down the line for copyright infringement. How could Lana and her boss resolve the issue when it wasn't even clear what the correct legal path was?

Depending on the industry, there may be significant legal consequences to business behavior that ignores agreed-upon ethical standards. Companies are responsible for following complex sets of laws and if they violate them, even unknowingly, their business may be in jeopardy. Violating the law deliberately can be the result of a lapse in emphasis and understanding of ethics and will have a serious impact on the future of the people inside the company and on the entire business community. In this section, we'll examine some of the dangers to a business of ignoring ethical conduct.

Legal Regulations and Legal Compliance

How is a company regulated legally? **Legal regulations** are the specific laws governing the products or processes of a specific industry. When enough people feel that a particular ethical standard is important, it eventually becomes law. For example, in 1962, the Consumer Bill of Rights was passed in Congress. This bill made the following ethical standards legal rights:

- the right to safety
- the right to choose
- the right to information
- the right to be heard[24]

Another example is the U.S. Department of Agriculture's (USDA's) Organic seal, which assures consumers of the quality and integrity of organic products. To have a product certified as organic, a company must meet conditions set by the USDA, including meeting annual and random inspections to check on standards.

Legal compliance refers to conducting a business within the boundaries of all the legal regulations of that industry. Government agencies like the Equal Employment Opportunity Commission (EEOC) and the Securities and Exchange Commission (SEC) provide guidance to companies to help them maintain legal compliance. The EEOC monitors compliance by investigating complaints of violations of federal law on issues such as discrimination, sexual harassment, or violations of the Americans with Disabilities Act. The Americans with Disabilities Act of 1990 requires companies to make a reasonable accommodation to the known disabilities of an applicant or employee, as long as it doesn't require undue hardship for the employer. The SEC governs the securities industry, making sure that all investors have the same access to information about companies.

Violations of governing laws can damage a company severely. We mentioned earlier how Archer Daniel Midlands, the agriculture giant, was involved in a large price fixing scheme in which it bilked its own customers out of millions of dollars. The company was later fined $100 million for its role in the price fixing. Likewise, in 2003, telecom giant MCI WorldCom was fined $750 million because of accounting fraud.

Don't companies often break the law and still make money?

There are plenty of cases in which companies have broken the law and seemed to benefit for a time. Take the case of Enron. With 21,000 staff members in more than 40 countries, Enron had grown to become America's seventh largest company. The company was lauded by *Fortune* magazine as the Most Innovative Company in America many times and was in the top 25 of *Fortune*'s 100 Best Companies to Work For. Enron had published its social and environmental positions, noting that the company made decisions based on the values of:[25]

- respect: mutual respect with communities and stakeholders affected by the company's operations
- integrity: examining the impacts, positive and negative, of the business on the environment and on society, and integrating human health, social and environmental considerations into the company's management and value system
- excellence: continuing to improve performance and encouraging business partners and suppliers to adhere to the same standards

But by October 2001, a series of scandals began to emerge when it was found that Enron's success had been largely based on fraudulent activities. The company had hidden debts totaling more than $1 billion to inflate its own stock price, had manipulated the Texas and California power markets, causing enormous hardship, and had bribed foreign governments to win contracts abroad. A few months later, the company dissolved in bankruptcy, and founder Kenneth Lay was convicted on 10 counts of fraud and conspiracy. He later died while awaiting sentencing. CEO Jeffrey Skilling was convicted of 18 counts of fraud and faces a sentence of 24 years in prison.

Even the accounting auditor that Enron had hired, the famous firm Arthur Andersen, collapsed as a result of its involvement. Andersen was convicted of obstruction of justice for destroying thousands of documents relating to its work with Enron and its knowledge of the criminal fraud taking place there. For Enron and Arthur Anderson, the flagrant violations of ethical conduct led to outside agencies levying huge penalties. It also led to the internal collapse of the company with the loss of the company's management and many of the employees within the firm. Most sadly, it led to the loss of the pensions of thousands of employees who had dedicated their lives to the company, not knowing management was participating in such illegal activities.

To avoid future occurrences such as these, the Sarbanes-Oxley Act was enacted. Under this act, CEOs are required to verify their companies' financial statements and vouch for their accuracy with the SEC.

Even though Lana's firm was not knowingly committing fraud on the scale of the Enron scandal, many of the same principles were at play. The temptation to ignore existing laws in order to make a profit, or even the chance for profit, was at the heart of both stories. For Enron officials, the penalties they paid for their unethical actions were devastating to thousands, if not millions, of people. At Lana's firm, future penalties could cripple the company, but the immediate penalty of knowingly violating her own personal code of ethics was the driving force for Lana. She was forced to decide whether she would refuse to work on the project and potentially lose her job, knowing that her manager would assign the work to another employee who would then be breaking the law. Lana decided to make her case to the company, urging it to not use the copyrighted DVDs. Ultimately, the company executives agreed with Lana's argument. They felt that the risk of future copyright infringement lawsuits was too great. Lana's persistence paid off, and she was able to maintain both her job security and her personal code of ethics.

Recovering from Weak Ethical Conduct

What if your company is breaking the law and you want it to stop? Some people risk their positions and future careers to stop corporate abuse when they see it in the workplace. A **whistleblower** is an employee who reports misconduct, most often to an authority outside the firm. Famous examples include Jeffrey Wigand, a vice president of a tobacco company who revealed on the television show *60 Minutes* in February of 1996 that his company was deliberately manipulating the effect of the nicotine in its cigarettes to promote addiction. Another example is Sergeant Joseph Darby, who sent to the U.S. Army Criminal Investigation Command an anonymous note and a set of images of the abuse taking place at Abu Ghraib prison in Iraq. It sparked an investigation that eventually revealed to the public the abuses at Abu Ghraib. Darby later received a John F. Kennedy Profile in Courage award, but he and his wife were forced to live in protective custody in an undisclosed location because of threats made against them.

Legal protection for whistle-blowers varies from state to state and industry to industry. For the people who take such a step, the pressure of the conflict between what they see and their own ethical standards forces them to make sacrifices.

" Companies do business in an ecosystem. Ultimately you can't have a great reputation unless everyone who comes in contact with you trusts you. And people don't trust you unless they think you do the right thing. " [26]

—Dov Seidman, CEO of LRN, a consultant firm specializing in legal compliance and ethical management

Can a company really recover from an ethical lapse?

Companies seeking to recover from publicized ethical lapses often face long battles once customer loyalty and the company's reputation have been lost. Recovery almost certainly requires pervasive change, and usually people who were not involved in the wrongdoing are involved in the efforts to forge a new image. For example, a major scandal broke at Tyco International in 2003. An SEC investigation had found that company president Dennis Kozlowski and chief financial officer Mark Swartz had swindled more than $170 million in illegal corporate loans and another $430 million by manipulating the company's stock price. Both Kozlowski and Swartz were convicted of fraud charges and later sentenced for up to 25 years in prison. Within a few months of being named the new CEO of Tyco, Edward Breen replaced the entire Tyco board and 290 employees.

Companies that are attempting to recover from scandal often follow some common strategies:

1. They work to find a leader who will set an example of the new ethical image of the company.

2. They restructure their internal operation to empower all employees to consider ethical implications of decisions and to feel free to speak up when they spot a concern.

3. They redesign internal rewards—for example, restructuring the incentive package for a sales department so that there is a financial reward for building an ongoing relationship with a client rather than just closing a sale one time.

By using creative thinking and adhering to clearly stated ethical principles, a company can actually turn a scandal into something good. For example, in 2004, many shoppers boycotted Target because the chain had a policy of not allowing solicitors to collect money outside its doors, including volunteers collecting for the Salvation Army. In fact, the Salvation Army claimed the ban cost them more than $9 million in possible donations. Target could have responded with a defensive attack on the Salvation Army. Instead, the company chose to work with the charity, first donating the lost $9 million directly and then by creating an online "Wish List" that shoppers could use to donate toys, clothes, and household items to needy families during the holiday season. By acting together with the Salvation Army in new ways, Target was able to turn a negative situation into something beneficial for both Target and the community.

▼ You have just read **Objectives 7 & 8**

Want to test your skills? Check out the Study Plan section @
www.mybizlab.com.

Business Opportunities Created by Ethical Needs pp. 82-84

At Bank of America, one of the world's largest financial institutions, it not only pays its employees for working, it pays them for shopping, too! That is, as long as this shopping involves the purchase of an environmentally friendly hybrid car. In June 2006, the company piloted a new program that offered over 21,000 associates in three cities—Boston, Charlotte, and Los Angeles—$3,000 toward the purchase of a new hybrid vehicle.[27] "The program continues to expand our commitment to the environment and offers our associates a way to participate in making a difference while cutting down on their commuting costs,"[28] said Anne Finucane, Bank of America's Global Marketing and Corporate Affairs executive and head of the company's environmental council. The program was a success; within a year, hybrid vehicle purchases by employees more than quadrupled, and Bank of America had plans to expand the offer. With this measure, Bank of America both helped bolster employee morale and reduce toxic emissions to the environment. How else might companies create opportunities from ethical needs? ➤

➤ So far we've paid attention to the extra work and the difficult decisions that are required to conduct business ethically. But there are also opportunities and the potential for gain by understanding and applying ethical standards to a business. Some companies focus on creating new markets with an ethical focus. Others redesign their business so that they no longer have a negative impact on the environment. Still others use ethical challenges as a tool to unite and empower employees.

Creating New Markets with an Ethical Focus

How can firms create business by acting ethically? By examining the world with an eye toward social responsibility, many firms have created opportunities with new types of products and services. Let's look at a few examples.

Offering Clean Fuel

Canadian-based Topia Energy has opened the first chain of "alternative fuel" stations, named GreenStop, which offer only renewable fuel blends, such as gasoline combined with corn ethanol. The gasoline products can be used in regular cars, and the stations themselves are constructed from renewable, chemical-free products. Inside you won't see the same lineup of cigarettes and candy, but you will have your choice of organic veggie wraps and coffee roasted using solar energy.[29]

Creating Medical Vaccines

Other companies have created business opportunities by addressing the world's most serious medical needs. Malaria kills up to 3 million people a year, mostly children, and is the leading cause of death in children worldwide, mostly in Africa. The disease is transmitted very easily, whereas the drugs currently used to treat it are becoming increasingly ineffective. Many businesses haven't found a way to balance the tremendous cost of research for creating a malaria vaccine with the anticipated meager profits. Enter Sanaria, a new pharmaceutical company founded by scientist Dr. Stephen Hoffman, whose mission is to create a malaria vaccine. Hoffman remarks, "I haven't spent 25 years working on diseases of the most disadvantaged and neglected people in the world to start a company that's just here to make money."[30] Already the company has secured government grants and a $29.3 million Gates Foundation grant.[31]

> Earth-friendly Topia GreenStop gas stations are popping up in Canada and the United States.

Fighting Censorship

Still other companies are creating business opportunities by fighting censorship. The Chinese government maintains a tight rein on the flow of information to its citizens, including controlling the accessibility of certain Internet sites. This censorship left Dynamic Internet Technology (DIT) company founder Bill Xia with a very skewed view of the world when he arrived in the United States from China. "I was a believer of the propaganda," he says.[32] Now DIT and similar companies provide a service to their clients in an effort to counteract the impact of censorship. When a site is placed onto the list of censored sites by the Chinese government, DIT quickly creates a new, uncensored Web address that points users to the same material. A list of the new accessible sites is then e-mailed to Web surfers who want full Internet access. Chinese censors often stamp out the new site within a few days, at which point DIT starts the process again, determined to override censorship through its business. These and other companies are showing there are ways to create business opportunities and tackle difficult ethical issues at the same time.

Businesses Going Green

How can businesses benefit by going green? While some businesses are tackling ethical issues and offering consumers more ethical choices through their businesses, others are attempting to reduce the impact they have on the environment. Take Interface, the world's largest commercial carpet manufacturer. The company was careful to follow all laws and regulations relating to its industry in its first 21 years of business, but it made no special commitment to stewardship of the environment beyond that. Then, in 1994, CEO Ray Anderson read *The Ecology of Commerce* by Paul Hawken.[33] He was so inspired by the book's message that he began the process of reorganizing his $1.4 billion company using the principles of **sustainability**—the process of working to improve the quality of life in ways that simultaneously protect and enhance the earth's life support systems.[34] Interface has a mission statement, nicknamed Mission Zero, which reads: "Our promise is to eliminate any negative impact our company may have on the environment by the year 2020."[35]

top

10 **"Greenest" Companies in the World**

1. Vestas Wind Systems (Danish)
2. Svenska Cellulosa (Swedish)
3. ABN-Amro (Dutch)
4. MTR (Hong Kong)
5. Ericsson (Swedish)
6. Westpac Banking (Australian)
7. Kingfisher (British)
8. Philips (Dutch)
9. BT Group (British)
10. Matsushita* (Japanese)
10. Sanyo* (Japanese)
10. ABB* (Swiss)

*These companies are tied for tenth place.

➤ In 2006, Starbucks stopped double cupping its hot drinks, saving some 78,000 trees a year. It also offers discounts to customers who use their own mugs when buying coffee.

Interface is considering all aspects of its business in its goal to run its business without having a negative impact on the planet. It is eliminating waste and toxic substances from its products, using renewable energy, and finding how to route its trucks for more efficient transportation routes. The grand goal of Mission Zero has resulted in a shift in the company's principles and the goals and expectations of shareholders.

COOL carpet is one product that demonstrates how Interface now operates. The "cool" part of COOL carpet is that it allows customers to choose to have an impact on global warming. Interface makes sure that all of the carbon dioxide emissions over the full life cycle of COOL carpet—from its manufacture through its delivery—are offset. Actions like purchasing energy from wind farms and choosing suppliers that are "green"—ecologically friendly—balance out the necessary carbon dioxide produced in other stages of carpet production. Anderson recognizes the choices Interface makes today will ultimately affect future generations and hopes his customers see the value in these choices and go green themselves.

Another large international company that has worked for over a decade to reduce its environmental footprint is coffeehouse giant Starbucks. In 1996, the company "double-cupped" every cup of coffee it sold, which meant using a second cup as insulation so customers could carry their steaming hot coffee drinks without burning their fingers. With the company selling some 1.9 billion cups a year, the director of environmental affairs led an effort to move instead toward a more environmentally-friendly cup. In 2006, began using a single "eco-cup," made from 10 percent recycled paper, and no longer doubles the cup but instead uses a sleeve made of recycled materials. This change alone save about 78,000 trees in just the first year.[36]

Companies can create opportunities based on ethical challenges in a number of different ways. New businesses are appearing, focused on addressing the ethical issues of our times. Other businesses redesign their business so that they leave no negative impact on the environment. Some, like Bank of America, respond to ethical needs in ways that both benefit the environment and boost employee morale. As many of today's most successful innovative companies have demonstrated, upholding ethical standards need not be a burden to businesses; it can instead be a portal to great opportunities.

▼ You have just read **Objective 9**

Want to quiz yourself? Check out the Study Plan section @ **www.mybizlab.com.**

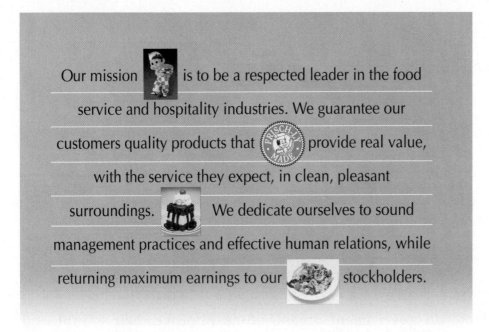

Our mission is to be a respected leader in the food service and hospitality industries. We guarantee our customers quality products that provide real value, with the service they expect, in clean, pleasant surroundings. We dedicate ourselves to sound management practices and effective human relations, while returning maximum earnings to our stockholders.

How Businesses Develop an Ethical Environment pp. 85-87

➤ Almost every business wants to promote an ethical environment, but sometimes managers find it difficult to know how to implement this successfully. Let's look at some different approaches being used by businesses to help their employees and the company decision-making processes become attuned to an emphasis on ethical conduct.

Ethical Focus from the Start

How can a business improve its own culture of ethical and responsible conduct? There are a number of steps businesses can take to make sure employees get off to an ethical start:

1. Managers can make sure a meaningful and current mission statement is in place and is clearly communicated throughout the many levels of the business. The mission statement should discuss issues of ethics and should be posted throughout the workplace.

2. Managers can focus on ethics themselves, setting clear examples for the standards of behavior expected at all levels of the organization.

3. The company can offer orientation programs to new employees to inform them of the ethical standards in place and the conduct expected of them right from the beginning of their careers.

If you were the CEO of a business, how would you ensure that your employees conducted business ethically? Consider the scenarios below. What steps would you take to improve the company's ethical environment?

Scenario 1: You've reminded your employees over and over about the company's code of ethics. However, you've found that employees are continually making decisions that do not adhere to the company's mission. What do you do?

Scenario 2: As the boss, you feel that you have a right to take home company supplies. However, you've noticed that many of your employees have begun taking home company supplies, too. You don't want this practice to continue. What do you do?

Scenario 3: You've recently hired many new employees. While they possess the basic skills required for their position, the new employees are not making the ethical decisions you'd like them to. What do you do?

Scenario 4: Your higher-level employees have a strong grasp of how to make ethical decisions, but you see that your lower-level employees are struggling with these issues. What do you do?

Do you know how you'd handle each situation? Do you have ideas for ways to avoid these situations in the future? Write a short paragraph explaining how you'd react to each scenario. To find out ways to respond to situations like these, pay particular attention to this section. ➤

On Target Playing the Ethics Game

A unique approach to ethics training is used by Cadbury Schweppes. The international confectionery and beverage company has created a board game called "Ethical Risk" that its employees play to help bridge the gap between the values the company wants to achieve and the day-to-day decision making and practices of its managers.[38] Scenarios are presented to teams, who are asked not to compete but to work together to rank the possible answers from most to least preferred. This approach promotes a stronger dialog within the company and builds insight into the practical ways to address the complex issues of corporate ethics and social responsibility.

4. Many companies employ ongoing **ethics training programs** designed to boost the awareness of their employees about ethical issues. Such training occurs at all levels of the organization. From top management that makes strategic and far-reaching decisions, to frontline managers who use their decision-making skills to put out fires, to sales people who work with vendors and must navigate ethical questions, to lower-level employees who make decisions regarding whether to follow the advice of their leaders, all levels of employees are involved in ethical training.

How do government organizations improve their ethical and responsible conduct? Private sector businesses are not alone in wanting ethics training programs for their employees. State and government organizations face similar challenges. Many law enforcement agencies—including local police, state police, and the FBI—have ethics training programs to help officers deal with cases in which there may be no clear response.[37] For example, when an officer responds to a domestic disturbance call but decides no crime has been committed, does he or she have a responsibility to try to prevent a potential escalation into a future criminal incident? By discussing, role-playing, and writing about these scenarios, the officers are more prepared for the ethical dilemmas facing them on the job.

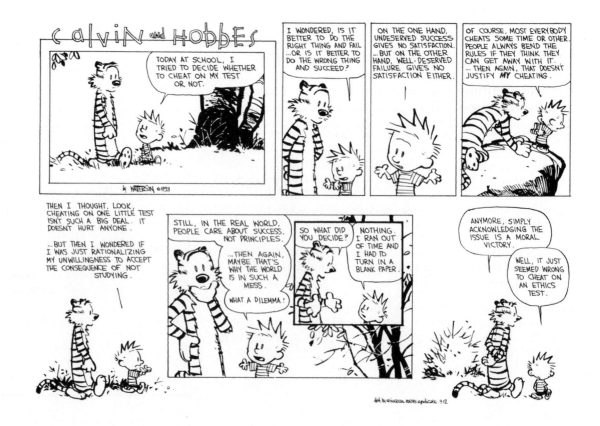

➤ Zhang Yue, chief executive of Broad Air Conditioning, discusses company ethics with new employees. Broad Air Conditioning manufactures energy efficient units sold to 30 countries worldwide and has developed the first solar air conditioning unit. The factory employs 3,000 people, most of whom live in factory dorms and eat organic food grown on the grounds.

Ethical Focus Every Day

How can a business maintain its policy of ethical conduct in the workplace? When employees are faced with unethical situations daily, adhering to a company's code of ethics can be very difficult. Business leaders must take steps in to make sure all employees are making ethical decisions. Frank Ross, a visiting professor at Howard University School of Business, has created a list of tips to help companies maintain ethics in the workplace. Ross believes that companies should:

- Develop a strict code of ethics and check sporadically to make sure the code is being followed.
- Create a hotline for employees to anonymously report violations of the ethics code and make sure the allegations are followed up on.
- Set the right tone at the beginning—show how serious the company is about ethics and act with the highest regard to ethical behavior.
- Communicate regularly about acceptable and unacceptable business practices.

Developing an ethical environment involves a number of components and often requires a concentrated investment of time and resources; however, it remains a priority for most businesses. Look back at the scenarios introduced on page 85. After reading this section, do you want to change your plan for addressing the situations?

▼ You have just read **Objective 10**

Think you got it? Check out the Study Plan section @
www.my*biz*lab.com.

1. What are ethics and different ethical systems? (pp. 63-64)

- **Ethics** (p. 63) are the moral choices people make.
- Ethical systems include:
  - **moral relativism** (p. 63), a perspective that holds that there is no universal moral truth but instead only individuals' beliefs, perspectives, and values
  - **situational ethics** (p. 64), which encourages people to make ethical decisions based upon the circumstances of a particular situation, not upon fixed laws
  - systems defined by religious traditions, such as **Judeo-Christian ethics** (p. 64), which refers to the common set of basic values shared across both Jewish and Christian religious traditions

2. How does a person create a personal code of ethics? (pp. 63-66)

- First, determine your base character.
- Next, make a list of all of the beliefs that influence your decision making.
- Next, think about how your behavior reflects these beliefs.
- Now think about where your beliefs and view of your character come from. Why do you hold these beliefs?

3. How might personal ethics play a role in the workplace? (pp. 67-69)

- Having a strong ethical foundation can help you achieve success in business and greater happiness in life.
- In the modern workplace, there is less distinction made between how you conduct yourself inside and outside the office. Telecommuting is one instance when a person's employer may influence how an employee behaves at home.
- Conflicts can emerge when your **personal ethics** (p. 63) are different than those of your company.

4. How can you evaluate a company's ethical code using available resources such as a mission statement? (pp. 69-70)

- Some companies may have a written **code of ethics** (p. 69), or a statement of their commitment to certain ethical practices.
- Many companies have a public **mission statement** (p. 69) that defines the core purpose of the organization and often describes its values, goals, and aspirations.

5. How do a company's policies and decisions affect its achievement of corporate social responsibility? (pp. 71-75)

- **Corporate social responsibility (CSR)** (p. 71) consists of five major areas: employment standards, ethical sourcing, marketing issues, environmental concerns, and community policies.
- A strong CSR plan allows a company to serve its local and global communities well. It also benefits the corporation in direct and indirect ways.

6. What challenges does a company face in balancing the demands of social responsibility with successful business practices? (pp. 75-77)

- Companies must balance their moral and ethical obligations to consumers with their need to respond to investors and produce a profit.
- It's also important for companies to show a strong commitment to their employees (by ensuring workplace safety), the local community (by responding to community needs, for example), and all the countries in which they operate (by upholding human rights policies). At times, it can be difficult to balance these commitments with the need to ensure that the business remains financially successful.

7. What is legal compliance, and how does it affect ethical conduct? (pp. 78-80)

- **Legal compliance** (p. 79) refers to conducting a business within the boundaries of all the legal regulations of that industry.
- Companies that establish and adhere to high ethical standards are more likely to maintain legal compliance.

8. What strategies can a company use to recover from ethical lapses? (pp. 80-81)

- The company can work to find a leader who will set an example of the new ethical image of the company.
- The company can restructure its internal operation to empower all employees to consider ethical implications of decisions and to feel free to speak up when they have concerns.
- The company can redesign internal rewards.

9. How can companies apply ethical standards to create new business opportunities? (pp. 82-84)

- While some businesses are tackling ethical issues and offering consumers more ethical choices through their businesses, others are attempting to reduce the impact they have on the environment.

10. What approaches can a company use to develop and maintain an ethical environment? (pp. 85-87)

- Managers can make sure a mission statement is in place and set clear examples for the standards of behavior expected at all levels of the organization.
- Companies can offer orientation programs to new employees to inform them of the ethical standards in place.
- **Ethics training programs** (p. 86) can boost the awareness of employees about ethical issues.

For an audio file of the Objectives and Chapter Summary, see the Student Resources section @ www.my*biz*lab.com.

Key Terms

amoral behavior (p. 64)

code of ethics (p. 69)

corporate philanthropy (p. 75)

corporate social responsibility (CSR) (p. 71)

ethics (p. 63)

ethics training program (p. 86)

Judeo-Christian ethics (p. 64)

legal compliance (p. 79)

legal regulations (p. 79)

mission statement (p. 69)

moral relativism (p. 63)

personal ethics (p. 64)

price fixing (p. 68)

situational ethics (p. 64)

social audit (p. 74)

socially responsible investing (SRI) (p. 77)

sustainability (p. 83)

unethical behavior (p. 64)

whistleblower (p. 80)

Self-Test

Multiple Choice Correct answers can be found on page 503.

1. **Amoral behavior means that a person**

   a. makes bad ethical choices.

   b. is a strictly moral person.

   c. behaves without thinking things through.

   d. has no consideration for the moral consequences of his or her actions.

2. **A corporation can behave in a socially responsible way by**

   a. having strong policies in place to help the community.

   b. acting to reduce the negative impact the company has on the environment.

   c. being truthful with consumers in its market.

   d. All of the above

3. **In cases when there is no formal charge of sexual harassment**

   a. there has been no ethical violation.

   b. there has been no legal violation.

   c. there still may be negative consequences for the individual and the firm.

   d. None of the above

4. **CSR can be measured by**

   a. the company's rate of growth.

   b. organizations that monitor and rank performance on social issues.

   c. the happiness level of employees in the company.

   d. businesses that have a high profit margin and gross sales.

5. **A business is in legal compliance if**

   a. it follows all the laws of which it is aware.

   b. it cannot be proven guilty of violating any laws.

   c. it meets all local, state, and federal regulating standards.

   d. it only hires employees who do not have criminal records.

6. **A whistleblower**

   a. harms the company by attracting negative publicity.

   b. is always valued by the company as an asset.

   c. can count on legal protection only in some states.

   d. seeks to be rewarded within the company.

7. **A mission statement**

   a. defines the core purpose of an organization.

   b. is a set of principles that guides your personal decisions.

   c. indicates how well a company is doing at meeting its social responsibilities.

   d. is the common set of basic values shared across both Jewish and Christian religious traditions.

8. **The theory of moral relativism asserts that**

   a. people should make ethical decisions based on a particular situation.

   b. there is no universal ethical truth.

   c. people should model their ethical code after important leaders.

   d. there is a set code of values shared across religions.

9. **Which of the following strategies is _not_ designed to help a company recover from an ethical lapse?**

   a. Ensuring that the whistleblower faces legal consequences

   b. Working to find a leader who will set an example of the new ethical image of the company

   c. Restructuring internal operations to empower all employees to consider ethical implications of decisions and to feel free to speak up when they have concerns

   d. Redesigning internal rewards—for example, restructuring the incentive package for a sales department so that there is a financial reward for building a relationship with a client rather than just closing a sale

10. **The book _The Power of Nice_**

    a. is a theory that has not yet had any serious business success.

    b. is a cautionary tale of how employees can take advantage of nice managers.

    c. states that success can be found by treating each other with empathy and assuming other people are trying to help you rather than hurt you.

    d. is a strategy that only works in advertising because advertising is a more friendly work environment by nature.

Self-Test

1. A mission statement details the plans of how a company will achieve profitability.
   □ **True** or □ **False**

2. Corporate philanthropy is the practice in which companies donate a portion of their profits or resources to charitable organizations.
   □ **True** or □ **False**

3. Ethics is the study of the general nature of morals and of the specific moral choices a person makes.
   □ **True** or □ **False**

4. In the real world of business, those who fail to make ethical compromises cannot succeed.
   □ **True** or □ **False**

5. Ethics training programs have proven to be unsuccessful in improving ethical codes in the workplace.
   □ **True** or □ **False**

Critical Thinking Questions

1. How can a person determine his or her personal ethical code? What is your personal ethical code? What forces have helped build your personal code of ethics?

2. Where are the boundaries between personal ethics and business ethics? Are there rules to indicate where one begins and the other ends? Should there be?

3. How does a corporation's responsibility to shareholders to produce a profit interact with its social responsibility? Name several areas of possible conflict and analyze them from both a short-term and long-term view.

4. Give an example of a situation in which a business can treat an ethical challenge as an opportunity.

5. How can both small and large businesses establish a common ethical framework for employees and executives?

Team Time

One Issue, Three Sides

Divide into three teams, one to represent each of the following:

a. pharmaceutical company executives

b. people with a catastrophic but treatable illness

c. people identified as having "unique" DNA

Scenario

Are there some things that can't be owned? Leukemia patient John Moore would answer yes. After Moore had his cancerous spleen removed at the University of California, the University kept the spleen and was eventually granted a patent for DNA removed from the organ. The value of the DNA was estimated to be more than one billion dollars. When Moore demanded that his cells be returned, the California Supreme court ruled against him, saying that he had no right to his own cells after they had been removed from his body. Pharmaceutical researchers, like those at the University of California, often hope to later license the DNA patterns or sell them to other companies so they may use them to develop drugs or tests for the presence of disease. Does the person or group of people who have that specific, perhaps unique, gene have ownership? Do they deserve payment? Do they have a right to a voice in the use of their genetic material?

Process

Step 1. Record your ideas and opinions about the issue presented in the scenario above. Be sure to consider the issue from your assigned perspective.

Step 2. Meet as a team and review the issue from the multiple perspectives. Discuss together what one best policy could be developed to address the concerns of all three groups.

Ethics and Corporate Social Responsibility

Personal and Business Ethics

As you've learned, sometimes a person's personal code of ethics does not fall in with the code of ethics used in his or her profession. What is your personal code of ethics? What profession do you hope to have in the future? How does your personal code of ethics match the code of ethics used in that profession? Would you be willing to ignore your personal ethical code for business?

Process

Step 1. Draft your personal code of ethics. Use the steps for analyzing one's own ethical system that is outlined at the beginning of this chapter.

Step 2. Think about a profession you'd like to have in the future. Visit http://ethics.iit.edu/codes/codes_index.html to find the code of ethics employed in this profession.

Step 3. Compare your personal code of ethics to the profession's code of ethics. Then, write a paragraph explaining how the two codes compare.

Web Exercises

1. **Happiness and That New Lexus**
   Do you need a new car every few years to be happy? International studies of happiness suggest that happiness is not tied to income or material wealth. Watch the BBC videos "Bhutan's happiness formula" (8 minutes, 39 seconds) and "The recipe for happiness" (8 minutes, 7 seconds) (both at http://news.bbc.co.uk/2/hi/programmes/happiness_formula/default.stm) and see if you think the idea of a Gross National Happiness measurement can be incorporated into the decision making of organizations.

2. **Identifying Your Strengths**
   Psychologist Martin Seligman's Web site, found at www.authentichappiness.sas.upenn.edu/Default.aspx, promotes the field of positive psychology. Visit the site and complete the VIA Signature Strengths Questionnaire. Consider how you can use your strengths each day in the work schedule you have right now.

3. **Social Issues: How Do These Companies Measure Up?**
   The Calvert Investment Company makes reviews of corporate performance on social issues available on its Web site. Visit www.calvert.com/sri_calvertratings.html, select one company, review its report, and discuss your reaction.

4. **Determining Your Personality Type**
   Complete the personality test at www.41q.com. Analyze the results to identify your Myers-Briggs personality type. What are your strengths? Are there any areas you would like to develop?

5. **Corporate Social Responsibility Report**
   Toyota posts an annual CSR report. Visit www.toyota.eu/04_environment/sust_report.aspx to view the latest abridged report. According to the report, which issues were considered to have to greatest significance for external stakeholders and Toyota alike?

Web Case

To access the Chapter 3 Web case and exercise, see the End of Chapter Assignments section @ www.my*biz*lab.com.

Video Case

To access the Chapter 3 Video case and exercise, see the End of Chapter Assignments section @ www.my*biz*lab.com.

Business in a Global Economy

p. 100

International Trade

▼ **Objective 3**

Large and small companies alike face foreign competition. Changes in foreign competitors' prices can be detrimental to businesses. What are the benefits of international trade? What are the costs?

p. 103

Trade Barriers and Protectionism

▼ **Objective 4**

Which is better—protectionist trade barriers or free trade? Factory workers in Ohio would say trade barriers, but consumers might say free trade. How do free trade agreements affect businesses and members of a community?

p. 110

Conducting Business Internationally

▼ **Objectives 5 & 6**

When conducting international business, many more factors come into play. What are the strategies of international business? How can you enter a foreign market? Which mode is best?

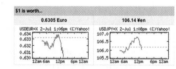

p. 115

International Business: Economic Factors and Challenges

▼ **Objectives 7 & 8**

Exchange rates encourage or deter countries from trading with one another, and other economic factors play a huge role in what products are exported overseas. Business owners are turning to countries with favorable exchange rates, like China, to import goods. How do exchange rates impact a nation's economy? What economic challenges does international trade create?

p. 95

International Business: What's It All About?

▼ **Objectives 1 & 2**

If you took an inventory of all your belongings, you'd probably see items from a wide array of countries that represent the global market. Products you use every day, like clothing, cars, and computers, are imported from countries around the globe. What is globalization, and why has it risen so rapidly?

p. 119

International Business: Sociocultural, Political, Legal, and Ethical Challenges

▼ **Objective 9**

How would you feel if a potential client from Brazil arrived late for a meeting? What challenges may you face when working with international business contacts? Knowing the answers to such questions is vital to running a successful global business.

International Business: What's It All About? pp. 95-99

➤ Former President Bill Clinton once said, "Globalization is not something we can hold off or turn off . . . it is the economic equivalent of a force of nature—like wind or water."[1] In recent years, the rise of globalization has made a dramatic impact on the lives of people around the world. People from the United States to Taiwan to Argentina are all connected and dependent on one another for a variety of goods and services. The United States and other nations are increasingly **importing**, or buying products from other countries, and **exporting**, or selling domestically produced products to other countries. This trend is why you'll notice that many products you own were made in countries other than the United States. Not only has globalization affected individual lives, it has also affected the way companies conduct business around the world.

Studying international business will make you a better employee, business owner, person, and citizen. It will broaden your horizons, requiring you to think outside your own domestic economic, social, and political box. Because the world is truly a global village, studying international business can also help you understand and appreciate the complex nature of the global economy, the rich diversity of world cultures, and the intricacies of international politics. At the very least, studying international business will give you the tools to answer questions inherent in many of today's headline-grabbing issues. For example, what can people do to enhance their country's ability to compete in the global economy? What can a country do to provide good-paying jobs for its citizens? How can U.S. companies increase their profitability in the face of foreign competition at home or enhance their market share overseas? When the U.S. dollar is stronger or weaker than other countries' currencies, how does it affect business in the United States? After studying this chapter, you'll be able to answer these and other questions.

Made in the USA? Not so fast. It's more likely that your belongings come from all over the world. Take this personal inventory and decide for yourself.

Check the labels on the following items to determine where in the world they were made.

- Shoes
- Shirt
- Pants
- Purse or backpack
- Technological device (cell phone computer, camera, MP3 player, etc.)

Calculate the number of countries, other than the United States, that are represented. If your personal belongings represent . . .

0 countries	Your goods are homegrown
1–2 countries	Your possessions have international flair
3 or more countries	Your goods truly reflect the growing trend of globalization ➤

Globalization

What is globalization? The old sayings "No man is an island" and "It's a small world, after all" can both be used to describe globalization. **Globalization,**[2] the movement toward a more interconnected and interdependent world economy, may be one of the most profound factors affecting people around the globe. Without a doubt, whatever happens today in the U.S. economy—the world's largest economy—will have a significant impact on people all around the world. It's also true that changing economic conditions in other countries can affect the U.S. economy and produce a ripple effect on U.S. consumers, businesses, and workers.

Consider an example: The booming economies of India and China are a major reason for the growing global demand for energy. Increased energy demand is one of the major causes of the world's rising oil prices, which have created higher prices at the gas pump for people around the world. As a result, people have less money to spend on other things, such as eating out. Local restaurants and other local businesses feel the pinch. Their sales fall. In response to lower demand, businesses curtail production and lay off employees. Higher energy prices can also drive up production costs and, in turn, can drive up the prices businesses must charge consumers. Businesses' sales and profits are squeezed once more. The consequences don't stop here, but you get the picture. People in the United States can be affected by events that have originated halfway around the world—events over which they have no control.

Facets of Globalization

Markets have not only become more interconnected, but they've also become more reliant on one another. You only have to inspect the tag on a department-store item—like a purse or a sweater like you did in the inventory of your possessions on page 95—to find that it may have been produced in China or in another foreign country. Many products consumed in the United States today, like laptop computers and cars, are often made from parts that have been manufactured in locations around the world (see ▼ **Figure 4.1**).

▼ **Figure 4.1**
Made in the USA?
Many brand name products are composites of components manufactured at different locations around the world. For example, most people think that Ford cars are made in the United States. But is it really "made in the USA" if most of its components are manufactured in other countries or assembled outside the United States?

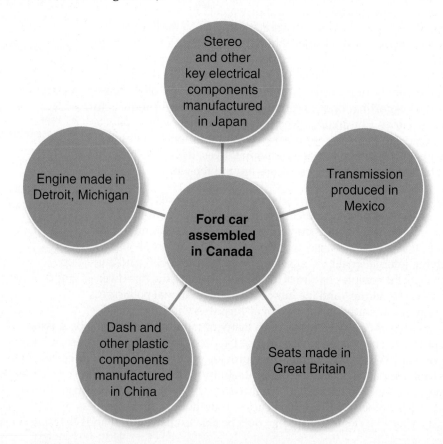

Globalization of Markets

Globalization has two main components: the *globalization of markets* and the *globalization of production*.[3] The **globalization of markets** refers to the movement away from thinking of the market as being the local market or the national market to the market being the entire world. Companies like General Electric, Dell, and Toyota are not just selling to customers in Dallas or Atlanta, California or Vermont, or Japan or Europe, they're selling to customers all over the globe. Even some relatively small companies find it profitable to sell their products abroad. ▼ Figure 4.2 shows that many U.S. corporations are benefiting from overseas markets.

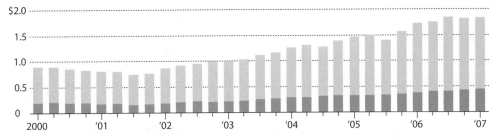

Help From Overseas

■ Receipts from overseas operations ■ Domestic operations

U.S. corporate profits are getting a boost from overseas...

In trillions; at a seasonally adjusted annual rate

Note: Corporate profits with inventory-valuation and capital-consumption adjustments (at current costs; quarterly data)

▼ **Figure 4.2**
Help from Overseas
Markets are increasingly becoming global markets. Notice the growing importance of foreign sales (receipts from overseas operations) to U.S. corporations.

The globalization of markets has become so widespread that more and more businesses are finding that they must "think globally and act locally." Companies often need to adjust their products or marketing campaigns to suit the unique tastes and preferences of their local customers, wherever they may be. For example, Coca-Cola often has to tweak its recipes to appeal to the tastes of consumers in different parts of the world. In India, Coca-Cola adapted its Minute Maid orange soda recipe to suit the taste of the majority of the Indian population, who prefer a sweeter version of the drink than is sold in the United States.[4] Similarly, many foreign-owned companies advertise or adapt their products for sale in the United States to attract consumers. As a result, it can be difficult to determine whether a company is U.S. owned or not. Look at the list of companies in ▼ Table 4.1 and see if you can figure out which are U.S. firms and which are foreign.

Globalization of Production

Globalization of production, the other facet of globalization, refers to the trend of individual firms moving production to different locations around the globe to take advantage of lower costs or to enhance quality. Globalization of production often involves *outsourcing*. **Outsourcing** is the assigning of certain tasks, such as production or accounting, to an outside company or organization. Currently, much outsourcing is *offshore outsourcing* (or *offshoring*), a term that describes the movement of production away from a domestic production site to a foreign location. When faced with intense foreign competition, firms may be forced to relocate at least some of their production to another country to realize lower costs so they can offer customers lower prices.

Globalization of markets and production is certainly nothing new. In fact, countries have been trading with each other since ancient times. What has raised so many eyebrows in the last several decades is the rapid pace at which globalization has been accelerating. Globalization of markets and production has resulted in some international firms becoming

▼ **Table 4.1**

Which Countries Are Home to These Companies?
Company
Adidas
Bayer
Shell Oil
Nokia
Samsung
Lamborghini
Purina (Alpo Dog Food)
Nestlé
Procter & Gamble
Jaguar

*Answers: Adidas—Germany; Bayer—Germany; Shell Oil—the Netherlands; Nokia—Finland; Samsung—Korea; Lamborghini—Germany; Purina—Switzerland; Nestlé—Switzerland; Procter & Gamble—United States; Jaguar—United States

so large that they generate more revenue than the gross domestic product (GDP) of most nations. This is reflected in ▼ **Figure 4.3**. Notice that if Wal-Mart were a nation, it would rank as the 30th largest country in the world in terms of the total revenue it generates.

Reasons for the Rise in Globalization

Why has globalization accelerated so rapidly? Two main factors seem to underlie the trend toward greater globalization.[5] The first is the dramatic decline in trade and investment barriers among countries since the end of World War II. The second is the role of technological innovations.

Decline in Trade and Investment Barriers

Trade and investment barriers are government barriers that prevent the flow of goods, services, and financial capital across national boundaries. (We'll discuss these barriers in more detail later in the chapter.) The lowering of trade barriers makes global business much cheaper and easier. The lowering of trade and investment barriers also lets international firms move their production facilities to the least-cost location for that activity, serving the world market from that location. A firm might design its product in one country, produce component parts in two or three other countries, assemble the product in yet another country, and then export it around the world. This is exactly what many companies, such as Ford, are doing today.

Technological Innovations

Technological innovations have also made it possible to manage the global production and marketing of products. Consider the dramatic advances in communications, transportation, and information technology. Using teleconferencing, a business manager in New York can meet with contacts at a firm's European or Asian operations without ever leaving his or her office. If a restaurant needs to purchase fresh Norwegian salmon, it can have the product flown in. People are also able to communicate and share information more rapidly and cheaply than ever before. BlackBerrys and wireless Internet access, which keep people in constant contact with the outside world, have significantly reduced the cost of doing business. Recent technological advancements have also been the great equalizer for small companies, enabling them to access customers worldwide through their Web sites at negligible expense so they can more effectively compete with huge global corporations.

▼ **Figure 4.3**
Company Revenue vs. National Incomes
Many international businesses today are larger than most countries in terms of economic activity generated.

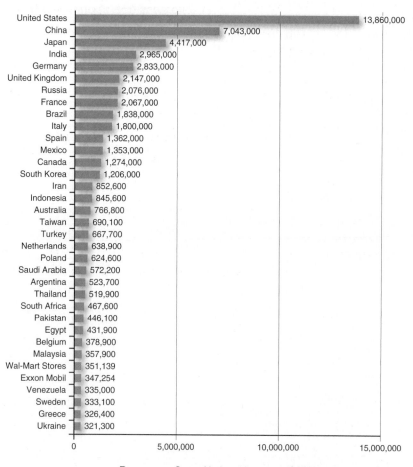

National Economies and the Fortune 500 in 2007

Country	Revenue or Gross National Incomes ($ Millions)
United States	13,860,000
China	7,043,000
Japan	4,417,000
India	2,965,000
Germany	2,833,000
United Kingdom	2,147,000
Russia	2,076,000
France	2,067,000
Brazil	1,838,000
Italy	1,800,000
Spain	1,362,000
Mexico	1,353,000
Canada	1,274,000
South Korea	1,206,000
Iran	852,600
Indonesia	845,600
Australia	766,800
Taiwan	690,100
Turkey	667,700
Netherlands	638,900
Poland	624,600
Saudi Arabia	572,200
Argentina	523,700
Thailand	519,900
South Africa	467,600
Pakistan	446,100
Egypt	431,900
Belgium	378,900
Malaysia	357,900
Wal-Mart Stores	351,139
Exxon Mobil	347,254
Venezuela	335,000
Sweden	333,100
Greece	326,400
Ukraine	321,300

Revenue or Gross National Incomes ($ Millions)

Global Business Trends

What are some important global business trends? Four noteworthy global business trends exist:[6]

1. **A growing role for developing nations.** Over the last several decades, U.S. dominance of world output and world exports has declined in relative terms due to the rapid economic growth of several other countries, most notably Japan, China, and India. This trend is expected to continue as developing nations such as China, India, Indonesia, Thailand, and many Latin American nations continue to grow and mature.

2. **A rise in non-U.S. foreign direct investment.** Over the last 30 years, U.S. dominance of **foreign direct investment**, which is the purchasing of property and businesses in foreign nations, has declined. Many other countries have begun to undertake foreign direct investment and have invested much of their money in companies in the United States. Consider the number of foreign companies merging or acquiring U.S. firms as reported in the media. Not only is more foreign direct investment flowing into the United States than ever before, but also more and more foreign direct investment is flowing into developing nations.

3. **A rise in non-U.S. multinational enterprises.** Over the last several decades, there has also been a rise in the importance of non-U.S. **multinational enterprises**, or businesses that manufacture and market products in two or more countries. Moreover, *mini-multinationals* (small and medium-sized multinational enterprises) have become prominent on the world stage. Garmin, the maker of Global Positioning System (GPS) technology, is a good example of a U.S. mini-multinational that has specialized in doing one thing very well. Garmin sells its GPS technology all over the world from its headquarters in Olathe, Kansas, and from its facilities in Oregon, Great Britain, and Taiwan.

4. **Increasing democratization.** With the movement toward democratization and the adoption of free-market economies around the globe, many more nations are becoming involved in the global economy. If this trend continues, broadening the scope of the global marketplace and opening more locations as potential production sites, the opportunities for international business will be enormous.

At the beginning of this section, you completed a personal inventory of some of your belongings to gauge how globalization has already affected you. As globalization of markets and production continue to affect the business world, it's likely these trends will continue to have an impact on your closet as well.

▼ **top**

10

Multinational Corporations in the World in 2007

Company	Sales (Millions)
1. Wal-Mart Stores (United States)	$351,139
2. Exxon Mobil (United States)	$347,254
3. Royal Dutch Shell (Netherlands)	$318,845
4. BP (British Petroleum) (Britain)	$274,316
5. General Motors (United States)	$207,349
6. Toyota Motor (Japan)	$204,746
7. Chevron (United States)	$200,567
8. DaimlerChrysler (Germany)	$190,191
9. ConocoPhillips (United States)	$172,451
10. Total (France)	$168,357

▼ You have just read **Objectives 1 & 2**

Think you got it? Check out the Study Plan section @
www.mybizlab.com.

International Trade pp. 100-102

Thomas McGovern was running a successful textile manufacturing firm, in which he provided high-quality clothing products to retail stores at reasonable prices. He was a dependable supplier with many satisfied customers who trusted his prices and overall advice on textile product offerings. However, over the years, cheaper foreign textiles began to flood the market, and his customers could not pass up the lower prices. His sales fell dramatically. Thomas tried to cut his costs to match the much lower prices offered by his new foreign competition, but he could not compete with the lower wages paid to foreign workers. After 38 years in business, McGovern's firm was forced to close up shop. ➤

➤ As the case to the left shows, competition in the international market may threaten domestic businesses like Thomas McGovern's firm that cannot keep up with the high-quality and low-cost products that international trade provides. International trade flourishes because it is in the best interest of the country. Thomas McGovern, however, might argue that international trade gives multinational corporations an unfair advantage over domestic businesses. But is he right? Let's take a closer look at why countries participate in international trade, how trade affects competitiveness, and what costs and benefits are associated with international trade.

Comparative Advantage

What is the theory of comparative advantage? Many theories apply to international trade. The best theory is the *theory of comparative advantage*. This theory states that specialization and trade between countries benefit all who are involved. The theory of comparative advantage suggests that a country should sell to other countries the goods that it manufactures most efficiently and effectively, and buy from other countries the goods it cannot manufacture as efficiently or effectively. If this method is practiced, each nation will have a greater quantity and variety of higher-quality products to consume at lower prices.

For this mutually beneficial system to work, each country must specialize in the production of those products for which it possesses a comparative advantage. To possess a **comparative advantage** means that a country can produce a good or service relatively more efficiently compared with other countries. A comparative advantage should not be confused with an **absolute advantage**, which is the ability to produce *more* of a good or service than any other country. Just because a large country can produce more of a good than a small country doesn't necessarily mean it is relatively more efficient at producing that good. What matters is relative efficiency, or comparative advantage—not absolute advantage.

When all countries focus on producing those products for which they have a comparative advantage, collectively they all have more production to share. This, in turn, creates higher standards of living for these countries. As you've probably guessed, countries export those products for which they have a comparative advantage and import those products for which they do not have a comparative advantage.

National Competitiveness

How can national competitiveness be fostered?

In many nations, governments focus on improving the nation's resources—natural resources, labor, capital (plant, equipment, and infrastructure), technology, and innovation and entrepreneurialism—to improve competitiveness.

Governments can't do much to improve a nation's natural resources; they have to work with what they have. Nations lucky enough to have abundant natural resources will likely have a comparative advantage in the production of goods that require these raw materials. However, governments do invest in health, education, and training designed to increase the productivity of their labor forces. All international businesses are constantly looking for good workers, and each country wants to attract businesses to enhance employment opportunities for its citizens. Moreover, high wages can only be sustained in a global labor market when justified by high productivity.

Many governments try to create incentives for private company investments in capital (plant and equipment). For example, governments may try to keep interest rates low so private companies will invest in the latest state-of-the art equipment, thereby giving them an edge over foreign competition. Governments also invest in *public capital*, which is sometimes called *infrastructure*. Infrastructure includes roads, bridges, dams, electric grid lines, and telecommunication satellites that enhance productivity. Governments also try to promote technological advances to give their nations a competitive edge. This can include investments in basic and applied research at state-funded higher educational institutions. Finally, governments might also promote innovation and entrepreneurialism.

Can a business create a competitive or comparative advantage?

The ingredients for national competitiveness are the same for a specific business. That is, successful firms try to gain access to cheap raw materials, invest in their workers' training, and purchase state-of-the-art capital (plant and equipment). Successful companies also invest in cutting-edge technology in their research and development departments. Finally, they promote innovativeness throughout their organizations.

Conversely, if a company, an entire industry, or even a nation has lost its comparative (or competitive) advantage, then it probably failed in one or more of these areas. What do you think can account for the demise of comparative advantage in the U.S. textile, steel, auto, or home electronics industries? Was it a lack of productivity on the worker's part, a lack of investment in the latest state-of-the art plant and equipment, a lack of investment in new technologies, or a lack of innovation? Or was it that the foreign competition (companies or nations) simply did a better job of improving in one or more of these areas? Remember, comparative advantage is really a relative advantage—relative to the competition.

➤ When foreign imports arrive in the United States, they increase the supply of the product, pushing its price down. Consumers welcome the competition and the lower prices, but domestic competitors are displeased.

The Benefits and Costs of International Trade

What are the benefits of international trade?
The theory of comparative advantage indicates that countries that participate in international trade will experience higher standards of living because of the greater quantity and variety of higher-quality products offered at lower prices. These results stem from the increased competition associated with more open trade. But these benefits are not without their costs.

What are the costs of international trade?
The costs of international trade are borne by those businesses and their workers whose livelihoods are threatened by foreign competition. Some domestic businesses may lose market share to foreign companies, stunting their profitability and ability to create jobs. Other firms, like Thomas McGovern's textile company, may be so clobbered by foreign competitors that they're driven out of business entirely.

Do the benefits of international trade outweigh the costs?
The answer to this question depends on the timing of the benefits and the costs and the extent to which they are felt within any given time frame. Obviously, the critics of more open border trade point to the costs, whereas the advocates point to the benefits. The costs are huge for the victims. After all, they might lose their livelihoods. The benefits, on the other hand, are not always easily recognizable, as they are spread out among millions of consumers. For example, a greater quantity and variety of higher-quality products to consume may not be easily traced to increased trade, because these benefits are often slow and subtle. Moreover, people benefit from lower-priced products, although the price reductions may only save people a nickel here and a dime there. But the sum of these lower prices for the public at large can be dramatic—especially over time.

Although international trade happens all the time in today's society, companies still have to abide by certain rules and regulations. Governments often impose restrictions on the quantity and types of goods that can cross national borders. We'll discuss both free trade and trade barriers in the next section.

▼ You have just read **Objective 3**

Want a review? Check out the Study Plan section @
www.mybizlab.com.

Trade Barriers and Protectionism pp. 103-109

➤ Countries implement trade barriers to protect domestic businesses from international competition that could put them out of business. As the NAFTA debate to the right illustrates, many people believe that trade barriers are the best way to protect a nation's economy; others are concerned about the possible negative side effects. In this section, we'll look at both sides of this sometimes controversial debate.

In 1994, the United States, Mexico, and Canada passed NAFTA, the North American Free Trade Agreement, which lifted most trade barriers between the three countries. Today, many politicians are beginning to scrutinize this agreement and are being questioned about job losses stemming from NAFTA. Since NAFTA began in 1994, nearly a million U.S. jobs have been lost, with 50,000 losses in Ohio alone. The Office of the United States Trade Representative, however, argues that NAFTA has not cost people jobs in the United States. In fact, U.S. employment rose from 110.8 million people in 1993 to 137.6 million in 2007. The office also reports that the average unemployment rate has lowered two percentage points over the last decade.[7] So, what are the true costs and benefits of free trade? Should trade barriers really be implemented to protect domestic workers? ➤

Free Trade

What is free trade? **Free trade** refers to the unencumbered flow of goods and services across national borders. That is, free trade is free from government intervention or other impediments that can block the flow of goods across borders. Virtually all economists are free-trade advocates because they argue that *over time* the benefits far outweigh the costs for the nation as a whole.

Still, even if virtually all economists are free-trade advocates, all real-world governments do have trade barriers in place to protect selected domestic industries from foreign competition.

Types of Trade Barriers

What are the different types of trade barriers? Types of trade barriers include:

- tariffs and subsidies,
- quotas and embargoes, and
- administrative trade barriers.

"Globalization and free trade do spur economic growth, and they lead to lower prices on many goods. "[8]

—Robert Reich, U.S. Secretary of Labor, 1993–1997

The most common trade barrier is the **tariff**, a tax imposed on an imported good or service like French wine. Governments prefer to impose tariffs because they raise tax revenues. The opposites of tariffs are **subsidies**, government payments to *domestic* producers, like California wine growers. A subsidy can take many forms. It can be a direct cash grant or a payment in-kind that could include tax concessions or a low-interest loan.

A **quota**, another common type of trade barrier, is a quantity limitation on the amount of an import allowed to enter a country. A quota on French wine might limit the quantity to 10,000 cases per day. The most heavy-handed government trade barrier is an **embargo**, a total restriction on an import (or export). The United States has imposed an embargo on most goods that could have otherwise been traded with Cuba since the 1960s. Embargoes are usually economic sanction tools designed to achieve an international political goal.

Several other types of trade barriers can be lumped under the heading of *administrative trade barriers*, which are government bureaucratic rules designed to limit imports. One example is a **local content requirement**, which is a requirement that some portion of a good be produced domestically. This usually drives up the cost of the import. Administrative trade barriers may also require an import to meet some technical standard or bureaucratic rule, effectively shutting the import out of the domestic market. For example, the European Union has banned the importation of all animal meats that use steroids to stimulate growth. This decision heavily impacted the U.S. beef and dairy industries. Although administrative trade barriers can be legitimate, they may be designed purely to protect domestic producers from international competition. It is sometimes difficult to determine the real motivation behind these barriers.

Protectionist Trade Barriers: Winners and Losers

Who benefits and who suffers from protectionist trade barriers? Without a doubt, trade barriers benefit domestic producers and their workers, and they hurt domestic consumers. How, you wonder? Trade barriers increase costs to foreign companies or restrict the supply of imports, driving up their prices and reducing their sales in the domestic market. As a result, the higher-priced imports increase the demand for domestically produced substitute goods or services. This higher demand also increases the domestically produced product's price, although it simultaneously increases domestic sales. And this is exactly what the trade barriers are designed to do—restrict sales of imports while stimulating sales for domestic firms. Because the domestic firms are selling more at higher prices, they are more profitable. This profitability also creates more job security for their employees. The undesirable outcome, however, is that both the imports and the domestically produced substitute products are now more expensive. Domestic consumers lose while domestic producers and their workers gain.

Trade barriers also hurt consumers because the overall quantity, variety, and quality of products are lower as a result of curtailing foreign competition. For any nation, the economic costs of protectionism outweigh the economic benefits over time. The result is the opposite of free trade. ▼ **Table 4.2** summarizes the economic benefits and costs of free trade and protectionism for a nation.

▼ Table 4.2

	Free Trade	Protectionism
Economic Benefits and Costs of Free Trade and Protectionism for a Nation		
Economic Benefits	A greater quantity and variety of higher quality products at lower prices	Increased sales at higher prices improves the profitability of the protected domestic companies, creating greater job security for their workers
Economic Costs	Reduced sales and lower prices for domestic firms that find it difficult to compete internationally, which reduces their profitability and lowers job security for their workers	Lower quantity and variety of lower-quality products at higher prices

What are common arguments in favor of protectionist trade barriers? Four main arguments emerge for protectionist trade barriers. The arguments include

- the national security argument,
- the infant-industry argument,
- the cheap foreign labor argument, and
- the threat of retaliation (bargaining chip) argument.

National Security Argument

The *national security argument* states that certain industries critical to national security should be protected from foreign competition. For example, the United States wouldn't want to become dependent on another nation for a critical component of national defense. However, rarely have protected industries using this argument proven critical to national defense.

Infant-Industry Argument

The *infant-industry argument* states that an undeveloped domestic industry needs time to grow and develop in order to acquire a comparative advantage in the global economy. The protected time to grow, the argument goes, will allow plenty of opportunities for the industry to make the investments needed to become innovative. Once the comparative advantage is captured, then protection from foreign competition will no longer be necessary. However, in practice, it can be very difficult to determine whether an industry legitimately holds promise of developing a comparative advantage. In addition, rarely do infant industries ever grow up, and the government protection can become addictive.

Cheap Foreign Labor Argument

The *cheap foreign labor argument* centers on the sometimes significantly lower wages paid to workers of foreign companies. How can domestic companies compete with these low wages? Sometimes they can't, but trying to protect these jobs creates still higher costs for the nation in the form of higher prices and a reduced quantity, quality, and variety of products from which to choose. Note also that what is relevant for costs of production is not just wages, but productivity in relation to wages. A company's costs of production can be lower even when it pays its workers twice as much if the productivity of workers is at least twice as high. It's no surprise that if a country wants to maintain high wages in a global marketplace, it needs to find a way to increase the productivity of its labor force.

Threat of Retaliation (or Bargaining Chip) Argument

The *threat of retaliation* (or *bargaining chip*) *argument* says that if a trading partner increases its trade barriers on your exports, or fails to reduce trade barriers as you reduce yours, then an uneven, unfair playing field is created. Domestic companies may also be put at a disadvantage if a foreign firm is dumping its product. **Dumping** refers to selling a product at a price below the price charged in the producing country; it is illegal and can be difficult to prove. The intent of dumping is to dominate an industry and then control it. The threat of higher trade barriers can be a bargaining chip in retaliation for dumping or for negotiating lower trade barriers for exports. However, the threat of trade barriers can be a risky policy. If it fails, the result can be a trade war—nations would implement higher trade barriers and leave everyone at a disadvantage.

How do economists feel about protectionist trade barriers? As noted earlier, most economists are free-trade advocates because they believe that the economic benefits of free trade outweigh the economic costs. Economists insist that the best way to address the concerns of those industries and their workers whose livelihoods are threatened by foreign competition is *not* to impose protectionist trade barriers. Instead, these displaced individuals need to be equipped with the education, training, and skills necessary to smooth their transition into a line of business or work in which the nation has a comparative advantage and demand is rising. Although all governments have protectionist trade barriers in place, they have been working to reduce them because they believe the economic benefits of doing so generally outweigh the costs. This political position explains the recent trend toward reduced trade and investment barriers that have fueled globalization.

International Organizations Promoting Free Trade

What are some international organizations promoting free trade? Countries realize that unilaterally reducing their trade barriers puts their businesses at an unfair disadvantage. The key for realizing the mutual benefits of international trade is to get all countries to lower their trade barriers simultaneously, which was the reason for creating organizations such as GATT and the WTO.

GATT

The **General Agreement on Tariffs and Trade (GATT)** was created in 1948 with 23 member nations and grew to a membership of 123 by 1994. Although GATT was not an organization with any real enforcement powers, its eight rounds of negotiated agreements or treaties were very successful in reducing tariffs and other obstacles to free trade on goods. This, in turn, spurred significant world economic growth.[9] However, GATT was not as successful in reducing trade barriers on services, protecting intellectual property rights, or enforcing agreements among member nations. As a result, the World Trade Organization replaced GATT in 1995 during the eighth and final round of negotiations (called the Uruguay Round because it was launched in Punta del Este, Uruguay).

WTO

The **World Trade Organization (WTO)** has strengthened the world trading system by extending GATT rules to services and increasing protection for intellectual property rights. But, perhaps of most significance, the WTO has taken on the responsibility for arbitrating trade disputes and monitoring the trade policies of member countries (see ▼ **Figure 4.4**).[10] The WTO operates as GATT did—on the basis of consensus—in the area of dispute settlement. However, unlike GATT, the

Map M2
WTO Members and Observers
(August 2005)

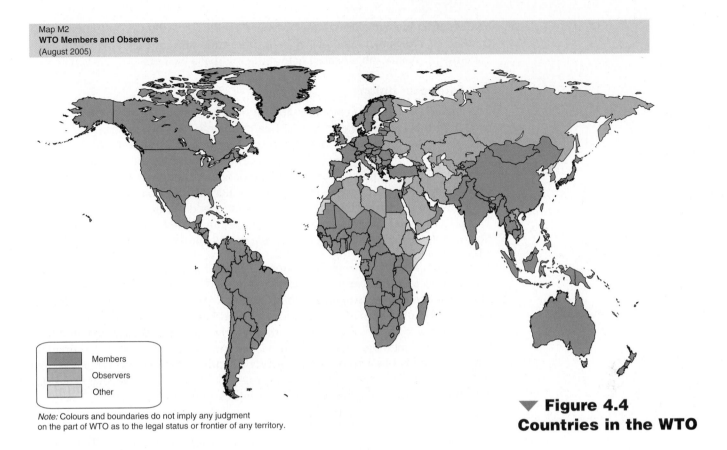

Members
Observers
Other

Note: Colours and boundaries do not imply any judgment
on the part of WTO as to the legal status or frontier of any territory.

▼ **Figure 4.4**
Countries in the WTO

WTO doesn't allow losing parties to ignore the arbitration reports of the WTO. The WTO has the power to enforce decisions, which gives the WTO something that the GATT never had: teeth.

Advocates of free trade argue that much remains to be done to reduce trade barriers in the global economy. The first round of talks under the umbrella of the WTO was launched in Seattle in 1999, but anti-globalization protestors disrupted and derailed these talks. The meetings were relaunched in 2001 in Doha, Qatar, in the Persian Gulf, with an agenda to curtail dumping, reduce protectionist trade barriers, protect intellectual property rights, and reduce government barriers on foreign direct investment.[11] The Doha round was slated to last three years, but had not yet concluded by spring 2008.

The 1999 demonstration in Seattle reflects an ongoing concern that free trade may encourage firms to shift their production to countries with low wages and lax labor standards. Critics argue that exploitation of workers can contribute to the gap between the rich and poor. Environmentalists have also expressed a growing concern that expanded international trade encourages companies to move production to countries in which they are freer to pollute and degrade the environment, which contributes to global climate change and all the problems that may stem from global warming. These concerns highlight the fact that the *economic* perspective on the benefits and costs of free trade is not the only perspective. Important social, ethical, political, and environmental concerns are also important.

Regional Free Trade Agreements

What are some regional free trade agreements? Many nations have been so eager to achieve the higher standards of living associated with free trade that they have struck out on their own by creating **free trade areas**, or compacts abolishing trade barriers among member countries. Although all current free trade areas still have some obstacles to free trade among their members, many have made considerable headway in reducing these barriers.

The European Union

The greatest free trade area exists among member nations of the *European Union (EU)*, which is the oldest and largest free trade area. The EU can trace its roots to 1957 with the creation of the European Economic Community (or Common Market), which consisted of the six founding countries of Belgium, France, Germany, Italy, Luxembourg, and the Netherlands. Although many obstacles had to be overcome, like the concern over the potential loss of national sovereignty, the EU has grown to its current membership of 27 independent states (see ▼ **Figure 4.5**). The EU's success is due, in large part, to its demonstrated commitment to the free flow of goods, services, capital, and people across borders in Europe.

The EU is currently the world's largest single market, surpassing the United States. It accounts for approximately one-third of the world's total production. The EU is the largest exporter in the world and the second largest importer.[12] In 1999, the EU also surpassed all other free trade areas with respect to economic integration by adopting a common currency—the euro. The euro is currently used by 15 of the 27 member states and has become a major currency in global financial markets. The EU has a population of nearly 500 million people and is likely to continue to grow as many other countries—like Croatia, the former Yugoslav Republic of Macedonia, and Turkey—apply to join the EU.

The European Union's economic power and political clout has a huge influence on international businesses worldwide. For example, some international businesses have been motivated to invest in production facilities within the EU to hedge against any potential trade barriers. The EU has also established many legal, regulatory, and technical standards for imports to the EU market. In addition, the EU's antitrust rulings have significantly affected U.S. businesses. For example, in 2004, the EU found Microsoft guilty of anti-competitive practices and levied a fine of $613 million on the company.[13]

NAFTA

As noted earlier, the **North American Free Trade Agreement (NAFTA)** is an ongoing agreement to move the United States, Mexico, and Canada closer to true free trade. NAFTA was established on January 1, 1994, after considerable political opposition. The experience of NAFTA so far indicates that earlier claims made by both advocates and critics were exaggerated. One big issue confronting NAFTA is the proposal to expand into a greater Free Trade Area of the Americas (FTAA) that would include most countries in the western hemisphere. Although meetings are being held for a workable FTAA, some countries like Brazil and Venezuela stand in opposition to such an agreement. As a result, much progress in the near future toward more free trade within the framework of FTAA is unlikely.

Other Noteworthy Free Trade Areas

Many other free trade areas exist in the world. For example, the *Andean Group* was formed in 1969 between Bolivia, Chile, Ecuador, Colombia, and Peru. *MERCOSUR* originated in 1988 as a free trade pact between Brazil and Argentina, but was expanded in 1990 to include Paraguay and Uruguay. In 1999, these two organizations began negotiating a merger that culminated in 2004 with a signed agreement to move toward integrating all of South America based on the European Union model. However, not much progress has been made to date. The *Association of Southeast Asian Nations (ASEAN)* includes Indonesia, Malaysia, the Philippines, Singapore, Thailand, Brunei, Vietnam, Laos, Myanmar, and Cambodia. Progress toward integration has been very limited. The *Asia-Pacific Economic Cooperation*

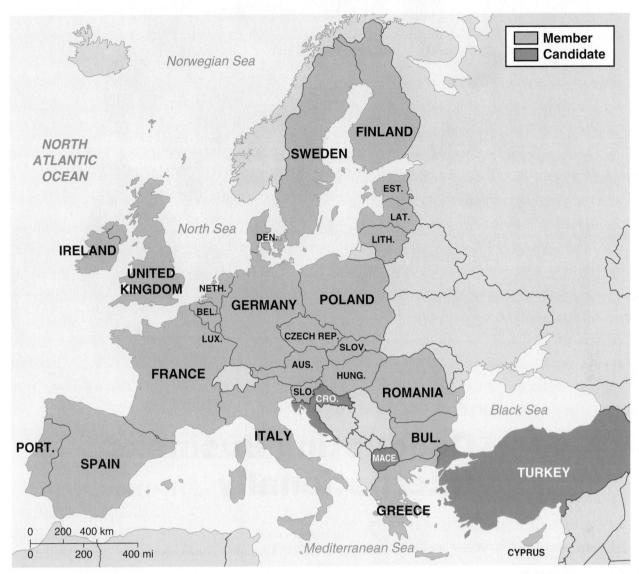

Member
Candidate

▼ **Figure 4.5**
As of 2008, the European Union consists of 27 countries. The EU is the most economically integrated free trade area in the world.

(APEC) was founded in 1989 at the suggestion of Australia and currently has 21 member countries, including economic powerhouses such as the United States, Japan, and China.

Most free trade areas haven't had the kind of success that the EU and NAFTA have had in reducing their trade barriers. However, it's clear that most countries are eager to come together to reduce trade barriers in an attempt to realize the economic benefits of greater free trade.

Now that you've had a chance to review both sides of the issues concerning trade barriers and free trade, what is your opinion? Can a balance be struck between protecting domestic businesses and offering customers the best services and products at affordable prices?

▼ You have just read **Objective 4**

Want to learn more? Check out the Study Plan section @
www.my*biz*lab.com.

Conducting Business Internationally pp. 110-114

Imagine you're sitting outside on a hot summer day. How would you like an ice-cold cucumber soda to cool you off? If you were in Japan during the summer of 2007, you were in luck. The cucumber-flavored soft drink was only available in the summer and maintained prime shelf space in stores nationwide.

Imagine you walk into your local McDonald's to order your favorite sandwich. Is it a salmon wrap? McDonald's and the Norwegian seafood company Marine Harvest joined together not only to promote Norwegian salmon, but also to provide a healthy alternative for customers. The salmon wrap was first offered in Norwegian McDonald's restaurants in August of 2007 and is being considered for a global launch.

Now imagine you own a popular restaurant chain that is flourishing. You want to expand globally, but aren't sure where. Pick a country where you think your business might be successful and create a menu that might appeal to the country's population. Think of ways that items such as pizza, ice cream, or soft drinks could be tailored to the population in your chosen country. ➤

➤ All business is undertaken within an economic, sociocultural, political, and legal environment wherever it operates. When doing purely domestic business, keeping up with environmental forces can be a huge challenge for even the savviest manager. However, managing an international business is even more complex because additional and different economic, social, and political environments must be considered. The rest of this chapter will explore some of the numerous important economic, sociocultural, political, and legal differences among nations. Knowledge of these differences is critical to conducting global business successfully. But first we'll begin with a look at the different strategies of international businesses and how firms enter foreign markets.

Three Strategies of International Business

What are three basic strategies of international business? Two major factors determine an international firm's strategy. The first factor involves how important it is for a business to keep its costs down and, therefore, its prices low. The second factor is how necessary it is for a company to customize or differentiate its product to adapt to different customer tastes and preferences around the globe.

Global Strategy

One basic strategy of international business is the **global strategy**—competing primarily on the basis of price while selling a standardized (or homogenous) product. Standardized products are basic products that meet universal needs. Examples of standardized products include agricultural products, oil, and raw material commodities. These goods are essentially the same from company to company—they are homogenous—because they are universally recognized and appeal to consumers across many cultures. When selling standardized products, firms compete aggressively on the basis of price. Firms pursuing a global strategy face strong cost pressures to keep their prices low *because* they are selling a standardized product. The company with the lowest price captures most market share. Sony and Boeing are companies that pursue a global strategy.

Multi-Domestic Strategy

A second basic strategy of international business is the **multi-domestic strategy**—competing primarily by customizing or differentiating the product to meet unique local needs, tastes, or preferences. Firms pursuing a multi-domestic strategy face relatively low pressures for cost reduction because the price is often of secondary concern to buyers. Instead, what is important to customers is whether the product meets their needs or is distinct from the product of competitors. Companies that pursue a multi-domestic strategy, such as Procter & Gamble and General Foods, all work to make their respective products appeal to different customers around the globe.

Transnational Strategy

A third basic strategy of international business is the **transnational strategy**—competing by offering a customized product while simultaneously selling at the lowest possible price. The strong cost pressures *and* strong pressures for differentiation that motivate this type of strategy are typically incongruent. Therefore, the successful pursuit of this type of strategy is extremely difficult in practice. Frito-Lay, American Express, MCI, Time Warner, and British Airways all pursue a transnational strategy.

Entering Foreign Markets

How do international firms enter foreign markets? In addition to determining a business strategy, international businesses must decide how they will serve foreign customers. Companies may:

- export their product
- implement a turnkey project
- undertake franchising
- enter into a licensing agreement, a joint venture, or a strategic alliance
- undertake contract manufacturing
- set up a wholly-owned subsidiary

Let's look briefly at these options.

Exporting

As noted above, *exporting* is the sale of a domestically produced good in a foreign market. Most businesses typically begin serving a foreign market by exporting and only later switch to another mode to expand sales abroad. Exporting has two advantages. First, exporting is relatively easy and inexpensive compared with establishing a physical presence in a foreign market. Second, exporting may help a firm realize lower costs because companies can move production to an inexpensive location and then export its product from that location around the world. Exporting also has a few disadvantages. It is not economical for heavy or bulky products with high transportation costs. Exporting may also become uneconomical if foreign trade barriers are unexpectedly imposed.

Turnkey Projects

When firms export their technological know-how in exchange for a fee, they have implemented a **turnkey project**. Turnkey projects are common in the production of sophisticated and complex manufacturing facilities like those involved in petroleum refining, steel, and hydroelectric energy production. Once the facility is up and running, the locals are trained, then the keys are turned over to the new foreign owners. Black & Veatch, an engineering firm in Kansas City, has built power plants in China as turnkey projects. Turnkey projects allow firms with specialized know-how, like Black & Veatch, to earn higher profits from their technical expertise. The drawback is that the firm may create a viable competitor if their technological expertise is easily accessible.

Franchising

Franchising involves selling a well-known brand name or a proven method of doing business to an investor in exchange for a fee and a percentage of sales or profits. The seller is the *franchisor*, and the buyer is the *franchisee*. Franchising, which we'll discuss in depth in Chapter 5, is popular both domestically and internationally. Examples of franchising abound in the fast food and entertainment industries. McDonald's and KFC restaurants are now found all over the world. Papa John's pizza has now opened its 50th restaurant in China.[14] Ruby Tuesday recently opened one of its restaurants in Jeddah, Saudi Arabia.[15] Walt Disney has recently franchised 150 stores in India.[16] Domino's Pizza has 500 stores in Mexico, 300 in the UK, 300 in Australia, 200 in South Korea, 200 in Canada, and many other stores around the world.[17] Undoubtedly, all of these franchises must be careful to adapt their goods and services to appeal to their different global customers.

▶ International franchising abounds in the fast-food industry.

The main advantage of franchising is that the franchisor shifts to the franchisee the costs and risks of opening a foreign market. Disadvantages include the enforcement of franchise contracts that ensure quality control over distant franchisees and ensuring that the product is properly adapted to appeal to customers.

Licensing

Licensing is an agreement in which the licensor's intangible property—patents, trademarks, service marks, copyrights, trade secrets, or other intellectual property—may be sold or made available to a licensee in exchange for a royalty fee. The advantage of licensing is the speed with which the *licensor* can enter a foreign market and the assumption of risks and costs by the *licensee*. The disadvantage is the loss of technological expertise to the licensee and the creation of a potential competitor. SRI International is a company that licenses its vast array of intellectual property around the world. Their technological specialty is patents in the biosciences, computing, and chemistry-related materials and structural areas.[18] IBM also licenses its software around the world.[19]

Joint Ventures

Joint ventures involve shared ownership in a subsidiary firm. International joint venture partners involve an international business teaming up with a local partner in order to enter a foreign market. The advantages of a joint venture include gaining local knowledge of the economic, social, and political landscape while sharing the costs and risks of accessing a foreign market. Entering into a joint venture, like entering into a marriage, requires considerable thought in the selection of a complementary partner. The disadvantage of joint ventures is losing control over the company because compromise with the partner is inevitable. The risk of losing proprietary technology in the event of dissolution or "divorce" of the joint venture is also a major drawback.

New United Motor Manufacturing, Inc., or NUMMI, is an example of a joint venture between U.S.-owned General Motors Corporation and Japanese-owned Toyota Motor Corporation. Both sides benefit from this partnership. GM workers learn how to build cars more efficiently using Toyota's unique production system, while Toyota has the opportunity to test its production methods in a U.S. setting.[20]

Strategic Alliances

Strategic alliances are cooperative arrangements between actual or potential competitors. Unlike a joint venture, each partner retains its business independence. Strategic alliances are typically agreements for a specific period of time or for only the duration of a particular project. The advantages of strategic alliances include the pooling of unique talents and expertise and the sharing of the costs and risks of a project for mutual benefit. The disadvantages include loss of technology and initial difficulty in finding a compatible partner.

The Intel Corporation, which is an international company based in California, has entered into a strategic alliance with Japanese-owned NMB Semiconductor Company. The companies hope to work together to manufacture an innovative computer chip for laptop computers. Intel will finance the project, while NMB will create the product.[21]

Contract Manufacturing

Contract manufacturing occurs when a firm subcontracts part or all of its goods to an outside firm as an alternative to owning and operating its own production facility. When doing international business, the subcontractor is a foreign firm. Therefore, contract manufacturing is really a form of offshore outsourcing. Contract manufacturing allows international business to enter a foreign market by placing its label on the good and selling it in the foreign market where it was produced. Contract manufacturing also enables a firm to test market its product in a foreign market with very little expense compared with the high startup costs of building its own facility. The disadvantage centers on the lack of quality control over the subcontractor.

Wholly-Owned Subsidiaries

A **wholly-owned subsidiary** involves establishing a foreign facility that is owned entirely by the investing firm. The advantages of this entry choice include total control over foreign operations and technological know-how. The disadvantage is that the parent company must bear all of the costs and risks of entering a foreign market.

The Advantages and Disadvantages of Each Entry Mode

Which mode of entering foreign markets is optimal? The optimal entry mode depends on many factors, including the firm's strategy. Companies must weigh the advantages and disadvantages of each when making a decision. ▼ **Table 4.3** summarizes the advantages and disadvantages of the various entry modes.

In the beginning of this section, you were asked to put yourself in the shoes of a restaurant owner considering global expansion. You revised a menu based on the tastes and preferences in a specific country, and you thought about how to customize your product so it would succeed in the global marketplace. After completing this section, you see that your approach is considered a multi-domestic strategy. What other tips did you pick up in this section that could help you expand your business to suit a more international palate?

▼ **Table 4.3**

Advantages and Disadvantages of the Various Entry Modes		
	Advantages	**Disadvantages**
Exporting	• Speed of entry • Production site in lowest-cost location	• High transport costs • Threat of trade barriers such as tariffs • Lack of access to local information
Turnkey project	• Increased profits for high-tech firms	• Loss of technical know-how to potential competitors
Franchising	• Costs and risks of opening the foreign market fall on the franchisee	• Difficulty in maintaining quality control over distant franchises
Licensing	• Speed of entry	• Licensee may become competitor • Loss of knowledge to potential competitor
Joint venture	• High potential for learning • Benefit of combined resources	• Shared control of business • Risk of losing specialized technology to partner
Strategic alliance	• Pooled talents and expertise • Shared costs and risks	• Risk of losing specialized technology to partner • Difficulty in finding a compatible partner
Contract manufacturing	• Speed of entry • Low test-marketing costs	• Lack of quality control over distant subcontractor
Wholly-owned subsidiary	• Total control over all operations • Preservation of proprietary technology	• Risks and costs of entering a foreign market

▼ You have just read **Objectives 5 & 6**

Want to test your skills? Check out the Study Plan section @ **www.mybizlab.com.**

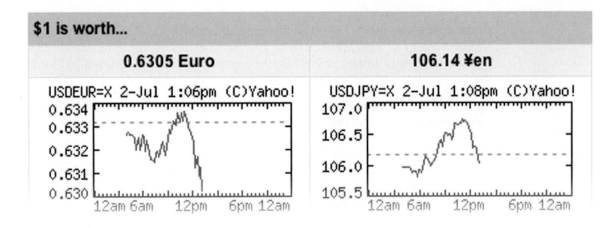

International Business: Economic Factors and Challenges pp. 115-118

➤ Businesses are impacted by fluctuating exchange rates every day. Transactions between international companies not only have to specify what each side will be paid, but also in which currency. In addition, multinational enterprises use foreign currency to pay foreign workers or to invest spare cash in other nations where interest rates may be more attractive. In this section, we'll look at exchange rates and how fluctuations in the value of currency affect the global economy. We'll also explore other economic factors and challenges that affect global business.

When Rachel Gao decided to expand her jewelry store to include handbags, she thought importing goods would be cheaper than purchasing them from a domestic company. Her initial thought was to go with a small European designer, but after she saw the exchange rate for the euro, she changed her mind. To make a profit, the retail price would be extremely expensive, and Rachel didn't think her customers would pay. She knew a lot of other business owners imported from China. Rachel looked into the exchange rate for the yuan and was surprised at how weak it was against the dollar. She was able to import a variety of handbags at a relatively inexpensive price. Not only would her customers appreciate the cheap prices, but she would also be able to make a decent profit. ➤

The Role of Exchange Rates

What are exchange rates? Foreign exchange markets determine **exchange rates**, the rates at which currencies are converted into another currency. Depending on a firm's perspective, it may prefer a strong or weak dollar. U.S. exporters prefer a weak dollar because their products will be more affordable to foreigners. However, U.S. importers prefer a strong dollar because the cost of importing foreign goods is cheaper. If goods are imported cheaply, then those savings can be either passed on to the consumer or kept as higher profits.

How do exchange rates affect international business? Changes in exchange rates can have important implications for international businesses. Suppose that the value of the dollar rises or gets stronger against the yen (the currency of Japan). What impact will this have on U.S. and Japanese businesses? Goods exported from the United States will become more expensive because the Japanese will now have to come up with more yen to purchase each dollar. This means, for example, the cost of a $40 pair of jeans made in the United States will increase in price for the Japanese consumer. Japanese consumers will buy fewer U.S. goods, like jeans, and exports to Japan will fall. U.S. businesses selling to the Japanese will be hurt through no fault of their own. At the same time, this stronger dollar will cause a decline in the relative price of Japanese goods for U.S. consumers, because fewer dollars are required to purchase each yen. Thus, due to the currency exchange rate change, the United States will import more Japanese goods and U.S. businesses will lose market share to Japanese companies.

The example of Japanese and U.S. trade illustrates that **currency appreciation**, an increase in the exchange rate value of a nation's currency, causes the relative price of imports to fall as the relative price of exports rises. When currency appreciates, the currency becomes stronger. **Currency depreciation**, a decrease in the exchange rate value of a nation's currency, has the opposite effect on the relative prices of exports and imports. A weak currency causes exports to become cheaper and imports to become more expensive.

Changes in exchange rates create other challenges for international business. In fact, rapid changes in exchange rates can create huge losses for some businesses. In the 1980s, Japan Airlines purchased several 747 jumbo jets from Boeing and agreed to pay in U.S. dollars. In the interim period between signing the contract and the delivery of the jets for payment, the value of the dollar rose dramatically. The airline company had to pay a lot more money than anticipated for the airliners, and it almost went bankrupt. This story illustrates a currency exchange rule: unanticipated exchange rate changes can pose huge risks for international businesses.

Changing exchange rates also affect multinational firms in other ways. Many companies like General Electric feel competitive pressure to shift production to countries with weak or low-valued currencies to take advantage of lower costs of production. For example, a weak Chinese currency reduces labor costs in China. If a firm doesn't shift more of its production to China and its competitors do, then its costs will be higher and the company will lose global market share.

Biz**Chat**

Which Is Better—A Strong Dollar or a Weak Dollar?

The answer to this question depends on the type of business a firm undertakes. Companies that do a lot of exporting—like auto companies, chemical manufacturers, and farmers—prefer a weak dollar because their product's price is lower in the global marketplace, so their sales and profits will be higher. On the other hand, companies that import components or finished goods for resale in the domestic market prefer a strong dollar because the relative price of their imports is lower.

From a consumer's perspective, a strong dollar is typically preferred because import prices are lower, which has a tendency to keep domestic competitors' prices low as well. As an employee, if you work for a company that exports much of its product, you would prefer a weak dollar to stimulate sales and ensure your job security.

The benefits of a strong dollar for a nation as a whole are lower priced imports, like oil, lower prices, and a lower inflation rate in general. However, a strong dollar creates a trade deficit. A weak dollar, on the other hand, is good for domestic international businesses because it stimulates employment and raises standards of living. The drawback of a weak dollar is the higher costs of energy and other imports that create higher rates of inflation. So, which is better—a strong dollar or a weak dollar? Like most real-world issues, the answer depends on your perspective.

For more information and discussion questions about this topic, check out the BizChat feature on www.my*biz*lab.com.

The Impact of a Changing Exchange Rate on a Nation

What impact do changing exchange rates have on nations?

Exchange rate changes can create trade deficits and trade surpluses for a country. For example, a stronger dollar will create a trade deficit for the United States because a strong dollar can cause export prices to rise as import prices fall.

Trade Deficit and Trade Surplus

A **trade deficit** exists when the value of a country's imports exceeds the value of its exports. A **trade surplus** occurs when the value of a country's exports exceeds the value of its imports. The United States has experienced significant trade deficits every year since the early 1980s. The advantage of a trade deficit for a nation is that it enables the country to consume more than it produces. However, the disadvantage is that domestic assets such as real estate or stocks and bonds must be sold to foreigners to pay for the trade deficit. This is similar to an individual who spends more money than he or she makes. The individual will go into debt and eventually have to sell off assets to continue to live beyond his or her means. The United States's experience with trade deficits helps explain the dramatic, news-making purchase of U.S. assets like U.S. businesses by foreigners.

Fixed and Freely Floating Exchange Rate Systems

Exchange rates can be manipulated or fixed by governments. For example, China has fixed its currency to a rate that is weak compared to the dollar. This means Chinese exports to the United States are cheap, and Chinese imports from the United States are expensive. As a result, the United States faces a huge trade deficit with China. The U.S. government is now calling upon the Chinese to allow their currency to "float," or to change in response to changing market conditions. Indeed, most countries operate under a *freely floating* (or *flexible*) *exchange rate system*, a system in which the global supply and demand for currencies determine exchange rates. Many specific factors affect the demand and supply of a nation's currency, such as changing interest rates, tax rates, and inflation rates. But generally, changes in exchange rates in a freely floating exchange rate system reflect the country's current economic health and its outlook for growth and investment potential. The problems with floating exchange rates are that they can create relative price changes outside the control of international businesses, as well as engender risks of losses due to rapid and unexpected changes in exchange rates.

Nonconvertible Currency and Countertrade

Governments also reserve the right to restrict the convertibility of their currency. For example, many developing countries have a *nonconvertible currency*, a currency that can't be converted into another currency in the foreign exchange market. These governments often fear that allowing convertibility will result in *capital flight*, the transfer of domestic funds into foreign currency held outside the country. Capital flight would deprive the nation of much-needed funds for investment and development.

Global companies can still do business with countries that have nonconvertible currencies through the use of countertrade. *Countertrade* is a form of international barter, the swapping of goods and services for other goods and services. Currently, countertrade may account for as much as 10 to 15 percent of total world trade. Companies do countertrade because of necessity and profitability. Examples of companies that have undertaken countertrade include General Foods, Goodyear, General Electric, Westinghouse, 3M, General Motors, Ford, Coca-Cola, and Pepsi-Cola.[22]

Other Economic Challenges to Conducting International Business

What are some other economic challenges to conducting international business? Changing exchange rates and nonconvertible currencies are not the only economic challenges to conducting international business. Companies must also consider how to adapt their products for sale in developing nations, how certain government policies might affect their business, and how the socioeconomic factors of an area impact the types of products they sell.

Economic Growth and Development

Many developing countries are experiencing more rapid growth than advanced economies are, and they have hundreds of millions of eager new customers ready to put their money into the global market. It is also true that many developing countries still lack the basic infrastructure necessary for effective transportation of goods and/or lack access to dependable electricity. They may also be lacking in modern communication systems. The implications are obvious. For example, the types of food products offered for sale would have to be altered and packaged differently. Makers of electric can openers would need to produce manual can openers for sale. The modes of advertising would shift from television to radio, and marketing a product via the Internet wouldn't be effective because few customers would own a computer.

Government Economic Policies and the Economic Environment

The degree to which markets are allowed to operate free from government intervention is another important economic consideration. International businesses prefer free market economies to state-run or socialized economies because the bureaucratic hassles associated with government intervention drive costs up. Other economic factors include the debt load of a nation, its unemployment and inflation rates, and its fiscal and monetary policies. *Unit labor cost*—a measure that divides a worker's wages by the average productivity of that worker—is also important. Global companies are concerned with labor costs when looking for lowest-cost locations to establish production facilities. In addition, the degree of competition that exists in a nation is important because it's more attractive to relocate to places with fewer competitors.

Socioeconomic Factors

Several socioeconomic factors also need to be taken into account, like the demographics of population density and age distribution. The birthrates of many developing countries are high and offer exciting opportunities to toy manufacturers like Mattel. Other socioeconomic factors that firms must consider include income distribution, ethnicity, and the cultural behaviors of a community.

As a business owner, Rachel Gao had to make decisions about her products based on exchange rates and the value of the U.S. dollar. She decided to import goods from China so she could sell her items for a more competitive price. While this business decision is a good one for her right now, she should continue to monitor exchange rates to be sure she is getting the best value. If the value of the yuan becomes stronger, Rachel will need to consider how those rising costs will affect her profits.

▼ You have just read **Objectives 7 & 8**

Want to quiz yourself? Check out the Study Plan section @
www.my*biz*lab.com.

International Business: Sociocultural, Political, Legal, and **Ethical Challenges** pp. 119-123

➤ When a business expands into an international market and lacks cross-cultural and political awareness, it's destined to fail. Along with cultural norms, political, legal, and ethical ideals vary from country to country. The role of government involvement in business is not universal, so knowing how specific government policies govern business activity is critical for business success. And because there is no global court to settle differences and disputes, businesses need to thoroughly study what is acceptable legally and ethically. In this section, we'll review the sociocultural, political, legal, and ethical concerns that can make or break a company working in the global marketplace.

Sociocultural Challenges

What is culture? **Culture** is the complex set of values, behaviors, lifestyles, arts, beliefs, and institutions of a population that are passed on from generation to generation. Culture impacts all aspects of business, from managing workers and production techniques to marketing and beyond. This section will explore a few of the most important components of culture that pertain to conducting global business successfully, including aesthetics, attitudes toward time and work, religion, and language.

Why is the study of culture important for international business? Most international businesses fail because they suffer from a lack of cross-cultural awareness. *Cross-cultural awareness* is an understanding, appreciation, and sensitivity to foreign culture. **Ethnocentrism**, a belief that one's own culture is superior to all other cultures, is a guaranteed recipe for disaster when undertaking international business.

Answer the following questions to determine your cultural IQ.

1. Between 1 and 4 P.M., business people in Spain are more likely to
   a. attend a lunch meeting with clients.
   b. return home for a family lunch and nap.

2. In Venezuela, it's common for business associates to
   a. maintain at least three feet of personal space.
   b. offer a handshake and pat on the shoulder upon greeting.

3. If you receive a business card from a Japanese business acquaintance, you should
   a. put it in your pocket without looking at it.
   b. receive the card with both hands and examine the information.

4. During a lunch meeting with a Muslim partner, you should avoid ordering
   a. lamb.
   b. pork.

5. If an Indian business acquaintance offers you a gift, you should
   a. politely decline the offer.
   b. open the present after your acquaintance has left.

If your answers are...
Mostly As – It's time to brush up on your cultural awareness.
Mostly Bs – Congratulations! With your high cultural IQ, you'll need to get your passport ready for global business encounters. ➤

Off the Mark
International Business Blunders

When selling products in the global marketplace, companies must research the cultural norms and language of the location in which they plan to sell. If not, the results could be disastrous, as illustrated by the examples below.[23]

- When American Motors introduced the Matador to the public, the company believed the car's name represented an image of courage and strength: the bullfighter. However, in Puerto Rico the name means "killer," so the car was not popular on the hazardous roads in the country.

- In many Latin American cultures, women do not order their husbands around, and people are very concerned with punctuality. Too bad a popular U.S. telephone company didn't know this. When the company showed a commercial in which a Latino wife tells her husband to call a friend and tell her they would be late for dinner, the commercial bombed.

- Procter & Gamble could not imagine the backlash it would receive when it used a popular European television commercial in Japan. The ad showed a man enter a bathroom and touch his wife while she bathed. The Japanese disapproved of this ad because the man's behavior did not adhere to the nation's cultural norms.

- When a golf ball manufacturing company tried selling its golf ball in packs of four in Japan, the campaign was unsuccessful. That's because pronunciation of the word for "four" in Japanese sounds like the word for "death," and items packaged in fours are unpopular.

Aesthetics

Aesthetics refers to what is considered beautiful or in good taste. Aesthetics encompasses etiquette, customs, and protocol. Few things are more embarrassing than violating a sense of good taste. For example, a company advertised eyeglasses in Thailand by featuring a variety of cute animals wearing glasses. The ad was a poor choice in Thailand because animals are considered a low form of life there, and no self-respecting Thai would wear anything worn by animals. Likewise, when former President George H.W. Bush went to Japan with the former Chairman of Chrysler, Lee Iacocca, and other U.S. business magnates to make explicit and direct demands on Japanese leaders, they violated Japanese etiquette. The Japanese considered this assertiveness rude and a sign of ignorance or desperation. Japanese businessmen don't condone lowering oneself to make direct demands. Some analysts believe this violation of cultural aesthetics severely damaged the negotiations and confirmed to the Japanese that U.S. citizens are barbarians.[24]

Attitudes Toward Time and Work

Attitudes toward time vary considerably across the world. Time is paramount to those in the United States, where people in general expect promptness and often insist on getting down to business. Some cultures view this as pushy and impersonal—a cultural turnoff. In addition, the U.S. time horizon differs markedly from the Japanese perspective. A long-term view to a U.S. citizen may be four to seven years into the future, while the Japanese may be preparing for decades in advance. Attitudes toward work also vary. The Germans argue that people in the United States live to work, while Germans work to live. Germans and other Europeans expect four to six weeks of vacation per year. Compare this to the two weeks on average a person in the United States gets, and it's clear which country values vacation time more.[25]

Religion

Religion plays a profound role in shaping a culture. International businesses are therefore well advised to educate themselves on varying religious value systems, customs, and practices if they don't wish to offend customers in marketing campaigns, among other things. For example, a soft drink was introduced into Arab countries with an attractive label that had stars on it—six-pointed stars. The Arabs interpreted this as pro-Israeli and refused to buy it. Another label was printed in ten languages, one of which was Hebrew—again the Arabs did not buy the product.[26]

Language

Language, both spoken and unspoken, is also extremely important. Consider a few more examples of international business blunders due to a lack of cross-cultural awareness.[27] A U.S. oil rig supervisor in Indonesia shouted at an employee to take a boat to shore. Since no one berates an Indonesian in public, a mob of outraged workers chased the supervisor with axes. In 2002, British sports manufacturer Umbro tried to market its new tennis shoe called the "Zyklon." The firm withdrew the marketing campaign immediately upon learning that the name of its tennis shoes was the name of the gas used by the Nazis to murder millions of Jews in concentration camps.

Unspoken language, or body language, also differs significantly around the world. Mountain Bell Company tried to promote its telephone services to Saudi Arabia. Its ad portrayed an executive talking on the phone with his feet propped up on the desk, showing the soles of his shoes—something an Arab would never do.

Although the world is getting smaller and a global culture is emerging, there are still profound and significant differences in culture. Cross-cultural awareness is a prerequisite to successful international business.

Political Challenges

What are the political challenges to conducting international business?
Generally, international businesses thrive in nations that have a firm commitment to free market principles with a stable, democratically elected government. However, some nations don't commit to free market principles, nor do they have democratic governments. The political differences among nations can sometimes pose a challenge when conducting international business.

Global companies often do business in government-controlled socialist economies, like China, Cuba, and North Korea; however companies

➤ Should you bow or shake hands when you visit a Japanese client in Japan?

prefer market-based or capitalist economies. Companies are better equipped to pursue their self-interests in a market-based or capitalist economy. However, even in market economies, governments must address *market failures*, or shortcomings associated with free markets. The extent to which government is involved in addressing market failures can vary dramatically from country to country, which can have very important implications for international businesses. ▼ **Table 4.4** summarizes the failures of markets and government attempts to address these shortcomings.

Government intervention in the process of determining which goods are undesirable and deciding whether goods should be regulated, taxed, or banned also varies from country to country. Many products that pollute the environment are deemed undesirable and have been regulated in one form or another by most governments around the world. The differences in these regulatory standards can impose big differences in costs of production for global businesses. There are also growing pressures on governments to address global climate change issues that will affect international business.

Just because governments intervene doesn't mean they succeed in improving market outcomes. Indeed, *government failure*—government intervention that fails to improve a market outcome—exists around the world. Government failure stems from corruption, ignorance, or pressure that special-interest groups place on politicians. International businesses prefer politically stable democracies because the probability of government failure is lower than for nondemocratic and unstable regimes.

Legal Challenges

What are the legal challenges to conducting international business? Laws, regulatory standards, and access to unbiased judicial systems based on a rule of law differ considerably around the world. No universal laws, regulatory standards, or global courts exist to settle disputes in the global economy. The different laws governing contracts, product safety and liability standards, and property rights are of particular importance when conducting global business. Property rights violations, including violations of patents and copyrights in the software, music, and publishing business, have cost businesses billions of dollars a year. Without adequate protection of intellectual property, technological developments could dry up as businesses think twice about funding expensive long-term research and development projects if others can easily steal the fruits of their labor.

▼ **Table 4.4**

Failures of Markets and Government Interventions	
Market Failures	**Government Intervention**
Growth of monopoly power	Government enforces anti-trust laws.
Undesirable and desirable social side effects from production and consumption	Government curtails the production and consumption of undesirable goods and promotes desirable products.
Lack of public goods and services	Government provides them.
Unfair distribution of income	Government redistributes income.
Macroeconomic instability	Government uses fiscal and monetary policies to stabilize the business cycle.

Different laws also govern bribes throughout the world. The United States passed the Foreign Corrupt Practice Act in the 1970s in response to questionable or illegal payments to foreign government officials to secure contracts or other favors. The Act was designed to restore public confidence in the business community in the United States. But Congress became concerned that U.S. businesses were put at a disadvantage with many foreign companies that routinely paid bribes and were even able to deduct the cost of bribes from their taxes as legitimate business expenses. The United States therefore pushed for the creation of the Organisation of Economic Co-operation and Development in 1988, which currently consists of 30 member nations committed to combating bribery. In many places in the world, however, bribes are not uncommon and may even be necessary to do business.[28]

Ethical Challenges

What are some ethical challenges to conducting international business? Bribery is just one of the many ethical dilemmas surrounding global business. But even when something isn't illegal, that doesn't mean it isn't unethical. Unique differences in economic conditions and cultural values give rise to many ethical dilemmas surrounding global business. For example, should a firm conform to its home country's environmental, workplace, and product safety standards—even though it's not legally required to do so—while operating in another country? Should a company do business with a repressive totalitarian regime? When conducting international business, companies must decide whether they're willing to defy their ethical codes to make a larger profit or even to survive.

Think back to the quiz that you took at the beginning of this section. What's truly important is to realize that you can't assume that people will behave in similar ways in various cultures. Understanding and respecting these differences in cultures will help you in life, whether you're hoping to work for a large international company or just hoping to visit foreign countries as a tourist.

▼ You have just read **Objective 9**

Think you got it? Check out the Study Plan section @
www.my*biz*lab.com.

1. What are the implications of the globalization of markets and the globalization of production? (pp. 97-98)

- The **globalization of markets** (p. 97) refers to the movement away from thinking of the market as being the local market or the national market, to the market being the entire world.
  - Businesses need to "think globally, but act locally," which means that companies must market their products so that they appeal to their local customers.
  - Determining whether a business is locally owned or foreign owned becomes more difficult because companies are putting local faces on their products.

- The **globalization of production** (p. 97) refers to the trend of individual firms to disperse parts of their productive process to different locations around the world to take advantage of lower costs or to enhance quality.
  - The globalization of production often involves **outsourcing** (p. 97), which is the contracting with another firm to produce part of a product that used to be produced in-house. Offshore outsourcing has become a significant concern for U.S. workers.
  - This trend helps increase profits and reduce the cost of production.

2. Why has globalization accelerated so rapidly? (pp. 98-99)

- The decline in trade and investment barriers, which are government barriers to inhibit the free flow of goods, services, and financial capital across national boundaries, is one factor that has led to increased globalization. This decline has:
  - encouraged developing nations to become involved in international trade
  - allowed companies to base production facilities at the lowest-cost location

- Technological changes that have also contributed to the rise in globalization include:
  - teleconferencing, which allows businesspeople to conduct meetings with contacts around the world
  - information technology, such as the Internet and cable and satellite TV systems, which allow companies to advertise and sell products on a global scale

3. What are the costs and benefits of international trade? (pp. 100-102)

- The **theory of comparative advantage** (p. 100) states that specialization and trade between countries benefits all who are involved. This is true because countries that participate in international trade experience higher standards of living due to the greater quantity and variety of higher-quality products at lower prices.

- The costs of international trade are borne by those businesses and their workers whose livelihoods are threatened by foreign competition. Businesses may lose their market shares to foreign companies, which in turn forces businesses to lay off workers.

4. What are the different types of trade barriers? (pp. 103-109)

- The different types of trade barriers are **tariffs**, **subsidies**, **quotas**, and **administrative trade barriers** (p. 104).
  - Tariffs are taxes imposed on a foreign good or service.
  - Subsidies are government payments to domestic producers in the form of a direct cash grant or a payment in kind.
  - Quotas are quantity limitations on the amount of an export allowed to enter a country.
  - Administrative trade barriers are government bureaucratic rules designed to limit imports. One example is a **local content requirement** (p. 104), which is a requirement that some portion of a good be produced domestically.

5. What are the three basic strategies of international business? (pp. 110-111)

- The three basic strategies of international business are the **global strategy**, the **multi-domestic strategy**, and the **transnational strategy** (pp. 111).

6. How can international firms successfully enter foreign markets? (pp. 111-114)

- There are eight common ways for a company to enter foreign markets. These methods include:
  - **exporting** (p. 111), the sale of domestically produced goods in a foreign market
  - **turnkey projects** (p. 112), which occur when firms export their technological know-how in exchange for a fee
  - **franchising** (p. 112), which involves selling a well-known brand name or business method in exchange for a fee and percentage of the profits
  - **licensing** (p. 112), an agreement in which the licensor's intangible property may be sold or made available to a licensee for a fee
  - **joint ventures** (p. 113), which involve shared ownership in a subsidiary firm
  - **strategic alliances** (p. 113), or cooperative agreements between competitors
  - **contract manufacturing** (p. 113), which occurs when a firm subcontracts part or all of its goods to an outside firm
  - **wholly-owned subsidiary** (p. 113), which involves establishing a foreign facility that is owned entirely by the investing firm

7. What are exchange rates and how do they affect international business? (pp. 115-117)

- An **exchange rate** (p. 115) is the rate at which one currency is converted into another.

- **Currency appreciation** (p. 116), or the increase in the exchange rate value of a nation's currency, causes the price of imports to fall and the cost of exports to rise. **Currency depreciation** (p. 116), or the decrease in the exchange rate value of a nation's currency, creates the opposite effect.

Chapter Summary (cont.)

8. What economic factors and challenges play a role in conducting business on a global scale? (p. 118)

- Economic growth and development present a challenge because some countries lack the infrastructure necessary to transport goods effectively.

9. What are the sociocultural, political, legal, and ethical challenges to conducting business in a global marketplace? (pp. 119-123)

- International businesses prefer stable, democratically elected governments with a firm commitment to free-market principles. However, many countries do not offer this kind of political and economic environment. This poses many challenges when conducting business internationally.

- **Ethnocentrism** (p. 119), the belief that one's own culture is superior to all others, can lead to conflict when conducting business globally. Other sociocultural challenges include differences in aesthetics, religion, and attitudes toward time and work.

- From a legal standpoint, the differences in laws and regulations around the world provide challenges for conducting business. There are no universal laws or policies for governing contracts, product safety and liability standards, or property rights.

- Government decisions about taxation, infrastructure investments, and antitrust law enforcement can all affect global business. Sometimes, government intervention fails to improve the market, and government failure occurs.

- Bribery is one ethical challenge facing international business. Decisions about whether to conform to a home country's environmental, workplace, and product-safety standards while operating in a foreign country are other ethical dilemmas.

For an audio file of the Objectives and Chapter Summary, see the Student Resources section @ www.my*biz*lab.com.

Key Terms

absolute advantage   (p. 101)

comparative advantage   (p. 100)

contract manufacturing   (p. 113)

culture   (p. 119)

currency appreciation   (p. 116)

currency depreciation   (p. 116)

dumping   (p. 106)

embargo   (p. 104)

ethnocentrism   (p. 119)

exchange rate   (p. 115)

exporting   (p. 95)

foreign direct investment   (p. 99)

franchising   (p. 112)

free trade   (p. 103)

free trade areas   (p. 107)

General Agreement on Tariffs and Trade (GATT)   (p. 106)

global strategy   (p. 110)

globalization   (p. 96)

globalization of markets   (p. 97)

globalization of production   (p. 97)

importing   (p. 95)

joint venture   (p. 113)

licensing   (p. 112)

local content requirement   (p. 104)

multi-domestic strategy   (p. 111)

multinational enterprises   (p. 99)

North American Free Trade Agreement (NAFTA)   (p. 108)

outsourcing   (p. 97)

quota   (p. 104)

strategic alliances   (p. 113)

subsidies   (p. 104)

tariff   (p. 104)

trade deficit   (p. 117)

trade surplus   (p. 117)

transnational strategy   (p. 111)

turnkey projects   (p. 112)

wholly-owned subsidiary   (p. 113)

World Trade Organization (WTO)   (p. 106)

Self-Test

Multiple Choice   Correct answers can be found on page 503.

1. **Globalization involves**

   a. making products that protect the environment.

   b. moving toward a more interconnected world economy.

   c. the use of aerospace technology.

   d. None of the above

2. **Which one of the following factors has <u>NOT</u> increased the trend toward globalization?**

   a. Falling trade and investment barriers

   b. Technological innovations in shipping

   c. The Web

   d. The rise of Communism in some nations

3. **The theory that states that specialization and trade is mutually beneficial to all economies involved in trade is called the**

   a. theory of comparative advantage.

   b. theory of beneficial trade.

   c. theory of absolute advantage.

   d. theory of relative trade.

4. **Which of the following are ingredients for national competitiveness?**

   a. Investments in health, education, and training

   b. Investments in capital (plant and equipment)

   c. Investments in technology

   d. All of the above

5. **Which of the following is true of a free trade economy?**

   a. Goods and services can be traded only at designated times.

   b. A tax is placed on all goods and services traded between countries.

   c. Goods and services can be traded without government intervention.

   d. A limit is placed on the amount of goods and services that can be traded.

6. **Which of the following international organizations is no longer in existence?**

   a. GATT

   b. EU

   c. NAFTA

   d. WTO

7. **If an international business is selling a standardized product and competing chiefly on price, the business is initiating a**

   a. transnational strategy.

   b. multi-domestic strategy.

   c. standard-price strategy.

   d. global strategy.

8. **Which of the following is an advantage to exporting?**

   a. It is good for transporting heavy and bulky products.

   b. It does not encounter foreign trade barriers.

   c. It is easier than establishing a physical presence in a local market.

   d. It allows local agents to do the marketing for the product.

9. **Which method of entering foreign markets has the advantage of allowing for test-marketing a product in a foreign market at the lowest cost?**

   a. Joint ventures

   b. Wholly-owned subsidiaries

   c. Exporting

   d. Contract manufacturing

10. **Ethnocentrism is**

    a. violating another country's ethical standards.

    b. understanding, appreciating, and being sensitive to cultural differences

    c. a belief that one's own culture is superior to all other cultures.

    d. an ingredient for international business success.

Self-Test

True/False   Correct answers can be found on page 503.

1. The globalization of production refers to a movement away from thinking of the market as being the local market toward the market being the entire world.
   ☐ **True** or ☐ **False**

2. Outsourcing sometimes involves moving the production of a product from a domestic location to a foreign location.
   ☐ **True** or ☐ **False**

3. Increasing U.S. dominance of foreign direct investments has helped accelerate globalization.
   ☐ **True** or ☐ **False**

4. International businesses prefer politically stable, democratically elected governments that have a firm commitment to free-market principles.
   ☐ **True** or ☐ **False**

5. There are no universal laws, regulatory standards, or global courts that exist to settle disputes in the global economy.
   ☐ **True** or ☐ **False**

Critical Thinking Questions

1. The text explains that sometimes an international business needs to modify its product to adjust to the specific needs or tastes of the local market. How would a company such as Hewlett-Packard adjust its laptop computers in order to market them to families in developing nations such as India?

2. Think about the technological advancements the world has embraced over the last 10 years. The Web, BlackBerrys, and wireless Internet connections have allowed businesspeople to have mobile offices. How does this technology reduce cultural distance and decrease business costs?

3. What are the advantages of increased competition in the global market? What are the disadvantages? Is foreign competition *always* good for the consumer? Is foreign competition *always* bad for the local business?

4. Review the three basic strategies of international business. Discuss the type of companies that would most likely pursue a global strategy, a multi-domestic strategy, and a transnational strategy.

5. Imagine you own a furniture store in the United States that specializes in handcrafted dining room tables and chairs. You would like to sell your product to countries in western Europe. What would be a good mode of entering the foreign market for your company?

Team Time

The Devil's Advocate

Read the following issues and questions. Which side of the issue do you believe is correct? Form a group with other students in the class who share your belief. As a group, play devil's advocate by creating a case for the opposing side of the issue. Now that you've considered both sides, you're ready to debate the opposition.

Issues and questions:

1. In the recent wave of globalization, developing countries have become the focus for many international businesses. Is this process of globalization the best way to strengthen developing countries and establish a level playing field, or does it keep them under the control of wealthy industries and drive income inequality?

2. Free trade versus protectionism is a heated debate in today's fragile economy. Which is better for the health of the U.S. economy over the next 10 years, free trade or protectionism?

3. Currently, the minimum age for a child to work in Indonesia is 12 years old. The minimum age for a child to work in the United States is 14 years old. If a garment company from the United States decides to outsource production to Indonesia, would it be ethical for the company to hire 12- or 13-year-old workers in the factory?

Process

Step 1. Meet as a group to discuss the issue. Remember that you must build a case for the side you chose. Look for problems with your own personal beliefs to develop a case for your side.

Step 2. Prepare an individual response that supports your side of the issue.

Step 3. Share your response with your group. Think of possible rebuttals for each response. Then, alter any responses that can produce a strong rebuttal.

Step 4. Determine who will be the group's primary spokesperson for the debate.

Step 5. Each group will be given 5 minutes to present its side of the issue. After each group has presented their argument, each team will be given 5 minutes to prepare a rebuttal and then 3 minutes to present the rebuttal.

Step 6. Repeat with other groups.

Step 7. After each group has debated, discuss whether anyone's personal views have changed after this assignment.

Ethics and Corporate Social Responsibility

Outsourcing

Workers in the United States often view outsourcing in a negative light. Many people believe that this practice is a way for companies to make more money by eliminating U.S. jobs. However, outsourcing is sometimes necessary for the survival of a company. Review the following scenario.

Scenario

You are the owner of a company that makes industrial sewing machines. Currently, your company's profits are decreasing because your competitors have lower prices. You cannot lower the price of your machines without losing a significant amount of money. The majority of your costs come from labor. You have 2,000 employees in your factory, and your company is a primary employer in the region. You could sell your product for a third of the price if you outsourced half your production to a foreign country. However, this would eliminate 1,000 jobs and devastate a community. Also, the country that you would be outsourcing to has a reputation for unsafe working conditions and practices. If you don't outsource some of your production, over time your company may be unable to compete and you will have to shut down your company.

Questions

1. As a business owner, what are the costs and benefits of moving half your production overseas?

2. Do the benefits of outsourcing outweigh the costs? Why or why not?

3. Are there any possible alternatives to consider? What other decision could you make so that each side (domestic and international) benefits?

Web Exercises

1. **Go Shopping**
   Think of a product you would like to buy. Use a search engine to find that product. How many options do you find? What is the cost? Which countries are exporting this product?

2. **Check out Foreign Web Sites**
   Go to the Web site of an international company such as Swedish furniture maker IKEA (www.ikea.com). Under the "select a location" option, choose the United States. Review the site and note the products and the design of the page. Then, go back to the home page and choose a different country. Look for differences in the appearance of the Web site and the products offered. Why do you think these sites are different for each county?

3. **Learning More about Foreign Trade**
   Go to www.wto.org to learn more about foreign trade. Click on Trade Topics and choose a topic that interests you. Write a paper about the issues surrounding this topic.

4. **Cultural Guidelines**
   Visit www.executiveplanet.com. Review the culture guides for travelers. Choose three countries and create a business "do's" and "don'ts" list for each country.

5. **You're the Trader**
   Imagine you're in charge of trading goods for a country. Would you focus on building wealth by selling commodities? Or on developing an industry by purchasing raw materials? Visit www.imf.org/external/np/exr/center/students/trade/index.htm and become the trader. Measure your success on the global economics conditions scale.

Web Case

To access the Chapter 4 Web case and exercise, see the End of Chapter Assignments section @ www.my*biz*lab.com.

Video Case

To access the Chapter 4 video case and exercise, see the End of Chapter Assignments section @ www.my*biz*lab.com.

Special Issues in
E-Commerce

In the past ten years, we've gotten used to seeing *e-* and *i-* before company and product names. E-mail has become so common that we have to specify when we refer to paper mail (i.e., snail mail). It's not just individual products like the iPhone that have gone *www*. Entire businesses are now being launched online. Most corporate retailers have online stores, and some, like Zappos, are exclusively e-commercial. In this mini-chapter, we'll discuss the rise of e-commerce within the business world, particularly the forms e-commerce takes, its impact on banking, and the challenges it creates.

Online Business

You've no doubt realized that the Internet has created markets that didn't exist before. A random assortment of everything from personal items and collectibles to cars and vacation homes are now available to a global market, thanks to eBay and similar Web sites such as uBid. Now anyone with Internet access can conduct business online, which makes for more consumer choices. Amazon.com, for example, has more books in stock than the biggest bricks-and-mortar bookstore chain in the country. Online stores can ship items straight from the warehouse to the consumer, bypassing the need to conform to space constraints in retail stores' storerooms. This phenomenon of online markets fostering easy access to hard-to-find items is often called the "Long Tail" effect.

Perhaps the most dramatic effect that the Internet has had on commerce is allowing businesses to go global. A company no longer requires a location or partner in another country to conduct business internationally. Thanks to the Internet, business communications move at lightning speed, allowing more opportunities than ever before for companies to establish a worldwide presence. The Internet has also increased outsourcing. This has allowed manufacturers to move production to cheaper locations, including over-seas. Many U.S. businesses began moving their back-office tasks, like data processing and information technology departments, to places such as India and the Philippines.[1] Others have relocated their helpdesk centers overseas as well.

Interaction between business and consumer has also changed radically since the introduction of the Internet. The most common modes of communication are business-to-business (B2B), business-to-consumer (B2C), and consumer-to-consumer (C2C), which are shown in ▼ **Figure 1** and which we discuss next.

| Business-to-Business B2B | Business-to-Consumer B2C | Consumer-to-Consumer C2C |

▼ **Figure 1**
Comparison of B2B, B2C, and C2C

to continue **mini 1** check out **www.mybizlab.com**.

Small Business and the Entrepreneur

p. 143

Buying Franchises and Existing Businesses

▼ **Objective 3**

Have you ever thought of owning your own business, but didn't know where to start? Aisha Lawrence had always dreamed of running a restaurant. Should she start her own from scratch? Or would buying a franchise or an established restaurant be the right move for her?

p. 149

The Risks of Small Businesses and Where to Get Help

▼ **Objectives 4 & 5**

There's a good reason why entrepreneurs are known for being risk takers: starting a small business is risky! More new businesses fail than succeed, especially in the first year or two. How can small business owners turn a failing business around? Where can they go for help?

p. 133

Entrepreneurs and the American Dream

▼ **Objective 1**

Do you detect *opportunity niches* everywhere you go? Are you a *system thinker*? Successful entrepreneurs must embody a number of different traits and master a variety of skills, including the use of a unique lingo. Do you have what it takes to be a successful entrepreneur?

p. 138

Small Business: The Mainstream of the American Economy

▼ **Objective 2**

Small businesses are an integral part of the American economy. What exactly is a small business? Why are they so important? And why do people start them?

p. 154

Financing Considerations

▼ **Objective 6**

All that stands between many would-be entrepreneurs and their pot of gold at the end of the rainbow is a way to finance their dream business—but as new business owners, which options should they consider? Which should they avoid?

Entrepreneurs and the **American Dream** pp. 133-137

➤ **What is an entrepreneur?** We've all heard of Starbucks, Nike, and Microsoft, but you probably don't associate these big-name companies with small business. But at one point, each of these companies started off as small businesses. They were all started by **entrepreneurs**—people who assume the risk of creating, organizing, and operating a business. Entrepreneurs most often start a business to satisfy a need in the market that is not being adequately fulfilled. This area of need is called an **opportunity niche**.

The brothers who started McDonald's spotted an opportunity niche. Realizing that the hamburger was the bestseller in their California restaurant, they created an assembly line that allowed them to produce burgers quickly and inexpensively, and business boomed. It expanded even more when businessman Ray Kroc, who was selling milkshake machines in California, convinced the brothers not only to use his milkshake machines, but also to let him open another McDonald's restaurant in Chicago. Seeing the opportunity niche in fast food, Kroc later bought the McDonald's restaurants from the McDonald brothers. The company now operates over 28,000 restaurants worldwide, generating more than $20 billion in revenue annually.[1]

The Traits of Successful Entrepreneurs

What are the traits of successful entrepreneurs?

Businessman Wayne Huizenga started Waste Management Inc., now a leader in the waste and environmental services industry, by buying a single garbage truck in 1968. He expanded the company by buying other trash collection services, and by 1983 the company had grown into the largest of its kind in the United States. But Huizenga didn't stop there. He also started Blockbuster Video, the nation's largest video rental company, as well as AutoNation, the behemoth automotive dealer.[2] How can some entrepreneurs like Wayne Huizenga begin successful businesses,

Becoming a successful entrepreneur involves a complex blend of skill, savvy, and luck. Before embarking on such an endeavor, however, you'll need to familiarize yourself with a few concepts. Test your entrepreneurial vocabulary with the following **quiz**.

1. "It's all about fulfilling an opportunity niche!" Liza, a budding entrepreneur, exclaims. Liza is likely referring to
   a. a need in the market.
   b. a storage nook.
   c. a sense of belonging.

2. A system thinker is someone who
   a. contemplates the technological side of a business.
   b. focuses on the entire process of turning an idea into a reality.
   c. designs methods of doing things.

3. Micropreneurs are likely to
   a. be petite.
   b. hire thousands of employees.
   c. enjoy running a small business.

4. When you hear the word *gazelle*, you think
   a. antelope.
   b. fast-growing business.
   c. graceful.

Are you confident in your understanding of entrepreneurial lingo? Or do you need a primer in the use of these terms? Whatever the case, read on for in-depth information on entrepreneur basics, types of entrepreneurs, and what it takes to be an entrepreneur. ➤

while others have a difficult time getting their ideas off the ground? How do successful entrepreneurs see an opportunity niche and know exactly what they need to do to seize the opportunity and succeed?

Although luck and timing play a large role in entrepreneurial success, research has also shown that successful entrepreneurs:

- are innovative
- take risks
- are motivated to succeed
- are flexible and self-directed
- work well with others and possess good leadership skills
- are "system thinkers," seeing the whole process rather than just individual pieces of it

How are entrepreneurs innovative? Successful entrepreneurs see problems to be solved or opportunities that aren't being addressed in the marketplace—they recognize opportunity niches. They also make improvements to existing products or systems, or they introduce something new and make profitable solutions out of problems. Renowned management and business thinker Peter Drucker noted that successful entrepreneurs "exploit change as an opportunity for a different business or a different service."[3] For example, Henry Ford turned his knowledge of engines into the first "horseless carriage," which he later improved to become the Model T.[4] His improvement was not only in creating a new machine, but also in developing an assembly line process by which his company could make multiple automobiles more efficiently. Ford's innovative assembly process became the standard for efficient manufacturing. Think about other entrepreneurs and the innovation behind their success. Ben Cohen and Jerry Greenfield of Ben & Jerry's Ice Cream didn't invent ice cream; rather, they capitalized on people's growing desire for high-quality food products and used the best and biggest chunks of nuts, fruits, candy, and cookies in their ice cream.[5] The McDonald brothers learned how to produce good hamburgers quickly and cost-effectively. ▼ **Figure 5.1** lists some other important innovations by entrepreneurs in the 20th century.[6]

How do entrepreneurs take risks? Being an entrepreneur involves risk, encompassing the risk of failure, the risk of losing one's career, and, of course, financial risks. Because entrepreneurs are often creating new and innovative products, the processes they develop are also often untried and therefore involve risk. Successful entrepreneurs are aware of these risks, recognize that they can influence events but do not have complete control over them, and are willing to accept the knowledge

▼ **Figure 5.1**
20th-Century Entrepreneurial Innovations

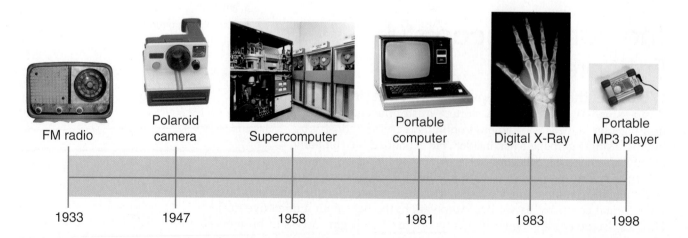

| FM radio | Polaroid camera | Supercomputer | Portable computer | Digital X-Ray | Portable MP3 player |

| 1933 | 1947 | 1958 | 1981 | 1983 | 1998 |

that they may fail. Successful entrepreneurs therefore take calculated risks—that is, they consider the likelihood of success before deciding whether to take a particular risk.

"If you take risks, you may still fail; but if you do not take risks, you will surely fail. The greatest risk of all is to do nothing." [7]

—Roberto Goizueta, *CEO of Coca-Cola* (1980–1997)

What makes entrepreneurs motivated to succeed?

Entrepreneurs are motivated by many different factors. Some entrepreneurs are motivated to provide for themselves or their families. These individuals may be driven to pursue multiple ventures before uncovering a successful idea. Other entrepreneurs are motivated to succeed by the personal fulfillment they feel upon successfully launching a business.

Entrepreneurs' keen desire to succeed has led one entrepreneur, Ted Kennedy, to start a company rooted in this notion. Kennedy noticed that many participants in the Ironman Triathlon Challenge were corporate executives. He also noticed that these executive triathletes sought above-average accommodations prior to and during their competition. So he formed CEO Challenges, a company that organizes luxury sports experiences for corporate executives. CEO Challenges provides luxury accommodations the night before a race, ensures family members and friends are positioned alongside the race so as to have the perfect view of their racer, and offers other amenities an executive might want when competing in physical challenges. Although Kennedy began his company focusing on triathlons, he has since expanded it to offer golf, sailing, tennis, and other competitive adventures to executives. He estimates that his company will have made over $5 million in revenue by 2010.[8]

Why do successful entrepreneurs need to be flexible and self-directed?

Because entrepreneurial ventures are subject to uncertainty and risk, entrepreneurs need to be able to react quickly to new and unexpected situations. And because entrepreneurs are their own bosses, they need to be able to make their own decisions. An entrepreneur must be able to wear many hats, acting not only as the executive, but also the sales manager, financial director, secretary, and mailroom person.

Why are people skills and leadership skills important to entrepreneurs?

They may come up with the initial idea behind their business, but entrepreneurs rarely work by themselves. As much as they have the capacity to wear many hats, at some point most entrepreneurs need other people with complementary skills to join them in their venture. If their business expands, they must hire employees and other managers to help them run it. Leadership and communication skills are therefore important traits of successful entrepreneurs who must motivate others to feel as passionately about the entrepreneurial enterprise as they do.

What does it mean for entrepreneurs to be "system" thinkers?

Although entrepreneurs develop companies from an idea, they must focus on the entire process of turning their idea into a business in order to succeed. Successful entrepreneurs are able to see the whole picture when they set up their businesses. They determine how to resolve a problem or to capitalize on an opportunity by developing a solid plan, including the production, financing, marketing, and distribution of the service or product. For example, Pete Slosberg, founder of Pete's Brewing Company, recognized the rise in popularity of microbreweries and brewpubs around the country. Slosberg saw the opportunity and began the process of creating his company not with just an idea but with a system: create a "great beer, a great name, and an interesting label. Have the name and the label to get people to try it for the first time, and a great beer so they keep coming back."[9] In 1998 Pete's Brewing Company had $19 million in sales before being sold to the Gambrinus Company.

Types of Entrepreneurs

Are there different types of entrepreneurs? Beyond the traditional entrepreneurs described in the previous sections, other entrepreneurial categories have begun to crop up, including:

- lifestyle entrepreneurs
- micropreneurs
- growth entrepreneurs
- intrapreneurs

What are lifestyle entrepreneurs? **Lifestyle entrepreneurs** look for more than profit potential when they begin their business. Some lifestyle entrepreneurs are looking for freedom from corporate bureaucracy or the opportunity to work at home or in a location other than an office. Others are looking for more flexibility in work hours or travel schedules.

What are micropreneurs? **Micropreneurs** start their own business, but are satisfied with keeping the business small in an effort to achieve a balanced lifestyle. For example, a micropreneur might open a single restaurant and be satisfied with running only that one restaurant, instead of expanding as Ray Kroc did with the McDonald brothers' restaurant. Micropreneurs, or small-business people, have no aspirations of growing large and/or hiring hundreds or thousands of employees. Businesses such as dog-walking services, painters, and special-occasion cake bakers would all be considered micropreneurial opportunities.

What are growth entrepreneurs? **Growth entrepreneurs** strive to create fast-growing businesses and look forward to expansion. The companies that these types of entrepreneurs create are known as *gazelles*. Typically, a gazelle business has at least 20 percent sales growth every year for 5 years, starting with a base of at least $100,000.[10] It's hard to recognize a gazelle business during its rapidly growing period, though companies such as eBay and Google can clearly be identified in retrospect as having been gazelles in their early years.

What are intrapreneurs? You don't necessarily have to leave your company to have an entrepreneurial experience. Some companies are fostering **intrapreneurs**—employees who work in an entrepreneurial way within the organizational environment. At the home appliance company Whirlpool, for example, developing intrapreneurs is an important part of corporate success. The company's success depends on producing creative solutions to household problems. Instead of relying solely on the traditional research and development (R&D) process, Whirlpool management is tapping the creative juices of their employees by encouraging them to generate ideas that will enhance the company's existing products. Although employees are not separately compensated for their ideas, they are pleased that the company asks for their ideas and have responded enthusiastically. By the end of the first year of the program, 60 ideas were in the prototype stage and 190 were close to entering the marketplace.[11,12]

What It Takes to Be an Entrepreneur

How do I know if I'd be a good entrepreneur? Look at the list of entrepreneurial traits described earlier in this section. Do you have these traits? If so, you may have what it takes to be an entrepreneur. However, if you don't possess all of these traits, it doesn't preclude you from starting your own business and becoming a successful entrepreneur. If you have an idea and really want to make it happen, you might want to think about assembling an entrepreneurial team.

What is an entrepreneurial team? An **entrepreneurial team** is a group of qualified individuals with varied experiences and skills that come together to form a new venture. The skills of the entrepreneurial team members complement one another so that as a group, the team has the necessary skills and traits to manage a successful project.

Entrepreneurial teams are also great for those who want to run their own business but perhaps lack the personal experience. For example, many college and business school students form entrepreneurial teams to get their first project launched. There are several examples of students who met in college and began to work on projects together that turned out to be successful businesses. Students from Stanford University have come together to create well-known companies such as Google, Hewlett-Packard, Cisco, Imagen, and Yahoo! Another example is the Big Bang competition at the University of California at Davis. In this year-long program, UC Davis students, alumni, staff, and faculty can join forces to construct and test their business plans.[13]

◎On Target Facebook

When Mark Zuckerberg, a Harvard student, came up with the idea for Facebook, he didn't realize that he was spearheading a billion-dollar organization. The idea behind "The Facebook," as it was originally called, was to provide a forum for students on the Harvard campus to network and display pictures of themselves and their friends. The site was launched on February 4, 2004, and within a month, half of the undergraduates on the Harvard campus were users of the site. Expansion came quickly, as Dustin Moskovitz and Chris Hughes joined Zuckerberg to help promote the site. Within two months, the entire Ivy League was included in the Facebook network. In September of 2005, these entrepreneurs decided to allow high schools to join the network. Finally, on September 11, 2006, the general public was allowed to join Facebook, so long as all potential members had a valid e-mail address were at least 13 years old.

Mark Zuckerberg's brainchild has become so successful that he reportedly turned down a $750-million offer to purchase Facebook. Media giants such as Google and Yahoo! have been attempting to outbid each other for ownership of Facebook, but Zuckerberg claims that he is not interested in parting with his creation. And why should he be? The site has over 70 million active users worldwide and is constantly expanding!

Perhaps you're part of an entrepreneurial team, an employee in an intrapreneurial company, or prefer to go it alone. Maybe you want to keep your business small or expand it like McDonald's. Entrepreneurial opportunities exist if you're up to the challenge.

Look back at the quiz at the beginning of the section. How did you do? As you've learned, opportunity niches, system thinking, micropreneurship, and gazelle businesses are just a few of the concepts that budding entrepreneurs must consider before starting their businesses. Which of these business ideas appeals to you most?

▼ You have just read **Objective 1**

Think you got it? Check out the Study Plan section @ **www.my*biz*lab.com.**

Small Business: The Mainstream of the American Economy pp. 138-142

Do the worries and hassles of everyday life leave you feeling tense and exhausted? Read more for five surefire solutions to life's stubborn stressors.

Stressor: You need a product or service, but no one offers it.
Solution: Start your own small business!

Stressor: You're tired of living paycheck to paycheck; you want to control your own financial destiny.
Solution: Start your own small business!

Stressor: Your boss drives you nuts.
Solution: Start your own small business!

Stressor: Workplace bureaucracy—you hate wading through it.
Solution: Start your own small business!

Stressor: You're unemployed.
Solution: Start your own small business!

Although starting your own small business might not be the answer to all your problems, it can mean independence, control, and flexibility. For many people seeking a new opportunity, it's a promising and attractive option. In addition, many new small businesses today are founded to solve a unique problem with an innovative solution and to ultimately provide a specialized service to other corporations. Small businesses often fill a niche that large companies do not. As a whole, small businesses in the United States play a major role in the economy.

Small Business and the Economy

What is a small business? The **Small Business Administration (SBA)**, an independent agency of the federal government that was formed to aid, counsel, assist, and protect the interests of small businesses, defines a **small business** as "one that is independently owned and operated and which is not dominant in its field of operation."[14] To qualify for governmental programs and benefits specifically targeted for small businesses, a small business must also meet employee and sales standards established by the SBA. In general, most small businesses must have fewer than 500 employees, though, as shown in ▼ **Figure 5.2**, nearly all small businesses have 20 or fewer employees. Also, to qualify as a small business, the SBA places restrictions on how much annual revenue a small business can earn. These limits on average annual revenue vary significantly by industry, but in the retail and service industries, which account for the majority of small businesses, the average annual revenue for a small business is $6.5 million.

Why are small businesses important to the economy? Because there are so many small businesses, they are very important to the economy and the job market. In fact, small businesses provide 40.9 percent of private sales in the country and account for more than half of America's economic output. In addition, they employ approximately 50 percent of the private workforce. This makes U.S. small businesses the world's fourth largest economy, preceded only by the entire U.S. economy, the European Union, and China, as shown in ▼ **Figure 5.3**.[15] Small businesses also represent 97 percent of all U.S. exporters.[16]

How do small businesses foster innovation? Small
companies often introduce new products or procedures that many large businesses do not have the flexibility, time, resources, or inclination to offer.[17] Smaller companies are also often better poised to take risks, more flexible to explore innovative techniques, and better equipped to push through inventions than larger firms.

The impact of small business innovations is well known in the computer, information science, and communications industries. For example, Michael Dell shook up the computer retail industry by marketing computers directly to customers via the Internet, rather than through retail stores. By taking direct orders from customers, Dell was able to order parts directly from suppliers on an as-needed basis, freeing his company from carrying large inventories of parts that could become outdated by the next technological innovation. Michael Dell's process improvement gave Dell an advantage over its competitors and helped Dell Computers, then a fledgling start-up company, take the lead in the personal computer retail market. The market responded favorably, and the competition responded in kind. Today, Dell's competitors—Hewlett-Packard, Toshiba, and Sony—all have online customized shopping options.

Other industries have also benefited from the innovative contributions of small businesses. For example, in the biotechnology industry, many small businesses have found innovative solutions to medical issues. One such company is the Insulet Corporation, which recently received an innovation award from the Smaller Business Association of New England for developing the OmniPod. This tiny instrument, weighing a little more than an ounce, sticks to the skin and delivers insulin at a constant rate based on instructions programmed into its wireless companion.[18] The flexibility inherent in small businesses such as these allows them to react more quickly than larger companies to changing market trends and needs. As such, small businesses play an important role in maintaining a healthy economy.

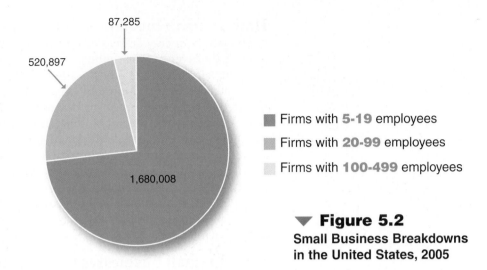

Firms with **5-19** employees

Firms with **20-99** employees

Firms with **100-499** employees

▼ **Figure 5.2**
Small Business Breakdowns in the United States, 2005

▼ **Figure 5.3**
U.S. Small Businesses vs. World Economies

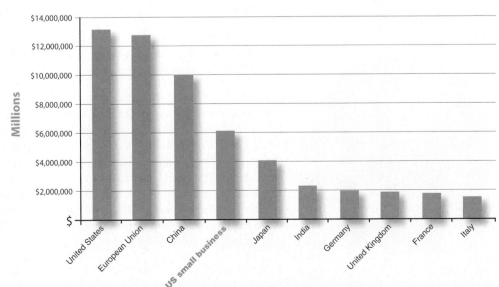

How do small businesses help bigger companies? Small businesses often operate in cooperative relationships with bigger businesses. At the beginning of the twenty-first century, over 40 percent of small businesses supplied goods or services to large businesses.[19] In the automotive industry, for example, small businesses are important because they make and supply parts that are required in large manufacturing processes. In fact, 3,200 small business suppliers worldwide provide General Motors with an average of 160,000 parts a day. Using small businesses to provide the small and specialized parts not only helps large manufacturers such as GM reduce their costs, but also helps with product design and innovation. Many of the latest features in cars, such as heated seats, were first developed by small companies and later sold to large automotive manufacturers. It is estimated that small-business suppliers now provide two-thirds of the value added in the production of the car through their increase in research and development.[20]

How do small businesses help consumers? Small businesses directly provide us with many of the specialized products and services we use every day. Service businesses such as hair salons, landscapers, and dry cleaners, as well as local restaurants, auto repair, and many other "mom and pop" stores provide the services and products larger businesses can't or don't want to provide.

Small Business and the Workforce

What kind of workers do small businesses employ? Almost all new businesses are small; therefore, they account for a substantial portion of the newly created jobs in the United States. In fact, small businesses create over 60 percent of net new jobs every year.[21] In addition, small businesses hire a larger proportion of younger workers, older workers, and part-time workers, so they help employ millions who do not fit into a traditionally corporate structure.[22]

Do small businesses provide opportunities for minorities? Many individuals see owning and operating their own business as a means of achieving the American dream. To that end, women, minorities, and immigrants are becoming more important players in the small business arena. According to a 2007 Small Business Administration report, 1.2 million African American-owned businesses and 1.6 million Hispanic-owned businesses accounted for 12 percent of all U.S. firms in 2002 (see ▼ **Figure 5.4**). Women owned 6.5 million businesses. And the number of minority-owned businesses is increasing. Between 1997 and 2002, the number of businesses owned by African Americans grew by 45 percent. The number of Hispanic-owned businesses grew 31 percent during this period, and firms owned by women increased by 20 percent. (Note: The Small Business Administration's 2007 report reflects the most recent data available.)

The infusion of foreign nationals and ethnic cultures in America has spawned more small business opportunities to provide services and products that cater to new needs and tastes. For example, Rajbhog Sweets, a small, family-owned, Indian sweets shop in Queens, New York, started to provide the Indian community there with authentic Indian sweets and snacks. As the Indian population increased in the area, so did the volume of items made and sold by Rajbhog Sweets. The company eventually expanded its operations to sell to 41 states and Canada, and caters to large weddings and conventions. In 2001, the company began to franchise its operations in other New York locations where large populations of Indians have settled.

▼ **Figure 5.4**
Small Business Ethnic Ownership, 2002

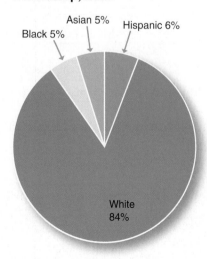

Black 5%
Asian 5%
Hispanic 6%
White 84%

The Impact of Technology on Small Businesses

How has technology affected new small businesses? Entrepreneurial success stories such as YouTube, MySpace, and eBay illustrate the vast opportunities that technology creates for new business start-ups. In addition to creating entirely new business opportunities, the personal computer and the Internet have made starting a new business much easier. Small businesses can flourish with an Internet connection, a modest Web site for marketing and communication, and a computer for financial, database, and research needs. Entrepreneur Nick Swinmurn, for example, went on a search for a new pair of his favorite boots one fateful day in 1999 and had a complete lack of success. He decided to form an Internet shoe store, www.shoestore.com. The site started small, but after Swinmurn realized the potential for advancement, he expanded the selection and shipping capacity of the site. The name of the site is now zappos.com, from the Spanish word for shoes, *zapatas*. Nick Swinmurn's small Internet shoe store is now a successful enterprise. Over 80 percent of small businesses have a home page, and nearly 25 percent take sales and orders online (see ▼ **Figure 5.5**). Almost 45 percent of small businesses promote their products on a company Web site and one-third of small businesses promote their products through e-mail marketing.[23]

▼ **Figure 5.5**
Businesses Often Use the Internet to Promote Their Products or Services

Reasons for Starting a Small Business

Why would I want to start my own business? People start small businesses for all kinds of different reasons.

1. **Opportunity Knocks.** An idea for a new company often starts with envisioning a product or service that isn't being offered yet. Other people create opportunities from their own obstacles. For example, a father frustrated at watching his autistic child try to communicate with others founded Animated Speech Corporation, a company that develops software-based conversational language learning systems to help autistic children communicate.

2. **Financial Independence.** Many begin a small business because they want financial independence. Still, most small businesses don't start out as profitable ventures. Traditionally, it takes three to five years for new businesses to become profitable.

3. **Control.** Many people starting their own business state that they want to take more control of business decisions than their current position allows. Others know that they wouldn't be satisfied working for someone else.

4. **Flexibility.** As illustrated in ▼ **Figure 5.6**, many view working in a small business as more rewarding than

Off the Mark iSmell

The dot-com era produced many businesses that just couldn't get off the ground. One example was the iSmell, a product that plugged into a computer's USB port and promised to enhance the user's Web surfing experience by generating different scents. Using the iSmell, you could smell a new perfume before buying it or conjure up the smell of a ballpark while playing a baseball videogame. Unfortunately, iSmell never made it beyond the prototype stage. Its parent company, DigiScents, shut its doors in 2001.[24]

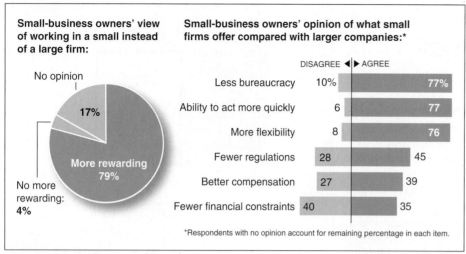

▼ **Figure 5.6**
Small Business Advantages, 2006

working for a larger company. Small-business owners believe their companies offer less bureaucracy and more flexibility than larger firms. With fewer channels to go through when decisions need to be made, business owners can react more quickly to take advantage of immediate opportunities. In addition, small business owners say running their own business allows them the flexibility to adjust their work to their particular situations.

5. **Unemployment.** Whereas most individuals start their own business for the reasons mentioned previously, some are "pushed" into starting their own business because they have no other employment opportunities. "Life begins when you get fired," muses Bruce Freeman, owner of Pro Line Marketing. Three months after being fired, he couldn't think of what to do next. Then, encouraged by a friend, Bruce started his own business. His first client was a company he worked with in his previous job. Now, eleven years later, he's making more money than he ever could have in his old job.[25]

Small Business Structures

What kind of structure should I choose for my small business?

Many small businesses start out initially as a one-person, individual business called a *sole proprietorship*. This is because sole proprietorships are the quickest and easiest way to start a business. However, there are five common types of business forms a small business can take:

- sole proprietorship
- general partnership
- limited partnership
- corporation
- limited liability company

We'll discuss these different structures in more detail in Chapter 6. As we'll see, the decision is centered primarily on two issues: legal liability and tax considerations. Depending on the nature of the business, owners may need to protect their personal assets should something go wrong with the business. Certain corporate structures protect owners' personal assets from claims against the company. Similarly, different corporate structures have tax advantages and disadvantages that are important for small business owners to consider.

Starting a small business is a sizeable challenge that, more often than not, creates as much stress as it eliminates. Nevertheless, it is a challenge to which many entrepreneurs, looking for their piece of the American dream, enthusiastically rise.

Places to Live and Launch a Small Business, 2008

1. Bellevue, WA
2. Georgetown, TX
3. Buford, GA
4. Marina del Rey, CA
5. Bethesda, MD
6. Portland, OR
7. Denver, CO
8. Charlotte, NC
9. Ft. Worth, TX
10. Franklin, MA

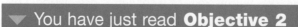

▼ You have just read **Objective 2**

Want a review? Check out the Study Plan section @
www.mybizlab.com.

Buying Franchises and Existing Businesses pp. 143-148

➤ Franchises have been around a long time. In the United States, Singer Sewing Machines was one of the first franchises, started in 1851. Today, they are a popular way for individuals like Aisha to enter the world of small business. In this section, we'll look at what it means to buy a franchise. We'll also discuss another small business option: buying an existing business and molding it into your own.

It was a desired change in lifestyle that prompted Aisha Lawrence to think about starting her own business. She had always dreamed of running her own restaurant, but she didn't have much business background or restaurant experience. What she did have was a lot of tenacity and knowledge of marketing. Additionally, she was a people person—a necessity for restaurant owners. Still, she was unsure of where to begin.

Aisha knew that the risks were way too high to start a restaurant on her own or to buy an existing restaurant. On the other hand, she felt that she could run a small, single-product food business, such as a coffee bar or ice cream shop, to give her the experience she would need to run her own restaurant some day. But Aisha was still uncomfortable starting from scratch. She felt that she needed the support of someone who had been through the process before her, so she looked into buying a franchise. The main question was, which franchise would be best for her? ➤

Franchising Basics

What is a franchise? A **franchise** is a method of doing business whereby the business (the **franchiser**) sells a company's products or services under the company's name to independent third-party operators (the **franchisees**).[26] In our example above, Aisha would be the franchisee using the franchiser's marketing methods and trademarked goods under the name of the business. In exchange, she would make monthly payments to the franchise.

What kinds of business opportunities are available as franchises?

Franchises play an important part in our economy. Over 750,000 franchised businesses are in operation, employing close to 10 million people with a combined annual payroll of nearly $230 billion.[27] More than half of all franchises are in the fast-food industry, including businesses such as McDonald's, Dairy Queen, and Subway, and another 13 percent are full-service restaurants. But franchise opportunities exist in nearly every industry. ▼ **Table 5.1** lists the top franchises from 2005 to 2008, illustrating the diverse industries that the most popular franchises are in.

Additionally, franchising provides a great opportunity to do business internationally. The franchise sector in China, for example, saw rapid growth in 2005. By the end of the year, China had 168,000 franchised stores, a 40-percent increase compared with about 120,000 the year before.[28]

▼ **Table 5.1**

Helpful Web Sites for Potential Franchisees	
sba.frannet.com	This site, sponsored by FranNet and the U.S. Small Business Association, features a video that explains what franchising is, how to determine if franchising is right for you, and how to select the right franchise.
www.franchisee.org	The American Franchisee Association's site offers advice on buying a franchise, legal resources, and opportunities to network with other franchisees.
www.ftc.gov	The Federal Trade Commission's site provides consumer information on franchise and business opportunities. The FTC's publication "Buying a Franchise: A Consumer Guide" outlines the steps to take before selecting a particular franchise, how to shop at a franchise exhibition, and what you should know before signing the franchisor's disclosure document.
www.entrepreneur.com/franchises/index.html	Entrepreneur.com's Franchise Zone allows users to search a directory of franchising opportunities and provides tips on buying a franchise. This site also ranks the top franchises in terms of growth, cost, global appeal, and other aspects.
www.franchise.org	The International Franchise Association provides answers to frequently asked questions about franchising and resources for potential and current franchisees. This site also hosts a directory of franchising opportunities in various industries.

Source: http://sbdcnet.org/SBIC/franchise.php and http://www.sba.gov/smallbusinessplanner/start/buyafranchise/index.html.

Pros and Cons of Franchising

What are the advantages of franchising? For many, franchising is an easier, less risky means of starting a business. Since the franchiser provides much of the marketing and financial tools needed to run the business, all the franchisee is expected to bring to the table is management and marketing skills, time, and money. In addition to a recognized brand name, there are many other advantages of owning a franchise.

- **It is a proven system of operation.**   Instead of wading through the muddy waters of new business ownership by themselves, franchisees benefit from the *collective experience* of the franchise company. The franchiser has determined, through trial and error, the best system of daily operations for the established business. New franchisees can therefore avoid many of the common start-up mistakes made by new business owners since they will be working with standardized products, systems, and financial and accounting systems.

- **There is strength in numbers.**   You are not alone when you buy a franchise. Because as a franchisee you belong to a group, you might benefit from economies of scale achieved by purchasing materials, supplies, and services at discounted group rates. In addition, it's often easier to get approved for business loans when running a franchise, as the lending institution views less risk associated with a franchise.

- **Initial training is part of the deal.**   The beauty of franchising is that you're in business *for* yourself but not *by* yourself. The franchiser offers initial training to ensure you have a successful opening and might offer ongoing training if new products or services are being incorporated into the franchise line.

- **Marketing support is provided.**   As a franchisee, you are often given marketing materials generated at the corporate level and have the benefit of any national advertising programs that are created. Although you are expected to run your own local marketing efforts, you have the support of other franchisees in the area to help you in your efforts.

- **Market research is often provided.** Good franchisers do considerable market research and can generally conclude whether there is demand for the product or service in the area before selling the franchisee a franchise. The franchiser should also help to identify the competition and offer strategies to differentiate the franchise from them.

What are the disadvantages of franchising? Although buying a franchise provides the franchisee with many benefits, there are some disadvantages too:

- **Lack of control.** There is not much opportunity to contribute creatively to the franchise since the franchiser often controls the look of the store and the product or service. The franchisee, however, is expected to bring the necessary drive and spirit to make the franchise a success.
- **Start-up costs.** As shown in ▼ **Figure 5.7**, over 70 percent of all franchises require more than $50,000 to start. In addition, franchisees must pay a monthly royalty fee to the franchiser. The royalty fees are due regardless of how the business is doing, and can be a huge overhead expense. Other costs the franchisee might incur include real estate purchase or rental, equipment purchase or rental, extra signage, and opening inventory.
- **Work load.** As with any new business owner, new franchisees shouldn't expect easy hours. Aisha Lawrence admits that she spends a lot more time running her franchise than she thought she would. However, because she can hire employees to run the day-to-day operations, her time is spent more on the business development and management end of the business.
- **Competition.** Some franchises do not restrict the location or number of their franchise locations. In those instances, franchisees could experience serious competition not only from another company, but also from other franchisees in the same franchise organization. In addition, some franchises do not offer geographic or demographic studies of the best location to open a new store and instead may expect the franchisee to have completed a good market analysis and be familiar with the surrounding competition.
- **Share common problems.** If the franchiser or another franchisee is having problems, all franchisees will feel its pain. For example, when a Wendy's restaurant was falsely accused of serving chili with a human thumb mixed in, business in all Wendy's restaurants plummeted.

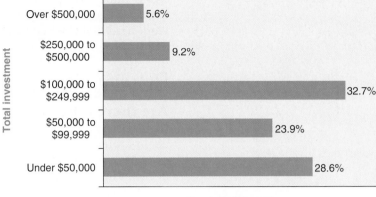

▼ **Figure 5.7**
Costs of Beginning a Franchise

Franchising Considerations

What are things to watch out for when considering buying a franchise? The most common piece of advice offered to anyone interested in buying a franchise is to do homework up front. Although a lot of the start-up process is done for you, you are still buying a business that will require your time and money and is not guaranteed to succeed. ▼ **Table 5.2** shows suggested questions to ask the company that you are buying the franchise from (franchiser) and other people who have bought franchises from the company (franchisees) before you take the plunge.

Aisha Lawrence ultimately decided that she wanted to open an ice cream franchise. There were many to choose from, so she spent months doing product research, visiting and tasting the various frozen treats offered by most of the ice cream franchises. Ultimately, Aisha has decided to buy a Cold Stone Creamery franchise because she thinks its product is superior. "Believe in your vision, and work hard to make that vision a reality," advises Aisha.

Buying an Existing Business

Are there other ways to start a business besides starting new or buying a franchise? While buying a franchise is a popular way to begin a business without starting from scratch, another way is to buy a pre-existing business. Just like buying a franchise or starting from scratch, the decision must be well thought-out.

What are the advantages of buying an existing business? Just as with buying a franchise, buying an existing business has certain advantages:

- It's often simpler than beginning one from scratch.
- There is a reduction in start-up time and energy if you are purchasing a business that is operational and without serious problems. This means that

▼ **Table 5.2**

Questions to Ask Before Buying a Franchise		
	Questions to Ask the Franchiser	**Questions to Ask Other Franchisees**
Competition	• What is the competitive advantage of the product/service? • What makes the business more attractive to an owner and more attractive to a customer?	• How is your system better than competitors'? • How does your business match up? • Who are competitors?
Franchise System	• How time tested and standardized is the franchise system? • What franchise system is used and how does it work? • How long has the franchise been in business and what improvements has it made recently?	• How long have you been in business? • Does your location meet your customers' needs? • Who selected the site?
Support and Training	• How much support does the franchiser give the franchisee? • What is the initial and ongoing training? • Are there toll-free help lines, field support, annual meetings, local meetings, purchasing programs, and marketing promotion?	• How is the relationship with franchiser? • How was the initial training and ongoing training and ongoing support? • How are the marketing, advertising, and promotional programs handled?
Financial Strength	• What is the financial strength of the company and the experience of management? • How much revenue comes from franchise fees and how much revenue comes from royalties? • How has the stock performed?	• Are you pleased with earnings? • Is volume growing?
Franchise Relationships	• How important is the franchisee to the franchise? • How can they describe the relationship with the franchiser? • Have there been lawsuits/arbitration? • If so, how have they been resolved?	• Do you have second thoughts (would you do this again)? • Would you own more units?

Adapted from: http://www.powerhomebiz.com/vol2/franchisechecklist.htm

suppliers, existing staff and management, and equipment and inventory are all in place to help facilitate taking over the business.

- An existing business may have an existing satisfied customer base. If no significant changes are made to drive away current customers, the business can continue to run and provide immediate cash flow.

- If the business has had a positive track record, it might be easier to obtain financing to purchase the existing business.

What are the disadvantages of buying an existing business?

There are also disadvantages to buying an existing business:

- Because you may need to buy the owner out of the business, the initial purchase price may be high. This can be more than the immediate up-front costs associated with a start-up, but not necessarily any different from a franchise. While you can easily determine the value of the physical business and its assets, it is more difficult to determine the true value of the previous owner's **goodwill**—the intangible assets represented by the business's name, customer service, employee morale, and other factors—that might be lost with a change in ownership. Often the intangible assets are overvalued, making the business cost more than it is worth.

- In addition, with a pre-existing business, you are sometimes stuck with the previous owner's mistakes. This means you might inherit dissatisfied customers, bad debt, and unhappy distributors or purchasing agents. You'll need to work to change the minds of people who have had a bad experience with the previous ownership.

- There is no guarantee that existing employees, management, customers, suppliers, or distributors will continue to work with the business once new ownership takes over. If staff does stay, you might be inheriting unanticipated problems.

What do I need to check before I buy a business? Existing businesses are sold for many reasons. Before buying an existing business, make sure you perform **due diligence**—research and analysis of the business to uncover any hidden problems associated with it. You want to avoid buying a company with a dissatisfied customer base or with a large amount of unpaid bills. ▼ **Table 5.3** provides a brief checklist of things you should look into before buying a business.

Not all businesses for sale have problems. For example, some family-run businesses run out of family members to pass the business on to. This was the situation that Dan Ratto, a business consultant in Texas, and Chris, his godson in California, came across. Chris knew of a restaurant near his home that was on the market. The restaurant had been part of a family business for many years, but no one in the family wanted to continue the business, so it was put up for sale. Dan and Chris did their due diligence and came up with their estimate of the restaurant's value. The owner's price was much less than Dan and Chris's estimate, so they scooped up the business. With only a few minor improvements, Dan and his godson exceeded initial sales expectations within the first year of ownership. They have since opened a few other locations and are considering the possibility of franchising the operation in other states.

Dan Ratto and his godson entered the restaurant business by buying an existing successful business and are pursuing franchising. Aisha Lawrence is taking a more cautious approach to entering the restaurant industry by buying into a franchise. Whether you buy an existing business or franchise or begin a business of your own, you'll be joining a large group of small business owners who make a significant contribution to the U.S. economy.

▼ **Table 5.3**

Things to Consider Before Buying a Business
Initial Questions to Ask
Why is the business for sale?
What do current customers say?
Are there opportunities for growth? How much time does the current owner put into the business?
Who is the competition?
Due Diligence Checklist
Get an independent valuation of inventory and equipment.
Have an accountant go over financial statements for the past 3 years.
Have a lawyer analyze pertinent business documents—property leases, employment contracts, etc.
Talk to suppliers to see if they will continue to supply the business when ownership changes hands.
Check for lingering or festering hazardous waste problems. They'll become your responsibility as the new owner.

Biz**Chat**

What's in a Name?

Naming a business should be fun, but it can be stressful, especially if you make some of the more common mistakes:

Mistake 1 | Involving friends, family, employees, or clients in the naming decision. You want to make the name communicate the key elements of your business, not the combined efforts of your friends and family.

Mistake 2 | Description + Product = Name. Although it seems catchy at the time, the result of company names that try to marry description with product is forced and often trite. A service franchise named QualiServe or a day spa named TranquiSpa ultimately aren't the right choices.

Mistake 3 | Using generic names. Gone are the days when General Electric or ACME Foods work as corporate names. In such highly competitive times when new products or servic-es are fighting for attention, it's best to choose a more unique name.

Mistake 4 | Making up a name. While using generic names may not be good, be careful to avoid names that are obscure, hard to pronounce, or hard to spell unless there is solid market research behind it.

Mistake 5 | Using geographic names. Unless you plan to stay local, including a specific geographic name may imply that you won't go beyond that regional territory.

- -

TIP: You might need to hire a company to create a name for you. Acura, Flixx, and Compac are all names that were created by experts.

- -

For more information and discussion questions about this topic, check out the BizChat feature on www.my*biz*lab.com.

▼ You have just read **Objective 3**

Want to learn more? Check out the Study Plan section @ **www.my*biz*lab.com.**

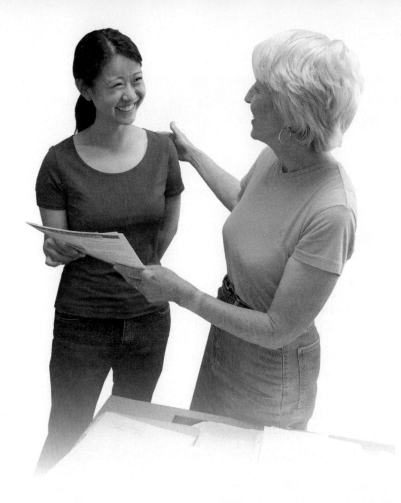

The **Risks** of **Small Businesses** and **Where** to **Get Help** pp. 149-153

➤ Not sure what SBA, SCORE, and EO stand for? Unclear as to exactly what business plans and business incubators are? Many new entrepreneurs are not as familiar with these concepts as they should be, just as they don't understand the risks they are going to incur and how much help they'll need in order to start up and maintain a business. In this section, we'll talk about what all of these terms mean, why so many businesses fail, and where owners can go for help.

Why So Many Small Businesses Fail

What are the risks of owning my own business?

Starting a business is a lot of hard work and comes with no guarantee for success. As shown in ▼ **Figure 5.8**, two-thirds of all start-ups fail in two years, and just over half survive after four years of operation.

Picture this: You've taken the plunge and poured your time, energy, and life savings into starting your own business. But a worsening economy and decreasing sales have brought your business to the brink of failure. Just when you think all hope is lost, you come across this:

How To Turn Your Business Around in 10 Days

- Days 1-2: Assume you can't afford professional advice and try to fix everything yourself.
- Day 3: Realize that you can't fix everything yourself; you need outside help.
- Day 4: Contact the SBA.
- Day 5: Attend an SBA workshop on tweaking your business plan.
- Day 6: Schedule a counseling session with a SCORE volunteer.
- Day 7: Get new ideas and fresh insights from a SCORE volunteer.
- Day 8: Learn about mentoring opportunities with EO.
- Day 9: Research business incubators in your area.
- Day 10: Realize it will take more than 10 days to turn your business around. But, also realize that by taking advantage of the many resources available to small business owners like yourself, it can be done. ➤

▼ Figure 5.8
Failure Rate of Businesses After Start-Up

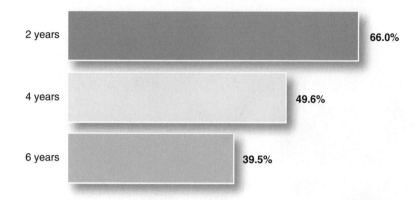

While many feel the benefits of owning their own business are worth the risks, it's important to be aware of why so many businesses fail. These reasons are shown in ▼ **Figure 5.9** and include:

- accumulating too much debt
- inadequate management
- poor planning
- unanticipated personal sacrifices

Let's look at each of these risks in a bit more detail.

Accumulating Too Much Debt One reason many new businesses fail is that they accumulate too much debt. Most begin a new business borrowing funds. Regardless of whether the loan comes from a bank, an outside investor, or a credit-card company, if the new business does not generate returns quickly enough to begin to pay back the initial loan, there is temptation to take on more loans to keep the business running. Interest on loans can accumulate too, causing an owner to become further entrenched in a potentially unrecoverable situation. What's worse is that some business owners borrow against their personal assets, putting them at risk of personal bankruptcy.

Inadequate Management Although entrepreneurs and small business owners are good at coming up with ideas, they may not be great at managing the books and their employees. The fact that so many businesses fail due to high levels of debt can be a sign of poor financial and business management. It's important that financial statements and budgets are created and adhered to honestly and

▼ Figure 5.9
Factors Contributing to the Failure of Many Small Businesses

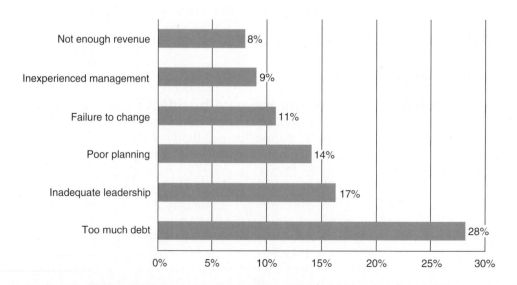

accurately each month, and that accounts receivable are religiously collected and accounts payable are aggressively managed. Take Jodi Gallagher, for example. Jodi owns a business designing and creating lingerie. In an effort to get her product into as many stores as possible, Jodi was lenient on the terms of collection. Rather than insisting on payment right away, she extended stores at least 30 days credit, and as a result it took her months to collect. Realizing that her mistake almost cost her the business, Jodi no longer extends credit.[29]

For other businesses, the challenge of managing growth has driven them under when they find that they cannot handle the increase in sales. This was a large part of many dot-com busts in the late 1990s. Many successful e-commerce businesses did not plan for rapid growth and therefore did not have sufficient inventory to fulfill orders when they came in. They also didn't take into consideration the subsequent impact this would have on dealers and retailers who were a part of their distribution channel.

Many business owners ignore the signs of a business beginning to fail or attribute the failure to the wrong reasons. In addition, although owners need to build a team, they can't hand over all control. Good management stays on top of all aspects of the business and makes the tough decisions, when necessary. As Nina Riley, CEO and founder of Water Sensations, a company that makes clear-liquid flavor enhancers for water says, "When things go bad—at the first indication—you gotta nip it in the bud, wrestle it to the ground to fix it. You just can't let it go. If this is your own company, you have to strive to be perfect."[30]

Poor Planning Accumulating debt and poor business management happen after the business has developed. One of the biggest reasons businesses fail is that there was no formal plan in place to begin with. The old adage "failing to plan is planning to fail" certainly applies to starting a business. Many budding business owners, in the excitement of starting something new, neglect to take the "boring" but necessary steps of building an effective business plan. A **business plan** is a formal document that states the goals of the business as well as the plan for reaching those goals. As shown in ▼ **Figure 5.10**, the plan includes the company's mission statement, history, and the qualifications of the owners and management team and any resources they might have to contribute to the business. It also includes a

▼ **Figure 5.10**
A Business Plan Outlines a Companys Goals and Strategies

Company Information
- Mission Statement
- Current Status
- History
- Management Team

Risk Analysis
- Risk Evaluation
- Risk Management Plan

Marketing Plan
- Competitive Analysis
- Pricing
- Distribution
- Promotion and Brand Development

Financial Plan
- Current Financing
- Funding Needs and Plan
- Financial History
- Financial Forecasts
- Valuation

Operational Plan
- Staffing
- R&D
- Manufacturing Plan
- IT Plan

marketing plan, an operational plan, a financial plan, a risk analysis, and identifies the competition and highlights opportunities for success. (You'll learn more about creating successful business plans in MiniChapter 2.) Neglecting to consider any of these factors can doom a business from the start.

Unanticipated Personal Sacrifices New businesses also may fail when owners do not adequately anticipate the many personal sacrifices—financial and otherwise—that new business owners are forced to make. For example, the cost of health insurance and retirement accounts falls solely on the shoulders of the new business owner. Additionally, the amount of time and effort owners must invest in the business, as well as the necessity to take on multiple responsibilities, makes running your own business not for the faint of heart.

Getting Help

Where do small business owners go for help? There are several sources of help that a small business owner can turn to.

The Small Business Administration As noted earlier, the *Small Business Administration (SBA)* is an independent agency of the U.S. government whose sole purpose is to cater to the needs of small businesses. The SBA offers assistance in the legalities associated with beginning and operating a business as well as education and training, financial assistance, disaster assistance, and counseling. The SBA holds events in major cities in all states, such as workshops in financial analysis, creating a business plan, and launching a business. It also offers free online courses and coordinates links to academic institutions that offer private online training. The SBA also acts as an advocate for small business owners to national and state policymakers. The agency works to reduce regulatory requirements and maximize benefits that small businesses receive from the government.

SCORE The nearly 11,000 volunteers who make up the SBA's Service Corp of Retired Executives (SCORE) offer workshops and counseling to small businesses at no cost. The volunteers are currently working in or have been in the field and can therefore provide advice to new or existing small business owners. They review business plans, help with tax planning, and offer new ideas and fresh insights. SCORE lists as some of its success stories such companies as Vermont Teddy Bear, Vera Bradley Designs, and Jelly Belly Candy.

Mentoring Sources SCORE is not the only source new business owners can turn to for mentors. Industry-related conferences or seminars often present new business owners with opportunities to find others who can serve as sounding boards and mentors. In addition, other organizations, such as the *Entrepreneurs Organization (EO)*, connect business owners with experts in their industry for individual mentoring. Although EO is for those who are currently in a viable operation (its requirements are that you must be a founder, co-founder, owner, or controlling shareholder of a business with a minimum of $1 million in annual gross sales and younger than 50 years old) such mentoring services can be helpful to second-stage small business owners.

Business Incubators One of the biggest overhead costs for any business is the support services required to run the business. **Business incubators** are organizations that support start-up businesses by offering resources such as administrative services, technical support, business networking, and sources of financing that a group of start-up companies share.

There are several benefits to incubation beyond sharing a receptionist and copy machine. Incubators create a synergistic environment where companies can act as peer-to-peer mentors, sharing both success and failures. Incubators also lend legitimacy to a beginning company as well as a more professional atmosphere than someone's home office. Studies show that a company that goes through an effective incubation period has about a 90 percent chance of success.[31]

Incubators can be either private organizations or public services. Over the past few decades, many cities as well as developed and developing countries have started public business incubators, often in conjunction with universities and research institutions, to promote new business development. Rensselaer Polytechnic Institute runs one of the oldest incubator programs in the country. Over the past 25 years, the incubator has provided support for 180 companies, creating some 2,000 jobs.

Advisory Boards and Partners As noted earlier, starting up a small business requires owners to take on multiple roles, acting not only as the chief executive officer, but also the chief operations officer, chief financial officer, and any other position that may need to be filled. Many owners quickly realize that their strengths lie in only one or a few of these areas, and therefore seek assistance from others. One option is to team up with *partners* who offer the company strengths that the new owner does not possess, and in turn share in its profits and liabilities. Forming an advisory board is another option. An **advisory board** is a group of individuals who offer guidance to the new business owner. Such boards are similar to boards of directors in publicly held companies, except that they generally do not have the authority to make decisions.

Remember the ideas presented in "How to Turn Your Business Around in 10 Days" at the beginning of this section? Unfortunately, many business owners don't look for outside help when they start their companies. Thinking that they couldn't afford professional advice, they rely on their own efforts, advice from friends and family, and trial and error. Often, they find that it takes more than a good idea and hard work to make a business successful. Knowing all of the resources available to fledgling businesses can help entrepreneurs avoid making the mistakes that eventually lead to the demise of their business. Careful financial decision-making, savvy management, meticulous planning, and the willingness to make significant personal sacrifices all play key roles in a successful business. Knowing when, where, and how to ask for help is also a factor critical to success.

▼ You have just read **Objectives 4 & 5**

Want to test your skills? Check out the Study Plan section @ **www.my*biz*lab.com.**

Financing Considerations pp. 154-155

How should business owners finance their ventures? Drain their personal savings accounts? Beg their family and friends for money? Max out their credit cards? All or none of the above? Before reading this section, complete the quiz below to find out what you already know about financing a business. Which of the following is a do and which is a don't?

When financing a business ...

1. Do or Don't: Give friends and family who you borrow from a document indicating how and when you intend to pay them back.

2. Do or Don't: Rely heavily on credit cards if you can't pay the balance completely every month.

3. Do or Don't: Borrow against your own assets without fully understanding the potentially severe personal consequences of business failure.

4. Do or Don't: Consider applying for a start-up loan or line of credit from a bank.

5. Do or Don't: Seek financing from a venture capitalist if the idea of relinquishing any control over your business does not appeal to you.

Answers: 1. Do; 2. Don't; 3. Don't; 4. Do; 5. Don't ➤

➤ The options, as well as the potential pitfalls, involved in choosing how to finance a business are numerous. In this section we'll look at the many sources of funding available to small business owners, and we'll discuss the problems associated with some of them.

Cash and Credit

Where can I get the money to start a business? Most business owners tap into their own personal savings when they initially invest in their business. Friends and family are generally secondary sources of cash. Such contacts are often good sources for financing because, unlike banks or other lending institutions, they often do not require a high rate of return or demand to see the business turn a quick profit. However, it's important when borrowing from friends and family that you treat them as professionally as possible. Make sure you give them a document with an indication of how you intend to pay them back and some sort of a contingency plan if things go wrong. In addition, they should be kept informed of any risks of the venture—upfront and ongoing.

Can I use credit cards to finance my business? Credit cards offer a convenient way to obtain funds quickly, especially with some of the zero percent financing available. If used wisely, credit cards are a convenient means of acquiring short-term cash, and nearly fifty percent of small business owners use personal credit cards as a source of financing for their small business. However, credit cards should be used only if you can pay the balance *completely* every month. The risk associated with using credit cards for your initial business financing is the high rate of interest charged on unpaid balances.

Bank and Other Loans

What if I need more money than what these sources provide? For larger amounts, new business owners sometimes borrow against their own assets, such as the equity in their house or against their retirement account, but the consequences of the business failing are very severe. If you're purchasing an existing business or a franchise, banks and savings and loan institutions often provide funding. In fact, roughly half of all small businesses use bank loans and lines of credit as part of their financing strategy. These institutions offer start-up loans and lines of credit to help businesses make payroll during slower periods as well as capital loans to buy equipment or machinery.

Venture Capital and Other Forms of Financing

What if I don't want to finance my business with loans? There are other sources of funding if you choose not to finance your business with loans.

Venture Capitalists Venture capitalists are another source of funding. Unlike banks, where there is a contractual agreement to pay back the money, **venture capitalists** contribute money to your business in return for some form of equity, or a piece of ownership. Venture capitalists are very picky about the projects in which they invest. They look for the potential of a public stock offering; therefore, such financing is generally only available to those businesses that have been operating for several years and that have the potential to become larger regional or national companies. To protect their investment, venture capitalists sometimes require that they play an active role in the management of the company, so business owners must be open to the idea of relinquishing control when they seek venture capital funding.

SBIC Program If venture capital is not available or suitable, an alternative is the **Small Business Investment Company (SBIC) program**. SBICs are private venture capital firms licensed by the Small Business Administration to make equity capital or long-term loans available to small companies. The size of the financing provided by SBICs is generally in the $250,000 to $5 million range.

Angel Investors Angel investors are another type of financing. **Angel investors** are wealthy individuals who are willing to put up their own money in hopes of a profit return later on. As indicated, angel investors tend to fund more projects with lesser amounts of money than venture capitalists. In addition, angel investors can be more patient and may take on a more active advisory role rather than a direct management role. Some angel investors, like venture capitalists, come in at the second stage of financing needs, after the company has been established and has shown some potential. Palmer "Pam" Reynolds, founder of Phoenix Textile Corp. in St. Louis, owes her success to an angel investor. Out of work with 13 years of experience in the textile business, Pam decided to start her own company. If not for an angel investor who put up $250,000, Pam would not be running a $43 million textile company today.

Funding a business is a task fraught with challenges and difficult decisions. When a great deal of money is on the line, the stakes—personal, professional, and financial—are quite high. Thorough research and careful planning are essential to navigating these tricky issues. By understanding the available options and being prepared to deal with financial predicaments, business owners give themselves the best chance at success.

▼ **You have just read Objective 6**

Want to quiz yourself? Check out the Study Plan section @ **www.mybizlab.com.**

1. What are the traits of an effective entrepreneur, and how do these characteristics often lead to business success? (pp. 133-137)

- An **entrepreneur** (p. 133) is someone who assumes the risk of creating, organizing, and operating a business.

- Entrepreneurs are innovative, risk-taking individuals who are motivated to succeed and who are flexible and self-directed. They work well with people, possess good leadership skills, and are "system thinkers."

2. What is the role and structure of the small business within the U.S. economy? (pp. 138-142)

- A **small business** (p. 138) is a business that is independently owned and operated, is not dominant in its field, and has fewer than 500 employees and less than $6.5 million in annual revenue.

- Small businesses are important to the economy for several reasons. They account for more than half of America's economic output; help foster innovation; supply larger companies with products and services that larger companies do not or cannot supply themselves; supply products and services to consumers that large companies cannot or will not provide; and employ approximately 50 percent of the private workforce.

3. What are the advantages and disadvantages of franchising within the context of entrepreneurship? (pp. 143-148)

- A **franchise** (p. 143) is a method of doing business whereby the business sells a company's products or services under the company's name to independent third-party operators.

- Advantages of franchising include that the business is a proven system of operation, that franchises benefit from economies of scale, and that the franchiser often offers training and marketing support as well as market research.

- Disadvantages of franchising include that there is a lack of control over the look of the store and the product or service being offered, that start-up costs and monthly fees must be paid to the franchiser, that operating a franchise often includes a heavy work load, and that franchises will be affected by negative news involving the franchiser or another franchisee of the same company.

4. Why is a business plan crucial to small-business success, and what factors lead to small business failure? (pp. 149-152)

- A **business plan** (p. 151) outlines the goals and strategies of a company, including company information, marketing plans, financial forecasts, a risk analysis, and an operational plan. Neglecting to consider any of these options can doom a business from the start.

- The reasons new businesses fail include accumulating too much debt, inadequate management, poor planning, and unanticipated personal sacrifices.

5. How do resources, including the Small Business Administration, mentoring sources, business incubators, and advisory boards provide assistance and guidance to small-business owners? (pp. 152-153)

- The **Small Business Administration** (p. 152) offers assistance in the legalities associated with starting and operating a business as well as education and training, financial assistance, disaster assistance, and counseling.

- **SCORE** (p. 152) volunteers provide free assistance by reviewing business plans, helping with tax planning, and offering new ideas and fresh insights. Other mentoring sources include industry-related conferences and other organizations, such as the Entrepreneurs Organization (EO).

- **Business incubators** (p. 152) support start-up businesses by offering resources such as administrative services, technical support, business networking, and sources of financing that a group of start-up companies share.

- **Advisory boards** (p. 153) offer guidance to new business owners but they generally do not have authority to make decisions.

6. What are the potential benefits and drawbacks of each major source of small-business financing? (pp. 154-155)

- The benefit of using cash borrowed from friends and family members is that unlike banks or other lending institutions, these contacts often do not require a high rate of return or demand to see the business turn a quick profit. However, the potential drawback is that these types of personal loans can sometimes be handled unprofessionally.

- The benefit of credit cards is that they are a convenient means of acquiring short-term cash. However, the risk associated with using credit cards for initial business financing is the high rate of interest charged on unpaid balances.

- The advantage of obtaining funding from **venture capitalists** (p. 155) is that these individuals contribute money to your business in return for some form of equity instead of a contractual agreement to pay back the money. However, venture capitalists sometimes require that they play an active role in the management of the company, so this funding option may not be attractive to business owners who aren't open to the idea of relinquishing control.

For an audio file of the Objectives and Chapter Summary, see the Student Resources section @ www.my*biz*lab.com.

Key Terms

advisory board   (p. 153)

angel investors   (p. 155)

business incubator   (p. 152)

business plan   (p. 151)

due diligence   (p. 147)

entrepreneur   (p. 133)

entrepreneurial team   (p. 137)

franchise   (p. 143)

franchisee   (p. 143)

franchiser   (p. 143)

goodwill   (p. 147)

growth entrepreneur   (p. 136)

intrapreneurs   (p. 136)

lifestyle entrepreneurs   (p. 136)

micropreneurs   (p. 136)

opportunity niche   (p. 133)

Service Corp of Retired Executives (SCORE)
   (p. 152)

small business   (p. 138)

Small Business Administration (SBA)   (p. 138)

Small Business Investment Company (SBIC)
   program   (p. 155)

venture capitalists   (p. 155)

Self-Test

Multiple Choice Correct answers can be found on page 503.

1. Which is *not* a key trait of an entrepreneur?

   a. Flexible

   b. Risk taker

   c. Procrastinator

   d. Creative thinker

2. Sally started her new business venture five years ago. It has grown, but only slightly, which is exactly what Sally had in mind. Which type of entrepreneur best describes Sally?

   a. Intrapreneur

   b. Micropreneur

   c. Slow growth entrepreneur

   d. None of the above

3. An entrepreneur is thinking of opening a business and is identifying the goals of the business as well as the plans for reaching those goals. This new business owner is writing a

   a. business plan.

   b. loan application.

   c. mission statement.

   d. franchise agreement.

4. Small businesses are important to the economy for which of the following reasons?

   a. They introduce new products and supply services to larger companies.

   b. They offer solutions specific to the needs of women, minorities, and immigrants.

   c. They provide specialized products or services and employ many people not suited for larger businesses.

   d. All of the above

5. Roger Conrad used to own a large auto parts retailer for many years and is now volunteering his services to advising new business start-ups. Roger is most likely a member of which organization?

   a. A business incubator

   b. Volunteers of America

   c. Small Business Development Corp

   d. Service Corps of Retired Executives

6. Which of the following is *not* a reason to start a new business?

   a. To be more of a decision maker

   b. To avoid having to report to someone else

   c. To offer a product or service that isn't offered yet

   d. To work fewer hours than you do at a traditional 9–5 job

7. Sharon just opened a Papa John's pizza franchise. Which is *not* a benefit Sharon receives as a franchisee?

   a. Supplies to make Papa John's pizza

   b. Signage and posters to help with advertising

   c. Retirement benefits from Papa John's

   d. Training and ongoing advice and assistance from Papa John's

8. Rebecca wants to start a pet grooming business in her home. Which is the most likely source of financing that Rebecca will use *first*?

   a. Venture capital

   b. Personal savings

   c. Funds from an angel investor

   d. Loan from a bank or savings institution

9. Which of the following factors commonly leads to small-business failure?

   a. Too much planning

   b. A small advertising budget

   c. Unanticipated personal sacrifices

   d. All of the above

10. Sarah Jones has developed an innovative software application. She is looking for space from which she can operate her business while sharing common resources with similar businesses. Sarah is looking to become a part of a(n)

    a. mentoring group.

    b. advisory board.

    c. business incubator.

    d. Small Business Association.

Self-Test

True/False   Correct answers can be found on page 503.

1. Being part of a franchise allows you to keep costs low through the benefits of group purchasing power.
   ☐ **True** or ☐ **False**

2. An angel investor is someone who provides funding for those in third-world countries who want to begin their own business but have no capital with which to do so.
   ☐ **True** or ☐ **False**

3. Hampton Computer Services has grown significantly over the years. It now has 450 employees and averages nearly $5 million in receipts. According to the Small Business Administration, Hampton Computer Services is still considered a small business.
   ☐ **True** or ☐ **False**

4. A lifestyle entrepreneur is best described as one who starts a business in an industry that promotes lifestyles that are more positive.
   ☐ **True** or ☐ **False**

5. The *biggest* risk of starting a new business and one of the primary reasons for failure is not generating enough revenue to cover business debt and expenses.
   ☐ **True** or ☐ **False**

Critical Thinking Questions

1. Bill Gates, Donald Trump, and Oprah Winfrey are some well-known successful entrepreneurs. What common traits do these individuals possess that have led to their success?

2. What are the reasons new businesses fail? What helps to make a new business venture successful?

3. Discuss the benefits of forming an entrepreneurial team when beginning a small business. Are there drawbacks to a team approach?

4. How has the Internet affected small businesses?

5. Discuss the different risks facing someone starting a business on his own and someone who is buying a franchise. What risks will both new business owners face?

Team Time

Starting a Business: Brainstorming

Assemble into groups of four or five.

1. Before meeting as a group, think about what you are passionate about, and whether there is a potential market involving your interests. Develop one or two ideas for potential businesses based on your passions. Do not consider any idea impossible at this stage.

   a. Consider if there is something missing in the current market. For example, are you passionate about locally grown organic vegetables but are frustrated that there isn't a place nearby to purchase these items? If so, you've developed an idea for a local farmers market.

   b. Consider combining two ideas together. When school has a half-day or full-day off, consider having high school students form a day-time child care service for elementary students.

   c. Consider business ideas that have potential but aren't doing very well now. Are there ways to make them better?

2. Gather your group and go over each other's ideas. Refine the list to two or three ideas.

3. Have each group member refine an idea even further, identifying the target market and outlining the business goals and objectives.

4. Meet as a team one more time to pick one business idea.

5. If time permits, the group can develop this idea further by using the Business Plan project template. See the Business Plan Mini Chapter for more information.

Ethics and Corporate Social Responsibility

Social Responsibility: Forming a Plan of Action

Milton Hershey, founder of Hershey Chocolate Company, dedicated himself to caring about his customers, his employees, and his community at large. Hershey felt that giving back to the community was not only his moral obligation, but also a crucial part of his success.

Step 1. Imagine that you operate a business in your community (choose from a restaurant, a landscaping service, or a beauty salon).

Step 2. As a class or in smaller groups, discuss the ways in which your business can contribute to customers, employees, and the community in socially responsible ways. Write down a list of ideas that your group came up with.

Step 3. Create a social responsibility plan for your company. In the document, describe your business and the ways in which your business can contribute to specific organizations in your community. Be as specific with your plan as possible.

Web Exercises

1. **A Closer Look at Franchising**
   Using the Internet, research a franchise that you think would be a viable investment opportunity for you. Put together a brief report that outlines the following information about your chosen franchise: fees (initial and ongoing), location/site assistance, training and ongoing support, marketing assistance, competition (both from other businesses and additional franchises within the organization), and the pros and cons of starting a business with this franchise.

2. **Micro-Financing: A Little $ Can Go a Long Way**
   Visit www.kiva.org and click on the "Lend" tab to view the list of entrepreneurs. Use the drop-down menus in the "Find Loans" search bar to locate an entrepreneur or entrepreneurial team to whom you would consider lending. In a brief report, discuss the entrepreneur or group you chose, including information on the loan amount requested, the percentage of funds raised, the entrepreneur's country of origin, and a summary of the entrepreneur's business venture. In your report, explain your reasons for choosing to loan to this particular entrepreneur.

3. **Do You Have What It Takes to Be an Entrepreneur?**
   In this chapter, you learned that there are several personality traits common to successful entrepreneurs. Do you possess any of these traits? Visit www.forbes.com and read

"Are You a Born Entrepreneur?" (www.forbes.com/2005/11/15/entrepreneur-personality-quiz_cx_bn_ 1116quiz.html). After reading the article, complete the entrepreneurial personality quiz. What aspects of your personality make you a good candidate to be an entrepreneur? What is holding you back?

4. **The Cost of Borrowing**
   How expensive is it to borrow funds for a new business? Using the Internet, research some of the new business loans and lines of credit offerings from local banks in your area. What kind of interest rates are banks charging? What are the terms of the loan or line of credit?

5. **Small Business Owners: Where to Go for Help**
   If you were a new small business owner, where would you go for help? Many colleges have a Small Business Development Center (SBDC). These centers, which are affiliated with the Small Business Administration, provide information and guidance to current and prospective small business owners. Use the SBDC Locator (www.sba.gov/aboutsba/sbaprograms/sbdc/sbdclocator/SBDC_LOCATOR.html) to identify the nearest SBDC in your area.

Web Case

To access the Chapter 5 Web case and exercise, see the End of Chapter Assignments section @ www.my*biz*lab.com.

Video Case

To access the Chapter 5 Video case and exercise, see the End of Chapter Assignments section @ www.my*biz*lab.com.

Forms of Business Ownership

p. **171**

Corporations
▼ **Objectives 3 & 4**
When some people hear the word "corporate," they think of corruption, greed, and big businesses like Enron. The energy giant had a very public fall from grace that left many jaded toward corporations. People use the word "corporation" frequently, but what *is* a corporation? What are the advantages of a corporation versus a sole proprietorship or a partnership?

p. **163**

Sole Proprietorships
▼ **Objective 1**
When an entrepreneur starts a business, choosing the proper business structure is vital to the company's success. When Jennifer Perez decided to start her own cleaning business, she became a sole proprietor. Her business began growing so fast she couldn't figure out if that was right for her. Would you know what business structure would be best for your company?

p. **180**

Alternative Business Arrangements
▼ **Objective 5**
Jeremy Perugia knew he wanted to make a difference in the world. He started by building parks and playgrounds in his community. He knew he wanted to expand to help more children, but he needed a corporate structure that would allow him to take his profits and put them back into communities nationwide. What type of alternative business structure would work best for him?

p. **166**

Partnerships
▼ **Objective 2**
Trying to do a job alone can sometimes be overwhelming. Because of this, businesses may partner together to share information and resources for the benefit of everyone involved. Even huge companies like AOL have partners. Recently AOL extended its partnerships with the financial Web site TheStreet.com and the sports-based ESPN.com. Why would a giant company like AOL partner with smaller Web sites like these?

"Are you thinking what I'm thinking?"

p. **182**

Business Combinations and Corporate Restructuring
▼ **Objective 6**
Companies constantly search for opportunities to expand by adding to their product lines, spreading into different geographic areas, or gaining a competitive advantage. Since research and development can take years for results, mergers and acquisitions are two ways companies can expand quickly. What is the difference between a merger and an acquisition? When do they occur?

Sole Proprietorships pp. 163-165

➤ Sole proprietorship is the most common form of business ownership because it's easy to set up. No legal paperwork needs to be filed to begin a sole proprietorship, and all the financial information can be reported on the owner's personal tax returns. Generally, if you start a business on your own, you're a sole proprietor.

Choosing the right legal structure for Jennifer's business may have initially seemed simple, but her business quickly outgrew its form. Should she have chosen a different form of ownership in the beginning? Could she have anticipated her immediate success? While Jennifer's rapid growth and success is not the norm for every start-up business, not having the right form of ownership can have significant consequences. So how do you know which form is best for your company? Choosing a form of ownership depends on many factors, including the type of business, the number of owners involved, current and future exposure to risks and liabilities, and the tax situations of the business and its owners.

Jennifer Perez was running a small cleaning business from her home. She had no employees, and the business's income and expenses seemed simple enough to report on her personal income taxes. However, the business grew so fast that Jennifer was concerned something could go wrong unexpectedly. She knew that as a sole proprietor she would be held responsible for any and all damages her company committed. Within another year, Jennifer's small business was one of the fastest growing businesses in her city. She soon realized that being the owner of her own company was more difficult than she had anticipated. ➤

The U.S. economy—as well as the global economy—is based on a variety of enterprises that range from *sole proprietorships*, businesses owned by one person; to *partnerships* where two or more people legally share ownership of a business; to *corporations*, businesses that are formed as separate legal entities. ▼ **Figure 6.1** shows these common forms of business ownership. In this chapter, we'll explore each of these forms of business ownership in greater detail.

Why is sole proprietorship the most common form of business ownership? A **sole proprietorship** is a business owned, and usually operated, by a single individual. Because no legal paperwork is necessary to establish a business as a sole proprietorship, many small-business owners are sole proprietors without even knowing it. Although a sole proprietorship has only one owner, it can have any number of employees. For example, you can be the owner of a plumbing business with several other plumbers working for you and still operate as a sole proprietorship. Other characteristics of a sole proprietorship are listed in ▼ **Table 6.1**.

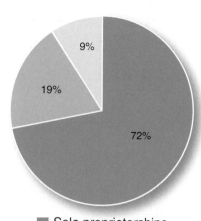

- Sole proprietorships
- Corporations
- Partnerships

▼ **Figure 6.1**
Businesses by Type of Ownership
Sole proprietorships are overwhelmingly the most common form of business ownership. Why might business owners be more inclined to set up this type of business?

Starting a Sole Proprietorship

How do I start a sole proprietorship? The minute you begin doing business by yourself—that is, collecting income as a result of performing a service or creating a product—you are operating as a sole proprietor. There are no special forms to fill out, nor any special filing requirements with the state or federal government. At a minimum, you might need to obtain local licensing or permits, or you might have to ensure that you're operating in an area zoned for such business activity.

Advantages and Disadvantages

Are there advantages of being a sole proprietor? There are several advantages to forming your business as a sole proprietorship, the first of which is ease of formation. With only one person making all the decisions and no need to consult other owners or interested parties, sole proprietors have greater control and more flexibility to act quickly. Another advantage is that there are no specific corporate records to keep or reports to file, including tax reporting. Since there is no legal distinction between the owner and the business, no separate tax return is required. As a result, the income and expenses of a sole proprietorship flow through the owner's personal tax return.

For example, imagine you run a landscaping business during the summer in addition to your regular job. If the lawn mower breaks down and needs to be replaced, that expense could be more than all the earnings you collected, generating a loss for your lawn mowing business. You can subtract that loss from the income earned from your regular job, reducing your income tax obligation. ▼ **Table 6.2** and ▼ **Figure 6.2** show the difference a business loss can have on your tax payment. A business loss of $150 reduces overall federal tax due by $23. In the beginning years of a business, this can be advantageous since business losses can offset other sources of income, thus reducing your overall tax burden.

Why wouldn't I want to begin my business as a sole proprietorship? If the type of business you're running has the potential for someone to sue you because of errors on your part, you may not want to operate as a sole proprietorship. A sole proprietor is personally responsible for all the debts and liabilities of the business. A **liability** is the obligation to pay a debt such as an account payable or a loan. A sole proprietor may also incur a liability if he or she becomes responsible for paying for any damages or personal injuries the owner's employees cause. While there may be an unlimited number of employees in a sole proprietorship, there is also unlimited

▼ **Table 6.1**

Characteristics of a Sole Proprietorship	
Characteristics	**Sole Proprietorship**
Preliminary paperwork	No special forms; no state or federal filing requirements
Period of existence	Proprietorship terminated when sole proprietor dies or ends business
Liability	Sole proprietor has unlimited liability
Operational requirements	Minimal legal requirements
Management	Sole proprietor has full control of management and operations
Taxation	Not a separate taxable entity; taxes paid through sole proprietor's personal returns
Reporting of income/loss	Income/loss reported on owner's personal income taxes
Raising capital	Outside sources of income difficult to raise; funding usually comes from owner contributions

liability for their actions. **Unlimited liability** means that if business assets aren't enough to pay business debts, then personal assets, such as the sole proprietor's house, personal investments, or retirement plans, can be used to pay the balance. In other words, the proprietor can lose an unlimited amount of money.

Imagine that you're running a catering business, and while you're preparing food in someone's house, the oven catches fire because you forgot to take the egg rolls off the paper tray. You are personally responsible, or liable, for paying for any damages if your business assets are not sufficient to cover the damages. If the damages are severe enough—perhaps your client's entire house burns down—you could lose all your assets, including your own home and savings.

Another drawback of a sole proprietorship is the potential difficulty in borrowing money to help your business grow. Banks will be lending to you personally, not to your business, so they will be more reluctant to lend large amounts, and the loan will be limited to the amount of your personal assets. Other business structures, which will be discussed later in the chapter, are more helpful should you need to raise large amounts of additional money.

Remember Jennifer Perez and her fast-growing cleaning business? Soon after starting her business, Jennifer realized that a sole proprietorship wasn't the best form of ownership for her because she didn't want to risk losing her personal assets in the event of an employee error. Jennifer, like many other small-business owners, learned that making decisions about choosing the correct corporate structure is complex. After getting advice from other business owners, Jennifer decided that her business needed to undergo some corporate restructuring so that the company's business form would be more conducive to her needs. What other forms of business ownership did Jennifer have to choose from?

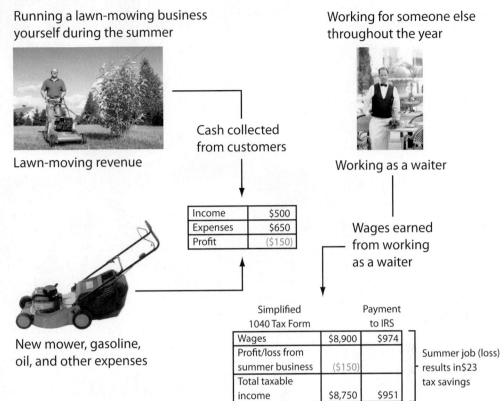

Running a lawn-mowing business yourself during the summer

Lawn-moving revenue

Cash collected from customers

New mower, gasoline, oil, and other expenses

Income	$500
Expenses	$650
Profit	($150)

Working for someone else throughout the year

Working as a waiter

Wages earned from working as a waiter

	Simplified 1040 Tax Form	Payment to IRS	
Wages	$8,900	$974	
Profit/loss from summer business	($150)		Summer job (loss) results in $23 tax savings
Total taxable income	$8,750	$951	

▼ **Figure 6.2**
The Effect of a Business Loss on Personal Income
Sole proprietors have the option of deducting businesses losses from their personal taxes, which reduces the personal taxes owed.

 **Table 6.2**

Personal Income with and without a Business Loss from a Sole Proprietorship		
	With business loss	**Without business loss**
Wage income	$8,900	$8,900
Business loss	-$150	
Net income	$8,750	$8,900
Tax due	$951	$974
		Difference: $23

▼ You have just read **Objective 1**

Think you got it? Check out the Study Plan section @
www.my*biz*lab.com.

Partnerships pp. 166-170

AOL Time Warner recently announced two new partnerships with TheStreet.com and ESPN. AOL is teaming up with financial Web site TheStreet.com and is increasing the amount of content taken from the site. Financial news from TheStreet will appear under AOL's Money and Finance section. ESPN is also partnering with AOL to include sports news, updates, and videos under AOL's Sports heading. These partnerships are beneficial for everyone; TheStreet and ESPN are paid for their reports, and AOL streams up-to-date news coverage from writers who are experts in their respective fields. What disadvantages can come from three established companies partnering together? ➤

➤ Running a business can be a hectic job, so sometimes a partner is needed to lend a hand. Even large companies like AOL find partnerships useful in keeping their business up-to-date and running at its best. In this section, we'll look at partnerships like AOL's in more detail.

Advantages and Disadvantages

When is it good to bring in another owner?

Sometimes, running a business by oneself can be a daunting task, and adding one or more owners can help share the responsibilities. A **partnership** is a type of business entity in which two or more owners (or partners) share the ownership and the profits and losses of the business. There are several reasons why joining with someone else in starting a business makes sense. More owners help contribute to both the starting and ongoing capital of the business. Multiple people are involved in partnerships, so there is more time available to increase sales, market the business, and generate income. Sharing the financial responsibility brings on more people who are interested in the company's overall profitability and are as highly motivated as you are to make the business succeed. Therefore, additional owners, unlike employees, are more likely to be willing to work long hours and go the extra mile.

Adding partners to help share the workload also allows for coverage for vacations or when a partner is out due to illness or personal issues. Moreover, if partners have complementary skills, they create a collaboration that can be quite advantageous. Partners can help discuss ideas and projects as well as make the big decisions. For example, if you're great at numbers but hate to make sales calls, bringing in a partner who loves to knock on doors would be beneficial for your business.

BizChat

How Do You Find the Right Business Partner?

Business partners are like spouses—finding each other is often through circumstance and happenstance. Because of the high financial stakes, many look to partner with those they trust most, turning to spouses, friends, or relatives. Hiring friends or relatives can have its benefits, but what do you do if your best friend doesn't do the job right?[1] You might instead want to turn to your casual acquaintance network—your gym buddy, a parent of your child's friend, a classmate—to find a business partner. If your network isn't turning up any promising leads, turn to others' networks. Similar to finding a job, write a description of the "perfect partner" and send it to as many people as you can. Make sure you interview the candidates and look for those who have similar goals but complementary skills. By all means, "date" the prospective partner before jumping into business marriage—there is too much at risk to proceed too quickly.

For more information and discussion questions about this topic, check out the BizChat feature on www.mybizlab.com.

Are there disadvantages to adding partners? For every advantage a partner can bring, adding the wrong partner can be equally problematic. Obviously, adding partners means sharing profits and control. A potential partner may have different work habits and styles from you, and if the partner's style isn't complementary, the differences can prove challenging. In addition, as the business begins to grow and change, your partner might want to take the business in a different direction than you do. Like entering into marriage, you want to consider carefully the person(s) with whom you will be sharing your business.

As a business form, how does a partnership compare to a sole proprietorship? Partnerships and sole proprietorships are very similar; in fact, the biggest difference between the two is the number of people contributing resources and sharing the profits and the liabilities. It's just as easy to form a partnership as a sole proprietorship. The government does not require any special forms or reports—although some local restrictions may apply for licenses and permits. For example, if you and your brother-in-law form a small partnership called "All in the Family Electricians," before you are able to do business you might have to apply for a license, but you do not need any special papers to create the partnership itself.

Also, like a sole proprietorship, partnerships do not file a separate tax return. All profits and losses of the partnership flow directly through each partner's own tax return. ▼ **Table 6.3** outlines other characteristics of a partnership.

Elements of a Partnership Agreement

What goes into a partnership agreement? Although no formal documentation is required to create a partnership, it's a good idea to draw up an agreement. A partnership can begin with a handshake, and many of them do, but it is best for all involved parties that a written document, called a **partnership agreement**, formalizes the relationship between business partners. Think of a partnership agreement as a business prenuptial agreement. It helps to settle conflicts when they arise and may discourage small misunderstandings from erupting into

▼ **Table 6.3**

Characteristics of a Partnership

Characteristics	General Partnership
Preliminary paperwork	No special forms required for state or federal filings; partnership agreement recommended
Period of existence	Partnership terminated upon death or withdrawal of a partner unless otherwise provided for in the partnership agreement
Liability	Partners have unlimited liability
Operational requirements	Minimal legal requirements
Management	Partnership agreement should specify management roles, though generally each partner has an equal voice
Taxation	Not a taxable entity; income flows through individual partner's tax returns, and each partner pays tax on his or her share of income; losses can be deducted against other sources of income
Reporting of income/loss	Income/loss reported on partners' personal income taxes
Raising capital	Capital primarily raised through partner contributions; additional raised as partners are added

larger disagreements. Many points can be included in a partnership agreement; however, the following items should always be included in the agreement:

1. **Capital Contributions.** The amount of **capital**, or investments in the form of money, equipment, supplies, computers, and any other tangible thing of value, that each partner contributes to begin the business should be noted in the partnership agreement. In addition, the agreement should also address how additional capital can be added to the business—who will contribute it, and whether there will be a limit to a partner's overall capital contribution.

2. **Responsibilities of Each Partner.** To avoid the possibility of one partner doing more or less work than others, or a conflict arising over one partner assuming a more controlling role than others, it's best to outline the responsibilities of each partner from the beginning. Unless otherwise specified, any partner can bind the partnership to any debt or contract without the consent of the other partners. Therefore, it's especially important to spell out the policy regarding who assumes responsibility for entering into key financial or contractual arrangements.

3. **Decision-Making Process.** It is important to consider how decisions will be made. Knowing whether decisions will be the result of mutual consent of all or several partners, or whether just one or two partners will make the key decisions is essential to help partners avoid disagreements. What constitutes a "key" decision should also be defined in the agreement. In a partnership of two, where the possibility of a deadlock is likely, some partnerships provide for a trusted associate to act as a third partner whose sole responsibility is to act as the tiebreaker.

4. **Shares of Profits or Losses.** Not only should the agreement specify how to divide profits and losses between the partners, but it should also specify how frequently this will be done. One partnership agreement might stipulate that the profits and losses will be proportional to each partner's initial contribution to the partnership, as reflected in ▼ **Figure 6.3**, whereas another partnership agreement might just split the profits evenly. It's also important to detail how adjustments to the distributions will be made—if any at all—as the partnership matures and changes.

5. **Departure of Partners.** Eventually, the composition of partners will change; original partners will leave and new partners will come aboard. The partnership

Shares of profits/losses

Capital contribution

Contributed $45,000

Contributed $30,000

50% Share

Contributed $15,000 of used office equipment

50% Share

Derrick Williams

Xiang Wu

80% of his time

20% of his time

80% of her time

20% of her time

Financial resources and record keeping

Selling services

Managing the office

Partner responsibilities

▼ **Figure 6.3**
Share of Profit and Loss in a Partnership
Partners' shares of profits and losses can be dependent on capital contribution and the assumed responsibilities of each partner.

agreement should have rules for a partner's exit, whether it's voluntary, involuntary, or due to death or divorce. Provisions to remove a partner's ownership interest are necessary so the business does not need to liquidate. The agreement should include how to determine the amount of ownership interest and to whom the departing partner is permitted to transfer his or her interest. It's important to consider whether a partner can transfer his or her ownership solely to the remaining partners or whether individuals outside the existing partnership can buy the departing partner's share.

6. **Addition of Partners.** The partnership agreement also helps spell out the requirements for new partners entering the partnership. How the profits will be allocated and whether there will be a "junior partner" period during which the new partner can prove him or herself before obtaining full partner status should also be included.

Types of Partnerships

What are the different types of partnerships? There are several types of partnerships. The distinction between the different types usually involves who accepts most or all of the business liability. The two most common partnership forms include *general partnerships* and *limited partnerships*.

General Partnership

A **general partnership** is the "default" arrangement for a partnership and is therefore the simplest of all partnerships to form. For instance, if two friends, Juan and Franklin, set up a lemonade stand on the side of the road, sell glasses of lemonade, and split the profits at the end of the day, they have created a general partnership. For Juan and Franklin, this is a logical arrangement, since they share the profits equally, and there is little worry about liability. In a general partnership, each partner has unlimited liability for the debts and obligations of the partnership, meaning every partner is liable for his or her own actions, as well as those actions of the other partners and the actions of any employees.

Limited Partnership

Sometimes, a business can bring on additional "limited" partners, mostly to provide capital and earn a share in the profits, but not to operate the business. To encourage investors to contribute capital to the business without risking more capital than they have contributed, a **limited partnership** is created. In a limited partnership, there are two distinctions of partners. The **general partners** are full owners of the business, are responsible for all the day-to-day business decisions, and remain liable for all the debts and obligations of the business. **Limited partners** are involved as investors and as such are personally liable only up to the amount of their investment in the business and must not actively participate in any decisions of the business. Limited partnerships can be very complex to form, so it may be worth exploring other business structures before deciding on this strategy.

What business structure is best when liability is a concern?

Although forming a general partnership for Juan and Franklin's lemonade business makes sense for them, it's not right for every business. In some situations, especially if liability is a concern, neither a sole proprietorship nor a partnership will protect the owner(s) from unlimited risk. For instance, if Sarah and Hannah decide to form Personal Training Partners, a personal training and fitness motivation company, they know that each partner is liable—not only for her own business debts and actions, but also for each other's business debts and actions. Therefore, they need a type of structure that would protect their homes and savings and other personal assets from being lost in case of a business disaster. If a client claims that Sarah mistreated him or her and the client sues the business, not only are Sarah's assets at risk, but so are Hannah's assets. Both partners want to be protected so only the business assets, like the building they bought for their gym, the exercise machines, and computers they use, are at risk and not any of their personal assets. In this case, a partnership is not the best business structure, because a partnership has unlimited liability and does not protect against losses of personal property. There are some options available for Personal Training Partners that are like partnerships in many ways, but that also help insulate an owner's personal liability from the business.

For AOL Time Warner, partnerships with TheStreet.com and ESPN have proven beneficial. AOL Senior Vice President Marty Moe says, "With TheStreet.com network continuing to deliver premium editorial content, plus our new Quotes & Portfolio pages, AOL is providing users a comprehensive package of information relating to their investments."[2] However, not all partnerships are as successful as AOL's partnerships. When this happens, what other options do small-business owners have?

▼ You have just read **Objective 2**

Want a review? Check out the Study Plan section @
www.my*biz*lab.com.

Corporations pp. 171-179

> U.S. writer Ambrose Bierce once defined a corporation as "an ingenious device for obtaining profit without individual responsibility." Unlike partnerships and sole proprietorships, *corporations* provide business owners with better protection of their personal assets. In the case of Enron, the owners of the company did not have to put up their personal assets to cover the failed business. Although not as common as sole proprietorships, corporations are a very popular form of business ownership. What is a corporation? Why might a business owner choose to form a corporation? What are the different types of corporations? In this section, you'll find the answers to these questions and more.

In 2001, Enron went from being the energy king just the year before to practically becoming a four-letter word in the corporate world. Enron hid losses in fictional partnerships, but eventually publicized a $638 million loss. The company subsequently filed for bankruptcy, and thousands of employees lost their retirement funds. Reviewing the scandal shows the complexities of large corporations. Thousands of people can invest in a corporation, whether it's through owning shares privately or by acquiring the shares by virtue of their jobs as directors, officers, or regular day-to-day employees. Because a corporation is considered its own entity, it's important that it has appropriate management. If not, anyone involved in the corporation can be ruined. >

What is a corporation? A **corporation** is a specific form of business organization that is legally formed under state laws. A corporation is considered a separate entity apart from its owners; therefore, a corporation has legal rights like an individual, so a corporation can own property, assume liability, pay taxes, enter into contracts, and can sue and be sued—just like any other individual. Other characteristics of a *common* or *C corporation* are listed in ▼ **Table 6.4**.

Advantages of Incorporation

When does it make sense to form a business as a corporation?

Some business owners incorporate just to be able to end the company's name with "company," "co.," "incorporated," or "inc." Having the "co." or "inc." at the end of the business name can give a start-up an air of legitimacy, which can be a perceived benefit to prospective clients and lenders, and potentially a greater threat to the competition. However, forming a corporation is a much more cumbersome process than forming a sole proprietorship or partnership. ▼ **Figure 6.4** shows the steps involved in forming a corporation.

▼ **Table 6.4**

Characteristics of a C Corporation

Characteristics	C Corporation
Preliminary paperwork	Paperwork required to file with both state and federal agencies
Period of existence	Corporations are separate entities; existence is not dependent on founders, owners, or partners; shares of stock are easily transferred
Liability	Shareholders are usually not personally liable for the debts of the corporation
Operational requirements	Must have a board of directors, corporate officers, annual meetings, and annual reporting
Management	Shareholders elect the board of directors that provides the global management of the corporation
Taxation	Taxed at the entity level; if dividends are distributed to shareholders, dividends are also taxed at the individual level (double taxation)
Reporting of income/loss	Corporations are separate entities; no income or loss reported on shareholder's tax statements
Raising capital	Capital raised through sale of shares of stock

More importantly, forming under a corporate structure provides many advantages not found with other business structures such as separated liability, extended life, and capitalization.

Separated Liability

Because a corporation is a separate legal entity and is responsible for its own debts and obligations, one of the main reasons owners incorporate their business is to protect the owners' personal assets. When a corporation runs into problems, only the corporate assets can be used to remedy the situation; the owners are not personally liable for business debts.

Extended Life and Ownership Transfer

Sole proprietorships and partnerships, by their nature, are dependent on their founding owners. When an owner dies or otherwise leaves, the partnership or sole proprietorship is usually terminated. On the other hand, shareholders own a corporation, so its existence doesn't depend on its founding members. Shares of ownership are easily exchanged, so the corporation will continue to exist should the owner die or wish to sell his or her interest in the business. A corporation is capable of continuing forever, in theory.

▼ **Figure 6.4**
Steps to Forming a Corporation

Forming a corporation is more complex than forming a sole proprietorship or a partnership. However, corporations provide owners with more protection than the other business structures.

Raising Capital

Incorporating offers a business greater flexibility when raising capital. Banks and venture capitalists are more likely to lend money to a business that is incorporated. In times when greater sources of funds are needed than venture capital or bank loans can raise, a corporation can extend its ownership by "going public"—selling shares of ownership in the corporation to the general public on the stock exchange. A stock certificate is tangible evidence of investment, and for some investors that is very important.

Choose a Name → Appoint Directors → File Articles of Incorporation → Draft Bylaws → Hold a Meeting of the Board → Issue Stock → Obtain Licenses and Permits

Corporate Benefits

Structuring a small business as a corporation allows the corporation to provide benefits to its employees. In a corporation, you can be the owner and the employee, and as the employee you can receive benefits. For example, if you started a computer repair and consulting business and structured it as a corporation, the corporation could hire you as the **chief executive officer** (**CEO**), or the top position of a company, pay you a salary, and provide benefits such as medical insurance premiums and life insurance. The corporation considers these legally deductible expenses—thus reducing the income of the company and consequently lowering the company's tax obligation—putting more money in your pocket as the owner.

Tax Benefits

A corporation is taxed at 15 percent for its first $50,000 in annual profits, whereas the same amount of profits from a sole proprietorship or partnership would be taxed at a rate of 28 percent through individual taxes. Although most large businesses will have more than $50,000 in annual profits, this advantage may well apply to those smaller businesses. Small-business owners might run the numbers to see which is a better fit.

Structure of a Corporation

What are the differences between a corporation and partnerships or sole proprietorships? The biggest difference between a corporation and other forms of ownership is liability. Sole proprietorships and partnerships do not provide limited personal liability for business debts, putting an owner's personal assets at risk. Because a corporation is a formal, separate, legal entity, the corporation is liable for its own debts, which shields the owner's assets. Corporations, as separate legal entities, must also file separate tax returns rather than having the profits and losses flow through to the owners' returns as is done with partnerships and sole proprietorships. Corporations are far more complicated than sole proprietorships and partnerships, with potential for many more layers of bureaucracy and reporting that are not necessary in the less formal business structures. For example, corporations are required to have shareholders, hold shareholder meetings, and maintain corporate records, which partnerships and sole proprietorships are not required to do.

How is a corporation structured?

A corporation's organizational structure is made up of three basic groups: shareholders, directors, and officers, as shown in ▼ **Figure 6.5**.

Shareholders

Shareholders are the owners of the company. Large **publicly owned corporations** are corporations whose stock is owned by more than 25 stockholders and is regulated by the Securities and Exchange Commission. While serving as the owners of the corporation, shareholders have no involvement in the direct management of the corporation. Instead, they influence corporate decisions by electing directors, overseeing bylaws and the *articles of organization* (the title of the document filed to create a corporation), and voting on major

▼ **Figure 6.5 Organizational Structure of a C Corporation**

In a C corporation, the shareholders have the power to elect a board of directors. The board, in turn, has the ability to hire (or fire) the company's corporate officers.

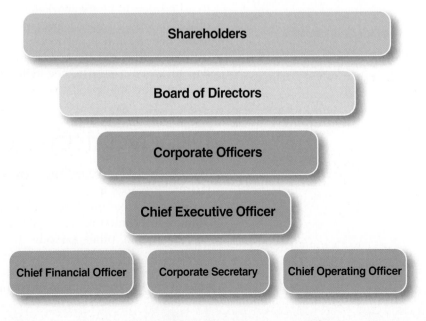

▼ top

10 U.S. Public Corporations by Profit in 2008

Company	Profit (in billions of dollars)
1. ExxonMobil	40.61
2. General Electric	22.21
3. Chevron	18.69
4. Microsoft	16.96
5. JP Morgan Chase	15.37
6. Bank of America	14.98
7. Berkshire Hathaway	13.21
8. Wal-Mart	12.73
9. AT&T	11.95
10. ConocoPhillips	11.89

corporate issues. In **privately held** or **closed corporations**—corporations owned by only a few people—there are fewer shareholders, and they are generally involved in the management and daily operations of the business, in which case they have more decision-making responsibilities than do shareholders of larger corporations. The shares of privately held corporations are not traded on public stock exchanges.

Directors

Directors—or the **board of directors**—usually set policy for the corporation and make the major business and financing decisions. Directors authorize the issuance of stock, approve loans to or from the corporation, and decide on major real estate transactions. In addition, the board of directors elects corporate officers and by doing so can influence the very nature of a business.

The board is also responsible for ensuring the corporate managers are doing their job, though this may be difficult, as has been demonstrated by such corporate scandals including the Enron, WorldCom, and Tyco debacles. Dennis Kozlowski, CEO of Tyco International Ltd., for example, scammed the company for years as he lavished hundreds of millions of dollars in illegal loans and expensive gifts on himself and his corporate officers.[3] Kozlowski's fraud bypassed the watchful eyes of Tyco's Board, the company's auditors, and even the Securities Exchange Commission. To prevent such situations from reoccurring, the *Sarbanes-Oxley Act of 2002*, a United States federal law, was enacted to provide a new set of standards of accountability for the board of directors. If the members of a board of directors ignore their responsibilities of managing the internal controls of a company, they incur the risk of long prison sentences and huge fines.

Officers

Officers are elected by the board of directors and are responsible for the daily operation and management of the company. The typical lineup of officers includes the president (or chief executive officer, CEO), secretary, and chief financial officer (CFO). Often there is a chief legal officer or general council, and depending on the needs of the company, there might also be a chief operating officer (COO) or a chief information systems officer (CIO). In actuality, any "officer" position can be formed if it makes sense for the company.

In large companies, the responsibilities of each officer are demanding enough that separate positions are necessary. In smaller companies, only one or two persons might perform the role of several different officers. After having worked as a yoga instructor for local gyms, Maureen Priest opened Breathe, her own yoga studio in a Philadelphia suburb. "I wanted to be an instructor, but found in my first year that I needed to be the marketing manager, finance director, and chief operating officer, as well. I had to learn quickly how to get my name and my new studio to many people; and I had to learn how to price my services and figure out my expenses so I could come close to breaking even, if not making a profit. Lastly, I had to locate a studio, negotiate a rental contract, and renovate the space to accommodate my specific business needs. I wore many hats that first year."[4]

Disadvantages of Incorporation

Are there disadvantages of structuring a business as a corporation? Because a corporation is a separate legal entity, there are many requirements that must be fulfilled in order to maintain the corporate status. For example, all companies must file an annual report and maintain written minutes of annual and other periodic board of director and shareholder meetings. Resolutions or consents of major decisions must be recorded, including decisions involving issuance of stock, purchase of real property, approval of leases, loans or lines of credits, the adoption or changes to stock options, and retirement plans. A corporation must also record financial transactions in a double-entry bookkeeping system and file taxes on a regular (quarterly or annually) basis.

Another disadvantage of the corporate structure is the idea of double taxation. **Double taxation** is the situation that occurs when taxes are paid on the same asset twice. The classic business example of double taxation is the distribution of dividends. Double taxation occurs because the corporation is first taxed on its net income, or profit, then distributes that net income to its shareholders in the form of *dividends*. The individual shareholder must then pay taxes on the dividends (which have already been taxed at the corporate level). Therefore, the same pool of money—corporate profits—has been taxed twice: once in the form of corporate profits and again as dividends received by the shareholders. Although this is a commonly mentioned disadvantage of corporations, it does not affect all corporations, since only 39 percent of publicly traded companies pay dividends.[5]

Can a business have the protection of a corporation but not pay corporate taxes? When choosing a legal structure for their business, most entrepreneurs will site two goals: protecting personal liability and flowing taxes through their individual tax returns. As has already been discussed, operating as a sole proprietorship or a partnership allows business profits and losses to flow through the owner's individual tax return, but the owner of a sole proprietorship or members in a partnership assumes the risk of personal liability exposure. A corporate structure offers the reverse; it protects the owner's personal assets from being touched if the corporation is in difficulty, as the corporation is taxed as a separate entity without flow-through to the owner's returns. Fortunately, there are two forms of business ownership in which both goals can be met: the *S corporation* and the *limited-liability partnership*.

S Corporation

What is an S corporation? An **S corporation** is a regular corporation (a C corporation) that has elected to be taxed under a special section of the Internal Revenue Service code called Subchapter S. S corporations are like C corporations in that there are shareholders and in that they must comply with all other regulations involving traditional C corporations.

What are the advantages of S corporations? Unlike C corporations, S corporations do not pay corporate income taxes. Instead, as in a partnership or sole proprietorship, the shareholders in an S corporation pay income taxes based on their proportionate share of the business profits and pay the taxes through their own individual tax returns. Passing taxes through personal tax returns is one of the primary advantages of forming a business as an S corporation. However, even though S corporations do not *pay* taxes like C corporations, they still must *file* a tax return every year. In addition, S corporations must comply with the meeting and reporting requirements established for C corporations. Other characteristics of an S corporation are shown in ▼ **Table 6.5**.

Does an S corporation have limited personal liability like a C corporation does? The beauty of an S corporation is that it offers the best of both worlds: profits and losses pass through to the shareholders, *and* the corporate structure provides some limitations on personal liability. However, the S corporation does not assume liability for an owner's personal wrongdoings. This is true for any corporate structure—whether it's a C corporation, an S corporation, or a limited-liability company (discussed later). So, if an owner directly injures someone or intentionally does something fraudulent, illegal, or reckless that causes harm to the company or someone else, he or she will be held personally responsible and is not protected under the corporate umbrella.

▼ **Table 6.5**

Characteristics	S Corporation
Preliminary paperwork	Forms required to file at state and federal levels
Period of existence	Corporations are separate entities; existence is not dependent on founders, owners, or partners; must observe IRS regulations on who can own shares of stock
Liability	Shareholders are typically not personally liable for the debts of the corporation
Operational requirements	Must have a board of directors, corporate officers, annual meetings, and annual reporting
Management	Shareholders elect board of directors, who provide the global management of the corporation
Taxation	No tax at the entity level
Reporting of income/loss	Income/loss is reported on the shareholders' taxes
Raising capital	Capital raised through sale of shares of stock

For example, suppose William is the owner of a boating business that offers day cruises in the San Francisco Bay. Unfortunately, one foggy day, William collided with another boat, causing his boat to capsize. Before leaving the dock that morning, William failed to provide sufficient life jackets for all his passengers and overloaded the boat. As a result, William would be held personally liable for his negligent actions, even though he had structured his company as an S corporation. William would not only be in danger of losing the business, but may also be forced into personal bankruptcy.

Can any business elect to be an S corporation? There are certain qualification requirements a business must meet to elect S corporation status. According to the U.S. Internal Revenue Code,[6] to be an S corporation, (1) the company must not have more than 100 shareholders; (2) shareholders must be U.S. citizens or residents; (3) the company must only issue one class of stock; and (4) the company must distribute proportionately all profits and losses to each shareholder based on each one's interest in the business. S corporations are the most appropriate business structure for small-business owners who want the legal protection of a corporation, but also want to be taxed as if they are the sole proprietor or partner of a business.

Limited-Liability Company

What is a limited-liability company? A **limited-liability company (LLC)** is a distinct type of business that, like an S corporation, combines the corporate advantages of limited liability with the tax advantages inherent in partnerships. LLCs are the relatively new kid on the block, and they are receiving quite a bit of interest in the business community because of their many benefits that suit a start-up company. Similar to creating an S or C corporation, an LLC requires articles of organization, so it is a separate legal entity. But an LLC is free of many of the annual meetings and reporting requirements imposed on a C or S corporation, so it's simpler to maintain. Because of the fewer corporate formalities, limited liability provisions, and the treatment of taxes, it is a popular choice of business structure for many new businesses.

Imagine, for example, that Joe owns a tree-cutting business. One day while Joe is cutting down a tree, the tree falls unexpectedly on his client's car. What liability protection would Joe receive if he structured his business as an LLC? An S corporation? A sole proprietorship? ▼ **Figure 6.6** shows how Joe would fare if he structured his business under each of these forms of business ownership.

It's good to note that some states may have restrictions on the types of businesses that can form as an LLC. Other characteristics of a limited-liability company are outlined in ▼ **Table 6.6**.

What's the difference between an LLC and an S corporation?
There are several distinctions between LLCs and S corporations:

- **Ownership:** S corporations are restricted to the number of owners the company can have, but LLCs can have an unlimited number of owners (called members). In addition, LLC members are not limited to just U.S. residents and are not subjected to other ownership restrictions imposed on S corporations.

- **Subsidiaries:** LLCs may have subsidiaries, but S corporations may not.

▼ **Figure 6.6**
Business Ownership and Liability Protection
Which form of business ownership provides Joe with the least protection?

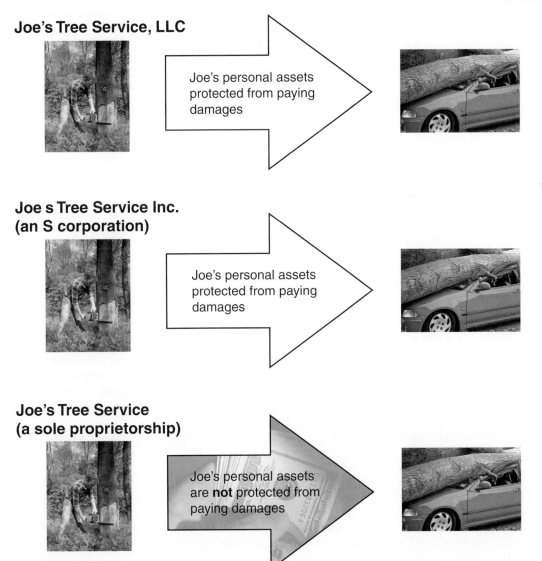

Joe's Tree Service, LLC

Joe's personal assets protected from paying damages

Joe s Tree Service Inc. (an S corporation)

Joe's personal assets protected from paying damages

Joe's Tree Service (a sole proprietorship)

Joe's personal assets are **not** protected from paying damages

▼ **Table 6.6**

Characteristics of a Limited-Liability Company (LLC)

Characteristics	Limited-Liability Company
Preliminary paperwork	Paperwork required to file with both state and federal agencies
Period of existence	Ongoing existence is determined by requirements imposed by the state of formation; transferability determined by operating agreement
Liability	Members are not typically liable for the debts of the LLC
Operational requirements	Fewer formal requirements than corporations
Management	Management details described in an operating agreement
Taxation	No tax at the entity level if properly structured
Reporting of income/loss	Income/loss is reported on members' taxes
Raising capital	Members may sell interests to raise capital; there may be operating agreement restrictions

- **Perpetual life:** When a member leaves an LLC, the LLC must dissolve. In addition, some states also require that a dissolution date be listed in the articles of organization, so an LLC has a limited life span.

- **Stock transfer:** Stock in an S corporation, like a C corporation, is freely transferable, while the ownership interest in an LLC is not and generally requires the approval of the other members.

- **Self-employment taxes:** LLC owners pay self-employment taxes on the entire share of profits, whereas S corporation shareholders pay only self-employment tax on monies received as compensation, but not all monies passed through as profits.

- **Profit and loss distributions:** LLCs may allocate profits in whatever manner best suits the owners, but profits of an S corporation are allocated in proportion to a shareholder's interest. So, if two members own a business, one contributes 75 percent of the capital but only does 20 percent of the work, and the other member contributes 25 percent of the capital but does 80 percent of the work, the two members decide that a fair allocation of profits is 50/50. This arrangement would be possible with an LLC, but with an S corporation, the profits would need to be distributed based on the 75/25 ownership interest.

- **Owner and employee benefits:** An S corporation may offer fringe benefits to its owners such as health insurance premiums and direct reimbursement of medical expenses, life insurance, and a company car. Since S corporations have stock, they can also offer their employees' stock options and other stock bonus incentives. LLCs are limited in the benefits their members can be offered, and since LLCs do not have stock, they cannot offer stock benefits to their employees.

What kinds of businesses are best suited as an LLC? There are many types of businesses in which an LLC structure is appropriate, but in particular, LLCs are often used by professional corporations formed by accountants, attorneys, doctors, and other similar professionals who want to separate themselves from partner liability, but still reap the other benefits of a partnership. As mentioned above, LLCs may be a good choice for start-ups, not only for the tax benefits, but also because it's easier to get financing since investors (owners) are not limited. Which form of ownership is best? See ▼ **Table 6.7** to see how the most common forms of ownership stack up to one another.

▼ **Table 6.7**

Comparing the Forms of Business Ownership				
	Proprietorship	**Partnership**	**Corporation (S or C)**	**LLC**
Best Suited For	• Single-owner business • Taxes or product liability are not a concern	• Business with partners • Taxes or product liability are not a concern	• Single- or multiple-owner business • Owners need company-funded fringe benefits and liability protection	• Single- or multiple-owner business • Owners need limited liability, but want to be taxed as a partnership
Type of Entity	• Inseparable from owner	• Inseparable from owner • Can have debt or property in its name	• Separate legal entity • Owners hired as employees • Owners called shareholders	• Separate legal entity • Owners hired as employees • Owners called members
Main Advantages	• Inexpensive to set up • Few administrative duties	• Inexpensive to set up • Few administrative duties	• Limited liability • Company paid fringes (C corp.) • Tax savings through income splitting (C corp.) • Capital easier to raise through sale of stock	• Limited liability • Pass-through entity • Unlimited number of owners • Capital easy to raise through sale of interests
Main Disadvantages	• Unlimited liability • No tax benefits • Business dissolves at death of owner • Profits increase owner's personal taxes	• Unlimited liability • Responsible for partner's acts • No tax benefits • Legally dissolves upon change or death of one owner • Profits increase owner's personal taxes	• Could be costly to form • More administrative duties • S corp. is limited to 100 shareholders	• Can be costly to form • More administrative duties • Profits increase owners' personal taxes
Taxes	• Flow-through entity • Owner is responsible for any taxes due	• Flow-through entity • Partners are responsible for any taxes due	• C corp. pays its own taxes • S corp. is flow-through	• Flow-through entity • Owners are responsible for any taxes due

Source: Forms of Business Ownership, Nevada Small Business Development Center, University of Nevada, Las Vegas, College of Business, 7/31/05.

A corporation is different from other business types because it is considered its own legal entity. It has its own tax return, and it can sue and be sued. Some businesses starting out become corporations to appear more stable and legitimate, which in turn helps them gain clients and lenders. Because a corporation is considered its own entity, it has its own debts and assets, which protects the owner. So, for example, the CEO of Enron did not lose $638 million of his own money; the corporation lost this sum. Corporations can keep business owners from experiencing major personal losses if the business is dissolved or fails.

▼ You have just read **Objectives 3 & 4**

Want to learn more? Check out the Study Plan section @
www.my*biz*lab.com.

Alternative Business Arrangements pp. 180-181

One day, Jeremy Perugia came up with an idea to provide inner-city children with more places to play. He decided to name his business PACS (Playing as Children Should), but he still had questions. Where would he get income? How could he structure his business to protect himself financially, gain credibility, and continue to serve the community?

➤ In some business ventures, the goal is not to generate a profit, but to make a difference in the lives of community members. When forms of business ownership, such as sole proprietorships, partnerships, and corporations don't fit, business owners must use alternative business arrangements. What are some alternative business arrangements? What are the benefits and drawbacks of using these forms of ownership? We'll answer these questions next.

Not-for-Profit Corporations

What is a not-for-profit corporation? Legally, a **not-for-profit corporation** (or *nonprofit organization*) is an incorporated business that does not seek a net profit and instead utilizes revenue available after normal operating expenses for the corporation's declared social or educational goals. Not-for-profit corporations must apply for tax-exempt status with the federal government and sometimes with the state in which they are incorporated. Incorporation is not necessary, but to receive limited liability protection, a nonprofit organization must file incorporation papers and become established as a separate legal entity.

Similar to a for-profit corporation, a not-for-profit corporation is required to hold board and director meetings and to keep complete books and records. The greatest difference from a for-profit corporation is that a nonprofit organization cannot be organized for any person's private gain. Nonprofit organizations do not issue shares of stock, and their members may not receive personal financial benefit from the organization's profits (other than salary as an employee). However, some nonprofit organizations do provide employee benefits such as health insurance. In addition, should the not-for-profit dissolve, the organization's assets must go to a similar nonprofit group.

Do not-for-profit corporations generate *any* **profits?** Not-for-profit corporations are not in the business to generate a profit, unlike for-profit organizations; however, they still need to generate even a modest profit to survive. Nonprofit organizations generate their revenues primarily through fund-raising and donations. To maintain their tax-exempt status, nonprofit organizations must demonstrate that a substantial portion of their income or revenue is spent on services to achieve their goals.

What are the benefits of being tax-exempt? As a corporation that has received 501(c)(3) status, the donations that are the organization's primary source of revenue are tax-deductible to the donor, which encourages funding. Other benefits of tax-exempt status are that the nonprofit is exempt from paying most federal and/or state corporate income taxes and may also be exempt from state sales and property taxes. Such organizations are able to apply for grants and other public or private distributions, as well as discounts on postal rates and other services.

Cooperatives

What are cooperatives? **Cooperatives** are businesses that are owned and governed by members who use its products or services, not by outside investors. Cooperative members can be individuals, such as individual farmers in an agricultural cooperative, or businesses, such as individual hardware stores, florists, or hotels that have come together to create cooperatives. Cooperatives are motivated to provide services to people with common interests and/or needs and not motivated by profits. Any profits made by a cooperative are returned to members in proportion to their use, not their investment or their ownership share.

How are cooperatives structured? Members are the most important part of a cooperative. They buy shares to help finance the cooperative, elect directors to manage the cooperative, and create and amend the bylaws that govern the cooperative. Cooperatives depend on their members to volunteer for projects supported by the co-op and serve on boards and committees. The board of directors in a cooperative appoints committees for specific purposes, such as member relations and special audits. The board of directors also hires the cooperative manager who handles the daily affairs.

What is the benefit of cooperatives? Cooperatives form because a group of individuals or businesses become dissatisfied with how the marketplace is providing the needed goods or services at affordable prices or acceptable quality. Cooperatives use the benefit of group power, individuals (people or companies) coming together for a single cause, to negotiate within their marketplace. Therefore, members enjoy reduced costs due to greater bargaining power and marketplace strength associated with a large member group.[7]

For example, Florida's Natural Growers is a cooperative of citrus growers who own their own groves in Florida. A group of growers formed the co-op in 1933 to market their crops. Today, the Florida Natural Growers Cooperative processes 129,000 boxes of fruit per day—an improvement from the original 3,000 boxes of fruit the co-op originally handled.

Some businesses don't fit the mold of sole proprietorship, partnership, or corporation. When this occurs, business owners might form nonprofit organizations or cooperatives. Jeremy Perugia, who we discussed at the beginning of this section, did not care about personal profit, so he found that forming a nonprofit organization was best for him.

▼ You have just read **Objective 5**

Want to test your skills? Check out the Study Plan section @
www.my*biz*lab.com.

"Are you thinking what I'm thinking?"

Business Combinations and Corporate Restructuring pp. 182-185

How much do you know about corporate restructuring? Read the statements below, then decide whether each statement is true or false to test your corporate restructuring expertise.

1. Exxon and Mobil merged in 1999 to form ExxonMobil.
2. IBM acquired iPhrase and renamed itself IBM Solutions.
3. In 1998, Amoco purchased BP for 56 billion dollars.
4. In 1999, Citicorp and Travelers Group merged to become TravelersCorp.
5. AOL purchased Time Warner and renamed itself AOL Time Warner.

Answers: 1. True; 2. False; 3. False; 4. False; 5. True

If you got...

0–1 answers correct: Good try. You're not savvy about corporate restructuring now, but don't worry. After reading this section, you will be.

2–3 answers correct: Good job. You're fairly up-to-date with major mergers and acquisitions. Read this section to get further acquainted.

4–5 answers correct: Congratulations! You are up-to-date on important corporate mergers and acquisitions. Read the section to learn even more. ➤

➤ Mergers and acquisitions are two quick ways companies increase their competitive advantage and gain synergy. Why do some companies decide to merge with another? Why do companies try to acquire other companies? What are advantages and disadvantages of mergers and acquisitions? We'll answer these and other questions in this section.

Mergers and Acquisitions

What are mergers and acquisitions? Sometimes, in the evolution of a business or in response to market forces, companies seek opportunities to expand by adding new product lines, spreading out into different geographic areas, or growing the company to increase their competitive advantage. Often product or market expansion is done gradually by slowly adding new product lines, or penetrating new areas. However, it takes time and investment to research and develop new products, or to locate and build in new areas. Sometimes, especially to remain competitive, expansion needs to happen more quickly. In that case, it's easier to integrate another established business through the process of mergers or acquisitions.

When two companies come together to form one company, a **merger** takes place. Generally, a merger implies that the two companies involved are about the same size and have mutually agreed to form a new combined company. When a "merger of equals" happens, both merging companies cease to exist and one new company takes over. For example, in 1998, Daimler-Benz, a German automobile manufacturer, merged with U.S. automobile manufacturer the Chrysler Corporation to form a new company, DaimlerChrysler.

An **acquisition**, on the other hand, occurs when one company completely takes over another company. The purchased company ceases to exist, and it operates and trades under the buying company's name. Often, acquisitions are friendly, as was the case when Robert Strauss's Noven Pharmaceuticals approached JDS Pharmaceuticals. JDS Pharmaceuticals, a privately held company, had two well-established products in its line, a third product in its last stages of testing and approvals, and a proven sales force. "We [would] now have the products, infrastructure and category expertise necessary to market and sell products ourselves," said Strauss of the acquisition.[8] Fortunately, Philip Satow, CEO and co-founder of JDS Pharmaceuticals, agreed that the acquisition would be beneficial to both sides. "By joining with the expertise and resources of Noven, we believe we can . . . more rapidly achieve the vision that we have been working toward," Satow remarked.[9]

Are all mergers and acquisitions mutually desired by both companies?

While many mergers are "friendly" and mutually agreed upon between companies, often acquisitions are "unfriendly." An unfriendly acquisition occurs when one company tries to take control over another company against its wishes. Unfriendly acquisitions are referred to as *hostile takeovers*. An unfriendly or hostile acquisition attempt occurs through a *tender offer*, where the acquiring firm offers to buy the target company's stock at a price higher than its current value, which is meant to induce shareholders into selling. For example, Pilgrim's Pride offered $20 a share to the shareholders of Gold Kist Inc., in an effort to acquire its Atlanta, Georgia-based rival. However, Gold Kist's CEO requested that stockholders take no action. Instead of giving in, Pilgrim's Pride launched a four-month campaign to appeal directly to Gold Kist's shareholders.[10] When Gold Kist shareholders had sold 67 percent of the company's stock to Pilgrim's Pride for $21 a share, the hostile takeover bid proved to be successful.

Another method of acquiring a company against its wishes is through a *proxy fight* in which the acquiring company tries to persuade the target company shareholders to vote out existing management and to introduce management that is sympathetic to the goals of the acquiring company.

Why do mergers and acquisitions occur?

Merger and acquisitions specialists estimate that there are nearly 300 friendly and unfriendly acquisitions a day.[11] *Synergy* is the business buzzword often used to justify a merger or an acquisition. **Synergy** is the achieved effect when two companies combine, and the result is better than each company could achieve individually. Synergistic value is created when the new company can realize operating or financial economies of scale. Combined firms often lower costs by trimming redundancies in staff, sharing resources, and obtaining discounts accessible only to a larger firm.

> " Nothing focuses the mind better than the constant sight of a competitor who wants to wipe you off the map. " [12]
>
> —Wayne Calloway, CEO of Pepsi (1986–1996)

Is competition a driving force for mergers and acquisitions?

Achieving a greater competitive advantage is one reason mergers and acquisitions take place. Often, companies join to become the dominant force in their market. In 1999, when Exxon and Mobil agreed to combine to form ExxonMobil, both companies felt there were efficiencies in coming together that would be mutually beneficial. At the time, crude oil prices were sharply lower due to an overabundance of oil in the market, and demand was stagnant resulting from an economic slump in Asia and a slowdown of world growth. The union of the two companies produced the world's biggest oil company and the largest corporation in terms of revenue. ExxonMobil's crude oil production would be the third greatest, behind Saudi Arabia and Iran.[13] The combination would allow the companies to reduce redundancies—estimating that $2.8 billion in costs would be saved due to the merger.

⊙On Target BP Buys Amoco

In 1998, British Petroleum (BP) purchased the U.S. oil company Amoco in a deal that was valued between $48 billion and $53 billion. When it took place, it was the largest industrial acquisition ever. Even though BP purchased Amoco, it was considered "an alliance of equals," according to then BP Chief Executive John Browne. Each company had its own strengths and weaknesses. BP was the more profitable company, but its exploration projects to find new sources of oil were struggling. On the other hand, Amoco was finding oil but wasn't able to translate that into increased profits. The combination of the two companies produced one mega company, BP Amoco PLC (Public Limited Company), which was the third largest oil producer in the world. Since 1998, BP Amoco PLC has acquired even more companies and retained its spot among not just the biggest oil companies in the world, but as one of the biggest companies in the world. According to Forbes' Global 2000 list, which ranks the 2000 largest global companies, BP is the seventh largest company in the world, with 2007 sales alone over $281 billion.

Do companies add value to their product line by mergers? Many times, larger companies acquire smaller companies for their innovativeness, and a smaller company will agree to merge or be acquired if they feel they wouldn't have the opportunity to go public and couldn't survive alone otherwise. IBM has long used the strategy of adding to its product line through acquisitions. Recently, IBM acquired iPhrase, a privately held company that specializes in making software, so IBM could "establish a new level of customer value for discovering and delivering actionable information."[14] IBM also acquired PureEdge Solutions Inc., one of the leading developers of electronic forms, so IBM could offer a seamless integration of electronic forms to IBM's customers. Both iPhrase and PureEdge Solutions Inc. have helped IBM in its quest to provide software that enables businesses to make sense of the consumer data they receive from online sales.

Are there different types of mergers? The rationale and strategy behind every merger is different, but, as illustrated in ▼ **Figure 6.7**, there are some consistencies, distinguished by the relationship between the two companies that are merging:

- **Horizontal merger:** Two companies that share the same product lines and markets and are in direct competition with each other, such as Exxon and Mobil and Daimler-Benz and Chrysler.

- **Vertical merger:** Two companies that have a company/customer relationship or a company/supplier relationship, such as Walt Disney and Pixar or eBay and PayPal.

- **Product extension merger:** Two companies selling different but related products in the same market, such as the 2005 merger between Adobe and Macromedia.

- **Market extension merger:** Two companies that sell the same products in different markets, such as when NationsBank, which had operations primarily in the East Coast and Southern areas of the United States, merged with Bank of America, whose prime business was on the West Coast.

- **Conglomeration:** Two companies that have no common business areas merge to obtain diversification. For example, Citicorp, a banking services firm, and Travelers Group Inc., an insurance underwriting company, combined to form one of the world's largest financial services group, Citigroup Inc.

Are there disadvantages with mergers? Nearly two-thirds of mergers don't succeed in achieving greater market value.[15] Often, managing a merger will force the top executives to take their eyes off business. Although cost-cutting may be the initial primary focus of some mergers, revenues and profits ultimately suffer because day-to-day activities are neglected. Additionally, corporate cultures may clash, and communications may break down if the new division of responsibilities is vague. Conflicts may also arise due to divided loyalties, hidden agendas, or power struggles within the newly combined management team. Employees may be nervous because most mergers result in the elimination of jobs, and more turnover may be created as those employees whose jobs may not be threatened by the merger seek employment in a more stable environment.

Review the corporate restructuring test you took at the beginning of this section. Are you familiar with some examples of corporate restructuring in the United States? Do you understand why companies merge with or acquire other companies? Can you explain why some mergers and acquisitions are unfriendly?

Horizontal Merger

 merges with

Vertical Merger

 merges with

Product Extension Merger

 merges with

Market Extension

 merges with

Conglomeration

 merges with

▼ **Figure 6.7**
Different Types of Mergers
Companies merge for different strategic reasons. Sometimes, companies merge to enter new markets, whereas others want to expand into new fields and save costs.

▼ You have just read **Objective 6**

Want to quiz yourself? Check out the Study Plan section @ **www.my*biz*lab.com.**

1. What are the strengths and weaknesses of a sole proprietorship? (pp. 163-165)

- A **sole proprietorship** (p. 163) is a business owned and usually operated by a single individual.

- Sole proprietorship is the most common form of business ownership because it is the easiest to set up, but there are both strengths and weaknesses inherent to this business form.

  - With sole proprietorships, there are no formal, legal requirements for starting the business, and the revenues and expenses are reported directly on the business owner's personal income tax report.

  - The primary disadvantage of a sole proprietorship is that personal and business assets are at risk in the event of a major business catastrophe.

2. What are the advantages and disadvantages of a partnership and a partnership agreement? (pp. 166-170)

- A **partnership** (p. 166) is another business structure that is easy to set up with no formal, legal requirements. Advantages and disadvantages of partnerships include the following:

  - Partnerships offer the benefit of two or more individuals sharing aspects of the business, including financial management and sales and marketing responsibilities. Income and expenses flow directly through each partner's individual tax return.

  - Partnerships also allow the partners to draw up a **partnership agreement** (p. 167), which is a formal document that outlines responsibilities for each partner and includes provisions when there are disputes among partners.

  - Problems can occur when partners do not agree on the nature of the business or have different work ethics.

  - Partners' personal and business assets are at risk, with each partner being solely liable for any part of the business. Responsibility is not limited to each partner's financial contribution to the business.

3. How is a corporation formed, and how does it compare with sole proprietorships and partnerships? (pp. 171-175)

- **Corporations** (p. 171) are businesses structured as separate legal entities. Corporations are structured with different levels of management, including shareholders, board of directors, corporate officers, such as the **chief executive officer** (p. 173), chief financial officer, corporate secretary, and chief operating officer.

- Corporations differ from sole proprietorships and partnerships because corporations

  - are difficult to set up.

  - require much paperwork, including annual reports, corporate minutes, and formal financial records.

  - must file separate tax returns.

  - can sue and be sued.

  - protect owner's personal assets.

4. What are the major differences between a C corporation, an S corporation, and a limited-liability company? (pp. 175-179)

- **S corporations** (p. 175) are like C corporations that offer the protection of limited liability, but S corporations allow the shareholders to flow the corporate revenues and expenses through their personal tax returns.

  - S corporations have certain restrictions, which include limiting the number of shareholders to no more than 100, requiring shareholders to be residents of the United States, allowing for the issuance of only one class of stock, and basing profits and losses on the proportional interest of each shareholder.

- The corporate structure of a **limited-liability company (LLC)** (p. 176) is similar to an S corporation that offers the protection of limited liability of a corporation. LLCs differ from S corporations because they can have unlimited members, must dissolve when any member leaves, and do not base distribution of profits on the direct proportion of a member's financial contribution.

5. What are the characteristics of not-for-profit corporations and cooperatives? (pp. 180-181)

- **Not-for-profit corporations** (p. 180) are corporations whose purpose is to serve the public interest rather than to seek to make a profit.

  - Not-for-profit corporations are tax-exempt, and donations to the organization are deemed tax-deductible.

- **Cooperatives** (p. 181) are businesses that are owned and governed by members who use its products and services, not by outside investors.

  - Cooperatives are motivated to provide services or goods to people with common interests or needs.

  - All profits generated by the cooperative are returned to the members in direct proportion to their share of ownership.

  - Cooperatives use the benefit of group power to negotiate within their marketplace.

  - Cooperatives are primarily in agriculture.

Continued on next page

Chapter Summary (cont.)

6. What are the different types of mergers and acquisitions, and why do they occur? (pp. 182-185)

- **Mergers** and **acquisitions** (pp. 182-183) are business practices that bring companies together (in two distinct manners) for the purpose of achieving better **synergy** (p. 183).

- A merger occurs when two companies of similar size mutually agree to combine to form a new company. Some types of mergers include the following:

  - **Horizontal mergers** (p. 184)—two companies that share the same product lines and are in direct competition with each other merge

  - **Vertical merger** (p. 184)—two companies that have a company/customer relationship or a company/supplier relationship merge

- Product extension merger (p. 184)—two companies selling different but related products in the same market merge

- Market extension merger (p. 184)—two companies that sell the same products in different markets merge

- Conglomeration (p. 184)—two companies that have no common business areas merge to obtain diversification

- An acquisition is the instance when one company decides to buy another company outright. The purchased company ceases to exist and starts to operate under the buying company's name and management.

  - Acquisitions can be friendly (mutually agreed upon) or unfriendly (one company buys the other against the wishes of the management and/or owner).

For an audio file of the Objectives and Chapter Summary, see the Student Resources section @ www.my*biz*lab.com.

Key Terms

acquisition (p. 183)

board of directors (p. 174)

capital (p. 168)

chief executive officer (CEO) (p. 173)

closed corporation (p. 174)

cooperatives (p. 181)

corporation (C corporation) (p. 171)

double taxation (p. 175)

general partners (p. 170)

general partnership (p. 170)

horizontal merger (p. 184)

liability (p. 164)

limited-liability company (LLC) (p. 176)

limited partner (p. 170)

limited partnership (p. 170)

merger (p. 182)

not-for-profit corporation (p. 180)

partnership (p. 166)

partnership agreement (p. 167)

privately held corporation (p. 174)

publicly owned corporation (p. 173)

S corporation (p. 175)

shareholder (p. 173)

sole proprietorship (p. 163)

synergy (p. 183)

unlimited liability (p. 165)

vertical merger (p. 184)

Self-Test

Multiple Choice Correct answers can be found on page 503.

1. A business has only one owner and several employees, and the owner reports income and expenses through personal tax returns. This business can best be described as

   a. a limited partnership.

   b. a sole proprietorship.

   c. a C corporation.

   d. a not-for-profit corporation.

2. Why might a potential business owner avoid setting up a business as a sole proprietorship?

   a. The owner must use personal assets to satisfy any business liabilities.

   b. The owner must take into consideration the opinions of other business owners.

   c. The owner must generate a separate tax report for business expenses.

   d. The owner must file legal paperwork to start up the business.

3. Which of the following reasons explains why it is helpful to bring partners into a business?

   a. Partners can contribute financially to the business, reducing the initial investment for a sole proprietor.

   b. Partners can offer complementary skills to the business and help create a synergy that helps the business succeed.

   c. Partners generally care more about the business and work harder than ordinary employees.

   d. All of the above

4. Alicia invested in her niece and nephew's partnership, but does not participate in the day-to-day business operations. Alicia is considered a(n)

   a. general partner.

   b. limited partner.

   c. owner.

   d. none of the above

5. Which of the following would *not* be a reason for creating a new business as a C corporation?

   a. The owner's personal assets would be protected.

   b. The owner could raise greater sources of funds by selling shares of ownership.

   c. Business profits and losses would flow through the owner's personal tax return.

   d. The corporation would continue to exist even if the owner left the business.

6. Which of the following types of business structures would be required to have a board of directors, corporate officers, and shareholders?

   a. Limited-liability company

   b. S corporation

   c. Not-for-profit corporation

   d. Sole proprietorship

7. LLC and S corporations are similar in many ways. Which of the following is *not* a common similarity between the two?

   a. Both LLCs and S corporations can have no more than 100 shareholders.

   b. Both LLCs and S corporations are separate, legal entities.

   c. Both LLCs and S corporations have limited liability protection.

   d. Both LLCs and S corporations allow taxes to flow through to the owners.

8. Which is a characteristic of cooperatives?

   a. They are owned and governed by members who use their products and services.

   b. They are exempt from paying federal and state taxes.

   c. They are set up to serve the public interest, rather than make a profit.

   d. They provide services to people with differing interests and needs.

9. If two large grocery store chains—named Mom's Grocers and Best Supermarkets—combined to form Mom's Best Grocery Stores, which best describes the type of transaction that occurred between the two companies?

   a. A vertical merger

   b. A product extension merger

   c. A horizontal merger

   d. A conglomeration

10. Which of the following is an advantage of mergers?

   a. Greater market share is always achieved through the merger of two companies.

   b. Communications tend to be much better due to the streamlined nature of the new corporation.

   c. Greater value is often created through the synergy that is achieved by combining two companies

   d. There is little turnover or elimination of jobs in a merged corporation.

Self-Test

1. When forming a partnership, partners are required to create a partnership agreement.
   ☐ **True** or ☐ **False**

2. The greatest difference between a not-for-profit corporation and a C corporation is that a not-for-profit corporation cannot be organized for any person's private gain.
   ☐ **True** or ☐ **False**

3. Cooperatives are the business form used only by groups of farmers.
   ☐ **True** or ☐ **False**

4. Partnerships are the most common form of business ownership.
   ☐ **True** or ☐ **False**

5. An S corporation cannot have shareholders who live outside the United States.
   ☐ **True** or ☐ **False**

Critical Thinking Questions

1. What are the advantages of sole proprietorships, partnerships, and corporations? What are the disadvantages of each form of business ownership? Which form of business ownership do you believe is best and why?

2. Discuss how different types and levels of financing can affect the type of organizational form a business can take.

3. What are the reasons why a company might want to be closely held or privately owned? Under what circumstances might its owners choose to become publicly traded?

4. Investigate a nonprofit organization in your area. What cause is it serving? What is the primary source of its income? What are its main expenses?

5. Colleges often offer good opportunities for cooperative businesses. Does your college currently have any cooperatives? If so, what are they? If not, discuss ideas for cooperatives that might be beneficial to your campus community.

Team Time

What's the Plan?

Imagine that you work for the Small Business Association and have the opportunity to advise new business owners on the form of ownership their business should take. Form groups of three to five people, and choose one of the business ideas below. Work as a group to create a business plan for the business idea you chose. What kind of business forms would you suggest and why? Be sure to consider the potential risks and liabilities, the potential income tax situations, and the current and future investment needs of each business.

Business Ideas:

- Roofing and siding company
- Ice cream parlor
- Yoga instruction
- Lawn mowing company
- Clothing donation company

Process

Meet as a group to discuss your business idea. Remember that you must prepare a business plan. Use what you know about forms of business ownership to create the business plan.

Step 1. Prepare an individual report that explains the form of ownership your business should take and outline why it should take this form.

Step 2. Determine who will be the group's primary spokesperson for your business plan.

Step 3. Your group will have 5 minutes to present your business plan. After you have presented, other teams will be given 5 minutes to ask questions about the proposed plan.

Step 4. After each group has presented, ask the class if anyone has changed his or her opinion about the best form of ownership for his or her business idea.

Ethics and Corporate Social Responsibility

Moving Offshore

The corporate income taxes in the United States are among the highest in the world. Under U.S. tax laws, multinational corporations must pay taxes on income earned in foreign countries. As a result, many U.S. corporations are coming up with inventive ideas to help them avoid paying high U.S. taxes. For example, in recent years, Tyco International, Ltd., a U.S. multinational corporation, has reincorporated abroad to save on paying U.S. taxes. Despite government attempts to intervene, Tyco voted to keep its address registered in Bermuda to increase company profits. Approximately two dozen other U.S. companies have followed Tyco's lead and have moved their companies offshore.

Questions for Discussion

1. Consider Tyco's reincorporation practices from the points of view of a Tyco employee, a government official, and an employee of a U.S. multinational corporation that has not reincorporated. Are Tyco's practices justified? Why or why not?

2. Imagine you are a government official. How would you respond to companies that reincorporate abroad?

Web Exercises

1. **Business Combinations**
   Look on the Internet for a current example of a business merger, takeover, or acquisition. Explain the circumstances of the event. What companies are involved? Was the event friendly or unfriendly? What are the reasons given for the combination? What is your opinion of this business combination? Do you think it is a good business decision? Why or why not?

2. **State Incorporation Requirements**
   What does it take to incorporate in your state? You read in the text that each state has its own requirements for incorporation. Go online and find a Web site that outlines your state's requirements for incorporation. What requirements does your state have? What assistance does your state provide for start-up businesses?

3. **The Perfect Partner**
   Go to www.inc.com/guides/leadership_strat/23041.html and read the advice for how to pick the perfect business partner. Using information you learned from this chapter

   and the Web site, write a list of rules for picking the perfect business partner. What factors should be taken into account? What can you do to avoid trouble in the future?

4. **Why Did It Fail?**
   Go online and research businesses that have been unsuccessful. Analyze the business's failure. What caused the business to fail? Would the business have been more successful had it adopted a different form of ownership? Write a paper analyzing why the business failed and explaining what you might have done differently as the owner.

5. **Preparing for Business**
   Think of a business idea you might like to pursue some day. Imagine that "some day" is today. Visit the SCORE (Counsel-ors to Small Businesses) Web site at www.score.org/business_quiz.html and take the quizzes there to see if you're prepared to start your business. Are you really ready to begin your business venture?

Web Case

To access the Chapter 6 Web case and exercise, see the End of Chapter Assignments section @ www.my*biz*lab.com.

Video Case

To access the Chapter 6 Video case and exercise, see the End of Chapter Assignments section @ www.my*biz*lab.com.

Constructing an Effective
Business Plan

From the moment you received money for mowing your neighbor's lawn or babysitting your neighbor's kid, you've been interested in starting your own business. But where do you begin? Do you purchase business cards? Do you create and pass out flyers? Although these might be good ways to get your business moving, they are not the first things you should do when starting a business. The Small Business Administration suggests the very first step in starting a business is *planning*.

Writing a formal business plan should be your first step in starting a business; however, this step is not required. In fact, *Inc.* magazine states that only 40 percent of the successful entrepreneurs they interviewed for the 2002 *Inc.* 500 list admit to writing a formal business plan before launching their business.[1] This does not make a formal business plan any less important. Regardless of when it is written, a business plan is a crucial part of a successful business operation.

Planning—It's Never Too Late

In 1958, college-aged brothers Dan and Frank Carney borrowed $600 from their mother to open a pizza parlor in Wichita, Kansas. This venture marked the inception of the Pizza Hut empire. The brothers had neither a formal business plan nor a clear vision of the path their business would take. In fact, the Carneys simply gave away pizza on their opening night to garner the public's interest. Although it was impulsive, their gimmick worked. Less than a year later, the boys incorporated and opened their first franchise unit in Topeka, Kansas.

Although Pizza Hut owners Dan and Frank Carney launched a successful business without a formal business plan, they soon found that planning was necessary for continued success.

Within the next 10 years, more than 150 franchises opened nationwide, and one international franchise opened in Canada. However, in 1970, the company's growth became explosive. Pizza Hut went public, and the brothers quickly became overwhelmed. "We about lost control of the operations," Frank Carney said in 1972. "Then we figured out that we had to learn how to plan."[2] Ultimately, Frank and Dan developed a plan that kept operations constant and under control. They also created a corporate strategy that enticed PepsiCo, Inc., to purchase Pizza Hut in 1977. At that time, Pizza Hut sales had reached $436 million a year.[3] The Carneys' story is a success; however, if they had developed a clear business plan from the beginning, they may have been better prepared to handle their company's incredible growth.

The **Purpose** of a **Plan**

A business plan is your "business story"—a story that you will tell to a wide variety of people, from personal friends and casual acquaintances to potential partners, suppliers, customers, and investors. Traditionally, a potential business owner should write a business plan *before* the business is launched. Writing down your business plan solidifies and defines your intentions. It forces you to think through many aspects of a business that might otherwise be overlooked. Writing a thorough business plan can take anywhere from one week to three months, depending on the intricacies of the business. A business plan should identify an existing opportunity and describe the manner in which the business intends to fulfill the opportunity. Of course, the goal of most businesses is to make money, so the plan should summarize how a business opportunity will translate into profits. A well-developed plan can also help in obtaining financing and attracting high-quality employees.

In some instances, and especially in industries in which change occurs rapidly, the business opportunity might be lost if you do not start operations immediately—you may not be able to take weeks or months to write a business plan. In this situation, you should still take the time to answer a few discrete and pointed questions, as shown in ▼ **Figure 1**. This will help determine whether the business you're pursuing will be worth the effort. Eventually, a formal business plan should be written to define the goals and objectives of the business and the means to achieve them.

to continue check out **www.my*biz*lab.com**.

Business Management and Organization

p. 195

The Foundations of Management

▼**Objective 1**

PepsiCo CEO Indra K. Nooyi has used her management skills to rise to the top of a multi-billion dollar corporation. What types of skills do successful managers need to have? And how do they use these skills to be effective?

p. 199

The Functions of Management: Planning, Strategic Management, and Organizing

▼**Objectives 2-5**

Planning and organizing are two of a manager's most important responsibilities. How a manager goes about accomplishing these tasks has a tremendous effect on every aspect of the company. Carrie and Mark have the same position at competing firms, and yet their day-to-day experiences differ greatly. Why is this?

p. 208

The Functions of Management: Leading and Controlling

▼**Objectives 6 & 7**

Leadership and *control*—they're both slippery terms that leave ample room for misinterpretation. And yet how managers apply these concepts plays a vital role in the success or failure of a business. How can managers use the means of effective leadership to ensure that the plans and strategies they have set in place are being properly carried out?

The **Foundations** of **Management** pp. 195-198

➤ What makes PepsiCo CEO Indra K. Nooyi (discussed in the box to the right) such a talented and effective manager? What skills does she possess, and how does she apply them? Read on to learn about what management is as well as the skills integral to successful management.

As Chairperson and CEO of PepsiCo, Indra K. Nooyi virtually defines management. She is the head of a corporation that includes three separate divisions: PepsiCo Americas Foods, PepsiCo Americas Beverages, and PepsiCo International. These divisions generate retail sales of more than 98 billion dollars each year in over 200 countries. Nooyi holds master's degrees from the Indian Institute of Management in Calcutta, India, and the Yale School of Management. Since assuming her role as CEO of PepsiCo, she has made efforts to further globalize the company, as well as increase its focus on health-conscious snacks and beverages. So far, she has been successful. *Fortune* named Nooyi the most powerful woman in business in 2007, in part due to PepsiCo's strong performance under her command. She is known for being an innovative thinker, brilliant business strategist, and powerful and persuasive speaker. Her motto for PepsiCo, "Performance with purpose," encapsulates her vision. ➤

Business Management

What is management? Have you ever been in a team situation in which one person has been instrumental in making the group work more effectively? That person could have been a peer or a superior, but somehow he or she knew exactly what had to be accomplished, assessed the resources that were available to achieve the goal, and organized and led other group members in such a way to accomplish the goal. If so, you've seen management in action.

Management is the process of working with people and resources to accomplish the goals of the organization. The organization can be a simple working group, a corporate department, or a multibillion-dollar company. The size of the group doesn't matter, but the skills of a manager and the process a manager goes through are similar across all management levels.

As illustrated in ▼ **Figure 7.1**, management involves four primary functions: planning, organizing, leading, and controlling. These functions integrate all of the company's resources, including human, financial, and technological. In the next section of this chapter, we'll look at each of these functions in a bit more detail.

The Skills of Successful Managers

What skills should a manager have? Since managerial tasks are so varied, a successful manager needs to possess a variety of skills, including *technical*, *interpersonal*, *conceptual*, *decision-making*, and *time management skills*. It is a rare person who is master of all these skills. Moreover, because they are responsible for a variety of jobs, and because these jobs can change quite rapidly, managers must

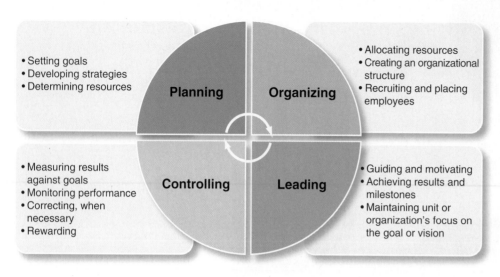

Planning
- Setting goals
- Developing strategies
- Determining resources

Organizing
- Allocating resources
- Creating an organizational structure
- Recruiting and placing employees

Controlling
- Measuring results against goals
- Monitoring performance
- Correcting, when necessary
- Rewarding

Leading
- Guiding and motivating
- Achieving results and milestones
- Maintaining unit or organization's focus on the goal or vision

▼ **Figure 7.1**
The Four Functions of Management

assess the skills that are required in any given situation. Managers must also be willing to acquire these skills quickly if necessary.

Technical Skills

Every job has a specific set of technical skills that are important for managers to possess. **Technical skills** include the abilities and knowledge that enable an employee to carry out the specific tasks required of a discipline or department, such as drafting skills for an architect, programming skills for a software developer, or market analysis skills for a marketing manager. Technical skills may also include how to operate certain machinery. Managers must be comfortable with technology and possess good analytical skills to interpret a variety of data. In addition to having the skills pertinent to their own jobs, managers must also know how to perform, or at least have a good understanding of, the skills required of the employees they supervise.

Interpersonal Skills

Managers achieve goals working with people both inside and outside the organization, so it's important that they possess good interpersonal or human relations skills. **Interpersonal skills** enable a manager to interact with other people in order to motivate them. It's important that a manager develop trust and loyalty with the people he or she interacts with often, and that the manager can motivate and encourage employees to work together.

Interpersonal skills are important skills at any management level. Top managers must be able to communicate with the board of directors, investors, and other leaders in the business community. They must also communicate with middle managers in order to understand clearly the goals and strategies of the organization. Middle managers must communicate with all levels of management and act as liaisons among groups. Lower-level managers must be able to motivate employees, build morale, and train and support those who perform the daily tasks of the organization. As workforce and business relationships continue to be more diverse, it is becoming increasingly important for managers to take into consideration the needs, backgrounds, and experiences of many different people when communicating with individuals and groups in an organization.

Decision-Making Skills

It is critical that a manager has good **decision-making skills**—the ability to identify and analyze a problem, examine the alternatives, choose and implement the best plan of action, and evaluate the results. When making important decisions, managers often go through a formal decision-making process similar to that shown in ▼ **Figure 7.2**. The steps in such a process are as follows:

1. Managers *identify problems* by analyzing data and searching for trends. Such problems may include poor growth in sales, an increase in customer dissatisfaction, or excess inventory buildup.

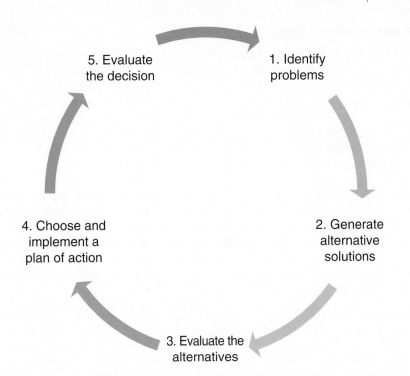

2. Once a problem is defined, managers then *generate alternative solutions*.

3. One they have identified several alternatives, managers *evaluate the alternatives* based on various criteria, such as cost, feasibility, time, resources needed, market acceptance, and compatibility with the company's mission, values, and goals. Managers often rank the evaluated alternatives by various criteria. This evaluation process can be tedious, but identifying and evaluating alternatives is critical to making a good decision. Many times the best routes are not taken because management has not taken the time to explore all alternatives thoroughly.

4. Once managers have evaluated all alternatives, they *choose the best plan of action*. As a final check, management may seek customer or market opinion on the chosen plan of action before completely committing to this choice. In some instances, if the market or customer feedback is not positive, management will look to pursue another alternative. When the final choice has been made, plans are put in place to *implement the plan of action*.

5. Managers also *evaluate the decision* to ensure it is carried out correctly and meets the goals of the organization.

If the goals are not being met, the decision-making process may possibly become cyclical, beginning again with *identifying problems*.

Conceptual Skills

To make good decisions, a good manager must also have **conceptual skills**—the ability to think abstractly in order to picture the organization as a whole and to understand its relationship to the rest of the business community. Such skills also include understanding the relationships between the parts of the organization itself. Whenever new market opportunities or potential threats arise, managers rely on their conceptual skills to help them analyze the impending outcomes of their decisions. Conceptual skills are extremely important for top-line managers and are often developed with time and experience.

Time Management Skills

Time management skills refer to the ability to achieve the maximum amount of productivity in a set amount of time. A manager may possess all the skills discussed above, but that may not be enough to manage a successful business. For example, say that the manager of a small deli built his business from humble beginnings; he had a vision and expanded from there. His knowledge of business logistics is superb, and every day he makes important decisions. He spends hours each day talking with his employees and has gained their respect. Taking all of this into consideration, you would think that his deli would be successful. But this is not the case.

Although this manager has the vision, the knowledge, and the interpersonal skills, he does not make efficient use of his time. For example, instead of socializing with his employees on Friday, he could manage a workshop to help them sharpen their customer service skills. Time management requires that managers have the ability to recognize specific ways in which they can make every task or situation productive. The following steps are crucial to effective time management for almost any manager:

1. *Determine the level of urgency of paperwork.*   Some paperwork, such as billing, may be more important than others, such as a quarterly report due in three months. Managers must therefore separate paperwork according to due dates and clearly label each pile. Keeping a schedule—either electronically or on a calendar—and crossing off each task when completed are important time management skills.

2. *Create folders for e-mail.*   Managers receive plenty of e-mail, which can be a tremendous time drain. To manage e-mail effectively, managers should filter spam to a specific folder and create other folders based on subject, such as "advertising samples," "employee requests," and so on. Effective managers leave the messages requiring an immediate reply in their in-box and address urgent messages right away. Otherwise, managers designate a time each day that they will address all other messages.

3. *Designate a time for telephone calls.*   Of course, as in the case with e-mail, there may be urgent calls that a manager must take immediately. However, effective managers have an office assistant take messages and allocate a specific time to return calls.

4. *Identify clear agendas for meetings.*   Time can be easily wasted if a meeting agenda is not clear and goals are not set. Effective managers therefore distribute an agenda to all attendees before a meeting that specifies the goals the meeting must achieve. An agenda helps everyone stay on task and end the meeting on time.

By following steps such as these, managers find that their productivity levels increase and more time is freed for completing other tasks required of the job.

Think back to Indra K. Nooyi. How might her education have equipped her with the technical skills she uses to achieve success? Do you think her success reflects strong interpersonal skills? What do the changes she has made at PepsiCo say about her decision-making and conceptual skills? How might time management skills come into play in her ability to manage three divisions of a giant corporation? Clearly, Nooyi's prominence and success in business demonstrate that a combination of management skills is vital.

▼ You have just read **Objective 1**

Think you got it? Check out the Study Plan section @
www.my*biz*lab.com.

The **Functions** of **Management: Planning, Strategic Management,** and **Organizing** pp. 199-207

➤ Carrie and Mark's jobs (described in the box to the right) seem similar, and yet their everyday experiences contrast significantly. Why is this? It's all about organization. Which organizational structure does Carrie's firm implement? Which one does Mark's firm use? Why are these structures necessary, and what are the benefits of each? Every company, regardless of its size or specialty, needs a solid organizational structure. Without one, employees may have trouble making decisions and assigning responsibility. But this doesn't mean there's just one way to organize a company. In this section, we'll explore the different aspects of strategic management and organization.

Carrie Witt and Mark Healy have a lot in common: they both graduated with degrees in business and they both acquired jobs as marketing associates at medium-sized firms that design solar energy panels for commercial use. Nevertheless, their professional experiences have been markedly different. At her firm, Carrie is part of the marketing department. She is training to become an expert in getting new clients within a specific region of the state. She reports directly to the department head, but her work is also overseen by several middle managers, including the marketing department supervisor and the marketing manager. They, in turn, take their orders from top managers: the executive vice president, the CEO, and the president. At his firm, Mark works in a team with individuals from a variety of areas, including marketing, research and development, finance, and operations. They work on a variety of projects as a comprehensive unit. One manager supervises his team and coordinates the team's efforts directly with the goals and instructions from the firm's CEO and president. ➤

Planning and Strategic Management

Why do managers need to plan? In today's busy world, it's easy to get distracted. Goals and plans help to keep you on task. **Planning** is the process of establishing goals and objectives and determining the best ways to accomplish them. **Goals** are broad, long-term accomplishments an organization wants to achieve within a certain time frame—in most companies, this is about five years. **Objectives** are the short-term targets that are designed to help achieve these goals.

Both goals and objectives are best set with deadlines and quantifiable measures. Managers should keep the acronym SMARTER in mind when designing and wording goals and objectives. Goals should be **S**pecific, **M**easurable, **A**cceptable (to those working to achieve the goals), **R**ealistic, **T**imely, **E**xtending (the capabilities of those working to achieve the goals), and **R**ewarding to them as well.[1]

Strategic Plans

Planning happens at all levels of an organization. A **strategic plan** is the main course of action created by top-level managers that sets the approach for achieving the long-term goals and objectives of the organization. A strategic plan serves as a framework for decisions and assists in setting corporate benchmarks. Simply put, a strategic plan points the organization to where it wants to be in the future and identifies how it's going to get there. It helps answer questions such as "Where are we going?"; "What do we want to focus on?"; and "What is the best means to get there?" A strategic plan is realistic and obtainable and looks at the big picture. Although individual goals sometimes contribute to the plan, the overall strategic plan is focused on the entire organization, or an entire department. Those making strategic plans must pay attention to the capabilities and resources of the organization, as well as changes in the environment.

How is a strategic plan developed? A good strategic plan reflects what is going on inside and outside the organization and how those conditions and changes will affect the organization in the future. There are several steps management takes while developing a strategic plan, as shown in ▼ **Figure 7.3**.

Vision and Mission Statement

As managers carry out the strategic plan, it's important that they make sure their decisions continue to match the overall objectives of the organization. The first step in creating a strategic plan is to establish a corporate purpose through a *vision* and a *mission statement*. A **vision** identifies what the business wants to be in the future. For example, the vision statement for Domino's Pizza is "Exceptional franchisees and team members on a mission to be the best pizza delivery company in the world."[2] Often times a company will not have one set statement defining its vision, but rather, the vision may be a series of goals and plans. The vision should be made clear to all employees and people investing in the company.

People often confuse the vision of a company with the mission statement. The **mission statement** is a more current description of the organization's purpose, basic goals, and philosophies. A mission statement not only helps management remain focused, but also lets employees understand the core values of the company for

▼ **Figure 7.3**
The Strategic Planning Process

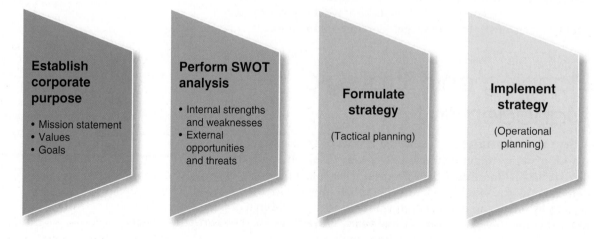

Establish corporate purpose	Perform SWOT analysis	Formulate strategy	Implement strategy
• Mission statement • Values • Goals	• Internal strengths and weaknesses • External opportunities and threats	(Tactical planning)	(Operational planning)

which they work. Because mission statements reflect the personality of a company, they can be very different in design and content. For example, compare the differences in mission statements of two major sports apparel corporations: Under Armour and Nike. As you'll see in ▼ **Table 7.1**, Under Armour's mission statement uses scientific jargon in a no-nonsense manner directed specifically to those who take athletic endeavors very seriously. Its products have been designed to "cover all seasons, climates, and conditions." In contrast, Nike's mission statement is directed toward a much larger target audience. After all, "if you have a body, you are an athlete." Nike refrains from technical jargon and relies on simplicity to inspire the average consumer—not the stereotypical athlete. Based on their mission statements, you would most likely envision Under Armour products on a serious and competitive athlete. In contrast, you might envision Nike being worn by anyone from a physical therapist, to a high school basketball player, to an Olympic gold medalist.

The two mission statements in Table 7.1 target different types of consumers. But this does not necessarily make one more effective than the other. Both statements clearly articulate what their mission is. An understanding of the company mission can help fuel employee enthusiasm. If employees feel the owner's passion for the business through the mission statement, their goals and objectives as employees of the business are incorporated into their daily work and passed onto customers and suppliers through their words and actions. This clarity tends to strengthen a company's position. Even simple mission statements have the power to say a lot about a company if they are written effectively.

Mission statements are not just for for-profit companies like Under Armour and Nike. The mission statements of non-profit organizations are not focused on investor return and therefore focus their outreach on the community or a specific public service. For example, the American Cancer Society's mission statement states, "The American Cancer Society is the nationwide community-based voluntary health organization dedicated to eliminating cancer as a major health problem by preventing cancer, saving lives, and diminishing suffering from cancer, through research, education, advocacy, and service."[3] This statement reflects the organization's commitment to serving the community.

Both the vision and mission statement are usually found on an organization's Web site. However, because the mission statement is directed toward customers—unlike the vision, which is directed toward employees—it is often used alone on advertising materials or on the actual product. The vision and mission statement are critically important as they help keep management on track, help inspire employees working for an organization, and indicate to investors or consumers what type of organization they are investing in. They also provide a guide for management as they evaluate alternative plans and strategies to ensure they are consistent with the organization's current and future direction.

▼ Table 7.1

Examples of Two Different Mission Statements	
Under Armour Mission Statement	**Nike Mission Statement**
"To make all athletes better through passion, science, and the relentless pursuit of innovation."	"To bring inspiration and innovation to every athlete in the world. If you have a body, you are an athlete."
Sources: underarmour.com and nike.com	

SWOT Analysis

Once the company's vision and mission statement have been articulated, management must assess the company's own strengths and weaknesses as well as its position among its competitors. In addition, management must assess what changes are anticipated to occur and determine whether the company is poised appropriately to respond to such changes. This analysis of strengths, weaknesses, and anticipated changes is called a **SWOT analysis** and helps determine the strategic fit between an organization's internal, distinctive capabilities, and external possibilities relative to the business and economic environments.

SWOT stands for **S**trengths, **W**eaknesses, **O**pportunities, and **T**hreats (see ▼ **Table 7.2**). In evaluating the company's strengths and weaknesses, management must analyze the company's internal resources, including finances, human resources, marketing, operations, and technological resources. A company's strength might be its strong marketing department, but the company's weakness could be an unfavorable location. To evaluate the company's business threats and opportunities, management needs to assess external elements, such as economic, political, and regulatory environments, as well as social, demographic, macroeconomic, and technological factors that could affect the company and industry. It also must perform analyses on the state of the industry and market as well as the company's competitors. For example, a recession could threaten an alternative energy company, whereas increasing awareness of global warming may provide greater opportunity for market growth.

Tactical and Operational Plans

What other kinds of planning does management do? Once the strategic planning process is complete and long-term goals and objectives have been determined, middle management generates *tactical plans* to carry out the goals determined by the strategic plan. **Tactical plans** specifically determine the resources and the actions required to implement particular aspects of the strategic plan. Whereas strategic plans have a long-term focus, tactical plans are made with a one- to three-year horizon in mind. Determining the company's annual budget, for example, is one function of a tactical plan. Say the strategic plan of a paper supply company is to sell more products to large offices on the East Coast. One part of this company's tactical plan might be to determine how much money should be allocated to advertising in that area.

The specifics of carrying out tactical plans are *operational plans*. In an **operational plan**, first-line managers precisely determine the process by which tactical plans can be achieved. Operational plans depend on daily or weekly schedules and focus on specific departments or employees. For example, once the paper supply company determines how much of its budget can be allocated to advertising, specific department managers might have to decide which employees will travel to advertise the product.

Tactical and operational planning are two methods that companies use to carry out plans, assuming there are no external factors affecting the business. But, sometimes, extreme circumstances occur that force the company to find alternative means to survive.

▼ **Table 7.2**

SWOT Analysis	
Internal Strengths	**Internal Weaknesses**
Potential assets that give a company a competitive advantage	Lack of capability or expertise compared to competition
External Opportunities	**External Threats**
Foreseeable changes that could favorably affect a company's competitive capability	Conditions that could negatively affect a company's competitive capability

Contingency Planning

We have seen all too frequently the effects that natural disasters can have on businesses. For example, two months after Hurricane Katrina, the Bureau of Labor Statistics reported the overall job loss to be approximately 35,000; many businesses were devastated.[4] We have also seen companies quickly fall into disfavor due to unexpected failures in product quality, such as the lead paint found on Mattel toys that resulted in millions of toys being recalled. All the best corporate strategies can be negated quickly if an unexpected crisis occurs and a plan is not in place to deal with it adequately. What happens if a company suddenly has more sales than production can handle, or if the best-selling product is recalled due to a defect? Who would run the company upon the unexpected death of the CEO or company owner? How should a company fight off an unpredictable takeover threat from a competitor or a rapidly spreading computer virus that threatens to shut down all internal and external lines of communication?

These are the sorts of questions answered through contingency planning. **Contingency planning** is a set of plans that ensures that the organization will run as smoothly as possible during an unexpected disruption. Such planning encompasses how management will communicate, both internally and externally. Internally, management must inform its employees how they should continue to do their jobs. Externally, an organization must have a plan in place to deal with requests for information either from employees, the families of employees, or even the media. Contingency planning involves determining what departments within the company are vital to the immediate needs of the organization when an unexpected crisis occurs. The particulars of each plan differ depending on the size and function of the company and the magnitude of crisis for which the plan is needed.

The Vanguard Group, an investment management company, has in place specific, formal business contingency plans to respond to a range of incidents—from worst-case scenarios such as loss of a data center, buildings, or staff, to more common occurrences such as power outages.[5] As important as it is to have plans in place, it's just as important to ensure the plans are tested and key individuals know exactly what is expected of them. Like fire drills in school, companies should periodically review and rehearse their plans. Vanguard officials put their contingency plans through rigorous testing, including full-scale practice drills in which the company closes a building and works from a remote location. The company also conducts mock disaster drills together with local, state, and federal authorities. Since Vanguard's business would be impacted significantly should a disruption in any of its technical systems occur, it also conducts tests to determine how quickly its information technology systems can become operational in the event of a disruption. ▼ **Table 7.3** summarizes the types of plans that companies such as Vanguard use to carry out their goals.

▼ Table 7.3

The Four Types of Management Plans	
Strategic Plan • Sets the approach for achieving an organization's long-term goals and objectives • Acts as a framework for decisions • Assists in setting corporate benchmarks	**Tactical Plan** • Determines resources and actions necessary to implement strategic plan • Made with a one- to three-year horizon in mind
Operational Plan • Involves planning the execution of the tactical plan • Depends on daily or weekly schedules • Focuses on specific departments or employees	**Contingency Plan** • Keeps an organization running in the event of a disruption • Details internal and external communication procedures for such an event • Determines which departments are most vital to an organization during a crisis

Organizing

How are plans put into action? Once goals have been finalized and plans have been made, the next step in the management process is to put those plans into action. **Organizing** is the process of structuring the capital, personnel, raw materials, and other resources to carry out the plans in a way that best matches the nature of the work. Part of organizing is to establish an organizational structure. Organizational structure depends on a variety of factors, such as the number of employees in the organization, the speed at which decisions need to be made, the subjectivity of the business to rapid change, and the collaborative nature of the work.

The Managerial Pyramid

All corporations are not organized in the same way. The traditional way of organizing management falls into a vertical, hierarchical structure. ▼ **Figure 7.4** shows a traditional vertically structured managerial pyramid.

At the peak of the pyramid, **top managers** are the corporate officers who are responsible for the organization as a whole. Most established corporations determine the corporate officers, especially the *chief executive officer (CEO)*, or *president*. Depending on the size and organizational complexity of the company, top management can also include the *chief financial officer (CFO)*, *chief operations officer (COO)*, and *chief information officer (CIO)*. Top managers generate the strategic plans, long-term goals, mission statement, and vision for the organization. They establish the culture of the organization and inspire employees to adopt senior management's vision of the organization. In smaller corporations, especially small start-up companies, top managers may also be responsible for planning and carrying out the day-to-day tasks of the company. But as the business grows, such companies will need to add more employees and divide the work into smaller tasks and areas of specialty.

▼ **Figure 7.4**
The Managerial Pyramid

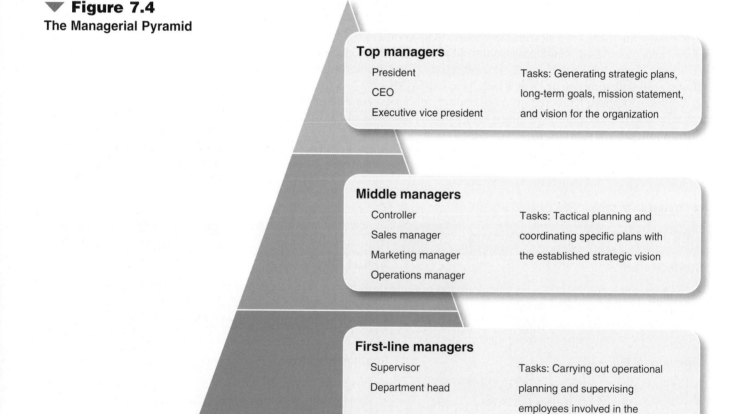

Top managers

President

CEO

Executive vice president

Tasks: Generating strategic plans, long-term goals, mission statement, and vision for the organization

Middle managers

Controller

Sales manager

Marketing manager

Operations manager

Tasks: Tactical planning and coordinating specific plans with the established strategic vision

First-line managers

Supervisor

Department head

Tasks: Carrying out operational planning and supervising employees involved in the daily operations of the company

Middle managers can be thought of as top managers but just for one division or a part of an organization. As such, they are responsible for the tactical planning and creating more specific plans that coordinate with the strategic vision set by the top managers. Included in this management layer are positions such as division managers (finance, marketing, sales, operations, and IT) or team leaders who are not arranged by function, but are responsible for a group of employees who must carry out specific tasks for the organization.

The bottom of the managerial pyramid includes **first-line managers** who carry out operational planning. These managers fill a supervisory role over those employees who carry out the day-to-day operations of the company.

Not all companies have all three layers of management—some have more, and some have fewer. Typically you'll find the "extra" layers are middle managers. However, the organizational pattern of a vertically structured business generally can be represented by the managerial pyramid.

Organizational Structures

Smaller companies that have relatively few employees tend to be organized differently than large corporations. Small companies tend to have much simpler structures compared with large companies. Regardless, to accomplish many tasks at the same time, organizations must have some division of labor and allocate work into smaller tasks. An **organizational chart**, like that shown in ▼ **Figure 7.5**, shows how groups of employees fit into the larger organizational structure.

Vertical and Horizontal Organizations In a **vertical organization** (or a *tall organization*), the company is organized by specific function, such as marketing, finance, purchasing, information technology, and human resources. In such organizational structures, levels of expertise within functions are developed and managers can better keep track of economic and environmental conditions that affect their functional area. Potential problems may arise, however, because integration between functions and divisions is not always easy. Vertical organization usually calls for long lines of communication and "reporting up." This makes it difficult for a company to respond quickly to changes in a market or to provide new innovation because keeping each division updated means spending time doing so.

Vertical organization has been the primary structure of business since the industrial revolution. Although such traditional pyramidal management has its benefits, in the early 1990s, vertical organizational structures were criticized as being overspecialized, fragmented, and inflexible. Some businesses, such as Ford

▼ **Figure 7.5**
Organizational Chart
An organizational chart is used to display the division of labor and organizational structure within a company.

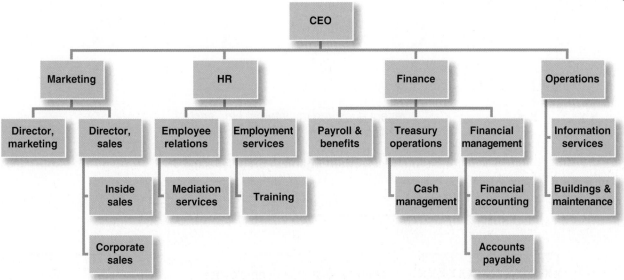

Motor Company, Xerox Corp., and Barclay's Bank, found that they were more successful when they organized in a horizontal structure and formed management groups around areas of specific production or product units.[6] In a **horizontal organization** (or a *flat organization*), the traditional managerial pyramid is flattened, and the management layers are collapsed. A horizontally structured organization still has some of the pyramidal aspects, including a CEO and perhaps another layer of middle management, but then the organization concentrates the majority of the remaining employees into working teams or groups. ▼ **Figure 7.6** illustrates the basic differences in organizational charts of a vertically structured organization and a horizontally structured organization.

The benefit of a horizontal organization is that each team has more responsibility for the outcome of its work. There are fewer layers of management, so fewer reporting issues arise, and, if needed, the bosses' approval can be sought and received much faster. The company can be more responsive since individuals in a horizontal organization are more empowered to make decisions. Horizontal structures have been deemed the "model for the knowledge age." They are suitable for industries that require rapid responses to quick changes.

Occasionally, when companies have grown so large that there are a variety of product lines, geographic regions, or manufacturing processes that can be difficult to manage, they restructure from a vertical organization to a horizontal one. In these circumstances, managers often try to streamline functions to make management easier. For example, they might structure the organization into divisions of employees who work on just one product line. Or they might divide the company into teams in which each team specializes in just one geographic region or works through just one manufacturing process. In essence, these divisions work like separate mini-companies. Each division has its own set of functional expertise, so separate managers are in charge of finance, marketing, human resources, informational technology, and so on. The groups work autonomously and are highly differentiated—so much so that they create barriers to coordination across functions. In today's business environment, there are fewer and fewer organizations structured vertically by function.

▼ **Figure 7.6**
Vertically and Horizontally Structured Organizations

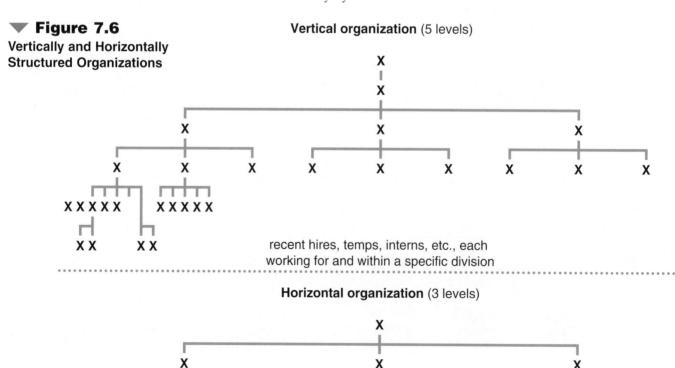

One company that made the shift from being a vertical organization to a horizontal one is Xerox, the document management company. It was once arranged in a traditional vertical structure, organized by function, such as research and development, manufacturing, and sales. To allow the business to become closer to the customer, in the early 1990s, the company realigned itself around individual business markets such as small businesses, office document systems, and engineering systems. Each individual group had its own set of financial reports, and factories were focused on individual product lines. "We've given everyone in the company a direct line of sight to the customer," says Paul Allaire, the CEO at the time of the restructuring.[7] Today, the company continues to maintain a flat organizational structure organized by product category, as well as by region, to take into consideration the company's global presence.

Network Organizations   Although the majority of companies are structured with the more traditional vertical structure or the group-oriented horizontal structure, a new business structure is emerging. Instead of the customary means of producing a product or service in which one company is responsible for all functions, **network organizations** are collections of independent, mostly single-function firms that collaborate on a product or service. For example, Boeing recently completed production of its latest airplane, the Boeing 787. In the past, airplanes were assembled in one hangar. This time, however, Boeing relied on the expertise of hundreds of manufacturers worldwide to independently manufacture the components of the plane and ship the individual pieces for assembly in its main plant. The wings and landing gear are assembled in Italy, and the nose and cockpit are assembled in Wichita, Kansas. Individual or combined elements are then shipped to Everett, Washington, where they are finally assembled into a single 787 plane.

In addition to Boeing, other companies are using a network arrangement, including Nike, which only owns one manufacturing plant, and Reebok, which only designs and markets but does not produce any of its products. A network structure is not suitable for every company, but it may be successful for those companies that need

- to be as flexible and innovative as possible;
- to respond quickly to threats and opportunities;
- to save time;
- to reduce costs and risk.

Reflect back on Carrie and Mark who were introduced at the beginning of this section. Carrie works under the supervision of the marketing department head and several middle managers in the same department, who in turn report to top management. Mark works on a team with people from various departments at his company. Is it clearer now as to why their experiences were so different despite the seeming similarity between their jobs? Carrie's company is a vertical, or tall, organization. The company is organized around specific business functions, and there are several levels of first-line and middle managers. Mark, on the other hand, works at a flat organization. There are fewer middle managers, and employees work in groups.

▼ You have just read **Objectives 2-5**

Want a review? Check out the Study Plan section @
www.mybizlab.com.

The **Functions** of **Management: Leading** and **Controlling** pp. 208-215

➤ An organization is often successful when employees have a leader to demonstrate what it takes for a company to achieve its goals. In this section, we'll look at what it takes to be a strong leader and how managers can maintain control of their teams and their companies.

Leading

Why does an organization need leaders? Leading is the process of influencing, motivating, and enabling others to contribute to the success and effectiveness of the organization by achieving its goals. Therefore, the quality of leadership exhibited by managers is a critical determinant of organizational success. Managers and leaders are not the same, though it is important for a manager to strive to be both a leader and a manager. Managers are task-oriented and focus on process and control, whereas leaders realize the importance of guiding and inspiring others to help accomplish a task. Sometimes, individuals prove that they can get the job done and are therefore considered effective managers. But they are not necessarily true leaders if they have not inspired others to contribute to the process. As illustrated in ▼ **Figure 7.7**, the best leaders are defined as those who

- *challenge the process* by not always accepting conventional beliefs and practices as the only way to accomplish tasks.
- *model the way* by serving as a living example of the ideals in which they are asking their employees to share.
- *inspire a shared vision* and appeal to people's values and motivate them to care about the corporate goals or an important mission.
- *encourage the heart* by showing appreciation, providing rewards, and so on, to motivate people in positive ways.
- *enable others to act* by giving people the access to information and empowering them to perform to their fullest potential.[8]

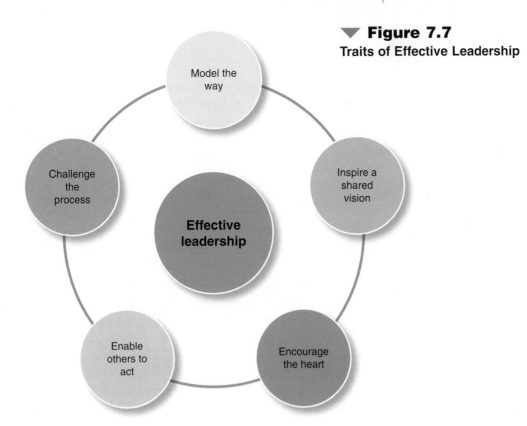

▼ **Figure 7.7**
Traits of Effective Leadership

The Traits of a Good Leader

In addition to these five means of effective leadership, there are several traits that most leadership analysts agree are common to good leaders:

- **Determination.** Leaders need to achieve and are constantly striving for improvement. They have a high energy level and are ambitious and persistent in the face of obstacles. Leaders don't give up easily. True leadership drive, however, does not come at the expense of others; therefore, leaders delegate authority and responsibility to others to promote their success also. They are the catalysts for positive action.

- **Inspiration.**   Leaders influence in a positive and moral way (rather than in a selfish and destructive way) and garner trust, respect, and commitment to their vision. They can communicate a vision throughout the organization and inspire others to adopt the same vision and work toward common goals.

- **Flexibility and empathy.**   Leaders are good listeners, can perceive the need for a change in tactics, and, if necessary, can adjust their leadership style to fit the current environment, people, and situation. Leaders must take into account the overall well-being of others and be mindful of their values and feelings.

- **Innovativeness.**   Leaders set goals and have a vision of the future that may be different from the norm. Leaders are not afraid to alter their methods, plans, or even thinking if the situation calls for change. Also, leaders exemplify resourcefulness as they continually brainstorm for solutions to problems and more effective ways of reaching goals.

- **Honesty.**   Leaders are honest and credible. Employees can trust that the leader will deal with them in a fair and equitable manner.

- **Self-confidence.**   Leaders have the confidence to overcome inevitable obstacles and to make tough decisions despite uncertainty. A leader's confidence promotes calm in stressful situations.

▼ **top**

10 **Companies for**

Cultivating Leadership Skills, 2007

1. General Electric
2. Procter & Gamble
3. Nokia
4. Hindustan Unilever
5. Capital One Financial
6. General Mills
7. McKinsey
8. IBM
9. BBVA
10. Infosys Technologies

Biz**Chat**

Do Successful Managers Need to Be Effective?

Although most people would agree that a manager's responsibilities center on planning, controlling, leading, and organizing, what do managers really do? According to a study by Fred Luthans at the University of Nebraska-Lincoln, there are two types of managers: successful managers and effective managers. Successful managers are those who are rapidly and consistently promoted, whereas effective managers are those who "get the job done and do it right." It might seem that to be successful, you must be effective, but according to the study, the two types have little in common. Luthans first determined that managers' activities may be assimilated into 11 behavior categories. He then further organized the behaviors into

four managerial activities, shown in ▼ **Table 7.4**.[9] After four years of observation, Luthans determined that the "successful" managers—those who were promoted relatively quickly—spent most of their time networking, whereas the "effective" managers—those who have satisfied subordinates and high-performing units—spent most of their time performing communication and human resources management activities. Interestingly, of the nearly 400 managers tracked, no more than 10 percent of the group fell into both "successful" and "effective" categories. What does this mean for management today? Managers should remember how important it is to pay attention to the human resources of business, and business should try to find a way to make effective managers successful.

For more information and discussion questions about this topic, check out the BizChat feature on www.my*biz*lab.com.

▼ **Table 7.4**

The Activities of Real Managers	
Real Management Activities	**Descriptive Categories**
Communication	Exchanging information
	Paperwork
Traditional management	Planning
	Decision making
	Controlling
Networking	Interacting with outsiders
	Socializing/politicking
Human resources management	Motivating/reinforcing
	Disciplining/punishing
	Managing conflict
	Staffing

- **Knowledge and competence.** Leaders have a good handle on their business and industry. They are willing to admit mistakes and constantly seek more information to make informed and reasoned decisions. Good leaders base their decisions on facts. They are well-organized and detail-oriented.

These traits are essential to effective leadership and are common to most good leaders.

➤ French chef Alain Ducasse, left, cooks with his aides in the kitchen of his restaurant Le Louis XV in Monaco. Chefs like Ducasse may use a variety of leadership styles, depending on the situation.

Leadership Styles

Henry Chang runs the kitchen of a five-star restaurant. While preparing for lunch and dinner, Henry allows his staff to offer opinions as he develops the menu. Prepping for the day's meals, the staff members can choose what area in which they want to work. He also lets them experiment with different recipes and food presentations and features their work on the main menu when possible. The kitchen staff members love working with Henry because he allows them to be creative and innovative. He also encourages them to cultivate the skills they need to run their own restaurant some day. However, Henry's restaurant often attracts important political dignitaries and famous entertainers. Sometimes, the restaurant becomes unexpectedly busy. In these circumstances, Henry doesn't leave anything to chance and dictates exactly what needs to be done and who should do it. Henry knows he might hurt someone's feelings, but, ultimately, his staff trusts him to make the right decisions to obtain the best results for the restaurant.

For the most part, Henry is a **democratic leader**, delegating authority and involving employees in decision making. Because Henry knows that by involving his employees they become more invested in the process, he feels the ultimate output is better. The trade-off, Henry recognizes, is that his democratic style of leadership requires more time and advanced planning. When such time is not available, Henry must take complete charge. In those instances, he becomes an **autocratic leader**, making decisions without consulting others. A good leader knows that autocratic leadership can be an effective style in certain circumstances when quick decisions need to be made or when it seems like the group cannot come to a consensus.

Some leaders take a more hands-off approach to management and act more as consultants rather than participants. **Laissez-faire leaders (or free-reign leaders)** are more advisory in style, encouraging employees to contribute ideas rather than specifically directing their tasks. This style of leadership is often best used with groups and teams. However, it is possible for the laissez-faire leader to lose too much involvement in the group's processes. Both employees and leaders should take caution to avoid this and to make sure that all goals are aligned. If the group or team members feel that management is virtually absent, team members may choose actions and strategies that are easy but inappropriate or unethical. Laissez-faire leadership implemented properly can give employees a sense of challenge, commitment, and renewed energy as they are left to handle tasks on their own. As businesses continue to reduce the layers of management, laissez-faire and democratic styles are becoming the leadership styles of choice.

As in the case with Henry and his restaurant, no one style of leadership will work in every situation. In reality, managers recognize that they need to be flexible and use whatever style works best for the particular situation. You can think of this adaptive style of leadership as **contingency leadership**. Contingency leadership places a range of leadership styles on a continuum, such as the one in ▼ **Figure 7.8**. Those who opt for contingency leadership recognize that forces in today's business environment change, and management may need to respond to different situations in different ways.

Controlling

Why does a company need good controls? As managers form the plans and strategies to carry out the goals of the organization, they must also determine whether their plans and strategies are adequate to generate the desired results. **Controlling** is the process that ensures that the plans and strategies set in place by management are properly carried out. Controlling helps to identify and correct weaknesses and errors in the system. Such weaknesses and errors, left uncorrected, can hurt an organization and have caused large companies to implode with illegal or immoral behaviors. Chapter 3 discussed the importance of running an ethical organization. Making sure that people are doing what they should and acting appropriately is a primary

▼ **Figure 7.8**
Continuum of Leadership Behavior

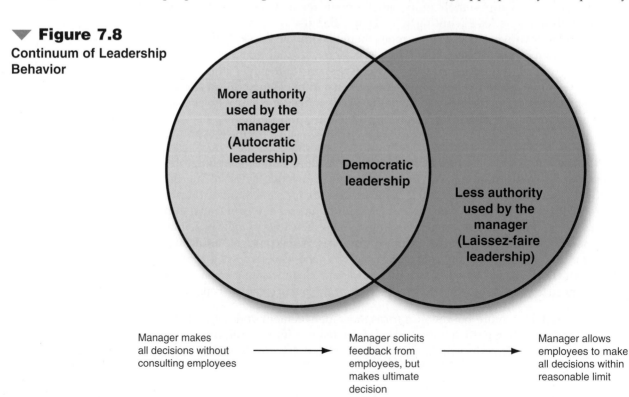

More authority used by the manager (Autocratic leadership)

Democratic leadership

Less authority used by the manager (Laissez-faire leadership)

Manager makes all decisions without consulting employees

Manager solicits feedback from employees, but makes ultimate decision

Manager allows employees to make all decisions within reasonable limit

◎ On Target Sausage Solution

In 1980, Johnsonville Sausage CEO Ralph Stayer was running a successful family business. Sales were good in the business' home state of Wisconsin and were rising in nearby Minnesota, Michigan, and Indiana. Competition from national sausage makers was always a problem, but Johnsonville had the potential to improve its performance. And even though the company was making enough money, Stayer knew they could do better. Employees were bored and making thoughtless mistakes; entire batches of sausage were thrown out because of improper handling or wrong seasoning.

Stayer knew in order for the company to fulfill its potential, he had to get employees to get motivated and care. So, over the course of the early 1980s, Stayer slowly gave employees more and more responsibilities. Until then, product quality was evaluated by senior management, not the people actually making the sausage. Stayer transferred quality control to the line workers making the product, telling them it was their responsibility to ensure good products left the plant. Line workers took control and created teams to handle problems related to taste and packaging. This one small change produced unexpected results; product rejects went from 5 percent to 0.5 percent. Line workers also took responsibility, ensuring that everyone in their department met performance standards. This was so successful that many personnel responsibilities, such as employee selection and training, were left up to line workers. Since people were taking on additional tasks, Stayer changed the company's policy for pay rates and bonuses. Additional responsibilities added additional pay to their income. Performance profits, similar to bonuses, were given every six months; calculations were based on an appraisal system and overseen by volunteers.

The true turnaround came when Stayer stopped owning problems and let his team members work them out on their own. He stopped attending meetings and reviewing product problems. He realized every word and action had meaning, whether symbolic or literal, so before reacting, he questioned whether what he was about to do or say would reinforce his vision for the company. His proudest moment came in the mid-1980s when an opportunity for extensive expansion was offered to the company. His executive board would have declined the offer because it was too risky, but Stayer posed the question to the entire company. Small groups discussed the deal, and over the course of a few days a decision was made: expansion was a go! Since the 1980s, Johnsonville Foods has expanded into 39 countries and has over 1,300 employees. Stayer maximized the company's success by reconsidering his own leadership style in favor of laissez-faire and democratic methods.[10]

---

rationale for instituting control functions in an organization. Controls also pick up errors in the system, so if a plan is not meeting its goals, it can be modified.

There are three broad control strategies that managers use either individually or in combination to achieve organizational control: bureaucratic control, market control, and clan control.[11] Each control strategy serves a different purpose:

- **Bureaucratic control** uses rules, regulations, and formal authority to guide performance. Budgets, statistical reports, and performance appraisals are all part of bureaucratic control.

- **Market control** involves evaluating workers on their attainment of specific objectives. Performance goals are set at various levels, and periodic reviews determine whether the goals have been achieved. Rewards (pay raises and promotions) are tied to goal attainment.
- **Clan control** assumes that employees and management have common goals and values and therefore will measure and monitor one another without the need for more formal external controls. Clan control is based on the concept that employees trust each other and, if invested in the same goals and values, will act for the best benefit of themselves, as well as the organization.

Most companies have control systems that help measure the plans they set in place to carry out the goals and objectives of the organization. In general, the control system forms a cycle, as shown in ▼ Figure 7.9: performance standards are set, performance is measured and compared against the standard, adjustments are made, and the cycle begins again.

Measuring Performance

To manage a business and ensure that the goals are being met, managers measure performance in a variety of ways. Bureaucratic reporting tools such as financial statements and sales reports are used to measure performance. These reports help determine whether the products are competitive, are using capital wisely, and are being produced as efficiently as possible. In addition to meeting financial, production, and sales measures, another measure of performance is quality so that the products or services the company provides meet or exceed customer requirements. Many managers use **total quality management**, an integrated approach to quality management that focuses on quality from the beginning of the production process up through managerial involvement to detect and correct problems. Another quality initiative that is receiving much attention is **Six Sigma**, a statistically based, proactive, long-term process designed to look at the overall business

▼ **Figure 7.9**
The Control Cycle

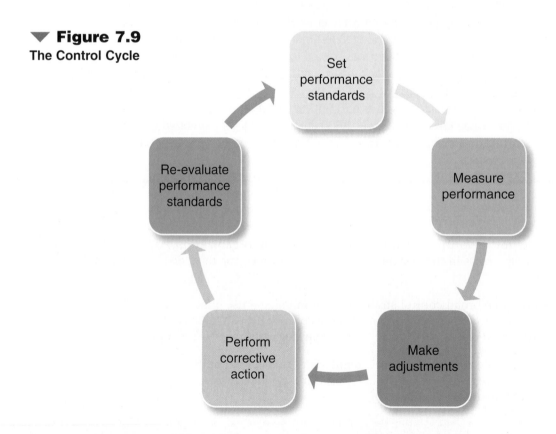

"I don't know how it started, either. All I know is that it's part of our corporate culture."

process to prevent problems. To achieve the Six Sigma standard, a business must not allow more than 3.4 defects per million opportunities.

Corporate Culture

As you have learned, management creates a mission statement and vision to keep them focused on corporate strategy and objectives. The mission statement and vision also help create the "feel" or workplace environment, also known as the corporate culture. The **corporate culture** is a collection of values, norms, and behavior shared by management and workers that defines the character of the organization. Google, for example, has a unique culture, set by a corporate philosophy that includes statements such as "You can make money without doing evil" and "Work should be challenging and fun."[12]

In a corporation in which the culture is not well defined, or even worse, it supports questionable behavior, problems result. This was the case for the natural-gas giant Enron, which eventually went bankrupt because of significant lack of control and poor ethical behavior from top management. On the other hand, when the corporate culture is strong, and all employees accept the culture as their own, they are motivated to maintain it and monitor their own behavior. Revisit the quiz at the beginning of the section. Are you more comfortable separating fact and fiction now? Although many myths and half-truths prevail concerning the complex roles of leadership and controls in business, at least one fact is fairly simple: strong leadership and effective controls are key components of business success.

▼ You have just read **Objectives 6 & 7**

Want to learn more? Check out the Study Plan section @
www.mybizlab.com.

1. In what ways do managers apply technical, interpersonal, decision-making, conceptual, and time management skills to business? (pp. 195-198)

- **Technical skills** (p. 196) include the abilities and knowledge that enable a manager to carry out the specific tasks required of a discipline.

- **Interpersonal skills** (p. 196) are those skills that enable a manager to communicate and interact with other people in order to engage and motivate them to achieve the organization's goals.

- **Decision-making skills** (p. 196) are those skills that enable a manager to identify and analyze a problem, examine the alternatives, choose and implement the best plan of action, and evaluate the results.

- **Conceptual skills** (p. 197) refer to the ability to think abstractly and to view the organization as a whole.

- **Time management skills** (p. 198) refer to the ability to achieve the maximum amount of productivity in a set amount of time.

2. What strategies do managers use to reach the corporate vision and mission statement and keep the company on task? (pp. 199-202)

- Managers use planning, goals, and objectives to help achieve the corporate vision and to stay on task.

  - **Planning** (p. 199) is the process of establishing goals and objectives and determining the best ways to accomplish them.

  - **Goals** (p. 199) are broad, long-term accomplishments an organization wants to achieve in about a five-year time frame.

  - **Objectives** (p. 199) are the short-term targets that are designed to help achieve goals.

- Top managers put together a **strategic plan** (p. 200), or a main course of action, that maps out the means by which the corporation will achieve its goals.

  - Before the strategic plan is in place, management must define the organization's purpose, basic goals, and philosophies through a **mission statement** (p. 200). The corporate **vision** (p. 200) describes why the company is in business and what the business will look like in the future.

  - Part of the strategic planning process is conducting a **SWOT analysis** (p. 202) to help management determine the strategic fit between an organization's internal capabilities and external possibilities. The SWOT analysis stands for **S**trengths, **W**eaknesses, **O**pportunities, and **T**hreats.

3. What are the implications of tactical plans, operational plans, and contingency plans within the context of management? (pp. 202-203)

- **Tactical plans** (p. 202) specifically determine the resources and the actions required to implement particular aspects of the strategic plan.

  - Tactical plans are made with a one- to three-year horizon in mind and are determined by middle management.

- **Operational plans** (p. 202) determine the process by which tactical plans can be achieved.

  - Operational plans depend on daily or weekly schedules and focus more on specific departments or employees.

  - Operational plans are determined by first-line managers.

- **Contingency planning** (p. 203) is a set of plans that ensures that the organization will run as smoothly as possible during a disruption and determines how management will communicate, both internally and externally.

  - Internally, management must inform its employees how they should continue to do their jobs.

  - Externally, an organization must have a plan in place to deal with requests for information from employees, the families of employees, or even the media.

4. What is the significance of organizing, and how is most management organized? (pp. 204-205)

- **Organizing** (p. 204) is the process of arranging capital, personnel, and other resources to carry out whatever plans management has in place.

- An organization traditionally is structured with **top managers**, **middle managers**, and **first-line managers** (pp. 204–205); this is known as the managerial pyramid.

5. What are the differences among vertical organizations, horizontal organizations, and network organizations? (pp. 205-207)

- A **vertical organization** (p. 205) is organized by specific function, such as marketing, finance, purchasing, information technology, and human resources.

  - Managers can better keep track of economic and environmental conditions that affect their functional area.

  - Potential problems may arise because integration between functions and divisions is not always easy.

  - Vertical organization usually calls for long lines of communication and "reporting up."

- A **horizontal organization** (p. 206) is flattened, and the management layer is collapsed. This type of organization

Continued on next page

concentrates the majority of the employees into working teams or groups.

- Teams have more responsibility for the outcome of their work.
- Bosses' approval can be sought and received much faster.
- **Network organizations** (p. 207) are collections of independent, mostly single-function firms that collaborate on a product or service.

6. What makes a good leader, and what are the various styles of leadership? (pp. 208-212)

- There are several traits that most leadership analysts agree make a good leader. These include:
  - determination
  - inspiration
  - flexibility and empathy
  - innovativeness
  - honesty
  - self-confidence
  - knowledge and competence
- The various styles of leadership are democratic, autocratic, and laissez-faire.
  - **Democratic leaders** (p. 211) delegate authority and involve employees in decision making.
  - An **autocratic leader** (p. 211) makes decisions without consulting others and dictates assignments.
- A **laissez-faire leader** (p. 211) is more hands-off and advisory in style and encourages employees to contribute and act on their own ideas.

7. What are the implications of control within a business? (pp. 212-215)

- There are three broad control strategies that managers use to achieve organizational control. These include:
  - bureaucratic control, which uses rules, regulations, and formal authority to guide performance.
  - market control, which involves evaluating workers on their attainment of specific objectives.
  - clan control, which assumes that employees and management have common goals and values.
- Most companies have a control system, which forms a cycle that helps measure the plans set in place to carry out the goals and objectives of the organization.
- Performance standards are measured with bureaucratic reporting tools such as financial statements and sales reports. Quality measures are also in place to ensure that products or services meet customer requirements.
- **Corporate culture** (p. 215), or the workplace environment, also helps set the tone for personnel to monitor themselves.

For an audio file of the Objectives and Chapter Summary, see the Student Resources section @ www.my*biz*lab.com.

Key Terms

autocratic leaders (p. 211)

conceptual skills (p. 197)

contingency leadership (p. 212)

contingency planning (p. 203)

controlling (p. 212)

corporate culture (p. 215)

decision-making skills (p. 196)

democratic leaders (p. 211)

first-line manager (p. 205)

goal (p. 199)

horizontal organization (p. 206)

interpersonal skills (p. 196)

laissez-faire (free-reign) leader (p. 211)

leading (p. 208)

management (p. 195)

middle managers (p. 205)

mission statement (p. 200)

network organizations (p. 207)

objective (p. 199)

operational plans (p. 202)

organizational chart (p. 205)

organizing (p. 204)

planning (p. 199)

Six Sigma (p. 214)

strategic plan (p. 200)

SWOT analysis (p. 202)

tactical plans (p. 202)

technical skills (p. 196)

time management skills (p. 198)

top managers (p. 204)

total quality management (p. 214)

vertical organization (p. 205)

vision (p. 200)

Multiple Choice   Correct answers can be found on page 503.

1. The four primary processes of management are

    a. planning, optimizing, leading, and controlling.

    b. organizing, controlling, planning, and leading.

    c. prioritizing, leading, controlling, and organizing.

    d. planning, leading, organizing, and controlling.

2. In business terms, a(n) _____ is a broad, long-range accomplishment and a(n) _____ is a specific, short-term target.

    a. goal; objective

    b. objective; goal

    c. objective; task

    d. task; goal

3. Julius has the reputation of being a great manager. He is able to interact well with his employees, as well as motivate and encourage them because Julius has good

    a. interpersonal skills.

    b. administrative skills.

    c. conceptual skills.

    d. marketable skills.

4. The organization you work for just hired a new CEO. Within the first week in her new position, the CEO drafted a memo for the board and members of senior management that defined the purpose of the business, as well as the basic goals and philosophies of the business. This document serves as a draft of a new

    a. vision.

    b. mission statement.

    c. goals and objectives statement.

    d. tactical plan.

5. A good strategic plan

    a. determines the best ways to accomplish goals of the organization.

    b. is specific and tactical.

    c. concentrates only on what is going on inside the organization, not outside the organization.

    d. is wide-ranging.

6. A businesses organized primarily by division or function is considered to be

    a. a horizontal organization.

    b. a vertical organization.

    c. a network organization.

    d. a tactical organization.

7. Stuart is a senior executive vice president of the information technology department in his organization. He has been in the IT field for nearly two decades and considers himself an expert in all areas of IT. Because of that, Stu dictates every assignment to each of the managers in his department, leaving very little room for them to make mistakes. Which of the following styles of leadership would best describe Stuart?

    a. Laissez-faire

    b. Democratic

    c. Autocratic

    d. None of the above

8. Bureaucratic controls are an important strategy for achieving organizational control. Which would not be considered a bureaucratic control?

    a. A financial budget

    b. A senior management performance appraisal

    c. A sales report

    d. A competitive analysis

9. Shauna is the sales manager for a regional chain of bookstores. Shauna reports to the executive vice president of sales and marketing, and each sales manager reports to Shauna. Shauna would be considered

    a. a top manager.

    b. a middle manager.

    c. a first-line manager.

    d. both b and c

10. Which would *not* be something that describes an organization's culture?

    a. The manner in which employees dressed

    b. How employees interact with each other

    c. The objectives of the corporation's strategic plan

    d. The ability for workers to have flexible hours

Self-Test

True/False Correct answers can be found on page 503.

1. A person who is a manager is also always a leader.
   ☐ **True** or ☐ **False**

2. A SWOT analysis is used to determine the strategic fit between the organization and its internal and external environments.
   ☐ **True** or ☐ **False**

3. When a company is organized primarily in teams or groups, it is considered a vertical organization.
   ☐ **True** or ☐ **False**

4. Every manager has only one style of leadership with which he or she is comfortable using in all situations.
   ☐ **True** or ☐ **False**

5. A good manager will use different styles of leadership in different circumstances.
   ☐ **True** or ☐ **False**

Critical Thinking Questions

1. Think back to your own personal working experience and the managers with whom you have had interaction. Discuss the qualities that define the best manager with whom you have worked and discuss the qualities that define the worst manager with whom you have worked.

2. Contingency plans are important in any business. Discuss what kinds of plans your school might have in place. How would these plans differ, if at all, from those of a local business in your area? What are a few possible scenarios that would require contingency plans in your school or at a local business?

3. How do you rank leadership qualities? Rank the following qualities and compare your results with your classmates: honest, loyal, competent, caring, determined, ambitious, inspiring, forward-looking, self-confident, and imaginative. What are the top three qualities?

4. Analyze your own ability to be a manager. What skills do you have now that are already polished? What skills would you need to improve? What skills would you still need to acquire? How could you go about acquiring or improving those skills you do not have?

5. What are some of the challenges management must face today due to changes in technology, globalization, and diversification?

Team Time

On a Mission

Research and print several mission statements. Be sure to choose statements from both nonprofit organizations and for-profit organizations. Bring these mission statements to class.

Process

Step 1. Assemble into groups of four or five.

Step 2. As a group, evaluate the mission statements you've chosen for similar components, such as a statement of the product, service, or primary market; an indication of commitment to quality; an indication of a commitment to social responsibility; and a declaration of corporate philosophy.

Step 3. Make notes of the components that are included in the majority of mission statements and those that are included in only a few mission statements.

Step 4. As a group, decide which mission statement is the most inspiring. Why? Which is the least inspiring? Why?

Step 5. As a class, compare the statements deemed most inspiring from each group and determine which of those is the most effective. Finally, openly discuss with your classmates how the winning statement would affect their inclination to work for this organization.

Ethics and Corporate Social Responsibility

Assessing Social Responsibility

One of the functions of management is control, which includes measuring financial performance. But how often and with what tools does a manager assess an organization's social responsibility?

Process

Step 1. As a class, in small discussion groups, discuss the following:

- the planning and organizational changes that might need to be implemented
- the controls that a manager might use to measure and monitor the results of his or her social responsibility initiatives
- any changes in leadership styles that might result from a focus on social responsibility

Step 2. After this discussion, research companies that are known for their social responsibility efforts. Then, discuss what impact their efforts have had on management.

Web Exercises

1. **What's the Mission?**
   Check the Web for a company that produces a product you particularly like and use often. What is their mission statement? Does it adequately reflect the company as you perceive it?

2. **Organizational Charts: The Big Picture**
   Check the Web for a company's organization chart, an organization chart for the company you work for, or the organizational chart for your school. Analyze the chart and determine whether the company or school is structured vertically or horizontally. Can you find an organizational chart for a competitor? Critique both organizational charts. Are the two company's organizational charts similar? Do you think your company or school could be structured in any other way? Why or why not?

3. **How Well Do You Manage Your Time?**
   Time management skills are important for a manager to have in order to work efficiently and accomplish all the tasks a manager is expected to handle on any given day. How are your time management skills? Even as a student, you are your own manager and can benefit from being more in control of your time. Find a quiz online that assesses your ability to manage your time. Write a brief report answering the following questions:
   - What online assessment did you find?
   - What were the results?
   - How can you improve your time management skills?

4. **Manager Wanted**
   Search the Web for a classified advertisement seeking a manager. What sort of qualities is the company looking for in a manager? What sort of leadership skills does the position require?

5. **Culture Shock**
   New employees often need at least a few weeks to feel comfortable in the corporate culture that comes with their new job. Search the Web for a corporate Web site. How specifically does the company describe their corporate culture? What does the description tell you about life as an employee at that company? Would you want to work there?

Web Case

To access the Chapter 7 Web case and exercise, see the End of Chapter Assignments section @ www.my*biz*lab.com.

Video Case

To access the Chapter 7 Video case and exercise, see the End of Chapter Assignments section @ www.my*biz*lab.com.

chapter 8

Motivation, Leadership, and Teamwork

p. **227**

Motivation: Business Applications
▼ Objectives 3-5
At Ana Gutierrez's public relations firm, the employees were suffering from a severe case of demotivation. Translating motivational theories into practical applications is a challenge many business managers face. How could Ana use abstract concepts about human behavior to inspire her workforce and turn around her struggling company?

p. **232**

Leadership
▼ Objective 6
True leadership comes when someone steps in and begins not just doing things right, but doing the right things. When Andrew Smithson purchased a leather goods store in 1997, the store was in terrible shape: sales were down, employees were bored, and the building housing the store was falling apart. Smithson had a clear vision of the future, and he knew that with hard work and determination he could turn the store around. What do you think Smithson did to create a successful business?

p. **223**

Motivation: The Basics
▼ Objectives 1 & 2
Feeling driven and inspired to complete a task—this is what it means to be motivated. Do you ever feel this way? Understanding personal motivation, recognizing the role of motivation in the workplace, and examining theories that explain it are important parts of business.

p. **237**

Teamwork
▼ Objective 7
Teamwork can bring about great success in business. This was the case with the development of the Motorola Razr. But effective teams must be created and managed thoughtfully in order for businesses to reap the benefits. How can managers accomplish this?

Motivation: The Basics pp. 223-226

We hear people use the word *motivation* often. When players stay on the field an extra 30 minutes after the end of practice to keep working on a skill, we say they are motivated athletes. When students seek out extra learning opportunities to go beyond a course's general requirements, they are described as motivated learners. But what does motivation have to do with working in a business? Are all of a business owner's actions motivated solely by profit? Does an employer who pays well always have strongly motivated employees? In this chapter, we'll examine motivation in detail and look at techniques used in the past and in the present to motivate employees.

Personal Motivation

What drives you to do your personal best? Even when pursuing personal goals, each of us retains and loses our motivation for very singular reasons. Think of times that you have pushed to be your best, whether at school, in sports, or in other activities. Is it easier for you to build enthusiasm for tasks that you're sure you can accomplish? Or do you set difficult goals and draw energy from the challenge of attaining them? Some people need immediate gratification or success in order to stay motivated. Others are able to postpone short-term success in pursuit of long-term gains. Do you need to be rewarded immediately for what you do, or are you more motivated by long-term benefits?

Now think about how hard you work when you receive a lot of positive feedback (either financial or emotional). Is getting praise or money for a job important to you? Or are you driven more by the values of the place where you work, your beliefs, or in doing a

Feeling motivated often involves the achievement of an intangible yet valuable state called *flow*. Are you a flow-stater? Or does the flow state float right past you? Take this quiz to find out.

1. When completing a task, I feel completely involved and focused on what I'm doing.
   a. Always
   b. Sometimes
   c. Never

2. I lose track of time when I'm working on a project or assignment.
   a. Always
   b. Sometimes
   c. Never

3. I feel like tasks are challenging yet doable.
   a. Always
   b. Sometimes
   c. Never

4. I feel like work isn't really "work"; it seems natural and effortless.
   a. Always
   b. Sometimes
   c. Never

5. I feel in control and content when tackling a project.
   a. Always
   b. Sometimes
   c. Never

Answers: If you answered . . .
Mostly a's . . . You are a flow-stater of the highest degree.
Mostly b's . . . You foray into flow state on occasion.
Mostly c's . . . Your familiarity with flow state is almost nonexistent.

job well? For some people, being part of the accomplishments of a team is what motivates them. You may not be sure what exactly motivates you. If so, there are tests you can take to determine your own motivational style.

Flow

Have you ever been working on a project and you were so immersed in what you were doing that when you looked at your watch, four hours had gone by? Psychologist Mihaly Csikszentmihalyi refers to this state of rapt attention as **flow**.[1] A flow state happens when you are completely involved and focused on what you are doing. Often people produce their best work, make the best use of their skills, and feel the most pleasure when they are in such a flow state. They feel a strong match between their own abilities and the challenge of a task—it is neither too difficult, which can lead to frustration, nor too simple, which can lead to boredom. They report a sense of control over what is happening and a feeling of effortlessness in their working. So how do you create this sense of flow? Creating a workplace that fosters this kind of motivation is the subject of **organizational psychology**—the study of how to create a workplace that fosters motivation and productivity among employees.

Motivation in the Workplace

How does a work environment encourage "flow"? The *Q12* is a twelve-question survey of employee engagement administered by the Gallup Organization. Based on respondents' answers to a series of questions, it classifies employees as "engaged," "not engaged," or "actively disengaged" (see ▼ **Table 8.1**). According to the survey's 2007 results, 73 percent of U.S. employees are not engaged or actively disengaged in their work.[2] This statistic makes clear that encouraging flow in the workplace is a challenge.

One company that has succeeded in creating an environment that engages workers and supports the creative experience of flow is SAS, a business software company located in North Carolina. With an incredibly low employee turnover rate of just 2 to 5 percent and revenues of over $1 billion, the company has created such an atmosphere in part thanks to the policies of CEO Jim Goodnight. Goodnight lists the following as ways in which SAS works to foster a creative environment:

- It keeps employees intellectually engaged.
- It removes distractions so employees can do their best work.
- It makes managers responsible for sparking creativity.
- It has managers eliminate the arbitrary distinctions between administrative "suits" and more abstract "creatives."
- It engages customers as creative partners.

▼ **Table 8.1**

Types of Employees		
Engaged	**Not engaged**	**Actively disengaged**
Work with passion	Work with minimal effort	Work in a disruptive manner
Feel connected and obligated to the company	Are indifferent to the company	Are unhappy with the company
Add to the success of the company	Make little or no contribution to the company	Combat the efforts of engaged workers

In addition to fostering strong professional lives, SAS supports its employees in their private lives as well. On the SAS campus, you'll find medical facilities for employees and their dependents, a Montessori day care center, and a cafeteria where families can eat lunch together. "The corporate philosophy is, if your fifth grader is in his first school play, you should be there to see it," says Goodnight. Such a philosophy has led to SAS earning a spot on *Working Mother* magazine's list of best companies.[3]

The Benefits of Keeping Employees Motivated

Both employer and employee benefit from a motivated workforce. Employers find workers are more productive, more creative, and have much better retention levels when care is taken to provide a motivating environment and tasks. Employees often spend the majority of their waking day at their jobs, and their quality of life and overall happiness are enhanced when they feel excited about the work they contribute. In fact, according to Gallup's calculations, the cost to the U.S. economy from disengaged employees is up to $350 billion a year in reduced productivity.[4] The results of a 1997 study commissioned by Sears Roebuck support the idea that employee motivation significantly influences company revenue. It found that increased employee-satisfaction scores at stores led to increased customer-satisfaction scores. This, in turn, led to a growth in revenue.[5]

Theories of Motivation

What are the different theories for what motivates people?

Several theories explain how and why people are motivated.

Maslow's Hierarchy of Needs

One early researcher in the area of human motivation was Abraham Maslow (1908–1970), who published the book *The Hierarchy of Needs* in 1954. In his theory of motivation, Maslow suggests that humans have a **hierarchy of needs**, and that primary needs are met first before higher-level needs are addressed (see ▼ **Figure 8.1**). The first needs to be met are inborn, basic needs—termed **physiological needs**—such as the need for water, food, sleep, and reproduction. This means that before we as humans can think about anything else in our lives, we must ensure that these basic physiological needs are met.

Once our physiological needs have been met, Maslow's theory holds that people strive to satisfy **safety needs**. This includes establishing safe and stable places to live and work. Once both physiological and safety needs have been met, we can consider social or **belonging needs**. This includes the need to belong to a group and to feel accepted by others. The next level in Maslow's hierarchy includes **esteem needs**. These are satisfied by the mastery of a skill and by the attention and recognition of others. Finally, at the top of the hierarchy are **self-actualization needs**. These needs include the desire to maximize your own potential through education, self-fulfillment, as well as experiences of

▼ **Figure 8.1**
Maslow's Hierarchy of Needs

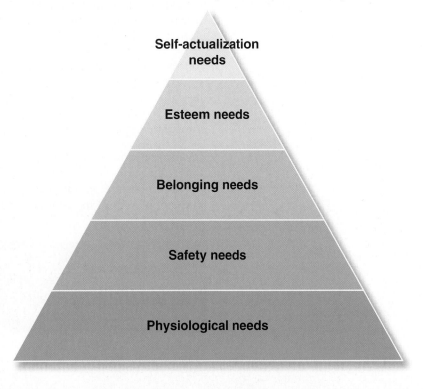

Self-actualization needs

Esteem needs

Belonging needs

Safety needs

Physiological needs

beauty and spirituality. These higher-level self-actualization needs cannot be addressed unless and until the lower level needs have been adequately met.

Maslow suggested that different people find themselves at different places in the hierarchy and so their motivations may be different. While an offer of overtime pay may be a successful motivator for a person concerned with safety needs, it might be the opposite of what someone working to satisfy their need for self-actualization finds motivating.

McClelland's "Three Needs" Theory

Other researchers have proposed different models to map human needs to motivation. Psychologist David McClelland's (1917–1998) **"three needs" theory** suggests there are three main motivators:

- *the need for achievement*—to accomplish something difficult on your own
- *the need for affiliation*—to form close personal relationships
- *the need for power*—to be able to control the behavior of others

According to McClelland, which need we try to satisfy depends on a variety of complex factors, including our cultural background. Although an individual may have multiple needs, McClelland suggests that one tends to be dominant over the others. In a workplace, this theory could account for differences in motivation among coworkers. For example, a person whose main need is for affiliation may have little motivation to perform a solitary task, whereas a person with a high need for achievement may be highly motivated to perform a difficult task alone.

Herzberg's Motivator-Hygiene Theory

In 1959, psychologist Frederick Herzberg (1923–2000) proposed a theory for job satisfaction called the **motivator-hygiene theory** (or **two-factor theory**). According to the theory, two factors influence a person's motivation. **Hygiene factors** are factors such as a safe working environment, proper pay and benefits, and positive relationships with co-workers. People rarely notice hygiene factors if they are present. However, if hygiene factors are absent or inadequate, people tend to be dissatisfied. Consider basic working conditions, benefits, or other company policies. If there suddenly is no heat in the place where you work or if your pay is cut, you may be motivated to find a way to meet these needs. But if these are already in place, they are taken for granted and may not serve to motivate you.

The second set of factors in Herzberg's theory are **motivator factors**. These factors include a sense of responsibility, recognition, promotion, and job growth. Consider the self-actualization needs from Maslow's hierarchy. If there is no path for growth in your job or little recognition of your achievements, you probably would not immediately quit, but it would create a set of conditions that fail to motivate you.

Review the flow state quiz you took at the beginning of the chapter. Do you understand now what a flow state is and why it is important? What are the benefits of flow state in the workplace? And how can the different theories of motivation account for your achievement, or lack thereof, of flow state?

▼ You have just read **Objectives 1 & 2**

Think you got it? Check out the Study Plan section @
www.mybizlab.com.

Motivation: Business Applications pp. 227-231

> Using motivational theories to address the practical matters of motivation in the workplace is no easy task. Finding a way to inspire employees often requires patience and persistence. Fortunately, motivational theories that specifically take into account the dynamics of the business environment abound, giving managers many options from which to choose.

Applying Motivational Theories

Do managers actually use theories of motivation? Theories of motivation can be very abstract. How can a manager of an assembly line at an automotive plant or a team leader of a software development company take what researchers know about human behavior and use it to increase productivity and the satisfaction of the employees? The theories of human motivation you have just read about have given rise to a number of different approaches to organize and motivate people in the workplace.

What could a manager do to enhance employee motivation? In the workplace, there are some external motivating factors that managers can control. These motivators, called **extrinsic motivators**, include such things as pay, promotion, and verbal praise. Other factors, called **intrinsic motivators**, are outside the set of factors under a manager's control because they are internal to each individual employee. These

"All of my employees were so . . . *uninspired*," Ana Gutierrez laments. "People seemed to be just 'showing up'; the sense of apathy in the office was almost palpable. The quality of our work was suffering. I wasn't sure what to do."

Ana, the founder and CEO of a small public relations firm, was facing a crisis of motivation within her workforce. The sales team hadn't scored a new account in months, and existing clients were complaining about their representation. "You're not delivering on your promises," one client, the leader of a local nonprofit, blurted during a particularly tense conference call. "A recent event was poorly advertised and poorly attended. There were errors in the latest press release. And your associates take two days to respond to my e-mails."

Ana had already tried a variety of tactics to motivate her employees. She dangled the possibility of additional bonuses and free dinners to the sales teams, to no avail. She instituted a new policy requiring all employees to work nine hours a day, plus two weekends a month. It didn't work. She told her associates she was prepared to promote at least three of the highest-performing employees among them to more lucrative positions within six months. No one was interested.

Ana's problem is not uncommon. Many managers struggle to motivate their employees effectively. How could Ana apply what she knows about motivational theories to light a fire under her employees and save her business? >

motivating influences are based on a person's actual interest in his or her work and stem from the sense of purpose or value a person derives from the work being done. In 2006, an educational study in England showed the differences between these two types of motivators.[6] Children from a boys' school and a girls' school were asked to make a poster about their lives. One group was told its poster would decorate a local hospital for sick children. The other group was told it would be paid for its work. Which group of children would produce the better work—those who perceived the task as being worthwhile or those who were promised payment? In this case, much more sophisticated and detailed work came from the group that was working for free. The children were motivated more by the knowledge that they would be helping sick children than by financial reward.

Different people have different balances between intrinsic and extrinsic motivators. So how can business managers best motivate all of their employees? An individual motivated intrinsically is working for his or her own satisfaction and may value challenging work he or she perceives as meaningful to the company more than extrinsic factors like pay. Intrinsic motivators also tend to be higher on Maslow's hierarchy. So, for example, a boss who offers unsatisfying work, even though he or she offers bonuses and promotions, will have difficulty motivating an intrinsically motivated worker.

Motivational Models Used in Business

In addition to the theories proposed by Maslow, McClelland, and Herzberg, several models have been developed that provide theoretical explanations of what motivates employees specifically in a business or workplace context.

Theory X and Theory Y Models In 1960, the social psychologist Douglas McGregor proposed the Theory X and Theory Y models (see ▼ **Table 8.2**). The **Theory X** model suggests a view of humans as inherently disliking work and wanting to avoid it. Because of this view, Theory X management suggests employees have to be coerced and controlled by management in order to be productive. This leads to an authoritarian, hard-line management style. In contrast, the **Theory Y** model suggests that people view work as being as natural as playing and resting. People are naturally motivated and will direct themselves to work for the aims of

▼ **Table 8.2**

Comparison of Theory X and Theory Y		
Theory X		**Theory Y**
Not motivated: People naturally dislike working and avoid it when given the opportunity.	**Motivation**	**Naturally motivated:** People see work as a natural part of life.
Authoritarian: Managers must use heavy controls to get people to work efficiently.	**Management**	**Democratic:** Managers need not use heavy controls. Managers allow employees to create their own motivation.
Followers: Employees would prefer to follow the direction of management than solve problems on their own.	**Leadership**	**Leaders:** People are creative problem-solvers whose ideas can be used in the workplace.
Avoiders: People do not want responsibility and avoid it when possible.	**Responsibility**	**Seekers:** People inherently seek responsibility and are willing to accept it when asked.
Security: People are not complex and mainly want security in their jobs.	**Needs**	**Creativity:** People need to be intellectually stimulated and feel their ideas are utilized.

the organization if they are satisfied with their jobs. Theory Y managers believe that, on average, people will accept and seek out responsibility. Such managers have a softer style of management that involves the participation of many.

Clearly, Theories X and Y would not work equally well in any given situation. Theory X-style management—which is authoritarian and hard line—is often seen in large-scale operations like mass manufacturing. In the knowledge industry, in which there is a mix of professionals working together to solve complex problems, Theory Y is more likely to be seen with a participative, gentler management style.

Theory Z Model In 1981, William Ouchi put forward a **Theory Z** model based on a Japanese management style that relied heavily on collaborative decision making. In many corporations in Japan in the 1980s, one person might be responsible for many different aspects of a single project. Employees tended to become generalists rather than specialists, who were trained in a very narrow set of tasks. Theory Z management offers long-term employment with an emphasis on individual responsibility. Workers tend to show a desire to cooperate and be loyal to the organization. As a result, companies that apply Theory Z management often reap the benefits of low turnover, high productivity, and strong morale among the workforce. Morale, a sense of purpose and enthusiasm toward one's work, is an important factor in an employee's level of motivation.

Vroom Model Although Maslow's hierarchy and other theories describe human motivation, they do so in terms of an overall model for all employees. In 1964, Victor Vroom proposed a theory named **expectancy theory**, which has been developed by other researchers since. Expectancy theory suggests an individual's motivation can be described by the relationship among three psychological forces. He put forward the following formula to describe the motivation a person feels in any given situation:

"We reward top executives at the agency with a unique incentive program. Money."

Motivation = Expectancy * Instrumentality * Valence

Expectancy is the idea that a person's effort has an appreciable effect on a situation's result, whether it is a success or failure. Does working harder lead to a more positive outcome for the employee and/or the company? Or does it not make a difference? This is what expectancy measures. **Instrumentality** refers to the idea that the outcome of a situation is related to rewards or punishment. For those who are extrinsically motivated, instrumentality answers the question, "What are the chances I'm going to be rewarded if I do a good job?" For those who are intrinsically motivated, instrumentality answers the question, "How good will I feel if I can accomplish this task?" **Valence** is the importance that the individual places on the expected outcome of a situation. It answers questions such as "How great a reward will there be if my performance is exemplary?" and "How serious a punishment do I expect if I underperform?" In common terms, Vroom's formulas for high and low motivations read as follows:

High Motivation = (My work actually affects the outcome) * (There's a good chance I'll get a reward if this works out) * (If it works out, it'll be a really big reward!)

Low Motivation = (Nothing I do is going to impact this situation) * (Even if it does go well, I probably won't see any benefit) * (The only reward from this is incredibly small)

The Vroom formula can be used to analyze factors including how satisfied employees are at their jobs, how likely it is they will remain at their jobs, and how hard they will work at their jobs. In addition, unlike Maslow's and McClelland's models, which address typical needs across large groups of people, Vroom's model, with its three independent variables measuring the specific levels of expectancy, instrumentality, and valence, can generate a much more specialized result, attuned to the mental state of a specific individual.

Strength-Based Management Management often works to help employees improve skills in areas in which they are weak. But is this the best investment of resources for a corporation? **Strength-based management** is a system based on the belief that, rather than improve weak skills, the best way to help employees develop is to determine their strengths and build on them.[7] This system is supported by research that shows that people can learn the most about areas in which they already have a strong foundation. Strength-based programs identify employees' current talents and skills and then provide additional training and support to develop them into areas of excellence.[8]

Evolution of Motivational Theories in Business

How have motivational theories changed? In the early 20th century, as the Industrial Age saw the creation of large corporations, issues of efficiency and labor costs became critical. Researchers like Frederick Taylor (1856–1950) began to study how to manage people optimally. In 1911, Taylor published his findings in *The Principles of Scientific Management*. Based on his research and experimentation, he proposed ways that managers could increase productivity. He encouraged managers to use scientific study to determine the best methods to complete tasks and then to train employees in these methods. Many of his ideas were implemented in factories. By the 1920s and 1930s, a field of academic study called **industrial psychology** was created to further address these issues. The objective of industrial psychology is to understand scientifically how to manage employees and work optimally. Other researchers, such as Frank and Lillian Gilbreath, used photography to study employee work patterns and then analyzed these patterns to increase productivity. For example, they used time-motion studies to analyze factory jobs and then train workers in the precise sequence of steps that would make them most productive.

Another famous study of the period was Harvard professor Elton Mayo's work at the Hawthorne plant of the Western Electric Company in Illinois. The study ran from 1927 to 1932 and examined physical influences on the workplace (such as lighting and humidity) as well as psychological aspects (such as group pressure and working hours). The major finding, known as the **Hawthorne effect**, was that *regardless of the experimental changes made*, the production of the workers improved. Researchers concluded that the increase in productivity was based on the attention the workers were receiving. Because they knew they were being studied, the employees felt special and produced more, regardless of the conditions Hawthorne studied. The Hawthorne effect is used now as a term to describe the increase in productivity caused by workers being given special attention. After World War II, the direction of research in management theory shifted from management of an individual worker toward management of the entire organization, its structure, and policies.

Motivational Theories for the Modern Workplace

The fields of organizational psychology and industrial psychology are still very active, and new theories of management practices continue to appear. These theories aim to better describe and understand the challenges in managing a modern, globalized, knowledge-based economy. One recent theory is the **uncertainty management theory**, which suggests that when people face increased uncertainty, fairness becomes more important to them. They have very strong reactions to actions and situations they judge to be unfair, which in turn influences their job satisfaction and performance.[9]

Another theory for motivating and organizing a modern workplace is based on the idea of **sociocracy**. Sociocracy is a system of organization and management in which the interests of everyone are served equally. In a sociocracy, all members of the organization are involved in decision making, and the final decision must be acceptable to all.[10] This doesn't mean everyone has to love the decision, but the goal is that no one finds the decision impossible to live with. Companies adopting a system of sociocracy find that workers feel they are treated fairly, are appreciated, and are respected. Proponents of sociocracy claim the system naturally fosters innovation, creativity, and a sense of belongingness among employees. One company using the concept of sociocracy is Ternary Software. The Philadelphia-based company has been named one of the best places to work in the Philadelphia region and is one of the fastest growing companies in the area.[11] Its founder, Brian Robertson, believes the model of "decision making by consent" has helped his company more efficiently develop software and has created a culture in which very highly motivated employees flourish. The system appears to be paying off: revenue at Ternary is increasing an average of 50 percent a year. "We could never have achieved this under a traditional management system,"[12] Robertson says.

Remember Ana Gutierrez and her team of uninspired public relations professionals? "I realized that extrinsic motivators didn't have much of an effect on my employees, nor did a hard-line management style based on the Theory X model," she says. "So I changed my approach, and I soon saw positive results." In an attempt to increase the level of intrinsic motivation among her employees, Ana met with her associates and asked them which accounts they found most meaningful and satisfying to work on. She modified her staff appropriately and found that levels of motivation increased when employees worked with clients with whom they felt a personal connection. Ana also eliminated the nine-hour day mandate, but soon found that many of her newly motivated employees voluntarily worked at least that many hours, if not more! The company, once struggling, now flourishes; sales are up, and clients are thrilled. With experimentation and careful thought, Ana achieved the goal of all business managers: translating motivational theory into business success.

Fortune's Top 10 Companies to Work For, 2008

1. Google
2. Quicken Loans
3. Wegmans Food Markets
4. Edward Jones
5. Genentech
6. Cisco Systems
7. Starbucks
8. Qualcomm
9. Goldman Sachs
10. Methodist Hospital System

▼ You have just read **Objectives 3-5**

Want a review? Check out the Study Plan section @
www.mybizlab.com.

Leadership pp. 232-236

Andrew Smithson is the owner of a leather goods store in California. When he bought the store in 1997, he had a rough start: only one or two pieces were being sold per day, employees were bored and underperforming, and the building itself was falling down around him. Smithson envisioned his business being more than just a store; it represented a fun lifestyle. He wanted to appeal to not just bikers but to anyone who wanted to live life on the wild side. He devoted time explaining his vision to his employees, and he expanded the space to include a bar. After shoppers leave the store, they can grab a drink and mingle next door. Since then, the combination has been a hit, and sales have taken off. How important is good leadership to a successful business? How can leaders inspire employees to perform at their best?

➤ Famed management researcher and author Peter Drucker once noted "management is doing things right; leadership is doing the right things."[13] Both leaders and managers strive to motivate people, but they have different scopes. Typically, managers spend their time making sure that specific tasks are done well and are completed on time. The leadership of the company, on the other hand, is focused on setting the long-term vision and strategies the company will need to survive and flourish. Truly great leaders are able to be both managers and leaders: they define a vision, foster agreement across the company, and then implement the strategy. In this section, we'll look at leadership and how it affects the workplace.

Leadership in Business

How do business leaders inspire? Naturally, many different leadership styles exist. ▼ **Table 8.3** lists six of the most common styles: Visionary, Coaching, Affiliative, Democratic, Pacesetting, and Commanding. Which one leaders employ depends on a complex mix of their own personality, the corporate culture, the type of company, the employees they manage, and the given situation. Often, a recognized leader knows how to shift between these styles as different situations present themselves.

Resonance and Styles of Leadership

One way of examining leadership is to consider the idea of **resonance**. This term was repeatedly used in 2002 in Don Goleman's book *Primal Leadership*. An experience resonates with you when it causes a distinctive emotional reaction and thus makes a lasting impression. A "resonant leader" is therefore highly aware of others' emotional states and skilled at inspiring people to feel more positive. A resonant leader also connects with others by being honest and open about their own ideals, concerns, and goals. In working with these types of leaders, people tend to feel secure and free to explore and share their creative ideas. Resonant leaders usually possess a high degree of **emotional intelligence**—the ability to

▼ **Table 8.3**

Styles of Leadership						
	Visionary	**Coaching**	**Affiliative**	**Democratic**	**Pacesetting**	**Commanding**
Leader characteristics	Inspires, believes in own vision, is empathetic, explains how and why people's efforts contribute to the "dream"	Listens, helps people identify their own strengths and weaknesses, acts as a counselor, encourages, delegates	Promotes harmony, is empathetic, boosts morale, solves conflicts	Is a superb listener, team worker, collaborator, influencer	Has strong drive to achieve, has high standards and initiative, has low empathy and collaboration, is impatient, micromanaging, numbers-driven	Is commanding, "do it because I say so," threatening, tight control, monitoring studiously, creating dissonance, contaminates everyone's mood, drives away talent
How style builds resonance	Moves people toward shared dreams	Connects what a person wants with the organization's goals	Creates harmony by connecting people to one another	Values people's input and gets commitment through participation	Meets challenging and exciting goals	Soothes fear by giving clear direction in an emergency
When style is appropriate	When changes require a new vision or when a clear direction is needed; radical change	To help competent, motivated employees improve performance by building long-term capabilities	To heal rifts in a team, motivate during stressful times, or strengthen connections	To build buy-in or consensus, or to get valuable input from employees	To get high-quality results from a motivated and competent team; sales	In a crisis, to kick-start an urgent turnaround, or with problem employees; traditional military

understand both one's own and others' emotions. It is a term for the set of skills including self-awareness, self-management, social awareness, and relationship management.

Corporate Leaders Who Exemplify Styles of Leadership

Visionary leaders are able to inspire others, believe in their own vision, and move people toward a shared dream. Other managers use different styles of leadership, with varying results.[14] For example, Robert L. Nardelli, who was named CEO of Home Depot in 2000, is known for his commanding leadership style. For example, Nardelli began requiring all aspects of store performance to be carefully measured, and he held executives responsible for meeting strict goals. He also implemented major cost-cutting measures, replacing thousands of full-time workers with part-time employees. Financially, Nardelli's style seemed a boon for the company; Home Depot sales rose from $46 billion in 2000 to $81.5 billion in 2005, an average annual growth rate of 12 percent. However, the strong numbers could not make up for an authoritarian leadership style that many experts say alienated both employees and customers. In January 2007, facing pressure from the board of directors, Nardelli resigned from the company.

In stark contrast to Nardelli is Jon Huntsman of the Huntsman, Corp., who uses coaching and affiliative styles of leadership. Huntsman started his petrochemical and plastics company in 1970, and by 2000, it had worldwide revenue of $8.5 billion. But in January 2001, the market saw some dramatic changes, and every

Leaders employ different leadership styles. For example, former Home Depot CEO Robert Nardelli is known for his commanding leadership style.

advisor advocated that the company file Chapter 11 bankruptcy. Huntsman refused, and the company rebounded. By early 2005, when the company went public, its annual revenues were more than $12 billion. Huntsman outlines the pillars of his innovative leadership style in his 2005 book *Winners Never Cheat*:

- Compete fiercely and fairly, but do not cut in line.
- Set the example for handling risk, handling responsibility, and demonstrating reliability.
- Revenge is unproductive—learn to move on.
- Operate businesses and organizations as if they are family-owned.[15]

Huntsman also emphasizes the importance of being ethical, respectful, and charitable in both business dealings and in life. And Huntsman practices what he preaches: the Huntsman Cancer Institute in Salt Lake City, which he founded in 1995, has received more than $225 million from the company.

Personality Traits

Are there systems for measuring personality? There are many models of personality in use today. While no one model is recognized as the perfect tool, all of these personality tests strive to give us a better understanding of the traits that are the foundation of successful leadership.

The "Big Five"

The "**Big Five**," also referred to as the *Five Factor Model*, is one of the most widely accepted models of personality.[16] The model categorizes most human personality traits into five broad dimensions and then assigns people a score for each dimension:

O Openness
C Conscientiousness
E Extraversion
A Agreeableness
N Neuroticism (Emotional Stability)

When this test is scored for individual feedback, it is usually presented in a percentile form. For example, if you score in the 30th percentile for Extraversion, you most likely have a tendency to shy away from social situations.

The Cattell 16 PF

The **Cattell 16 personality factors (16 PF)** is another widely used model of personality.[17] According to this model, each of us has a consistent and constant underlying personality. However, the way we see ourselves is influenced by our intelligence, our upbringing, and our education. These influences may have taught us to suppress or emphasize certain aspects of our personality.

If we can understand our basic personality type, this model suggests, we can make better use of our natural strengths and weaknesses. The 16 PF is often used in hiring or in promotion recommendations as well as to improve relationships. Some sample reports the 16 PF can produce are shown in ▼ **Figure 8.2**.

The Tat

The **Thematic Apperception Test (TAT)**, developed by Morgan and Murray of Harvard University in the 1930s, is another personality test. Similar to the well-known Rorschach, or ink blot test, the TAT presents a person with a series

16PF Profile

(a)

Sten	Factor	Left meaning	1	2	3	4	5	6	7	8	9	10	Right meaning
4	Warmth (A)	Reserved				◆							Warm
1	Reasoning (B)	Concrete	◆										Abstract
5	Emotional stability (C)	Reactive					◆						Emotionally stable
2	Dominance (E)	Deferential		◆									Dominant
5	Liveliness (F)	Serious					◆						Lively
5	Rule-consciousness (G)	Expedient					◆						Rule-conscious
4	Social boldness (H)	Shy				◆							Socially bold
5	Sensitivity (I)	Utilitarian					◆						Sensitive
3	Vigilance (L)	Trusting			◆								Vigilant
6	Abstractedness (M)	Grounded						◆					Abstracted
6	Privateness (N)	Forthright						◆					Private
5	Apprehension (O)	Self-assured					◆						Apprehensive
4	Openness to change (Q1)	Traditional				◆							Open to change
6	Self-reliance (Q2)	Group-oriented						◆					Self-reliant
5	Perfectionism (Q3)	Tolerates disorder					◆						Perfectionistic
5	Tension (Q4)	Relaxed					◆						Tense

(Low: 1–3, Average: 4–7, High: 8–10)

16PF Profile

(b)

Client 1	Client 2	Factor	Left meaning	1	2	3	4	5	6	7	8	9	10	Right meaning
4	4	Warmth (A)	Reserved				◇							Warm
1	6	Reasoning (B)	Concrete	◆					◇					Abstract
5	4	Emotional stability (C)	Reactive				◇	◆						Emotionally stable
2	4	Dominance (E)	Deferential		◆		◇							Dominant
5	5	Liveliness (F)	Serious					◇◆						Lively
5	2	Rule-consciousness (G)	Expedient		◇			◆						Rule-conscious
4	5	Social boldness (H)	Shy				◆	◇						Socially bold
5	5	Sensitivity (I)	Utilitarian					◇◆						Sensitive
3	4	Vigilance (L)	Trusting			◆	◇							Vigilant
6	7	Abstractedness (M)	Grounded						◆	◇				Abstracted
6	5	Privateness (N)	Forthright					◇	◆					Private
5	6	Apprehension (O)	Self-assured					◆	◇					Apprehensive
4	4	Openness to change (Q1)	Traditional				◆◇							Open to change
6	5	Self-reliance (Q2)	Group-oriented					◇	◆					Self-reliant
5	7	Perfectionism (Q3)	Tolerates disorder					◆		◇				Perfectionistic
5	4	Tension (Q4)	Relaxed				◇	◆						Tense

(Low: 1–3, Average: 4–7, High: 8–10)

▼ **Figure 8.2**
Sample 16 PF Charts
The 16 PF personality test generates reports like these. a) Would this person be your choice for a position in Human Resources or in the sales department? b) The 16 PF can also help with analyzing relationships. Would these two people work well on a team? Where might there be conflicts?

Biz**Chat**

Do You Have to Be Tall to Be a Leader?

What does height have to do with successful leadership in business? A lot, according to many industry experts and observers. Lara Tiedens, an organizational behavior professor at the Stanford University Graduate School of Business, cites height—or in some cases, the illusion of

height—as a tool business leaders use to appear powerful. Several studies have also found positive correlations between height and salary.[18] What do you think? How much does appearance affect success in business, and more specifically, as a leader? Do top CEOs tend to be taller than average? Or is the idea that DNA, rather than skills and talents, seals one's leadership fate a myth?

For more information and discussion questions about this topic, check out the BizChat feature on www.my*biz*lab.com.

of images and interprets his or her responses. However, instead of ambiguous blots of ink, the TAT shows pictures of persons participating in various activities, such as riding a bike or playing a guitar, to a subject. The subject is asked to make up a story about the individuals in the pictures to explain why the pictured persons are engaged in particular acts. These stories are supposed to reveal the subject's needs. If the subject explains that the woman riding a bike is trying to get exercise, that subject might carry a need for physical activity. Another subject may suggest that the woman is riding the bike to save money on gasoline. That subject might carry a need for financial stability.

While no one model is recognized as the perfect tool, all of these personality tests can help to give us a better understanding of the traits that are the foundation of successful leadership.

Before establishing his leather goods store, Andrew Smithson used the Big Five to determine that while he had high scores for extraversion and agreeableness, he needed to work on his openness. This knowledge helped him improve his leadership, he says. "The personality test made me aware that I needed to be more open. I made sure to let my employees and customers know I was interested in their opinions. It's made a huge difference." Before you assume a leadership role, you might also consider using one or more of these tests to achieve greater self-awareness and an improved management style.

▼ You have just read **Objective 6**

Want to learn more? Check out the Study Plan section @
www.my*biz*lab.com.

Teamwork pp. 237-243

It's challenging to develop effective teams, but the benefits can be extraordinary. While different personalities have the potential to create conflict within a team, they can also create unique ideas. In this section, we'll discuss teamwork and how it affects organizations.

The Advantages of Teams in the Workplace

What is the value of using teams in the workplace? In good, working teams, there's agreement on the objectives at hand and on the best approach to solve the problem.[20] Teammates depend on one another's ideas and efforts to successfully complete tasks. There is a sense of accountability, and members are committed to one another's success. You've already read about Motorola's productive use of teams. Another company that makes use of teams is MasterCard. From 1987 to 1997, the company implemented five different advertising campaigns, yet was still eclipsed by rival company Visa.[21] In an attempt to change this pattern, MasterCard commissioned advertising agency McCann Erikson to come up with a new campaign. The agency enlisted the skills and talents of a seasoned creative team to tackle the project. After much brainstorming and debate, the team came up with a new tag line: "There are some things money can't buy. For everything else, there's MasterCard." The team then worked on developing ideas for commercials based on the tag line. By combining their creative talents, the team members came up with a "priceless" idea. Their commercials started by listing the prices of ordinary items, such as popcorn or soda. Then, they ended by mentioning an item that is priceless, such as spending time with your family. The "priceless campaign" was a great lead in

Have you ever seen a Motorola Razr cell phone? If so, you've seen the product of true teamwork in action. At the start of the project, Motorola began with a modest goal: to design a phone that celebrities would be happy to show off during the Academy Awards, generating a lot of publicity and buzz for Motorola products. A special team of 20 engineers was formed and given the task of creating the thinnest phone ever released. Would they be able to do it?

For almost a year, the team met daily, often for hours at a time, to work on the top-secret project. The team struggled to come up with a practical yet innovative design, often engaging in spirited debate over such matters. Despite the many challenges, the hard work paid off. The team that created the Razr not only created one of the best selling technology products of all time, but also contributed to creating a new Motorola.[19] In fact, Motorola reported that in 2006, its Razr cell phone even outsold the popular Apple iPod.

> Not every team performs at its best.

to MasterCard's new tag line. Since then, commercials based on this theme have been shown in 105 countries and translated into 48 languages. Most importantly for MasterCard, it has issued U.S. credit cards at nearly twice the rate Visa has since 1997.

Another company making effective use of teamwork is Ford. In the early 1980s, Ford was struggling with pressures to compete with Japanese imports Toyota and Honda. In 1980, the company lost $1.5 billion. Its response was to create a team to design a new model from the ground up. "Team Taurus" was nearly 400 people strong, including engineers, designers, and marketers. The team was given freedom from the traditional model of work flow at Ford, where isolated groups made only one part of the car and then "passed it over the wall" to the next group. Over five years, the push to design Taurus required an investment from Ford of over $3 billion.[22] Team Taurus worked as an integrated group, and in 1985 released the Ford Taurus. It proved to be the model that took the company back into the black, selling over 7 million cars over 21 years.[23] The risk Ford took to redesign the basic processes in place for work flow and production and to foster more creative thinking brought about terrific results for the company.

The Challenges Teams Face in the Workplace

Some people suggest that teamwork does not always bring more creative output. A 2006 study conducted by Barry Staw at University of Berkeley found that when college students were asked to think of business ideas either individually or in teams, the individuals came up with more ideas than did the teams. In addition, the individual's ideas were voted as more creative than were the teams' concepts. Staw concluded that collective thinking does not lead to increased creativity and can, in fact, hamper it. One possible reason, Staw proposes, is that team members often want to "fit in" rather than "stand out," and true creativity and original thinking is largely dependent on one's willingness to stand out and take risks.[24]

Selecting teams for optimum performance is another challenge. If a team is not carefully selected, a type of narrow-mindedness can emerge. This is the phenomenon referred to as **groupthink**. People who are from similar backgrounds and from similar sectors of the company tend to have a set of familiar ideas and work with the same set of unspoken assumptions. These may lead to rejecting different ideas without fair examination. The impact of groupthink can be chilling to the creative output of a team, although this challenge can be minimized with thoughtful design of the team membership.

In the twenty-first century, another challenge to successful workplace teams is the fact that there is now a wide mix of generations in the workforce (see ▼ **Table 8.4**). In fact, it is possible for there to be three or even four generations assigned to a single team. People from separate generations have grown up with social and educational experiences that are so different that they take on distinct styles in the workplace.

In their book *Millennial Rising*, researchers William Strauss and Neil Howe discuss the three dominant generations in the workplace today: the baby boomers, those born between 1943 and 1960; the Gen-Xers, those born between 1961 and 1981; and the Millennials, those born between 1982 and 2002. The baby boomers are the veterans in the workforce, and many have been with the same company for more than 30 years. Gen-Xers, who are known for their independent thinking and hankering for change, are the first generation of workers to value family life over work life. Like Gen-Xers, Millennials want their jobs to accommodate their personal lives, but they also have very high expectations for achievement in their careers. Millennials, who are now entering college campuses and the workforce, believe in their self-worth and value, whether deserved or not.[25] They feel they have the capability to change the company they work for and the world. According to Strauss and Howe, members of this generation expect to make their greatest marks in society by using technology to empower the community. Also important to note is that this generation is the focus of marketing efforts because they are the biggest youth spenders in history, most often in "co-purchases" with their parents. Teamwork, good behavior, and citizenship are much more important to Millennials than to earlier generations, and they see equality between different races and genders. How will this affect business? Strauss predicts, "Young workers will demand that employers adjust to the needs of workers who wish to build careers and families at the same time and to lead lower-stress lives than their parents did. Older employees will admire their skills, confidence, and team spirit, but will question their creativity and toughness."[26]

◎ Off the Mark
Barry Bonds, Team Player: A Miss!

On August 7, 2007, San Francisco Giants slugger Barry Bonds hit his 756th career home run, surpassing Hank Aaron's record. It was one of the most celebrated individual achievements in sports history. Unfortunately for the rest of the team that night, the Giants lost. During Bonds quest to beat Hank Aaron's record, every time at bat was an opportunity to inch closer to his goal. Baseball is not a game that revolves around home runs though; they're fun for fans, but hitting home runs doesn't win games. Teams that win games put small accomplishments together to get the job done.[27] Bonds' home runs didn't help his team win that night or the entire 2007 season: the Giants were last in their division by a significant amount.[28]

▼ Table 8.4

Four Generations in the Workplace			
Generation	**Birth Years**	**Famous Man**	**Famous Woman**
Silent	1925–1942	Colin Powell	Barbara Walters
Boomer	1943–1960	Steven Spielberg	Oprah Winfrey
Gen-X	1961–1981	Matt Damon	Jennifer Lopez
Millennial	1982–2002	LeBron James	Miley Cyrus

Sources: William Strauss and Neil Howe, Generations: The History of America's Future, 1584 to 2069

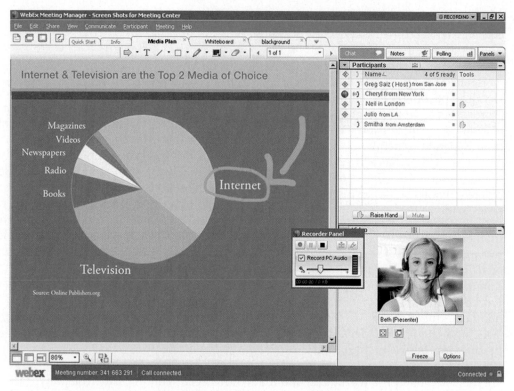

➤ Through the use of Web conferencing software, teams with people in various countries can work together seamlessly.

Best Practices for Teams

What kinds of practices set the stage for the best team performance? Psychologist Mihaly Csikszentmihalyi has extended his idea of flow into the team setting. **Group flow** occurs when a group knows how to work together so that each individual member can achieve flow. The characteristics of such a setting include:

- Creative spatial arrangements: Pinning ideas on the walls and using large charts to combine ideas from the entire group tend to lead to open consideration of ideas. Tables are used less since working while standing and moving promotes more discussion and interaction.

- Playground design: This begins with creating a "safe space," agreeing it is safe to bring out ideas that normally one might just keep to himself or herself. Often a large number of charts display information inputs, graphs, and the project summary. Wall space can be used to collect results and lists of open topics.

- Constant focus on the target group for the product.

- Heavy use of visualization and prototyping to construct early models. These are then refined to make models more efficient.

The environment itself can also be fine-tuned to help promote the success of the team. Management must also be sure to praise team accomplishments. The Razr team, for example, was asked to come to company headquarters for a meeting of top executives. What was the purpose of the meeting? The company's top executives wanted to thank the team members; they did so by giving them a standing ovation as well as stock options.[29]

How Managers Can Form the Best Teams

Some important aspects a manager should consider in forming a team include the following:

- **Size.** A team that is too large may struggle with cohesiveness. At the same time, a large group can offer the benefit of diverse perspectives.
- **Time.** Some teams may be formulated to work on a specific problem or project within a short time frame, while others may work together for longer time periods on everyday tasks.
- **Status.** A team that is formally created by a company may be required to provide progress reports and updates, and it often has access to company resources. Less formal teams may need to take initiative in maintaining lines of communication.

According to business writer and theorist R. M. Belbin, effective teams are made up of people with diverse skills, talents, and points of view. Team members' respective skills and talents should complement one another in order for the team to perform at the optimum level. For example, what might happen if everyone on a team was extremely creative, yet inexperienced in effective time management? Or if five of six team members were all aggressive leaders? Clearly, a balance of people who embody different "team roles" is key in the success of a team.

Belbin's model of nine team roles is outlined in ▼ **Table 8.5**. Considering both these roles and the personality traits of potential members can be helpful when designing teams.

The Effect of Technology on the Design of Teams

In a **virtual team**, members are located in different physical locations but work together to achieve a goal. The need for virtual teams grows out of the increased globalization of business. Familiar tools like conference calls and e-mail have evolved to include video conferencing and live broadcasting of key meetings and

▼ Table 8.5

Belbin's Nine Team Roles

Role	Personality Traits
Plant	Creative and imaginative
Resource investigator	Extroverted and communicative
Coordinator	Mature and confident
Shaper	Challenging and dynamic
Monitor evaluator	Serious and strategic
Teamworker	Cooperative and diplomatic
Implementer	Disciplined and reliable
Completer finisher	Painstaking and conscientious
Specialist	Dedicated and self-starting

Source: http://www.belbin.com/content/page/731/Belbin_Team_Role_Descriptions.pdf

events over the Web. Web casts can now support interactive participation of the viewing audience. In real time, audience members can ask questions, exchange their own electronic files with the group, and record the presentation for repeated viewing. Web conferencing software like WebEx and Microsoft Office Live allow participants in any geographic location to brainstorm together in real time on a common "virtual whiteboard," to watch demos and presentations live, and to record and annotate these discussions for later playback.

The promise of much higher-speed Internet transfer is also being explored. Internet2, a group of educational institutions and some technology companies, is using high-speed transfer of information to create events such as "America Reads the Constitution."[30] At the event in 2006, students from 43 different schools across the nation read the Constitution together. The Washington State School for the Blind read its portion from Braille, and the Scranton State School for the Deaf performed its section in sign language. After the reading students asked each other questions. This process helps students learn early on that distance does not have to keep people from communicating and working well together. The potential to connect students and workers from many parts of the world may lead to exciting new possibilities for synergy.

The best practices for creating strong virtual teams are emerging as virtual teams become a more accepted and useful teaming solution.[31] Most successful virtual teams include some face-to-face meeting time periodically. Very few virtual teams are 100 percent virtual. Although technology allows teams to communicate without ever meeting face to face, it is still important to have the group occasionally meet with each other in the same space to build social connections. Keeping the team connected is a key priority to a virtual team, and it can be difficult to keep contacts strong from a distance. There can be communication delays from working across time zones or using e-mail as a primary mode of communication. Establishing team rules, such as agreeing to respond to e-mail messages within a certain window of time or initiating global office hours, can minimize these problems.

Your Role on a Team

How can I be a valued team player? It is important to begin now to build the skills that will make you successful in team settings. As we have seen, the best teams are carefully planned and selected and can be the place where some of the most exciting and innovative work in the company is happening. Preparing yourself to contribute in a team setting may be the most important thing you can do to increase your value to an organization, no matter what position you hold.

The Seven Habits Model

There are many skills that you can build to enhance your success as a member of a team. One model that organizes these skills is the **Seven Habits model** developed by famed management author Stephen Covey.[32] He has found that there are seven habits of behavior that are exhibited by successful people:

1. **Be proactive.**   This is the ability to control your environment rather than have it control you. Proactive team members are constantly looking "down the road" in terms of their time management, work, and obstacles coming that may impede the success of the project.

2. **Begin with the end in mind.** This means that you are able to see the desired outcome and concentrate on activities that help in achieving it. Staying focused on the ultimate goal allows you to avoid taking the team in directions that will cause divisiveness and will waste resources and energy.

3. **Put first things first.** This skill works together with habit #2 in pushing you toward success in your team role. Manage your time and energy so that the required tasks are prioritized. Covey thinks of habit #2 as a mental creation and habit #3 as a physical creation.

4. **Think win-win.** This is the most important aspect of interpersonal leadership because most achievements are based on cooperative effort, therefore the aim needs to be win-win solutions for all.

5. **Seek first to understand and then to be understood.** In communicating with other members of the team, it is critical to develop and maintain positive relationships. This style of communication recommends listening and working to give your teammates the feeling they have been heard as key to your own success in being understood and contributing.

6. **Synergize.** This is the habit of creative cooperation—the principle that collaboration often achieves more than could be achieved by individuals working independently toward attaining a purpose.

7. **Sharpen the saw.** This catch phrase comes from the metaphor of chopping down a tree. If you are constantly sawing and never take time to stop and sharpen the saw, you'll feel you're investing tremendous energy, but the results will not be what they could be if you just stopped to sharpen the saw first. Strong team contributors avoid the work mode of continually reacting to crisis. Instead, they take time to step back and develop skills and to analyze the task at hand so that they can work more efficiently.

Work to develop and use these habits in your role on teams and you will find that your teams become more successful—and that you are in demand for the next team. Effective teamwork involves a complex blend of personalities, skills, and actions. Achieving this blend in the business environment can be a great challenge. As the Motorola Razr team demonstrated, however, it can be done. Its success is the kind to which all managers and team members aspire.

▼ You have just read **Objective 7**

Want to test your skills? Check out the Study Plan section @
www.my*biz*lab.com.

1. How do motivation and work environment encourage "flow"? (pp. 223-225)

- **Flow** (p. 224) is a state of feeling completely involved and focused on a task.

- Managers can increase motivation and foster flow by keeping employees intellectually engaged, removing distractions, encouraging creativity and flexibility, and supporting employees in all aspects of their lives.

2. What are the intricacies of Maslow's hierarchy of needs, McClelland's "three needs" theory, and Herzberg's motivator-hygiene theory? (pp. 225-226)

- Maslow's hierarchy describes motivation as a response to a progressive set of needs for **physiology** (p. 225), **safety** (p. 225), **belonging** (p. 225), **esteem** (p. 225), and **self-actualization** (p. 225).

- McClelland's **"three needs" theory** (p. 226) states the main motivators are the need for achievement, affiliation, and power.

- Herzberg broke the idea of motivation into two categories, **hygiene factors** (p. 226) and **motivators** (p. 226).

3. What are the distinguishing factors between extrinsic and intrinsic motivators? (pp. 227-228)

- **Extrinsic motivators** (p. 227) are external factors that generate engagement with the work, such as pay or promotion.

- **Intrinsic motivators** (p. 227) are internal drives that come from the actual interest of the work, or from a sense of purpose and value in the work being done.

4. What are the implications of Theory X, Theory Y, Theory Z, and the Vroom model? (pp. 228-229)

- **Theory X** (p. 228) posits that humans inherently dislike work and will try to avoid it if they can. As a result, managers should adopt a hard-line, authoritarian style.

- **Theory Y** (p. 228) proposes that people view work as natural and will be motivated to work as long as they are satisfied with their jobs. Thus, managers should implement a softer style that involves ample employee participation.

- **Theory Z** (p. 229) suggests workers want to cooperate and be loyal to an organization. It emphasizes collaborative decision making.

- **The Vroom model** (expectancy theory) (p. 229) states that an individual's motivation can be described by the relationship between expectancy, instrumentality, and valence.

5. How have motivational theories and industrial psychology changed the work environment since the early 20th century? (pp. 230-231)

- **Industrial psychology** (p. 230) is a field of academic study developed to understand scientifically how to manage people and work optimally.

- A 1932 study by Elton May concluded that when workers are made to feel important, productivity increases. This is called the **Hawthorne effect** (p. 230). After World War II, research began to focus on management of entire organizations rather than individual workers.

- Modern workplaces are influenced by new ideas including the **uncertainty management theory** (p. 231) and **sociocracy** (p. 231).

6. What are the various identifiable leadership styles and personality traits, and how do they affect business leadership? (pp. 232-236)

- Visionary, coaching, affiliative, democratic, pacesetting, and commanding describe different leadership styles. Many top executives demonstrate one or more of these styles in their business dealings.

- The **Big Five traits** (p. 234), a widely accepted model of personality, categorize personality traits into five broad dimensions: Openness, Conscientiousness, Extraversion, Agreeableness, and Neuroticism (Emotional Stability).

- The **Cattell 16 PF** (p. 234) is another model of personality. It proposes that we have an underlying personality and the way we see ourselves is affected by our intelligence, upbringing, and education.

- Leaders can maximize their potential, support conflicts, and resolve conflicts by understanding their personality type.

7. What are the best ways to create, manage, and participate in teams, taking into account factors such as technology, group flow, Belbin's nine team roles, and Covey's Seven Habits model? (pp. 237-243)

- Teams can benefit the workplace, allowing creative exchanges, organization, and positive competition.

- Effective teams must be designed and managed thoughtfully. The modern workplace includes workers spanning many generations, and it takes care and insight to make them mesh well in a single team.

- **Group flow** (p. 240) is achieved when a group knows how to work together so that each individual member can achieve flow. Best practices for creating strong teams include considering the size, life span, and status of the team.

Continued on next page

Chapter Summary (cont.)

- R. M. Belbin outlined a model of nine team roles. An effective team requires a variety of roles, and the members must be matched carefully to the team needs.

- Technology allows for virtual teams in which members are in different locations around the country or the world. Web casts, electronic file exchange, and Web conferencing software make this more effective each year.

- Stephen Covey's **Seven Habits model** (p. 242) can help employees enhance their success as members of a team.

For an audio file of the Objectives and Chapter Summary, see the Student Resources section @ www.my*biz*lab.com.

Key Terms

belonging needs (p. 225)

"Big Five" traits (p. 234)

Cattell 16 personality factors (16 PF) (p. 234)

emotional intelligence (p. 232)

esteem needs (p. 225)

expectancy (p. 229)

expectancy theory (p. 229)

extrinsic motivators (p. 227)

flow (p. 224)

group flow (p. 240)

groupthink (p. 238)

Hawthorne effect (p. 230)

hierarchy of needs (p. 225)

hygiene factors (p. 226)

industrial psychology (p. 230)

instrumentality (p. 229)

intrinsic motivators (p. 227)

motivator factors (p. 226)

motivator-hygiene theory/two-factor theory (p. 226)

organizational psychology (p. 224)

physiological needs (p. 225)

resonance (p. 232)

safety needs (p. 225)

self-actualization needs (p. 225)

Seven Habits model (p. 242)

sociocracy (p. 231)

strength-based management (p. 230)

Thematic Apperception Test (TAT) (p. 235)

Theory X (p. 228)

Theory Y (p. 228)

Theory Z (p. 229)

"three needs" theory (p. 226)

valence (p. 229)

virtual team (p. 241)

uncertainty management theory (p. 231)

Self-Test

Multiple Choice   Correct answers can be found on page 503.

1. **Flow is a psychological state characterized by**

   a. a lack of interest in the world as it "flows" by.

   b. anxiety and sometimes depression.

   c. an intense desire to compete and win.

   d. being so involved and focused in an activity you may not realize time has passed.

2. **Maslow's hierarchy of needs**

   a. organizes the needs that motivate human beings.

   b. lists all of the most important theories of motivation.

   c. presents a system to motivate workers.

   d. is no longer valid because it was introduced in 1954.

3. **The Vroom model of motivation**

   a. disagrees with Maslow's hierarchy.

   b. uses three factors to compute the motivation of a person in a situation.

   c. was developed to address the Hawthorne effect.

   d. was displaced when Theory Z was introduced.

4. **The Big Five are**

   a. the top five qualities of successful leaders.

   b. the five most important styles of leadership.

   c. five broad dimensions of personality.

   d. the most famous five accounting firms in the country.

5. **Teams improve creativity**

   a. when the phenomenon of groupthink sets in.

   b. no matter what the makeup of the team.

   c. when best practices for selecting the team members and roles are followed.

   d. when individuals work with others who are just like them.

6. **An example of ineffective behavior in a team is**

   a. open-mindedness.

   b. groupthink.

   c. being proactive.

   d. supporting synergy.

7. **The Cattel 16 PF model is used to determine**

   a. a person's underlying personality.

   b. the best floor plan for an office.

   c. a person's level of motivation.

   d. how well a team works together.

8. **Virtual teams are teams that**

   a. are incomplete and need to be established.

   b. only communicate through face-to-face meetings.

   c. primarily focus on technology-based projects.

   d. work in different physical locations.

9. **Group flow can be encouraged by**

   a. making sure everyone has a comfortable chair.

   b. using tables less frequently so people stand and move more in discussions.

   c. creating a "safe space" where anyone is free to gossip.

   d. discouraging visualization that leads to daydreaming and lost time.

10. **Extrinsic motivators include such things as**

    a. knowing your supervisor cares about you.

    b. believing your opinion matters.

    c. knowing there is a large financial bonus for good work.

    d. working for a company whose mission is meaningful to you.

Self-Test

True/False Correct answers can be found on page 503.

1. Organizational psychology studies how people organize their work materials.
   ☐ **True** or ☐ **False**

2. The Gallup Q12 survey was a study of the salaries of different leaders in industry.
   ☐ **True** or ☐ **False**

3. Intrinsic motivators come from a sense of purpose and value in the work employees are doing.
   ☐ **True** or ☐ **False**

4. Strength-based management believes the best way to develop talent is to help employees add skills and knowledge that build on their existing strengths.
   ☐ **True** or ☐ **False**

5. There is one perfect style of leadership that brings people together and achieves business success.
   ☐ **True** or ☐ **False**

Critical Thinking Questions

1. Consider the responsibilities and risks of a management position in a national firm. What do you feel is a reasonable salary ratio between the highest paid manager of a company and the lowest paid employee? Does it depend on the industry?

2. Is it better for a business to respond to a changing climate by hiring a different style of leader or to expect the current leadership to adapt its style to what is required?

3. What factors are the most important to creating a team that works efficiently together? What problems have you seen in your own academic career when working in group settings, and how could they be prevented?

4. Are there personality differences between genders? Between generations? Explain your answers.

5. Stephen Covey's Seven Habits model is focused on making you a more successful, efficient person. What impact would these seven habits have on your relationships with your friends and family?

Team Time

Forming a Successful Team

A shoe retailer's sales and earnings have a history of lagging during the spring and summer months. The company wants to reverse this trend by appealing to young people, a rapidly growing consumer base with increasing amounts of disposable income. The company has decided to give one team almost unlimited resources and freedom to develop a flip-flop sandal for modern, gadget-loving youth. You need to apply the principles of best practices in team formation to determine the personalities and strengths of each member and assign roles in which the members will be motivated and contribute.

Process

Step 1. Break up into teams of three or four individuals.

Step 2. Begin by deciding what tool you will use to evaluate each member for personality traits, strengths, and weaknesses.

Step 3. Develop a strategy for assessing what work needs to be done and then how your team will assign appropriate responsibilities to each member.

Step 4. How will you evaluate the level of motivation and creativity for the team? What changes can be made if the team's performance is not adequate?

Step 5. Present your findings to the class for discussion.

Conclusion

Teamwork can lead to creative, exciting results, but only if the team is designed well and managed well. It takes a combination of technical skills, emotional intelligence, and leadership to create a team that motivates people to contribute and thrive.

Ethics and Corporate Social Responsibility

Ethics in Teamwork

Being a member of a team means you are accountable for your actions and the actions of your fellow teammates. Review the following scenario.

Scenario

Imagine you work at an advertising firm. You're on a team that is developing an ad campaign proposal for a chain of fitness centers. The firm has been struggling and needs your team to land this account. At a meeting, one of your teammates reveals that he has hacked into a competing firm's network and has a draft of its proposal for the same account. Your teammate wants to steal the idea and use it in your team's proposal. Most of your teammates agree with this idea, but you think it is unethical.

Questions

1. How would you handle this situation? Would you voice your objection or go along with the team?

2. If you decide to voice your objection, do you address the entire team or speak to members individually? Why?

3. How would you reconcile your role as a loyal employee and team player with your need to uphold ethical standards?

Web Exercises

1. **Testing 1, 2, 3 . . .**
   Find three online leadership, team roles, and/or personality assessment tools. See www.psychtests.com/tests/alltests.html for examples. How consistent are the results in describing your personality or tendencies? How accurate would you rate the results?

2. **Great American Leaders**
   Visit www.hbs.edu/leadership/database/index.html, the 20th Century Great American Leaders database, maintained by the Harvard University Business School. Select one leader from your state, one of your gender, one leader of the same ethnicity, and two additional people profiled from different industries. What similarities and differences do you see in this group of five great leaders?

3. **Running the Family Business**
   Locate two Web resources that offer an analysis of the special challenges and rewards of a family-run business. Validate the sites with additional references for statements made.

4. **Your Emotional IQ**
   Review your strengths in areas of emotional intelligence by taking an online emotional IQ quiz. What roles in a business would take advantage of your emotional IQ strengths? Which role on a team would be best fit for you?

5. **Evaluating Leadership Styles**
   Using the Internet, research a person heading a national business that exhibits three of the six leadership styles presented in Table 8.3. What evidence can you locate to decide whether that style is effective in his or her business setting?

Web Case

To access the Chapter 8 Web case and exercise, see the End of Chapter Assignments section @ www.mybizlab.com.

Video Case

To access the Chapter 8 Video case and exercise, see the End of Chapter Assignments section @ www.mybizlab.com.

Human Resource Management

p. 262

Compensating, Scheduling, Promoting, and Terminating Employees
▼ Objectives 3 & 4
To attract high-caliber applicants, companies need compensation packages that are comparable with their competitors or better. Companies like Google promote a fun atmosphere with their work/life benefits to maximize performance and efficiency. What types of benefits are important in a good compensation package?

p. 268

Managing Workplace Diversity
▼ Objective 5
Company demographics are changing to include a variety of cultures, religions, genders, and ages. Diversity is encouraged because it benefits the company, but it has been a challenge for some large businesses like Texaco, which was forced to pay millions of dollars to settle discrimination lawsuits. What issues do companies face when managing diversity?

p. 251

Human Resource Management
▼ Objective 1
H and R—two simple letters that, when taken together, represent a vital component of any successful business. Indeed, a well-managed human resources department is essential to the smooth operation of all organizations. HR managers like Leslie Booth are responsible for many tasks, from hiring to firing, and everything in between. Why is human resource management so important?

p. 271

Labor and Union Issues
▼ Objective 6
Workers form unions in an effort to protect their interests. If management makes a decision to reduce health care or salaries, union leaders are there to fight for the rights of workers. In 2007, when GM was planning on cutting labor costs, workers feared their jobs were at risk. For two days, 73,000 workers went on strike in an effort to solidify job security. Did it work?

p. 257

Training and Evaluating Employees
▼ Objective 2
Have you ever worked at a fast-food restaurant or an ice-cream shop? What kind of training did you get? At Cold Stone Creamery and other businesses, training comes in a very different—and fun—format. Why is training necessary to the success of a business?

Human Resource Management pp. 251-256

➤ When you think about the resources required to run a business, you probably think about things like money, space, equipment, and supplies. Although financial and material resources are key aspects of a business, the resource often taken for granted, but which is arguably the most important, is the "human" resource—or people. People provide the ideas, creativity, knowledge, and ingenuity that make a business run. An organization can have all the money and materials in the world, but without the right people doing the right things, it will not be successful.

When human resource manager Leslie Booth was given the task of finding a new senior account executive, she weighed her options carefully. To fill such a senior position required patience. She hired a recruiter to find outside candidates to interview for the position, and, to keep her options open, she also placed job postings online and in newspapers. What other methods could Leslie have used to fill the position? What else is involved in the hiring process? ➤

Human resources (HR)—the people in an organization—need to be managed just as carefully as the material and financial resources of a business. **Human resource management (HRM)** is the organizational function that deals with the people in the business: the executives and the managers, as well as the frontline production, sales and administrative staff. HRM encompasses every aspect of the "human" in a business, including hiring, training, motivating, evaluating, and compensating personnel, as shown in ▼ **Figure 9.1**. In addition to the traditional functions, HRM also works through the many challenges in today's society, such as diversity issues, work/lifestyle preferences, and global business considerations. In this section you'll learn the ins and outs of human resource management.

Manpower Planning and Recruiting

Doesn't having the right number of employees happen naturally?
As you learned in Chapter 6, an entrepreneur may initially serve as the company's chief executive officer and financial manager, as well as the sales executive and

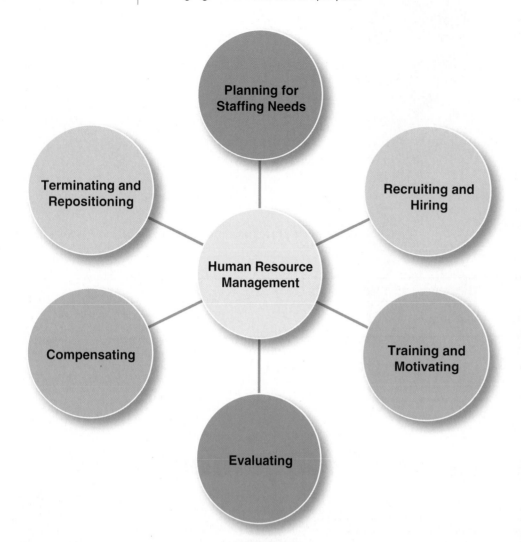

marketing director. As a business expands, new people are brought into the organization. At that point, the owner may still serve as the HR director, hiring, firing, and realigning employees to fill the growing needs of the expanding business. Although keeping track of HR needs at small businesses can be fairly simple, companies that add employees and continue to grow require more specific HR planning. Poor staff planning can be costly. Being overstaffed burdens a company with the unnecessary expense of maintaining salaries, benefits, and training for surplus employees. An understaffed organization can lead to loss of sales and competitiveness if customer needs are not met. Planning staffing needs is therefore comprised of two components: 1) assessing the supply of and demand for current and future employee resources, and 2) evaluating job requirements.

▼ **Figure 9.1**
The Functions of Human Resource Management

How does a company determine whether it has all the employees it needs? The first component of HR planning is to assess the current supply of and demand for employees. Current supply of employees is determined by developing a workforce profile. A **workforce profile** is a personnel "inventory" that includes information about each employee, such as age, education, training, experience, specialized skills, and current and previous positions held within the company. Future demand for employees is determined in a process called **forecasting**. Forecasting is based on several factors, such as predicted sales of the company's goods or services, current workforce skill level, the effect of technology changes on staff needs, and changes in employment practices (such as using more or less temporary staff). In addition, staffing changes that are expected to occur through normal turnover, retirement, and any planned reassignments are also taken into consideration. If forecasting indicates an imbalance between the supply of and demand for employees, further action must be taken. Such actions may include recruitment, training, retraining, labor reductions, or changes in workforce utilization.

How do companies identify the right people for a particular job? Before making shifts in manpower levels, the HR department completes an analytical study of the tasks to be performed within the organization. A **job analysis** defines in detail the particular duties and requirements of the tasks and responsibilities an employee is required to perform. In a job analysis, each task is defined by a **job description**, a formal statement that summarizes what the employee will do in that role. It includes the job responsibilities, the conditions under which the job will be performed, and its relationship to other functions in the organization. Job descriptions are important because they define job objectives that are used later in performance appraisals. They also can become a part of the legal contract between the employee and the employer. To assist in recruiting the right person to fulfill the job's requirements, **job specifications** are also defined in the job analysis. Job specifications are the skills, education, experience, and personal attributes that candidates need to possess to successfully fulfill the role. ▼ **Figure 9.2** shows a sample job description and job specifications.

Company: Nelson Wireless	
Position title: Marketing manager	
(a) Job description	**(b) Job specifications**
Join a team of marketing professionals focused on mobile technologies in the consumer market segment. The marketing manager is responsible for coordinating and/or implementing marketing projects designed for the consumer market segment. Working in cooperation with the sales team, product offers, and other headquarters marketing teams, the marketing manager will coordinate public relations projects and other promotional activities to drive Nelson Wireless brand awareness and product demand and generate consumer purchases. The marketing manager will provide strategic oversight for regional-level industry events, and be responsible for planning and executing customer events. The marketing manager will be responsible for coordinating budgets and timelines, maintaining accurate records of expenditures, and compiling reports of activity results. Additionally, he/she will be responsible for managing a team of 8-10 marketing associates. The marketing manager role will also include administrative elements such as invoice processing, event scheduling, and maintenance of a promotional calendar.	• College degree required with emphasis in marketing, business administration, or communications preferred • 3+ years marketing/communications experience required • Excellent demonstrated verbal and written communication skills • Demonstrated experience in event execution • Demonstrated ability to coordinate cooperative working relationships across multiple parties • Ability to work well under pressure • Extremely well organized, strong project management and time management skills and strong ability to multi-task • Proven ability to operate in a fast-paced, high-growth professional environment

▼ **Figure 9.2**
A Sample (a) Job Description and (b) Job Specifications

How is the right person found for each job?

Matching the right person for each job depends on a well-devised recruiting plan. **Recruitment** is the process of finding, screening, and selecting people for a specific job. The recruitment process uses a variety of methods and resources. **Internal recruiting**, or filling job vacancies with existing employees from within the business, is the first choice of many companies. Often, companies post job openings on the company intranet, staff notice boards, in-house newsletters, and in staff meetings. Internal recruitment has several advantages. It tends to be a morale booster for employees because they know that the company has an interest in promoting their own. In addition, because employer and employee have established a working relationship, there is a reduced risk of selecting an inappropriate candidate for the desired position. Additionally, choosing from within is potentially quicker and less costly as it reduces costs associated with outside recruiting and shortens the length of training time.

However, there are disadvantages to solely looking internally and not considering outside sources. This includes the possibility of not getting the best candidate due to a limited search process. In addition, another internal vacancy is created that must be subsequently filled. Moreover, relying on internal employees may discourage new perspectives and ideas and eventually make the business resistant to change. As a result, businesses also rely on external recruiting to meet staffing needs. **External recruiting** looks outside the business to fill vacancies using various resources and methods (see ▼ **Figure 9.3**).

Depending on the type of position, employment agencies or consultant firms are often used. Employment agencies often specialize in specific sectors such as accounting, sales, or clerical services. Employment agencies provide a screened pool of candidates, which reduces the hiring company's administrative burden of recruitment. However, they can be costly. Recruitment consultants, often referred

▼ **Figure 9.3**
**External Recruitment
Resources**

to as "headhunters," conduct more specialized searches, usually for senior management or key employees. Recruitment consultants are often expensive, but the costs of finding the wrong candidate can be even higher. Posting ads in local newspapers, on Internet job sites, or in specialized trade magazines can be advantageous methods because they are not expensive and reach a wide audience.

BizChat

What Is Recruiting 2.0?

You're probably familiar with social networking sites such as MySpace and Facebook. The same concept is applied to the professional community through sites such as LinkedIn (www.linkedin.com), ZoomInfo (www.zoominfo.com), and Spoke (www.spoke.com). LinkedIn is an online network of more than 20 million[1] experienced professionals from around the world whose connections are made through college, graduate school, or professional affiliations. Most people would like to hire or work with someone

they know, and LinkedIn can provide helpful colleague and customer recommendations. Additionally, LinkedIn may assist job seekers by providing insiders' information on companies and employees. If you've scheduled an interview, you might find a LinkedIn page for the person with whom you are meeting. This can give you some information on that person's professional background, including where he or she went to school, as well as information on hobbies. Knowing these details may provide for good conversation starters during the interview.

For more information and discussion questions about this topic, check out the BizChat feature on www.my*biz*lab.com.

What are the challenges in recruiting? One of the newer challenges facing recruiting specialists is the use of technology. As noted above, online job and resume posting sites, Web and video blogs, virtual job fairs, and podcasts are all being used by both those looking to find a job and those looking to fill a position. When the use of technology was new, these methods were often highly successful and cost effective. The dramatic growth of job and résumé postings has made the efficient and effective use of technology in recruitment more challenging. While online job postings yield many responses and thus a large pool of candidates, sifting through these responses to find the right person for the job can be time-consuming for HR professionals. In fact, one of the greatest recruiting challenges cited is the difficulty finding qualified candidates for critical positions.[2] Therefore, HR managers must know how to use technology skillfully. At a basic recruiting level, this means learning how to make a posted job description appeal to the most qualified candidates as well as stand out from competitors in the online environment so the right person can find the open position more readily. It also means becoming familiar with the new social networking technologies and Web 2.0 techniques to post jobs and to find recruits.

Hiring

What happens in the hiring process? As shown in ▼ **Figure 9.4**, hiring is a multistep process. The first step is to narrow down the group of applicants to form a select pool of candidates. To do this, HR managers compare the candidates' qualifications to the job specifications. In addition, many companies use special applicant-tracking system software to sort through résumés and job applications quickly. HR managers also use systems that build assessments into the application process to help prescreen for certain personality traits. For example, Kay Straky, senior vice president of human resources at Universal Studios Hollywood, needed a system to manage the recruiting efforts required to fill high-turnover positions at the studio. In addition, rampant theft from employees demanded that Straky find a way to hire more responsible and honest employees. Her solution was to use an applicant-tracking and workforce-optimizer system by Unicru (now Kronos). This system allowed her to build a job application that included a dependability assessment to screen candidates who were inclined to steal or skip work. The changes in the application and screening process improved the turnover rate from a high of 40 percent down to 10 percent.[3]

After identifying a small pool of appropriate candidates, department and HR managers interview them to gauge a candidate's personality, to clarify information in the candidate's résumé, and to determine whether he or she is the best match for the position. The candidate might also need to complete one or more skills-related tests. If necessary, a candidate will be brought back for follow-up interviews.

Before offering a candidate a position, it's important that the company completes thorough background and reference checks. It's not uncommon to hear stories about companies that failed to conduct background checks and hired someone who

▼ **Figure 9.4**
The Hiring Process

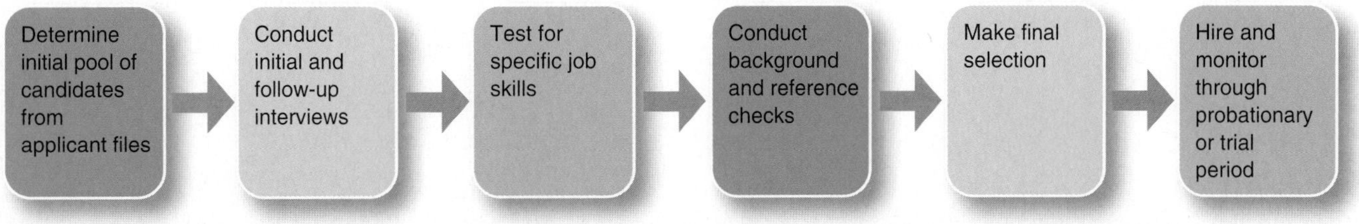

| Determine initial pool of candidates from applicant files | → | Conduct initial and follow-up interviews | → | Test for specific job skills | → | Conduct background and reference checks | → | Make final selection | → | Hire and monitor through probationary or trial period |

Fortune's Top 10 Most Diverse Companies to Work For

1. Baptist Health South Florida
2. Four Seasons Hotels
3. Methodist Hospital System
4. Marriot International
5. Station Casinos
6. Qualcomm
7. Erickson Retirement Communities
8. Scripps Health
9. Navy Federal Credit Union
10. Stew Leonard's

falsified his or her educational or professional experiences or who had been in trouble with the law. For example, the Treaty Group, Inc., relied on a large global personnel and training firm to help with its hiring needs. Unfortunately, the person whom Treaty hired to assist with bookkeeping functions defrauded the company of over $250,000. It was discovered later that the hired bookkeeper had been convicted of defrauding a former employer prior to joining Treaty.[4]

What legalities must be considered when hiring? Several federal laws must be observed during the hiring process:

1. **Federal Equal Employment Opportunity.** Established in 1965, the Federal Equal Employment Opportunity Commission (EEOC) works to "ensure equality of opportunity by vigorously enforcing federal legislation prohibiting discrimination in employment." This legislation is comprised of a number of different acts and laws, known as Equal Employment Opportunity (EEO) laws. As part of this mission, the EEOC investigates claims of discrimination and files lawsuits against companies when necessary.[5]

2. **The Civil Rights Act of 1964.** The Civil Rights Act of 1964 prohibits discrimination based on race, color, gender, religion, and national origin. Title VII of the act also established the EEOC to enforce anti-discrimination laws.

3. **Americans with Disabilities Act.** The Americans with Disabilities Act of 1990 (ADA) prohibits discrimination based on disabilities (or perceived disabilities). It also requires employers to make reasonable accommodations to the known disability of a qualified applicant or employee as long as it does not impose an "undue hardship" on the operation of the employer's business. Reasonable accommodations might include providing wheelchair accessibility, modified equipment, or interpreters.[6]

4. **Age Discrimination in Employment Act.** The Age Discrimination in Employment Act of 1967 (ADEA) makes it unlawful to discriminate against a person because of his or her age with respect to employment. It also prohibits the inclusion of age preferences in job notices or advertisements, except in specific circumstances where age is considered necessary to the job's function.[7]

HR departments take care of a company's biggest resource—its employees. HR managers like Leslie Booth must possess a variety of skills in order to oversee a wide array of complex tasks capably. Although these tasks—planning, recruiting, and hiring—may not seem directly related to the overall success of a company, they are, in fact, closely entwined.

▼ You have just read **Objective 1**

Think you got it? Check out the Study Plan section @ **www.mybizlab.com.**

Training and Evaluating Employees pp. 257-261

➤ Employee training is important for many reasons, as it often contributes to:[9]

- Increased job satisfaction, motivation, and morale among employees
- Greater efficiency in work, resulting in financial gain
- More effective use of new technologies and methods
- Development of new strategies and products
- Lower employee turnover
- Fewer interpersonal conflicts and better communication

Companies that emphasize training and development experience greater employee productivity, loyalty, and retention, all of which are good for the bottom line. In this section, you'll learn about how training can enhance the success of a business and ensure that employees stay in top form.

Have you ever worked at a fast-food restaurant or an ice-cream shop? If so, what kind of training did you receive? Some companies like Cold Stone Creamery are turning once-dull training into a good time by taking advantage of "serious games" to train their employees. Stone City[8] is a training game used by new Cold Stone Creamery frontline employees that focuses on portion control and customer service. Other companies are offering simulation training that allows their employees to really get a taste for their jobs. At the Institute for Simulation & Training at the University of Central Florida, students like the one shown in the photo above interact with virtual students in a classroom simulation program. For employees who are accustomed to playing video games, learning through computer simulation programs is an attractive option. Would you want to try it? ➤

Training Methods and Requirements

What kind of training do new employees receive? Initially, when an employee is hired, the organization uses an **orientation program** to integrate the new employee. Orientation can be as simple as an overview of the organization and the distribution of basic information, such as company procedures and expectations. Today, however, many companies are going beyond the traditional orientation program of explaining rules and regulations, as reflected in the orientation checklist in ▼ **Table 9.1**. Orientation is more effective if it becomes a means of familiarizing the employee with the company's mission, discussing how the new employee's contribution can add to the company's success. In addition, employees should be introduced to associates in their department so they feel at ease and can quickly become as productive as possible. Failure to integrate new hires into a company adequately leads to low retention rates.

▼ **Table 9.1**

New Employee Orientation Checklist

Action	Reason
Before the New Employee Arrives	
Create a proper workspace.	The employee will need an area and the necessary supplies to start work.
Contact the company's IT facilitator to set up e-mail and access codes for the new employee.	The employee may need to receive important e-mails and access certain password-protected computer drives immediately.
Inform current employees about the new employee's arrival and update them on the role the new employee will fill and how it affects the team.	Current employees will need to be made aware of any changes in workflow so that the new employee's arrival will not cause confusion.
Appoint an orientation mentor.	Having a go-to person for the new employee will increase productivity.
The New Employee's First Day	
Welcome the new employee and introduce him/her to the current staff and appointed mentor.	A warm introduction will help the employee feel more comfortable in the new environment.
Show the new employee his/her new workspace and give a tour of the facilities.	The employee will need to know where he/she should work and how to access the appropriate facilities.
Review the job description and indicate responsibilities and expectations.	The employee should be aware of what he/she is expected to do and agree to those responsibilities.
Provide the employee with a copy of the company handbook and explain all key policies.	The employee will need to be familiar with all of the company's policies before he/she is expected to follow them.
Have the employee review the company's benefits.	The employee should be aware of any health or financial benefits that are available.
Explain and give examples of general administrative practices used by the department.	Giving the employee the proper templates, scripts, and forms will help him/her abide by the department's practices.
Give the employee an opportunity to ask questions.	Giving the employee an opportunity to ask questions the first day will avoid confusion later.
The New Employee's First Week	
Schedule brief daily meetings with the new employee to explain his/her responsibilities for the day.	Since priorities may change daily, it is good to review and clarify the employee's responsibilities.
Set up times for the new employee and appointed mentor to meet.	Meeting with a mentor throughout the week will create more opportunities to discuss issues or problems.
Have a meeting at the end of the week to discuss any professional questions or personal concerns the employee may have.	This will present an opportunity to understand how the employee feels about the job and if he/she feels comfortable moving forward.

What other training is required of new and present employees?

Training begins where orientation ends. Training should teach employees skills or ways to improve on existing skills. For example, a salesperson might know how to sell a product but may not know all the intricacies of selling a new product. Often, other employees in the department or the recent hire's mentor can conduct **on-the-job training**. In on-the-job training, employees learn skills by performing them. Sometimes, however, an apprentice training program is required. An **apprentice training program** trains individuals through classroom or formal instruction and on-the-job training. Some jobs are more readily learned through a **programmed learning approach** in which the employee is asked to perform step-by-step instructions or to respond to questions. These often come in the form of computerized multiple-choice tests, which provide immediate feedback. The benefit of programmed learning is that the employee can progress at his or her own pace, picking up information piece-by-piece. The downside of these programs is the cost, as they tend to be delivered via computer programs.

What kind of impact has technology had on training? Improvements in technology provide companies with other training options such as simulated training and interactive multimedia training. **Simulation training** (or **vestibule training**) provides realistic job-task training in a manner that is challenging, but does not create the threat of failure. It is most suitable to airline pilots, astronauts, and surgeons for whom making mistakes during training is not an option or is too costly.

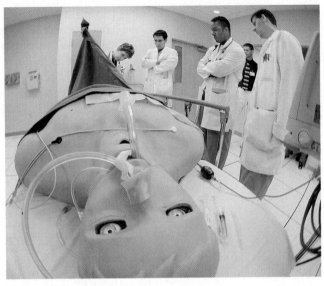

Online training, or distance learning, allows employees to take college classes on the Internet at their convenience, enabling them to obtain specific job-related education or to pursue a degree. Other forms of Internet-based distance learn-

▶ Robots are used in simulation training for medical students.

ing training have instructors in a centralized location teach groups of employees at remote locations via television hookups (*teletraining*) or through a combination of audio/video equipment (*videoconferencing*). Electronic Performance Support Systems (EPSSs) provide employees with information, advice, and training when they need it, automatically, so they can accomplish specific tasks quickly. EPSSs are especially useful to train and support help-desk and on-call operators as well as to act as an in-house help-desk alternative. When Pitney Bowes, a provider of mail and messaging management equipment, previously upgraded its information management system, few employees took advantage of the half-day instructor-led training programs the company offered. Instead, employees inundated the company's help desk with their questions, which turned out to be a very inefficient and costly result. With their next software upgrade, Pitney Bowes implemented an EPSS mentor program and found that the volume of help-desk call requests declined by over 2,000 calls per week, saving the company an estimated $50,000 per week.[10]

Do managers need training? Because of their roles in the organization, managers require different training than their frontline co-workers. Manager training focuses on leadership, communication, teamwork, and relationship-building skills. In addition, managers need to keep abreast of the changes in employment laws such as discrimination and harassment, as well as updates in the use of electronic communication resources. In addition to training for current managers, many companies offer **management development programs** that prepare management-trainees to become managers within the organization. These programs may have the trainees participate in an on-the-job training program, which might include *job rotation,* in which the employee rotates through different departments to learn firsthand the various aspects of the business, or a *coaching/understudy program,* in which the employee works directly with senior management in planning and other managerial functions. *Action learning*, another management development training approach, focuses on solving real problems on actual work projects. Action learning allows trainees to work together in teams to analyze real-time corporate problems that extend beyond their areas of expertise. Companies such as General Electric and Johnson & Johnson have successfully implemented action-learning teams as part of their management development programs.[11]

Some companies use **off-the-job training and development** techniques that require employees to participate in outside seminars, university-conducted programs, and corporate universities. Hamburger University, McDonald's corporate training facility, trains restaurant managers and mid-level managers. Management hopefuls enroll in extensive classroom and field instruction and can earn credit that can even be applied toward a two-year or four-year degree.[12]

Senior managers often use *executive coaches* to further develop their effectiveness. Executive coaches identify the manager's strengths and weaknesses by interviewing those who work closely with the manager. They then meet with the manager to work on eliminating weaknesses and further developing strengths. *Mentoring* is another option that companies use to enable their experienced managers to work closely with inexperienced managers. **Mentors** are experienced individual employees who help a less experienced person by explaining how to perform specific tasks, creating opportunities to learn new skills, and counseling about the consequences of particular actions and decisions. Like other forms of training and management development, mentoring increases employee performance, satisfaction, and loyalty.

Performance Appraisals and Alternatives

Why are performance appraisals necessary? A **performance appraisal** is an evaluation of an employee's performance that gives feedback about how well the employee is doing, as well as where changes and improvements are needed (see ▼ **Figure 9.5**). Managers use the results of performance appraisals in decisions about promotion, raises, additional training, or reassignments. The performance appraisal process is important for both employees and the organization as a whole. The process includes:

1. Determining standards that employees should aim for in their work.

2. Evaluating the employee's performance in comparison with these standards.

3. Providing feedback to reduce and eliminate poor performance and improve or enhance positive performance.

When employees are hired, they should have a good understanding of what is expected of them. These expectations become the performance standards upon which they'll be measured. Appraisals act as a confirmation of these standards and help employees establish quantifiable and measurable goals for improvement in the upcoming year.

Are there problems with performance appraisals? Although performance appraisals, when conducted properly, are very helpful to the employee and ultimately the organization, they are often not effective. Since appraisals often lead to criticism, many managers shy away from them because they are uncomfortable handing out bad or harsh comments. Additionally, some managers have a difficult time quantifying performance, and fear not being able to defend their ratings if questioned. Although performance appraisals often suggest means to improve weak performance or to enhance solid performance, the process does not always offer the opportunity to follow up and ensure that such means have been acted on. Often, it's not until the next performance

▼ **Figure 9.5**

A Sample Performance Appraisal

Kayse Optics
2653 N. Dayton Ave.
Memphis, TN 38110

Annual Employee Performance Evaluation

Employee's Name:		Supervisor:	
Job Title:		Date Hired:	
Department:		Date of Review:	

Evaluation

This form is design to assess your current performance and to help in setting goals for the future. This form is considered confidential and will only be reviewed by you and your supervisor(s).

Overall Job Knowledge/Experience Level

	Consistently meets requirements
	Generally meets requirements
	Does not meet requirements
Comments:	

Quality of Work

	Exceeds expectations
	Meets expectations
	Does not meet expectations
Comments:	

Attendance

	Rarely tardy or absent
	Sometimes tardy or absent
	Frequently tardy or absent
Comments:	

Cooperation

	Consistently participates and contributes to the team
	Generally participates and contributes to the team
	Does not participate or contribute to the team
Comments:	

Future Goals:

appraisal that it is recognized that such training and development have not happened. And when the next appraisal can be a year away, the benefits of appraisals become diluted.

Do alternatives exist for performance appraisals❓ An alternative to a performance appraisal is performance management. **Performance management** is an approach that combines goal setting, performance appraisal, and training and development into a unified and ongoing process. As such, it is more of a cyclical and fluid process than the single occurrence of a performance appraisal. Employees are constantly receiving feedback and given opportunities for training and development to ensure that they have the right tools with which to perform their job. ▼ **Table 9.2** summarizes several aspects of the performance management process. The concept, while often applied to employees, is also applicable to other components of the organization, including an entire department, a product or service, or the organization as a whole.

▼ **Table 9.2**

Aspects of Performance Management	
Direction sharing	Communicating organization's higher-level goals such as vision, mission, values, and strategy
Role clarifying	Defining roles in terms of daily work tasks
Goal setting and planning	Redefining organizational or departmental goals into specific employee goals, which includes the employee's development of the steps necessary to achieve goals
Ongoing performance monitoring and feedback	Periodic performance reports regarding progress on meeting goals as well as feedback regarding progress toward goals
Coaching and support	Ongoing as a part of the feedback process
Performance assessment (appraisal)	An element in performance management process that offers specific defined knowledge on how employee's performance is improving company results
Rewards, recognition, and compensation	Given as appropriate to motivate employee toward achieving current and future goals
Workflow, process control, and return on investment management	Making sure employee's measurable performance is linked to measurable goals of company

Source: Dessler, Gary. Human Resource Management, 11th edition. Upper Saddle River, NJ: Prentice Hall, p. 338

Performance management, appraisals, and training can play a significant role in keeping a business productive and efficient. Although they often require an investment of time and money, the investment often pays off. For Cold Stone Creamery, which is pursuing a fresh new approach to employee training, although the initial cost to develop its Stone City game may have seemed high, in the end, such games are often more cost effective than a centralized approach.[13] Moreover, games don't need to take up valuable work hours—employees can log in at home during their free time. And they're fun!

▼ You have just read **Objective 2**

Want a review? Check out the Study Plan section @
www.my*biz*lab.com.

Compensating, Scheduling, Promoting, and **Terminating Employees** pp. 262-267

How would you like to go to work and play beach volleyball during your lunch break? Or how about a game of table tennis to prevent the afternoon slump? Well, if you work at Google's Mountain View, California, campus, you can. Google strives to make its workplace culture fun and relaxed to help facilitate creativity and energy to get the job done. It ranked #1 in 2007 on *Fortune* magazine's "Best Companies To Work For" list. Perks such as being able to bring your dog to work, a swimming pool, and the choice of 11 free gourmet cafeterias all aim at boosting workers' morale.[14] How important are Google's work/life benefits compared with salary? Is one preferable to the other?

Having the right pay system in place is very important for a company to become and remain competitive. A fair and comparable compensation package attracts high-quality employees and keeps them from leaving. Moreover, employees have a greater incentive to work harder and more efficiently if they know their compensation is tied to their efforts and to the overall success of the company. A low turnover rate and a productive workforce help to keep costs low, which has a positive impact on the company's profits. But, as is clear from the Google example, compensation is not just monetary rewards. In today's workplace, employees frequently receive compensation in a variety of forms, including work/life benefits, health insurance, and retirement plans. Because there are many ways to structure compensation, the decision is not an easy one. It's often a delicate balance between paying to attract and keep the best and not jeopardizing the financial security of the company. In this section, you'll learn about payment structures, as well as two more functions of the HR department: promotions and terminations.

Compensation Strategies

Are all employees paid in the same way? There are many ways to pay workers for their time and effort. **Compensation**, payment for work performed, is generally offered through *direct financial payments* in the form of fixed **salaries** (annual pay for a specific job) or **wages** (payments for hourly work). Usually on an annual basis, the employee's compensation level has the potential to increase based on the results of employee evaluations. Some positions, such as those in sales, are better compensated with an **incentive-based payment** structure that has a lower base salary enhanced with **commissions**, compensation based directly on the employee's performance. Incentive-based compensation motivates employees to perform at their best. **Bonuses**, compensation based on total corporate profits, help tie employees' efforts to the company's bottom line. Higher corporate profits mean higher bonuses.

What types of retirement plans and other financial incentives do companies offer employees?

The most popular retirement plan offered today is the 401(k) plan. A **401(k) plan** is a defined contribution plan in which pre-tax dollars are invested in a bundle of investments that are generally managed by an outside investment company, such as the Vanguard Group. The amount of the annual contribution is determined by the employee as a percentage of salary up to a specified legal limit. In some cases, the company matches a portion of the employee's contribution to the account.

Some companies offer their full-time employees the opportunity to participate in a pension plan. **Pension plans** are programs that provide income to individuals in their retirement. There are two categories of pension plans. With *defined benefit plans*, employees know ahead of time how much pension they will receive when they retire. Defined benefit plans are not popular with employers, as the company takes on the financial risk if the fund's investments do not perform as expected. *Defined contribution plans* specify the annual amount employees will contribute to their pension plan through payroll deductions. With defined contribution plans, the actual amount received at retirement is dependent on the amount contributed and the fund's investment earnings. The burden of risk falls on the employees with defined contribution plans, and there is no way they can determine how much will ultimately be available until they actually retire.

A **profit sharing plan** is a retirement plan for businesses in which the employer alone makes contributions. The business owner can contribute and deduct between zero and 25 percent of the eligible employee's combined compensation. In spite of its name, profit sharing plans aren't dependent on a company making a profit. Profit sharing plans are usually offered as a part of executive compensation in larger companies, but in many small companies, they are a way to motivate employees, especially during the start-up phase when cash is tight and salaries may be low.

Stock option plans offer shares of company stock to employees for purchase on a set date. The shares can be purchased at the value of the stock when it was originally offered or at an agreed-upon price. Thus, if the stock value increases over time, the employee reaps financial rewards. If not, however, the employee gains little. **Employee stock purchase plans** allow employees to buy company stock at a discount (usually 85 percent of market value). Companies typically provide payroll deductions for these purchases and limit amounts to 10 percent of total pay. **Employee stock ownership plans (ESOPs)** are a form of defined contribution plan that allow employees to own part of the company without purchasing stock. Instead, the company contributes its stock to the plan. An advantage of providing employees with ownership in the company via stock transactions is that employees feel more connected to the business and are motivated to ensure that the business succeeds.

Benefits

What are non-cash compensation payment structures?

An important part of the business planning and management process is determining the type and amount of **employee benefits**, or indirect financial and nonfinancial payments an employer offers that supplement cash compensation. Benefit compensation often enables a company to attract, motivate, and retain the best employees. Benefits come in many forms, including health and disability insurance, vacation and sick pay, and retirement plans. Some companies offer **flexible benefit plans** (or **cafeteria plans**) that permit the employee to pick from a "menu" of several choices of taxable and nontaxable forms of compensation. Flexible benefit plans allow employees to choose the benefits that are most important to them, while reducing the cost of offering all benefits to all employees. Vacation, holidays, and pensions, once referred to as "fringe benefits," constitute a significant percentage of total compensation. Other non-cash benefits help employees balance the demands of their professional and personal lives.

What are work/life benefits? Work/life benefits are benefits that help an employee achieve a balance between the demands of life both inside and outside the workplace. Work/life benefits include flexible schedules, relaxed atmospheres, and child care and fitness/gym programs. For example, the SAS Institute, the largest privately held software developer in the United States, offers employees an on-site fitness club with indoor pool, on-site car detailing, massages, and a hair salon. Although seemingly expensive, this strategy of keeping its employees happy saves the company approximately $70 million per year because it experiences low turnover. In fact, compared with an industry average of 20 percent turnover, SAS has kept its turnover rate at around 2 percent.[15]

What are some other trends in employee benefits? In the early 80s, the *Village Voice*, a free alternative weekly newspaper in New York City, began offering *domestic-partner benefits*. These benefits provide for an employee's unmarried partner of the same or opposite sex. Since then, domestic-partner benefits have become increasingly common components of compensation packages. The Phoenix Companies, Inc., a life insurance and wealth management corporation, recently enhanced its employee benefits package with *paternity and adoption benefits* that allow time off for new fathers, and reimbursement and paid leave for adoption. The company is following a trend that, according to the Families and Work Institute and the Society for Human Resource Management, is represented by approximately 15 percent of companies in the United States that offer paternity benefits.[16] In addition to these voluntary benefits, the Family and Medical Leave Act states that companies with more than 50 employees must allow all eligible employees to take up to 12 weeks of unpaid time off to be with family because of medical issues, births, or adoptions. Upon the employee's return, the act guarantees that the employee can return to his or her job or a comparable job.

Alternative Scheduling Arrangements

What work arrangements are possible for those who choose not to work a traditional workweek? An increasing number of employees are finding that managing the demands of work and personal life results in doing neither well. The added stresses that face employees today from child care, elder care, commuting, and other work/life conflicts have led to a decrease in productivity and an increase in employee absenteeism and tardiness. As a result, more and more employers are offering alternatives to the traditional 9 AM to 5 PM, Monday to Friday workweek. In fact, according to the U.S. Bureau of Labor and Statistics, over one-quarter of U.S. employees take advantage of some form of flexible work arrangement.[17] The most popular flexible work arrangements include the following:

1. **Alternative Scheduling Plans (Flextime).** In *alternative scheduling plans or flextime*, management defines a total number of required hours as a core workday and is flexible with starting and ending times. Managers must rise

to the challenge of ensuring that required hours are met and monitoring employee performance. However, overall, flexible arrangements allow for increased productivity due to reductions in absenteeism and tardiness.

2. **Permanent Part-Time. Permanent part-time employees** are hired on a permanent basis to work a part-time week. Unlike temporary part-time workers who are employed to fill short-term needs, permanent part-time employees enjoy the same benefits that full-time employees receive.

3. **Job Sharing**. **Job sharing** is an arrangement in which two employees work part-time sharing one full-time job. Those who share a job have been found to be very motivated to make this flexible situation work, so productivity and employee satisfaction increase. On the other hand, conflicts may arise if the job sharers don't have a clear understanding of who is in charge of what or if there is confusion from other employees about whom to contact and when. Therefore, job sharers must carefully coordinate and communicate both with one another and their employer to ensure that all responsibilities are met.

4. **Compressed Workweek**. A **compressed workweek** allows employees to work four 10-hour days instead of five 8-hour or nine days (not ten) in a two-week schedule for 80 hours. Such arrangements can reduce worker overtime, make more efficient use of facilities, and provide employees with longer blocks of personal time and less commuting time. The disadvantages are a potential increase in employee fatigue and conflicts with state labor laws that cite overtime requirements for hours worked in excess of eight a day.

5. **Telecommuting. Telecommuting** allows employees to work in the office part-time and work from home part-time, or to work completely from home, making only occasional visits to the office. Telecommuting reduces commuting costs and allows employees to take care of home needs while also fulfilling work responsibilities. Telecommuting arrangements are also necessary for those employees dealing with clients, colleagues, or suppliers who are on the other side of the globe. Taking calls at 2 AM is much easier at home than at the office. The disadvantages of telecommuting include monitoring employees' performance at a distance, servicing equipment for off-site employees, and communication issues. Additionally, employees who telecommute may become isolated from other employees.

➤ UPS offers a permanent part-time package handler position in which employees work 3.5 to 4 hours, Monday to Friday, with no weekend or evening work required. In addition to traditional health insurance, vacations, and a stock purchase plan, UPS offers tuition assistance as an additional benefit, which makes this type of position perfect for the working student.

Despite the costs associated with designing and implementing flexible working arrangements, employers can expect positive bottom-line results due to increases in employee satisfaction, decreases in absenteeism, and increases in worker productivity. Similarly, reductions in employee turnover lead to a decrease in time and costs associated with employee recruiting and replacement training.

Temporary and Contingent Workers

Why does a company hire temporary workers? Contingent workers are persons who are hired on an as-needed basis and lack status as regular, full-time employees. These workers often fulfill important and specific functions. Contingent workers are most likely to be hired by companies in business and professional services, education and health care services, and construction industries. Companies hire temporary workers to fill in for absent employees or to augment the staff during busy periods. Long-term temporary staff is often hired for indefinite periods of time to work on specific projects. In many cases, temporary staffing is part of a company's human resource "temp to perm" strategy.

Independent contractors and **consultants** are another form of contingent worker who are generally self-employed and who companies hire on a temporary basis to perform specific tasks. Often, contractors are hired for those jobs that are commonly hard to fill that involve state-of-the-art skills in construction, financial activities, and professional and business services. For example, it might be most cost efficient to hire a Web-page developer as an independent contractor rather than keeping one on staff permanently. Consultants are hired to assist with long-term projects, often at a strategic level, but also with a specific end in sight. For example, a company that is reviewing its executive management compensation arrangements might hire a compensation consultant.

Why would someone want to be a temporary worker? Temporary staffing is a $70-billion industry, represented by companies such as Kelly Services, Manpower, Accountemps, and Spherion. Many people cite flexibility and variety as a benefit of working for a temporary agency. Because their assignments are short-term, temporary workers are able to experience working in many different companies, doing different jobs, and meeting numerous people. In many instances, temporary workers are hired permanently. Recent college graduates and college students find temporary work as a means to gain real-world experience in an industry they are interested in pursuing on a full-time basis. Other temporary workers are retired professionals who want to do something productive in their free time, but still maintain some flexibility. Also, parents who need to earn income but also require a flexible schedule find that temporary work enables them to accomplish both.

Promotions and Transfers

How can employees increase their level of responsibility in the firm? After performing successfully in a position, many employees look to increase their level of responsibility and stature in the firm or department through a promotion. Usually, a promotion means more pay and responsibility. Employers like to promote from within because they can reward exceptional behavior and fill positions with tested employees. However, promotion may not always result in a positive situation if it is seen as being draped in secrecy, unfairness, or arbitrariness. Therefore, management must ensure that promotions are based on a distinct set of criteria such as seniority or competency.

Do promotions need to be geared toward management positions? Consider an engineer who succeeds on the job but has no desire to manage. Some companies provide two career paths: one toward management and the other for "individual contributors" with no management aspirations. Therefore, engineers, for example, with a desire to manage can pursue one track, and other engineers without managerial aspirations or capabilities can be promoted to a position such as "senior engineer." Alternatively, it's always possible to keep employees in their same job but give them more responsibility, thus enriching their experience while continuing to prepare them for further advancement.

Is there a set age when employees retire? It used to be that employees retired when they reached the age of 65. **Retirement** is the point in one's life where he or she stops participating full-time in his or her career. Although nearly three-fourths of all workers would like to retire before the age of 60, a survey by the John J. Heldrich Center for Workforce Development at Rutgers University[18] indicates that nearly 7 in 10 workers plan to keep working past retirement age. While some survey respondents indicated that the reason for staying on the job was to remain active, the major factor contributing to this shift is financial need. One impact of this shift in workforce demographics is more competition for younger employees to be promoted into certain jobs. For employers, an aging workforce may present other challenges such as decreasing morale among workers or age-discrimination lawsuits if they aggressively lay off older workers. Therefore, to encourage older workers to retire, companies have offered financial incentives, known as **worker buyouts** (or *golden parachutes*). This was the case at the Chrysler Group in 2007. After losing $1.5 billion in 2006, the automaker began cutting jobs. Its strategy included offering workers aged 62 and older three months' pay for retiring early, and full medical benefits for retiring early to workers aged 53 and older.[19]

Terminating Employees

Why do companies lay off workers? At times it is necessary to reevaluate an employee's contribution or tenure at the company, or to reevaluate the composition and size of the workforce altogether. Downsizing and restructuring, the growth of outsourcing and offshoring, the pressures of global competition, and the increased uses of technology are all reasons companies look to reduce the number of employees. Reducing the number of employees takes place through a process called **termination**—permanently laying off workers due to poor performance or a discontinued need for their services.

When faced with the need to lay off employees, companies often offer outplacement services such as résumé writing and career counseling. Terminating employees due to poor performance or illegal activities is much more complex. Most states support **employment at will**, a legal doctrine which states that the employer can fire an employee for any reason at any time. Likewise, the employee is equally free to resign at any time for any reason. Exceptions to the employment-at-will doctrine include the inability for employers to discriminate and fire someone because of legally protected characteristics or activities, such as race, religion, age, gender, national origin, or disability. In addition, companies cannot terminate employees because of whistle-blowing, filing a worker's compensation claim, jury service, or testifying against the company in a legal proceeding.

Before firing an employee for wrongful doings or incompetence, managers must take steps to avoid a wrongful discharge lawsuit. These steps include maintaining solid records so that they can build a case for dismissal with sufficient documentation and evidence. Courts have sided with the terminated employee, especially when not enough evidence of poor behavior is brought forth. Written evidence is the only material evidence accepted, which makes building an employee's personnel file with documented proof of poor performance critical. Hearsay and rumors do not stand up in legal proceedings.

Compensation, scheduling, promotions, and termination comprise an important part of HR management. Companies such as Google, profiled at the beginning of this section, have revolutionized the way that businesses approach these issues with their implementation of innovative work/life benefits and a dynamic, employee-friendly work environment. Indeed, many of the highest-quality applicants nowadays expect companies to offer these perks. Such is the nature of the modern workplace.

▼ You have just read **Objectives 3 & 4**

Want to learn more? Check out the Study Plan section @ **www.mybizlab.com.**

Managing Workplace Diversity pp. 268-270

With changing demographics, diversity has become more and more prevalent in the workplace. Companies need to address diversity with training in order to be successful. Failure to do this can lead to lawsuits and embarrassment. Look at the following statements, and think about what your reactions to the statements tell you about yourself.

1. Everyone, including white males, benefits from diversity training.
2. Diversity training only includes race and gender.
3. Certain ethnic groups are smarter than others.
4. Talking about diversity just makes people uncomfortable.
5. Some professions are not suited for older people.

 In this section, you'll learn about what makes the modern workplace so diverse and how diversity introduces both challenges and benefits to organizations.

Managing Workforce Diversity

What demographic changes are presenting management challenges? Look around you. Most likely, you work, study, and socialize with people who are of different gender, age, religion, race, sexual orientation, mental and physical ability, and educational background than you. Several demographic changes have brought forth HR challenges—some new and some that have existed for many years.

Advancements in technology have made it possible for businesses to operate with relative ease on a global basis. It's not unusual to read about companies that are offshoring work to other countries to lessen labor costs, or establishing operations in other countries to broaden their market reach. Moreover, companies are hiring workers who have emigrated from other countries to the United States, where greater opportunities exist. European and Middle Eastern companies are experiencing similar increases in immigration. As we discuss below, many companies are seeking to increase the cultural diversity of their workforce because it has been proven to have positive results on the bottom line.

A more culturally diverse population naturally brings about a wider variety of religious beliefs and practices, with more employees trying to integrate their religious practices into their workday. As employers struggle to accommodate workers' religious needs, they must also try to avoid the potential friction that open demonstrations of religious practices might provoke. Many employers strike a balance by allowing employees to take prayer breaks, enabling employees to take time off to observe religious holidays, catering to dietary requirements, and permitting differences in dress. Value City Department Stores, for example, have set up quiet prayer rooms for Muslims. Some employers encourage workers to form religious-based support groups such as Bible-study groups.

More women are entering the workforce than ever before. However, statistically, there are substantially fewer women top executives than you would expect given the increase in women's numbers in the workforce. In addition, women are still battling some of the same issues that their mothers and grandmothers faced: sexism, salary inequities, and sexual harassment. Historically, women in similar positions as their male counterparts are paid less and have experienced fewer promotions, despite documented higher performance ratings. Many gender-discrimination and sexual harassment lawsuits continue to receive national press and indicate that gender-related challenges have not gone away.

Baby boomers, those born between 1946 and 1964, make up about one-third of the U.S. workforce. As discussed earlier, many baby boomers are indicating that they would like to and need to work beyond the traditional retirement age. This aging demographic group creates several workforce challenges. Compared with younger workers in the same position, older workers often expect higher salaries and better benefits. Health care costs, for example, are higher with an older workforce. However, many employers find that hiring and retaining older employees has several benefits, including less turnover and absenteeism, lower training costs, and a willingness to learn new skills and to help and train younger co-workers. These benefits offer enough savings to a company to negate the higher costs in retaining more senior workers.

Impact of Diversity

How is a diverse workforce beneficial? As discussed earlier, diversity is an important component of the modern workplace. For many companies, hiring to diversify the workforce initially meant fulfilling an **affirmative action** requirement by filling positions with a certain number of women, Hispanics, or African Americans. Some criticized this strategy as unfair and bad for the company if the best candidate was not hired in favor of meeting such a requirement. Over time, however, many companies have come to embrace the idea of diversity beyond just satisfying a requirement. It's now becoming clear that companies should embrace diversity as a strategy and resource to become more competitive in the global market. Promoting diversity in the workplace is more than affirmative action that prescribes a company to employ a certain number of minorities and women. Instead, diversity should be aggressively pursued as a means to improve a company's competitiveness and its bottom line. A diverse workforce helps companies offer a broad range of viewpoints that are necessary to compete in a world that is more globalized. Such variety in viewpoints promotes creativity in problem solving with improved results. Products and services need to cater to customers and clients with diverse

▶ Harley-Davidson realized that in order to remain competitive, it needed to understand the needs and wants of customers beyond the traditional stereotype of the white male. Since then, the motorcycle manufacturer has made a significant effort to hire and retain women and minority managers.[20]

Off the Mark
One Diversity Training Does Not Fit All

Because promoting diversity is a priority for most companies in today's global marketplace, so too is the implementation of diversity training programs. These often-costly programs typically involve workshops and seminars that teach managers about the benefits of a diverse workforce. And yet, according to a 2007 study, most of them simply don't work.[21] After analyzing years of national employment statistics, they concluded that standard diversity training rarely had an effect on the number of women or minority managers employed at companies where it was used. Why not? Some theorize that mandatory training inevitably leads to backlash; others say altering people's inner biases is a nearly impossible task. Hope for promoting diversity in the workplace is not lost; however, the study also found that two techniques had significant, beneficial effects on workplace diversity. The first, the appointment of a specific person or committee who is specifically accountable for addressing diversity issues within the company, led to 10-percent increases in the number of women and minorities in management positions. The second, mentorships, increased the number of African American women in leadership positions by 23.5 percent.

backgrounds, and if you have a workforce that does not understand the nuances of different cultural needs, you might be missing some opportunities.

PepsiCo's Frito Lay launched a Doritos Guacamole Flavored Tortilla chip to appeal especially to Latino consumers. The Latino Employee Network at PepsiCo's Frito Lay division provided valuable feedback on taste and packaging to ensure that these chips would be regarded as authentic in the Latino community. The product generated more than $100 million in sales in its first year, making it the most successful product launch in the company's history. Additionally, a diverse staff helps strategize ways to handle markets that have become segmented, both culturally and demographically.[22]

What issues do companies face while managing diversity?

Unfortunately, a diverse workforce can have its obstacles. Cultural differences can create misunderstandings and conflict, even over the most well-intentioned behaviors. Therefore, it's important that employers provide effective diversity training for their employees. It's also important for co-workers to learn to look at situations from a perspective that's different from their own. While implementing a diversity plan, it's important to ensure that the white men who have been instrumental in the company do not feel tossed out or undervalued if they are passed up for promotion in lieu of someone from a more diverse background. Ultimately, managing diversity is developing a workforce that has a capacity to accept, incorporate, and empower the diversity of human talents and perspectives.

Review the self-inventory at the beginning of this section. Have your feelings on the importance of diversity changed? What challenges, and benefits, have you encountered or do you anticipate encountering in the workplace?

▼ You have just read **Objective 5**

Want to test your skills? Check out the Study Plan section @ **www.my*biz*lab.com.**

Labor and Union Issues pp. 271-273

➤ Have you ever passed a picket line and wondered why the workers were on strike? A **strike** occurs when workers agree to stop work until certain demands are met. In this section, you'll learn about the role of organized labor in the workplace and how this role is changing in today's global economy.

Unions are formed to protect the interests of workers. When General Motors workers became concerned about job security, union and GM representatives negotiated to no avail. In September 2007, more than 73,000 employees for GM went on strike. Before this, the United Auto Workers (UAW) union hadn't led a strike on GM in over 35 years. Issues of contention included job security and retiree health benefits. In an effort to be competitive and reduce the cost of vehicles, GM wanted to cut labor costs. Workers knew these cuts could have a potentially profound effect, so they took action.[23] ➤

Organized Labor

What is a labor union? A **labor union** is a legally recognized group dedicated to protecting the interests of workers. Unions represent many types of workers in public-sector industries such as teachers, nurses, and firefighters, in manufacturing industries such as the automotive industry, and in construction specialty "craft" groups such as engineers, plumbers, and roofers. Entertainers and supporting industries, such as actors and writers, also have unions. Labor unions negotiate employment issues such as salary, benefits, and working hours.

What are the objectives of organized labor? Labor unions began as a means to protect workers from the terrible injustices employers inflicted upon their workers in the 19th century during the U.S. Industrial Revolution. During that time, employers took advantage of workers, subjecting them to long hours, low pay, and health risks. Women and children were often treated even worse and paid less. Labor unions formed to fight for better working conditions and employee rights. These individual labor unions, by joining together, proved to be more effective in bettering working conditions. Two of the more influential unions were the **American Federation of Labor (AFL)**, founded in 1886 to protect skilled workers and the Industrial Workers of the World, founded in 1905 to represent mainly unskilled workers.

The **Congress of Industrial Organizations (CIO)** was formed in 1935 to represent entire industries, rather than specific workers' groups. The CIO was initially a separate organization within the AFL, but soon split to form its own organization. In 1955, the two were reunited to form the AFL-CIO, which is still in effect today as a federation made up of 56 member unions. The Change to Win Federation, formed in 2005 as an alternative to the AFL-CIO, is the newest member to organized labor. Other prominent unions include the United Auto Workers, the International Brotherhood of Teamsters, and the Service Employees International Union.

How are labor unions structured? To form a union, a group of workers must either have their employer voluntarily recognize them as a group or have a majority of workers form a **bargaining unit** for union representation. A bargaining unit is a group of employees that negotiate with the employer for better working conditions or pay. When a union forms, workers join and pay membership dues. Most unions have paid, full-time staff who are often supplemented with substantial volunteer workers. In addition to dues, some unions create strike funds that help support workers should they strike. Union members elect officers and shop stewards who make decisions for the entire body and represent the members in dealings with management. So that unions can better represent specific interests, union **locals** are created by workers of the same industry, company, region, or business sector.

Collective Bargaining

What is the collective bargaining process? One of the primary roles of a union is to negotiate with the employer for better work conditions and terms of employment. This generally is done through a **collective bargaining** process. Negotiation is between union representatives and employers usually over concerns including wages, benefits, working hours, and grievance procedures. A collective bargaining agreement is the result of such negotiations and forces the employer to abide by the conditions specified in the agreement. Change can only be made through subsequent negotiations.

What happens if an agreement cannot be reached through collective bargaining? If negotiating does not produce a collective bargaining agreement, and both parties seem to be at an impasse, then other means to settle the dispute are used before workers go on strike. **Mediation** is a process that involves a neutral third party that assists the two parties both privately and collectively to identify issues and to develop proposals for resolution. The mediator works with both sides to understand their genuine interests and helps each side generate proposals that address those interests. In **arbitration**, the dispute is sent to an arbitrator for a decision. Arbitrators hear both sides of the dispute and the parties involved agree in advance that the arbitrator's decision is final. Sometimes, arbitration is nonbinding, meaning that neither party is required to accept the arbitrator's decision.

What happens when negotiations break down? When negotiation reaches an impasse, union workers can take several actions to prompt management to accept union demands. Union members and those who are sympathetic to their cause can stage a **boycott**, in which supporters refuse to buy or handle the company's products or services. On the other hand, companies can use a **lockout** in which management refuses to allow union members from entering the premises. Lockouts are legal only if negotiations have come to an impasse and the company is defending a legitimate position.

As a last resort, union workers may vote to go on strike and agree to stop working. Strikes jeopardize the productivity of the organization, so they are used to force management into making concessions that they might not have made otherwise. Strikes also gain considerable media publicity, especially when the workers **picket** the workplace by walking outside the company's entrances with signs that reflect the employee's grievances. Workers do not easily make the decision to strike, as they risk losing income throughout the strike period. For example, a six-week strike would cost a worker earning $700 per week a total of $4,200 in lost wages. Assuming the new contract negotiated a weekly wage increase of $1, it would take about two years to recover the lost wages. Additionally, strikers might be fired or replaced as management has the authority to hire replacement personnel, known as **strikebreakers**, or scabs. Some states prohibit public safety workers such as police officers, and hospital workers to go on strike. In those cases, workers often have "sick-outs" during which union members are not officially on strike but instead call in sick, refusing to come to work.

The State of Labor Unions

Are labor unions still effective today? In the United States, the role of labor unions is declining. As of 2006, 15.4 million people representing 12 percent of employed workers[24] were union members (see ▼ **Table 9.3**). Many private-sector unions such as the automobile workers and construction trade unions have experienced dramatic reductions in membership. This decline is the result of several factors, but arguably, the most prominent reason is a reaction to their own success by fighting for better working conditions, higher wages, and more benefits. Additionally, the introduction of technology has resulted in a shift from blue-collar–based industries to professional white-collar service-based industries, for whom unions are less common. Despite declining numbers, labor unions continue to be influential in many industries, as well as in other countries.

What is the future of unions and labor-management relations?
In response to a more globalized working community, unions have begun to build alliances with unions in other nations. They recognize that when multinational corporations make decisions to move production abroad, for example, there might be a negative impact on local and international workers. Consequently, in an effort to protect their interests, they must broaden their reach and make a commitment to international labor solidarity. Immigration is another issue affecting unions as immigrant workers are crossing borders, threatening to take jobs traditionally supported by labor unions. Unions, especially in California and Florida, continue to grapple with integrating and embracing these potential new members into the organization. Lastly, and perhaps most importantly, unions, will need to transform themselves to survive the effects of globalization.

It was through bargaining that the UAW strike discussed at the beginning of this section was ultimately resolved. After a long bargaining session, an agreement was reached that ended the two-day strike. As part of the agreement, the union agreed to shoulder the responsibility for more than $50 billion in retiree health costs. The changing economy has made the relationship between management and unions in the United States increasingly complex. The precise role unions will play in the global workplace remains to be seen.

▼ **Table 9.3**

Union Membership in the United States 2000–2007	
Year	Members of unions as percentage of employed workers
2000	13.4
2001	13.3
2002	13.3
2003	12.9
2004	12.5
2005	12.5
2006	12.0
2007	12.1

Source: http://www.bls.gov/ webapps/legacy/cpslutab1.htm

▼ You have just read **Objective 6**

Want to quiz yourself? Check out the Study Plan section @ **www.mybizlab.com.**

1. What processes are involved in human resource management? (pp. 251-256)

- **Human resource management** (p. 251) covers every aspect of managing the people resources in a company.

- Staff planning involves determining how many employees a company needs. A **workforce profile** (p. 252) is compiled as a form of "personnel inventory" and includes information about each employee.

- **Recruitment** (p. 253) is the process of finding, screening, and selecting people for a job.

- Hiring begins by narrowing down candidates that have been identified in the recruiting process to a select group of applicants.

- Companies that emphasize training and development experience greater productivity, loyalty, and retention.

- An **orientation program** (p. 257) integrates new employees into an organization. Other forms of training include **on-the-job training** (p. 258), **simulation training** (p. 259), and **online training** (p. 259).

- **Management development programs** (p. 259) prepare management trainees to become managers within the organization by having them participate in on-the-job training programs.

- **Off-the-job training and development** (p. 259) require the employee to participate in outside seminars, university-conducted programs, and corporate universities.

2. Why is the performance management process proven to be more effective than performance appraisals? (pp. 260-261)

- A **performance appraisal** (p. 260) is an evaluation of an employee's performance that gives feedback and suggestions for improvement. They are useful when done properly, but many managers avoid performance appraisals because they do not feel comfortable critiquing employees harshly.

- **Performance management** (p. 261) is an alternative to performance appraisals. It approaches employee evaluations as ongoing and systematic.

3. What are the main components of compensating and scheduling employees? (pp. 262-265)

- **Compensation** (p. 262), or payment for work performed, consists of financial and nonfinancial payments.

- **Salaries** (p. 262) and hourly **wages** (p. 262), **bonuses** (p. 263), **commissions** (p. 263), and retirement **pension plans** (p. 263) constitute financial compensation.

- *Defined benefit plans* define the amount of retirement benefit the employee will receive and *defined contribution plans* define the contribution the employee must make to the plan. **401(k) plans** (p. 263) allow employees to contribute pre-tax dollars to their retirement plan.

- Non-cash **employee benefits** (p. 263) come in many forms including health and disability insurance, vacation and sick pay, and retirement plans.

- **Work/life benefits** (p. 264) such as gym memberships are important for those employees who are trying to balance busy lives both in and out of work.

- Alternative scheduling arrangements enable employees to have more flexibility in their workday times. **Flextime** (p. 264), **job sharing** (p. 265), **permanent part-time** (p. 265), **telecommuting** (p. 265), and **compressed workweeks** (p. 265) are alternative scheduling methods.

4. How does employee status change through promotions, transfers, retirement, and termination? (pp. 266-267)

- Employees increase their level of responsibility through promotion—taking on a job that has more responsibility and stature in the company or department.

- When vertical advancements are not available or possible, employees can transfer laterally to another department to learn more skills.

- **Retirement** (p. 266) occurs when employees decide to stop working on a full-time basis or stop working altogether. Financial security, staying active and engaged, and learning something new are reasons seniors cite for deferring their retirement.

- **Termination** (p. 267) is when companies permanently lay off workers due to poor performance or a discontinued use for their services. Downsizing and restructuring, outsourcing and offshoring, pressures of global competition, and increased uses of technology are reasons companies look to reduce the number of employees through termination.

5. How does incorporating diversity affect the workforce? (pp. 265-270)

- Companies hire **contingent workers** (p. 265) on a temporary or contingent basis to fill voids due to absent employees or to supplement existing staff during busy times.

- The workforce today is comprised of employees from many different cultures and religions, which can lead to challenges in helping employees to understand one another.

- More women are entering the workforce, but few are reaching executive management levels. Sexism, salary inequity, and sexual harassment remain prominent issues.

- The workforce is getting older as more baby boomers work beyond typical retirement age. An aging workforce increases health care costs, but also increased productivity and decreased training costs.

- A diverse workforce has proven to be more creative and innovative. Diversity keeps companies competitive in a global business community.

Continued on next page

Chapter Summary (cont.)

6. What are the objectives, structures, and future of labor unions in the global business environment? (pp. 271-273)

- A **labor union** (p. 271) is a legally recognized group dedicated to protecting the interests of workers. Labor unions typically negotiate issues such as salary, health benefits, and work hours.

- Representatives of the labor union form a **bargaining unit** (p. 272) that negotiates with employers in a **collective bargaining** process (p. 272) in hopes of reaching an agreement that is satisfactory to both sides.

- If satisfactory terms cannot be agreed on by both sides, often the process is turned over for **mediation** (p. 272), in which a neutral third party assists both sides and generates a proposal that addresses each party's interests.

- In the **arbitration** (p. 272) process, a third party settles the dispute after hearing all the issues.

- If negotiations break down, unions may choose to **boycott** (p. 272) the company.

- As a last resort, union members may vote to go on **strike** (p. 271) and agree to stop working altogether.

- As the business community continues to expand globally, unions will need to change their definition of membership to handle the increase in immigration workers.

For an audio file of the Objectives and Chapter Summary, see the Student Resources section @ www.my*biz*lab.com.

Key Terms

401(k) plan (p. 263)
affirmative action (p. 269)
apprentice training program (p. 258)
arbitration (p. 272)
American Federation of Labor (AFL) (p. 271)
bargaining unit (p. 272)
bonus (p. 263)
boycott (p. 272)
collective bargaining (p. 272)
commissions (p. 263)
compensation (p. 262)
compressed workweek (p. 265)
Congress of Industrial Organizations (CIO) (p. 272)
consultants (p. 266)
contingent workers (p. 265)
employee benefits (p. 263)
employee stock ownership plan (ESOP) (p. 263)
employee stock purchase plan (p. 263)
employment at will (p. 267)
external recruiting (p. 253)
flexible benefit plan (cafeteria plan) (p. 264)
flextime (p. 264)
forecasting (p. 252)
human resources (HR) (p. 251)
human resource management (HRM) (p. 251)
incentive-based payment (p. 263)
independent contractors (p. 266)
internal recruiting (p. 253)
job analysis (p. 252)
job description (p. 252)
job sharing (p. 265)

job specifications (p. 253)
labor union (p. 271)
locals (p. 272)
lockout (p. 272)
management development programs (p. 259)
mediation (p. 272)
mentor (p. 260)
off-the-job training and development (p. 259)
online training (p. 259)
on-the-job training (p. 258)
orientation program (p. 257)
pension plan (p. 263)
performance appraisal (p. 260)
performance management (p. 261)
permanent part-time employee (p. 265)
picketing (p. 272)
profit sharing plan (p. 263)
programmed learning approach (p. 258)
recruitment (p. 253)
retirement (p. 266)
salary (p. 262)
simulation training (vestibule training) (p. 259)
stock option plan (p. 263)
strike (p. 271)
strikebreakers (p. 273)
telecommuting (p. 265)
termination (p. 267)
wages (p. 262)
worker buyout (p. 267)
workforce profile (p. 252)
work/life benefits (p. 264)

Self-Test

Multiple Choice   Correct answers can be found on page 503.

1. Sally McGowan, the HR director for her company, is assessing whether the company has adequate staff. To do so, Sally needs to compile

   a. a job analysis.

   b. a workforce profile.

   c. a job description.

   d. a job specification.

2. Walter Thompson will be interviewing candidates for an administrative assistant's job. Which of the following interview questions would be legally inadvisable for him to ask?

   a. What church do you attend?

   b. What are your strengths and weaknesses?

   c. What are your hobbies?

   d. Who do you think will win the Super Bowl?

3. Billy Gofinsky didn't mind the training his new company was asking him to complete. "It's like playing one of my video games at home," he commented. Most likely, Billy is using

   a. online training.

   b. programmed learning.

   c. simulation training.

   d. teletraining.

4. As an alternative to an annual performance appraisal, which of the following ties goal setting, training, and development into the performance review process?

   a. Workflow evaluation

   b. Performance assessment

   c. Role clarifying

   d. Performance management

5. Amit Patel, as part of his compensation package, was given the offer to purchase company stock at a later date but valued at the current, lower price. Which of the following is Amit given?

   a. Stock option

   b. Stock ownership plan

   c. Stock purchase plan

   d. None of the above

6. James Rodriguez wants to spend more time at home with his two-year-old daughter by shifting his work schedule to work nine consecutive days in a two-week period. Of which of the following flexible work arrangements would James take advantage?

   a. Flex time

   b. Permanent part-time

   c. Job sharing

   d. Compressed workweek

7. Which one of the following is NOT a reason to hire a contingent worker?

   a. To fill in for absent employees

   b. Not enough office space for a full-time employee

   c. To supplement staff during particularly busy times

   d. To evaluate how a person performs on the job before hiring permanently

8. Which of the following is an issue companies face while managing diversity?

   a. Cultural differences create misunderstandings and conflict.

   b. The traditional "white male" employee might feel undervalued if passed up for promotion in lieu of a more culturally diverse individual.

   c. Co-workers and managers are not always comfortable working with individuals whose beliefs and practices are different from their own.

   d. All of the above

9. The employees of General Motors recently walked off the job and picketed the entrances of their plant in an effort to get management to take their grievances seriously. These employees participated in a(n)

   a. strike.

   b. arbitration.

   c. collective bargaining process.

   d. mediation.

10. Which of the following are actions that management can take when threatened with disgruntled employees walking out on their jobs?

    a. Hiring strikebreakers

    b. Boycotting the employees

    c. Imposing a lockout

    d. Both *a* and *c*

Self-Test

True/False Correct answers can be found on page 503.

1. Frontline employees are the only employees who need training.
   ☐ **True** or ☐ **False**

2. Affirmative action plans are the only way to diversify a workforce.
   ☐ **True** or ☐ **False**

3. Some managers are uncomfortable conducting performance appraisals with their employees because they find it hard to quantify or rate performance.
   ☐ **True** or ☐ **False**

4. On-site car detailing, dry-cleaning pickup and delivery, child day care, and a health facility are considered work/life benefits.
   ☐ **True** or ☐ **False**

5. A diversified workforce adds creativity and a variety of viewpoints to the workforce, which often helps improve a company's competitiveness and its bottom line.
   ☐ **True** or ☐ **False**

Critical Thinking Questions

1. Human resources is a separate function in most large companies. Explain how HR concepts and techniques can be useful to all employees in a company.

2. Discuss how human resource management can help a company achieve or maintain a competitive advantage. How does human resource management help a company maintain a healthy bottom line?

3. Discuss the various types of training you have had as an employee. What suggestions would you make to improve the training? What parts of the training did you find to be most effective? How important is training employees to a company's overall goals and strategies?

4. Discuss the purpose of a performance appraisal. What kinds of problems might an employee and manager encounter during a performance appraisal? Discuss some strategies that could be used to get both the employee and manager to communicate with each other most effectively.

5. Describe the "perfect" benefits package that would be most important to you when applying for a job. What kinds of questions could you ask to determine how and when those benefits will be offered to you? How does salary/pay level affect your decision? Would you accept a lower salary/pay level for better benefits?

Team Time

Seeing Both Sides

Wal-Mart has been both praised and criticized for many of its human resource policies. Assemble into teams of four students. Break each team into two subgroups.

a. Subgroup 1: Good HR Practices: Going back no more than five years, research articles about the positive human resource policies and practices Wal-Mart has implemented. Prepare a summary paper outlining your findings.

b. Subgroup 2: Bad HR Practices: Going back no more than five years, research articles about the negative human resource policies and practices Wal-Mart has implemented. Prepare a summary paper outlining your findings.

Process

As a group, compile your findings, comparing the positive and negative policies. Were there instances where a policy started out as a positive and ended up as a negative, or vice versa? How did their policies work with Wal-Mart's strategic goals? How have their policies affected Wal-Mart's stock price and bottom line?

If you were employed as an HR consultant for Wal-Mart, what kind of advice would you give the company based on your findings?

Ethics and Corporate Social Responsibility

The Ethics of Interviewing

The interview and hiring process is fraught with ethical concerns. Form a small group and discuss the ethical implications of the following scenario.

Scenario

Where does a candidate's right to privacy end and a company's right to know begin? As you learned in this chapter, federal laws protect potential employees from discrimination. Hiring managers must observe these laws by refraining from asking certain questions during the interview process, such as direct questions about age and physical disabilities. However, to find out about these topics while still staying within the bounds of legality, managers have devised alternative questions.[25] For example:

Instead of asking. . .	They ask this legal alternative. . .
Which religious holidays do you observe?	Can you work our required schedule?
Do you have kids?	What is your experience with "X" age group?
Do you have any disabilities?	Are you able to perform this position's specific duties?

Process

With your group, discuss your opinions on the use of these "legal alternatives" as an HR strategy. They are legal, but are they ethical? Do managers undermine the laws by finding ways around them? Or does the company have a right to know about these topics in order to make the best hiring decision?

Web Exercises

1. **Analyzing Annual Reports**
   Using the Internet, access annual reports of three companies in different industries. How is HR handled in the annual report? What kind of issues do these companies discuss that relate to HR? What is similar and different between the companies?

2. **International Recruiting**
   Research a multinational company of your choice. What is the nature of its business? In what countries does this company operate? Describe how the company recruits and manages employees internationally. What kind of HR training does the company do as a result of its multinational presence?

3. **Organized Labor**
   Explore The American Federation of Labor and Congress of Industrial Organizations Web site (www.aflcio.org).

   What are its current concerns and causes? How does one become involved in this organization? What about its history? Which historical, political, and social forces propelled the organized labor movement?

4. **HR Career Possibilities**
   Use the Internet to investigate the field of HR management. Search career sites such as Monster.com for job postings in this field. What are the job specifications for an HR manager? What education and experience is required? What skills sets?

5. **Legal Matters**
   Visit the ACLU Action Center (http://action.aclu.org) to find information about current issues concerning employee rights, anti-discrimination laws, or other HR concerns. What are the circumstances of theses cases? What is your opinion on them?

Web Case

To access the Chapter 9 Web case and exercise, see the End of Chapter Assignments section @ www.mybizlab.com.

Video Case

To access the Chapter 9 Video case and exercise, see the End of Chapter Assignments section @ www.mybizlab.com.

chapter 10

Business Technology

▼ Objectives 1-5

1. What are the functions of a company's **chief information officer (CIO)** and **information technology (IT)** department? (p. 281)

2. How are **information technology**, **information systems**, **information**, and **data** interrelated within a business? (p. 283)

3. How are major types of hardware, software, and **networks** used in business? (p. 286)

4. What are the benefits and risks of technology in the workplace, taking into account safety, creativity, communication, productivity, privacy, and ethics? (p. 292)

5. What is the impact of technology on the international business environment based on off-shoring, outsourcing, and alternative methods of communication? (p. 296)

For more chapter resources, go to www.my*biz*lab.com.

p. **286**

Computer Systems in Business
▼ Objective 3

Frank Ordoqui is an IT specialist and an expert when it comes to advising businesses on how to use technology. He has seen the costs of failing to use technology, as well as the costs of using technology in ways that don't benefit a business. How can companies best take advantage of technology while avoiding its pitfalls?

p. **292**

The Benefits and Challenges of Technology
▼ Objective 4

Mark Dagostino has worked as an IT specialist at an insurance firm for 15 years. Now, more than ever, he is on call around the clock and even monitored by his boss electronically. How has business technology affected employees? How has it affected the bottom lines of businesses?

p. **281**

Information Technology Basics
▼ Objectives 1 & 2

When Melissa McGregor started working for a hardware store, she was amazed that the technology it used was so outdated. There was no Web site or e-mail account, and the cash registers weren't even connected to an information system. How could advancements in technology benefit the store?

p. **296**

The Global Impact of Business Technology
▼ Objective 5

Peggy Best left the business world 11 years ago to raise her children. She's reentering the pharmaceutical industry and finding the differences between now and when she left shocking. Not only does she spend most of her day at her office in Pennsylvania using teleconference programs to communicate with her clients in China, but she also has to make sure that her work can be picked up seamlessly at the end of the day by the pharmaceutical team in India. How is the new global landscape affecting employees, businesses, and countries?

Information Technology Basics pp. 281-285

➤ Try to imagine a type of business that doesn't use computer systems for some primary functions—it's hard to do! Any modern business must be able to reach consumers via electronic communication media such as e-mail and Web sites. Accounting information can be managed electronically so that taxes are filed easily, and word processors and databases are vital to any business. In retail, point-of-sale terminals collect information that is fed into inventory and sales computer systems so that stock can be reordered, fast-moving products can be identified, and accounting information can be kept current and accurate. At Apple's retail stores, employees roam the store with mobile "cash registers" in hand. They complete credit card transactions, e-mail sales receipts, and have customers in and out of the store in no time. Now, many grocery stores, as well as Home Depot warehouses, provide self-service automated checkout systems, reducing the need for cashiers. It's clear that technology is changing fundamental aspects of how business is conducted.

When Melissa McGregor began working for a hardware store, she thought all she'd be doing was updating a Web site and maintaining the computer system. But when she saw the outdated technology it used, she was amazed it was still in business. There was no Web site or e-mail account, and the cash register was simply a calculator. The store owner told her that he wanted to give the store a makeover and update the technology so he could increase his profits. Melissa didn't know where to begin. What role does information technology play in business? ➤

In this chapter we'll take a look at how information technology is changing the way we do business. Whether it's a small family-owned business getting its first electronic accounting system or a huge corporate conglomerate launching a new interactive Web site, the business world is getting more technologically advanced every day.

IT Professionals and the IT Organization

Who is in charge of business technology? Information technology (IT) is the design and implementation of computer-based information systems. In many organizational structures, the person responsible for such technology is the **chief information officer (CIO)**. This is typically a position at the same level as the chief financial officer of the firm, for example. As ▼ **Figure 10.1** shows, the CIO is in charge of information processing, including systems design and development and data center operations. He or she is responsible for updating or replacing the computer systems and the software the company uses. The CIO

▼ **Figure 10.1
The Many Functions
of a CIO**
Because technology is
spread across all
divisions and across all
major functions of a modern
business, a CIO requires
excellent leadership and
organizational skills.

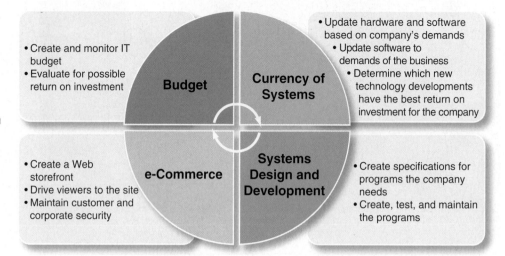

- Create and monitor IT budget
- Evaluate for possible return on investment

Budget

Currency of Systems

- Update hardware and software based on company's demands
- Update software to demands of the business
- Determine which new technology developments have the best return on investment for the company

- Create a Web storefront
- Drive viewers to the site
- Maintain customer and corporate security

e-Commerce

Systems Design and Development

- Create specifications for programs the company needs
- Create, test, and maintain the programs

must also manage a budget that balances the benefits of technology against the ever-rising costs of upgrading to the latest systems. In addition, CIOs are involved in creating business and e-business opportunities.

What happens in an IT department? The IT department is made up of a number of professionals responsible for everything from hardware components and software programs to networking strategies. Members of this department are also responsible for security both in response to computer virus attacks and emergency recovery from power outages and system failures. In addition, the department keeps all of the computers, printers, and other equipment operational and current. The IT department manages the design of the company's networks and databases where information is stored. The department is also responsible for selecting the appropriate software programs as well as often providing training to employees. Sometimes, IT professionals must also create custom software to bridge the gaps between the products available and the needs of the firm. The IT department also maintains and manages the use of mobile computing throughout the company. Equipment includes notebook computers, tablet PCs, smartphones, and other

▼ **top**

10

Questions to Ask Before Adopting a New Piece of Technology

Question	Reason for Asking
1. Who makes it?	Adopting new technology is like adopting a new partner, so you want to make sure that the partner is strong and reliable.
2. Who supports it?	If something goes wrong, you want to know who will fix it.
3. What are *all* the costs?	The initial cost of new technology can double once installation, training, and customization are calculated.
4. What other technology is required to make it work?	Some software might require certain hardware, and vice versa.
5. What services are required to make it work?	Additional communication partners, like telephone, cable, or Internet providers, might be needed to connect new technology to outside systems.
6. How long has it been around?	A new system might still have some glitches, and an old system might be out of date.
7. Who else is using it?	It is valuable to know if your competitors are using the same product.
8. How will it generate profits for my company?	You must know if the cost of the system will be recouped by increased profits.
9. Can I take a test-drive?	It is important to know and see how the technology works.
10. Will it speak to my other systems?	An incompatible system can hinder, rather than help, operations.

devices. Finally, the IT department is responsible for implementing remote access to computing resources, such as employees' access to work files or e-mail when they are working outside the office.

Information Systems

What's an information system? The main difference between information technology (IT) and **information systems (IS)**, also called **management information systems (MIS)**, is that MIS is focused on applying IT to solve business and economic problems. For example, the payroll department may come to MIS asking for an upgrade to a new accounting system or software package. It is the role of MIS to be able to investigate the impact of that change on the other technology systems in the company and to rate the amount of gain against the cost required for the new software. So, MIS professionals bridge the gap between purely technical knowledge and how it will impact a business.

What is the difference between data and information? In common usage the terms *data* and *information* are often used interchangeably, but they have different meanings. **Data** are the representations of a fact or idea. They may be a number, a word, an image, or a sound. **Information**, however, is data that have been organized or arranged in a way that make them useful (see ▼ **Figure 10.2**). The extraction of information from raw data is critical to the success of many business enterprises. Businesses try to use all the resources at their disposal to gather raw data. For example, media, credit bureaus, and information brokers often purchase

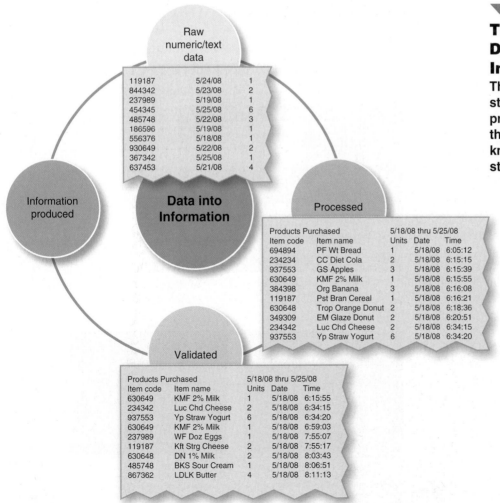

▼ **Figure 10.2**
The Processing of Data into Useful Information
The raw data from a grocery store's sales log can be processed into information that will help the storeowner know when to schedule the store's milk shipments.

data made public in court proceedings. These data are processed into useful information for that business or later resold to other companies. So, a health club in Massachusetts may request a list of recently divorced women from family court. The health club's plan is to process that raw data into a mailing list of a specific target audience for its membership services.[1]

How can collecting data help an organization?

Businesses can easily collect and store large amounts of data, but turning them into useful information is a challenging task. A number of software systems help in this regard. **Decision support systems (DSSs)** are software systems that enable companies to analyze collected data so they can predict the impact of business decisions. A DSS can also retrieve data from external sources and display results tied to the decision making of the business. **Executive information systems (EISs)** are software systems that are specially designed for the needs of management. These systems can consolidate and summarize the transactions within an organization by using both internal and external sources. The terms DSS and EIS are sometimes used interchangeably, but usually an EIS has a more graphical interface compared to a DSS, which often uses spreadsheets and can only show one department or product at a time.

Business intelligence software can also assist managers in reporting, planning, and forecasting workforce performance. Business intelligence packages allow managers to analyze financial states, customer satisfaction, sales analysis, and supply chain status. Managers can quickly display the answers to several questions:[2]

- Who are my top 10 revenue-generating customers?
- What factors (e.g., regions, products, or customers) are the greatest contributors to bad debt?
- Which vendors have unpaid invoices, and how much money do these vendors owe?
- How many days' worth of inventory is in each warehouse?
- Which plants have completed the highest number of work orders on time?

➤ Many businesses use software programs to organize and analyze the data they collect.

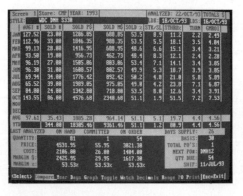

Information on receiving, on-hand and sales is expressed month by month, in either numerical or graphical form, clearly showing important market trends.

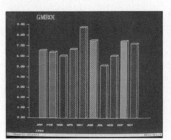

Five primary statistics are constantly monitored and always available: GMROI, Turn, Stock to Sales, Sell-through and Days of Supply.

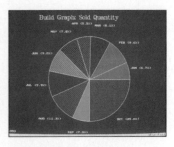

Information graphically displayed helps you quickly interpret the real situation.

➤ The IT department is responsible for everything from hardware to software to networking.

How can companies make sense of all their data? Data are stored in database management systems (DBMSs). **Database management systems (DBMSs)** are collections of tables of data that organize the data and allow simple analysis and reporting. As companies begin to store vast amounts of data in database systems separate from their production databases, **data warehouses** are created. These can hold terabytes (thousands of gigabytes) of transaction data. Sometimes, subsets are created to isolate one product or one department. These smaller data sets are called **data marts**. The process of exploring and analyzing the data mart to uncover the relationships and patterns that will help a business is referred to as **data mining**. Data mining can be used in many ways. For example, suppose a supermarket uses data mining to help decide whether to restock a product that isn't selling well. If data mining reveals that the few people who typically buy the product are among the supermarket's most profitable customers, it will most likely be worth keeping the product on the shelves to retain their business. Although data mining has not yet lived up to its full potential, new advances in hardware and software are making it a larger part of business decision making.

Even small businesses like the hardware store Melissa McGregor works for need someone with IT experience to bring their business into the modern age. Melissa's boss recognized that the success of his business was dependent upon upgrading the technology used at his store, but he wasn't sure where to begin. That's where IT professionals like Melissa come in. By creating a company Web site and e-mail account, Melissa showed her boss that he would better be able to stay in touch with his customers by using this technology. She also recommended that the store upgrade to computerized cash registers, which would help employees process the sale and exchange of goods more efficiently. As the store's business improves, Melissa may have the opportunity to make additional IT changes.

▼ You have just read **Objectives 1 & 2**

Think you got it? Check out the Study Plan section @
www.my*biz*lab.com.

Computer Systems in Business pp. 286-291

A marketing firm contracted Frank Ordoqui to act as an IT advisor to help upgrade the company's systems. The firm's CIO wanted the company to have up-to-date technology, so he proposed issuing all members of the sales staff the latest mobile devices. He wanted each salesperson to be issued a smartphone, global positioning system (GPS) monitor, mobile projector, and a portable printer. Frank advised that issuing all of these devices to every salesperson would be wasteful. The excessive devices would cost the company a lot of money and not necessarily increase its profits. The previous year, Frank served as an advisor for a company that wanted to keep business simple and incorporate only minimal technology. In this case, instead of wasting money, the company was wasting potential because it was limiting itself by not being maximally accessible to its customers and its employees. ➤

➤ With advancements in technology happening daily, what role do modern technologies like mobile devices play in business? Is there such a thing as too much technology? In this section, you'll learn about the various types of business technology and what these different technologies accomplish in the workplace.

Hardware

Is business computing the same as personal computing? You're probably familiar with the hardware basics of a home computing system. A well-designed personal computer has a balance between the amount of (slow) hard disk storage, the amount of (faster) volatile memory called random access memory (RAM), and the speed of the central processing unit (CPU). In a business computing setting, these measurements are still critical to the design of a system, but there is a different emphasis. Entertainment features, like powerful video graphics processing for video games or 7.1 channel sound cards, are typically not part of a business system. Hard disk storage, however, becomes incredibly important. If a hard drive with critical information fails, it can impact an entire organization. For this reason, business systems often use a hard disk backup design called *RAID* (short for *redundant array of independent drives*). RAID 1 systems use two disk drives instead of one and copy each piece of information stored onto both drives at the same time, making a perfect backup on a completely separate drive. There are other types of RAID that are more efficient, but the idea of using multiple drives to increase data security is the same.

Depending on the type of analysis being done on a particular business workstation, the processing power and speed of the CPU may need to be more advanced than that of the typical home computer. Because the amount of RAM is also related to the overall processing speed of the system, business workstations often have more memory. The exact speed of the processor and the amount and speed of memory vary dramatically each year as new systems are introduced. To be able to understand and compare specifications, it's useful to be familiar with the common units used in computing, shown in ▼ **Table 10.1**.

What role do mobile devices play in a modern business strategy? Although the availability of Internet access enables workers to make decisions and conduct meetings virtually, business travel is still in huge demand. Business travelers, whether they are salespeople or field engineers, no longer need to be out of touch with their workplace when spending time in cars, airports, and hotels. Cell phones and more fully featured **smartphones** like the BlackBerry 8800 or the iPhone allow employees to access their e-mail and the Internet from virtually anywhere. Furthermore, smartphones running the Windows Mobile operating system enable users to read Microsoft Word, Excel, and Access files as well. Devices like the Garmin Nüvi use a GPS to provide turn-by-turn directions to travelers and can locate the nearest restaurant, hospital, or gas station. Projectors and printers are available in mobile sizes as well. Projectors as light as one pound make it easy to bring your own complete presentation that is ready to play at any location. Mobile printers are small enough to tuck into a carry-on bag, and they allow users on the go to print documents.

➤ Mobile devices, such as smartphones, GPS devices, and portable printers and projectors, enable business travelers to stay in touch when they're out of the office.

As more and more devices appear on the market and as prices continue to drop, CIOs find they need to have a consistent policy to manage mobile devices. The requests for IT support can quickly cause a quagmire of technical support demands. One approach some companies are using is to restrict mobile devices to only those issued by the company itself. At Tastykake, a snack food company, CIO Brendan O'Malley makes it a point to provide the leading-edge connected handheld devices so users aren't tempted to get their own devices. "We figure out what people need and give it to them," he says.[3]

▼ **Table 10.1**

Common Units Used in Computing

Unit	Number of bytes	Equivalent to	Common measures
Kilobyte (KB)	1,000	1 k	Small files
Megabyte (MB)	1,000,000	1,000 KB	Video card memory
Gigabyte (GB)	1,000,000,000	1,000 MB	Hard drive storage
Terabyte (TB)	1,000,000,000,000	1,000 GB	Large server farms of stored data, data warehouse

Software

What analytical software is common in business? Managers need to make decisions driven by data. Earlier we discussed different software products business may use to analyze the large amounts of data they need to make business decisions. In addition to these programs, a variety of analytical software packages are used to support numerical analysis, such as the following:

1. **Spreadsheet Programs. Spreadsheet programs** like Microsoft Excel can run hundreds of different statistical and financial functions with no programming required. They support "what if?" calculations, allowing managers to change one or two variables and easily interpret the results.

2. **Database Programs.** Database programs allow businesses to quickly enter data, filter and sort information, and generate reports. Forms can be easily designed so that data can be entered and validated for accuracy. These forms—such as weekly timecards or customer surveys—can be delivered through e-mail, and the responses automatically added into the database. The collected data can be queried to create lists of data that meet specific conditions, such as the addresses of all employees who worked overtime in the past week.

3. **Online Analysis Packages. Online analysis packages (OLAPs)** are software applications that enable very quick analysis of combinations of different business factors. OLAP systems are designed to help analysts combine multiple pieces of information into a clear picture of the state of the business. These software applications are used for tasks such as reporting sales figures and budgeting and forecasting. OLAP products in the marketplace include MS Analysis Studio, the open-source product Openi (pronounced "open eye"), and Jedox Palo software.

What software applications help manage the details of a business effectively? Software packages can help businesses make strategic decisions about the use of resources, the direction of new marketing campaigns, or daily operations. Software can also help with the mechanics of the business world—

➤ Spreadsheet on a computer monitor.

such as payroll, accounting, and tracking benefits for individual employees. For example, many companies use software that allows employees to check the number of remaining personal leave days they have available, the insurance options they have selected, the amount of money they have placed into retirement, and other aspects of their benefits package. QuickBooks is a very popular accounting package used by small businesses worldwide to handle accounting and budgeting needs. It can also handle many other common business tasks such as processing UPS and FedEx shipments or paying income taxes from payroll. In addition, QuickBooks can help a business become more tech-savvy with the package's full service Web storefront program that allows businesses to set up an online store, take credit card payments, and automatically record all transactions into the accounting system.

Human resource management systems are software tools that organize people-related management tasks such as employee reviews, compensation calculations, and applicant management. Packages like PeopleTrak and eAppraisal make it easier to execute and document the management of employees from the hiring process through performance evaluations. These tools help employers know when to offer additional training and how to assist employees in achieving their future career goals.

What communications technology is commonly used in businesses?

E-mail and instant messaging aren't the only forms of business communication using modern technology. The following are other communications technologies frequently used by businesses today:

1. **VoIP.** Standard telephone communications have evolved through the use of the *Voice Over Internet Protocol (VoIP)*. VoIP technology lets users check their voicemail messages from any Internet browser. Products like Skype use VoIP to allow national and international calls to be made for free over the Internet instead of over traditional phone networks.

2. **Remote Conferencing. Remote conferencing** allows many people to join a common discussion regardless of their physical location. Conferences can be conducted with or without video cameras at each workstation, and participants can each work collaboratively on a single document using a common virtual whiteboard. Some products even allow a participant to take control of another's desktop to demonstrate software to the group or to make a presentation. With more attendees participating in virtual meetings, the environmental impact of such a shift in business practices is significant. For example, one business person moving her sales presentation online in place of flying from New York to London saves 2,690 pounds of carbon dioxide emissions. This shift across large sections of the business world could have a powerful, positive impact on the environment.

3. **Marketing Technologies and Services.** Marketing is an aspect of business that has responded to changes in business technology by redefining itself. In today's world, a marketing department must consider the Internet as a tool both for collecting information on its customers and distributing information about its products and services. Companies such as Lyris, Topica, and Constant Contact can organize and control mass e-mail campaigns by providing templates for e-mail newsletters or advice on how to create e-mail surveys. They also provide services that generate reports to track

▶ With applications like WebEx, presenters can see and hear others as well as run software applications, exchange files, and take control of others' workstations.

the number of people who read the e-mail message, how many followed the links inside, and how many forwarded the e-mail to another contact.

Networks

Why are business networks created? In many homes, a family may have more than one computer but only one printer or Internet connection. Each computer user in the household can share accessories or connections by implementing a home network—a set of communication links between computer systems that allows an exchange of information. This means a printer can receive printing jobs from multiple computers, and scanners can send files to multiple computers. This sharing capability helps households save on expensive resources that are only needed for brief periods of time. In business, companies want to utilize resources efficiently as well. Expensive devices such as color laser printers or important collections of secure, protected data may need to be accessed by numerous employees in the organization. The most efficient way to provide needed resources to everyone is to create a network. In business, a **network** is a system of computers and other devices joined together using cables, fiber optic links, or wireless connections.

But only techies need to know about networks, right? Some employees may be interested enough in networking to follow that as a career path, but even those who do not work in the IT department need to have a basic understanding of networks. In most workplaces, employees use networks to access shared files and documents, to access their private personnel data, and to communicate with others in the firm. Understanding the basic structure and operation of networks helps employees do their jobs more efficiently. Managers need to know about networking because the use and maintenance of networks as a company resource are important in their decision making.

What types of networks are in the workplace? There are two types of networks commonly used. An **intranet** is a network that is accessible only to employees or others with authorization. An intranet's Web site looks just like any other Web site. However, specialized firewall software surrounding an intranet keeps unauthorized users from gaining access to the site. An **extranet** is an intranet that is partially accessible to authorized outsiders. Customers or vendors with a valid username and password are able to see certain parts of the network. Extranets are becoming a very popular means for business partners to exchange information.

Do networks come in different sizes? Some networks include only machines in close physical proximity to one another, such as the computers in one office building. These are known as **local area networks (LANs)**. The different computers on the network may be joined by physical cables, run through the walls and floors of a building, or by using a Wi-Fi (wireless fidelity) signal. If the LAN is connected wirelessly instead of with cables, it is referred to as a **wireless LAN (WLAN)**. Often, **Wi-Fi hotspots**, places where access to a wireless LAN is available, are advertised in airport terminals, coffee houses, and hotels trying to appeal to business travelers who need to reach server files or e-mail using the Internet while traveling. A collection of LANs can be joined into one network, forming a **wide-area network (WAN)**.

As networks grow and begin to link sites very far apart geographically, **virtual private networks (VPNs)** are often used. A VPN may connect some of its systems by cables that the company owns, but other sections of the network will be joined using the public Internet. This requires the encryption of information so that the company's private information is kept secure as it travels across public sections of the network. For example, if a company merged offices in two different cities into one network, a VPN would ensure secure flow of information.

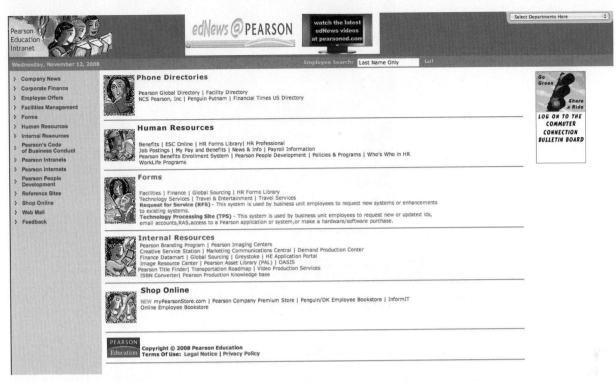

Phone Directories

Pearson Global Directory | Facility Directory
NCS Pearson, Inc | Penguin Putnam | Financial Times US Directory

Human Resources

Benefits | ESC Online | HR Forms Library| HR Professional
Job Postings | My Pay and Benefits | News & Info | Payroll Information
Pearson Benefits Enrollment System | Pearson People Development | Policies & Programs | Who's Who in HR
WorkLife Programs

Forms

Facilities | Finance | Global Sourcing | HR Forms Library
Technology Services | Travel & Entertainment | Travel Services
Request for Service (RFS) - This system is used by business unit employees to request new systems or enhancements
to existing systems.
Technology Processing Site (TPS) - This system is used by business unit employees to request new or updated ids,
email accounts,RAS,access to a Pearson application or system,or make a hardware/software purchase.

Internal Resources

Pearson Branding Program | Pearson Imaging Centers
Creative Service Station | Marketing Communications Central | Demand Production Center
Finance Datamart | Global Sourcing | Greystoke | HE Application Portal
Image Resource Center | Pearson Asset Library (PAL) | OASIS
Pearson Title Finder| Transportation Roadmap | Video Production Services
ISBN Converter| Pearson Production Knowledge base

Shop Online

NEW myPearsonStore.com | Pearson Company Premium Store | Penguin/DK Employee Bookstore | InformIT
Online Employee Bookstore

Copyright © 2008 Pearson Education
Terms Of Use: Legal Notice | Privacy Policy

➤ An intranet, such as this one for Pearson Education is available only to employees and others with authorization.

Is the Internet just a network? Put simply, the **Internet** is a large network that connects millions of computers internationally. The **Internet2**, a network of networks that can communicate at speeds a hundred to a thousand times faster than Internet1, is a collaboration of over 200 universities and 120 companies. Internet2 has been running since 1996, exploring projects that require incredibly high-speed transfer of data, like real-time high-definition video applications. The showcase archive of Internet2 projects includes international communities in biomedical research, fully immersed virtual reality medical simulators, and a global Internet telescope.[4]

As you may know, the Internet and the World Wide Web are not the same thing. The **World Wide Web (WWW)** is a way of accessing information available on the Internet. The Web uses a specific protocol, named hypertext transfer protocol (HTTP), to send data between systems. **Protocols** are the different "languages" that are used to transfer information across the Internet. Some examples of other protocols include FTP, a file transfer protocol to move files, and SMTP, simple mail transfer protocol, which handles outgoing e-mail.

As you read at the beginning of this section, Frank Ordoqui has seen both ends of the spectrum when it comes to advising companies on the types of computer systems and mobile devices that would be most beneficial to their businesses. New technology can be both exciting and overwhelming to business managers. Some executives are tempted to incorporate every piece of new technology into their business operations, regardless of actual need, while others resist new technology, even though it could prove helpful, because they fear it could overcomplicate their business. Frank advises all of his clients to incorporate new technology at a pace that follows the individual needs of the company, not the latest and greatest program or device.

▼ You have just read **Objective 3**

Want a review? Check out the Study Plan section @
www.my*biz*lab.com.

The Benefits and Challenges of Technology pp. 292-295

Mark Dagostino has been a successful IT specialist at an insurance firm for 15 years. He was excited by the prospect of being able to access his work files from home, because he figured it would allow him to spend more time with his family. However, Mark now finds that the office is in constant contact with him. The insurance agents work shifts around the clock, processing claims from clients, and Mark is frequently asked to work at all hours to solve technological problems. He even had to work on a computer crisis on Christmas morning one year, much to the chagrin of his family. Mark has reached a new level of frustration with his job, and he is strongly considering taking a pay cut at a new job in exchange for a less chaotic schedule. ➤

➤ Is the ability to work from home beneficial to employees? Is it beneficial to employers? Does constant connection to the workplace increase employee productivity or employee frustration? In this section, we'll discuss the benefits and risks of IT.

IT Benefits and Challenges for Employees

What are the benefits and challenges of IT for employees? There are aspects of technology that clearly benefit employees. In rescue operations, robots and robotic assistance have relieved human rescue personnel of dangerous tasks. In automotive plants, robots have taken over most of the very monotonous, unfulfilling work, freeing humans for more creative positions. But some uses of technology in the workplace have brought about difficult changes. The increasing volume of e-mail can contribute to a breakdown in communication as fewer personal exchanges take place. Communication experts agree that in face-to-face discussions, up to 93 percent of the meaning of the messages exchanged is communicated in nonverbal ways—through gestures, glances, body position, and facial expression.[5] As more office discussions take place in e-mails, the chance of misunderstandings and errors starts to rise.

The boundary between work and home has also blurred dramatically because of the increase of technology. Once a worker has access from home to office files, and the office has access to the employees through smartphones or live video conferencing, the workday can extend dramatically.

Has technology increased productivity? What is the business value of IT? Many studies have been conducted to answer this question, and their findings differ widely. Some conclude that corporate investment in IT has led to increased output from employees, whereas others find that the investment has actually led to a drop in productivity. It's a complex question, and some of the discrepancies depend on the actual definition of productivity. Are they looking at knowledge workers only, or blue-collar workers as well? How was the impact of the overall strength of the economy factored into the measurement of productivity? Other researchers question whether profitability, consumer benefit, and productivity are actually related. Although employees certainly have more access to information through technology, it is up to the individual to use that information appropriately. If you cannot guarantee that new technology is going to make a workforce more productive, then the task of selecting the IT solutions and tools that will yield enough benefit to outweigh the investment of purchase, training, and maintenance becomes all the more difficult.

How do intellectual property laws affect knowledge workers?

With more technology in place at businesses, more employees are becoming "knowledge-based" workers. Their contribution to the company is measured by their creativity and originality. But who owns the idea that an employee has while at work? In most businesses, the idea is the property of the company, even if it is a brainstorm that occurred during lunch instead of during an afternoon meeting. For example, a software engineer working at a health information management center is struggling to come up with a way to store large files of hospital records on one drive. Suddenly, an idea for the design of a microchip comes to her while she is driving to work. Even though the idea was formed outside the work environment, the idea belongs to the company because it was based on previous work. Intellectual property and copyright law are constantly evolving. As technology creates a higher percentage of knowledge workers, the issue of ownership of ideas will affect more and more employees.

How does technology affect employee privacy?

At home, U.S. citizens are guaranteed specific levels of privacy and freedoms. In the workplace, however, the expectation of privacy is quite different. **Electronic monitoring** is commonly used to track employees' keystrokes and e-mails, examine their Internet browsing histories, and even monitor their cell phone and instant messaging usage.[6] Camera surveillance can be conducted with recording devices so small that employees do not realize they are being recorded. Used appropriately, these technical tools can help a company eliminate a drain of business resources for personal use. But to some employees, the work environment then begins to feel so monitored that they no longer produce their best work. In a study conducted at Bell Canada, a telecommunications company, researchers found that 50 percent of employees in the customer service department reported an increase in stress and anxiety when their calls were being monitored. Employee stress can lead to job dissatisfaction and prompt health problems.[7] Finding the balance between an appropriate level of monitoring and an optimal work environment is a continuous challenge.

Can technology support ethical conduct?

Part of the Sarbanes-Oxley Act, which took effect in 2003, mandates that all public companies have procedures for handling the concerns of whistle-blowers—persons who report on illicit activities. Several corporations now use their intranet to allow whistle-blowers to make anonymous reports. Organizations such as the Occupational Safety and Health Administration (OSHA) and the American Civil Liberties Union (ACLU) also have designed their Web sites to allow people to file reports easily and safely, shielding them

Off the Mark
Hewlett-Packard Spying Scandal

Hewlett-Packard (HP) crossed the ethical lines of employee privacy in 2006 in an attempt to discover the source of an anonymous article that leaked private company information. Chairman Patricia Dunn hired private investigators and allegedly authorized them to use illegal tactics to uncover the source of this leak. The private investigators used pretexting, or lying about one's identity, to gain access to phone records, tracer e-mails containing spyware, and the surveillance of journalists. Placing physical spies in a newsroom was even discussed. Dunn resigned from HP in 2006, as well as board member George Keyworth, who was discovered to be behind the information leak. The scandal ended up costing the company several board members, millions of dollars, and bad press.

Employee privacy concerns are a big issue today, as technology makes it easier to spy on employees. Although HP engaged in illegal methods of observation, companies can legally screen the e-mail and Internet histories of employees, raising ethical concerns about the right of companies to do so.

from possible retaliation. This type of reporting system is common in hospitals and medical centers. Staff members can report "near misses"—mistakes that could have occurred but were caught and corrected—through the organization's intranet. This allows the organization to learn from possible mistakes, but safeguards the employee from embarrassment or disciplinary action. Without the benefit of anonymity, many mistakes and unethical actions might go undetected.

IT Benefits and Challenges for Management

What risks does technology pose for management? Although the increase in IT has allowed many advances for businesses, it also has added risks. The stability of the business can be jeopardized if technology is not implemented reliably. Even a short blackout of vital services, like internal e-mail or customer access to the corporate Internet presence, can damage a company's reputation and value. In June 2007, the Hawaiian airline Go! attempted to sell 1,000 tickets for $1. The promotion caused so many people to access the company's Web site that it crashed, and customers could not get tickets. The company was forced to double the number of $1-tickets it was offering to assuage upset customers.[8] One survey of managers in the United Kingdom found that 70 percent said IT failure was the top threat to their organization, whereas only 2 percent cited a concern over terrorism disrupting their business.[9]

Another challenge IT brings to management is security. With so much of the value of a modern business stored in electronic material—whether as documents, software programs, or e-mail files—a company can be vulnerable to hackers. **Hackers** are individuals who gain unauthorized entry into a computer system. Their goal may be to disrupt the operation of the system or to gain access to protected data. In 2007, a hacker or hackers broke into the accounting systems of the retail stores T.J. Maxx and Marshalls, both owned by TJX Cos. The company reported to the Security and Exchange Commission that data from at least 45.7 million credit and debit cards were illegally accessed, making it the largest hacking case to date.[10] Risk of a security breach becomes even greater if unprotected wireless networks are in use. If no encryption scheme is used, then the data traveling through a wireless network are available to anyone in range.

How a Simple Mistake Can Lead to a Major Data Breach

In May 2006, the U.S. government experienced the second largest data breach to date. This occurrence wasn't attributed to savvy hackers though. Rather, an employee for the Department of Veterans Affairs (VA) went against policy and took a laptop home, and it was stolen during a burglary. The laptop contained the names and Social Security numbers of over 26 million veterans. According to Bill Conner, CEO of Entrust, a digital security company, lost or stolen laptops are the number-one way to compromise a company's security. Web sites like http://breachalerts.trustedid.com are dedicated to detailing security breaches that affect millions of people. The VA breach prompted the House of Representatives and the Senate to speed up bills waiting to be passed. These bills mandate criminal penalties for data breaches and disclosure agreements for consumers. The VA laptop was eventually recovered in July 2006. Fortunately for the VA and the vets involved, sensitive information on the computer had not been accessed.

For more information and discussion questions about this topic, check out the BizChat feature on www.mybizlab.com.

Does keeping pace with technology put a financial burden on businesses? Another challenge IT poses for business is the financial burden placed on companies trying to stay up to date. The full cost of any new piece of technology includes not only the purchase of the software and hardware itself, but also potential hardware upgrades required to make the new product useful. For example, say management decides it wants to upgrade the operating system that runs on the company's computers. This requires that the firm buy not just licenses for the operating system software, but also memory upgrades for computer systems. In addition, the IT department will need to take time to test the software prior to deployment, establish a support staff, install the software, and train users on how to interact with the programs. Before adopting new technology, business managers must evaluate whether the benefits of new technology will exceed the costs.

Sometimes, management may feel pressure to upgrade software or hardware because the entire market has switched to a new product or because customers or vendors have already moved to a new version of a program or device. In such circumstances, the CIO must evaluate the available workforce and determine whether there are sufficient people trained with the new software or hardware to make the return on investment significant and worthwhile. Occasionally, software products are released and working, but they are not yet supported by other companies' software products. For example, when Microsoft released the Windows Vista operating system, many mid-size companies found they would be required to upgrade their hardware, adding hard disk drives, more memory, or possibly even buying completely new computers because their existing processors were too slow for Vista.[11] However, Microsoft predicted a savings of $340 a year per machine in IT labor and support costs. In these cases, the CIO must evaluate whether adopting a new piece of technology is in the best interest of the company.

What are the pros and cons of conducting business online? Taking advantage of cyberspace storefronts is a major benefit of increased technology in business. But it does bring with it a set of concerns that managers must be prepared to face. Because customers are justifiably worried about possible online threats to their privacy, every aspect of an online store must be secure and inspire consumer trust. This can create some complicated decisions for management. For example, some companies use **cookies**, small text files written to a user's hard disk that track customer preferences and Web clicks, or they store previous responses to online forms. This allows a company to customize its Web storefront for each customer. For example, an estimated 131 million users visit Yahoo! each month.[12] By using cookies, Yahoo! collects a significant amount of data about its users—almost 12 terabytes of data a day. Sophisticated analysis programs try to predict consumer behavior when processing those data. This valuable information can then be sold to marketing firms or used to justify high prices for Yahoo! ad space. Some people feel this practice compromises their security. Just that perception, whether it is truthful or not, can cost a company business. So, should a company use cookies or not? Some companies, like Yahoo!, say yes. Others, like Google, refuse to collect such information about their users.[13]

The rapid advancement of technology has brought about many changes in the workplace. As in the case of Mark Dagostino, discussed in the beginning of this section, those changes can have both positive and negative effects. Finding an appropriate balance between the benefits and challenges of new technology can be a daunting task for business owners, CIOs, and employees alike.

▼ You have just read **Objective 4**

Want to learn more? Check out the Study Plan section @
www.my*biz*lab.com.

The Global Impact of Business Technology pp. 296-299

When Peggy Best worked at a pharmaceutical company 11 years ago, her main clients were all located within 100 miles of her company's main office in Pennsylvania, and all of her co-workers worked on-site. When Peggy returned, she found the company, and business in general, had changed dramatically. Now most of the company's clients are located in foreign countries, and many of her co-workers work outside the office. She even has co-workers in India. Peggy has found adapting to new technology the most difficult part of the transition. She has to be trained in a variety of virtual communication programs so she can speak to her international clients, and she needs to become familiar with the company's information network so she can share information with her counterpart in India. Peggy is enjoying learning about new technology and other cultures, but at times she feels overwhelmed.

➤ Earlier in this chapter, you learned how business technology can impact companies. But how does technology affect business on a global scale? In this section, you'll read about the ways in which technology is changing where businesses are located, what goods are produced, how goods and services are marketed, and what will be expected of employees in the new global marketplace.

Off-shoring

How has technology impacted international business? One impact of technology has been the increase in **off-shoring**, a practice in which work is shifted from the United States to other nations. In the past, this practice was employed primarily for production and manufacturing. The North American Free Trade Agreement (NAFTA) of 1994 made it easier for companies to shift work from the United States to Mexico and opened the door to expanding off-shoring. As technology provided secure and simple means to transmit data files, white-collar off-shoring began to take off. Workers in many sectors of the economy that had been insulated from foreign competition began to see change. For example, in 2001 and 2002, the unemployment rate for computer programmers rose significantly above the national average, despite remaining well below it for the previous 20 years. The financial services industry—retail banking, investment banking, and insurance—has also been very aggressive in moving call center jobs and clerical jobs offshore.

Location has become much less important, and countries that have educated, English-speaking citizens can bid for work that has previously taken place in the United States. With a population of more than one billion, India graduates 350,000[14] engineers each year, compared to 60,000 graduated in the United States.[15] This has fueled 10 years of double-digit increases in salary in India for many technology workers, as U.S. firms send a variety of programming and support positions to Indian companies. Although the income of Indian workers has risen, the economic advantage of off-shoring to India is fading. Now China is beginning to show it has the necessary infrastructure and pool of talent to become an off-shoring destination for knowledge work.

Although countries in Asia are seeing the most off-shoring activity, some U.S. companies like to keep their business a little closer to home. **Near-shoring** is a form of off-shoring in which a company moves jobs to a foreign location that is geographically close or linguistically and culturally similar to the domestic country. Sending work from the United States to countries such as Canada, the United Kingdom, and Australia could be considered near-shoring. Google, Yahoo!, and Hewlett-Packard all have offices in Dublin, which is where they send a portion of their IT work. Although labor in these countries may not be as low-cost as labor in some Asia countries, similarities in geography, language, and culture make it easier to integrate foreign workers into the daily operations of the original location.

What changes might off-shoring bring for U.S. companies and employees?

The drastic difference in wages between offshore countries and the United States is the key ingredient in making off-shoring profitable for a business. A U.S. technology worker averages a $2000-a-month income, whereas his or her counterpart in China earns $100 a month.[16] As the international pool of technical talent becomes the new marketplace, U.S. workers can expect to see a slowing of wage growth. It will be important for U.S. workers to have increased language skills and to shift their view of their careers and opportunities toward the reality of a global economy.

It is also useful to point out that U.S. workers will see benefits from off-shoring. As middle-class jobs appear in India and other developing countries, the middle class in those countries will expand. Companies and workers in the United States will benefit in the long run when more countries are politically stable and the demand for U.S. products increases. Another benefit comes from the time zone differences. For example, there is almost an 11-hour time difference between India and the United States. As the workday ends in New York, people begin to wake up and head to work in Bangalore and Hyderabad. By using teams of workers that are divided between both locations, companies can conduct business almost 24 hours a day. If a well-designed and well-managed team can exploit the time zone difference, it holds the possibility of great success for the team and for the business overall.

What is the difference between outsourcing and off-shoring?

Outsourcing takes place when a company contracts with an outside firm to handle a specific part of its daily business activities. *Off-shoring* is the relocation of part of a business to a lower-cost location, typically a foreign country. Sometimes, the terms *outsourcing* and *off-shoring* are mistakenly used interchangeably. Outsourcing, for example, includes a real estate company hiring a graphic design firm to create a special layout for a sales brochure. Most companies outsource work to outside firms that can do a job or project better, faster, or cheaper than the company could do on its own.

The International Business Environment

How does technology change marketing in a global marketplace?

Internet technology allows every company with a Web site to advertise to the entire world. The site must support multiple languages, but more importantly, it must also make sure the content for different countries is culturally customized. Every marketing campaign

▶ Companies like GE Capital employ people in Delhi, Bangalore, and other cities in India to answer calls from credit card customers, perform accounting tasks, and manage computer systems.[17]

▶ Thanks to Internet technology, every company with a Web site is now capable of advertising globally. This page, for the American investment company Charles Schwab, is designed for Chinese-speaking investors.

is now global. In 2007, when Hewlett Packard launched its new Print 2.0 Web printing service, it began with a $300 million global marketing campaign.[18] The campaign used interactive Web technologies to create "achiever experiences" designed to give customers printable content they could customize with their own images and text. HP also established two print communities for consumers and small businesses and wikis to allow customers to collaborate on print projects, marketing, and branding. HP found it needed to use Internet technologies joined with excellent content to deliver its worldwide marketing message.

How can technology redefine boundaries of business cooperation?
Business technology has helped fuel the collapse of fixed boundaries between international divisions of a business. Time and distance are no longer barriers between the collaboration of two parts of a business. Instead, different countries can bring the energy needed to foster breakthrough, high-impact innovation.[19] It can be challenging to take the necessary risk to create new ideas, especially once executives and business units have a record of proven success. The use of international, high-stakes competitions within a firm can ignite new designs. Mazda used this approach when it designed the Miata sports coupe in the 1990s. Two teams, one from the United States and one from Japan, were tasked with the job of designing an affordable sports car reminiscent of the classic British roadsters of the past. Technology allowed them to communicate easily and keep an eye on what the other team was doing, leading to a healthy competitive environment that resulted in one of the most successful sports car designs in the industry.

How is technology affecting the world's production and design centers?
For several decades, China has grown as a production center for the world. "Made in China" is stamped on products from clothing to machinery. But the design centers drafting the products have been traditionally located in the United States and western Europe. As business technology and education continue to blossom in China, design is shifting there as well. General Motors owns a plant in a suburb of Shanghai. The design of the latest model Buick LaCrosse was left to an open internal competition between U.S. and Chinese designers in design studios 6,000 miles apart. Both teams excelled in the competitive environment. Ultimately, the Chinese GM design team was given the redesign for the LaCrosse interior and overall flow, and the U.S. team worked on the exterior. The teams reported in for reviews with the Chinese employees in Shanghai and GM management using a virtual reality "suite" in the GM offices near Detroit.[20]

Technology Creates a Global Village

Where will the next generation of workers live? On one hand, employees with skills that stand out in the global talent pool will be able to live anywhere. With employees relocating often and internationally, the demand for workers with language and communication skills will increase. On the other hand, the introduction of millions of talented knowledge workers worldwide may cause workers who have only average or marginal skills to be displaced.

What skills will be expected in the global workplace? Flexibility on the part of employees will be expected in the global workplace. Communication skills and social understanding of a range of cultures will be invaluable, as will mathematical skills, which transcend language boundaries. Demonstrated fluency in learning new technologies will let employers know a prospective employee can be counted on to handle a multitude of projects.

Knowledge of other languages in addition to English will be a key asset to business technology employees. Currently, over 110 million Chinese students are studying English, while only 50,000 U.S. students are studying Chinese.[21] Considering the fact that the population of China is 1.3 billion and growing, the demand for Chinese-language speakers is increasing. As other developing countries continue to grow, so will the demand for foreign language skills.

How does an understanding of digital culture help in business? Those raised with Internet access, digital media, and easily available computer-processing power have developed a different set of skills, strengths, and demands than the generations that preceded them. In today's workplace, three different generations are often working on the same project; being able to understand and adapt between the different styles of each generation is key to a successful team. It is also critical to understanding the marketplace, which is also composed of both "digital natives" and "digital immigrants."

Improvements in business technology have allowed for greater coordination between countries in business. Peggy Best, after returning from an 11-year absence from the workforce, is seeing this firsthand. Companies like Peggy's employer commonly use practices such as off-shoring and outsourcing to lower costs. These practices allow companies to pay lower wages for work and choose from a greater pool of skilled employees. Workers within the United Sates, like Peggy, are challenged to compete in an international skills market. Advances in business computing allow for global marketing campaigns, and consumers expect interactive Web media. Telecommuting to work has become increasingly popular, as employees can complete tasks from home while being able to care for their children or parents. The spread of work to foreign countries will force employees to develop greater communication skills and cultural awareness.

▼ You have just read **Objective 5**

Want to test your skills? Check out the Study Plan section @ **www.mybizlab.com.**

Chapter Summary

Find your Study Plan and Study Guide @ **www.my*biz*lab.com.**

1. What are the functions of a company's chief information officer and information technology department? (pp. 281-283)

- A company's **chief information officer** (p. 281) is the executive in charge of information processing, including systems design and development and data center operations. He or she is also responsible for the following:

  - updating or replacing the computer systems and the software the company uses

  - managing a budget that balances the benefits of technology against the ever-rising costs of having the latest systems

  - creating business and e-business opportunities

- The IT department consists of a number of professionals responsible for everything from hardware components to software programs to networking strategies. The IT department also

  - maintains security both in response to computer virus attacks and emergency recovery from power outages and system failures.

  - keeps all of the organization's computers, printers, scanners, and other equipment operational and current.

  - designs networks used within the company and databases where information is stored.

  - selects or creates the software programs used by the business and sometimes provides software training to employees.

  - maintains and manages the use of mobile computing throughout the company.

  - implements remote access to computing resources, such as employees' access to work files or e-mail when they are working from home.

2. How are information technology, information systems, information, and data interrelated within a business? (pp. 283-285)

- **Information technology** (p. 281) is the design and implementation of computer-based information systems.

- **Information systems** (p. 283) focuses on applying IT to the solution of business and economic problems. Information systems professionals bridge the gap between purely technical knowledge and how it will impact business.

- Raw **data** (p. 283) must be organized and arranged into useful **information** (p. 283). Information systems professionals and other decision makers can then use this information to determine which IT solutions to implement.

3. How are major types of hardware, software, and networks used in business? (pp. 286-291)

- Types of hardware, such as hard drives, are used for data storage. CPU speed is also important in business, depending on the type of analysis being done on a particular computer workstation.

- Software packages are used to drive decision making for executives, human resource personnel, and accounting functions. Communications software allows remote conferencing, instant messaging, and mass e-mail marketing campaigns.

- Business **networks** (p. 290) allow multiple users to work with limited resources. Networks can be organized to allow access to only internal employees or a mix of internal and external people. They can be joined locally or across distance using encryption schemes to ensure security of data.

4. What are the benefits and risks of technology in the workplace, taking into account safety, creativity, communication, productivity, privacy, and ethics? (pp. 292-295)

- Among the risks of technology in the workplace is an increased chance of corporate espionage.

- One of the benefits of technology in the workplace is that it frees up employees to spend more time on creative tasks.

- Although technology allows employees to stay connected even when they aren't physically in the office, it also introduces risks related to communication.

  - The increasing volume of e-mail can contribute to a breakdown in communication as fewer personal exchanges take place.

  - With remote access to work files and features such as live video conferencing, the workday for employees can extend round the clock.

- In terms of productivity, the risks and benefits of technology are unclear. Some studies conclude that corporate investment in IT has led to increased output from employees, whereas others find that the investment has actually led to a drop in productivity.

- Electronic monitoring and other advances can help companies by eliminating a drain of business resources for personal use. However, these practices also carry the risk of invading employees' privacy.

- One of the benefits of technology is that it can support ethical conduct within the workplace. Several federal organizations have Web sites that allow people with complaints or allegations of misconduct to file reports easily and safely, shielding them from possible retaliation.

Continued on next page

Chapter Summary (cont.)

5. **What is the impact of technology on the international business environment based on off-shoring, outsourcing, and alternative methods of communication? (pp. 296-299)**

- **Off-shoring** (p. 296) and outsourcing allow many types of work to be located outside the United States. This shift in production and design centers requires employees to develop communication skills and social understanding of different cultures as well as demonstrating fluency in new technologies.

- Technology has allowed more people from around the world to interact, therefore increasing the demand for foreign-language skills.

For an audio file of the Objectives and Chapter Summary, see the Student Resources section @ www.my*biz*lab.com.

Key Terms

business intelligence software   (p. 284)

chief information officer (CIO)   (p. 281)

cookies   (p. 295)

data   (p. 283)

database management system (DBMS)   (p. 285)

data mart   (p. 285)

data mining   (p. 285)

data warehouse   (p. 285)

decision support system (DSS)   (p. 284)

electronic monitoring   (p. 293)

executive information system (EIS)   (p. 284)

extranet   (p. 290)

hackers   (p. 294)

information   (p. 283)

information systems (IS)/management information systems (MIS)   (p. 283)

information technology (IT)   (p. 281)

Internet   (p. 291)

Internet2   (p. 291)

intranet   (p. 290)

local area network (LAN)   (p. 290)

near-shoring   (p. 297)

network   (p. 290)

online analysis package (OLAP)   (p. 288)

off-shoring   (p. 296)

protocols   (p. 291)

remote conferencing   (p. 289)

smartphone   (p. 287)

spreadsheet program   (p. 288)

virtual private network (VPN)   (p. 290)

Wi-Fi hotspot   (p. 290)

World Wide Web (WWW)   (p. 291)

wireless local area network (WLAN)   (p. 290)

wide-area network (WAN)   (p. 290)

Self-Test

Multiple Choice Correct answers can be found on page 503.

1. **The CIO is responsible for**

   a. corporate internship opportunities and community-relationship building.

   b. company-wide investigations of office conduct.

   c. building and executing a plan for the flow and use of information.

   d. fiscal accountability to shareholders.

2. **Intranets allow**

   a. hackers to enter secure parts of corporate operations.

   b. employees to check their health benefits and access work documents.

   c. a company to be connected to the World Wide Web.

   d. All of the above

3. **DSSs are used most often by**

   a. managers who make decisions based on current data.

   b. employees to decide how to solve technical problems.

   c. clerical staff to organize and format documents and reports.

   d. trainers to teach staff and employees new software products.

4. **RAID and data warehousing**

   a. have nothing to do with each other.

   b. are different names for the same thing.

   c. are related because RAID keeps the stored data secure.

   d. are related because RAID is the technique used to get data into warehouse storage.

5. **Electronic monitoring in the workplace**

   a. is illegal in the United States.

   b. allows a company to monitor employees' usage of its technology resources.

   c. is using surveillance cameras to watch employees' behavior and track their location.

   d. None of the above

6. **Hackers can infiltrate systems**

   a. only if they use cookie files to store information.

   b. unless the systems are isolated as a single corporate extranet.

   c. All of the above

   d. None of the above

7. **Which one of the following initials is related to using encryption to keep information safe as it travels?**

   a. WWW

   b. WLAN

   c. OLAP

   d. VPN

8. **The speed of Internet2 is *most* useful for**

   a. e-mailing.

   b. the real time exchange of holographic images.

   c. downloading music files.

   d. saving files to your desktop.

9. **Outsourcing of knowledge work**

   a. is dangerous to national security.

   b. works to improve global stability.

   c. is difficult because of different levels of commitment to the protection of intellectual property in different countries.

   d. Both *b* and *c*

10. **The global workplace requires workers to**

    a. be flexible.

    b. have fluency in new technology.

    c. have the ability to communicate with a variety of cultures.

    d. All of the above

Self-Test

True/False Correct answers can be found on page 503.

1. Data and information are just different words for a set of letters and numbers.
   ☐ **True** or ☐ **False**

2. Business intelligence software supports decision making by presenting visual, interactive views of the state of the business.
   ☐ **True** or ☐ **False**

3. Some corporate networks allow customers and vendors access.
   ☐ **True** or ☐ **False**

4. Data mining allows marketing teams to predict future customer behavior.
   ☐ **True** or ☐ **False**

5. Near-shoring is the process of sending work to a foreign country that is geographically far and culturally different.
   ☐ **True** or ☐ **False**

Critical Thinking Questions

1. Many large international corporations are hesitant to place large development centers in China because of a history of disrespect for intellectual property rights. Pirated CDs and DVDs are everywhere as you walk down the street in any major city. How can IT companies use technology to ensure the protection of their own intellectual property? Might IP protection improve with additional regulation from the Chinese government? How might the hunger for more U.S. outsourcing fuel a change in behavior?

2. There are many differences between "digital natives" and "digital immigrants." From your experiences, how would you define each term? What experiences have you had, at school or in the workplace, with the different attitudes of the two groups? Different skills? Different approaches to problem solving?

3. How does electronic monitoring impact your life as a student? Should the IT resources of the college be monitored? How might the goals of the institution come into conflict with the needs of the students on this issue?

4. Discuss the impact of off-shoring of knowledge-based work. Is it in the interests of the nation to try to stop the export of certain types of work? Is it possible to do that? What benefits might arise from a more global structure for a business?

5. Think about how a CIO can determine whether the business will benefit enough from a specific hardware/software upgrade to justify its purchase. What information would he or she need? How might past experience benefit the decision that needs to be made today?

Team Time

The Winds of Change

Assemble into groups of three. Each member of the group should select one of the following areas:

a. Business hardware/software/networking

b. Ethical impact of business technology

c. Global impact of business technology

Process

Step 1. As a group, determine what innovation in business technology will have the most impact over the next year, five years, and ten years. Once the group has selected a specific innovation, each member will create a short presentation on why that particular technology change will be significant in his or her area.

Step 2. Evaluate the innovation by asking the following:

- How many businesses will be impacted?
- How many aspects of business activity will be impacted?
- How many consumers and/or vendors will be impacted?
- Will the innovation lead to additional changes in the business in the future?

Step 3. Optional: As a class, compare the group results. Decide which innovation has the most likelihood of coming to fruition. How will it change your career and the world you will be part of in the future?

Ethics and Corporate Social Responsibility

Computer Hacking: A High Price to Pay

Read the following case study. Then, as a class, discuss the questions that follow.

One night 21-year-olds Brian Salcedo and Adam Botbyl were driving around in Adam's car with a couple of antennas hanging out the window and a laptop powered up looking for open wireless networks they could access. As they drove past the Lowe's home improvement store, they found one. Lowe's had set it up so that scanners and other devices could connect to its network without cabling. Six months later the pair decided to place a modified program onto Lowe's computer system. Now, when credit card transactions were processed, a copy of the number would be sent to a special file they could use later. The FBI investigated and arrested them before they ever saw a single credit card number. They pleaded guilty and worked with Lowe's to boost its security. Even so, Brian Salcedo was sentenced to nine years in prison, the longest sentence in U.S. history for computer hacking, and Adam Botbyl was sentenced to 26 months.

Questions

1. Who holds responsibility for Lowe's customers?

2. How can consumers know their purchases are safe?

3. Were the sentences given to the pair appropriate? Why or why not?

Web Exercises

1. **Cookies: A Privacy Threat?**
   Using resources on the Web, evaluate the risks and benefits of the use of cookies by business Web sites. Would you argue the benefits outweigh the risks or not? Describe how to find which cookies are on your computer and how to delete them.

2. **The Great Firewall of China**
   Check the Web for information on the Golden Shield of China. As technology brings businesses into a more global arena, the position of the Chinese government on censorship seems difficult to maintain. How might the Golden Shield give Chinese businesses an advantage in the global economy? What disadvantages does it bring as China works to compete in the global marketplace?

3. **Locating Language Resources**
   What can be done in the United States to foster the growth of Chinese-speaking U.S. citizens? What Web resources are there available for learning Chinese? What

policies and procedures would help speed the development of bilingual U.S. citizens in the workplace?

4. **Data Breach!**
   Visit http://breachalerts.trustedid.com/ and review the recent data breach reports posted on the homepage. Select one of these reports and note relevant information about the breaches, such as the source(s) of data loss, the date(s) of the occurrence, the sizes of loss, and the individuals or geographic area(s) affected. How did the loss occur? How might it have been prevented?

5. **Meeting Online**
   Visit three or four remote conferencing sites such as www.webex.com, www1.gotomeeting.com, www.dimdim.com, or www.webhuddle.com. Do all sites offer cross-platform meetings (Windows, Mac, etc.)? Which sites offer free meetings? How many participants may be included in each meeting?

Web Case

To access the Chapter 10 Web case and exercise, see the End of Chapter Assignments section @ www.my*biz*lab.com.

Video Case

To access the Chapter 10 Video case and exercise, see the End of Chapter Assignments section @ www.my*biz*lab.com.

Production and Operations Management

p. 313

Facility Location
▼ **Objective 3**
Your furniture company has had great success in northern California, and you're considering expanding your operations. What factors do you need to consider before deciding on a new location?

p. 307

The Production Process and Technological Influences
▼ **Objectives 1 & 2**

Although the concept was not new, the automated assembly line was made famous by the Ford Motor Company. Ford's system of mass production also made a huge economic impact because it transformed the car from a luxury item to an affordable product.

p. 318

Production Management
▼ **Objective 4**
IKEA has developed a streamlined production process that allows the company to produce inexpensive, high-quality goods for its franchised stores around the world. The "build it at home" concept allows for great reductions in shipping costs, as the packaging takes up a great deal less space than preassembled products would.

p. 324

Quality Control
▼ **Objective 5**
The Bridgestone/Firestone tire company was at the center of a major controversy in the year 2000. Due to a lack of quality control, a large batch of defective tires hit the road and caused many accidents. Some drivers were killed, and the company had to pay massive amounts of money to settle consumer lawsuits and to recall the defective tires.

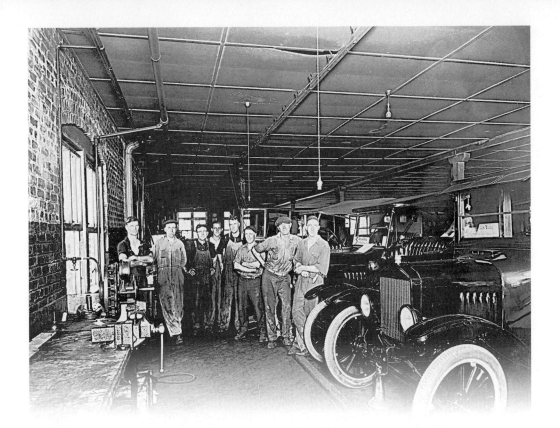

The Production Process and Technological Influences pp. 307-312

Every business that produces goods or provides services has a specific production process. A series of links in a production chain makes up the entire production process. In other words, the production process is how things get made. Many people think of production in terms of producing goods ("things"), but do not consider the fact that even services require some form of production. In this chapter, you'll learn about the various concerns for both the production of goods and the production of services.

In 1908, the Model T Ford was less expensive than most other cars on the market. However, it still wasn't affordable "for the great multitude,"[1] which was Henry Ford's ultimate goal. The changes that Ford introduced during the production process—division of labor, interchangeable parts, precise speed and motions, and, most famously, the use of an assembly line—allowed the Ford Motor Company to produce an automobile that truly was affordable for a great number of people.

The Production Process

Why is the production of goods and services a critical component of any business? Companies strive to make a profit by providing goods or services to consumers. To increase their profits and decrease production costs, businesses must find the most efficient production process possible. If a business utilizes a production process that's inefficient or costly, the company might go bankrupt, even if there is demand for its product. Companies that spend too much on production have to raise prices to break even, which can drive consumers away. A cost-efficient production process is crucial to a successful business.

What types of production processes are usually used by businesses? There are several types of production processes that businesses can use. The type that is chosen depends on the company and what types of goods or services it produces. The most common types of production processes are *mass production*, *flexible production*, and *customer-driven production*.

Mass Production

The method of producing large quantities of goods at a low cost is called **mass production**. This method relies on machines and automated assembly lines to mass-produce goods that are identical and adhere to certain standards of quality. Mass-produced goods are usually manufactured along an **assembly line** (or production line), in which partially complete products are moved from one worker to the next on a conveyor belt.

The cost to run an assembly line is kept low because machines do the majority of the work and the laborers don't need to be especially skilled to perform their repetitive tasks. This method also cuts down on production time, allowing a large quantity of goods to be produced very quickly. Because machinery is the main component, risk of human error is virtually eliminated. A major disadvantage, however, is that mass production is inflexible. After a production line is established, it's very difficult to change or alter the process if an unexpected problem occurs.

Flexible (Custom) Production

A solution to the rigid system of mass production is a different method of production called *flexible production*, or *custom production*. It's also known as a **flexible manufacturing system (FMS)**. In this system, several machines are linked together by one central computer. All the machines in the system can process different part types simultaneously. Unlike a mass-production system, an FMS can adapt to changes in schedules and product specifications. There are four components to a flexible manufacturing system:[2]

- *Processing machines* are arranged in stations according to their tasks. They perform various operations, like assembling and inspecting parts. These automated workstations keep the products moving through the entire system until completion.
- The *material-handling system* is what moves the products from one workstation to the next. It's often a conveyor belt or automatic rail that delivers parts to the various processing machines.
- The *central computer* controls all of the components in the FMS. It coordinates the actions of the processing machines and the material-handling system, directing product parts to the appropriate machines.
- Although machines are an essential part of an FMS, *human labor* is still needed to manage the system, correct any problems, and repair machinery.

Flexible production is appropriate when demand for the goods is low to medium, when changes in demand are frequent, and when a wider variety of customized products are necessary to satisfy customers. Cars, for example, will always be in high demand, so mass production of a large volume of essentially identical models makes sense for the automobile industry. On the other hand, a cosmetics manufacturer might choose to use flexible production because it generates many customized products that have slightly different formulas and packaging. An FMS is ideal

► A flexible manufacturing system includes four components: processing machines, a material-handling system, a central computer, and human labor.

for this because it provides the flexibility to make products with many
slight variations.

Customer-Driven Production

The methods of production discussed so far revolve around the
manufacturer and the type of product. **Customer-driven production**,
as the name suggests, revolves
around the customer. In today's
competitive market, it's necessary
to plan production with the consumer in mind.

Companies like Dell have taken
the concept of customer-driven
production beyond simply offering customizable products with
optional features. In 2007, company founder Michael Dell launched
IdeaStorm,[3] an online forum where
Dell customers can offer input about
the development of new products.

➤ Vehicles designed to meet the needs of physically disabled drivers are one example of
customer-driven production.

Customer-driven production, when implemented well, can have many advantages in each stage of the prospect-to-cash process. **Prospect-to-cash** is a core
business process that outlines the steps from identifying a new business prospect
to receiving payment for the product. Once a business opportunity has been identified, the next step is to develop a quote or fill the product order. Engineering,
order management, and production then lead to the ultimate goal of the business:
cash. Here are the steps in this process:

1. First, the sales and marketing teams are responsible for *prospecting*, or finding
   potential customers and new business opportunities. The sales team must
   determine whether the business prospect is within the realm of the company's
   capabilities and whether the contract is cost-effective.

2. Engineering provides information to the other departments so they can
   process the quote or fill the order. A company that uses customer-driven
   production sets customization limits that allow the product to be designed
   according to customer specifications, while also making it cost-effective.
   The goal is to make the production as cost-effective as if it were a standardized or homogenous product.

3. Order management includes order processing, transaction management,
   inventory control, and shipping. In customer-driven production, the process
   is designed to streamline the operations that affect the consumer directly. The
   goal is to get the product from the manufacturer to the customer as quickly
   and cheaply as possible. The order-management process also includes gathering market information, such as changing trends and promotions, to keep the
   company aware of consumer demand. It standardizes sales and marketing
   tasks, making those departments more efficient.

4. Production occurs when the materials are assembled into a product based
   on the quote, engineering, and order management. The product must be
   manufactured according to the customer's requirements, so factory instructions are linked electronically to the order. This reduces the risk of errors
   and wasted materials. Clear communication and accurate instructions are
   crucial during the production stage to ensure that the product is made correctly and efficiently.

5. The conclusion of the prospect-to-cash process is when a business bills its customers and collects money. Direct interaction with the customer is very important, so it's vital for the company to have a strong financial-management team. Invoice errors can be costly, since payments will be delayed if there are mistakes in the bill. This will also affect customer satisfaction, which can impact future business opportunities.[4]

When products are customized to the specifications of the consumer, it's key to make every step of the prospect-to-cash process as efficient as possible. The overall goals of this type of production are to reduce the time it takes to process an order, to create a customized product at almost the rate of mass production, and to achieve customer satisfaction. With IdeaStorm, Dell is able to involve customers from the ground up in the prospect-to-cash process.

Technological Influences on the Production Process

What is the role of technology in the production process? With thousands of goods to produce at a given time, you might guess that technology plays an integral role in facilitating the flow of any production process. When managed efficiently, the technological aspect of a production process should lead to increases in production and reductions in costs. Technology may also improve the quality and increase the variety of products, which influences the customer's buying decisions. Customers are more likely to buy a product that's not only low-priced compared to other similar products, but also of high quality and readily available in many varieties. It's essential for businesses in today's globally competitive environment to be up-to-date on new technologies that can improve any or all aspects of the production process. In this section you'll look at two specific areas of technology—robotics and computer-aided design and manufacturing—and their roles and impact on the production process.

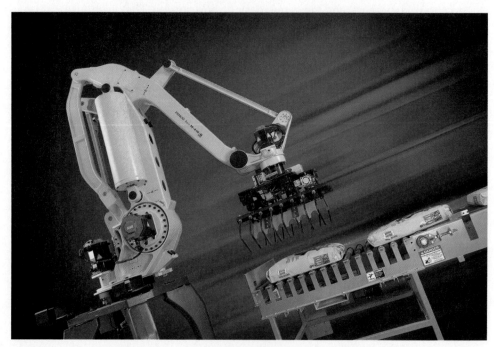

▶ FANUC Robotics America, Inc., supplies many of the industrial robots used in North and South America. The company's range of products include assembly robots, material-handling robots, painting robots, dispensing robots, and welding robots.

Robotics

An *industrial robot* is any device that performs automatically, typically completing repetitive tasks.[5] Humans are sometimes a disadvantage when it comes to performing a task repetitively for many hours and with great precision and accuracy. This is where robots come in. Not only can robots work around the clock with accuracy, but they can also work in potentially hazardous conditions, thereby protecting human workers from dangerous environments. The two biggest areas utilizing robot applications are the automotive industry—which uses robots for welding, painting, assembly, and handling various materials—and the household appliances industry—which requires sealing, painting, and installation of goods such as microwave ovens.

Robots offer consistency in reducing production costs, raising productivity, and producing high-quality products. Industrial robots may take away some jobs, but they also create many new jobs for technicians and engineers. Companies that can effectively apply robotic technology in their production process are more likely to gain an economic advantage in the global marketplace.

Computer-Aided Design and Manufacturing

Computer-aided design (CAD) refers to the use of a computer to create two-dimensional or three-dimensional models of physical parts. With CAD systems, the models displayed on screen can be modified in size or shape, viewed internally, and rotated on any axis. CAD also enables testing of a part by simulating real-world environments. CAD, however, cannot design a model of a product on its own. A designer must first translate the design into a geometrical model for the CAD system to display. Once the model data are received, the CAD system provides the designer with tools and a flexible environment. By programming a simple design change into the CAD system, a manufacturer can produce custom-designed products such as clothing and cars without incurring higher costs. CAD is not only used to design smaller products; it can also be used to design houses, machinery, tools, and commercial structures.

Some manufacturing processes that are more complicated, such as those for motor vehicles, airplanes, and ships, need more than one CAD program to design and incorporate all the different model parts. For instance, the design of a ship may require one CAD application for the steel structure and another CAD program for the propeller. A disadvantage to this method is that it requires knowledge of all the different software applications used as well as knowledge of how to integrate them in the end. On the other hand, the Boeing Company's 757 model is a good example of how integration can be achieved. Because the 757 model is composed of parts from 50 different firms, Boeing's CAD system effectively integrates all of the parts, ensuring a precise fit. This system then effectively reduces the number of prototypes needed and the working hours for assembly.[6]

Once a design is approved, **computer-aided manufacturing (CAM)** uses the design data to control the machinery used in the manufacturing process. The integration of the CAD and CAM systems with the various aspects of a firm's production process is referred to as *simultaneous engineering*. Ford Motor Company's engine division, for example, successfully integrated all its production and design systems into one database that could be accessed by PCs and workstations of employees and suppliers involved with design and production.[7] This type of facilitated communication is a huge benefit for firms with complex systems. One of the main disadvantages of using CAD/CAM systems is that they require considerable time and investment to set up and to learn the necessary software, hardware, communications, and integration.

Computer-integrated manufacturing (CIM) goes even further. CIM systems combine design and manufacturing functions with other functions, such as order taking, shipment, and billing. For example, the printing company VistaPrint uses CIM not only to manufacture its products, but also to help customers create and place orders for custom-designed business cards, brochures, and even T-shirts. Through the use of CIM, the company has expanded its business and is able to serve more customers while continuing to offer affordable prices.[8]

More than any other factor, CAD, CAM, and CIM have dramatically improved the process of producing goods by reducing the time between design and manufacturing, thus making a sizable impact on productivity. These systems have also increased the scope of the use of automated machinery in the production process. Through the rapid pace of technological advancement, the use of CAD, CAM, and CIM is not limited to large mass-production facilities, but is entering smaller companies as well.

Innovations in the production process have been the key to producing more goods at a lower cost, such as the example shown by Henry Ford and his automobile "for the great multitude." These innovations, along with changes in technology, have helped many businesses achieve success with mass production. The ability to produce standardized goods in mass quantities allows businesses to fill large customer demand. In addition, modern technology has allowed for the mass production of goods to become much safer and more efficient. The use of robots for automated assembly has cut down on the need for human labor, but has opened up new jobs for the production of the robots and the monitoring of the production process. Computers play a major role in new product design, allowing designers to get a better idea of how a product may work before building an expensive prototype. Although modern technology is expensive, the benefits of its use can make it quite profitable in the long run.

▼ You have just read **Objectives 1 & 2**

Think you got it? Check out the Study Plan section @
www.my*biz*lab.com.

Facility Location pp. 313-317

➤ What factors should be considered before choosing a manufacturing location? Although it's necessary to consider an area's availability of raw materials, there are also other concerns, such as transportation costs, human factors like labor availability, and even physical factors like electrical power, water, and communication capabilities that impact a location decision. In this section, we'll look at some of the more important factors that a company must consider when looking for the ideal location that will minimize costs and maximize profits.

Imagine you own a furniture company in northern California. Your company has enjoyed a great deal of success—its close proximity to natural resources and a large employee base has allowed it to produce large quantities of high-quality furniture. Shipping has been efficient, as the factory is located 3 miles from a major highway and 20 miles from a port for international delivery. Due to the success of your first location, you are considering opening a new location in Europe to expand your business internationally. The European factory is in a remote area of Switzerland near the Alps. Natural resources are amazingly abundant—they are what have drawn you to the area—but the area is not densely populated, and finding an adequate quantity of skilled employees may be difficult. Shipping is also a concern, as the area is not centrally located. Weighing the pros and cons, what should you do? ➤

Transportation Factors

What are the transportation factors a company must consider? Say an automotive company is looking to start its operations in the United States. The company finds a good potential location that is close to three major highways, one international airport, two domestic airports, and several waterways. This could be a dream location for this business, but why? Transportation costs for supplies coming in and goods going out are one of the major costs that many manufacturing companies need to consider. In fact, transportation costs can amount to as much as five times the cost of operating a production facility.[9] Many automotive companies outsource their transportation systems to logistics companies that plan and execute this complex operation through logistics networks. For example, Ford Motor Company partners with Penske Logistics to manage the delivery of millions of dollars worth of goods and parts to Mexico.[10]

Transportation systems become more complex and costly when a company's supply chain is global. For example, in October 2006, CNH (Case New Holland) Global N.V., a top manufacturer of agricultural and construction equipment, hired the software company Oracle as part of its plan to help the company gain control of spiraling transportation costs.[11] Previously, CNH had outsourced its transportation operations, but then the company realized it could significantly lower costs if the transportation system was operated in-house. With the help of the software application Oracle Transportation Management, CNH was able to efficiently plan and control its manufacturing cycles, manage and adjust for unexpected supply chain events, and help customers know when a product left the factory and when it would reach the end user. Global companies like CNH that learn how to reduce transportation costs, manage transportation processes more efficiently, and improve customer service are more likely to have a competitive edge over other large-scale companies that have less efficient and more costly transportation operations.

Some of the more important transportation factors a company must consider include proximity to the market, the cost of transporting raw materials, and the presence of highways and other transportation systems.

Why is it important to be close to the ideal market? Some businesses
such as restaurants, supermarkets, and service businesses must choose their locations based on the potential customer base in an area. A restaurant that's easily visible to passing cars and pedestrians has more of an advantage in attracting business than a restaurant tucked away in a remote part of town where few people visit. In 1988, two college graduates and a 70-year-old master brewer worked out of an apartment in San Diego to create the perfect recipe for handcrafted microbrewed beer.[12] They later opened the Karl Strauss Brewing Company in the densely populated market of downtown San Diego. Locals lined the streets on opening day, and soon local bars and restaurants became interested in offering the product to their own customers. By choosing a downtown location, they were able to save time and money with little transportation. As it continued to grow, the company needed to move to a larger brewing facility in the San Diego area. Today it has breweries at many locations around Southern California close to targeted customers.

What about transporting raw materials? For some businesses, the
costs and logistics of transporting raw materials is a bigger issue than proximity to the market. Easy access to natural resources helps a business keep transportation costs low, especially when the business relies heavily on natural resources. Businesses such as steel producers and oil refineries would likely be found in an area with rich sources of iron ore or oil. Tata Steel is one of the world's leaders in steel making. Importantly, one of Tata's success factors is its proximity to raw-material sources.[13] Although the company headquarters is located in India, Tata Steel operates in 24 countries around the world. Not only has Tata secured the iron ore mines in India, its overseas operations in Southeast Asia, Australia, and parts of Africa are focused on securing raw-material sources at these locations as well.

What's the best mode of transportation? Businesses
look to different transportation methods when receiving materials from suppliers and delivering orders to customers. A business might rely on one method of transportation or a combination of methods. Each type of transportation comes with its disadvantages and advantages.

The most common transportation mode used by suppliers and businesses is road transport. Not

▶ The Karl Strauss Brewing Company started out of an apartment in San Diego. Today it delivers beer to 2,500 restaurants and bars in the area.

only is this method cheaper than other transportation modes, the delivery time is relatively quick, and the goods can be tracked easily by communicating with the driver. This method is especially ideal for delivering perishable goods such as fresh fruit and vegetables. The disadvantages of transporting by road include possible damage to goods from rough driving, delays due to heavy traffic or bad weather, the effects of high gas prices, and vehicle breakdowns or accidents.

Another cost-effective transportation mode is rail transport, which may be the choice mode for delivering heavy goods such as coal or steel. Railroads provide a quick and safe mode of transportation. However, rail schedules may be inflexible and wrought with unexpected delays. Some areas may not be close to a rail station either, meaning longer delivery times and higher costs due to additional forms of transportation to and from the rail station.

When businesses receive supplies from abroad or when they export goods to foreign markets, sea transportation is usually the preferred mode for heavy, bulky goods like stone slabs. Sea tankers are also used to carry goods such as oil and coal. Transportation by sea naturally takes more time, entails higher costs, and is subject to delays from bad weather.

Another transportation option for companies with distant suppliers and customers is air. Although this option may not be ideal for huge or bulky goods, businesses that want to transport fragile goods are likely to use transportation by air as opposed to land. The rapid delivery time also improves service, satisfying customers who are in a rush. This method is usually the most costly. Like other transportation modes, it can be affected by bad weather, which can cause flights to be canceled or delayed.

Human Factors

What else impacts location selection? The second consideration when deciding on a location for production is the **human factor**, which refers to how the location decision affects the people in a surrounding community and vice versa. Companies need to hire employees to maintain their operations, but they also need to be aware of how their presence affects the community overall. The human factor has three separate, though interrelated, components:

- Labor availability
- Living conditions
- Laws and regulations

What labor factors must a company consider? One component of the human factor is the availability of labor. After all, labor is one of the factors of production necessary for a company to operate successfully. Choosing a location for virtually any business requires finding an area with an abundance of workers who possess the necessary skills. California's famed Silicon Valley became a top hub for the tech industry's software and hardware manufacturing businesses because of its proximity to Stanford University, its abundance of local engineers, and the area's history in developing technology.[14]

However, seeking skilled workers is only part of the decision-making process. Many businesses need to find a workforce that they can afford financially as well. One of the reasons some corporations send their manufacturing operations outside of the United States is because those countries contain highly skilled workers who require lower wages than their U.S. counterparts. India is the number-one destination for outsourced high-tech labor because it offers an experienced, skilled, and affordable labor pool.[15]

> Providing "green collar" jobs is what solar-panel manufacturer SunPower does. Here, a 150-acre solar installation uses panels that follow the sun's path across the sky to generate more electricity than conventional systems. The solar system delivers electric power to approximately 8,000 homes.[16]

How is an organization mindful of impacting living conditions in a community? Another way the human factor figures into selecting a manufacturing location is through its impact on living conditions. These conditions can either be altered positively or negatively by manufacturing. On the one hand, a business brings opportunities to citizens of a community by creating jobs and a higher standard of living. Similarly, many businesses seek out areas where the quality of life is already high (good schools, pleasant weather, low crime rates, etc.) before settling on a location. Some social entrepreneurs might take it upon themselves to locate their businesses in an impoverished area to revitalize the local economy. Environmentally aware politicians advocate "green collar" jobs precisely for their ability to rejuvenate economically depressed communities.

Conversely, a business could also have negative effects on the surrounding area. Some corporations have been accused of bringing down a community's living conditions by exploiting workers or polluting the environment. In 2006, Apple was accused of poor working and living conditions at an iPod manufacturing plant in China.[17] Apple responded to the charges by launching an investigation of the accusations. Its internal audit concluded that although no workers' rights were being abused, some violations of its code of conduct had taken place.[18] This example illustrates the need for companies to be mindful of their impact on a community.

Does the government have a say in location? To try to maintain a balance between business and community interests, governments have created many laws and regulations to protect individuals and the environment. The U.S. Department of Labor is one federal government agency responsible for monitoring many laws and regulations affecting workers. Each state also has its own labor department responsible for enforcing local labor laws and regulations. Consider the minimum wage. Since the 1930s, the U.S. government has determined the minimum wage a worker must be paid. The federal minimum wage, though, is only applicable for jobs that fall under the Federal Fair Labor Standards Act. Since July 2007, the federal government has mandated the minimum wage be set at $5.85. However, many states—such as Rhode Island and Massachusetts—set their

minimum wage at a higher rate than the federal standard, while others—such as Washington and Vermont—set their minimum wage to rise with inflation.

Federal and state governments also regulate how businesses interact with the environment. The U.S. Environmental Protection Agency (EPA) and other environmental agencies regulate, implement, and enforce environmental laws. Many of these environmental regulations specifically apply to the business world. These agencies assist businesses in complying with specific requirements and federal regulations.

Physical Factors

What are the physical factors a company must consider? When selecting a location for production, a company must also consider physical factors such as hazardous-waste disposal and utility supply (which we'll discuss next). These factors are often determined by local ordinances that may vary from state to state—and even from city to city.

Why is it important to consider utility supply when determining location? The **utility supply** refers to the availability of public infrastructure services such as power, water, and communications. For example, a company that is establishing a large facility—like a bottling plant or a warehouse—wouldn't want to situate it in a remote location with little public infrastructure, even if the land is cheap. Because such a large facility requires ample amounts of electricity or running water to operate properly, the cost to establish this infrastructure could be enormous. Moreover, locating manufacturing operations in an area where easy access to these utilities and resources is inexpensive greatly reduces costs. Another common public utility—waste management—is also essential for business operations. Just as being "off the grid" wouldn't make much sense in terms of selecting a business location, a remote location would also render waste disposal and treatment difficult.

Why is hazardous-waste disposal important? Knowing how to handle hazardous waste is a must. Regardless of the type of business, understanding how to dispose of unwanted material—and the regulations involved—is an important factor to consider when selecting a location. Even everyday materials like paint and cleaning fluids are considered hazardous waste and must be disposed of properly.[19] Many businesses, as part of their day-to-day operations, create large amounts of hazardous waste. The proper disposal of this waste has ramifications on a business's immediate vicinity. Each state, county, municipality, and other local government will have its own guidelines and procedures for dealing with hazardous waste. Responsible organizations must be aware of the disposal options that are available in their areas.

Taking transportation, human, and physical factors into consideration, businesses ultimately choose a manufacturing location in order to remain competitive. These decisions are influenced and measured by their efficiency and practicality. Selecting a proper facility for operations is just the first step for a successful business owner. The next step involves determining and developing a proper production-management plan. Think back to the furniture company example that starts this section. Given what you know now about choosing a manufacturing location, is Switzerland the best bet for the company?

▼ You have just read **Objective 3**

Want a review? Check out the Study Plan section @
www.mybizlab.com.

Production Management pp. 318-323

Swedish furniture manufacturer IKEA has mastered the production process to produce high-quality products at a low cost. The factories purchase mass quantities of production resources, driving down the consumer cost of the finished product. What sets IKEA apart from other furniture companies is the packaging and storage of its products. Most of the furniture it produces is shipped in flat packs to be assembled at the consumer's home. These condensed packages minimize shipping and storage costs, which in turn lowers the retail cost of IKEA products. The company has many factories worldwide and is constantly opening new locations to supply its growing number of franchised stores. IKEA is a great example of a company that uses intelligent production management to enhance its business.[20]

➤ Goods and services don't exist in a vacuum; therefore, the whole point of production is to provide the process through which those products are created and given value. Therefore, **production management**—sometimes called **operations management**—refers to the organized structure used to convert resources into finished products. The act of production gives these finished products value, or **utility**, by satisfying consumers' wants or needs.

To ensure that a product provides utility, production managers must successfully develop and carry out a production plan. A well-thought-out plan will ensure a smoothly run operation process. A production manager, also called an operations manager, can either be an individual or a team of employees. Production managers are in charge of setting schedules, making buying decisions, overseeing quality control, and other important issues. The scope of production planning includes making decisions involving the design and management of the many factors that affect operations. These decisions include, but are not limited to, designing the size and layout of a facility; determining what to produce, where to locate that facility, what processes and machinery to use to minimize costs, the number of products that need to be produced each month, and how to meet the needs of all employees; and maintaining quality control. Managers who plan effectively are able to increase productivity, reduce costs, and improve customer satisfaction.

Determining Facility Layout

Why is facility layout important? A production manager must be responsible for determining the layout of a facility. **Facility layout** refers to the physical arrangement of resources and people in the production process and how they interact. The design of a facility's layout is important to maximize efficiency and satisfy employees' needs. It involves everything from the arrangement of cubicles in an office space to the position of robotic arms in an automobile-manufacturing plant. When determining or renovating a facility layout for maximum effectiveness, business owners must also consider many operational factors. For example, facilities should be designed so that they can be easily adjusted to meet changing production needs. Having to undergo extensive renovations or completely relocate as a company's operations change or expand can be a costly endeavor; therefore, managers need to be prepared to factor possible growth at the planning stage. Additionally, the facility layout should be in accordance with Occupational Safety and Health Administration guidelines to ensure worker safety.

How does facility layout affect production? A facility layout should also be able to handle materials orderly and efficiently to ensure a smooth flow of production. To do so, designers need to utilize available space effectively. Warehouses, for instance, need to have enough space to stack goods. Moreover, these products need to be easily accessible for workers using equipment such as fork-lifts and conveyor belts. Employees at Amazon.com's UK division warehouse

➤ Many new office layouts take into consideration a more "horizontal" management structure where there are open work areas. Some offices also give employees spaces where they can meet to share ideas and work together as teams.

must work with equipment efficiently to ensure a smooth process flow. When an order is placed online, Amazon's warehouse design allows workers to find the shortest possible route to assemble, sort, and process each component of the order.[21]

The distance that a work in progress must travel within a facility must also be taken into account. This is not only true for the production of goods, but in service industries as well. For example, the layout of a fast-food restaurant can help the employees involved in the different parts of the process—preparing food and serving customers—to work in a more integrated fashion.

Does facility layout affect employees? Facility layout may even affect the productivity of individual employees. Some layout designs, such as spacious cubicles, ergonomic chairs, or window views, can greatly improve the morale of office workers. The happier a company's employees are, the more productive they'll be. Other layout options that could improve employee productivity include providing a break room, cafeteria, or on-site child-care services. However, when planning, a company must decide whether the increase in productivity outweighs the cost of including such features.

Working with Suppliers

What is a make-or-buy decision? When starting the production process, one of the first decisions that must be made is what needs to be manufactured and what needs to be purchased from outside suppliers. This is commonly called a

make-or-buy decision. If a company plans to manufacture a product that will carry both the company's name and reputation, it has to decide if it will make the entire product in-house or if the product will be assembled from a combination of parts manufactured in-house and other parts purchased from suppliers. It's not always necessary for a company to make everything in-house, so how does a company decide what to make and what to buy? A company needs to consider factors such as cost and quality. If it's less expensive to outsource the production of certain parts elsewhere, that may be the best decision. However, it's important that a manager can trust the quality of any parts that are produced elsewhere and that appropriate quantities are delivered in a timely manner.

How does a company decide which suppliers to use? Selecting suppliers is a significantly less complicated task than making a make-or-buy decision, but that doesn't mean that deciding which suppliers to use should be made with any less consideration. After all, establishing a business relationship with a supplier is like entering into a partnership. Customers don't see a product that is supplied by one company with parts provided by different suppliers; they see a total product. Customers will hold the company responsible even if an individual supplier is to blame for making a faulty part or missing a deadline and causing a delay. For example, in 2007, Mattel had to recall close to one million toys because its supplier in China had coated the toys in lead paint.[22] Such recalls can be costly and damaging to a company's reputation. So having a good supplier that meets the company's needs and cares about the company's customers as if they were its own is an invaluable asset.

A company's first step in finding suppliers involves clearly defining and understanding its needs so that it can find suppliers that truly fit its requirements. Cost is always a factor, but it should never be the sole factor. For example, if several potential suppliers offer similar products with similar prices, other factors will come into play: the company may need a supplier that is reliable or one that is fast. Likewise, one supplier may offer a part for significantly less, but of such poor quality that later repairs or recalls would end up costing the company more than the cost of quality parts, as well as its reputation. Understanding these needs before choosing a supplier will make the process easier and more beneficial in the end.[23]

There's a vast collection of resources designed to help businesses connect with suppliers. These resources include the Better Business Bureau, the local chamber of commerce, exhibitions, trade magazines, the Internet, and old-fashioned recommendations from friends and business acquaintances. The challenge is in finding the best people for the job and determining which of those suppliers offer optimal solutions for production needs. A company might use a process similar to the following to come to a decision:

1. Research potential suppliers and develop a short list of three to five suppliers that best fit the company's needs.

2. Put together a summary explaining what the company needs, including how much of it and how often. Provide this summary to potential suppliers and ask for quotes and, if possible, samples. If necessary, meet the potential suppliers face-to-face and tour their facilities.

3. When all of the information is gathered and only the strongest suppliers are left, a decision can be made regarding which ones to use. Generally, it's a good idea to have more than one supplier. Having a good working relationship with a few suppliers is a good way to keep things manageable and personal without relying entirely on any one supplier. When deciding, it's important to measure each supplier's strengths and weaknesses against what is most important and necessary for the company. This will likely produce those two or three suppliers that best meet or exceed the company's needs. Then all that is left is to discuss contracts.

Maintaining Inventory Control

How does a company maintain inventory control? Inventory control includes the receiving, storing, handling, and tracking of everything in a company's stock, from raw materials to finished products. Inventory often makes up a large portion of a business's expenses. Therefore, proper management is not only just a way to stay informed, it's necessary to keep costs low while ensuring that all necessary materials are in stock and stored in the proper place. There are four main types of stock: raw materials, unfinished products, finished products, and consumables like pens and paper. Maintaining each of these kinds of stock helps determine where money should and shouldn't be spent. Proper maintenance keeps track of things such as products that have shelf lives that could deteriorate or products that have become obsolete, or where more stock than necessary is being purchased. Ensuring an adequate supply of finished products or other types of stock is further complicated when customer demand is variable.

What's the best way to manage inventory control? Managing stock can be achieved in a number of different ways, and no single method works best for every business. Factors like the size of the business, the amount of inventory necessary, the amount of inventory storage space, and the proximity to suppliers all contribute to which inventory control method will work best for an individual company.

The least involved way to manage inventory is to simply eyeball it. This method works really well for smaller companies or companies that don't maintain large amounts of stock. When accuracy is a necessity, a **stock book solution**, where stock on hand is tallied in a book along with stock on order and stock that has been sold, would probably work best. Another less complicated management system is called the **reserve stock system**. This is where stock is set aside in reserve so that it cannot be used. The company goes through its inventory as it regularly would, and when it has to dip into the reserve stock, it knows it is time to reorder that item. It is important for managers to keep in mind when using this system that however much stock is in reserve should be enough to last the amount of time it takes to resupply.[24]

Whereas these systems can work well with smaller businesses, larger businesses generally require a more complicated inventory-management system. A **just-in-time (JIT) inventory control** system keeps the smallest amount of inventory on hand as possible, and everything else that is needed is ordered so that it arrives just in time to be used. Storing fewer items and using items right away can reduce storage costs. This system, however, is not without its drawbacks. To work properly, a company must have a very good relationship with its suppliers to ensure that appropriate quantities arrive on time and where they are needed. Even then, if a supplier is far away, there may be shipping delays due to weather. The shipping costs, too, may become quite high.

How is technology used to streamline the process? Many organizations rely on a computerized inventory system that uses a barcode or **radio frequency identification (RFID)** on each item, allowing a computer to keep track of the status and quantity of each item. Each item is logged and classified when it is stocked and an identifying barcode or RFID is attached to the item. Both barcodes and RFIDs store all the specific information for each item, such as cost, stock number, and storage location. Using this system, items in inventory can just be scanned when they are used or sold, and the computer can continuously update the information for each item. Depending on the system used, computerized inventory makes it easier to analyze the quantitative factors of managing stock, such as how quickly each item is sold, how much really needs to be held in inventory at once, and when it's time to restock items.

► With the use of barcodes and RFIDs, items can be scanned and inventory can be monitored electronically.

What is materials requirement planning (MRP)? More appropriate to the production side of inventory management is **materials requirement planning (MRP)**, a computer-based program used for inventory control and production planning. When an order is made, the specifics of that order are put into the MRP. The MRP then determines which parts will be needed to finish the job and compares these findings to the current inventory. Based on this information, it highlights what needs to be obtained, either through production or a supplier, as well as when the parts will be needed. It uses previous manufacturing data to break the job into parts. A process is input into the system, and the MRP portion of the system determines which components are needed when to meet customers' order quantities and due dates. The end result should be the best estimate based on previous data. Knowing these estimates helps determine both part and labor shortages before a project even starts. There are many limitations to MRP, the biggest being that it is only as effective as its data. So if its data are not well maintained, the estimates that it provides will only become increasingly useless. Another limitation to MRP is its scope: it only focuses on the management of needed component parts in the *manufacturing* processes of a company.

What is enterprise resource planning? One way around this limitation is to use **enterprise resource planning (ERP)**[25] instead of MRP. ERP systems can do the same inventory control and process scheduling that MRP can do, but they can integrate these functions with all the other aspects that business management would like to tie together, such as finance and human resources. Through various types of computer software and hardware, the usual ERP system consolidates information into a central database that is accessible to various system modules. Companies that specialize in ERP systems include Oracle, SAP, and Microsoft.

ERP systems allow companies the ability to streamline the various workflows and share information across departments. This allows for improved productivity from all employees. With an ERP system in place, the various aspects of an organization can work together without worrying about compatible software. Unfortunately, there are disadvantages for a business that fails to fully invest in an ERP system. These problems can range from inadequate tech support to limited customization of the system.

With everything properly coordinated electronically, though, consumers also have more options in the products they purchase. Customers can choose how they want to receive their products—like Amazon's Super Saver shipping options—and even what kind of product they wish to buy. The sneaker company Puma has a special "Mongolian BBQ" Web site that allows consumers to choose different materials and "assemble" their very own shoe.[26]

Controlling the Production Process

How can production managers best manage the process? One of the most important aspects of the production process is making sure that work gets done as efficiently as possible. Increased efficiency helps work get done faster, cheaper, and sometimes with better quality. Although efficiency has always been a concern, the success of lean production has made efficiency a primary focus for many companies. **Lean production** is a set of principles concerned with reducing waste and improving flow. This system was first defined and utilized by Toyota in the 1980s with great success. Although lean production originally was used for manufacturing, the principles behind it are highly flexible and can be used in every step of the production process.

How does scheduling shape the production process? When it comes to production, **scheduling** refers to the efficient organization of equipment, facilities, labor, and materials. There are two different types of scheduling: *forward* and *backward*. With *forward scheduling*, you start with the date that materials are available, create the most efficient schedule, and then determine a shipping date based on that schedule. *Backward scheduling* is the exact opposite, where you are given a shipping or due date and you have to determine the start date and the most efficient schedule based on when everything has to be finished.

There are two major components that go into making an effective schedule: loading and sequencing. *Loading* is assigning a job to a specific machine or entire work center. *Sequencing* is assigning the order in which jobs are processed. There are numerous pieces of software and systems that are designed to put together a cohesive schedule of loading and sequencing to ensure that all of the right tools are working on the right jobs at the right times. But no matter how complex the system, all configurations are just estimates based on the data input in the system and the rules it uses. Having a person to oversee scheduling is still invaluable because that individual can bring experience and judgment that cannot be programmed into a computer.

What goes into proper routing? Product transportation is yet another area where the expense involved is significantly large and takes up a huge portion of a business's overall budget. Just as with technology, labor, and material expenses, transportation costs can only be limited to a certain point before they start to affect a business negatively. **Routing** is simply the way in which goods are transported, via water, rail, truck, or air. It includes transporting goods to a client, transporting materials from suppliers, or any of the other many combinations. The management of routing ensures that any transportation of goods, be it with a company's own equipment or through a courier, is done at a minimum of cost, time, and distance without sacrificing quality. The best way to understand all the variables of all the transportation options pertinent to a specific company is to put together a comprehensive routing guide. A *routing guide* is a unique and thoroughly researched document that provides detailed routing solutions for every shipping situation involving a company.[27]

The production process plays a major role in determining the profitability of a business. Efficiency and low production costs are essential in successfully producing any product. The IKEA furniture company of Sweden is a prime example of a streamlined production process. IKEA has gained worldwide recognition for its high-quality, inexpensive furniture, and is always striving to improve its production process.

▼ You have just read **Objective 4**

Want to learn more? Check out the Study Plan section @ **www.my*biz*lab.com.**

Quality Control pp. 324-327

➤ The use of techniques, activities, and processes to guarantee that a certain good or service meets a specified level of quality is referred to as **quality control**. Quality control has evolved from the formation of craftsmen's guilds in medieval Europe to improving methods of total quality management in the twentieth century.[29]

The Bridgestone/Firestone tire company had to endure a major crisis as a result of poor quality assurance. Millions of its ATX, ATX II, and Firestone Wilderness radial tires had to be recalled in the year 2000 due to tire tread separation, which caused SUV rollovers. These tires had not been adequately tested for quality and safety, and they caused numerous accidents due to their defects. Many people were injured and some were killed as a result of this lack of quality management, and Bridgestone/Firestone had to pay the Ford Motor Company $240 million to settle claims from injured motorists.[28] This crisis could have been prevented had the company taken greater quality-control measures in the production of these tires. ➤

Product Inspection

Has quality control always been part of the production process? The old method in the United States was to delegate quality control to a separate department that would test the products for flaws. The inspection method of quality control involves checking work at the end of the process before products are delivered. Unfortunately, several problems arise using this method. For one, this method is expensive in terms of time, labor, and employee confidence. Because inspection is performed by outside people instead of by the workers, each inspector can pass or fail a product using his or her own standards and procedures. Moreover, inspecting finished products and discovering defects means some of these defects have to be scrapped or reworked. This can be costly.

What is total quality management (TQM)? Merely controlling for quality through inspection and monitoring employees is like visiting the doctor for treating symptoms as opposed to the source of an illness. So, since the 1980s, firms have been focusing on building quality into every step of the production process instead of merely taking action to scrap or fix defects. This concept of "total quality" at every stage of a production process was only fully embraced by U.S. companies after Japanese manufacturers implemented company-wide quality-improvement methods and strengthened their presence in the global market.[30] The Japanese produced exports not only at lower prices, but also at higher levels of quality. Finally, by the 1980s, companies in the United States began to implement the *total quality management (TQM)* approach in their production processes. Unlike the old inspection method of quality control, in which products are reviewed at certain points of the process (usually the end), total quality management involves every factor in producing high-quality goods—management, customers, employees, and suppliers. At any point, employees and leaders are aiming to produce high quality.

Total quality management involves ongoing improvement of products, services, and processes. This can be accomplished by undertaking a Plan, Do, Check, Act (PDCA) cycle, created by American statistician W. Edwards Deming.[32] Using the PDCA, organizations first formulate a plan to reduce potential errors, carry out the plan on a small scale, check the outcome and effectiveness of the change, and then implement the plan on a larger scale while monitoring results continually. One popular tool used to check or measure if quality goals are being met is **statistical quality control (SQC)**, or the continual monitoring of each stage of the entire production process to ensure that quality standards are being met at every stage. **Statistical process control (SPC)** uses statistical sampling of products at every phase of production and displays the results on a graph to show potential variations that need to be corrected. A common SPC tool is *six sigma*, a method that seeks to eliminate defects by removing variation in outcomes and measuring and analyzing manufacturing processes to see if standards are being met. As you learned in Chapter 7, a company with six sigma quality produces at a low defect rate of just 3.4 defects per million opportunities.

How does TQM cater to the customer? It's not enough to simply implement quality-management tools. A significant aspect of TQM is catering to the customer's needs and desires. SGL Carbon, a manufacturer of graphite specialties, emphasizes adherence to a TQM approach by giving its customers the final say in determining whether a product meets the requirements of high-quality standards. Although firms may define in the beginning what makes their products high quality or low quality, those companies that learn how to simultaneously emphasize quality throughout the production process and incorporate the desires of customers will make a greater presence in the global marketplace.

ISO Standards

What is the ISO? The International Organization for Standardization (ISO) is an organization dedicated to creating worldwide standards of quality for goods and services. ISO was created in 1947 and is headquartered in Geneva, Switzerland. Between 1951 and

> " Quality is not something you install like a new carpet or a set of bookshelves. You implant it. Quality is something you work at. It is a learning process. " [31]
>
> —W. Edwards Deming, American statistician

On Target Six Sigma Takes Organizations to the Top

Six sigma was developed in the 1980s by Bill Smith, an engineer at Motorola. It involves using the statistical analysis of SPC and also builds in the TQM ideas of finding assignable causes for variations and always striving for *continuous improvement*. Motorola managed to achieve six sigma quality in 1992 after adopting continuous quality improvement methods in the 1980s.[33] Other large corporations, such as General Electric and Honeywell, have followed suit. Over the past several years, Motorola has taken the concept of six sigma even further by adapting it to the innovation involved in creating new products. At Motorola, designers are free to develop new products, and "project hoppers" are on hand to ensure that new projects meet quality standards.[34] As a result, innovation is encouraged, and at the same time, projects are monitored at every step to uphold quality and increase profitability.

1998, the organization published more than 10,000 standards. The objective of ISO is to develop production processes that are equal in quality and capability in all participating countries.[35] The ISO standards apply not to the products themselves, but to the production methods and systems used to manufacture them, as well as other areas, such as communication within the company and leadership. Such a standardized system is necessary to avoid trying to comply with various conflicting systems.

The **ISO 9000** quality assurance standards were first published in 1987. Since then, more than 90 countries have adopted these standards, and thousands of companies require their products to be ISO 9000 certified. Some industries have even developed their own industry-specific set of ISO standards. Certification is usually done by a third-party registrar who conducts an assessment of the company's quality-assurance manuals and practices. First, a pre-assessment must be conducted, during which the registrar reviews the documents that outline the company's standards and processes. If the manual and other printed documents pass the review, the company can proceed with the rest of the assessment. If the registrar finds errors in these documents, further review will have to be delayed until the mistakes are corrected.

During the formal assessment, the registrar reviews the corrected documents and interviews the employees and administrators of the company. The goal of this part of the assessment is to ensure that written policies and procedures are being implemented in the company's production methods. Finally, the registrar issues an audit report summarizing the results of the assessment and listing any areas that need improvement. If corrections are required at this stage, the company can make them and document them in a report to the registrar. After satisfactory corrections have been made, the registrar can then award certification to the company. Once it has earned certification, the company can put the ISO 9000 seal in advertising and on letterhead.

After certification, the registrar returns to the company twice a year to make sure the company is still in compliance with the ISO standards. These spot checks are conducted without advance warning, and the registrar focuses on areas that were notably weak during the initial assessment. Every three years, the registrar will complete another assessment and issue a new audit report. The company must also establish an internal auditing program that is responsible for keeping the ISO standards in practice.

PERT and Gantt Charts

What is a PERT chart? The **program evaluation and review technique (PERT)** was first used in the development of submarines in the 1950s. This method maps out the various steps involved in a project, differentiating tasks that must be completed in a certain order from tasks that may be completed simultaneously. The result is a Weblike diagram similar to the example shown in ▼ **Figure 11.1**.

In creating a PERT chart, time estimates are assigned to each task. Creating the chart helps identify the **critical path**, or the path of sequential tasks that will take the longest amount of time to complete. This helps managers determine an overall timeline for completing a project or, from a manufacturing standpoint, producing a particular good or service. However, because delays can cause the critical path in a project to change, PERT charts are limited in their ability to predict project completion times.

What is a Gantt chart? Another method for keeping tabs on the progress of a given project is a **Gantt chart**, a tool developed by Henry Gantt in the 1920s. A Gantt chart is formatted similarly to a horizontal bar graph. It's used to lay out

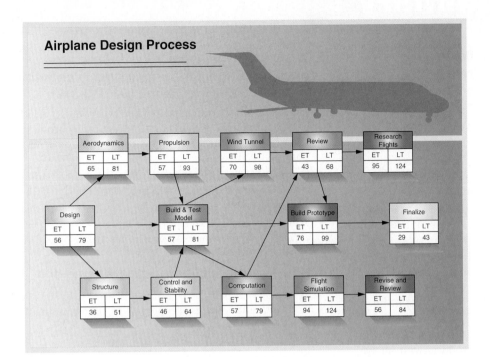

Figure 11.1
Sample PERT Chart

each task in a project, the order in which these tasks must be completed, and how long each task should take. (See ▼ **Figure 11.2**.) Originally used for large-scale construction projects, such as building the Hoover Dam in the 1930s, Gantt charts are still used today to manage a variety of both large-scale and small-scale projects. At any point in the process, project managers and manufacturers can see at a glance which tasks have been completed and whether these tasks were completed on schedule.

Quality control is essential in maintaining both the reputation of a business and consumer safety. A lack of effective quality control can be disastrous, as in the case of the Firestone tire recall. Many consumers were injured or killed due to a lack of effective quality control. Although not all cases of poor quality are this tragic, consumers have come to expect a certain level of quality when purchasing a product.

Remodeling Project

Remodeling Project Job No.: 980015.05	Jul '09			Aug '09				Sep '09					Oct '09	
	15	22	29	5	12	19	26	2	9	16	23	30	7	14
Project Summary														
Soft Demo														
Soft Demo-Structural														
Structual Steel-Fab														
Framing-Rough														
Skylights														
Roof Curbs & Patch														
Electrical-Rough/Finish														
Overhead Doors														
Inspection-Structural Rebar														
Structural Concrete-Pour														
Service/Repair Elevator														
Pluming Rough														
Data/Phone Cabling														
Structural Steel-Install														
T-bar Grid Repair														
Inspection-Walls														
Inspection-Drywall Screw														
Mud & Tape														
Mezzanine Demo														

Figure 11.2
Sample Gantt Chart

▼ You have just read **Objective 5**

Want to test your skills? Check out the Study Plan section @
www.mybizlab.com.

Chapter Summary

Find your Study Plan and Study Guide @ www.mybizlab.com.

1. What are mass production, flexible production, and customer-driven production, and what are the benefits and challenges of each? (pp. 307-310)

- **Mass production** (p. 308) is the method of producing large quantities of goods at a low cost.
  - Benefits of mass production include low cost, decreased production time, and virtually no human error, due to the reliance on machinery.
  - A major disadvantage is that mass production is inflexible, making it very difficult to change or alter the process if an unexpected problem occurs.
- Flexible production utilizes a **flexible manufacturing system** (p. 308)—a system in which machines are programmed to process different part types simultaneously—allowing a manufacturer to mass produce customized products.
  - The primary benefit of flexible production is that it provides the flexibility to make products with many slight variations.
  - A challenge of flexible production is that it is not well-suited for goods that are in high demand.
- **Customer-driven production** (p. 309) is a method of production that revolves around the customer.
  - When applied during the **prospect-to-cash** (p. 309) process, this method allows the manufacturer to set customization limits to keep production cost-effective. It also keeps the company up to date on consumer demand and helps streamline operations, such as delivery, that directly affect consumers.
  - A key challenge is making this process as efficient as possible, including reducing the time it takes to process an order, create a customized product at almost the rate of mass production, and achieve customer satisfaction.

2. How does technology influence the production process? (pp. 310-312)

- Robots offer consistency in reducing production costs, raising productivity, and producing high-quality products.
- **Computer-aided design**, **computer-aided manufacturing**, and **computer-integrated manufacturing** (pp. 311-312) have dramatically improved the process of producing goods by reducing the time between design and manufacturing, thus making a sizeable impact on productivity. These systems have also increased the scope of the use of automated machinery in the production process.

3. What are the transportation, human, and physical factors that are involved in choosing a manufacturing location? (pp. 313-317)

- The major transportation factors a company must consider include proximity to market, the cost of transporting raw materials, and the presence of highways and other transportation systems.
- **Human factors** (p. 315) that should be considered include labor availability, living conditions, and laws and regulations.
- When selecting a location for production, a company must consider physical factors such as hazardous-waste disposal and **utility supply** (p. 317).

4. How is a production plan developed and controlled? (pp. 318-323)

- A production plan is developed by determining the following:
  - the ideal size and layout of a facility
  - what to produce
  - where to locate that facility
  - what processes and machinery to use to minimize costs
  - the number of products needed to be produced each month
  - how to meet the needs of all employees
- Effective **scheduling** and proper **routing** (p. 323) can help managers control the production process.

5. What is quality control and how do ISO standards help companies produce high-quality goods and services? (pp. 324-327)

- **Quality control** (p. 324) is the use of techniques, activities, and processes to guarantee that a certain good or service meets a specified level of quality.
- The International Organization for Standardization (ISO) has created worldwide standards of quality for goods and services. The ISO standards apply not to the products themselves, but to the production methods and systems used to manufacture them, as well as other areas, such as communication within the company and leadership.

For an audio file of the Objectives and Chapter Summary, see the Student Resources section @ www.mybizlab.com.

Key Terms

Self-Test

Multiple Choice Correct answers can be found on page 503.

1. **The advantages of mass production include which of the following?**
   a. Large quantities of goods produced at a low cost
   b. Standardization of goods
   c. Low consumer costs due to low production costs
   d. All of the above

2. **A flexible manufacturing system is characterized by**
   a. several machines linked by one central computer.
   b. a process run entirely by human labor.
   c. a process run entirely by mechanized labor.
   d. None of the above

3. **The steps of the prospect-to-cash process of customer-driven production are**
   a. prospecting, engineering, order management, production, and cash.
   b. prospecting, analyzing, interpreting, managing, and cash.
   c. cash, cost-benefit analysis, production, and prospecting.
   d. cash, engineering, production, and profit.

4. **CAD is used to**
   a. market new products.
   b. find customers for a product.
   c. create two-dimensional or three-dimensional models of physical parts.
   d. analyze the market value of a product.

5. **All of the following are important factors in selecting a location for production EXCEPT**
   a. proximity to raw materials.
   b. impact on community of location.
   c. availability of labor.
   d. humid climate.

6. **An effective plan by a production manager should lead to**
   a. increased productivity.
   b. reduced costs.
   c. improved customer service.
   d. All of the above

7. **All of the following are factors in the make-or-buy decision EXCEPT**
   a. situational factors.
   b. quantitative factors.
   c. common factors.
   d. qualitative factors.

8. **Radio frequency identification is used to**
   a. keep track of the status and quantity of each item.
   b. keep track of the customer base for an item.
   c. stay in touch with other workers in a factory.
   d. manufacture stereo systems.

9. **Selecting the best routing for the shipment of goods is important because**
   a. transporting goods can be expensive.
   b. quality can be compromised in the shipping process.
   c. rapid delivery is essential in maximizing business.
   d. All of the above

10. **Total quality management is geared toward**
    a. producing the largest quantity of goods in the time allotted.
    b. catering to the customer's needs and desires.
    c. eliminating humans from the workplace.
    d. meeting government standards for emissions.

True/False Correct answers can be found on page 503.

1. Robots can work around the clock with good accuracy and in potentially hazardous conditions.
   ☐ **True** or ☐ **False**

2. CAD and CAM have dramatically reduced the time between the design and manufacturing stages of production.
   ☐ **True** or ☐ **False**

3. Selecting a location in close proximity to skilled workers is not necessary in establishing a business.
   ☐ **True** or ☐ **False**

4. A facility's layout is important in maximizing efficiency and satisfying employees' needs.
   ☐ **True** or ☐ **False**

5. The just-in-time method of inventory control consists of keeping a large amount of inventory in the warehouse to be sure that all deliveries will be made on time.
   ☐ **True** or ☐ **False**

Critical Thinking Questions

1. How did the advent of mass production and the mechanized assembly line change the role of human labor in manufacturing? Did this shift eliminate jobs, or did it create new ones? How did it change the face of the consumer market?

2. You have decided to open a company that produces wooden furniture, and you must select a suitable location for production. The first option is in a remote region of Montana with easy access to abundant raw materials, but far away from a skilled worker base. The second option is in Southern California in close proximity to many skilled workers as well as several major highways for distribution. Which location would you choose for your business and why?

3. A sports equipment company is known for a special grip on its tennis rackets that is imported from South America. The cost of shipping these grips has grown steadily more expensive, and the business would like to produce the grips in-house. What factors does the business need to consider before adding another step to the production process?

4. How does a business decide what the best method of shipment is for its products? What factors, other than cost, are important in this decision?

5. Give an example of what the process of total quality management would involve in the production of automobiles. What steps can manufacturers take to ensure that a high level of quality is maintained consistently in their production processes?

Team Time

To Outsource or Not to Outsource . . . That Is the Question

Divide into two teams to represent both sides of the issue.

    a.   group that thinks the company should make the component

    b.   group that thinks the company should outsource the component

Scenario

The Grindstone Supply Company of New Jersey is attempting to expand its manufacturing of large wall clocks. In years past, the company has outsourced the manufacturing of clock springs to a company in Nebraska. This has been cost-effective in the past, but now that demand for the springs has increased, Grindstone is considering manufacturing the springs in-house. Although the cost of producing the springs in-house is lower, it is unclear whether it will be profitable in the long run, as the manufacturing process will change greatly. New machines for the production of springs will be needed, as the factory works exclusively in wood and plastic. With the new machines comes the need for new technicians to monitor and service them. Should the Grindstone Supply Company alter its manufacturing process to include the production of clock springs, or should it continue outsourcing to Nebraska as it has in the past? What factors contribute to this decision? Will this be more profitable in the long run? How will it affect employee morale and relations?

Process

Step 1. Record your ideas and opinions about the issue presented in the scenario above. Be sure to consider the issue from your assigned perspective.

Step 2. Meet as a team and review the issue from both perspectives. Discuss together why the position of your group is the best decision.

Ethics and Corporate Social Responsibility

Environmental Shipping Concerns

You have just been promoted to head of the shipping department for your office supply company, and it is now your responsibility to determine routing. The company is located on the eastern seaboard, near major highways as well as the ocean. In the past, trucking has been the preferred method of shipping, as it was deemed the most cost-effective. Shipping the freight by boat, however, would greatly reduce the negative effects on the environment caused by truck emissions. After calculating the cost on paper, you realize that shipping by sea would have a negative effect on the overall profit margin, but the company would still generate solid profits.

Questions

1. What decision would you make in this situation, land or sea?
2. If you were told that you would take a personal pay cut from switching to the more environmentally friendly route, how would that affect your decision?
3. What kind of impact do you think one company switching to less environmentally damaging practices could have on the general atmosphere of the shipping world?

Web Exercises

1. **Leaders in the Industrial Robot Industry**
   Search the Internet for several industrial robot production companies. What kinds of functions are robots being used to perform? In what kinds of industries are these robots best suited to perform?

2. **Shipping Goods by Land**
   Shipping products can be quite expensive, depending on the distance that needs to be covered. Go to www.freightnshipping.com/quote.php for an instant shipping quote from several companies. Type in several items of different sizes, weights, and shipping locations, and see what the price would be to ship through each company. How do these variables affect the cost of shipping, and how can this shape a business plan?

3. **Radio Frequency Identification**
   The use of chips to track goods during the shipping process is becoming more widespread. Use the Internet to research options for radio frequency identification.

   What are some of the options for tracking goods? What kind of range can these products cover?

4. **Efficiency in Production**
   Research the Toyota Production System on the Internet. Why do you think this system has been so effective for Toyota? What are the major concepts that set the Toyota system apart from the competition? Write a short paragraph considering the system and these questions.

5. **Quality Control**
   Quality control is a major issue in the mass production of goods. Many systems have been used to assure quality control in manufacturing. Find two different systems of quality control on the Internet. What are the merits and downfalls of each? If you were in charge of the production of a product, which system of quality control would you choose? Write a paragraph comparing and contrasting these two quality-control systems.

Web Case

To access the Chapter 11 Web case and exercise, see the End of Chapter Assignments section @ www.mybizlab.com.

Video Case

To access the Chapter 11 Video case and exercise, see the End of Chapter Assignments section @ www.mybizlab.com.

Business Communications

We communicate and interact with others all day. In fact, people in organizations spend at least 75 percent of their time in interpersonal situations, whether it's one-on-one, in groups, intra-organizational, or with customers, suppliers, investors, and advisors.[1] Communicating effectively is critical in the business world, yet can present significant challenges. When you consider the impact poor communication can have on business—such as loss of customers from poor customer service, lack of focus on business objectives, and stifled innovation—it becomes clear why effective communication is an important business goal. In this mini chapter, we'll discuss how you can improve your communication skills at the workplace.

Improving Your Speaking Skills

In business, you often need to persuade, educate, or inform a group about your ideas. If you don't have good speaking skills, your audience won't be receptive. Good presentation skills begin with good oral communication skills, so you need to make sure you speak loudly and clearly. Change your voice intonation to add emphasis or interest when appropriate. It's important to engage the audience members by looking directly at them, often changing your focus to different individuals around the room. Relax and smile, just as you would if you were talking to your friends.

In many instances, presentation software, such as Microsoft's PowerPoint, can be a great addition to a presentation if it's used correctly. We have all sat through boring presentations where the presenter has read directly from the slides, or has been distracted by too many graphics, animations, or blinding color schemes. However, when used to its best capabilities, PowerPoint can be a very effective tool. On the next page you'll find some tips to make your next PowerPoint presentation successful.

The complement to good oral communication skills is active listening skills. To ensure that you're being attentive when listening, repeat back or summarize the points that you believe were being made. Good listening also means asking good questions, but avoid becoming distracted by trying to think of what you're going to say next. If you need clarification, try to respond with statements such as "Tell me more." Finally, keep an open mind to others' ideas and suggestions. You do not necessarily want to have a solution or outcome defined in your mind before you hear what everyone else has to say.

PowerPoint Tips

➤ Delivering effective PowerPoint presentations requires planning and practice.

1. **Keep it simple.** Just because the software is capable of doing amazing things, don't feel like you have to use all the bells and whistles. Keep the design clean and charts simple and easy to understand. Limit the number of animations and special effects. In addition, use graphics to illustrate or highlight what you're saying, not serve as the focus.

2. **Follow the 6 × 6 × 24 rule.** Remember, PowerPoint is merely an outline of your presentation, not the entire presentation. Therefore, only place those key words or thoughts you want your audience to remember on your slides. You'll fill in the other details as you speak. To help keep the content of your slides to a minimum, some presentation experts suggest you aim for no more than six words in a bullet point, six bullet points on a slide, and the words formatted in no less than 24-point font. Also, try to keep the total number of slides to a minimum.

3. **Use graphics and media to convey ideas.** Most of us are visual learners, which is why PowerPoint is an effective presentation tool. We can better remember what someone is saying if we see key words at the same time. We remember even better when the right graphic or image is used to convey an entire idea. There are terrific short video pieces available on the Web that can be embedded easily into the presentation to add a bit of humor, bring in a different "speaker," or convey a message in a different way.

4. **Use color sparingly, but effectively.** A light background with dark text is the best color combination for most light conditions. Adding color sparingly will help add visual interest and bring special attention to key areas of the presentation. Too much color can be distracting.

5. **Edit, edit, and edit.** Typographical or spelling errors make you look like you didn't care enough about the material or your audience to spend time reviewing your presentation. It's also important that you run your presentation beforehand in SlideShow mode to catch any problems with animations or transitions.

6. **Practice makes perfect.** Practice giving your presentation several times aloud before giving it live in front of an audience. If you find yourself stumbling through a part, think about how you want to communicate that idea and change your slides accordingly. When you are nervous, it will be even more difficult to work with slide content that is unnatural or uncomfortable.

to continue   check out **www.my*biz*lab.com**.

chapter 12

Marketing and Consumer Behavior

▼ Objectives 1-7

1. How has **marketing** evolved over the production concept era, the sales concept era, the marketing concept era, and the customer relationship era? (p. 337)

2. What are the benefits of marketing to customers, sellers, investors, employees, and society at large, and what are the criticisms of marketing? (p. 340)

3. What are the two basic elements of a marketing strategy and the 4 Ps of the marketing mix? (p. 343)

4. How do firms implement a marketing strategy by applying the five steps of the marketing process? (p. 346)

5. How do the various factors in the **marketing environment** influence a firm's ability to manipulate its **marketing mix**? (p. 348)

6. What are the five steps of the **marketing research** process and the four elements of a good **marketing plan**? (p. 352)

7. How do the buying decisions and marketing processes in **business-to-business markets** compare to those in the **consumer market**? (p. 358)

For more chapter resources, go to www.my*biz*lab.com.

p. 343

Marketing Tactics
▼ **Objectives 3 & 4**
Aaron Hoffman has a business idea to start a mobile pet-grooming service. Aaron was told he needs to create a "marketing strategy." What is a marketing strategy? Why is it necessary?

p. 348

The Marketing Environment
▼ **Objective 5**
Amelia Russo runs a store selling inexpensive dress shoes that she imports from overseas. The value of the U.S. dollar has gotten so low that she needs to raise her prices. Her marketing environment is forcing her to change the way she does business. What is a marketing environment? How can it pose constraints on a business?

p. 352

Marketing Research and Planning
▼ **Objective 6**
Tiara Watson has decided to start a salon supply business. She knows that there is a demand for her products, but she wants to draw up a carefully organized marketing plan to ensure the success of her business. There are over 30 salons in her city, and Tiara has the connections to offer them products at a lower cost. What steps must she take to get her name known in the salon supply world? What can she do to ensure success in her new business?

p. 337

Marketing Fundamentals
▼ **Objectives 1 & 2**
How ethical is the energy drink product name "Cocaine"? The product isn't being marketed to children, but the name still raises moral concerns. The drink obviously does not contain cocaine, but does contain a lot of caffeine as a stimulant. What relationship does the marketing team behind this have to the message being sent?

p. 358

Consumer Behavior
▼ **Objective 7**
If you were opening your own business, how would you figure out who would be the ideal customer? Doing market research would be a good place to start. The goal of your research is to identify consumer behavior and choose your target market from there. What is consumer behavior? How does a consumer make the decision to buy something?

Marketing Fundamentals pp. 337-342

> The American Marketing Association (AMA) defines **marketing** as "an organizational function and a set of processes for creating, communicating, and delivering value to customers and for managing customer relationships in ways that benefit the organization and its stakeholders."[1] Marketing departments serve a variety of functions. First and foremost, marketers are responsible for keeping an eye on what people need and want, then communicating these desires to the rest of the organization. Marketing departments help establish desirable pricing strategies and promote the organization by persuading customers that their products are the best. A **product** is any tangible good, service, or idea available for purchase in a market, as well as any intangible benefits derived from its consumption, such as the brand. Marketing departments are also responsible for distributing products to customers at a place and time most suitable to the customer. But perhaps the most important aspect of marketing is to successfully establish meaningful relationships with customers to instill loyalty and ensure repeat business. Marketing is one of the most visible functions of any organization; however, the public only sees the tip of the iceberg.

Members of the American Marketing Association follow a code of ethics to ensure that their marketing practices are fair to consumers. But how responsible are marketers who work with products that may do a disservice to society? For example, what is the moral responsibility for a caffeinated energy drink called "Cocaine"? Does this glamorize drug use, or is it just a cheeky, attention-grabbing name created by marketers to generate buzz? >

The Evolution of Marketing

How does marketing address the customer? In its broadest sense, marketing can be thought of as identifying and meeting human needs and wants. However, the degree to which marketers have identified and met people's needs and wants has changed over time, as has the AMA's official definition of marketing. In 2004, the organization revised the definition to reflect a new focus on value for customers and to recognize the importance of managing customer relationships. Certainly, an organization-wide consumer orientation is of paramount concern to all businesses today. However, this intense focus on customer satisfaction was not always the case.

How has marketing evolved over time? The nature of marketing has evolved over four general eras (see ▼ **Figure 12.1**):

1. The production concept era

2. The sales concept era

3. The marketing concept era

4. The customer relationship era

Although each concept experienced a peak in popularity during a specific time period, some companies still use marketing concepts from an earlier era. Today's most successful marketing campaigns are a sophisticated combination of the best of each of these times.

The Production Concept Era

From the Industrial Revolution until the 1920s, most companies focused solely on production. The prevailing mindset was that a good-quality product would simply sell itself. This approach worked for many organizations during this era because of a strong demand and a limited supply of products. Whenever demand outstrips supply, it creates a "seller's market." This may have motivated Henry Ford to remark in relation to his Model T cars that customers could have any color they wanted, as long as it was black. At the time, black was the only color available.

The Sales Concept Era

From the mid-1920s through the early 1950s, technological advances meant that production increased more sharply than demand for goods and services. The competition for customers became more intense, and businesses began to undertake aggressive sales tactics to sell or "push" their products. The use of heavy public advertising in all available forms of media became prevalent. During this era, marketing generally took place after the product was developed and produced. Heavy emphasis was placed on selling existing products. Even today, many people associate marketing with selling or advertising; however, it has become much more than that.

The Marketing Concept Era

By the 1950s, production continued to expand more quickly than the growth in demand for goods and services, creating a "buyer's market." Soldiers returning from World War II were getting married, starting families, and were willing to spend their money on goods and services. Businesses began to realize that simply producing quality products and pushing them onto customers through clever advertising and promotional campaigns didn't guarantee sales. Companies needed to determine what customers wanted and then produce products, as opposed to produce products and then try to convince customers to buy them.

▼ **Figure 12.1 Timeline of the Four Evolutionary Marketing Periods**

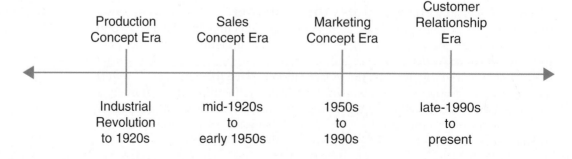

The **marketing concept** changed the focus from finding the right customer for a product to producing the right product for a customer and doing it better than the competition (see ▼ **Figure 12.2**). More specifically, the marketing concept focuses on:

1. identifying customer needs before the product is designed and produced;

2. aligning all functions of the entire organization to meet or exceed these customer needs through superior products and customer service;

3. realizing a profit (not just sales) by satisfying customers over the long term.

This requires constantly taking the pulse of changing customer needs and wants, and then quickly adapting to meet them. Moreover, it may mean anticipating customers' changing preferences—before they are expressed or even known by consumers—and satisfying these preferences before competitors. For example, Apple has become a master of anticipating customers' desires and fulfilling them with its range of iPods, iPod accessories, and the iPhone.

The Customer Relationship Era

Since the late 1990s, organizations have tried to build on their marketing concept successes by intensifying the entire organization's focus on customer satisfaction over time. The result has been the creation of **customer relationship management (CRM)**, the process of establishing long-term relationships with individual customers to foster loyalty and repeat business. The marketing concept is good for *acquiring* customers by offering customized products, among other things, but customer relationship management goes one step further by trying to please customers *after the sale*. It combines computer information technology with customer service and marketing communications to *retain* customers in order to stimulate future sales of similar or supplementary products. Several popular clothing stores, including Gap, Banana Republic, and Old Navy, offer coupons to customers who join their mailing lists. Customers on the list also receive information about sales and promotions to keep them up to date on the latest deals at the store.

The idea is to learn as much as possible about customers and create a meaningful one-on-one interaction with each of them. In practice, CRM often involves the sales force gathering information about specific customers to create a customer database. CRM software allows e-mail or other communications to be personalized. It enables the company to offer products tailored to these specific customers' needs and desires. CRM databases also mean that customers visiting the organization's Web site or customer service call center can be quickly and easily recognized, and offerings can be adapted to their preferences. Customer relationship management is part of why airlines offer frequent flyer programs to selected customers and why credit card companies offer customized services and low-interest balance transfer to certain targeted customers.

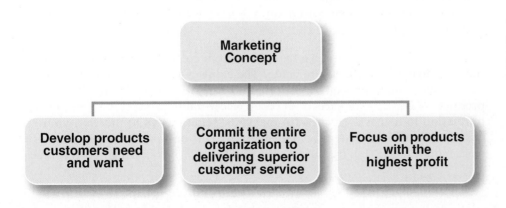

▼ **Figure 12.2
The Marketing
Concept**

Nontraditional Marketing

What is nontraditional marketing? To understand nontraditional marketing, let's first be clear about the definition of traditional marketing. The objective of traditional marketing is to generate a profit. However, many not-for-profit organizations also have an interest in marketing. Rather than a product or service, these organizations look to market an event, cause, place, or person. This is nontraditional marketing. For example, environmental organizations like the Sierra Club, the National Wildlife Federation, and the Nature Conservancy, and other nonprofits like the Red Cross, the American Cancer Society, and the Peace Corps rely on marketing to raise awareness of and increase donations to their causes. Likewise, churches and other civic organizations market their missions to attract new membership. Countries, states, and cities also run marketing campaigns to attract tourists and businesses to their locations. Museums and zoos also undertake "place marketing" by emphasizing the value of visiting their locations.

What about marketing people? Politicians and political parties market candidates for elected office. Agents for athletes, movie stars, television personalities, and musicians market their clients. We market ourselves when we interview for a job. You may have marketed yourself for acceptance to your college or university. To a certain extent, we're all marketing ourselves everyday at work and play. Regardless of what is being marketed—an event, a cause, a place, a person, a good, or a service—the essence of marketing remains the same. The only difference between nontraditional and traditional marketing practices is the stakeholders involved and their objectives.

How Marketing Benefits Stakeholders

How does marketing benefit stakeholders? *Stakeholders*, or interested parties, include customers, sellers, investors, employees, and society at large. Each group of stakeholders has a different set of motives for their interest in the success of the business.

Customer and Seller Benefits

As consumers, we have many needs—food, clothing, housing, medical care, and transportation, among others. Marketers don't really *create* needs. Instead, they *respond* to them. Indeed, many businesses have become extremely profitable by finding a need and satisfying it. Although marketers do not create needs, they do work very hard to convince you to choose their specific product over competing products. Subway and Quiznos go to great lengths to convince you to buy their sandwiches to satisfy your need for food, just as Toyota and Ford try to convince you to purchase their vehicles to gratify your transportation needs. If a company is unable to convert customer need into a desire for its product, then that company will not succeed.

Whenever a business satisfies a need or want, it creates value for the customer. But how do customers measure value? The **value** of a product equals the ratio of the product's benefits to its costs (value = benefits/costs). With a high-value product, its benefits far exceed its costs. A low-value product has few benefits in relation to its costs. Successful marketing finds ways to increase value to customers—to increase real or perceived benefits of a product or to minimize customers' costs by reducing the price or maximizing convenience.

Organizations that offer the highest-valued products win the most customers and thrive. Those organizations that offer low-value goods and services lose market share or go out of business entirely.

There are four kinds of utility that marketing provides to customers:

1. When a company produces a product from raw materials, like a designer swimsuit from fabric and raw materials, it creates **form utility**. The product takes on a form that pleases the customer.

2. When the store sells the swimsuit, it transfers ownership from the store to the customer, creating **ownership utility**. The buyer derives satisfaction from owning the latest swimwear.

3. When the business makes the swimsuit available in time for summer, it creates **time utility** because the swimwear is available for sale at a time when it's most needed.

4. When the swimsuit is stocked and placed on display at your local department store, it creates **place utility** by making the product available for purchase at a place that's convenient for buyers.

Of course, the benefits of marketing to customers can only be achieved when organizations can sustain themselves. This requires organizations to generate at least as much revenue as cost. Successful organizations generate more revenue than cost, creating a profit. Hence, sellers, as stakeholders, benefit from successful marketing because their profits enable the organization to not only sustain itself, but to prosper and continue to provide value to customers.

Investor and Employee Benefits

Investors, as stakeholders, receive profits to reward them for devoting their financial resources to organizations that are successful. Indeed, more and more investment flows to those businesses that are most successful in satisfying customers because investors are rewarded with higher profits. Employees benefit from successful marketing as well because their jobs and livelihoods are more secure. In addition, new job opportunities are created as production expands to satisfy the growing demand for high-value products.

Societal Benefits

Society at large benefits from successful marketing because scarce resources are more efficiently allocated or channeled into the production of those goods and services most desired by society. Resources, such as raw materials and labor, flow into the production of those goods and services in greatest demand and away from low-value products with falling demand. The market mechanism ensures it. For example, if the public demands more of Research in Motion (RIM)'s BlackBerrys, then RIM's profits rise and RIM has a huge incentive to produce more BlackBerrys. Because more resources are required to produce more BlackBerrys, the demand for resources and labor used in BlackBerry production rises, raising prices and wages, and more resources flow into the production of BlackBerrys.

Profitable businesses that satisfy public needs and wants, like RIM, attract more resources. Unsuccessful businesses and their unsuccessful products use fewer resources. The market mechanism benefits society by shifting scarce resources away from less desired products into more desired products. When resources are utilized more efficiently, society is able to consume more products, increasing the average standard of living.

Criticisms of Marketing

What are the criticisms of marketing? Over time, certain social short-comings have emerged from marketing techniques. Some of the questionable tactics criticized include price gouging (asking for a price that is widely considered unfair), high-pressure selling, the production of shoddy or unsafe products, planned obsolescence (the product becomes obsolete after a period of time planned by the manufacturer), poor customer service, misuse of customer information, confusing and deceptive labeling, and other deceptive practices, such as hidden fees and charges.

Let's consider a few examples of the costs to society of questionable marketing.

➤ Was it ignorance of the harm their product could have on society or a conscious effort to deceive the public for selfish gain that motivated tobacco companies to undertake promotions like this one in the 1950s? Many believe that ad campaigns such as this one fall under the heading of unscrupulous marketing.

- **Misuse of personal information.** Marketing often involves the collection of personal information about customers. Companies conduct marketing surveys to find out the marital status, annual income, age, sex, race, and other characteristics of their primary customers. Many of us feel violated when this personal information is not adequately protected or is resold without our permission, especially in the age of identity theft.

- **Hidden fees.** Many of us feel taken advantage of when we must pay "hidden" fees and charges not included in the advertised price. Products that require additional parts or shipping and service fees often make customers upset.

- **Consequences of purchase.** Unscrupulous marketing may take advantage of less sophisticated members of society. To what extent is it reasonable to hold buyers responsible for being aware of the consequences of their purchases? This is especially important when purchasing expensive or sophisticated goods and services, such as a car or a mortgage on a home. Similar concerns emerge when marketing is directed at children.

The many criticisms of marketing should not be taken lightly. These concerns may help explain the strong support for consumer protection laws and other regulations governing business behavior. Too often the social costs of marketing stem from unethical business behavior. As we discussed in Chapter 3, all companies should have a code of ethics and policies in place to curb unethical behavior within their organizations. However, not all companies do, which allows for questionable products, like the "Cocaine" energy drink, to be marketed. The American Marketing Association has a code of ethics that contains guidelines on ethical norms and values for marketers. You can visit the AMA's Web site to review this code at www.marketingpower.com.

▼ You have just read **Objectives 1 & 2**

Think you got it? Check out the Study Plan section @
www.mybizlab.com.

Marketing Tactics pp. 343-347

➤ All organizations can benefit from a well-developed marketing strategy. In this section, we'll look at the factors that are involved in the marketing process.

Marketing Strategy: The 4 Ps of Marketing

What is a marketing strategy? A marketing strategy consists of two major elements: the organization must determine its *target market* and then develop a *marketing mix* to meet the needs of that market. The **target market** is a specific group of potential customers on which a firm focuses its marketing efforts. (We'll discuss target marketing in more detail later in the chapter.) The **marketing mix** is the combination of four factors, called the "4 Ps" of marketing, designed to serve the target market:

- product
- price
- promotion
- place

The idea is to provide the *product* that customers need and want at an appropriate *price* and to *promote* its sale and *place* or distribute the good or service in a convenient location for the customer to purchase (see ▼ **Figure 12.3**). The 4 Ps of the marketing

Aaron Hoffman is determined to work for himself, and he knows he can do that with his own mobile pet-grooming service. Since he worked as a pet groomer for seven years, he has enough experience to branch out on his own. Aaron has already found a van to hold all of his equipment and he knows a few of his previous customers are interested, but he isn't sure what the next step should be. Someone suggested he come up with a marketing strategy to help him get organized. What does a marketing strategy do? And how should Aaron apply it to his new business? ➤

▼ **Figure 12.3**
The Marketing Mix
The marketing mix consists of the 4 Ps: product, price, promotion, and place. Effective marketing requires the appropriate blend of the 4 Ps directed at targeted customers. This blend is constrained by forces outside the firm's control that are found within the broader market environment.

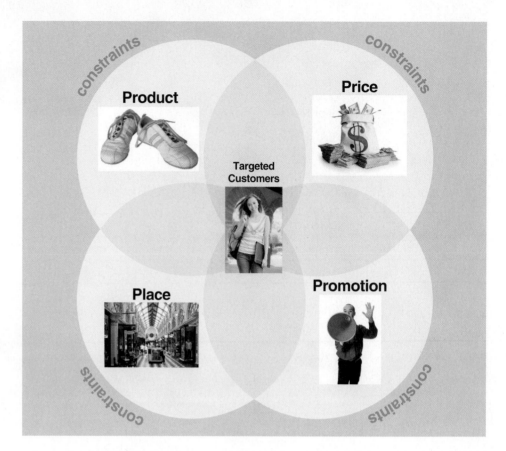

mix need to be blended in the most appropriate manner to best meet the needs of the target market. Finding the best blend of the 4 Ps is constrained by environmental factors outside the firm's control. We'll discuss these constraints found within the broader market environment later in this chapter. Let's look at each of the 4 Ps in a bit more detail.

BizChat

Is There a Fifth P?

Although the "4 Ps" of marketing are the accepted criteria for the marketing mix, there has been some discussion of adding a fifth "P" to the mix. In today's competitive business world, some say it's necessary to have a "purple cow" factor—something that makes your business or product stand apart from the competition. A company that has attained success using a "purple cow" is the Geek

Squad computer service. An affiliate of Best Buy, the Geek Squad provides a wide range of technical services to customers. What makes it stand apart is its image. Geek Squad employees make house calls, driving PT cruisers with Geek Squad logos. The IT world is considered a nerdy field, and the Geek Squad embraces that image and runs with it. As a result of its unique marketing approach, Geek Squad is one of the most recognizable technical service businesses.[2]

For more information and discussion questions about this topic, check out the BizChat feature on my*biz*lab.com.

Product

Distinguishing your product from that of your competitors is critical. If you don't do something that's different from and superior to the competition, why should customers buy from you? *Product differentiation* is the creation of a real or perceived difference in a product designed to attract customers. Product differentiation is one of the most critical ingredients to success for most businesses and will be discussed in greater detail in Chapter 13. Product differentiation can take the form of functionality, styling, quality, safety, packaging, warranty, accessories, or brand name image. A **brand** is a name, term, symbol, or design that distinguishes a company and its products from all others.

> "We read advertisements to discover and enlarge our desires. We are always ready—even eager—to discover, from the announcement of a new product, what we have all along wanted without really knowing it." [3]
>
> —Daniel J. Boorstin, U.S. historian (1914–2004)

Price

There's a lot to consider when deciding on the price for a product. Of course, the price will have to be sufficient to cover costs if you wish to make a profit. However, the product must be competitively priced to appeal to customers. We'll investigate the price component of the marketing mix in more detail in Chapter 13.

Promotion

The **promotion** part of the marketing mix consists of all the methods to inform and persuade targeted customers to buy a product and to build positive customer relationships. Communicating the benefits of your good or service to customers includes advertising, sales promotions, personal selling, public relations, direct marketing, and publicity. We'll explore promotion more fully in Chapter 14.

Place

The **place** (or **distribution**) component of the marketing mix refers to all the methods involved in getting the product into the hands of customers. A product isn't beneficial to a customer if it can't be purchased when and where it is needed. When a business is providing a good instead of a service, the delivery component is often more complicated. Many goods, like grocery store items, go through a *distribution channel*, which is a series of firms or individuals that participate in the flow of a product from manufacturer to consumer. The middlemen in a distribution channel are sometimes called *distributors* or *wholesalers*. Some goods, such as food products, go through many wholesalers before reaching a retail outlet (like a grocery store) and, finally, the consumer. Other goods, such as automobiles, typically move from the manufacturer to just one wholesaler, the car dealership, and then on to the consumer. Still other goods bypass wholesalers altogether and move from the manufacturer directly to the consumer, such as L.L.Bean clothing products, which are ordered from a catalog and shipped directly to consumers.[4] In Chapter 14, we'll examine finding the appropriate distribution channel and managing it efficiently in order to get the product to the right place at the right time, in the proper quantity, and at the lowest cost.

➤ Costco offers its warehouse members a more direct distribution channel and therefore saves them money.

The Marketing Process

What are the steps in the marketing process? There are five steps in the marketing process, as outlined in ▼ **Figure 12.4**.

1. **Identify a Market Need.** Let's think back to Aaron Hoffman's mobile pet-grooming service. Aaron has his own pets, and before he became a groomer himself, he used to take his dogs to the pet-grooming service at which he was later employed. Transporting his dogs was a huge hassle, and he felt horrible about leaving them in a cage for part of the day. He didn't know it at the time, but Aaron had identified an unfilled market need: a *mobile* pet-grooming service that eliminated the hassle and guilt that trouble pet owners when they take their pets to a grooming service. This is the first step in the marketing process.

2. **Conduct Market Research and Develop a Marketing Plan.** The next step is to conduct research on the profitability of a potential business. As Aaron researches, he discovers that many other people share his desire for a more convenient pet-grooming service. It appears sufficient demand already exists for the services of his potential business. We'll discuss how to conduct market research and how to develop a marketing plan in more detail later in the chapter.

3. **Identify Target Customers.** The third step is to select a target market. Without this focus, Aaron will waste effort and money promoting a service to individuals not interested in his product. When selecting a target market, Aaron visualizes his ideal customer. Aaron thinks about what his ideal customer does, thinks, and wants, and uses that image to inform his marketing decisions. We'll discuss target marketing in more detail later in the chapter.

4. **Implement the 4 Ps.** Once Aaron selects a target market, the fourth step is to implement the marketing mix, or the 4 Ps of marketing—product, price, promotion, and place. Once an unfilled customer need has been identified, it's important to develop a product that not only meets that need, but fulfills it better than the competition. For Aaron's product, he should start by coming up with a memorable brand to distinguish his business and services from all others. Having a memorable brand name will make it easier to find investors and to attract customers.

Having developed a set of goods and services and a brand that distinguishes his business from all others, Aaron will now want to contemplate his pricing strategy. What price are people willing to pay, and how sensitive are customers to price changes? Will different hourly rates be charged for grooming during a weekday compared to Saturday or Sunday? Will seasonal differences influence prices? Will Aaron charge more for larger pets?

Promotion is the most visible part of the marketing mix. It can be very expensive, yet very fruitful. How should a mobile pet-grooming service be promoted?

The place component of the marketing mix often involves finding the best location for the business. The mobility of Aaron's business affords him great flexibility with location; he can bring his business to his customers, within a reasonable distance. Although his business is providing a service, the "place" (or delivery) component of the marketing mix is equally important.

5. **Nurture Customer Relationships.** The final step in the marketing process is to manage customer relationships. As we noted earlier, the goal of customer relationship management (CRM) is to establish long-term trusting relationships with individual customers to foster loyalty and repeat business. Aaron must develop a rapport with his customers and their pets. He should know which customers are returning clients and note any particular grooming preferences. He might even offer discounts for select customers. Aaron should not only solicit but also respond to suggestions by customers on how to improve his services. To build customer trust, he should also offer customers their money back if they are unsatisfied. To maintain and foster interest in his services, he may want to create a mailing list for select customers. Aaron may also want to establish relationships with veterinary clinics and dog breeders. Above all, it's critical to personalize and maintain good customer relationships. Marketing is an ongoing process of tweaking a business to satisfy customers in order to ensure quality, value, and repeat business.

The marketing process may seem simple when it's written on the page, but it's as much art as it is science. Aaron Hoffman's mobile pet-grooming service would have a completely different marketing strategy than a non-mobile standalone business producing a good. Each product needs to be looked at individually in order to tailor an appropriate marketing plan.

▼ **Figure 12.4**
The Five Steps in the Marketing Process

▼ You have just read **Objectives 3 & 4**

Want a review? Check out the Study Plan section @
www.mybizlab.com.

The **Marketing Environment** pp. 348-351

Amelia Russo runs a successful shop selling inexpensive dress shoes for women. She gets most of her stock from France, so the value of the U.S. dollar makes a big difference in her total costs. However, the value of the dollar has gotten so low that Amelia is considering limiting her overseas orders and using domestic distributors. This would save money on purchasing shoes and delivery; however, the quality and style would be different than what her customers expect. If she keeps the same stock, she'll be forced to raise her prices, and her sales may fall significantly. What other types of environmental influences are affecting Amelia's business?

➤ The 4 Ps in the marketing mix are variables under the direct control of an organization. However, the **marketing environment** includes environmental influences outside the firm's control that constrain the organization's ability to manipulate its marketing mix. These environmental influences include the competitive, economic, technological, and sociocultural environments as well as the political, legal, and regulatory environments (see ▼ **Figure 12.5**).

Marketers must be keenly aware of the marketing environment when selecting their marketing mix. In fact, one of the key responsibilities of managers in any organization is to undertake **environmental scanning**, the process of surveying the market environment to assess external threats and opportunities. A successful business detects changes in the market environment and adjusts its marketing mix (product, price, promotion, and distribution) quickly and appropriately, inasmuch as the overall market environment will allow it to do so. Let's look at each of the elements of the marketing environment in a bit more detail.

The Competitive Environment

Assessing the competitive environment, or the degree of competition facing the firm, is critical to creating an effective marketing mix. You may recall from Chapter 2 the four basic market environments with respect to the varying degrees of competition facing firms: perfect competition, monopolistic competition, oligopoly, and monopoly. The degree of competition impacts the firm's production, pricing, promotion, and place (distribution) strategies in many ways. A successful business must be aware of competition and always try to stay one step ahead. Amelia Russo's shoe store had an edge on the competition due to her low prices. As a result of the dollar's weakness, Amelia is going to lose her competitive pricing advantage and be forced to come up with new marketing ideas.

The Economic Environment

The economic environment can affect customers' willingness and ability to spend their money on a firm's product. Therefore, marketers must keep abreast of changes in inflation, interest rates, unemployment, and economic growth rates over the course of the business cycle. Part of this is keeping up with changes in consumer confidence levels and government fiscal and monetary policies. Moreover, because of globalization, prudent firms follow global economic trends as well. This is especially important if the firm is involved in international business.

The economic environment impacts the firm's marketing strategy in many ways. For example, a rising inflation rate reduces the purchasing power of money, and sales may fall. A recession will reduce the demand for most products. Even the best-laid marketing plans will fail when customers can no longer afford to buy your product. If interest rates are high, then the cost of borrowing is up, and consumers who buy on credit will purchase less and your sales may fall. As a final example, suppose the value of the dollar falls (gets weaker) in foreign exchange markets. This will cause imported goods to become more expensive, like Amelia Russo's French dress shoes. Importing firms may need to raise their prices, which could significantly reduce sales. Savvy marketers try to keep their fingers on the changing pulse of the economy to forecast looming problems or potential opportunities and make the necessary adjustments.

▼ **Figure 12.5**
The Marketing Mix and the Marketing Environment
The marketing mix (the blend of the 4 Ps) can be controlled by marketing managers. The marketing environment represents external forces that can't be controlled by managers and impose constraints on managers' ability to blend the 4 Ps.

The Technological Environment

The technological environment can also influence the marketing mix. Indeed, advances in communications and transportation technologies may be one of the most influential factors affecting modern business. The Internet alone has enabled many small businesses to compete with large corporations around the world by marketing and selling their products online. Moreover, modern, sophisticated manufacturing innovations have enabled many firms to more easily customize their products and to offer them at dramatically reduced prices to satisfy the varying tastes of targeted customers. The availability of mass-produced, inexpensive dress shoes and expedient shipping allowed Amelia Russo to make her shoe store a profitable venture. Successful marketing requires use of the latest technologies to reach and satisfy target customers wherever they may be. This also includes the use of computer databases to enhance customer relationship management.

Off the Mark Would You Buy Dog Food Online? The Tale of Pets.com

The Pets.com sock puppet signaled an advertising frenzy for a brief period in the late 1990s. These ads were so popular that the company's spokesperson, a sock puppet dog, ended up being the company's best-selling product. Unfortunately, sock puppet sales alone were not enough to sustain the business. Selling dog food and other pet products online did not pan out the way that the young Pets.com entrepreneurs had hoped, or the way that the venture capitalists who supplied them with $110 million had counted on. Pets.com made the crucial error of buying expensive advertising slots and going public before the company had generated significant revenue. In the fall of 2000, Pets.com announced that it was selling all of its assets, including the rights to the sock puppet. What is to be learned from this? Perhaps that running a successful business takes more than producing catchy sock puppet commercials. With a little more thought about the target market—did people really want to buy pet food online?—maybe this company wouldn't have ended up in the doghouse.[5]

The Sociocultural Environment

In Chapter 4, we examined the critical role that the sociocultural environment has on international business. We saw that most international business blunders have resulted from a lack of sensitivity or understanding of cultural differences. Domestic businesses must also realize that culture is dynamic, and effective marketers must be able to adapt to different attitudes and keep up with changing social trends. Demographic shifts—such as age, gender, ethnicity, and marital status—and changing values can signal opportunities for businesses. For example, we can expect the demand for medical care, pharmaceuticals, and nursing homes to increase as the average age of the population increases. We've also observed greater demand for convenience foods and restaurant services over the years as lifestyles have changed. Amelia Russo recognized the demand for inexpensive, high-quality dress shoes from a younger crowd and took advantage of the opportunity.

The Political, Legal, and Regulatory Environments

It has been said that in a democracy, the squeaky wheel gets the grease. Special-interest groups try to influence the political process in various ways. Businesses are no exception. They try to wield political influence through contributions to political parties, individual candidates, and political action committees (PACs) because government laws and regulations significantly impact business interests. In addition, a variety of regulatory agencies enforce laws and regulations constraining marketing efforts. These include the Environmental Protection Agency (EPA), the Consumer Product Safety Commission (CPSC), the Food and Drug Administration (FDA), and the Federal Trade Commission (FTC). Businesses are forced to consider the political and legal environment in making marketing decisions, as these factors can play a major role in overall success.

Store owner Amelia Russo judged her options and decided to buy domestically until the dollar gets stronger. Her customers were generally satisfied with the domestically produced substitute dress shoes, so Amelia was able to stay in business. Successful businesses like Amelia's are constantly on the lookout for changes in the market environment and are prepared to adjust accordingly.

▼ top 10 Corporate Contributors to Political Parties

LEGEND: 🐘 Republican   🫏 Democrat   ▦ On the fence

▦ = Between 40% and 59% to both parties

🐘 = Leans Dem/Repub (60%–69%)

🫏 🫏 = Strongly Dem/Repub (70%–89%)

🐘 🐘 🐘 = Solidly Dem/Repub (over 90%)

Rank	Organization Name	Total	Contribution Tilt 1989-2008	Contribution Tilt 2005/2006 Only
1.	AT&T Inc	$38,473,085	▦	🐘
2.	Goldman Sachs	$27,172,482	🫏	🫏
3.	Citigroup Inc	$23,033,490	▦	▦
4.	Altria Group	$22,923,875	🐘 🐘	🐘
5.	United Parcel Service	$21,508,040	🐘	🐘
6.	FedEx Corp	$21,288,684	▦	🐘
7.	Time Warner	$17,483,375	🫏	🫏 🫏
8.	JP Morgan Chase & Co	$16,970,798	▦	▦
9.	Microsoft Corp	$16,653,584	▦	▦
10.	Verizon Communications	$15,975,908	🐘	🐘

▼ You have just read **Objective 5**

Want to learn more? Check out the Study Plan section @ **www.mybizlab.com.**

Marketing Research and **Planning** pp. 352-357

Tiara Watson decided that opening a salon supply business in her city would be a great investment. The next closest supplier is over 70 miles away, so salons have to pay unnecessarily high shipping costs. If her business is in the city, the shipping costs for salons will be nominal compared to the other company. Tiara started researching and found over 30 salons around the city, so she has a strong target market. She's already met with a few of the owners to see if they'd be willing to switch suppliers, and they seem interested. She knows she can't start out selling supplies to every salon in the city, but she isn't sure where to start. How can she figure out which salons to target for her startup? ➤

➤ Look back at the five-step marketing process shown in Figure 12.4. You'll notice that after a market need is identified, a firm needs to conduct *market research* to determine the profitability of a venture, develop a marketing plan, and determine its target market. In this section, we'll explore each of these processes in more detail.

The Marketing Research Process

What is market research and what are the steps involved in the process? Market research is the process of gathering and analyzing market information for making marketing decisions. The marketing research process consists of five steps:

1. Define the marketing information need, problem, or objective.

2. Collect the relevant data.

3. Analyze the data.

4. Interpret analytical results and reach conclusions.

5. Act on research conclusions.

1. **Define the Need, Problem, or Objective.** Marketing managers and researchers need to work together to clearly define the objective of the research. They should determine the exact nature of the business need, problem, or opportunity, and the information desired. They should also determine why that information will be helpful to the manager. This step will help the researcher collect relevant and appropriate data for analysis. Tiara has defined the need for a salon supply company that is in close proximity to city salons.

2. **Collect Relevant Data.** Determining which types of data will be collected and how the information will be collected is the next step. Two general types of data exist: primary and secondary. **Primary data** are raw data collected by the researcher. The data are frequently collected through observation, questionnaires, surveys (via mail, e-mail, or telephone), focus groups, interviews, customer feedback, samples, and controlled experiments. A **focus group** is typically a group of eight to ten potential customers who are asked for feedback on a good or service, advertisement, idea, or packaging. They're often used in test-marketing an idea or new product. For example, Apple used focus groups to help develop its line of iPods. The iPod wristwatch with a time display never made it to market as a result of input from focus groups.[6] Apparently, the groups didn't like this particular product idea.

   Secondary data are data that have already been collected and processed. An example of secondary data is census data. This information is usually much cheaper to obtain. Tiara Watson has collected secondary data about the location of the closest salon supply companies and primary data about the interest of the salon owners in changing to a closer, cheaper supplier. Examples of primary and secondary data sources are summarized in ▼ **Table 12.1**.

3. **Analyze Data.** Analysis of data requires knowledge of appropriate statistical techniques that are beyond the scope of this textbook. Nevertheless, honest analysis is necessary. You should never adjust your data to get the results you want. For example, Apple's honest assessment of marketing data led the company not to introduce the iPod wristwatch.

4. **Interpret Results.** Statistics never speak for themselves. Careful analysis will lead to conclusions about marketing strategies that have more favorable benefits in relation to their costs. For example, a company's profit numbers for the previous year might appear to indicate a lack of growth, but when inflation and the falling value of the dollar are taken into account, the statistics may actually show that the company expanded its business.

5. **Act on Conclusions.** The whole purpose of marketing research is to point managers toward better marketing decisions. Marketing research should therefore be ongoing. Changing market conditions require businesses to continually adapt and constantly search for better ways to provide value to customers. Part of acting on the conclusions of marketing research is creating a marketing plan, which we'll discuss next.

The Marketing Plan

What is a marketing plan? A **marketing plan** is a written document that specifies marketing activities designed to reach organizational objectives. A marketing plan is typically a *written* document because details about tasks to be performed by employees can be lost easily if communicated orally. Moreover, written objectives can be compared with actual measurements to see whether objectives are being met.

▼ **Table 12.1**

Examples of Sources of Primary and Secondary Data	
Primary Sources of Data	**Secondary Sources of Data**
Observation Questionnaires Surveys Focus groups Interviews Customer feedback Sampling Controlled experiments	**Government publications** • U.S. Bureau of Economic Analysis, Survey of Current Business - http://bea.doc.gov • U.S. Bureau of Labor Statistics - http://www.stats.bls.gov • U.S. Census Bureau - http://www.census.gov • U.S. CIA - World Fact Book - https://www.cia.gov/library/publications/the-world-factbook • U.S. CIA - Handbook of International Economics - http://www.cia.gov/cia/di/products/hies • US. Department of Commerce - Links to National and International Governmental Databases - http://www.fedworld.gov • U.S. Federal Reserve - http://research.stlouisfed.org/fred • U.S. Government Materials - http://www.fedstats.gov • U.S. Office of Trade and Economic Development - http://www.ita.doc.gov/tradestats • U.S. Statistical Data International and National Stat-USA - http://www.stat-usa.gov
	Commercial Publications Marketing Resources Links, provided by Decision Analyst, Inc. - www.SecondaryData.com AC NielsenCompany – http://www2.acnielsen.com/site/index.shtml Information Resources, Inc - http://us.infores.com Gallup - http://www.gallup.com
	Organizational Publications Chamber of Commerce - http://www.chamberofcommerce.com/public/index.cfm Pew Research Center - http://pewresearch.org/about Trade Organizations
	Magazines *BusinessWeek, Time, Fortune, Forbes Inc., Fast Company, Advertising Age, Entrepreneur*
	Newspapers *Wall Street Journal, Washington Post, New York Times*
	Internal sources Accounting records

What are the elements of a good marketing plan? Four elements emerge from all good marketing plans:

- a clearly written marketing objective
- performance of situational (SWOT) analysis
- selection of a target market
- implementation, evaluation, and control of the marketing mix (4 Ps)

A **marketing objective** is a clearly stated goal to be achieved through marketing activities. It should be realistic, quantifiable, and time specific.[7] A marketing objective of having every home in the United States purchase a specific product is unrealistic. Selling 100,000 units in a year is a more realistic, quantifiable, and time-specific marketing objective. When objectives are realistic, they are attainable and can motivate employees toward their goal. When they are measurable, the firm can determine whether they are being achieved. If deadlines are also imposed, then firms know whether they are reaching their goals in a timely manner.

Situational (SWOT) Analysis

What is situational (or SWOT) analysis? Creating clearly stated objectives is the first step in any good marketing plan. The next step is conducting a *situational (or SWOT) analysis*. As you learned in Chapter 7, this is an evaluation of

the organization's internal *strengths* and *weaknesses*, as well as the *opportunities* and *threats* found in the external environment.

What do we mean by internal strengths? In terms of marketing, a company's internal strengths refer to the competitive advantages or core competencies that the company has at its disposal to meet a specified marketing objective. Core competencies provide customer benefits and are not easily imitated by other companies, setting the company apart from the competition. For example, John Deere has been very successful in expanding its business by transferring the strength of its brand-name reputation of superior-quality agricultural products into lawn tractors and mowers for urban dwellers and earth-moving equipment for the construction industry. Indeed, a significant portion of John Deere's revenues now come from its non-agricultural sales.[8]

How does a company assess its weaknesses? Assessing internal weaknesses means that a company must perform an audit of current managerial expertise, manufacturing and financing capabilities, and the organization's execution of the 4 Ps in the marketing mix. By honestly assessing its weaknesses, a company can determine a realistic marketing objective. For example, a company that makes handmade watches and has only three employees cannot expect to produce 75,000 watches a week.

Why look to the external environment? The dynamic and ever-changing external environment offers many opportunities and creates many threats. Changes in the degree of competition facing firms, the economy, technology, sociocultural forces, as well as changes in the political, legal, and regulatory environments have caused some firms to thrive while damaging others. This is especially true for international businesses because the number of market environments compounds the analysis. Rapid changes in technology create new opportunities, like expanding sales over the Internet, but pose new threats, like requiring additional technological expertise to protect against hackers. Successful companies continually evaluate environmental factors as part of their SWOT analysis to match their strengths with opportunities and to address their weaknesses to avoid threats.

Target Markets

How are target markets determined? Once an organization has evaluated its internal strengths and weaknesses, as well as the external opportunities and threats of the market environment, then it is ready to select its target market. If a business doesn't focus its marketing efforts, it will likely waste time and money promoting its product to individuals who are not interested. In fact, some firms focus so much on one specific market that they undertake **niche marketing**, or marketing a product to a very narrowly defined set of potential customers. A company that sells specialized gear shifters for racing bicycles is operating in a niche market.

How do you find a target market? Finding a target market begins with **market segmentation**, the process of separating the broader market into smaller markets (or market segments) that consist of similar groups of customers. A **market segment** is a subgroup of potential customers who share similar characteristics and therefore have similar product needs and preferences. Marketers choose those market segments that offer the greatest profit potential, and these become the target markets. For each target market, the company tries to blend the 4 Ps of the marketing mix to best satisfy the targeted customers. The process of developing a unique marketing mix that best satisfies a target market is known as **positioning**.

Consumer markets can be segmented based on many variables or characteristics of consumers. Four of the most common consumer market segmentation classifications are geographic, demographic, psychographic, and behavioral. These types of market segmentations are summarized in ▼ **Table 12.2**.

Geographic Segmentation

Geographic segmentation is market segmentation according to geographic characteristics (see Table 12.2). For example, clothing apparel, skis, snow blowers, four-wheel drive vehicles, air conditioning, and heating needs differ by regional climate differences. Taste in food products also varies by region. For example, Cracker Barrel restaurants commonly serve grits at their locations in the South, but are less likely to serve them elsewhere. For Tiara Watson's salon supply company, the prominent hairstyles in some parts of the city may require specialized products that are not as popular in other locations.

Demographic Segmentation

Demographic segmentation is market segmentation according to age, race, religion, gender, ethnic background, and other demographic variables (see Table 12.2). For example, it's estimated that by the year 2020, one in five Americans will be of Hispanic origin.[9] Few businesses want to miss out on this growing market segment. It's now common to find labels published in Spanish, Spanish language television stations and newspapers, and companies marketing their products to this growing community in the United States.

Automobile companies also use demographic segmentation. They are keenly aware of how important it is to position their models to appeal to different age groups, income levels, and differences in gender. The salon supply company that Tiara is starting focuses primarily on African American women's hair product needs.

Psychographic Segmentation

Psychographic segmentation is market segmentation based on lifestyles, personality traits, motives, and values (see Table 12.2). Harley-Davidson offers a wide variety of motorcycles, and each model attempts to cater to a particular lifestyle.[10] Cat food advertisements are cleverly focusing on "cat lover" personalities, whereas many beer commercials target specific personality types. When motives are used to determine the appropriate market, marketers focus on why consumers make a purchase. For example, Volvo has been very successful in selling cars to consumers motivated by safety concerns, and Gold's Gym sells memberships to customers concerned with their health. Salons that will purchase Tiara's products are motivated by the need to supply customers with high-quality beauty products.

▼ **Table 12.2**

Consumer Market Segmentation			
Geographic	**Demographic**	**Psychographic**	**Behavioral**
• Region • Suburban • Rural • City • County • Population density • Climate • Terrain	• Age • Race • Religion • Family size • Ethnicity • Gender • Income • Education	• Lifestyle • Personality traits • Motives • Values	• Benefit sought • Volume usage • Brand loyalty • Price sensitivity • Product end use

Sophisticated marketers closely examine their customers' lifestyles, personality traits, motives, and values because, unlike geographic and demographic variables, these psychographic variables can be manipulated by marketing efforts. Whatever consumers may value, whether it be quality, social status or affiliation, safety, health, privacy, technology, or appearance, you can bet that businesses will offer a good or service to satisfy that real or perceived need. They will be rewarded with profits for doing so.

Behavioral Segmentation

Behavioral segmentation is market segmentation based on certain consumer behavior characteristics, such as the benefits sought by the consumer, the extent to which the product is consumed, brand loyalty, price sensitivity, and the ways in which the product is used (see Table 12.2). For example, a company that produces herbal supplements is appealing to the specific benefits sought by its consumers.

Brand loyalty is another kind of behavioral segmentation. It can impact price sensitivity—the more loyal the customer, the less sensitive he or she is to a price increase. If a customer has been using the same brand of toothpaste for 12 years and has had no cavities in that time period, a small price increase will most likely not be an issue to that customer. Finally, knowing how the product is actually used can help companies develop packages that appeal to customers. For example, when pills are taken daily, having pills placed in a package where the day of the week is written below each pill can be useful for consumers.

➤ What personality traits and motives would marketers target when marketing a gym membership?

The marketing process may only involve five steps, but each of these takes some time and plenty of focused effort. Tiara Watson has given much thought to whom she wants to target as customers. However, without doing a SWOT analysis, she wasn't sure where to start. Once she stepped back and took time to go through the research process, she knew where to begin. Tiara is off to a good start, but still has some work ahead of her in implementing her marketing mix and in nurturing good customer relationships. The next two chapters explore the implementation of the marketing mix in more detail to nurture good customer relationships.

▼ You have just read **Objective 6**

Want to test your skills? Check out the Study Plan section @
www.my*biz*lab.com.

Consumer Behavior pp. 358-361

➤ The term **consumer behavior** refers to the ways individuals or organizations search for, evaluate, purchase, use, and dispose of goods and services. Notice that consumer behavior involves the study of individual consumers or business organizations as buyers in the market. Most of us intuitively think of a market as being a consumer market. Consumer markets are the markets we, as consumers, are most familiar with. In a **consumer market**, individuals purchase goods and services for personal consumption. But there are also business-to-business markets. In **business-to-business (B2B) markets**, businesses purchase goods and services from other businesses. In this section, we'll explore both markets and examine the buying behavior differences between consumer markets and business-to-business markets.

Consumer Markets

Why study consumer behavior? Knowledge of consumer behavior helps marketers select the most profitable target markets and guides the implementation, evaluation, and control of the marketing mix (4 Ps) for selected targeted markets. For example, consumers are becoming increasingly concerned about gas mileage. Automobile companies that realize this can create more gas-efficient cars or drop the prices on less-efficient models to compensate for poor gas mileage.

How does a consumer make a buying decision? The consumer buying process involves five steps: (1) need recognition, (2) information search, (3) evaluation of alternatives, (4) purchase or no purchase decision, (5) post-purchase evaluation

Not all consumers go through each step in the process, and the steps do not need to be completed in the same order. The process can be interrupted at any time with a "no purchase" decision.

Consider your decision to purchase the educational services of your college or university. You first recognized the need for higher education. You likely obtained information about colleges from many sources, including your friends, family, counselors, and maybe even *U.S. News & World Report*'s annual college rankings.[11] You may have also visited a few college campuses to gather firsthand information. You then evaluated your choices based on a number of factors, including the tuition (price), geographic location, or maybe where your friends were going to college. Your final choice may have been based on "rational analysis" or the result of an emotional decision (based on some "gut feelings"). After making a purchase, we also evaluate our decision in terms of how well our expectations are being met. You'll likely continue to evaluate your college choice long after you graduate.

What influences consumer decision making❓
The five-step consumer decision-making process is part of a broader environmental context that influences each step. These environmental forces are shown in ▼ **Figure 12.6**.[12]

1. **Sociocultural Influences.** *Sociocultural influences* on buying decisions include the buyer's culture, subculture, social class, family, and peers. Culture is the set of learned attitudes, beliefs, and ways of life that are unique to a society and are handed down through generations. Subcultures are specific groups within a culture that share attitudes and life experiences. Some examples of subcultures include churches, community organizations, and online communities like Facebook and MySpace. Cultural values change over time. For example, many people today value healthier lifestyles. Social class refers to a combination of factors such as education, income, wealth, and occupation common to a group of people. Social class can have an impact on purchasing decisions, as some possessions are considered status symbols.

2. **Personal Influences.** *Personal influences* on a buyer's consumption choice are often shaped by his or her age, economic situation, lifestyle, and personality. A person who enjoys spending time outdoors hiking is more likely to purchase a tent than a person who spends time playing video games.

3. **Psychological Influences.** *Psychological influences* include differences in the buyer's motivation, perception, attitudes, and learning. One goal of marketing is to shape the perception of a product in the minds of consumers. Attitudes toward a product put customers in a frame of mind that either predisposes them to favorably view the product or not. For example, changing attitudes toward the environment have increased the demand

▼ **Figure 12.6**
Major Influences Impacting a Consumer's Buying Decision
Many factors influence consumer buying decisions. Effective marketing attempts to help consumers with their information search and the evaluation of alternatives.

for hybrid cars. Learning refers to changes in buying behavior based on experience. Good experiences with brands result in repeat business. Bad experiences stunt future sales.

4. **Situational Influences.** *Situational influences* include the physical surroundings, social surroundings, and the type of product purchased. Complex, expensive, and infrequently purchased products, like a new home, will elicit a greater degree of information searching and evaluation of alternatives than a frequently purchased product that has few substitutes, such as table salt.

5. **Marketing Mix Influences.** *Marketing mix influences* (4 Ps) include the product, price, promotion, and place (distribution) aspects of purchases. As stressed throughout this chapter, marketing is interested in producing a product that buyers want at an affordable price, promoting awareness of the attributes of the product, and placing the good or service in a timely and convenient location for consumers to buy.

Knowledge of consumer buying behavior and the influences on the buying decision is critical to effective marketing. Some of these influences, like personal influences, are outside the control of marketers, while other influences, like psychological influences, can be impacted by businesses. All of these influences should be kept in mind when selecting a target market, implementing, evaluating, and controlling the marketing mix, and building customer relationships.

Business-to-Business (B2B) Markets

What is the difference between consumer markets and business-to-business markets? The difference between consumer and B2B markets hinges on who's doing the buying. If a good or service is purchased in a B2B market, it is purchased by a business for further processing or for resale or to facilitate general business activity. The B2B market is significantly larger compared to consumer markets because virtually all consumer products go through a number of distributors or wholesalers before reaching the final consumer at a retail outlet. In fact, each time an unfinished product is bought and sold through the many stages of a product's development, a separate B2B market exists. Think of all the transactions involved in producing a car. Most of the components are produced by separate firms. Moreover, each of these firms derives its inputs from different businesses.

There are several key differences between consumer and B2B markets.[13] The more important characteristics of B2B markets include the following:

1. **A few buyers that purchase in large quantities.** Business-to-business markets typically involve a few buyers that purchase very large quantities. For example, there are only a few airline companies that buy most of Boeing's jets.

2. **Highly trained buyers.** Most business purchasing agents are highly skilled at their jobs. They often weigh the benefits and the costs in a more systematic fashion and are less influenced by emotional factors than buyers in consumer markets. This requires sellers to pitch their products at a much more sophisticated level.

3. **Group purchasing decision.** A team of individuals within purchasing departments usually collaborate in making a purchasing decision in B2B markets. This means marketers must be prepared to be patient and mindful of all decision-makers' concerns to seal a deal.

4. **Close customer relationship.** Because there are only a few sophisticated buyers that purchase large quantities, marketers find it necessary to establish a much closer relationship with customers compared to the relationship with buyers in consumer markets. As a result, B2B marketing is more focused on personal selling compared to the mass advertising campaigns that typify consumer markets.

5. **Geographically concentrated buyers.** Most buyers in B2B markets are concentrated in a few of the most industrialized states where most large businesses are located. This reduces the costs of reaching buyers.

6. **Direct purchasing.** Often buyers in B2B markets purchase directly from sellers, as opposed to consumer markets, where products typically go through many wholesalers before the product arrives to the end user.

These key differences between consumer and B2B markets are summarized in ▼ Table 12.3. These differences can be organized by differences in market structure, the nature of the buying unit, and the purchasing process.

How does a business make a buying decision, and what influences that decision? The five-step consumer decision-making process is equally applicable to business purchasing decisions. Businesses begin by recognizing a need; they seek out information to aid them in the purchase decision; evaluate alternatives; decide to either purchase or not to purchase; and undertake a post-purchase evaluation. However, business purchases are generally more rational, reasoned, objective decisions based on influences such as the state of the economy, technological factors, the degree of competition, political and regulatory concerns, and organizational objectives, policies, and procedures.

Is the marketing process different for B2B markets? The marketing process remains the same for all markets: identify a need, undertake research to come up with a marketing plan, select a target market, implement and control the marketing mix, and nurture customer relationships.

Think back to the quiz you took at the beginning of this section. Would you ace the quiz now based on what you've learned? Understanding consumer behavior and the buying and marketing process is essential for marketers when selecting a target market and managing the marketing mix.

▼ Table 12.3

Differences Between Business-to-Business and Consumer Markets		
	Business-to-Business Market	**Consumer Market**
Market Structure	• Few customers • Large-volume purchases • Geographically concentrated	• Many customers • Small-volume purchases • Geographically dispersed
Nature of the Buying Unit	• More professional and rational purchase decision	• Less sophisticated and more emotional purchase decision
Purchasing Process	• Highly trained buyers • Group purchasing decision • Complex buying decisions • Formalized buying procedures • Close and personal selling relationship between marketer and buyer • Personal selling • Geographically concentrated	• Untrained buyers • Individual purchasing decision • Relatively simple buying decisions • Informal buying decision • Impersonal relationship between marketer and buyer • Mass advertising • Geographically dispersed

▼ You have just read **Objective 7**

Want to quiz yourself? Check out the Study Plan section @
www.my*biz*lab.com.

1. How has marketing evolved over the production concept era, the sales concept era, the marketing concept era, and the customer relationship era? (pp. 337-339)

- During the production concept era (from the Industrial Revolution until the 1920s), most companies focused solely on production. Demand was often greater than supply, and the prevailing mindset was that a good-quality product would simply sell itself.

- During the sales concept era (from the mid-1920s through the early 1950s), technological advances meant that production increased more sharply than demand for goods and services. The use of heavy public advertising in all available forms of media became prevalent.

- During the marketing concept era (from the 1950s through the 1990s), production continued to expand more quickly than the growth in demand for goods and services. The **marketing concept** (p. 339) changed the focus from finding the right customer for a product to producing the right product for a customer and doing it better than the competition.

- During the customer relationship era (from the late 1990s to the present), organizations have worked to establish long-term relationships with individual customers to foster loyalty and repeat business.

2. What are the benefits of marketing to customers, sellers, investors, employees, and society at large, and what are the criticisms of marketing? (pp. 340-342)

- **Marketing** (p. 337) identifies and satisfies human needs and wants. It provides value to customers by providing benefits that exceed their costs. In turn, sellers benefit because marketing enables firms to survive.

- Businesses that are most successful in satisfying customers generate higher profits, and investors benefit from the profits earned. Employees benefit from successful marketing as well because their jobs and livelihoods are more secure.

- Society at large benefits from marketing because scarce resources are more efficiently allocated to those goods and services most desired by society.

- Criticisms of marketing include price gouging, the production of shoddy or unsafe products, and confusing and deceptive practices. The criticisms of marketing should not be taken lightly. All companies should have a code of ethics and policies in place to curb unethical behavior within their organizations.

3. What are the two basic elements of a marketing strategy and the 4 Ps of the marketing mix? (pp. 343-345)

- The two basic elements of a marketing strategy are the **target market** (p. 343) and the **marketing mix** (p. 343).

- The 4 Ps of the marketing mix are **product** (p. 337), price, **promotion** (p. 345), and **place** (p. 345).

4. How do firms implement a marketing strategy by applying the five steps of the marketing process? (pp. 346-347)

- Five steps emerge from the marketing process: (1) identify a need, (2) conduct market research and develop a marketing plan, (3) determine a target market, (4) implement the 4 Ps of the marketing mix, and (5) nurture good customer relationships.

- The application of the marketing process is as much an art as a science. Producing a high-quality product with a unique brand properly promoted and consistently delivers value to customers at a "fair" price, and when and where they want the product are common ingredients for marketing success.

5. How do the various factors in the marketing environment influence a firm's ability to manipulate its marketing mix? (pp. 348-351)

- The **marketing environment** (p. 348) includes environmental influences such as the competitive, economic, technological, and sociocultural environments as well as the political, legal, and regulatory environments. Because these factors are outside the firm's control, they constrain the organization's ability to manipulate its marketing mix.

6. What are the five steps of the marketing research process and the four elements of a good marketing plan? (pp. 352-357)

- **Marketing research** (p. 352) is an ongoing process of gathering and analyzing market information to gauge changing market conditions that may suggest better ways and opportunities to provide services to customers.

- Five steps emerge from the marketing research process: (1) define the marketing information need, problem, or objective; (2) collect the relevant data; (3) analyze the data; (4) interpret analytical results and reach conclusions; and (5) act on research conclusions.

- A **marketing plan** (p. 353) is a written document that specifies marketing activities designed to reach organizational objectives.

- Four elements emerge from all good marketing plans: (1) a clearly written marketing objective; (2) performance of situational (SWOT) analysis; (3) selection of a target market; and (4) implementation, evaluation, and control of the marketing mix (4 Ps).

7. How do the buying decisions and marketing processes in business-to-business markets compare to those in the consumer market? (pp. 358-361)

- In a **consumer market** (p. 358), buyers are households that purchase final consumer goods. In a **business-to-business**

Continued on next page

Chapter Summary (cont.)

(B2B) market (p. 358), businesses buy from other businesses. There are many more B2B markets compared to consumer markets. In B2B markets, purchases are often undertaken by a small group of highly trained individuals who buy in large volumes and have a much closer relationship with marketers. B2B buyers are also more geographically concentrated and often avoid distributors.

- Consumers and businesses undertake the same five-step decision-making process when making a purchase. However, some of the influences that impact the business purchase are different.

- The marketing process remains the same for all markets: identify a need; undertake research to come up with a marketing plan, select a target market, implement and control the marketing mix, and always remember to nurture good customer relationships.

For an audio file of the Objectives and Chapter Summary, see the Student Resources section @ www.my*biz*lab.com.

Key Terms

behavioral segmentation   (p. 357)

brand   (p. 345)

business-to-business (B2B) market   (p. 358)

consumer behavior   (p. 358)

consumer market   (p. 358)

customer relationship management (CRM)   (p. 339)

demographic segmentation   (p. 356)

environmental scanning   (p. 348)

focus group   (p. 353)

form utility   (p. 341)

geographic segmentation   (p. 356)

market research   (p. 352)

market segment   (p. 355)

market segmentation   (p. 355)

marketing   (p. 337)

marketing concept   (p. 339)

marketing environment   (p. 348)

marketing mix   (p. 343)

marketing objective   (p. 354)

marketing plan   (p. 353)

niche marketing   (p. 355)

ownership utility   (p. 341)

place (distribution)   (p. 345)

place utility   (p. 341)

positioning   (p. 356)

primary data   (p. 353)

product   (p. 337)

promotion   (p. 345)

psychographic segmentation   (p. 356)

secondary data   (p. 353)

target market   (p. 343)

time utility   (p. 341)

value   (p. 340)

Self-Test

Multiple Choice   Correct answers can be found on page 503.

1. The notion that products would simply sell themselves was the prevailing thought during the

   a. production concept era.

   b. sales concept era.

   c. marketing concept era.

   d. customer relationship era.

2. When a car is purchased, form utility refers to the value customers receive from

   a. owning the car.

   b. the styling and function of the automobile.

   c. ready availability and speed with which the dealer made the car available for purchase.

   d. close proximity to the car dealership.

3. Which of the following is part of the marketing mix?

   a. Finding a market need

   b. Conducting market research

   c. Identifying target customers

   d. Establishing a price

4. Which of the following correctly describes the steps involved in the marketing process?

   a. It begins with identifying a target market, followed by market research and developing a marketing plan, identifying a market need, implementing the marketing mix, and nurturing good customer relationships.

   b. It begins with market research and developing a marketing plan, followed by identifying a target market, identifying a market need, implementing the marketing mix, and nurturing good customer relationships.

   c. It begins with market research and developing a marketing plan, followed by identifying a market need, identifying a target market, implementing the marketing mix, and nurturing good customer relationships.

   d. It begins with identifying a market need, followed by market research and developing a marketing plan, identifying a target market, implementing the marketing mix, and nurturing good customer relationships.

5. Which of the following is part of the marketing environment?

   a. Personal influences

   b. Psychological influences

   c. Political, legal, and regulatory influences

   d. Situational influences

6. Which of the following is true of SWOT analysis?

   a. The strengths and weaknesses of an organization stem from the external market environment.

   b. The opportunities and threats facing an organization stem from within the organization.

   c. An organization's strengths, weaknesses, opportunities, and threats depend on the selected marketing objective.

   d. SWOT analysis should be undertaken before a clearly stated marketing objective is determined.

7. Market segmentation based on lifestyles, personality traits, motives, and values is

   a. geographic segmentation.

   b. demographic segmentation.

   c. psychographic segmentation.

   d. behavioral segmentation.

8. Which of the following is a common criticism of marketing?

   a. Price gouging

   b. Confusing and deceptive practices

   c. The production of shoddy or unsafe products

   d. All of the above

9. Environmental scanning is

   a. market segmentation according to geographic characteristics.

   b. market segmentation based on certain consumer behavior characteristics.

   c. the process of developing a unique marketing mix that best satisfies a target market.

   d. the process of surveying the market environment to assess external threats and opportunities.

10. An example of secondary data is

   a. census data.

   b. customer feedback.

   c. surveys and questionnaires.

   d. data collected through controlled experiments.

True/False   Correct answers can be found on page 503.

1. The marketing mix consists of form, ownership, time, and place.
   ☐ **True** or ☐ **False**

2. The fifth element of the marketing mix is known as the "purple cow" factor.
   ☐ **True** or ☐ **False**

3. A market segment is a group of eight to ten potential customers who are asked for feedback on a good or service, advertisement, idea, or packaging.
   ☐ **True** or ☐ **False**

4. Employees benefit from successful marketing because new job opportunities are created as production expands to satisfy the growing demand for high-value products.
   ☐ **True** or ☐ **False**

5. Purchases made in consumer markets and purchases made in business-to-business markets undertake the same decision-making process.
   ☐ **True** or ☐ **False**

Critical Thinking Questions

1. Can you think of an example of how a specific organization (for-profit or not-for-profit) tried to establish a better customer relationship with you? What did the organization do? Was it effective? Why or why not? What recommendations would you make to these organizations?

2. Does ethical marketing make good business sense if it reduces profits?

3. You're interested in starting a limousine service in your community. How might you best segment the market for your services? What is your target market and why? What marketing mix strategies would you employ? How would you nurture customer relationships?

4. Why should a marketing plan be a written document?

5. Think of the last major purchase you made. Discuss how the sociocultural, personal, psychological, situational, and marketing mix influences impacted this purchase.

Team Time

Tobacco Wars

Divide into two even teams, one to represent each of the following:

    a.   tobacco company employees; pro-cigarette advertising in magazines

    b.   anti-tobacco advertising activists

Scenario

Does a company have a fundamental right to market its products wherever it wishes? Cigarette advertising in magazines has been a topic of great controversy. The large tobacco companies provide publications with a great deal of revenue by purchasing expensive advertising space, but many anti-smoking groups and some magazine publishers are questioning the ethical nature of this. Anti-smoking groups argue that these advertisements appeal to children and glamorize smoking. Tobacco companies claim that they are merely making attractive advertisements with no intention of encouraging children to use their products. The European Union has banned tobacco advertisements from magazines entirely, and many U.S. publications have stopped selling ad space to tobacco companies. Do tobacco companies have the right to advertise their products as they see fit? Is it morally wrong to advertise a product that is known to cause health problems?

Process

Step 1. Collaborate with team members to discuss both sides of the issue, analyzing the arguments from each perspective.

Step 2. Prepare the most effective argument for your team's perspective, and think about counterpoints to arguments that the other team may raise.

Ethics and Corporate Social Responsibility

Subprime Mortgage Crisis

Subprime loans are home loans made available at temporarily reduced or zero interest rates that adjust or increase to much higher interest rates over time. These allowed many people to qualify for loans to buy expensive homes that they otherwise would not have been qualified to buy. Because of the long-standing expectation that home prices would continue to rise over time, as they have historically, and that recipients of subprime loans would be able to refinance their loans into traditional fixed-interest loans, many people thought these subprime loans were going to turn out to be great deals. However, when the price of homes began to fall in 2006 and 2007, it became difficult to refinance these subprime loans. At the same time, the temporary low interest rates on subprime loans were rapidly adjusting upward as specified in the loan contracts. Some people found themselves unable to make their monthly house payments, and they couldn't sell their homes because they owed more than the homes were worth. Many people were forced into foreclosure and lost their homes. Foreclosures also hurt many banks, and this downturn has negatively affected the U.S. economy as a whole.

Questions

1. Do you feel that it is unethical to offer loans at "teaser" low rates that adjust upward rapidly over time to people who may not fully understand the consequences of increased house payments, or to allow people to purchase homes that they otherwise would not be able to afford?
2. As a bank owner, do you feel that the benefits of giving subprime loans outweigh their potential risks?
3. Do you think the banks that gave the loans should take responsibility for their payment?
4. Should the government provide assistance at taxpayers' expense to those people who received these subprime loans and now have trouble keeping their homes?

Web Exercises

1. **Apple's Marketing Mix**
   Go to Apple's Web site that focuses on the iPhone: www.apple.com/iphone. Describe Apple's marketing mix strategy: product, price, promotion, and place. How does Apple attempt to foster good customer relations? What marketing recommendations would you make to Apple?

2. **SWOT Analysis**
   Go to www.marketingteacher.com/SWOT/walmart_swot.htm to see a SWOT analysis for Wal-Mart. What strengths, weaknesses, opportunities, and threats would you add or delete? Why? How could Wal-Mart take advantage of its strengths in terms of its marketing mix? How do Wal-Mart's weaknesses impact its marketing mix? What market environmental forces do you think gave rise to its opportunities and its threats? How much control does Wal-Mart have over its market environment? What recommendations would you make for Wal-Mart? Why?

3. **Mission and Values as Marketing Tools**
   Go to the Phillip Morris Web site at www.philipmorrisusa.com/en/cms/Company/Mission_Values/default.aspx?src=top_nav. What kind of advertising techniques does this site use? Do you feel that this company is genuine in its concerns about public health?

4. **Freebies: Long-Term Gain or Loss?**
   Go to www.sephora.com. This company gives three free samples with every purchase from its Web site. Do you think that this strategy will be profitable for the company in the long run, or will it cause it to lose money?

5. **The Jeep Experience**
   The Jeep brand uses a nontraditional marketing approach by offering Jeep owners invitations to special events. Go to www.jeep.com/en and research the events that this company offers to its customers. How effective do you think engaging customers in ongoing events is in getting them to be repeat buyers?

Web Case

To access the Chapter 12 Web case and exercise, see the End of Chapter Assignments section @ www.my*biz*lab.com.

Video Case

To access the Chapter 12 Video case and exercise, see the End of Chapter Assignments section @ www.my*biz*lab.com.

chapter 13

Product Development and Pricing Strategies

▼ Objectives 1-7

1. What are the definitions of a **product** and a **total product offer**? (p. 369)

2. What is **product differentiation**, and what role does it play in product development? (p. 370)

3. What are the different classifications of **consumer products** and **business-to-business products**? (p. 372)

4. Why is **branding** beneficial to both buyers and sellers, and what are some different types of brands? (p. 375)

5. What steps take place during new product development, and what is the **product life cycle**? (p. 382)

6. What are some pricing objectives, and how do they relate to the marketing mix? (p. 386)

7. What are the three major approaches to pricing strategy, and what are some pricing tactics used to launch a new product, to adjust prices, and to impact price perceptions? (p. 387)

For more chapter resources, go to www.my*biz*lab.com.

p. 375

Branding
▼ Objective 4

When you go shopping, how important is the brand of a product? Do you go out searching for Nike tennis shoes or just tennis shoes? Branding is an important tool that a company uses for product differentiation that not only benefits sellers, but buyers as well. What is branding? How does it affect your purchases?

p. 382

New Product Development and the Marketing Mix
▼ Objective 5

Jessica Smith wants to open a yoga studio in her neighborhood. She also wants to sell yoga supplies like clothing, mats, and other props. The closest studio is 15 miles away and in poor condition, so she thinks her location would be great. What else does Jessica need to do to fully develop her studio? What steps are involved in the product development process?

p. 369

Developing Goods and Services
▼ Objectives 1-3

How can companies like Coca-Cola keep developing products when they already have a slew of successful ones? Instead of creating completely new products, companies can modify an existing product to appeal to a new audience. That is exactly what Coca-Cola did when it launched Coke Zero in 2006. What is a product? What is a total product offer? How important is product differentiation?

p. 386

Pricing Goods and Services
▼ Objectives 6 & 7

When Eugene Whitaker wanted to increase profits at the department store he managed, he looked at sales data. He learned that people purchasing items for newborn babies were more likely to buy premium priced items as opposed to the more economical selections. How can these data help Eugene increase his profits? What are pricing objectives?

Developing Goods and Services pp. 369-374

➤ In Chapter 12, we saw that successful marketing requires the identification of a need, use of market research to determine a target market, and implementation of a marketing mix plan that satisfies customers over the long run. This may sound easy, but it's not. The application of the marketing process is as much an art as a science. Making a high-quality product with a unique, properly promoted brand that consistently delivers value to customers at a "fair" price, when and where they want it, presents significant challenges to marketers all over the world. This chapter focuses on the product and price components of the 4 Ps of the marketing mix. Chapter 14 will focus on promotion and distribution to get the product to the right place at the right time. We begin with a focus on the product, because all marketing begins with a product. Most businesses must regularly modify their product offerings or offer entirely new products to meet rapidly changing market conditions. The idea is to distinguish, or differentiate, your product from your competitors' products.

Which do you prefer: Diet Coke or Coke Zero? You may think they're the same, but they're not. They have different flavors, marketing strategies, and targeted demographics. After having moderate success with flavored versions of Coke products, the company came up with an idea to differentiate Diet Coke to appeal more to men.[1] Coke Zero's marketing strategy reflects this new target market. The can is darker to convey a bigger flavor, and advertisements for the beverage are male dominated, with plots built around sports like auto racing. The Web site for Coke Zero also includes pages with information on fantasy football and the NCAA tournament. Coke Zero shows it's not only important to differentiate products from their competitors, but also to differentiate current products to meet the needs of a broader market. How important is product differentiation? ➤

The Total Product Offer

What is the total product offer? A **product** is any good, service, or idea that might satisfy a want or a need. An Apple iPhone, a Toyota Sienna, a college education, E*Trade financial services, a doctor's advice, and even a Caribbean vacation package are all products. Consumers buy products for a number of tangible and intangible benefits. The **total product offer** consists of all the benefits associated with a good, service, or idea that impact a consumer's purchasing decision. When you buy a car, you're not just buying a mode of transportation; you're also buying some intangible benefits, such as style or an image. Marketers know this, and when planning a total product offering, they think about products on three levels: the *core product*, the *actual product*, and the *augmented product*. Each level adds more value to a product.

➤ Ben & Jerry's Homemade Ice Cream differentiated itself from other ice cream makers by offering original and unique flavors and product names such as Goodbye Yellow Brickle Road, Cherry Garcia, and Phish Food.

The Core Product

The **core product** provides the core benefit or service that satisfies the basic need or want that motivates the consumer's purchase. For a car, that core benefit is the convenient transportation it provides. For a soft drink, it's the product's thirst-quenching capability. For a camera, it's the ability to capture and share memories. Notice that the core product is intangible. You can't touch it. This is because the core product is the basic *benefit* the product provides. Companies use the benefits of their products to lure customers. That is why car companies such as Toyota use "Moving Forward" as an advertising slogan. Similarly, the soft drink Sprite uses "Obey Your Thirst," and camera conglomerate Kodak once used "Share a Moment, Share a Life" to draw in customers.

The Actual Product

Of course, an actual product must be developed in order to provide the core benefit or service desired. The **actual product** is the tangible aspect of the purchase that you can touch, see, hear, smell, or taste. It provides core benefits when it is used. Consumers often assess the tangible benefits of actual products by comparing brands, quality (often associated with a brand's reputation), features, styling, or packaging. For a car, the actual product is the automobile itself. Benefits of an actual product such as a Volvo station wagon could be a high-quality brand, numerous safety features, seating for seven passengers, or leather seats. For a soft drink, the actual product might provide a refreshing taste, desirable color, or pleasant aroma. The product could even provide the "pick-me-up" caffeine buzz that consumers are looking for when they purchase some sodas. For a camera, the actual product may provide features such as an LCD screen or a lightweight design.

The Augmented Product

The **augmented product** consists of the core product and the actual product *plus* other real or perceived benefits that provide additional value to the customer's purchase. These benefits might include customer service and support, delivery, installation, a warranty, or favorable credit terms. The value-enhancing elements of an actual product are an important part of the total product offering because they help provide a more satisfying customer experience. For a product like a car, augmented benefits might include a reasonable price, an easy payment plan, a 10-year warranty, or just the security of owning a brand-new car.

➤ For a Caribbean vacation package the core product is an opportunity to take a break from your everyday life. The actual product includes airplane tickets and accommodations at a resort. Together, these products aim to produce an augmented product that includes benefits such as having fun, resting, and relaxing.

▼ **Figure 13.1** summarizes the three levels of a product. Remember that when developing products, marketers must begin with a basic customer need or want to be satisfied by a product. Then marketers develop an actual product to satisfy that need for targeted customers. Successful product developers then augment the product to create a total product offering that provides a benefit package superior to that of the competition. This is the essence of successful *product differentiation*, which we'll discuss next.

Product Differentiation

How important is product differentiation? **Product differentiation** is the process of distinguishing a product from its competition in real or perceived terms to attract customers. A company can distinguish a product from its competitors by establishing concrete or intangible differences between similar products. For example, a luggage company might offer suitcases in unique colors or shapes. It might also offer a lifetime guarantee on certain models. Product differentiation is critical for a product's success. If a product doesn't possess qualities that make it stand out, then customers will not be motivated to buy that product instead of a competitor's product.

How does consumer input affect product development?

Companies rely on customer input and feedback to help shape their products. Listening to customers and incorporating their suggestions are effective ways to foster good customer relationships, which is a critical component in establishing repeat business and long-term success. In fact, listening to customers is one of the most important elements of sound customer relationship management. You have to know what your customers want to tailor a product offering that best satisfies their needs.

Consumer input often provides information that prompts companies to segment a large market and focus on narrowly defined targeted customers. For example, a breakfast cereal company might find that most consumers buy its cereal because it is high in fiber. That company can differentiate its product from competing products by labeling the cereal "a good source of fiber" and target the product to health-conscious adults. Companies might also use consumer input to differentiate their products by improving an existing product or creating an entirely new product. SC Johnson, makers of popular cleaning products like Windex, Pledge, and Fantastik, found consumers were using a competing product, Lysol Disinfectant Spray, because they thought the spray killed bacteria in the air, when in fact the spray only kills bacteria on surfaces. SC Johnson used this information to create a new product, Oust Air Sanitizer, and differentiated it from competing products by stating that Oust Air Sanitizer is different because "it kills odor-causing bacteria in the air. Most disinfectant sprays are designed to kill bacteria on surfaces only."[2] Product differentiation is therefore the result of carefully segmenting markets into clearly defined targeted customers and developing a variety of total product offerings that best meet these varying customer needs—and doing it better than the competition.

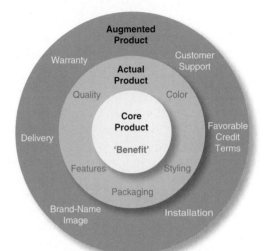

▼ **Figure 13.1**
Three Ring Model
The three levels of a product define the benefits to be derived from a total product offering.

The Three Levels of a Product

Product Lines and the Product Mix

What are a product line and a product mix? Customer feedback guides product development and product differentiation. It also gives rise to the creation of a **product line**, a group of similar products marketed to one general market. A **product mix** is the combination of all product lines offered for sale by a company. For example, Coca-Cola has many product lines, including its soft drinks, energy drinks, and sports drinks, which collectively make up its product mix. Toyota offers a full line of automotive products, which can be broken down into various product lines, including its cars, minivans, trucks, SUVs, motorcycles, ATVs, and vehicle-related parts and accessories. Toyota also offers a financial-services product line to dealers and their customers for the purchase or lease of Toyota vehicles. Toyota is involved in a number of other non-automotive business activities as well. One of these product lines is the manufacture and sale of prefabricated housing.[3] All of Toyota's combined activities constitute its product mix.

An important marketing decision involves product line length. *Product line length* is the number of items in any given product line. Product line length is determined by how the addition or removal of items from a product line affects profits. Coca-Cola has found it very profitable to pursue a long product line length given the huge variety of drinks it offers for sale. Although Coca-Cola is the biggest-selling soft drink in history, the company still offers 450 different types of beverages in order to satisfy the specific tastes of the 1.5 billion customers it serves each day.[4] Consumers who like Coca-Cola but desire a low-calorie alternative can purchase Diet Coke. Consumers who want a low-calorie soda without caffeine can purchase Caffeine-Free Diet Coke. Those who do not want a soft drink can choose from one of Coca-Cola's many beverage offerings that appeal to the various wants and needs of the company's wide consumer base.[5]

Product mix width refers to the number of different product lines a company offers. This, too, is determined by profitability. General Electric (GE) has hundreds of product lines, ranging from light bulbs and home appliances to jet engines and medical machinery.[6] GE aims to achieve maximum profitability by stretching the company's capabilities across multiple markets. Product line length and product mix width are the result of companies striving to offer differentiated products to satisfy targeted customers.

Consumer and Business-to-Business Products

What's the difference between consumer products and business-to-business products? In Chapter 12 we explored the differences between consumer markets and business-to-business (B2B) markets; now we'll explore the differences between consumer products and B2B products. **Consumer products** are goods and services purchased by households for personal consumption. They are traded in consumer markets. **Business-to-business (B2B) products** (sometimes called *industrial products*) are goods and services that are purchased by businesses for further processing or resale or are used in facilitating business operations. They are traded in B2B markets.

Most products can be classified as either consumer products or B2B products. The distinction depends on their use. For example, if a homeowner purchases a lawn mower for personal use, then it would be a consumer product. If a landscaper purchases the same lawn mower but uses it to run his business, then it would be a B2B product. It's convenient for marketers to classify various consumer and B2B products because the buying behavior is different between these two categories. This behavior impacts how the marketer prices, promotes, and distributes the product.

Consumer Product Classifications

Four classifications of products emerge from strategic marketing mix plans for consumer products. These classifications are

- convenience goods and services;
- shopping goods and services;
- specialty goods and services;
- unsought goods and services.

Let's look at each of these consumer product classifications in a bit more detail.

Convenience Goods and Services **Convenience goods and services** are those that the customer purchases frequently, immediately, and effortlessly. Convenience goods are typically *nondurable goods*—goods that are normally used or consumed quickly. Gum, soap, tobacco, and newspapers are all considered convenience goods, as are common grocery items such as ketchup and milk. A car wash is an example of a convenience service. These purchases are usually based on habitual behavior, meaning consumers routinely purchase a particular brand with which they're familiar and comfortable. Convenience goods and services are relatively low-priced items. They're usually promoted through brand awareness and image (which we'll discuss shortly) and are widely distributed through convenience stores or local grocery stores. Consumers make purchasing decisions for these goods based on the convenience of location and brand-name image.

Shopping Goods and Services **Shopping goods and services** are products that are purchased less frequently than convenience goods and services and typically require more effort and time for comparison. Consumers usually base their comparison on attributes such as suitability, quality, price, and style. Shopping goods are typically *durable goods*—goods that can be used repeatedly over a long period of time. Examples of shopping goods include clothes, shoes, televisions, cameras, stereos, bicycles, lawn mowers, furniture, and major appliances. These products are often sold at shopping centers that allow for easy comparison between stores, such as Best Buy, Circuit City, Sears, Home Depot, Kohl's, and Lowe's. Examples of shopping services include hotels and airline services. Since consumers carefully compare brands, companies that sell shopping services compete on the basis of price, quality, and brand-name image.

Specialty Goods and Services   **Specialty goods and services** are unique to the point that buyers are willing to spend a considerable amount of time and effort searching for particular brands or styles. Customers know exactly what they want and they will not accept substitutes. Examples of specialty goods and services include Ferrari sports cars, Rolex watches, high-fashion designer clothing, and the services of prestigious medical and legal experts. Because there are no suitable substitutes, buyers of specialty products do not comparison shop. They already know the specific good or service they want, and they are willing to seek it out regardless of its price and location. Businesses that successfully differentiate their product to the point that it is considered a specialty good or service can set a much higher price than similar products that are considered shopping goods or services.

Unsought Goods and Services   **Unsought goods and services** are products buyers don't usually think about buying, don't know exist, or buy only when a specific problem arises. We don't usually think about or want to think about buying some products such as life insurance or cemetery plots. These goods and services require a lot of persuasive advertising and personal selling to encourage consumers to buy products that will help them prepare for life's uncertainties. Other unsought goods and services are products that are completely new to consumers. New and innovative products, such as pharmaceutical drugs, must be introduced to consumers through promotional advertising before consumers can actively seek out these products. Emergency medical services and automobile repairs are also unsought purchases where pre-purchase planning is rarely considered. In these cases, resolving the immediate problem is more important than comparison shopping based on price or other features. Notice that sales of unsought products require personal selling or promotional advertising, and price may not be an important consideration if the good or service is urgently needed.

Business-to-Business Classifications

What are the different business-to-business product classifications?
B2B products (or industrial products) can be divided into five categories:

- equipment
- maintenance, repair, and operating (MRO) products
- raw and processed materials
- component parts
- specialized professional services

Each of these types of products has unique pricing, promotion, and distribution strategies.

> Pharmaceutical companies have stepped up their direct-to-consumer advertising efforts because they realize their products are unsought until consumers become aware of them and their benefits.

Equipment *Equipment*, also known as *installations* or *capital items*, includes all the physical facilities of a business, such as factories, warehouses, office buildings, heavy equipment, and other less costly equipment like computers, printers, and copiers. Many of these capital items are expensive, unique, and intended to last for a long time; therefore, they may require special negotiations involving top management that can stretch out over many months or even years. Marketers frequently offer a variety of services to help sell this type of equipment, including financial assistance with the purchase, maintenance, and repairs after the sale.

Maintenance, Repair, and Operating (MRO) Products *MRO products* facilitate production and operations, but do not become a part of the finished product. They include printing paper, pens, cleaning materials, tools, and lubricants for machines. They are often marketed based on convenience, just like consumer convenience goods and services.

Raw and Processed Materials *Raw and processed materials* are the basic inputs that become part of a finished good. Many raw products and some processed farm products, such as eggs or butter, go into the production of our grocery items. Raw materials like wood and processed materials like steel are used to make a variety of products, such as buildings or bridges. Raw and processed materials are usually purchased in large quantities at prices that are based on the quality of the materials.

Component Parts *Component parts* are assembled portions of the finished product. Examples include brakes, engines, transmissions, and steering columns for a car, or lumber, cement, drywall, and electrical wire for a house. Businesses purchasing component parts make their decisions based on quality and brand-name recognition, because, ultimately, the quality of a business's product will be based on the quality of its component parts.

Specialized Professional Services *Specialized professional services* help support a firm's operations. They include advertising, management consulting, legal, accounting, and information technology services. Managers compare the costs and the quality of these specialized services with their in-house operations before deciding whether to *outsource* these activities. For example, a local grocery store owner might assess his or her ability to handle the business's financial records before hiring an outside accounting firm.

Considering the variety of types and classifications of products, it's clear that product development is an exciting yet challenging area of business. As Coca-Cola showed with the development of Coke Zero, new product development can lead to great success. The key is considering and understanding the many complex factors involved in creating a differentiated product.

▼ You have just read **Objectives 1-3**

Think you got it? Check out the Study Plan section @
www.my*biz*lab.com.

Branding pp. 375-381

➤ Why do companies use logos? What does the logo say about the brand? What are the benefits of a brand? These questions are important components of another complex aspect of product development: branding. We'll discuss branding in this section.

Branding Benefits

What are the benefits of branding? A *brand* is a name, term, symbol, or design that distinguishes a company and its products from all others. Branding is one of the most important tools of product differentiation, and it benefits both buyers and sellers. For buyers, well-recognized brands reduce the shopping time necessary to find the quality and consistency they desire in a product. Branding also reduces the risks involved in some purchases for which buyers are unable to determine quality objectively. We rely on established brand names to deliver an expected level of quality consistently. Imagine the frustration you'd feel if all the products in your grocery store were packaged with generic labels. How would you decide what type of peanut butter or frozen pizza to buy? Comparing product descriptions and ingredients takes a lot longer than simply picking up your favorite brand. Consumers are also able to express themselves by buying brand names with which they wish to be identified. For example, some buyers seek prestige by buying exclusive brands like Mercedes-Benz, Rolex, or Dom Pérignon.

Branding also helps sellers define their products' special qualities, thus promoting repeat purchases as well as new sales at higher prices. Because certain brands, like Coca-Cola, are associated with quality and value, these companies are able to introduce new products quickly and at a relatively low cost. In doing so, they add length to their product lines, widen their product mix (also known as *brand extension*), and enhance their profitability. Because Coca-Cola has a large amount of diversity in its product mix, the company can market its brand to just about any person in the world. To those who don't enjoy cola, Cola-Cola claims it is "so much more than soft drinks. Our brands also include milk products, soup, and more so you can choose a Coca-Cola Company product anytime, anywhere for nutrition, refreshment or other needs."[7] Well-branded companies usually establish a trademark so their products are easily identifiable. A **trademark**, a legally protected brand, can also benefit sellers by distinguishing them from competitors' *knockoff brands*, or illegal copies or cheap imitations of a product.

Brand Loyalty and Brand Equity

What is brand loyalty? Another major benefit of branding for sellers is the creation of **brand loyalty**, the degree to which customers consistently prefer one brand over all others. In fact, companies hope their brands are not just recognized (*brand recognition*) and then preferred (*brand preference*), but that customers will eventually insist on their brand name (*brand insistence*). Brand insistence is the highest degree of brand loyalty. It can turn a product into a specialty good or service that can command a much higher price. Ultimately, the degree of brand loyalty depends on satisfied customers. Perhaps the most significant contemporary example of brand loyalty is the fervent devotion of many Mac users to Apple and its products.

What is brand equity? Strong brand loyalty contributes to **brand equity**, the overall value of a brand's strength in the market. Perceptions of quality contribute significantly to brand equity. Quality products are not just free from defects; they consistently perform at high levels. For example, many of Toyota's customers will purchase another Toyota vehicle because of the brand's high quality. This adds significantly to Toyota's brand equity. *Interbrand* and *BusinessWeek* annually rank the top 100 brands in the world based on their brand equity. ▼ **Table 13.1** lists the top 10 brands by brand equity.

Perceptions of *brand awareness* and *brand association* also contribute to brand equity. **Brand awareness** refers to the extent to which a particular brand name is familiar within a particular product category. Companies participate in mass

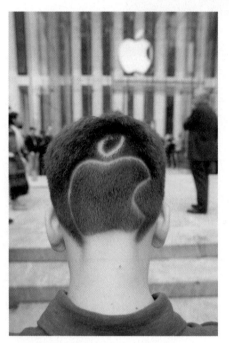

➤ One benefit of branding for sellers is brand loyalty, such as that displayed by many Mac users for Apple products.

▼ **Table 13.1**

The World's Most Valuable Brands[8]			
Rank	**Brand**	**2007 Brand Value ($ million)**	**Country of Ownership**
1	Coca-Cola	65,324	United States
2	Microsoft	58,709	United States
3	IBM	57,091	United States
4	General Electric	51,569	United States
5	Nokia	33,696	Finland
6	Toyota	32,070	Japan
7	Intel	30,954	United States
8	McDonald's	29,398	United States
9	Disney	29,210	United States
10	Mercedes-Benz	23,568	Germany

advertising as a way to help their product's brand name become synonymous with the actual name of the product. For example, what brand first comes to mind when you think of diapers? If it's Pampers, then Procter & Gamble has succeeded in its brand awareness campaigns for its disposable diapers.

Brand association involves connecting a brand with other positive attributes, including image, product features, usage situations, organizational associations, brand personality, and symbols. Hiring celebrities to endorse a product can be an effective tool for nurturing brand associations. Nike was so successful with Michael Jordan's endorsement that it launched its Air Jordan line of sport shoes. Nike later joined forces with Tiger Woods to enter the golf category with its apparel, equipment, and accessories. Disney has been successful in associating its brand with wholesome family values. The images invoked by symbols and slogans can also be very powerful brand association techniques.

What does a brand manager do? Branding has become such an important part of marketing that businesses have created brand manager (or product manager) positions within their organizations. A *brand manager* is responsible for the 4 Ps of marketing a specific product or product line. Brand managers attempt to increase the product's perceived value to customers in order to increase brand equity. Brand managers are also responsible for new product development.

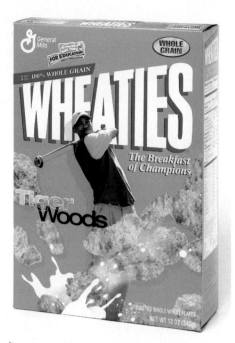

➤ Since 1934, the breakfast cereal Wheaties has featured professional and Olympic athletes on the cover of its box. These images allow the Wheaties brand to associate itself with desired values like athleticism and success.

Branding Strategies

What strategies are employed in branding products? Branding strategies are important to building brand equity. Six types of brands emerge from branding strategy.

Generic Brand

A **generic brand** is a product that has no brand at all. The product's contents are frequently identified by black stenciled lettering on white packages. A generic brand may mimic a branded product, but the generic brand is not associated with the branded product's manufacturer. For example, a generic brand of cream-filled sandwich cookies may look like Oreo cookies, but they are not associated with Nabisco Cookies. Generic brands are typically lower in price and do not advertise.

Manufacturer's Brand

A **manufacturer's brand** is a brand created by producers. Manufacturer's brands are also known as *national brands* even though they may be distributed globally. Well-known brands such as Levi's jeans, Dell computers, Ford, IBM, McDonald's, and Bank of America are considered manufacturer's brands.

Private Brand

A **private brand** is a brand created by a distributor, or middleman. These middlemen can be wholesalers, dealers, or retail stores. As a result, private brands are also called *distributor, wholesaler, dealer, store,* or *retail* brands. The key characteristic of a private brand is that the manufacturer is not identified on the product. Examples include Sears's line of DieHard batteries, Kenmore appliances, and Craftsman tools. Wal-Mart, Ace Hardware, and RadioShack also have their own private brands. The advantage of private branding is that the individual distributor has more control over the product's price and promotion. The competition—sometimes called the "battle of the

Characteristics of a Good Brand Name

· ·

1. Copyright protected
2. Pronounceable
3. Memorable
4. Recognizable
5. Eye-catching
6. Beneficial
7. Image-promoting
8. Distinguishable
9. Attractive
10. Standout

BizChat

Who's Behind Those Catchy Slogans?

The Advertising Council is a nonprofit public service advertising organization that markets many causes. Funding is received strictly through donations. A main goal of this volunteer organization is to address important social issues with public service campaigns. Much of its work is probably familiar to you. It is behind the "Friends don't let friends drive drunk" and "Buzzed driving is drunk driving" campaigns for the prevention of drunk driving. It created Smokey the Bear and "Only you can prevent forest fires." The Ad Council also helps to further high school dropout prevention for the United Negro College Fund with "A mind is a terrible thing to waste," and crime prevention for the National Crime Prevention Council with "Take a bite out of crime."[9]

For more information and discussion questions about this topic, check out the BizChat feature on www.my*biz*lab.com.

---

brands"—is heating up between manufacturer's brands and private brands, as many private brands have gained national recognition.

Family Brand

A **family brand** is a brand that markets several different products under the same brand name. Consumers are more likely to try new products from an established brand that is familiar and trusted. These established companies are able to penetrate new markets successfully with their brand names. This is known as **brand extension**, marketing a product using the same brand-name image in a different product category. Sony home and portable electronics, Keebler snack food products, Kodak photo and film offerings, and Fisher-Price toys are examples of companies that have experienced successful brand extension. Bic successfully extended its disposable ink pen brand when it added Bic disposable razors and Bic lighters to its family brand. Family brands, as opposed to private brands, have the advantages of brand awareness and brand association. This can foster more brand loyalty and still greater brand extension. However, an unsuccessful extension can dilute an established brand name or create a negative brand image.

Individual Brand

An **individual brand** is a brand assigned to each product within a company's product mix. For example, Sara Lee uses individual brands among its many food, beverage, household, and personal care products. Many of these brands may be familiar to you: Ball Park hot dogs, IronKids bread, Hillshire Farm meat products, Prodent toothpaste, Kiwi shoe polish, and, of course, Sara Lee's frozen and packaged foods. A major advantage of individual branding is that if a new product fails, it won't damage the image of the other products.

Co-Brand

A **co-brand** is the use of one or more brands affiliated with a single product. Examples include Intel and Dell, AT&T Universal MasterCard, Healthy Choice Cereal by Kellogg's, and Gillette M3 Power shaving equipment with Duracell batteries. The objective is to combine the prestige of two brands to increase the price consumers are willing to pay.

Co-branding is also used to foster brand loyalty for one product while extending to the contributing product.

Brand Licensing

Brand licensing is an agreement between the owner of a brand and another company or individual who pays a royalty for the use of the brand in association with a new product. Brand owners use licensing to extend a trademark or character onto different products. The Walt Disney Company is a good example. Characters like Mickey Mouse appear on toys, books, and clothing that are not made by Disney. The NFL, NBA, NASCAR, and Major League Baseball are also big licensors and leading retail sellers of licensed products.

➤ The slogan "Got Milk?" released in 1993 became so popular it spawned endless parodies such as "Got Faith?" and "Got Soy?"

The Packaging

How does packaging affect a brand? How a product is packaged sends a message about the product and the brand. Packaging serves four functions:

- to contain and protect the product
- to facilitate use and convenience
- to promote the product
- to be environmentally friendly

Effective packaging is crucial to the success of a product, because the customers typically see the packaging before they see the product.

How does packaging protect the product? Packaging should preserve and protect the product. This is the most obvious purpose of packaging. Most products are handled several times as they are distributed from the manufacturing site to the final consumer. Many of these products need to be protected from heat, cold, light, spoilage, infestation, and many other conditions. Packaging must also protect the product from tampering. Many products such as ibuprofen or infant formula need to be tamperproof and must meet the minimum requirements set by the Food and Drug Administration. The U.S. Consumer Product Safety Commission has also established guidelines concerning packaging.

Why is convenient packaging so important? Packaging should facilitate use and convenience. Sellers want packages that are easy to ship, store, and stock on shelves. More importantly, consumers want products that handle easily, open and reseal, store conveniently, and have a long shelf life. We dislike bulky, heavy packages that are difficult to handle and open. Packages that don't reseal or result in easy spoilage are also unpopular.

Packages that are convenient to use and are also physically attractive sell better. Heinz ketchup experienced a significant increase in sales when it began offering ketchup in a squeezable bottle. Hellman's mayonnaise now offers a similar squeezable bottle for its product. Campbell's soup is responding to changing consumer tastes and preferences for greater convenience by offering

On Target AND Off the Mark
Q-tips Brand Cotton Swabs

Branding acts as a tool to help differentiate a product from other similar products. However, what happens when the brand itself becomes the category? When was the last time you purchased a box of cotton swabs? How about Q-tips? Well if you bought cotton swabs that didn't display the brand name Q-tips, then you didn't buy Q-tips. The Q-tips brand has been so effective in establishing itself that the brand name has become synonymous with its product category. Someone shopping for Q-tips may actually buy another brand of cotton swabs. The competitor's price and/or packaging could convince a consumer to choose that particular brand over the Q-tips brand. Perhaps the issue Q-tips hasn't made clear is explaining why a box of Q-tips cotton swabs is better than a competitor's brand. Nevertheless, all companies want to guard against their brand name becoming a generic description for a product category because then their brand name becomes public property, which means the owner loses all rights to it! This not only happened to Q-tips, but *aspirin*, *yo-yo*, *cellophane*, *escalator*, *shredded wheat*, *kerosene*, *jello*, *band-aid*, and *thermos* as well. If these companies trademarked their brand names, they could have prevented them from becoming public property and preserved their product differentiation.

➤ The Association for Dressings & Sauces named Hellman's Easy Out! mayonnaise squeezable bottle the 2007 package of the year.[11] However, the product values consumer-friendly packaging over economy. Consumers will pay about $.03 more an ounce for the Easy Out container than Hellman's original squeeze bottle.[12]

sippable soups, microwave soup lines, and ready-to-serve soups. Campbell's Soup at Hand line has expanded to 13 varieties, and the microwave bowl soup line now offers 10 varieties. These products account for about $250 million of Campbell's $2.7 billion in North America soup sales.[10] Many sellers also offer different sized packages dependent on frequency of use. For example, salt, sugar, and breakfast cereal packages come in many different sizes for added convenience.

How does packaging help promote the product? Getting the consumer to notice a product and pick it up from crowded shelves is extremely important. The package design, shape, color, and texture all influence buyers' perceptions and buying behavior. Luxury items such as jewelry or high-end cosmetics typically package their products to create an impression of extravagance, sophistication, and exclusiveness. The little blue box from Tiffany & Co. is an example of an iconic package that promotes both a brand and a lifestyle. The robin's-egg blue jewelry box has been a symbol of elegance and excitement since it was introduced in 1837. The packaging is so desirable that some consumers simply want to buy the box. However, it is an ironclad rule of the company that no Tiffany & Co. blue box can leave the store unless it encloses a purchased item.[13]

What about the environment? A growing concern among many consumers is whether a product and its package are environmentally sound. Landfills contain discarded products and packaging materials, which are often not biodegradable. For example, some people have been critical of the excessive and wasteful packaging of products like Oscar Mayer's Lunchables. Consequently, many companies are going "green." Increased effort is being placed on recycling and in developing new products that are eco-friendly. This is true even for companies that are selling services. For example, the Fairmont

Hotels & Resorts luxury chain is advertising green luxury packages. With the help of the World Wildlife Fund (WWF), Fairmont hopes to reduce its impact on climate change through the use of renewable energy resources and environmentally friendly business practices.[14]

The Importance of Labels

What does the government have to say about product labels? Labeling serves two functions: to inform and to persuade. The Fair Packaging and Labeling Act of 1966 requires companies to identify

- the product;
- the name and place of business of the manufacturer, packer, or distributor;
- the net quantity of the contents.

➤ The Tiffany Blue color is used on Tiffany & Co. boxes, catalogues, shopping bags, brochures, and advertising to promote the idea of luxury and sophistication associated with the company and its products.

Other government attempts to make labels more useful for consumers to evaluate products include the Nutrition Labeling and Education Act of 1990. This legislation requires all nutrient content claims, such as "high-fiber" or "low-fat," and health claims to be consistent with agency regulations. Clearly, labels should inform consumers about the product, its uses, and any safety concerns. However, labels can be confusing and misleading. For example, what does the label "organic product" really mean? Are all ingredients in that product organic, or just one ingredient? Businesses that wish to foster good customer relationships must be careful to label their products ethically.

Why is labeling important to establishing a brand image?

Labels are also used to promote and to persuade customers to buy the product. Labels can educate consumers of the features and other benefits of the product. Many companies label their products with their brand logo to distinguish their product from their competitors'. If the label comes to represent consistent quality and dependability, then the label can perpetuate a positive brand-name image.

So how many logos can you think of? If you are able to easily identify a brand represented by a logo, then the company that owns the logo successfully branded its product. Companies pour millions of dollars into developing brands, logos, and slogans for their products. Making products memorable and appealing is a priority for all companies, and branding plays an important role in achieving this goal.

▼ You have just read **Objective 4**

Want a review? Check out the Study Plan section @
www.mybizlab.com.

New Product Development
and the **Marketing Mix** pp. 382-385

Jessica Smith had a dream: to open the best yoga studio in her hometown. At the time, the closest studio was 15 miles away and terribly run-down. Jessica used to teach classes there, but quit because it was so poorly run and maintained. There weren't enough mats for students, the locker rooms were tiny, and the paint on the walls was peeling off. It was not a place for relaxation and meditation. So Jessica decided it was time to open her own studio. Not only did she want to teach classes, she also wanted to sell equipment. She knew quality was important, so everything she planned to use and sell needed to be of the highest quality she could afford to buy. How important is product quality? Does product quality relate to customer satisfaction?

We've already explored how the perception of quality contributes to brand equity. Quality products are not just free from defects, but they consistently perform at high levels. The production of a high-quality product is critical for marketing success because it's closely linked to customer value and satisfaction. Quality experts tell us that quality doesn't cost companies more. Instead, higher quality reduces costs because of fewer defects that cause a product to be scrapped or reworked. In addition, higher-quality products require fewer recalls or warranty costs associated with fixing defects after the product is sold. Moreover, higher-quality products result in greater customer satisfaction and repeat sales. It is much cheaper to retain customers than to acquire new ones.

As Jessica soon found in starting her business, developing quality products is a multi-step process that requires a great investment of resources. Once the product is developed, the product life cycle begins. As Jessica will also find out, monitoring a product's progress through this cycle is a significant factor when determining the best marketing mix.

New Product Development

What are the steps in new product development? As outlined in ▼ **Figure 13.2**, developing new, high-quality products involves five steps:

1. **Idea Generation.** Ideas for entirely new products or improved versions of existing products are often obtained by listening closely to customers or focus groups. In fact, customer complaints may signal a need for a new product. Suppliers, employees, and salespeople also generate ideas by assessing the competition and through trade shows.

2. **Idea Screening.** The objective of idea screening is to eliminate unsound concepts before devoting costly resources to their development. Screening involves estimating the level of consumer demand for the product, its profitability, and its production feasibility given the company's current technical capabilities.

3. **Product Analysis.** Product analysis estimates costs of production, selling price, sales volume, and profitability. Costs of production depend on the features of the product deemed necessary to meet the targeted customers' needs. The selling price, sales volume, and profitability may depend on the degree of competition in the market.

4. **Product Development and Concept Testing.** At this stage, product ideas that survive the screening and analysis steps are analyzed further. This often begins with a physical prototype of the good. Computer-aided design systems are helpful in quickly making design changes even before a physical prototype is manufactured. In the testing phase of a new service offering, management determines the details concerning staffing needs and equipment requirements to ensure the service is delivered properly. Concept testing involves soliciting customer responses to a new product idea. Potential targeted customers are asked to evaluate different features, prices, packages, and a host of other factors surrounding the product. The idea is to come up with the best, most profitable total product offering.

5. **Commercialization.** If a product makes it this far in the process, it is ready to be launched. Commercialization is the decision to market a product. Introducing a new product can be costly due to manufacturing investments, advertising, personal selling, and other promotional activities. The returns from such investments can take time. This may explain why many companies introduce their new products in one region at a time—sometimes called *rolling out the product*.

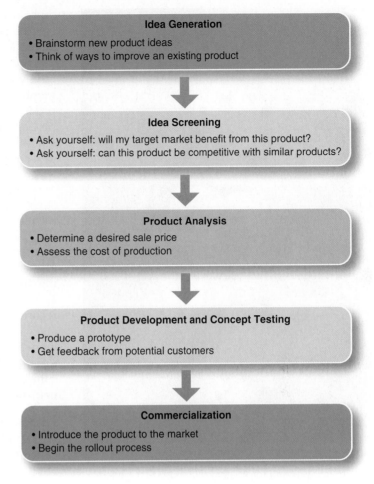

**▼ Figure 13.2
The Five Steps in
the New Product
Development Process**

Despite the scientific nature of new product development, a large proportion of new products still fail. In contrast to the success of Coke Zero discussed earlier, one of the most interesting cases of a new product failure was Coca Cola's "New Coke," launched in 1985. In an attempt to revitalize its brand, the company toyed with the formula of its popular soda and almost destroyed it. People didn't want their favorite soft drink to be modified, and New Coke was pulled from the shelves only three months after the product was introduced.[15] Coca-Cola returned to its original formula and renamed the cola Coca-Cola Classic.

Product Life Cycle

What is a product life cycle? Once a product is developed, it begins the product life cycle. A **product life cycle** is a theoretical model describing a product's sales and profits over the course of its lifetime. During this cycle, a product typically goes through four stages: an introductory stage, a growth stage, a maturity stage,

Crocs footwear was originally marketed as an outdoor shoe that was useful for boating, but in 2007 it gained popularity as an everyday casual shoe. Crocs have been considered a fad, but only time will tell if this product will continue to grow or hit a declining stage.

and a declining stage. The product life cycle can be applied to a specific product or to an entire product category. However, like all models, it is a simplified version of reality and should not be used prescriptively. This is because the duration of time associated with stages of a product's life can be as short as a few months, as is often the case for fad items like Beanie Babies. The product's life can also be as long as a century or more for some products like automobiles. In addition, not all products strictly follow these stages. Some products are introduced but never grow in sales, whereas others never seem to decline.

You can see how the theory works if you consider the life cycle of vinyl musical recordings. Vinyl records were first introduced in 1930 by RCA Victor, but became popular in the 1950s as a replacement for the brittle and easily broken 78-rpm records. This was their introductory stage. Sales grew rapidly in the 1950s and through the 1960s, representing the product's growth stage. They came in the 33 and 1/3-rpm long playing records, or LPs, and the 45-rpm single records. In the early 1970s, vinyl records hit their maturity stage. By the late 1970s and early 1980s, cassette tapes gained wide acceptance and caused sales of vinyl records to drop drastically, representing their declining stage. After compact discs, or CDs, were introduced, the decline continued. Vinyl records are now sold mostly as collectors' items.

How do marketing decisions affect the product's life cycle ? The product life cycle model may be useful as a general description of a product's sales and profits over time, but it should be used with caution when forecasting or predicting future sales and profits. All products don't strictly follow these stages, and the time frame involved with each stage can vary dramatically. In fact, marketing decisions can affect each of the phases of a product's life cycle, while knowledge of a product's life cycle stage also helps determine the appropriate marketing mix strategy for that stage. ▼ **Figure 13.3** summarizes the characteristics, marketing objectives, and strategies for each of the four stages of a product's life cycle.

Because most products eventually decline and may have to be withdrawn from the market, companies must continuously seek to develop new products to replace older ones. At the same time, marketers work hard to extend the life of existing products to milk as much profit from them as possible. Some auto companies have used discounted prices, rebates, and low-interest loans to extend the life of their models. Arm & Hammer, a company that produces baking soda, extended its product's life by advertising and *creating a new use* for its product as a refrigerator deodorizer. Home Depot and Lowe's tried to *create new markets* for their businesses by expanding into do-it-yourself training on home projects within their stores. Jell-O extended its knowledge (*extended technology*) of raw gelatin to create puddings and other snacks. *Repackaging*, or using new labels or different container types, is another popular method to extend a product's life. For example, Coca-Cola switched from 6-ounce glass bottles to 8-ounce cans. A company can also *reposition* its product as Oldsmobile attempted with its "This isn't your father's Oldsmobile" campaign. These strategies are not always effective—the Oldsmobile, for example, has been discontinued.[16]

As you've just learned, developing a high-quality product is not so much an end in itself as it is a beginning. After a product is developed, the product life cycle begins, and appropriate marketing strategies must be conceived and implemented accordingly. Jessica Smith is experiencing this now. Three years after

▼ **Figure 13.3**
The Product Life Cycle Model

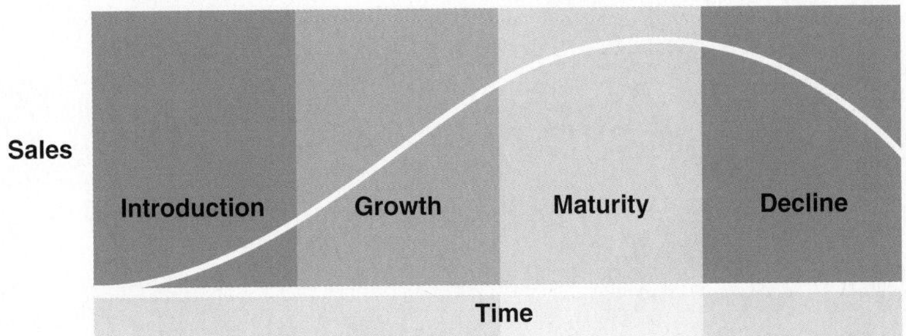

	Introduction	Growth	Maturity	Decline
Characteristics				
Sales	Low sales	Radically rising sales	Peak sales	Declining sales
Costs	High cost per customer	High cost per customer	Low cost per customer	Low cost per customer
Profits	Negative	Rising	High	Declining
Customers	Innovators	Innovators	Middle majority	Laggards
Competitors	Few	Growing number	Stable number beginning to decline	Declining number
Marketing Objectives				
	Create product awareness and trial	Maximize market share	Maximize profit while defending market share	Reduce expenditure and milk the brand
Strategies				
Product	Offer a basic product	Offer product extensions, services, warranty	Diversify brands and models	Phase out weak items
Price	Charge cost-plus	Price to penetrate market	Price to match or beat competitors	Cut prices
Distribution	Build selective distribution	Build intensive distribution	Build more intensive distribution	Go selective; phase out unprofitable outlets
Advertising	Build product awareness among early adopters and dealers	Build awareness and interest in the mass market	Stress brand differences and benefits	Reduce to level needed to retain hard-core loyals
Sales Promotion	Use heavy sales promotion to entice trial	Reduce to take advantage of heavy customer demand	Increase to encourage brand switching	Reduce to minimal level

opening her yoga studio and equipment store, she started offering discounts on products that were experiencing declining sales. At the same time, she expanded offerings of her most popular classes to maximize profits during the critical growth and maturity stages. As Jessica quickly learned, a dynamic market calls for dynamic product development.

▼ You have just read **Objective 5**

Want to learn more? Check out the Study Plan section @
www.mybizlab.com.

Pricing Goods and **Services** pp. 386-391

When store manager Eugene Whitaker wanted to increase profits at the store where he worked, he examined sales data. He noticed that premium newborn baby items were being purchased more often than less expensive choices. After getting approval from his supervisor, he raised prices for all newborn-related products. At the end of the quarter, store revenues were up. Whitaker found that the rise in prices did very little to reduce the quantity of newborn-related sales, so store executives implemented a slow increase in prices over the course of the next year at other locations, and Eugene Whitaker got a raise.

➤ Pricing is so important to consumers and producers alike that it ranks as one of the 4 Ps in the marketing mix. We conclude this chapter with an overview of the pricing component of the marketing mix. We'll discuss promotion and distribution strategies in the next chapter.

Product Pricing and Pricing Objectives

Why is price an important component in the marketing mix? Price is what must be given up in order to acquire a total product offering. Prices are sometimes called *fees*, *fares*, *tolls*, *rates*, *charges*, or *subscriptions*. Price is the only revenue-generating component of the marketing mix—product, promotion, and distribution strategies are all cost components. In fact, *revenue* to a business equals the price multiplied by the number of units sold or services performed. *Profit* equals total revenue minus total costs. So, you can see that the pricing decision has a huge impact on profitability.

Trying to set the right price can be a real challenge for marketers. The price of a product has to be low enough to generate enough value to customers to motivate sales, yet high enough to enable the company to cover costs and earn a profit. Setting the right price is challenging because market conditions are always changing. As a result, companies must constantly tweak prices to remain competitive. Moreover, some companies operating in very competitive markets may have little to no control over their price. Instead, price is determined in the market through the interaction of demand and supply. These companies may therefore be *price-takers* (not *price-setters*). For example, farmers have virtually no control over the prices of their agricultural commodities. However, most companies have at least some control over the price they charge.

What are some pricing objectives? Some of the most common pricing objectives include the following:

1. **Maximizing profits.** This occurs when price is set so that total revenue exceeds total cost by the greatest amount.

2. **Achieving greater market share.** A company's market share is the percentage of total industry sales or revenues it is able to capture. Unfortunately, achieving greater market share does not always translate into higher profits.

3. **Maximizing sales.** Maximizing sales often means charging low prices that can result in losses. Firms cannot survive for long with losses. However, maximizing sales may be an appropriate short-run objective to rid the company of excess inventory, such as last year's models.

4. **Building traffic.** Many retail stores, like grocery stores, pharmacies, hardware stores, and department stores, may advertise a sale price on a few goods to increase traffic in their stores and build a stronger customer base. They also hope customers will purchase other, more profitable items while they are shopping for the bargains.

5. **Status quo pricing.** The objective of status quo pricing is simply to match competitors' prices, possibly to avoid a price war that could be damaging to everyone. The airfare wars of the past hurt all of the airline carriers, so they have chosen to compete on nonprice factors instead.

6. **Survival.** If a company is struggling to build a customer base, it may choose to set prices to generate just enough revenues to cover costs. However, this is not a suitable long-term objective. Survival prices might generate sales, but they will not generate profits.

7. **Creating an image.** Some products are priced high because firms hope that consumers will associate high prices with high quality. This is the case for many specialty goods such as luxury cars, perfume, and designer jewelry.

8. **Achieving social objectives.** Some companies may charge low prices to enable the poor to afford their products. For example, many governments have been involved in ensuring that staple food products such as grains are affordable to all.

Marketers must develop their pricing strategies in coordination with their product branding, packaging, promotion, and distribution strategies as well. Indeed, price is only one element in the marketing mix.

Pricing Strategies

What are the major pricing strategies? Although there is no one right way to determine the price of a good or service, there are a number of strategies a seller can use. The most common pricing strategies include *cost-based pricing*, *demand-based pricing*, and *competition-based pricing*. We'll discuss these strategies next, along with some popular alternative pricing strategies.

Cost-Based Pricing

Cost-based pricing (also known as *cost-plus pricing*) is charging a price in relation to the costs of providing the good or service. It is the simplest and one of the more popular pricing strategies. Suppose you manufacture 100 units of a product at a total cost of $2,000. The average (or per unit) total cost would be $20. If you want to make a unit profit margin, or *markup*, of 20 percent, which is $4 (0.20 × $20), you would price the product at $24. Total revenue would equal $2,400 and profit would equal $400, or 20 percent above costs.

There are many advantages of cost-plus pricing. Besides being easy to calculate and easy to administer, it requires a minimum amount of information. However, it has several disadvantages as well. It ignores whether the price is compatible with consumer demand or expectations and the prices charged by competitors. It also provides little incentive to be efficient and to hold costs down. Many pharmaceutical companies undertake cost-plus pricing to recoup their expensive research and development costs associated with a new drug and to earn a targeted profit level. The monopoly power granted by patents on new drugs means there is no competition, and pharmaceutical companies find little need to consider consumer demand when setting prices on drugs.

Cost-based pricing can be facilitated by **break-even analysis**, which determines the production level for which total revenue is just enough to cover total costs. Total costs equal total fixed costs plus total variable costs. *Fixed costs* (sometimes called *overhead costs*) are any costs that do not vary with the production level. Total fixed costs typically include salaries, rent, insurance expenses, and loan repayments. *Variable costs* are costs that vary with the production level. Examples include wages, raw materials, and energy costs. *Average variable costs* (or *per unit variable costs*) equal total variable costs divided by the production level. A convenient formula for calculating the break-even production level is

$$\text{Break-even volume of production} = \frac{\text{Total Fixed Costs}}{\text{Price} - \text{Average Variable Costs}}$$

For example, suppose that the total fixed costs equal $600, the selling price is $24, and average variable costs are $14. The break-even volume of production is therefore $600/($24 − $14), or 60 units. Any production level below the break-even volume will result in losses, and any production level above the break-even level will result in profits. Any changes in fixed or variable costs, as well as changes in the price, will affect the break-even volume of production.

Demand-Based Pricing

Demand-based pricing (sometimes called *value-based pricing*) is pricing a good or service based on the demand for the product or its perceived value. A high price will be charged when demand or the perceived value of the product is high, and a lower price will be charged when demand or perceived value is low. This pricing strategy assumes firms can accurately estimate perceived value or the demand for their goods or services. Sometimes this is the case, but it's usually very difficult to do in practice. Nevertheless, many firms try.

One of the specific demand-based pricing strategies that firms employ is target costing. *Target costing* estimates the value customers receive from a product and therefore the price they are willing to pay, and then subtracts an acceptable profit margin to obtain a desired cost. Firms then work to get costs down to this targeted level. The Boeing Company, Caterpillar, DaimlerChrysler, and Continental Teves (a supplier of automotive brake systems) have successfully used target costing as a pricing strategy.[17]

Another demand-based pricing technique is **price discrimination**, charging different prices to different customers when these price differences are not a reflection of cost differences. Successful price discrimination charges higher prices to targeted customers who are price insensitive and lower prices to other targeted customers who are more price sensitive. Price discrimination requires firms to be able to successfully segment customers based on their differences in demand and price sensitivity, and it requires that the product cannot be easily resold among customers. One example of price discrimination includes hotels and resorts charging different rates based on different days of the week or seasonal variations. Movie theaters may also charge higher prices to view a movie during the evening showing as opposed to the matinee viewing time. Airline companies also price discriminate on the airfares they charge. Those who place their reservations well in advance pay less than those who book a flight on short notice. Restaurants price discriminate with early bird specials and discounted happy hour rates. Grocery stores price discriminate by offering clip-out coupons that price-sensitive customers may use to buy grocery items at lower prices. In some cases, even salespeople charge different prices to customers based on their perceived demand for big-ticket items like cars and furniture, so don't tell them how much you value or love their good or service! Many organizations price discriminate because it's profitable to do so.

Competition-Based Pricing

Competition-based pricing is a pricing strategy based on what the competition is charging. Revenues and costs are secondary. The degree of competition in markets affects a company's price-setting ability. As you saw in the last chapter, competitive markets, including agricultural and raw material commodity markets firms, have little, if any, control over their prices. They charge prices equivalent to all others' prices. *Monopolistically competitive markets*, markets in which many firms compete on the basis of doing something unique, have some firms that charge higher prices if they are successful in their product differentiation strategies. Other companies may charge lower prices to get an edge on the competition. *Oligopolies*, a market with a few dominant sellers like those in the airlines and oil industries, often avoid competing on the basis of price to avoid price wars. Instead, they compete aggressively on product differentiation and charge higher prices if their total product offerings are unique. However, periodically, a *price leader* may charge a different price and all other firms follow with similar price changes. Finally, a *monopoly*, a market that is controlled by one dominating firm, possesses the greatest price-setting ability because there is no competition. In some extreme cases, monopolies may have captured their markets through *predatory pricing*, the practice of charging very low prices with the intent to destroy the competition. Predatory pricing is illegal, but that hasn't prevented it from occurring. Most real-world competition rests on product differentiation and customer's perception of value. Companies like Harley-Davidson have successfully differentiated their products and can charge higher prices for comparable models produced by Honda, Yamaha, and Kawasaki.

Alternative Pricing Strategies

When launching a new product, companies may need to use a different type of pricing strategy than they would on an existing product. One pricing strategy for introducing a new product is **price skimming**. It involves charging a high price for a product initially, then lowering the price over time. Price skimming coincides with the introductory stage of a product's life cycle during which there are few, if any, competitors. The idea is to skim off as high a price as possible to recoup the expensive new product development costs. However, the high price may encourage competitors to enter the market at a lower price.

At the other end of the spectrum is **penetration pricing**, a strategy of charging the lowest possible price for a new product. This pricing strategy is designed to build market share for the product quickly. If the increased production to satisfy growing sales results in lower per unit costs, then profits can actually rise even though the price is lower. Penetration pricing is appropriate during the growth stage of a product's life cycle and when customers are price sensitive. It may also create goodwill among consumers and inhibit competitors from entering the market. Its drawbacks include the establishment of low price expectations or a poor-quality image for the brand and the company. This may make it difficult to raise prices later.

Adjusting Prices and Price Perceptions

What are common types of price adjustments? Most businesses adjust their prices to promote their products. Several tactics are used. One way is to use **discounts**, a deduction from the regular price charged. Discounts come in many forms:

- quantity discounts (a lower price for buying in large quantities)
- cash discounts (a reduced price for paying with a method that does not require processing)
- seasonal discounts (a price reduction if you buy out of season)
- forms of allowance, like a trade-in allowance (a reduced price if you trade your old good for a new good)

Another way to adjust prices is to use rebates. **Rebates** are partial refunds on what a customer has already paid for a product. An example is mail-in rebates, where the manufacturer writes a check to the customer after the customer provides proof of purchase.

Bundling is another type of price adjustment. In **bundling**, two or more products that usually complement one another are combined and sold at a single price. To be attractive, the single price is usually lower than the sum of the individual products' prices. Bundling is quite common in the fast-food industry where products are bundled to make a complete meal. Bundling also occurs with cable or satellite TV sales, when a package of channels is sold at a single price. Many vacation packages are also bundled products consisting of airfare, car rental, hotel accommodations, and other amenities bundled together.

Dynamic pricing is another price-adjustment technique. In **dynamic pricing**, prices are determined directly between the buyer and seller, unlike the more traditional fixed pricing in which prices are set by the seller. Auctions are a traditional form of dynamic pricing. More recent examples exist in e-commerce, like eBay and Priceline.com. Dynamic pricing often results in quick price adjustments.

▶ In dynamic pricing, prices are determined directly between the buyer and the seller, a practice seen in traditional auctions such as the one shown here.

Finally, some retail stores choose not to adjust their prices at all, but instead offer **everyday low pricing (EDLP)**, a strategy of charging low prices with few, if any, special promotional sales. Wal-Mart has successfully used this strategy because it has been able to give the impression that its brand means everyday low cost. However, it risks taking the excitement out of shopping for bargain hunters.

What are some strategies used to impact price perceptions?

For many consumers, a high price indicates good quality. Although this is not always the case, many consumers make this association when products are complex, do not have a strong brand identity, or are services with which they are unfamiliar. The less they know about a product, the more consumers rely on price as an indicator of quality. Many businesses have to be careful not to lower their prices too much or the product may be perceived as low quality. This is certainly not the case with prestige pricing. **Prestige pricing** (also known as *premium pricing*) is the practice of charging a high price to invoke perceptions of high quality and privilege. For those brands for which prestige pricing may apply, the high price itself is a motivator for consumers. The higher perceived value because of the higher price actually increases demand and creates a higher price that becomes self-sustaining. Some people have called this the *snob effect*. Examples of this strategy include the pricing of cars made by Mercedes-Benz, Lexus, and Rolls-Royce.

➤ Mercedes-Benz uses the pricing strategy known as prestige pricing to invoke perceptions of high quality and privilege.

Another pricing strategy that impacts price perceptions is **psychological pricing** (sometimes called *odd* or *fractional pricing*), the practice of charging a price just below a whole number to give the appearance of a significantly lower price. For example, charging $9.99 as opposed to $10.00 is an example of psychological pricing. Gas stations often use psychological pricing.

A **loss leader** is a product that is priced below its costs. Stores use loss leaders to attract customers and motivate them to buy more expensive items as well. Reference pricing is another strategy used to attract customers. **Reference pricing** refers to listing an inflated price (the "regular retail price" or "manufacturer's suggested retail price") that is then discounted to appear as if it is a good value. A variation of this strategy occurs when stores provide both a more expensive "gold-plated" version of a product and a lower-priced alternative. This makes the alternative appear to be a bargain.

These are just a few pricing strategies—many others exist. Indeed, the pricing component of the marketing mix is one of the most difficult for marketers to grapple with. Although Eugene Whitaker was able to raise prices on products for newborns without significantly affecting sales, this approach might not work in all cases. In those instances, marketers must go back to the drawing board to figure out a strategy that will lead them to success.

▼ You have just read **Objectives 6 & 7**

Want to test your skills? Check out the Study Plan section @ **www.my*biz*lab.com.**

1. What are the definitions of a product and a total product offer? (pp. 369-370)

- A **product** (p. 369) is a good, service, or idea offered for sale or use. A **total product offer** (p. 369) consists of all the tangible and intangible benefits associated with a good, service, or idea. Marketers know this, and when planning a total product offering, they think about products on three levels. Each level adds more customer value. These three levels of a product are the following:

- A **core product** (p. 370) satisfies the basic need or want that motivates the purchase. Because it is the basic benefit provided by the product, you can't touch it; it is intangible.

  - An **actual product** (p. 370) is the tangible aspect of a purchase that you can touch, see, hear, smell, or taste. It provides the core benefits from its use.

  - An **augmented product** (p. 370) consists of the core and actual product plus other real or perceived benefits that provide additional value to the customer's purchase.

2. What is product differentiation, and what role does it play in product development? (pp. 370-372)

- **Product differentiation** (p. 370) is the process of distinguishing a product from its competition in real or imaginary terms to attract customers.

- Customer input and feedback guides product development and product differentiation. It also gives rise to the creation of a **product line** (p. 371), a group of similar products marketed to one general market. A **product mix** (p. 371) is the combination of all product lines offered for sale by a company. Product lines and mix result from trying to tailor total product offerings to unique targeted customers.

3. What are the different classifications of consumer products and business-to-business products? (pp. 372-374)

- The four classifications of **consumer products** (p. 372) are convenience goods and services, shopping goods and services, specialty goods and services, and unsought goods and services.

  - Customers purchase **convenience goods and services** (p. 372), such as gum, soap, and milk, frequently, immediately, and effortlessly.

  - **Shopping goods and services** (p. 372) are products that are less frequently purchased and require more time and effort to compare for the consumer. Examples include clothes, electronics, and furniture.

  - **Specialty goods and services** (p. 373) have unique characteristics and have no suitable substitutes. Examples include designer clothing or the services of prestigious lawyers.

  - **Unsought goods and services** (p. 373) are products buyers don't usually think about buying, don't know exist, or buy only when a specific problem arises. An example is funeral services.

- There are five categories of **business-to-business (B2B) products** (p. 373): equipment; maintenance, repair, and operating products; raw and processed materials; component parts; and specialized professional services. Successful marketers adapt to different markets.

4. Why is branding beneficial to both buyers and sellers, and what are some different types of brands? (pp. 375-381)

- **Branding** (p. 375) reduces shopping time for buyers and helps consumers express themselves. Branding helps sellers define their product's special qualities, encouraging repeat purchases and new sales at higher prices.

- For sellers, branding creates **brand loyalty** (p. 376) among consumers. Brand loyalty contributes to **brand equity** (p. 376), the overall value of a brand's strength in the market.

- Seven different types of brands include generic brands, manufacturer's brands, private brands, family brands, individual brands, co-branding, and brand licensing. Appropriate packaging and labeling can enhance a brand.

5. What steps take place during new product development, and what is the product life cycle? (pp. 382-385)

- The steps in new product development are idea generation, idea screening, product analysis, product development and testing, and commercialization.

- The **product life cycle** (p. 383) is a theoretical model describing a product's sales and profits over the course of its lifetime. It is a general description that traces a product's sales and profits over time. Stages in the product life cycle include introduction, growth, maturity, and decline.

6. What are some pricing objectives, and how do they relate to the marketing mix? (pp. 386-387)

- Common pricing objectives include maximizing profits, achieving greater market share, maximizing sales, building traffic in stores, matching the status quo prices, covering costs to survive, creating an image, and ensuring affordability to all.

- Price is the only revenue-generating component of the marketing mix. Marketers must carefully consider their pricing objectives in order to develop the best pricing strategy.

7. What are the three major approaches to pricing strategy, and what are some pricing tactics used to launch a new product, to adjust prices, and to impact price perceptions? (pp. 387-391)

- The major approaches to pricing strategy are **cost-based pricing** (p. 387), **demand-based pricing** (p. 388), and **competition-based pricing** (p. 389).

Continued on next page

Chapter Summary (cont.)

- **Price skimming** (p. 389) and **penetration pricing** (p. 389) are tactics used for launching new products.
- **Everyday low pricing** (p. 390), **discounts** (p. 390), **rebates** (p. 390), **bundling** (p. 390) and **dynamic pricing** (p. 390) are common types of price adjustments.
- In addition, **prestige pricing** (p. 391), **psychological pricing** (p. 391), the use of **loss leaders** (p. 391), and **reference pricing** (p. 391) are pricing strategies that impact price perceptions by consumers.

For an audio file of the Objectives and Chapter Summary, see the Student Resources section @ www.my*biz*lab.com.

Key Terms

actual product (p. 370)

augmented product (p. 370)

brand association (p. 377)

brand awareness (p. 376)

brand equity (p. 376)

brand extension (p. 378)

brand licensing (p. 379)

brand loyalty (p. 376)

break-even analysis (p. 388)

bundling (p. 390)

business-to-business (B2B) products (p. 372)

co-brand (p. 378)

competition-based pricing (p. 389)

consumer products (p. 372)

convenience goods and services (p. 372)

core product (p. 370)

cost-based pricing (p. 387)

demand-based pricing (p. 388)

discounts (p. 390)

dynamic pricing (p. 390)

everyday low pricing (EDLP) (p. 390)

family brand (p. 378)

generic brand (p. 377)

individual brand (p. 378)

loss leader (p. 391)

manufacturer's brand (p. 377)

penetration pricing (p. 389)

prestige pricing (p. 391)

price discrimination (p. 388)

price skimming (p. 389)

private brand (p. 377)

product (p. 369)

product differentiation (p. 370)

product life cycle (p. 383)

product line (p. 371)

product mix (p. 371)

psychological pricing (p. 391)

rebates (p. 390)

reference pricing (p. 391)

shopping goods and services (p. 372)

specialty goods and services (p. 373)

total product offer (p. 369)

trademark (p. 376)

unsought goods and services (p. 373)

Self-Test

Multiple Choice   Correct answers can be found on page 503.

1. The level of a product that satisfies the basic need or want that motivates the purchase is the

   a. total product offering.

   b. augmented product.

   c. actual product.

   d. core product.

2. Product mix width refers to

   a. a total product offer.

   b. a group of similar products marketed to one general product market category.

   c. the number of product lines a company offers.

   d. the number of items in a product line.

3. When companies compete aggressively on the basis of price, quality, and brand-name image because consumers carefully compare brands, then these businesses are most likely selling

   a. convenience goods and services.

   b. shopping goods and services.

   c. specialty goods and services.

   d. unsought goods and services.

4. When businesses hire celebrities to endorse their products and connect their brands with positive attributes, they are focusing on enhancing their brand

   a. loyalty.

   b. awareness.

   c. association.

   d. extension.

5. A brand that markets several different products under the same brand name is a

   a. manufacturer's brand.

   b. family brand.

   c. private brand.

   d. co-brand.

6. Which of the following correctly describes the order of the five steps of new product development?

   a. Idea generation, idea screening, product analysis, product development and testing, and commercialization

   b. Idea screening, idea generation, product analysis, product development and testing, and commercialization

   c. Idea generation, idea screening, product development and testing, product analysis, and commercialization

   d. Idea screening, idea generation, product development and testing, commercialization, and product analysis

7. Which stage of a product's life cycle do the following conditions describe: Sales and profits rise; the marketing objective is to maximize market share; the product strategy is to offer product extensions, services, and warranties; and the price strategy uses penetration pricing?

   a. Introduction

   b. Growth

   c. Maturity

   d. Decline

8. Suppose a firm's fixed costs of production equal $1,000, its average variable costs equal $50, and it sells its product for $70. Its break-even production volume is

   a. 150 units.

   b. 67 units.

   c. 50 units.

   d. 14.28 units.

9. Which two kinds of pricing strategies are often used for launching new products?

   a. Discounts and rebates

   b. Bundling and dynamic pricing

   c. Price discrimination and predatory pricing

   d. Price skimming and penetration pricing

10. A pricing technique that requires firms to segment customers successfully based on their price sensitivity is

   a. predatory pricing.

   b. price discrimination.

   c. target costing.

   d. psychological pricing.

Self-Test

True/False Correct answers can be found on page 503.

1. Augmenting products is an important method of product differentiation.
   ☐ **True** or ☐ **False**

2. Brand extension lengthens an existing product line.
   ☐ **True** or ☐ **False**

3. Prestige pricing is most common for shopping goods and services.
   ☐ **True** or ☐ **False**

4. MRO business-to-business products are marketed much like consumer convenience goods and services.
   ☐ **True** or ☐ **False**

5. A disadvantage of an individual brand is diluting an established brand name with an unsuccessful product extension.
   ☐ **True** or ☐ **False**

Critical Thinking Questions

1. Why is it important for marketers to think of a good or service as a total product offering?

2. What types of consumer products are sold by a gas station? By an automotive repair shop? By a shoe store? By an orthodontic dentist? How might these goods and services be best differentiated in terms of the "product" and "price" components of the marketing mix?

3. How are brand loyalty, specialty goods and services, and prestige pricing related?

4. What are the differences between cost-based pricing, demand-based pricing, and competition-based pricing?

5. Describe the conditions when it might be appropriate to use each of the following pricing strategies: discounting, rebates, bundling, dynamic pricing, prestige pricing, psychological pricing, loss leader pricing, and reference pricing.

Team Time

Developing a Product

Divide into teams of three or four. As a team, use what you have learned in this chapter to discuss how you would develop a new product.

Process

Step 1. Begin with Step 1 in the five steps in the new product development process: idea generation. Work as a group to decide what your new product will be.

Step 2. Proceed through the idea screening, product analysis, product development and testing, and commercialization steps. What do you estimate the consumer demand and production feasibility for this product to be? How much will it cost to produce, and what should be its selling price? How might you concept-test this product? How will it be marketed? Discuss the answers to these questions as you address their corresponding steps.

Step 3. Prepare a summary of your findings and present them to the class.

Ethics and Corporate Social Responsibility

The Ethics of Rx

The pharmaceutical drug industry is an ethical minefield. The development of prescription medications is one topic among many that can present significant ethical challenges. Consider the questions raised by the following scenario. If possible, discuss your thoughts with a classmate or participate in a group debate on the topic.

You are an executive at one of the top drug companies in the United States. At the most recent product development meeting, two teams of scientists reported that each is within one year of having a new drug ready for clinical trials. Team A is developing a drug to cure a rare but fatal bone disease. Team B is developing a drug to treat a common, non-life-threatening skin condition. In order to make the deadline, however, both teams need an additional 10 million dollars in funding. You know that the company can only afford to fund one team. According to the product analysis, Team A's drug will be expensive to produce, difficult to market, and will yield only modest profits. Team B's drug has the potential to yield massive profits.

Questions

1. Which team would you recommend the company fund? Why?
2. How do the potential profits of Team B's drug affect your stance, from both financial/business and medical/ethical perspectives?
3. What about pricing? How might you reconcile the need to keep the drug company profitable with the ethical responsibility to make medications affordable for those in need?

Web Exercises

1. **The iPhone as a Product**
   Go to Apple's iPhone Web site: www.apple.com/iphone. Describe Apple's marketing mix strategy for its product and its price. When would an iPhone be a consumer product, and when would it be a B2B product? What does Apple do to augment its product? What type of branding strategy is Apple pursuing? What stage of the product life cycle is the iPhone experiencing? Is Apple undertaking the appropriate strategies, given this stage of the product's life cycle?

2. **Strategic Product Development and Pricing at Toyota**
   Toyota has gained the reputation of being a leader in producing high-quality products. Visit www.toyota.com. How does Toyota use its site to communicate its product? How does it augment its product to differentiate the brand from the competition? Can you gain any information about Toyota's pricing strategy from this site? What type of product and pricing strategy would you recommend to Toyota?

3. **Research a Brand**
   Choose a favorite brand of clothing or food and use the Internet to gather information about it. What type of brand is it—a manufacturer's, private, individual, or other? Is it part

of a brand extension? Is it associated with a co-brand or a licensing arrangement? How do packaging and labeling affect the image the brand projects? Summarize your findings in a brief report.

4. **The Pricing of Prescription Drugs**
   Visit Merck's Web site to explore the issue of the pricing of prescription drugs (www.merck.com/about/public_policy/pricing/home.html). According to Merck, how are the prices of medications determined? Does it offer discounts? To whom and why? Are these policies fair? How would you describe Merck's pricing objectives? You might visit other drug company Web sites to compare policies and investigate the matter in more depth.

5. **The Dynamics of Dynamic Pricing**
   Visit an online auction Web site such as www.ebay.com. Choose a few products and compare their prices on the Web site with their prices at a retail store. What do the higher or lower prices on eBay indicate about supply and demand? How does dynamic pricing differ from fixed pricing? What other factors must buyers take into account when purchasing products from eBay?

Web Case

To access the Chapter 13 Web case and exercise, see the End of Chapter Assignments section @ www.my*biz*lab.com.

Video Case

To access the Chapter 13 Video case and exercise, see the End of Chapter Assignments section @ www.my*biz*lab.com.

Promotion and Distribution

One way to influence someone to buy a product is through a memorable advertising campaign. Some of the most effective campaigns of all time began over 50 years ago and are still used today. What effect does advertising have on business as well as on the culture in which we live?

Keith Jefferson works for a trucking company and is going on his first sales pitch alone. When his potential client asks a question about shipping rates, Keith freezes. He has no idea how to answer the question. What is personal selling? What traits do good salespeople have?

When Danny Perez started his own catering business, he thought having a special offer would help him get his name out there. He wanted to get people's attention, so he set up a booth in a busy commercial area of the city during lunchtime. He gave away free samples of his food and pamphlets advertising his specialties. Is this an effective promotional strategy?

Think about the last time you bought a bottle of cough syrup. Did you ever wonder how many miles the bottle traveled to be on the shelf? How many stops did the cough syrup make before it finally arrived at the store? What is a middleman? Is a middleman necessary in the distribution process?

When Ichiro Satou was hired to manage a packing supply wholesaler, he was told the company was in need of a major makeover. The company was doing well, but the previous manager did a terrible job of keeping it profitable. The biggest expenditure of all was transportation costs. What is a wholesaler? What factors need to be weighed when choosing a mode of transportation?

Promotion and the **Promotional Mix** pp. 399-401

> While Danny's plan to promote his catering business was well intentioned (see the box to the right), it didn't work out quite the way he had hoped it would. What should he have done differently? What other options does he have? In this chapter, you'll learn about the promotion and distribution (or place) components of the 4 Ps of the marketing mix.

Danny Perez dreamed of having his own catering business. When he decided to take the leap and switch careers, he was nervous but excited. He wanted to get people to taste his food, so he thought he should come up with a special offer. He decided to rent a food cart and set up a tasting stand during lunch in a busy commercial area. Not only would he give away samples of some of his best dishes, but he also created pamphlets that listed his other dishes and their prices. He ended up being rushed with people who were in a hurry to get back to work. Since he was by himself, he could barely keep up. In the end, he was out $400 in food and only gave away half of his pamphlets. >

Promotion

What is promotion? Few products—no matter how well developed, priced, and distributed—will sell well if they are not properly promoted. **Promotion** involves all of the techniques marketers use to inform targeted customers of the benefits of a product and to persuade them to purchase the good, service, or idea. Promotion is designed to increase brand awareness, brand loyalty, and sales, and is therefore one of the most visible components of the marketing mix. Finding the best way to communicate the benefits of a product and to persuade consumers to buy it is a critical job of marketers. Should the product be advertised, or is personal selling more appropriate? If advertising is used, is it best to advertise through newspapers, magazines, radio, television, or another source? Beyond advertising and personal selling, what types of public relations activities might be most appropriate? These are just a few of the questions that marketers must ask themselves when promoting a product.

What are the most popular tools marketers use to promote a product? Four basic promotional tools are used to promote a good or service: advertising, public relations, personal selling, and sales promotions. The **promotional mix** is the strategic combination of promotional tools used to reach targeted customers to achieve marketing objectives. These elements of the promotional mix are illustrated in ▼ **Figure 14.1**. Notice that the product itself can be a promotional tool because its features may be promoted by giving away free samples of the good or service.

▼ **Figure 14.1**
The Promotional Mix
The promotional mix consists of advertising, public relations, personal selling, and sales promotions. The product itself can also be considered part of the promotional mix—especially if samples are given away to promote the product.

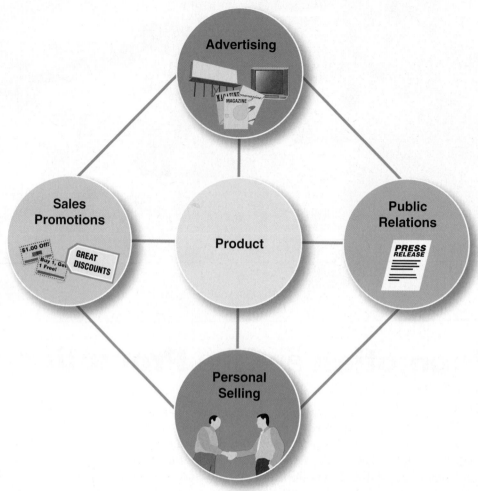

Efficient organizations search for the optimal or most cost-effective promotional mix, given their marketing objectives and their budgetary constraints. If a firm's major objective is to maximize profits, then it will juggle the amounts of advertising, public relations, personal selling, and sales promotion until a mix is found that maximizes profits, given the company's limited promotional budget. The optimal, or best, promotional mix for a given product will vary depending on the goals of the business.

What are the steps involved in a promotional campaign? Six steps emerge from all effective promotional campaigns:

1. **Identify target market.** Recall from Chapter 12 that a *target market* is a specific group of potential customers on which to focus marketing efforts. Identifying these customers is the first step in any promotional campaign.

2. **Determine marketing objectives.** Is the business trying to maximize profits, sales, or market share? Is the goal to build traffic, brand awareness, or brand image? Is the business trying to introduce a new product or respond to an attack by a competitor? Whatever the marketing objective is, the goal should be clearly understood and measurable.

3. **Design the message.** The message should inform customers of the benefits of the business's product and be echoed by all elements of the promotional mix to give a unified message.

4. **Determine the budget.** The best combination of promotional activities can be determined by finding that mix with the biggest bang for the buck.

5. **Implement the promotional mix.** Businesses must always integrate and coordinate all promotional efforts. For example, public relations, sales promotions, and direct marketing efforts should try to produce results at the same time advertisements are scheduled to appear.

6. **Evaluate and adjust as needed.** The effectiveness of any promotional mix depends on clearly understood and measurable objectives. Each element of the mix, as well as the entire combination of the mix, will need to be adjusted as necessary for growth, for changing marketing objectives, or to correct ineffective promotional techniques.

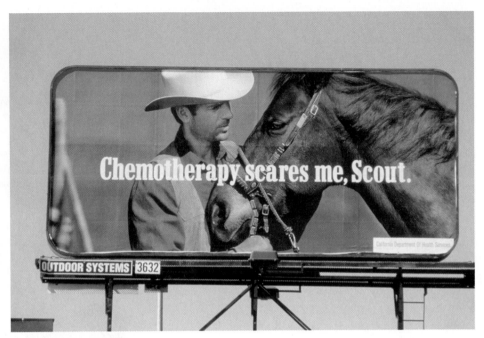

➤ Billboards like the one shown here may be part of an integrated marketing campaign strategy.

Integrated Marketing Communication

How do companies make sure they are consistent across the entire promotional campaign? An **integrated marketing communication (IMC)** is a strategy to deliver a clear, consistent, and unified message about the company and its products to customers at all contact points. This strategy contrasts with allowing members of the organization to develop their own communication with customers in isolation. This could give rise to conflicting messages, consumer confusion, and a loss of sales. It is essential that all members of the marketing team—whether they are involved with advertising, public relations, personal selling, or sales promotions—work together to foster and sustain a consistent and compelling message to create a positive brand image. Consistency nurtures good customer relations and repeat business. In short, everyone in the organization needs to be on the same page and communicate with one voice.

Promoting a product involves choosing the best combination of promotional tools to persuade customers to purchase the good, service, or idea. As Danny Perez's experiences show, achieving this blend can be a great challenge. After all his time and efforts, he only received two calls related to his catering business from giving out free samples from a cart. Having learned his lesson, he is now putting careful thought into each of the six steps of developing an effective promotional campaign in order to determine the best promotional mix for his business.

▼ You have just read **Objective 1**

Think you got it? Check out the Study Plan section @
www.my*biz*lab.com.

Promotional Techniques: Advertising and **Public Relations** pp. 402-409

Below are some of the most successful advertising campaigns of all time. Can you connect each advertising campaign to its product?[1]

1. "Have it your way" 1973
2. "When it rains it pours" 1912
3. "Takes a licking and keeps on ticking" 1950s
4. "Good to the last drop" 1959
5. "Ring around the collar" 1968
6. "Reach out and touch someone" 1979
7. "Breakfast of champions" 1930s
8. "Be all that you can be" 1981
9. "When you care enough to send the very best" 1930s
10. "Snap! Crackle! Pop!" 1940s

A. Maxwell House coffee
B. AT&T
C. Morton's Salt
D. U.S. Army
E. Burger King
F. Hallmark
G. Wisk Detergent
H. Timex
I. Kellogg's Rice Krispies
J. Wheaties

Answers: 1. E; 2. C; 3. H; 4. A; 5. G; 6. B; 7. J; 8. D; 9. F; 10. I

How did you do? Did these campaigns succeed in making a lasting impression on you? Some of these campaigns date back over 50 years and are still used today. In this section, you'll learn about the roles of advertising and public relations in the promotional mix. ➤

➤ Advertising

What is advertising? Advertising is paid, impersonal mass communication from an identified sponsor to persuade or influence a targeted audience. When we think of advertising, many of us first think of television commercials, like those during the Super Bowl. But as we shall see, advertising is much more than this.

What role does advertising play in business and society? Advertising plays a huge role in business as one of the promotional tools designed to communicate with targeted customers. It is especially important in the introduction and growth stages of a product's life cycle, as it helps build mass brand awareness and brand association. In the maturity stage, advertising is often used to stress product differentiation. Effective advertising also builds brand loyalty and brand equity. Although it is costly, advertising also often leads to lower prices for consumers. This is because advertising is a mass-marketing tool. The more people know about a product and like it, the higher its sales and the greater its production level. Given the frequent economies of scale associated with increased volumes of production, we, as consumers, get lower per-unit costs and lower priced products. Advertising can also inform consumers of the value inherent in products and educate the public in their uses. However, critics argue that advertisers are less concerned about informing or educating consumers and are instead more interested in misleading the public into perceptions of value that may not really exist. This debate continues. It echoes the need for ethical business behavior and can explain the existence of government laws and regulations that constrain advertising and other marketing practices.

Advertising also impacts the economy because of the huge sums of money spent on it. This creates many jobs in advertising agencies as well as related and supporting industries. Companies spend so much on advertising because it is economically in their best self-interest to do so. It doesn't just cost, it pays! For example, a business that advertises online with Google can exponentially increase traffic to its company Web site, leading to more sales. ▼ **Table 14.1** lists the top ten companies in terms of advertising expenditures in the United States.

Types of Advertising

What are the different types of advertising? Advertising is undertaken by virtually all organizations in one form or another. Different organizations use different types of advertising. The following are some of the more common types of advertising:

- **Product advertising**—advertising that promotes a specific product's uses, features, and benefits. This is the type of advertising we most often think of.

- **Corporate (or institutional) advertising**—advertising that focuses on creating a positive image toward an organization or an entire industry as opposed to a specific product. The campaign "Beef, It's What's for Dinner," sponsored by the Cattlemen's Beef Board and National Cattlemen's Beef Association, and the pharmaceutical industry's advertisements for treatments for leukemia and other diseases are examples of industry-wide institutional advertising. Government

▼ **Table 14.1**

Rank	Advertiser	U.S. Advertising Spending ($ millions)
\multicolumn{3}{l}{**Leading National Advertisers, 2007**}

Rank	Advertiser	U.S. Advertising Spending ($ millions)
1.	Procter & Gamble Co.	5,230.0
2.	AT&T	3,207.3
3.	Verizon Communications	3,016.1
4.	General Motors Corp.	3,010.1
5.	Time Warner	2,962.1
6.	Ford Motor Co.	2,525.2
7.	GlaxoSmithKline	2,456.9
8.	Johnson & Johnson	2,408.8
9.	Walt Disney Co.	2,293.3
10.	Unilever	2,245.8

Source: "National Marketers Ranked 1 to 50," Advertising Age Data Center 2007 Marketer Profiles Yearbook: 100 Leading National Advertisers, June 25, 2007, 10, at http://adage.com/datacenter/datapopup.php?article_id=127910

On Target Dove Ads Break the Model Mold

It's no secret that women frequently compare themselves to models in magazines, and that in order to sell products, advertisers often emphasize beauty and sexuality. Models with smooth, clear skin; long, shiny hair; perfect teeth; and very thin figures are used to sell just about everything. Dove went against the grain in 2005, though, when it launched its Campaign for Real Beauty. Instead of using traditional models, Dove recruited women of all different ages, shapes, and sizes to appear in advertisements for its products. The goal of the Campaign for Real Beauty is to broaden people's perception of beauty. While the campaign has had its critics, it has been a success overall, generating a great deal of publicity and sales for Dove and its products.[2]

entities can also undertake institutional advertising. For example, state governments do it when they run advertisements that promote their states.

- **Comparative advertising**—advertising that compares a brand's characteristics with those of other established brands. Examples include television commercials comparing toothpaste, pain relievers, and detergents.

- **Retail (or local) advertising**—advertising that focuses on attracting customers to a fixed location like a department store or a grocery store.

- **Business-to-business advertising**—advertising that is directed to other businesses rather than to consumers. For example, Caterpillar, the earth-moving equipment company, advertises to construction companies.

- **Nonprofit advertising**—advertising that focuses on promoting not-for-profit organizations like the Red Cross and the Nature Conservancy.

- **Public service advertising**—advertising that communicates a message on behalf of a good cause, like the prevention of wildfires.

- **Advocacy advertising**—advertising that promotes an organization's position on a public issue, like global warming or immigration. We are familiar with advocacy advertising undertaken during political campaigns by organizations that are independent of a political party or candidate.

- **Interactive advertising**—advertising that uses interactive media, like interactive video catalogs on the Internet or at kiosks at shopping malls, to connect directly with consumers in a personal and engaging way.

- **Internet advertising**—advertising that uses pop-up and banner ads and other techniques to direct people to an organization's Web site. Internet advertising is growing rapidly. Revenues to businesses from this type of advertising are expected to continue to grow.[3]

Types of Advertising Media

What are the different types of advertising media? Advertising media are the means of conveying a message about a product. Media conveying informative and persuasive messages exist all around us, including on seats of grocery carts, on sides of buses and trucks, on billboards, in magazines, in newspapers, and in brochures. Advertisements are also heard on telemarketing and telephone hold messages, on in-store public address systems, and on the radio. And of course we see ads on television, on the Internet, in movies, in video games, and in our mailboxes every day. Advertising is pervasive and has also been around for many years. Some of the more modern, traditional media for advertising include television, newspapers, magazines, radio, the Internet, and outdoor media. Outdoor media include billboards; signs in sports arenas; ads painted on the sides of cars, trucks, and buses; and even skywriting. ▼ **Figure 14.2** illustrates the relative importance of these types of media by expenditures.

Beyond these advertising media, *direct mail advertising* remains one of the largest forms of advertising. You're probably familiar with direct mail advertising; you just have a different name for it—junk mail. Direct mail advertising comes in many forms, ranging from coupon offers to brochures and catalogs. However, it continues and may even grow because it's generally a very effective advertising tool.[4] Direct mail advertising allows companies to target their advertising dollars to customers who are most likely to buy their products and to offer customized product offerings to these customers. Besides direct mail, the Yellow Pages are also frequently used to advertise. This medium is particularly important for small businesses.

What are the advantages and disadvantages of the different types of advertising media? Many advantages and disadvantages accompany each of these advertising media. For example, television advertising reaches a huge audience, but it's very expensive. In fact, TV commercials are so effective that networks can command huge sums of money for commercial airtime during popular or prime-time TV events. For example, as of 2007, a 30-second spot during the Super Bowl now commands over $2.5 million.[5] But remember, the marketer's task is to find the most effective and efficient medium for transmitting his or her message to targeted customers—given marketing objectives and budget constraints. ▼ **Table 14.2** lists some of the advantages and disadvantages of each major medium.

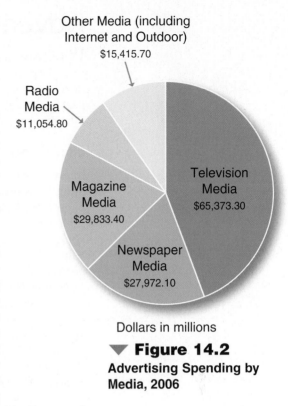

Dollars in millions

▼ **Figure 14.2**
Advertising Spending by Media, 2006

▼ **Table 14.2**

Advantages and Disadvantages of Advertising Media

Media	Advantages	Disadvantages
Television	Good mass-market coverage; low cost per contact; combines sight, sound, and motion; good attention span	High cost; low recall; channel surfing or digital video recorders skip over ads; short exposure
Newspaper	Timing and geographic flexibility; good local market coverage; high credibility and acceptability	Short life span; lots of competition for attention; poor-quality reproductions
Magazine	High market segmentation; high-quality color; long life; longer attention span; high credibility	Declining readership; lots of competition for attention; high cost; long ad-purchase lead time
Radio	High geographic and demographic selectivity; low cost; creative opportunities with sound	Low attention span; short exposure time; information overload; limited coverage
Internet	Global and interactive possibilities; ease of segmentation; high audience interest; easy to measure responses	Audience controls exposure; clutter on each site; skewed demographically to surfers
Outdoor	Able to select key geographic areas; low cost per impression; high frequency on major commuter routes	Short exposure time; brief messages; creative limitations; little segmentation possible
Direct Mail	High levels of segmentation; allows personalization; high flexibility; ad can be saved; measurable impact	High cost; can be rejected as "junk mail" and viewed as a nuisance
Yellow Pages	Inexpensive; commonly used and accessible; good local coverage and segmentation possible; long life	Costly for very small businesses; lists the competition as well

Advertising Trends

What are some important recent trends in advertising? One of the most important trends to have emerged from modern advertising has been the development of Internet advertising. In fact, it is one of the fastest-growing media in part because it allows firms to focus their advertising dollars on targeted customers. Other trends include product placement, infomercials, and global advertising.

Internet Advertising

Internet advertising includes spam ("junk" e-mail), pop-ups, banner ads, and other links found at Web sites to attract potential customers to a company's Web page. Google, Yahoo!, and other search engine sites can determine customers' perceived needs and wants based on their searches. If you search for a vacation package, for example, then Disney or Norwegian Cruise Lines may pay Google or Yahoo! to have its banner ad appear on your search. Once customers have been persuaded to visit a firm's Web site, the company can learn a lot about potential customers depending on where and how many times they click within the company's Web site. Businesses then attempt to interact with their customers through videos or even through starting a chat based on their perceived needs and wants. The idea is to work with customers to create a customized product offering that best meets the customers' unique tastes and preferences. If the business is able to consistently deliver high-quality value using these modern techniques, then Internet advertising can help businesses maintain positive customer relations.

Product Placement and Infomercials

The placement of products in TV shows, movies, and video games where they will be seen by potential customers has become much more common. This is known as **product placement**. For example, the superhero in the movie *Iron Man* drives an Audi R8, while his leading lady cruises around in an Audi S5.[6] The advent of digital video recorders (DVRs), which allow viewers to record shows and then fast-forward through advertisements, has driven product placement on TV. Another variant of strategic placement is the banners of brand names, symbols, and slogans found on the walls of professional sports stadiums so that camera shots of the televised games will frequently display the banners' messages.

Another significant trend on TV is the use of **infomercials**, television commercials that run as long as regular TV programs. Infomercials typically appear as actual television programs, often in the form of a talk show, with little direct reference to the fact that they are actually advertisements. Unlike normal commercials, infomercials are designed to elicit a specific, direct, and quantifiable response from viewers. The pitches are similar to "call this toll-free number and order yours today" or "if you call within the next few minutes we will also . . ." Infomercials often use "experts" or celebrities as guests or hosts to endorse and push their products. Infomercials have the advantage of showing the features of the products in great detail. Some of the most successful infomercials include Bowflex Home Gym, Carlton Sheets's Real Estate Tutorial, Proactiv Solution Acne Treatment, Showtime Rotisserie Pro Electric Rotisserie Oven, and Ionic Breeze Air Purifier.[7]

Global Advertising

The globalization of advertising is another important trend. Most products have to be customized to satisfy foreign customers. This means that products are tailored to meet the unique local tastes, preferences, and cultural sensitivities of foreign customers or to satisfy the regulatory standards of different governments around the globe. Likewise, some advertising campaigns can be exported intact, while others have to be changed. Advertisers prefer to use the same message

BizChat

Brand Name Movie Fame

Good product placement can help catapult a product. In 2004, the film *Sideways* featured a wine connoisseur with a deep affection for pinot noir. Sales of pinot noir jumped 16 percent in the United States following the film's release.[8] Before HBO's *Sex and the City*, how many people were familiar with Manolo Blahnik shoes? And now with online video sites like YouTube attracting so much

attention, product placement agencies such as Brandfame have been created to connect online-video producers with the best brands for their products. If people see a character they want to emulate, they may go out and buy the same brand of shampoo that character uses or the same jacket the character wears. The next time you watch a movie or television show, try to pick out possible product placements.[9]

For more information and discussion questions about this topic, check out the BizChat feature on www.my*biz*lab.com.

because it is cheaper, it allows for a more globally integrated communication message, and it allows for the pooling of talent to design the most compelling advertising message. But transferring domestically successful advertising messages abroad can be tricky. As we discussed in Chapter 4, marketers have to carefully consider the interpretations of their messages in the underlying cultural context of the foreign market. Increasingly, marketers are realizing that customized advertising campaigns to globally segmented markets work much better, just as domestic market segmentation is more effective.

Public Relations

What is public relations? Another important part of the promotional mix is public relations. **Public relations** is the management function that establishes and maintains mutually beneficial relationships between an organization and its stakeholders.[10] All organizations—for-profits, not-for-profits, and even governments—are interested in public relations. Stakeholders for businesses include all interested parties, including consumers, stockholders, employees, suppliers, the government, and the public in general.

What steps are involved in developing public relations plans? The idea behind public relations is to create and maintain a positive image of the organization in the minds of stakeholders. This begins with assessing public attitudes and perceptions of the organization. Sometimes, public opinion may be based on perceptions that have little to do with facts. Nevertheless, an honest audit of public opinion is necessary before specific public relations programs can be implemented to shape the image and reputation of the organization. Once an organization has listened carefully to public concerns and interests, it needs to respond by changing its behavior or by correcting misperceptions. Finally, the organization needs to inform the public of any changes it has made or educate the public about the facts associated with the organization.

What are some common public relations tools? Several specific types of public relations tools exist to build a positive business image. They can be classified by whether the news transmitted is controlled, semicontrolled, or uncontrolled by the organization.[11] The degree of control hinges on how and when the message is delivered. *Controlled messages* include corporate (or institutional) advertising, advocacy advertising, and public service advertising. The company may also disseminate annual reports, brochures, flyers, and newsletters, or provide films or speakers to send a controlled message to targeted audiences. *Semicontrolled messages* are placed on Web sites, in chat rooms, and on blogs. In these forums, what people say about the company is not strictly regulated. Other semicontrolled messages include sponsorships of sporting events and other special events, because the participation by the press and stakeholders is not under the control of the sponsoring company. In addition to controlled and semicontrolled messages, a company also may use uncontrolled messages. *Uncontrolled messages* generally take the form of publicity.

Publicity

Publicity is information about an individual, organization, or product transmitted through mass media at no charge. Publicity has two advantages over advertising. First, it is free. Second, it is more believable because it is often presented as a news story. However, publicity is *not* controlled by the seller—it is controlled by the media, and this is its disadvantage. If, when, and how a news release, a press conference, a captioned photograph, an appearance on a talk show, or a staged event will be covered by the media is outside the control of public relations managers.

How does a company generate positive publicity? Naturally, keeping friendly relations with the press increases the probability that a "newsworthy" story will be covered and treated with a favorable spin.

▶ The names of companies and brands on NASCAR drivers' clothes and cars demonstrate companies undertaking event sponsorship.

Nevertheless, public relations managers need to ensure that publicity releases are timely, interesting, accurate, and in the public interest. For example, in May 2005, GE launched its "ecomagination" campaign to portray itself as an environmental leader. Was General Electric sincere about the environment, or was it just jockeying for a favorable marketing impression? The consensus was that GE was sincere. This may explain why the campaign won the prestigious 2006 Silver Effie Award in the category of Corporate Reputation, Image & Identity.[12] GE's publicity releases were timely, interesting, accurate, and in the public interest.

It appears green business is good business, and not just for GE. For example, Home Depot, the world's largest seller of lumber, now gives preference to vendors that offer FSC-certified wood. The FSC (Forest Stewardship Council) determines whether lumber is grown and harvested responsibly to preserve environmental integrity. Shoppers can identify FSC-certified lumber by its greentree logo. IKEA, based in Sweden, where nearly half the forests are certified, produces as much furniture as possible from FSC-certified wood. These companies received a lot of publicity when the documentary *Buyer Be Fair* first aired on Public Television in March 2006. You can bet these companies appreciate the publicity for their efforts.

Another example of positive publicity is the favorable press that McDonald's Ronald McDonald House Charities receive for providing families with temporary living quarters while their children are in the hospital. Corporate philanthropy is generally good publicity, especially if it results in getting your name on a building, an annual event, a scholarship, or volunteer programs that are visible to the community. Many smaller companies give to local schools, hospitals, and arts programs.

➤ Companies like Avon generate positive publicity through philanthropic efforts, such as hosting a Walk for Breast Cancer.

Some of the larger corporations renowned for their philanthropic and charitable efforts include Microsoft, Target, Avon, Hewlett-Packard, AOL, and Timberland.[13]

Whether motivated by publicity needs or a sense of social responsibility, giving back to the community doesn't just *cost* companies, it *pays* them. Most of us like buying products from companies if we believe that some of our money will be used to give back to the community or to reward companies for doing the right thing.

How does a company respond to negative publicity? A final role of public relations personnel is managing a crisis. *Damage control* is a company's effort to minimize the harmful effects of a negative event. Negative publicity can, in a matter of days, tear down a firm's image that took decades to build up. For example, ExxonMobil still suffers from the *Exxon Valdez* oil spill accident that occurred over two decades ago. Sometimes, bad news doesn't come from the media but from word of mouth. In the event of bad news, a company must stand ready to react, and react quickly. No easy remedies exist for crises, but being honest, accepting responsibility, and making other ethical responses are the first steps toward regaining credibility and re-establishing a positive image.

Advertising, public relations, and publicity are important elements in the promotional mix. Review the ad campaign quiz at the beginning of the chapter. You're probably familiar with many of the ads, which means that they were highly successful, well-crafted campaigns. These campaigns were effective because they resonated with customers, created memorable brand awareness, and made people want to buy the products. In doing so, they demonstrated the power of promotion.

▼ You have just read **Objectives 2 & 3**

Want a review? Check out the Study Plan section @
www.mybizlab.com.

Promotional Techniques: Personal Selling and Sales Promotion pp. 410-416

Keith Jefferson is nervous about giving his first big sales pitch alone. He's trying to convince an electronics wholesaler to switch from its current trucking company to his company. Despite his nerves, the presentation goes well, and the client seems receptive. After the presentation, the client asks him how fluctuating oil prices will affect shipping rates. Keith has no idea what to say. How could he have been more effective with his potential client?

Personal selling is more complicated than simply telling a customer to buy your product. It's a complex process that involves a number of steps, each of which must be executed with great thought, planning, and care. In this section, you'll learn about personal selling as well as yet another promotional technique, sales promotion.

Personal Selling

What is personal selling and why is it important? Personal selling is direct communication between a firm's sales force and potential buyers to make a sale and to build good customer relationships. For example, a laboratory supplies company may deploy a representative to a research facility to demonstrate new products. Good salespeople don't just want to sell their products; they want to serve customers. A salesperson should help customers with their buying decisions by understanding their needs and presenting the advantages and disadvantages of a product. Salespeople most effectively represent their companies by establishing good customer relationships that foster repeat business and long-term company success.

The sales staff is often the first contact point for many customers. To build good customer relationships, a salesperson should be customer oriented, competent, dependable, honest, and likeable. Good salespeople are also able to listen carefully to customer needs. They possess knowledge of the company's total product offerings and make the buying process as easy as possible for the customer. In many business-to-business or industrial sales, millions of dollars may be involved in a single purchase, such as buying an airplane or building an office building. You can see why businesses want nothing less than truly professional salespeople—people who can deliver carefully prepared presentations, establish rapport with customers, and negotiate details with skill. In fact, the demand for well-educated, well-trained professional salespeople today explains why some salespeople earn more than the CEOs of their companies. It also explains why sales positions still account for approximately one in ten jobs in the United States. The unflattering stereotype of the backslapping, fast-talking salesman of the past certainly doesn't depict the modern sales consultant. Today's sales consultants are highly skilled professionals.

Obtaining and keeping good salespeople is expensive. This helps explain why personal selling is the most expensive part of the promotional mix for most companies, along with the fact that sales, unlike advertising, is labor-intensive and deals with only one buyer at a time. Generally, personal selling is preferred over advertising when selling a high-value, custom-made, or technically complex product. Advertising is more cost-effective when selling a low-value, standardized product that is easily understood.

Types of Salespeople

There are three general types of salespeople. Of course, some salespeople, especially in smaller businesses, may be required to fulfill all three roles.

Order Getters. An **order getter** is a salesperson who increases a company's sales by selling to new customers and by increasing sales to existing customers. This task is sometimes called *creative selling*. It requires recognizing customer needs and providing information to potential buyers of a product's uses and features. Many companies—such as real estate, insurance, appliance, automobile, and heavy industrial equipment firms—depend on new sales. To enhance repeat sales, salespeople stay in touch with current customers to ensure satisfaction. Salespeople also use current customers as sources for leads on new prospects. Examples of order getters include car sales representatives, real estate and insurance agents and brokers, manufacturing and wholesale sales representatives, and securities and financial services sales representatives.

Order Takers. An **order taker** is a salesperson who handles repeat sales and builds positive customer relationships. One of the major jobs of order takers is to ensure buyers have sufficient quantities of products when and where they are needed. This is especially true in business-to-business sales like selling grocery items to grocery stores, or selling shoes to shoe stores. Order takers generally handle routine orders for standardized products that do not require a lot of technical sales expertise. It is becoming more common for orders to be placed electronically using the Internet, so the role of order takers is changing more toward identifying and solving problems. Some of the same people who are order getters are also order takers. Most of us encounter order takers as retail sales clerks and cashiers.

Support Personnel. **Support personnel** are salespeople who obtain new customers but also focus on assisting current customers with technical matters. They are most common in business-to-business sales where manufacturers assist wholesalers and retailers with the best ways to sell and promote their products to ultimate consumers. We'll discuss the role of wholesalers and retailers in greater depth later.

All salespeople, whatever their specific role at any given time, are ambassadors for the business. They need to listen carefully, act as sounding boards, and relay customer feedback to the organization. This allows firms to improve existing products or create new products to better meet customer needs and preferences. Serving customers better is a large part of what building good customer relationships and promotion is all about.

The Personal Selling Process

What are the steps in the selling process? The best way to understand the personal selling process is to look at an example. Suppose your company sells a sophisticated global positioning system (GPS) for use in the trucking industry. Your latest model allows trucking firms to keep track of their tractor-trailer rigs via a password-protected Web site that features a digital map display of vehicle location and speed, engine use, refrigerated load temperature, door alarms or other motion-sensing devices that have been activated, cargo weight, and odometer reports. You can imagine the benefits of such a system for trucking companies. Although this is a business-to-business (B2B) example, the steps involved in the selling process are essentially the same for selling a consumer product, even though selling a B2B product is usually more complex. In all cases, the salesperson has to be knowledgeable about his or her product and competitors' products.

No two salespeople are alike, and no two selling situations are the same. However, six steps emerge from all personal selling: prospecting, approaching the prospect, presenting, overcoming objections, closing the sale, and following up. This six-step personal selling procedure is outlined in ▼ **Figure 14.3**.

Prospecting.   The first step in the personal selling process is to identify qualified potential customers. This is known as **prospecting**. Notice that businesses need to not only find potential customers, they need to identify those who are qualified to buy. To be qualified to buy means that the potential customer has the ability and the authority to purchase, plus the willingness to listen to the sales message. Prospecting can be a daunting task. Good salespeople find leads at trade shows from those who have scouted the company's Web site, or, better yet, from currently satisfied customers who are willing to recommend the salespeople to others for their superior product and service.

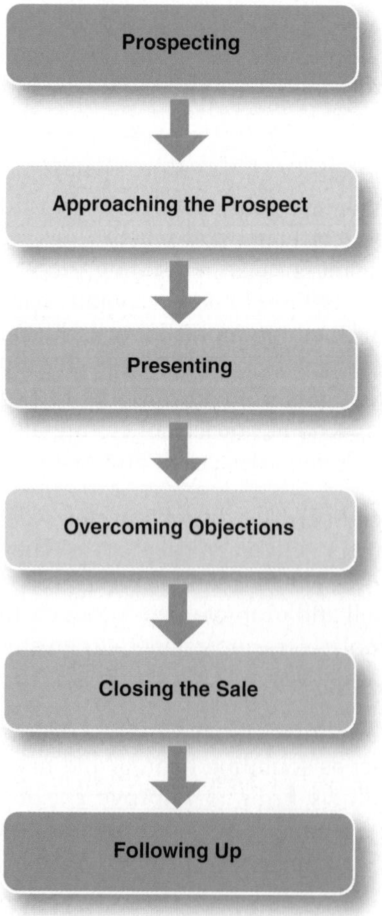

Approaching the Prospect.   This step divides into two parts: the pre-approach and the actual approach. The pre-approach involves salespeople doing their homework. This is especially critical if they are trying to sell a B2B product like a GPS device. Salespeople must learn as much as possible about their potential customers to determine their likely needs and think about how they might be able to satisfy those needs. In our trucking example, you would need to determine the people in the trucking firm who would be most interested in buying your GPS product and learn as much about them as you can. Are they currently using a GPS system? If so, what brand is it? How is your product better? You should also decide on the best approach. Should you phone them, send a letter, or make a personal visit? The timing decision of the actual approach should also be carefully planned to not catch the prospect at a busy time.

▼ **Figure 14.3
The Personal Selling
Process**

- Prospecting
- Approaching the Prospect
- Presenting
- Overcoming Objections
- Closing the Sale
- Following Up

In the actual approach, the idea is to meet, greet, and put the prospect at ease. First impressions are lasting impressions! This is the salesperson's first chance at building a long-lasting relationship. Good salespeople present themselves as knowledgeable and friendly professionals who are genuinely interested in serving customers. The first impression is followed by asking some questions to learn about the potential customers' needs. Then, the salesperson must listen carefully to those responses. In our example, because GPS hardware and software is often complicated, you may want to remind them that your product is not only superior, but your service is better than that of the competition as well. You can offer to help install the system, train employees in its use, and offer free 24-hour service and upgrades when necessary.

Presenting. In the actual presentation of the GPS technology, you'll need to tell your product's "story" and detail how your product can help the trucking firm. You should demonstrate the product and let the prospect use it as well. Your presentation should be carefully planned using the most advanced presentation technologies that allow for the full use of multimedia effects. Most importantly, you should ask probing questions during your presentation and listen carefully to answers. Listening is more important than talking. You can't serve the customer until you fully understand his or her needs or problems.

Overcoming Objections. Objections to buying are common. Good salespeople anticipate them and are prepared to counter them. Once objections surface, you should use this opportunity to provide more information on your GPS product and turn these objections into reasons to buy. You may invite others from your company to join in at this point to address any objections via a teleconference or a virtual meeting. This provides an opportunity to establish a rapport based on trust between you, your company, and the prospect. Overcoming objections can be the beginning of a mutually beneficial and lasting relationship.

Closing the Sale. After overcoming objections, the next step is to close the sale and ask for a purchase. You should look for physical cues, comments, or questions that signal the time to ask the buyer for an order. You may want to review points of agreement, ask the buyer which model he or she prefers, ask how many units are needed, or sweeten the deal by offering more favorable credit terms or by throwing in an extra quantity free of charge. Closing the sale is an art that is learned with practice.

Following Up. To ensure a long-term relationship and repeat business, be sure to follow up with the customer to ensure he or she is happy with his or her new GPS product. Stand ready to promptly help him or her with any problems after the sale. Ask for feedback. Relay that feedback to your company as input for improving existing products or for designing new ones. Periodically check up on customers by phone or by sending birthday cards. Good follow-up service and rapport can give rise to referrals or testimonials that can be used to enhance future sales. Following up is all about building and nurturing relationships.

Sales Promotion

What is sales promotion? The final element of the promotional mix is sales promotion. **Sales promotions** are short-term activities that target consumers and other businesses for the purpose of generating interest in a product. Sales promotions encompass all those activities designed to inform, to persuade, and to remind targeted customers about the product—and that have not already been undertaken by advertising, public relations, or personal selling. As consumers, we see sales promotions almost everywhere: from clip-out coupons in our newspaper, to rebate offers on a new car purchase, to e-mail announcements offering discounted prices on airline tickets, to end-of-aisle displays of potato chips at our local grocery store tempting impulse purchases.

What are two general types of sales promotions? Most companies' products go through a distribution system before they ever reach the final consumer. These companies encourage the middlemen (like wholesalers) to push their products on through the distribution channel to end users. Any incentives to push a product through the distribution system to final consumers are called **trade (or business-to-business) sales promotions**. In addition, **consumer sales promotions** are incentives designed to increase final consumer demand for a product. The whole idea behind all sales promotions is to generate interest and excitement around a product. Businesses need to create a reason why stores should not only carry their product, but encourage its purchase by consumers. Companies want consumers to be so excited about their products that they seek the products out and ask for them by name. In short, companies want to create a tipping point so that all involved will opt for their products instead of the competitors' alternatives.

Consumer Sales Promotion Tools

Consumer sales promotions are aimed at the end users, or final consumers. Consumer sales promotions are intended to increase demand for a good or service, or at least provide that extra incentive to tip consumers in favor of a specific brand. Sales promotions are also aimed at providing customers with another reason to feel good about their purchases. Timing of consumer sales promotions is important to get maximum impact. They need to be strategically coordinated with the other elements in the promotional mix. Here are a few of the most common consumer promotional tools.

- **Coupons.** Coupons are discount certificates that reduce the price of a product and are redeemable at the time of purchase. Coupons are found in print ads, on packages, in direct mail, at checkout counters, and on the Internet. They are used to encourage the purchase of a new product or to generate repeat sales. Coupons are the most common consumer promotional tool. They are popular because consumers like the sense of getting a bargain.

- **Rebates.** Rebates provide for a reduced price if the rebate form is mailed in along with a proof of purchase. Unlike coupons, the discounted price is not realized at the point of purchase. Because most people do not redeem the rebates, they are an inexpensive way for businesses to promote sales.

- **Frequent-user incentives.** Some credit card companies encourage customers to use their credit cards for purchases that accumulate points redeemable for merchandise. Airlines sometimes offer frequent-flyer miles redeemable for free tickets for additional travel. Some merchandise-buying clubs, like Sam's Club, also offer points redeemable for cash back at the end of the year. These incentives encourage customer loyalty and repeat business.

- **Point-of-purchase (POP) displays.** These are displays strategically located to draw attention and encourage impulse purchases. Examples are items placed in racks close to checkout counters at grocery stores and end-of-aisle stacks of soft drink bottles. Studies indicate that POP displays really work.[14]

- **Free samples.** Free samples are an effective way to introduce a new product, to get nonusers to try it, or to get current users to use it in a new way—especially if the samples are made available where the product is sold. Most of us have sampled small portions of foods at our local grocery stores. Some companies also mail samples of products such as cereal and shampoo directly to consumers.

- **Contests and sweepstakes.** Many companies use contests and sweepstakes to increase the sales of their products. As a reward for participating, consumers might win cash, free products, or vacations.

- **Advertising specialties.** Companies frequently create and give away everyday items such as bottle or can openers, caps, and key rings with their names and logos printed on them. Companies prefer to use inexpensive handouts that will yield constant free advertising when used by the recipient.

Other consumer sales promotion tools include bonuses (buy one, get one free), catalogs, demonstrations, special events, lotteries, premiums, and cents-off deals. Consumer sales promotions are becoming more common because they help segment markets and they are cost-effective.

Trade Sales Promotional Tools

If you want other businesses to become interested and excited about carrying your product, then you must first generate in-house enthusiasm. You will need to educate your entire staff, especially your sales staff, about your product and its many uses, features, and benefits. This may require some formal training of your sales staff on how to best present your product. In order to generate leads, you may need to send your sales staff to trade shows equipped with sophisticated multimedia presentations, full-color brochures, shirts, hats, coffee mugs with your product logo, and a lot of excitement. You have to create some internal buzz and excitement for your product before you can ever expect other businesses to be interested in carrying and promoting your product. Once your staff is energized, then you can work on creating the same level of energy and excitement for distributors. Some of the specific tools used to promote a product to other businesses include the following:

- Trade shows and conventions
- Trade allowances (deals and price reductions to wholesalers, dealers, and retailers)
- Cooperative advertising (a manufacturer agrees to pay for some of the advertising costs of the retailer)
- Free merchandise
- Sales contests (e.g., a free trip to Hawaii for those who sell the most)
- Dealer listings (advertisements of your product that mention retail outlets where it can be found)
- Catalogs and store demonstrations
- In-store displays
- Quantity discounts
- Training and support programs

When it comes to trade sales promotional techniques, firms have many options from which to choose. If one doesn't work, they can easily adopt new strategies until they find the best combination.

Technology's Effect on Sales Promotions

Technology has also had a huge impact on sales promotions. More and more companies are using the Internet to promote their products by using their companies' Web sites to offer all kinds of deals. Moreover, many businesses post positive comments about their products and their companies on Internet blogs to generate positive publicity for their products. The idea is to create a positive image and use word of mouth to generate enthusiasm for a product and stimulate sales. In addition, the technology of *podcasting* allows companies to promote their products directly to targeted customers by providing audio and video feeds for download. We can expect the further use of technology and the Internet for sales promotions in the future.

Advantages and Disadvantages of the Promotional Mix

What are the advantages and disadvantages of the promotional mix? As you've learned, when developing the best promotional mix for a product, companies must weigh the advantages and disadvantages of each of the four main options—advertising, public relations, personal selling, and sales promotions. ▼ **Table 14.3** summarizes some of these key advantages and disadvantages.

▼ **Table 14.3**

The Advantages and Disadvantages of Promotional Tools

Promotional Tool	Advantages	Disadvantages
Advertising	• Builds brand awareness and brand loyalty • Reaches a mass audience	• Expensive • Impersonal • Not good at closing a sale
Public Relations	• Often seen as more credible than advertising • Inexpensive way of reaching many customers	• Risk of losing control • Cannot always control what other people write or say about your product
Personal Selling	• Highly interactive communication between the buyer and seller • Excellent for communicating a complex product, information, and features • Good for building customer relationships and closing a sale	• Expensive • Not suitable if there are thousands of buyers
Sales Promotions	• Can stimulate quick increases in sales by targeting promotional incentives on particular products • Good short-term tactical tool	• If used over the long term, customers may get used to the effect • Too much promotion may damage the brand image

Recall Keith Jefferson, who wasn't prepared to answer questions about the service he was offering when giving his sales pitch to a potential client. As a result of his lack of preparedness, he wasn't able to land the account. As Keith's story shows, determining which promotional tool to use is merely half the battle. Effective execution—whether it is an ad campaign, a public relations event, a sales pitch, or a sales promotion—is equally important.

▼ You have just read **Objectives 4 & 5**

Want to learn more? Check out the Study Plan section @ **www.my*biz*lab.com.**

Distribution: The Basics pp. 417-419

➤ **Distribution** is the process that makes products available to consumers when and where the consumers want them. Managing the entire process of getting products out the door and eventually into the hands of final consumers is known as *supply-chain management*. Although somewhat limited in scope, this is still a very complicated process in the real world of business today. Most of us don't think about the transfer and storage of the products we buy—unless something goes wrong and we are unable to get the products we want, when and where we want them. You can imagine the challenges companies face trying to guarantee that customers have access to the products at the right time and in the right quantity and place. Despite proper distribution being critical and extremely complicated in practice, the distribution function of the 4 Ps of marketing is often overshadowed by the more visible product, pricing, and sales promotional strategies. In this section, you'll learn some of the basics about distribution.

Imagine walking through a drugstore, looking for cough syrup. Did you ever wonder how far the products on the shelves have traveled? Consider that cough syrup you're looking for. After it was bottled, it had to travel to a wholesaler and then to the retailer. If you cut out all the traveling and middlemen, how much would the cough syrup actually cost? What are wholesalers and middlemen? Why are they needed? And how do they affect the price of a product? ➤

Marketing Intermediaries and Distribution Channels

What are marketing intermediaries and distribution channels?
A **marketing intermediary**, or middleman, is a business firm that operates between producers and consumers or business users. Intermediaries are sometimes referred to as *middlemen* or *resellers* because they pass along products from manufacturers to end users. A **distribution channel** is a set of marketing intermediaries who buy, sell, or transfer title (or ownership) of goods as they are passed from manufacturers to consumers. Some distribution channels involve more intermediaries, while others are shorter with fewer intermediaries.

What are the different types of intermediaries? There are three types of intermediaries:

- **Wholesalers** are intermediaries that buy and resell products to other wholesalers, to retailers, and to industrial users. For example, your local grocery store probably purchased the Tide laundry detergent on its shelves from a wholesaler who bought it from Procter & Gamble, the manufacturer.

- **Agents/brokers** are intermediaries that facilitate negotiations between buyers and sellers of goods and services but never take title (ownership) of the products traded. Examples include real estate agents and brokers, stockbrokers, and agricultural brokers. Even eBay, which never owns the various items it sells, can be considered an agent/broker because the company facilitates the transfer of ownership from sellers to buyers.

- **Retailers** are intermediaries that buy products for resale to ultimate consumers. As consumers, we buy most of our products from retail outlets, like the Tide laundry detergent from our local supermarket.

Why are intermediaries needed? You might wonder why we need all of these intermediaries and whether they serve to only drive up prices. It's certainly true that each link in the distribution channel incurs costs, and intermediaries must cover these costs and earn a profit to remain in business. However, these costs and the higher prices we must pay are usually less than the time and money we would otherwise spend to obtain the products directly from the manufacturer. In short, intermediaries add costs, but these costs are offset by the value added.

To examine the efficiencies provided by intermediaries, review ▼ **Figure 14.4**, which shows five manufacturers and five retail outlets. Without an intermediary, each retailer would have to contact each manufacturer to order desired goods. That would entail 5 times 5, or 25, exchange relationships. Now suppose a wholesaler is established to stock and resell each of the five manufacturers' products to each of the five retailers. Now the five manufacturers and five retailers have only one intermediary to deal with. This reduces the number of exchange relationships from 25 to 10. Intermediaries reduce the time and costs of providing products to customers. Of course, the wholesaler will incur some costs that will be pushed onto the consumer. But these costs are less than the costs without the involvement of the intermediary. The most efficient intermediaries get most of the business and survive in a competitive environment. This is why intermediaries are always looking for more advanced technologies to facilitate their operations. The modern distribution system is high-tech business.

▼ **Figure 14.4**
The Efficiencies of Intermediaries
The introduction of an intermediary reduces the number of exchange relationships between manufacturers and retailers.

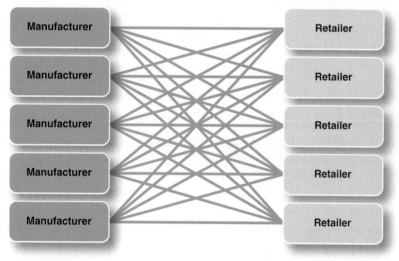

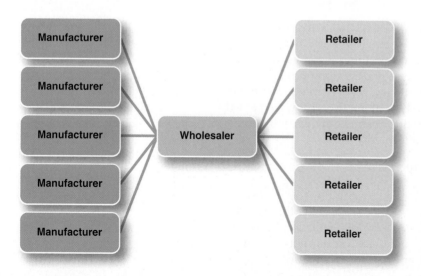

Types of Distribution Channels

What are the different types of distribution channels? Many distribution channels exist, as illustrated in ▼ **Figure 14.5**. As you can see, the type of distribution channel used varies depending on the type of product that is being brought to the consumer. The number of intermediaries depends on whether greater efficiency or adding value is possible by adding another link to the chain in the distribution system. If greater efficiency is possible, then another link will be added in order to increase profits. Competitive markets determine what number of intermediaries will be most efficient.

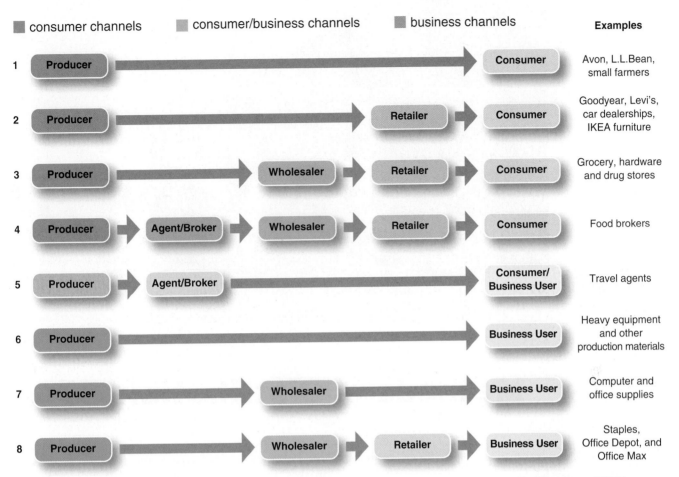

▼ **Figure 14.5 Different Channels of Distribution**

An important recent development in the distribution of products has been the increased use of **e-commerce**, buying and selling on the Internet. It is now possible for consumers to buy thousands of products online. Businesses are also using the Internet to buy and sell to other businesses. For example, customer relationship software can be purchased and downloaded online for sales to other businesses. These direct channels (channels 1 and 6 in Figure 14.5) bypass all intermediaries.

E-commerce is prevalent in all distribution channels, not just the direct channel. Almost all firms—whether they are manufacturers, agents, brokers, wholesalers, or retailers—have Web sites that allow customers to shop, place an order, and pay. Many sites also use interactive videos to enable customers to explore the features of products from their homes or offices. E-commerce is expected to continue to grow because of the convenience it provides.

Remember the questions you had about the cough syrup in the drugstore? You now know that the cough syrup likely traveled from the manufacturer to a wholesaler and then to a retailer before landing in your hands. You also know that although intermediaries do add costs to products, these costs are offset by the value they add. As you purchase your cough syrup, consider that while it may at first seem cheaper to buy products directly from the producer, the time and money it would take to do so would ultimately make it more expensive.

▼ You have just read **Objective 6**

Want to test your skills? Check out the Study Plan section @
www.mybizlab.com.

Methods of Distribution pp. 420-427

When Ichiro Satou was hired to manage a packing supply wholesaler, the owner told him it was going to be a big job. Ichiro had managed wholesalers before, so he wasn't worried about his new position. In his experience, as long as everything was organized, a wholesaler practically ran itself. Unfortunately, Ichiro's first few weeks at the company were a nightmare. The inventory wasn't properly organized or under control, and transportation costs were so enormous, the warehouse couldn't make a profit. The first thing Ichiro needed to do was either change the transportation companies he worked with or try to renegotiate the company's contracts. What are the benefits and costs of various transportation modes?

In this section, we'll examine the role of wholesalers like Ichiro, as well as that of agents/brokers and retailers, in the distribution process. In addition, we'll look at the issues of physical distribution, warehousing and inventory control, and transportation modes, issues that wholesalers like Ichiro wrestle with on a daily basis.

Wholesaling

What services do wholesalers provide? As we've already discussed, wholesalers are intermediaries that buy and resell products to other wholesalers, to retailers, and to industrial users. They are different from retailers because retailers only sell products to final consumers. It can be confusing because some of us, as households, purchase products at wholesale distributors like Sam's Club, Costco, or Office Depot, which also sell to other businesses. One of the most effective ways to distinguish wholesalers from retailers is to remember that wholesalers *primarily* sell business-to-business products, while retailers sell *only* consumer products. Nevertheless, wholesalers provide a host of services to their customers. Some of these are listed in ▼ **Table 14.4**.[15]

What are the different types of wholesalers? Wholesalers are technically known as **merchant wholesalers**, independently owned businesses that take ownership (title) of the products they handle. They are sometimes called *jobbers*, *mill supply firms*, or *distributors*. Merchant wholesalers include

▼ **Table 14.4**

Services Provided by Wholesalers

Service	Description
Bulk Breaking	Wholesalers save retailers money by buying in bulk and breaking bulk packages down into smaller quantities.
Financing	Wholesalers finance retailers by giving credit, and they finance manufacturers by ordering early and paying bills on time.
Management Service and Advice	Wholesalers often help retailers train their sales clerks, improve store layouts and displays, and set up accounting and inventory control systems.
Market Information	Wholesalers give information to manufacturers and retailers about competitors, new products, and price developments.
Risk Bearing	Wholesalers absorb risk by taking title to merchandise and bearing the costs of theft, damage, spoilage, and obsolescence.
Selling and Promoting	Wholesalers' sales forces help manufacturers reach many smaller retailers at a low cost. The wholesaler has more contacts and is often more trusted by the retailer than the distant manufacturer.
Transportation	Wholesalers can provide quicker delivery to buyers because they are closer than the producers.
Warehousing	Wholesalers hold inventories, thereby reducing the inventory costs and risks of suppliers and retailers.

full-service wholesalers and *limited-service wholesalers*. Full-service wholesalers provide a full line of services: carrying stock, maintaining a sales force, offering credit, making deliveries, and providing management assistance. There are two types: *Wholesale merchants* sell primarily to retailers. *Industrial distributors* sell to manufacturers and institutions like hospitals and the government. As intermediaries, limited-service wholesalers offer fewer services than full-service wholesalers. There are four major types:

- **Cash-and-carry wholesalers** carry a limited line of fast-moving goods and sell to small retailers for cash. They normally do not deliver. For example, a small fish store may drive to a cash-and-carry fish wholesaler, buy fish for cash, and bring the merchandise back to the store.

- **Truck wholesalers** (or truck jobbers) perform primarily a selling-and-delivery function. For example, soft-drink trucks that deliver to supermarkets and restaurants are truck wholesalers.

- **Drop shippers** don't carry inventory or handle the product. On receiving an order, they select the manufacturer, who ships the merchandise directly to the customer. Drop shippers assume title and risk from the time of the order to delivery. They operate in bulk industries like lumber, coal, and heavy equipment.

- **Rack jobbers** serve grocery stores and drug retailers, mostly in nonfood items. They send delivery trucks to stores, where the delivery people set up racks or displays within the stores. Rack jobbers retain title to the goods and bill the retailer only for the goods sold to consumers.

Because of their limited functions, these limited-service wholesalers usually operate at a lower cost than wholesale merchants and industrial distributors.

Agents/Brokers

What distinguishes agents and brokers, and what are some common types of agents? Agents and brokers are unique among intermediaries because they do not take title to the products traded. They merely facilitate the buying and selling of products and earn a commission on the selling price. What distinguishes agents from brokers is that agents represent the buyers or sellers who hired them on a more permanent basis than brokers do. Three common types of agents are manufacturers' agents, selling agents, and purchasing agents.[16]

- *Manufacturers' agents* represent two or more manufacturers of complementary lines. A formal written agreement with each manufacturer covers pricing, territories, order handling, delivery service and warranties, and commission rates. Manufacturers' agents are often used in such lines as apparel, furniture, and electrical goods. Most manufacturers' agents are small businesses with only a few skilled salespeople. Small manufacturers may hire an agent if they cannot afford their own field sales force, while larger manufacturers rely on agents to open new territories or to cover territories that cannot support full-time salespeople.

- *Selling agents* have contractual authority to sell a manufacturer's entire product line. The manufacturer is either not interested in the selling function or feels unqualified. The selling agent serves as the sales department for the manufacturer. Selling agents are common in the industrial machinery and equipment businesses as well as for coal, chemicals, and metals.

- *Purchasing agents* generally have long-term relationships with buyers and make purchases for them, often receiving, inspecting, warehousing, and shipping the merchandise to the buyers. They provide helpful market information to clients and help them obtain the best goods and prices available.

Retailing

What are three important retail strategies? Retailers primarily sell their products to final consumers. All companies need to decide how intensively they wish to cover any geographic market. Should the product be sold through all available retail outlets? If so, then the company is undertaking an **intensive distribution**. This seems most appropriate when selling convenience goods like tobacco, newspapers, soft drinks, chewing gum, potato chips, bread, and milk. Companies want these products to obtain the widest possible exposure in the market. As a result, they try to make these products convenient for purchase at as many convenience stores and supermarkets as possible.

Selective distribution uses only a portion of the many possible retail outlets for sale of a product. This approach is appropriate for the sale of shopping products and durable goods like stereos, TVs, and furniture. Buyers spend more time comparing competitors' prices and features when buying shopping products. A sale often depends on providing buyers with information on these features to successfully differentiate one brand's product from another. Naturally, producers want to selectively determine where their products will be sold to ensure successful differentiation. Moreover, customers often want other services like installation to be properly distributed. Again, producers are selective in determining outlets and may provide training to outlets to ensure the best service.

At other times, sellers want to undertake **exclusive distribution**, the use of only one outlet in a geographic area. This is most appropriate when selling specialty products like expensive, high-quality sports cars; jewelry; or high-fashion clothing. Because these products carry a certain degree of prestige, sellers often require distributors to carry a full line of inventory, offer distinguished high-quality service, and meet other exclusive requirements. Another common form of exclusive distribution exists with franchises like McDonald's and Subway. Only one outlet is chosen in a given geographic area, and the retail distributors are required to meet strict quality and service standards to protect brand-name integrity.

Types of Retailers

What are the different types of retailers? Retailing constitutes a major sector of our economy. Although around a half million wholesalers exist in the United States, there are well over a million retail stores that employ approximately 15 million people.[17] You're likely familiar with retail distributors because most of your personal shopping experiences have occurred at retail stores. ▼ **Table 14.5** describes the major types of retail stores and lists some examples of each.

Little has drawn as much attention in modern retailing than the growth of nonstore retailing. **Nonstore retailing** is a form of retailing in which consumer contact occurs outside the confines of a traditional brick-and-mortar retail store. Examples include the use of electronic shopping, vending machines, at-home personal selling, and catalogue buying.

▼ **Table 14.5**

Types of Retail Stores

Type of Store	Description	Examples
Specialty Store	A retail store that carries a wide selection of products in one category	Gamestop, Foot Locker
Department Store	A retail store that carries a wide variety of products organized by departments	Nordstrom, Saks, Neiman Marcus, JCPenney
Supermarket	Large, low-cost, high-volume grocery stores that also sell household products	Safeway, Albertson's, Kroger
Convenience Store	Small stores located near residents that are open long hours seven days a week and carry the most frequently purchased convenience goods	QuikTrip, 7-Eleven
Discount Store	Stores that offer lower prices by accepting lower profit margins and sell at a higher volume than department stores	Target, Wal-Mart
Category Killer	Large specialty stores that specialize in selling a particular product line and are staffed by knowledgeable sales staff	Dick's Sporting Goods, Toys "R" Us, Best Buy, Barnes & Noble, Bass Pro Shops
Factory Outlet	Stores owned and operated by a manufacturer that normally carries surplus, discontinued, or irregular goods	Nordstrom Rack, Neiman Marcus Last Call Clearance Centers
Warehouse Club	Stores that sell a limited selection of brand-name food and nonfood items at deep discounts that usually require an annual membership fee	Sam's Club, Costco

The rapid growth of technology and especially the Internet has made it possible for consumers to shop online—comparing prices, ordering, and paying for a product from the convenience of their homes. **Electronic retailing**, or the selling of consumer goods and services over the Internet, is a fast-growing trend. This poses many risks for some businesses that don't adapt to this trend. Online shopping offers many benefits as well. In fact, many small businesses have found the Internet to be the great equalizer. They can establish Web sites offering an interactive environment that allows for the full use of state-of-the-art multimedia to attract sales. In fact, some small businesses are entirely online. The increased competition from online retail sales has pushed larger, more traditional brick-and-mortar retailers to improve their Web sites to complement their in-store sales. Since more of their store traffic is online, these companies can gather information about current and potential customers to establish more personalized customer relationships. Some are able to offer customized product offerings that suit customer interests based on where the customer clicks within the company's Web site and from information gathered from the search engine queries. Internet shopping also allows for companies to go global because products can be sold all over the world from a company's single Web site.

Many other forms of nonstore retailing exist beyond electronic retailing. You have seen vending machines, kiosks, and carts before. Vending machines provide many convenience goods, like soft drinks, at locations where they are most often desired, such as airports, swimming pools, and college dorms. Kiosks are familiar in shopping malls. They are an inexpensive way to sell many goods, as are carts that often sell food on the street. Here are some other important nonstore retailers:

▶ Mall kiosks are a relatively inexpensive way to sell goods and services in a nonstore retail environment.

- **Telemarketing** is selling products over the phone. Sometimes the sales pitches are recorded messages. Many people, annoyed by telemarketers, sign up for the National Do Not Call Registry. However, many consumers do use the telephone to place orders, even though these sales may not have been solicited by phone.

- **Direct selling** is selling goods and services door-to-door at people's homes and offices, or at temporary or mobile locations. Avon and Mary Kay cosmetics, Pampered Chef kitchen products, and Herbalife health products are sold through direct selling.

- **Direct marketing** refers to any aspect of retailing a good or service that attempts to bypass intermediaries. It includes catalog sales, direct mail, and telemarketing. You may have bought products through a catalogue, like clothing from L.L. Bean or Lands' End. Sales from infomercials are also examples of direct marketing.

Retail Organization

There are several different organizational approaches to retailing. The increased competition from nonstore retail sales among companies has forced many businesses to seek out more cost-effective ways to distribute their products. This has resulted in the development of **corporate chain stores**, two or more retail outlets owned by a single corporation. Corporate chain stores attempt to realize economies of scale because their size enables them to buy large volumes at reduced prices. Corporate chains appear in all types of retailing like department stores, drugstores, shoe stores, and women's clothing stores. Specific examples include Safeway (grocery stores), Sears, and Wal-Mart.

In response to the success of corporate chains, other *independent* companies have voluntarily banded together to buy in bulk and to experience other economies of scale that reduce costs. Examples of wholesalers who have banded together to buy in bulk and have agreed to common merchandising include the Independent Grocers Alliance (IGA) and True Value (hardware stores). Examples of independent retailers that have banded together and have created jointly owned, central wholesale operations include Associated Grocers (groceries), and Ace (hardware stores).

Another way to organize retailers is to use a franchise, like McDonald's, Subway, KFC, Pizza Hut, Jiffy Lube, and Holiday Inn. Recall from Chapter 5 that a franchise is a distribution system where a *franchiser* sells a proven method of doing business to a *franchisee* for a fee and a percentage of sales or profits. Franchisees are typically required to purchase necessary items from the franchiser and must meet strict rules and regulations to ensure consistency and quality.

Physical Distribution

How important is physical distribution? It's often much easier to sell products than to get them to their destinations. This is especially true when selling products globally. We mentioned earlier in this chapter that *supply-chain management* involves the logistics of obtaining all the necessary inputs that go into a production process (*inbound logistics*), managing the actual production process (*materials handling* and *operations control*), and managing the **physical distribution** (or *outbound logistics*) of getting the proper quantities of produced products to customers when and where they want them. It is also important to properly manage *reverse logistics*, bringing products back to the producer because they are defective, overstocked, outdated, or being returned for recycling.

Unfortunately, there are tradeoffs between maximizing customer service and minimizing physical distribution costs. Increasing customer service requires rapid delivery and large inventories to reduce the probability of being understocked. But this is expensive. On the other hand, lowering distribution costs can cause slower deliveries and lower inventory levels that increase the risk of being out of stock of a desired product. Given these tradeoffs, the goal of any physical distribution system should be to first determine the desired level of customer service and then work toward achieving that level of customer service at the lowest cost. Those companies that are most efficient at this survive and prosper. Inefficient businesses lose market share and risk failure.

Warehousing and Inventory Control

How important are warehousing and inventory control? Warehousing, or storing products at convenient locations ready for customers when they are needed, is critical for customer service. Two types of warehouses emerge from marketing products. *Storage warehouses* store goods from moderate-to-long periods of time. *Distribution warehouses* (or distribution centers) are designed to gather and move goods quickly to consumers. For example, Wal-Mart operates around 100 distribution centers in the United States. Each center is over 1 million square feet of space (about 29 football fields) under one roof. Warehousing today uses sophisticated technologies to effectively store and distribute products.

There are a host of technologies that allow companies to more effectively manage their entire supply-chain systems. As you learned in Chapter 11, one of the challenges in managing a supply chain is managing inventory levels to ensure there is neither too much nor too little inventory on hand.

Benefits and Costs of Transportation Modes

What are the benefits and costs of various transportation methods? Transportation is the most expensive distribution cost. If a company wants one of its products to remain price competitive, then the selection of the most effective transportation mode is obvious. When deciding on transportation modes, companies also have to consider other factors beyond cost—like speed, dependability, flexibility in handling products, frequency of shipments, and accessibility to markets. ▼ **Table 14.6** outlines

▼ **Table 14.6**

Benefits and Costs of Various Transportation Modes						
Mode	Percentage of Freight[18]	Cost	Speed	Dependability	Flexibility in Handling Products	Frequency of Shipments	Accessibility to Markets
Railroads	42.5%	Moderate	Average	Average	High	Low	High
Trucks	28.2%	High	Fast	High	Average	High	Very High
Waterways	16.5%	Very Low	Very Slow	Average	Very High	Very Low	Limited
Airways	13.2%	Very High	Very Fast	High	Low	Average	Average
Pipelines	0.4%	Low	Slow	High	Very Low	Very High	Very Limited

➤ The pros of using pipeline as a transportation mode include its low cost, but it is not a flexible mode (not many products can travel by pipeline) and its speed is slow.

the benefits and costs of the five major types of transportation according to these criteria. Businesses have to carefully weigh these benefits and costs in making a mode-of-transportation decision.

Recall the story about Ichiro Satou at the beginning of this section. After weighing the advantages and disadvantages of the various modes of transportation, Ichiro decided to make a change. The company had been using trucks to ship its goods. While the speed was fast and the dependability high, so too were the costs. By switching to railroads as the primary mode of transportation, Ichiro was able to cut costs and increase profits to keep the business alive. Ichiro, like all business leaders, was faced with some tough decisions when it came to the distribution component of the marketing mix. Having the knowledge to make these decisions wisely—whether they concern promotion or distribution—plays an important role in the success of any business.

▼ You have just read **Objectives 7 & 8**

Want to quiz yourself? Check out the Study Plan section @ **www.my*biz*lab.com.**

Chapter Summary

1. What is a promotional mix, and what is its function in a promotional campaign? (pp. 399-401)

- A **promotional mix** (p. 399) is the strategic combination of promotional tools used to reach customers to achieve marketing objectives. It includes advertising, public relations, personal selling, and sales promotions.
- Implementing the promotional mix is part of an effective promotional campaign. Promotional campaigns involve six steps:
  - Identify target market.
  - Determine marketing objectives.
  - Design the message.
  - Determine the budget.
  - Implement the promotional mix.
  - Evaluate and adjust as needed.

2. What are the different categories of advertising, and what role do these categories play in business and society? (pp. 402-407)

- **Advertising** (p. 402) is paid, impersonal mass communication from an identified sponsor to persuade or influence a targeted audience.
- Advertising plays several important roles in business.
  - It helps businesses build brand awareness and product differentiation.
  - Advertising has economic benefits as well. It can lower the costs and prices of products. It also provides many jobs.
- Advertising also plays a societal role.
  - Society benefits from advertising because it informs and educates us of new and different products.
  - Advertising can also persuade us in ways that can have positive or negative social ramifications.
- Many categories of advertising emerge from marketing: **product** (p. 403), **corporate** (p. 403), **comparative** (p. 404), **retail** (p. 404), **B2B** (p. 404), **nonprofit** (p. 404), **public service** (p. 404), **advocacy** (p. 404), **interactive** (p. 404), and **Internet advertising** (p. 404).

3. How are the various public relations tools essential to the marketing mix? (pp. 407-409)

- **Public relations** (p. 407) is the management function that establishes and maintains mutually beneficial relationships between an organization and its stakeholders.
- Public relations tools consist of controlled, semicontrolled, and uncontrolled news messages. **Publicity** (p. 408) is uncontrolled and can be a powerful public relations tool.
- Damage control is the effort to minimize the harmful effects of a negative event. It is critical to respond to crises honestly to re-establish a positive image.

4. What are the six steps in the personal selling process? (pp. 410-413)

- **Personal selling** (p. 410) is direct communication between a firm's sales force and potential buyers to make a sale and to build good customer relationships. Establishing and maintaining good customer relationships through personal selling is critical for a firm's success.

- Six steps are involved with personal selling.
  - **Prospecting** (p. 412) is identifying qualified potential customers.
  - Approaching the prospect has two parts. In the pre-approach, the salesperson learns as much as possible about potential customers to determine their likely needs and think about how those needs might be satisfied. In the actual approach, the idea is to meet, greet, and put the prospect at ease.
  - Presenting involves telling the product's story, demonstrating its use, asking questions, and listening to the customers' answers.
  - Overcoming objections involves countering customers' reasons for not buying with reasons to buy.
  - Closing the sale is when the salesperson asks for a purchase.
  - Following up is when the salesperson ensures the customer is happy with the product and asks for feedback. Following up is critical to the establishment and maintenance of good customer relationships that are conducive to new and repeat business.

5. What are the two main types of sales promotions, and what types of tools are commonly used as incentives? (pp. 413-416)

- **Sales promotions** (p. 413) are short-term activities that target consumers and other businesses for the purpose of generating interest in a product—and that have not already been undertaken by advertising, public relations, or personal selling.
- One type of sales promotion is **consumer sales promotion** (p. 414).
  - Tools used for consumer sales promotions include coupons, rebates, frequent-user incentives, point-of-purchase displays, free samples, contests and sweepstakes, and advertising specialties.
- **B2B (or trade) sales promotion** (p. 414) is another type of sales promotion.
  - Tools used as incentives for trade sales promotions include trade shows, trade allowances, cooperative advertising, free merchandise, sales contests, dealer listings, store demonstrations, quantity discounts, and training programs.

6. Why are marketing intermediaries and distribution channels important elements in marketing? (pp. 417-419)

- **Marketing intermediaries** (p. 417) are middlemen in the distribution process. Wholesalers, agents/brokers, and retailers constitute the different types of intermediaries.
- A **distribution channel** (p. 417) is a whole set of intermediaries. There are many different types of distribution channels, including consumer channels, consumer/business channels, and business channels.
- Intermediaries are important because they reduce the costs of products to consumers by increasing the efficiency of the distribution of goods and services.

Continued on next page

Chapter Summary (cont.)

7. What types of services do agents/brokers and wholesalers provide? (pp. 417-422)

- **Wholesalers** (p. 417) provide many services that add efficiency to the distribution of merchandise. These include selling and promoting, warehousing, transporting, financing, and providing market information.
- **Agents/brokers** (p. 418) are intermediaries that facilitate negotiations between buyers and sellers of goods and services but never take title (ownership) of the product traded.
  - Manufacturers' agents represent two or more manufacturers of complementary lines.
  - Selling agents have contractual authority to sell a manufacturer's entire product line and serve as the sales department for the manufacturer.
  - Purchasing agents make purchases for buyers and receive, inspect, warehouse, and ship merchandise to buyers.

8. Why are retailing and physical distribution key aspects of distribution? (pp. 422-427)

- Retailers can cover their markets using an **intensive**, (p. 422) **selective** (p. 422), or **exclusive distribution strategy** (p. 423).

- Several types of retailers exist: specialty stores, department stores, supermarkets, convenience stores, discount stores, category killers, factory outlets, and warehouse clubs.
- In **nonstore retailing** (p. 423) consumer contact occurs outside a traditional retail store. Examples include electronic retailing, vending machines, kiosks, carts, telemarketing, direct selling, and direct marketing.
- **Physical distribution** (p. 425) involves getting products to customers when and where they want them.
- Physical distribution is one of the most expensive parts of marketing a product. In the broadest sense, it entails the management of the entire supply chain.
- Transportation options include railroads, trucking, waterways, airways, and pipelines. Careful measurement of the advantages and disadvantages of these options is important before selecting a mode of transportation.

For an audio file of the Objectives and Chapter Summary, see the Student Resources section @ www.my*biz*lab.com.

Key Terms

advertising   (p. 402)

advocacy advertising   (p. 404)

agents/brokers   (p. 418)

business-to-business advertising   (p. 404)

cash-and-carry wholesalers   (p. 421)

consumer sales promotion   (p. 414)

comparative advertising   (p. 404)

corporate (or institutional) advertising   (p. 403)

corporate chain stores   (p. 425)

direct marketing   (p. 424)

direct selling   (p. 424)

distribution   (p. 417)

distribution channel   (p. 417)

drop shippers   (p. 421)

e-commerce   (p. 419)

electronic retailing   (p. 424)

exclusive distribution   (p. 423)

infomercials   (p. 406)

integrated marketing communication (IMC)   (p. 401)

intensive distribution   (p. 422)

interactive advertising   (p. 404)

Internet advertising   (p. 404)

marketing intermediary   (p. 417)

merchant wholesalers   (p. 420)

nonprofit advertising   (p. 404)

nonstore retailing   (p. 423)

order getter   (p. 411)

order taker   (p. 411)

personal selling   (p. 410)

physical distribution   (p. 425)

product advertising   (p. 403)

product placement   (p. 404)

promotion   (p. 399)

promotional mix   (p. 399)

prospecting   (p. 412)

publicity   (p. 408)

public relations   (p. 407)

public service advertising   (p. 404)

rack jobbers   (p. 421)

retail (or local) advertising   (p. 404)

retailers   (p. 418)

sales promotion   (p. 413)

selective distribution   (p. 422)

support personnel   (p. 411)

telemarketing   (p. 424)

trade (or business-to-business) sales promotions   (p. 414)

truck wholesalers   (p. 421)

wholesalers   (p. 417)

Multiple Choice   Correct answers can be found on page 503.

1. **Which of the following is NOT part of the promotional mix?**

   a. Personal selling

   b. Selecting the appropriate transportation mode

   c. Advertising

   d. Public relations

2. **Advertising that promotes a specific product's uses, features, and benefits is**

   a. corporate advertising.

   b. retail advertising.

   c. comparative advertising.

   d. product advertising

3. **Which of the following describes advantages for television as a medium for advertising?**

   a. Global and interactive possibilities; ease of segmentation; high audience interest; easy-to-measure responses

   b. Good mass-market coverage; low cost per contact; combines sight, sound, and motion

   c. Short life span; lots of competition for attention; poor-quality reproductions

   d. High levels of segmentation; allows personalization; high flexibility; ad can be saved; measurable impact

4. **Which of the following statements is true about publicity and advertising?**

   a. Positive organizational publicity is preferred over advertising because publicity can be controlled by the organization.

   b. Positive organizational publicity is preferred over advertising because publicity is free and is more believable.

   c. Advertising is preferred over publicity because it is cheaper and the message can be controlled.

   d. Advertising is preferred over publicity because it is cheaper and more believable.

5. **A salesperson who handles repeat business and builds positive customer relationships is**

   a. a rack jobber.

   b. support personnel.

   c. an order taker.

   d. an order getter.

6. **The last step in the personal selling process before following up is**

   a. approaching the prospect.

   b. closing the sale.

   c. overcoming objections.

   d. presenting.

7. **Which of the following would most likely be an advantage associated with the sales promotional element of the promotional mix?**

   a. Highly interactive communication between buyer and seller

   b. Excellent for communicating a complex product, information, and features

   c. Good short-term tactical tool to stimulate sales

   d. Reaches a mass audience

8. **Limited-service wholesalers that do not carry inventory or handle the product are called**

   a. drop shippers.

   b. cash-and-carry wholesalers.

   c. truck wholesalers.

   d. rack jobbers.

9. **The use of only one retail outlet in a given geographic area is called**

   a. intensive distribution.

   b. selective distribution.

   c. exclusive distribution.

   d. monopoly distribution.

10. **A giant specialty store that specializes in selling a particular product line and is staffed by knowledgeable salespeople is which type of retail store?**

   a. Category killer

   b. Convenience store

   c. Factory outlet

   d. Department store

Self-Test

True/False Correct answers can be found on page 503.

1. The product itself can be considered part of the promotional mix because samples of the product could be given away to demonstrate its features.
   ☐ **True** or ☐ **False**

2. Advertising can reduce the costs of production and lower product prices.
   ☐ **True** or ☐ **False**

3. A good public relations plan starts with educating the public about the organization's initiatives.
   ☐ **True** or ☐ **False**

4. Retailers sell products to other intermediaries.
   ☐ **True** or ☐ **False**

5. E-commerce is prevalent in all distribution channels.
   ☐ **True** or ☐ **False**

Critical Thinking Questions

1. Why might companies need to devote larger advertising expenditures to new products as compared to advertising expenditures on established brands with larger market share?

2. How might digital video recorders (DVRs) impact media selection for advertising?

3. Discuss how different forms of sales promotions may build or erode brand loyalty.

4. Describe which distribution strategy—intensive, selective, or exclusive—would be most appropriate for each of the following products, and explain why: laundry detergent, cigarettes, Mercedes sports cars, and Snickers candy bars.

5. Suppose you are the distribution manager for a high-tech producer of big-screen televisions. Which mode of transportation would you select in distributing your products to customers and why?

Team Time

Developing a Promotional Mix

The company you work for, FitFoods, is launching a new product: Shine Breakfast Bars, all-natural, vitamin-fortified granola bars. The company has enlisted you and your teammates to design an optimal promotional mix for this product.

Process

1. Assemble into teams of four. Each team member should be assigned as the "lead" for one of the four components of the promotional mix—advertising, public relations, personal selling, and sales promotions.

2. Use the knowledge gained from this chapter to develop a promotional mix for Shine Breakfast Bars that integrates each of the four components. What will be the key aspects of the advertising campaign? What media will be used? What public relations tools will be used? What will a sales pitch for this product consist of? How will sales promotions be implemented?

3. Summarize the key points of the promotional mix plan in a poster or PowerPoint presentation.

4. Present your findings to the class for discussion.

Ethics and Corporate Social Responsibility

Just What the Doctor Ordered?

In Chapter 13, you considered the ethics involved with the pricing of prescription drugs. Now turn your attention to the promotion of these products and the ethical issues raised by such advertising. Read the following scenario and then discuss the questions that follow in a small group.

Currently, the United States and New Zealand are the only two countries in the world that permit widespread use of direct-to-consumer (DTC) advertising for prescription drugs. Such advertising has become big business in the United States—from 1996 to 2005, expenditures on DTC advertising of pharmaceuticals increased a whopping 330 percent.[19] Some people argue that DTC advertising is unethical as it encourages the overuse of medications, preys on the elderly and/or chronically ill, and does not fully inform consumers of drugs' risks and side effects. Others say that DTC advertising puts the power where it belongs—in the hands of the consumers—and allows people to be advocates for their own health.

Questions

1. If you were a legislator voting on a bill that proposed a ban on DTC advertising of pharmaceuticals in the United States, would you vote for it or against it? Why?
2. Is DTC advertising more appropriate for certain drugs? For example, is it more ethical to advertise cholesterol-lowering drugs or antidepressants? Why?
3. Consider the tactics used in print and television ads for pharmaceuticals. What type of style is typically employed? Why? When and/or where are the side effects mentioned? Are these ads helpful in raising awareness of certain illnesses and treatments, or are they irresponsible in giving false hope and/or incomplete information about powerful medications? Explain.

Web Exercises

1. **The Perks of Internet Advertising**
   Go to www.google.com and click on "Advertising Programs." What are the benefits of advertising on Google as opposed to in a nationally circulated magazine like *Newsweek*, a nationally circulated newspaper like the *New York Times*, or a national television network?

2. **Sweet Success?**
   Ensuring ethical behavior is a constant challenge for all businesses, including international businesses. Visit the American Marketing Association (AMA) at www.marketingpower.com and review the AMA's Statement of Ethics. What recommendations would you make to a candy company as it begins to distribute its candy in developing countries?

3. **Read All about It**
   Search the Web sites of a variety of large companies for recent press releases. For example, visit Apple's press release library (www.apple.com/pr/library) or GE's

updates about ecomagination (www.ge.ecomagination.com/site/index.html#press). What type of language is used in these press releases? How does this publicity advance promotional goals? Do you think it is effective? Why or why not?

4. **Personal Selling**
   Read what the U.S Department of Labor has to say about careers in sales at www.bls.gov/oco/oco1004.htm. What are the pros and cons of a career in sales? Is this a field you are interested in entering? Why or why not?

5. **Tracking a Product**
   Use the Internet to research the likely distribution path of a product of your choice. Where was it produced? Through which countries and/or states did it travel? Which intermediaries were involved in its distribution? Make a chart or diagram tracing its channel of distribution.

Web Case

To access the Chapter 14 Web case and exercise, see the End of Chapter Assignments section @ www.my*biz*lab.com.

Video Case

To access the Chapter 14 Video case and exercise, see the End of Chapter Assignments section @ www.my*biz*lab.com.

Finding a Job

According to the U.S. Department of Labor, the average American will have 10 different jobs between the ages of 18 and 38.[1] Clearly, finding a job that best fits your talents, skills, and needs will likely be an important concern throughout your life. In this mini chapter, you'll learn how to effectively market yourself, search for jobs, and interview and negotiate with a company so that your future job searches will be successful.

Marketing Yourself

In order to get your dream job, you need to be able to sell yourself. It all starts with developing a resume and writing a cover letter.

Developing a Resume

A **resume** is a fact sheet that outlines your work history, experience, and accomplishments. It lets an employer know what you've done and what you want to do. There are two main types of resumes: chronological and functional. A *chronological resume* lists jobs in order, beginning with the present. Use this type of resume if you're staying in the same field or just getting started in the job market. *Functional resumes* detail your work history by pointing out your skills and achievements, not your titles and the companies you've worked for. This is a good type of resume to use when you're switching fields. Your skills show employers what you can do for them since your previous job experience may not relate.

Getting Started

Before you start typing, take some time to evaluate yourself. Consider the following:

- What are your strengths and weaknesses?
- What types of skills do you possess?
- What do you want from an employer?

Aside from technical skills, think about your soft skills. Soft skills include personality traits and interpersonal skills, such as honesty, responsibility, leadership, and teamwork. Some employers find these traits more desirable than technical abilities because technical skills can be taught, while soft skills are an innate value.

When you begin your resume, remember that organization is key. Employers generally spend about 15 seconds reviewing a resume,[2] so you need to make a good first impression. Organize your resume clearly, with bold headings and bulleted information; no one is going to take the time to read a lengthy paragraph about your achievements. The following headings can help you organize a basic chronological resume: Contact Information, Objective, Education, Experience or Work History, Skills/Interests, and References.

Contact Information

Contact information is typically centered at the top of the page, with your name in the largest font. Include your mailing address, phone number, and e-mail address. Remember that prospective employers may be hearing your outgoing phone message, so be sure it's appropriate.

Objective

An **objective** is a short summary of the job you're seeking and how your skills will apply to that job. Objectives need to be specific to the job for which you're applying. Generalized objectives don't tell the employer anything about you.

Read the following objective and look at it from an employer's perspective.

> **OBJECTIVE: To utilize my advertising knowledge by working for a successful company that will help me get experience to kick-start my career.**

What position is the applicant applying for? This objective doesn't specify. It's also describing what the applicant wants the job to do for him, not what he can contribute to the company. Employers already know that you want to learn and gain experience; reiterating it only makes you look selfish.

A good objective is specific and short. Here's an example.

> **OBJECTIVE: To obtain a position at Doyle and Associates as an entry-level graphic designer where my creativity and technical ability will add value to operations.**

With this objective an employer knows what position you want and why you think you're the right person to fill the opening. It also shows you're serious about the position because you took the time to tailor your resume to this specific opening.

to continue **mini 4** check out **www.mybizlab.com**.

Financing and Tracking Business Operations

For more chapter resources, go to www.my*biz*lab.com.

p. 442

Financial Needs

▼ Objectives 2 & 3

Ginny McIntyre runs a small business out of her home tailoring clothes. She is so overwhelmed with business that she doesn't have enough space for her orders and equipment. She wants to expand her business into a small shop, but she doesn't have enough money. Where can Ginny find financing for her business?

p. 447

Accounting Functions

▼ Objectives 4 & 5

Arnold Sawyer always thought he was good with figures, and for years he was able to help his niece manage the books for her catering business. Then, after an appearance on a local newscast, sales went through the roof. Could the company mobilize quickly enough to fill the requests? Where was the money going to come from?

p. 437

Financial Management

▼ Objective 1

In an effort to remain competitive, the company that Chief Financial Officer Cindy Li worked for needed to launch a new device to quickly match its competitor's latest gadget. Li was asked to assess the company's ability to pull this off. What kind of financial information does she need to pull together? What are her company's options to finance such a project?

p. 453

Financial Statements

▼ Objective 6

Financial statements help provide insight into a business for management, creditors, and investors. In a previous section you learned about the primary accounting equation; a balance sheet reflects this equation in more detail. Aside from showing whether both sides of the equation are balanced, what else might a balance sheet reveal about a company such as Wal-Mart?

Financial Management pp. 437-441

➤ Financial managers are key to the success of a company. In this section, you'll learn about what financial management entails, what responsibilities a financial manager must fulfill, and how financial managers help guide their companies to success.

The Financial Manager

What is financial management? By now, you should understand that a business is created to sell a good or service, and, of course, to make a profit. Producing, marketing, and distributing a product are important aspects of generating a profit. Even more important, however, is the company's ability to *pay* for the resources required to accomplish these tasks. Without management of finances, there is no business! Situations like the one at Cindy Li's company can arise quickly. Without good financial controls and planning, a company will not be able to respond to unexpected challenges or planned expansion. **Financial management** involves the strategic planning and budgeting of short- and long-term funds for current and future needs. Tracking past financial transactions, controlling current revenues and expenses, and planning for future financial needs of the company are the foundation of financial management.

In most companies, the finance department is comprised of two divisions: accounting (which we'll discuss later in the chapter) and financial management. Just as you might save money to ensure that you can pay the next month's rent, or make plans for a big purchase such as a car or home, businesses must also plan and save. To remain competitive, businesses must make large strategic

Cindy Li had no idea how her company was going to pull this off. In the past, board members had come up with some far-reaching projects, but this one was the most aggressive by far. As a part of the strategic plan, the board was suggesting the company launch a new kind of portable handheld computer to keep up with its competitor's latest gadget. Putting this together would require significant cash and capital investments. As chief financial officer, Cindy was asked if the company currently had the resources to pull off this venture, and, if not, what its options to finance such a project were. Cindy knew that her days would be full for the next few months. ➤

investments such as buying or building a new factory or investing in more advanced machinery or technology. At the same time, they also must ensure that they can pay their monthly bills. Financial management involves setting up and monitoring controls to make certain the plans and budgets are monitored sufficiently so that the business can reach its financial goals.

What is the role of a financial manager? A **financial manager**, sometimes referred to as a chief financial officer (CFO), oversees the financial operations of a company. Generally, a financial manager assumes accounting responsibilities for the company. A financial manager is responsible for planning and managing the company's financial resources, including the following:

- developing plans that outline the company's financial short-term and long-term needs
- defining the sources and uses of funds that are needed to reach goals
- monitoring the cash flow of a company to ensure that obligations are paid in a timely and efficient manner and that funds owed to the company are collected efficiently
- investing any excess funds so that those funds can grow and be used for future developments
- raising capital for future growth and expansion

Although not all companies have a CFO, all successfully run businesses have some person or persons designated to manage the financial needs of a company. In smaller companies, the financial manager may have other business-related responsibilities as well. Some entrepreneurs might serve as both owner and financial manager of a company.

Planning for Financial Needs

How does the financial manager plan for financial needs? A company's financial needs are both short term and long term in nature, and a financial manager must plan for both. In addition, he or she must ensure that funds are used optimally and that the firm is ultimately profitable. In order to meet these objectives, a financial manager oversees three important processes: forecasting financial needs, developing budgets and plans to meet financial needs, and establishing controls to ensure that the budgets and plans are being followed.

What is involved in forecasting financial needs? In most large companies, the executive management team and the board of directors formulate a strategic plan that sets out corporate goals and objectives. For example, among the goals and objectives that Cindy Li's company's board of directors and management team discussed, a priority was to produce a new device to go head-to-head with a competitor's product. As the CFO and head financial manager, it was Cindy Li's responsibility to manage revenues and expenses for this plan. In addition, she also had to develop short- and long-term financial forecasts to ensure that the strategic goals and objectives were financially feasible. Financial managers coordinate with other areas of the company to formulate answers to certain questions: How much product do we need to sell? Do we need to expand to meet demand? Do we have the resources to expand our product line? Financial forecasts are especially important when strategic goals include large capital projects, such as acquiring new facilities, replacing outdated technology, or expanding into a new product line. It's critical that such forecasts are relatively accurate, as erroneous forecasts can have serious consequences.

In developing forecasts, the financial manager takes many factors into consideration, including the current and future plans of the company, the current and future state of the economy, and the current and anticipated actions of the competition. In addition, the financial manager must anticipate the impact such factors will have on the company's financial situation. If, for example, national economic forecasts predict a recession in six months, a financial manager knows such a forecast will affect the company in many ways. Therefore, additional planning is required during general economic downturns to handle the possibility that payments might be harder to collect or that sales could be lower. Because of the result from either or both of these possibilities, plans for expansion of buildings or equipment might need to be postponed.

How does a company know it has enough resources to meet forecasted needs? The accounting area of the finance department generates financial statements. These statements include the income statement, balance sheet, and statement of cash flows. We'll discuss financial statements in more detail later in the chapter, but for now just understand that together they create a financial landscape that explains where the company has been over the current and past years. Moreover, they serve as a basis for management to develop expectations of where the company will be in future periods. Using these expectations, a financial manager puts together a **budget**, a financial plan that outlines the company's planned cash flows, expected operating expenses, and anticipated revenues. An **operating (master) budget** includes all the operating costs for the entire organization, including inventory, sales, purchases, manufacturing, marketing, and operating expenses. The operating budget maps out the projected number of units to be sold and estimated income for the coming year, in addition to all anticipated costs of operating the business to manufacture and sell the estimated level of business.

How are funds made available for large projects? Another component of the budgeting process is the capital budget. The **capital budget** considers the company's long-range plans and outlines the expected financial needs for significant capital purchases such as real estate, manufacturing equipment, plant expansions, or technology. Since capital projects are often financed with borrowed money or money raised through the sale of stocks or bonds, it is important to plan ahead to ensure that necessary funds are available when needed. During the capital budget process, each department in the organization puts together a list of its anticipated capital needs. Then senior management and the board evaluate these needs to determine which

➤ For financial managers, ensuring that the business stays within the budget is a priority.

will best maximize the company's overall growth and profitability. Some requests are routine replacement of equipment or technology and may not need much evaluation. Other requests might be necessary in order to move the company in a new direction and should be evaluated closely.

For example, according to its annual report, capital expenditures anticipated in 2008 for Apple included "approximately $400 million for expansion of the company's retail segment, and approximately $700 million to support normal replacement of existing capital assets, including manufacturing related equipment, enhancements to general information technology infrastructure, and real estate acquisitions."[1] Keep in mind that **assets**, which we will discuss in further detail later, are the things a company owns, which include cash, investments, buildings, furniture, and equipment.

Addressing the Budget

What helps plan for short-term needs? Cash flow is the money that a company receives and spends over a specific period. The **cash flow budget** is a short-term budget that estimates cash inflows and outflows and can predict a business's cash flow gaps (▼ **Figure 15.1**). Cash flow gaps occur when cash outflows are greater than cash inflows.[2] Cash flow budgets help financial managers determine whether the business needs to seek outside sources of funds beyond sales to manage anticipated cash shortages. Cash flow budgets also indicate future investment opportunities due to surges in cash inflow, as well as show whether a business will have enough cash to grow. Moreover, the financial manager uses the cash flow budget to help plan for debt repayment or to cover unusual operating expenses.

Why is monitoring cash flow important? A company can have the best-selling product on the market, but if the flow of funds coming in and going out of the company is not managed properly, the company can easily fail. Monitoring cash flow is important because it measures a company's short-term financial health and financial efficiency.

Cash flow specifically measures whether there are sufficient funds to pay outstanding bills. For seasonal businesses such as ski shops and pool installation companies, cash management is critical to carry a business through the slow months. Dennis Vourderis, co-owner of an amusement park in Coney Island, New York, relies on cash flow to carry his company through the less busy winter months, as his maintenance, taxes, and equipment financing are all on a 12-month schedule. He also needs a buffer of cash to help manage years when unfavorable weather conditions may affect business.[3] Although many investors focus on a company's profitability as an indicator of strength, a company's *liquidity*—how quickly an asset can be turned into cash—is often a better indictor. After all, companies go bankrupt when they cannot pay their bills, not because they are unprofitable.[4] As you'll read later on in this chapter, accountants also play a big role in helping financial managers monitor cash flows.

▼ **Figure 15.1**
Business Cash Flow

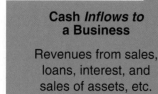

Cash *Inflows to* a Business

Revenues from sales, loans, interest, and sales of assets, etc.

Cash *Outflows from* a Business

Payment for raw materials, stock, labor, insurance, rent, etc.

How does a company know if it's staying on budget? After the budget is developed, it must be compared periodically to the actual performance of the company. It is very important that management compare actual performance regularly to the budget. This generally occurs every month. Without such a comparison, it's hard to determine whether the company is actually performing as expected. For example, let's say you decide to save some money, and at the end of the month, you have $50 in your savings account. Is that good or bad? It all depends on what you originally planned on saving. If you intended on saving only $35, then ended up with $50, that's great. If you intended on saving $75, then the outcome is not as good.

The same is true with the financial performance of a company. If the actual numbers generated by the company closely match the budget, this shows the company is fulfilling its plans. On the other hand, if the actual numbers differ greatly from those projected by the budget, this indicates that corrective actions must be taken. Businesses strive to stay on budget and fund needs through monies generated by business operations. However, there are many situations, even with the best planning, when a financial manager needs to consider funding operations with internal cash sources or finding outside sources to fund large projects.

What must a financial manager consider when seeking outside funds? In your personal life, you most likely have different types of financing to help you manage your financial needs. For example, you may have a credit card to pay for expenses. In addition, you might also have loans to pay for bigger, long-term expenses such as school, a car, or your home. Like you, a company may have several different types of borrowing needs to finance small operating costs as well as large projects. There are many sources of outside funds available to a company. How does a financial manager evaluate the best financing option? The financial manager must first match the length of the financing to the length of the need. Then, the financial manager must evaluate the cost of obtaining the funds and determine whether it is best to finance by raising *equity*—ownership interest in the form of stocks—or issuing debt.

Financial managers or CFOs like Cindy Li have myriad responsibilities. In order to determine the feasibility of the company's launch of a handheld computer device, Cindy developed short- and long-term financial forecasts. Taking into account the state of the economy and the future plans of the company, Cindy found that while producing the new product would be challenging, it could be done. Next she would need to take a close look at the capital budget and evaluate funding options. We'll take a closer look at some of these options in the next section.

▼ You have just read **Objective 1**

Think you got it? Check out the Study Plan section @
www.mybizlab.com.

Financial Needs pp. 442-446

➤ As you've probably heard before, it takes money to make money. When businesses, both large and small, find it necessary to expand, they must make some important decisions regarding financing. In this section, you'll learn about what options are available for short- and long-term business needs, and how business leaders decide which option is best for their companies.

Financing Short-Term Business Needs

How are the operations of a company financed? You may recall from Chapter 6 that different forms of business ownership have varying short-term needs. It's important that all companies have a plan to finance those needs. As was mentioned above, cash flow budgets are prepared to predict a company's cash flow gaps—periods when cash outflows are greater than cash inflows. When these gaps are expected, depending on the size of the business and the cash flow gap, there are several short-term sources available to help fill the temporary gap.

Short-term financing is any type of financing that is repaid within a year or less. It is used to finance day-to-day operations such as payroll, inventory purchases, and overhead (utilities, rent, leases). Smaller startup businesses often fund cash flow gaps first by appealing to friends and family. This is not a recommended strategy as it can lead to severed relationships if loans are not paid back promptly. However, when it is used, it's important that both parties understand and agree to formal payment arrangements. Another approach that many smaller businesses take to fund cash flow gaps is the use of credit cards. Credit cards are a good way to defer payments, but they can become very expensive if credit balances are not paid off completely every month.

Larger businesses with good credit and an established relationship with their suppliers take advantage of another credit relationship to help bridge the temporary gap. Companies will often purchase inventory and supplies on trade credit. **Trade credit** is the ability to purchase inventory and supplies on credit without interest. Suppliers will typically request payment within 30, 60, or 90 days. Deferring payment with trade credit is a good strategy to bridge a temporary cash flow gap because it does not tie up cash unnecessarily. Moreover, using trade credit keeps debt levels down, which is always attractive to outside investors and lenders. However, there are disadvantages associated with using trade credit. Sometimes, buyers are offered a discounted rate if they pay their creditor early. Trade credit will negate this early payment discount. Additionally, if payments extend beyond the trade credit period, delinquency penalties are charged, and, if allowed to accrue, can be very costly.[5] Financial managers must weigh the costs and benefits of paying early for a discount or paying on time without a discount so that their cash is available longer. ▼ **Figure 15.2** illustrates this decision.

In addition to trade credit, often companies will rely on commercial banks, savings and loans institutions, or other commercial lenders for interim credit arrangements and other banking services.

How do commercial banks help with financial management?

Commercial banks are financial institutions that raise funds from businesses and individuals in the form of checking and savings accounts and use those funds to make loans to businesses and individuals. Small startup businesses rely on commercial banks for savings and checking services to pay bills and to store excess funds. Checking and savings accounts are a form of **demand deposit**, funds that can be withdrawn (or demanded) at any time without prior notice.

As a business develops and establishes a good relationship with a bank, the business owners may seek to open a line of credit. You can think of a business **line of credit** like credit on hand, which a manager can access at any time up to an amount agreed upon between the bank and the company. The funds can be withdrawn all at once or in multiple withdrawals during the stated period. This is a common way of covering cash flow shortages, purchasing seasonal inventory, or financing unforeseen operating expenses.

Many commercial banks also offer loans for the purchase of equipment, property, or other capital assets. A **secured loan** requires collateral, which is generally the asset that the loan is financing, to guarantee the debt obligation. For example, if a bank were to give a loan to a company so it could purchase a building, the building would serve as the collateral. If

▼ **Figure 15.2**
Trade Credit
Using trade credit can be advantageous, but always must be evaluated and monitored carefully.

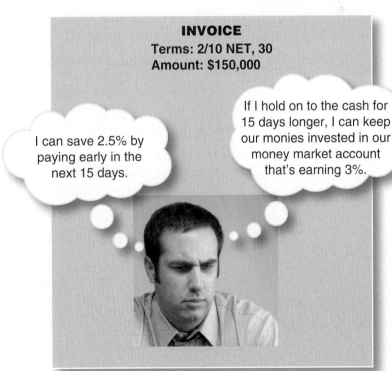

INVOICE
Terms: 2/10 NET, 30
Amount: $150,000

I can save 2.5% by paying early in the next 15 days.

If I hold on to the cash for 15 days longer, I can keep our monies invested in our money market account that's earning 3%.

the company was unable to pay down the loan, the bank would then take possession of the building as a substitute for the remaining loan payments. If the firm has an excellent credit history and solid relationship with the lending institution, it may get an **unsecured loan**, which doesn't require collateral.

Are there other short-term financing options?

Sometimes, a company is unable to secure a short-term loan from a commercial bank. In these cases, an alternative source of financing is a **commercial finance company**, a financial institution that makes short-term loans to borrowers who offer tangible assets as collateral. Commercial finance companies, such as General Electric Credit Corporation, provide businesses with loans but are not considered banks. Soon after starting his own clothing manufacturing business, Ken Seiff needed additional short-term financing. He was looking to expand his product line for the next season, but he had no cash—it was tied up in receivables (money he is owed by customers) and other business expenses. Commercial banks were not interested in helping him because of his perceived risk as a young startup business. Being in the apparel industry added even more risk. On the advice of his accountant, Seiff turned to a commercial finance company, which ultimately helped him through his short-term cash crunch.[6]

One of the strategies that the commercial finance company used in Seiff's case was factoring. **Factoring** is the process of selling accounts receivable for cash. The finance company agreed to give Seiff money, and in exchange it would collect the accounts receivable and keep the money that was owed Seiff's company. The money given to Seiff is equal to the amount his company would have received had he waited to collect the funds directly, minus a fee charged by the factoring agent. The fee applied is dependent on how long the receivable has been outstanding, the nature of the business, and the economy. While costly at times, factoring can be an important strategy for companies to bridge cash flow gaps.

Do larger corporations do anything differently for short-term financing?

Large corporations have the advantage over smaller startup companies in that they have a greater ability to establish a credit or debt rating. Those companies who have a high-quality debt rating can issue commercial paper. When a company has a high-quality debt rating, it means it is looked upon favorably by lenders as being a company that has a good or excellent likelihood of paying off its debt. **Commercial paper** is an unsecured (that is, it does not need collateral) short-term debt instrument of $100,000 or more, typically issued by a corporation to bridge a cash flow gap created by large accounts receivable, inventory, or payroll. Commercial paper comes due (matures) in 270 days or less and is not required to go through the same registration process as other longer-term debt and equity instruments, which we'll discuss next. When companies have extra cash, they may choose to buy commercial paper from other companies that need cash. The company that purchases the commercial paper will make money from the interest that is charged to the debtor. Therefore, commercial paper can be a means of short-term financing for companies in need of cash, and for other companies, commercial paper can be a short-term investment.

Financing Long-Term Business Needs

Why do companies need long-term financing solutions?

Remember that in order to grow, new or small companies need expansion projects such as establishing new offices or manufacturing facilities, developing a new product or service, or buying another company. These projects generally cost millions of dollars and may take years to complete. **Long-term financing** is needed because it provides funds for a period longer than one year. In most cases, a company will use several sources of long-term financing, even for one project.

What are the different types of long-term financing?

In general, a company can choose from two different types of long-term financing: debt financing and equity financing. **Debt financing** occurs when a company borrows money that it is legally obligated to repay, with interest, by a specified time. Contrary to debt financing, the funds for **equity financing** are generated by the owners of the company rather than an outside lender. These funds might come from the company's own savings or partial sale of ownership in the company in the form of stock. The choice depends on many factors, including the maturity and size of the company, the number of assets a company already owns, and the size and nature of the project being financed.

➤ Construction of large capital projects often requires long-term financing.

What kinds of debt financing are available?

For larger projects that demand big loans and long payment terms, long-term financing is available from financial institutions such as insurance companies and pension funds, as well as large commercial banks and finance companies. Most long-term loans require some form of collateral, such as real estate, machinery, or stock. Often, as in a home mortgage, the asset being financed serves as the collateral. Large long-term loans usually have a higher interest rate because of the added risk associated with a large project and the longer term of the loan. The rate of interest is also determined by the prevailing market interest rates and the general financial worthiness of the borrower.

Are there other ways besides loans to raise funds?

Loans are easiest to obtain, especially when a firm has established a relationship with a bank or other financial institution and has a good credit standing. However, there are times when loans aren't obtainable or are not the most economical option; perhaps the rates are too high or the project requires a greater amount of financing than loans can provide. In these cases, some companies have the option to issue bonds. We'll talk more about bonds in Chapter 16, but for now think of a bond as a type of loan; however, rather than borrowing from a bank, the firm is borrowing from investors. There is a formal contract between the firm and the investors that outlines the project, the term of the bonds, and the interest due the investors. **Secured bonds** require some form of collateral pledged as security. **Unsecured bonds**, also called **debenture bonds**, are issued with no collateral. They are only backed by the general creditworthiness and reputation of the issuer.

What kinds of equity financing are available?

If a company is successful, finding long-term funding can be as simple as looking at its balance sheet for *retained earnings*, or *accumulated profits*. Using retained earnings is an ideal way to fund long-term projects because it saves companies from paying interest on loans or underwriting fees on bonds. Unfortunately, not all companies produce enough retained earnings to fund large projects. In particular, startup businesses find themselves with few options for long-term financing. Each business owner can contribute money to the company for expansion, purchases, operations, etc. However, at some point the individual owners contribute as much as they can or are willing to and still need additional funds to keep their business growing.

Without an established credit history, it is difficult to obtain a loan from a financial institution. Raising capital through owner's equity is one of the few options available to a startup operation. Offering shares of ownership in the company to the general public—in other words, "going public"—can be a great option. A company can choose to go public when it feels it has enough public support to attract new shareholders.

If a company does not feel it is ready to go public, it may look for long-term financing in the form of venture capital. **Venture capital** is an investment in the form of money that includes a substantial amount of risk for the investors. Because of the high level of risk, the group of outside investors, called venture capitalists, command an active role in the management decisions of the company. Venture capitalists seek their return in the form of equity, or ownership, in the company. They anticipate a large return on their investment when the company is sold or goes public. Venture capitalists are willing to wait longer than other investors, lenders, or shareholders for returns on their investment, but they expect higher than normal results. We'll explore stocks and equity ownership further in Chapter 16.

How do companies decide between debt and equity financing?

Most companies use debt to finance operations, which increases the company's leverage. **Leverage** is the amount of debt used to finance a firm's assets with the intent that the rate of return on the assets is greater than the cost of the debt. Using leverage wisely is beneficial because a company can invest in business operations without losing equity and increasing the number of owners in the company. For example, if a company formed with $3 million from five investors (who become the company's shareholders), the equity in the company is $3 million. If the company also uses debt financing to borrow $17 million, the company now has $17 million to invest in business operations without having to take on more shareholders. This creates additional opportunities for the original shareholders to make more money. Although there is a cost to borrowing, the intention is that the project or company expansion will ultimately have a positive rate of return after paying for the cost of the debt. However, it can be risky to take on too much debt, so lenders consider how much debt a company has relative to the amount of equity (or assets) a company owns before they issue a loan. A common leverage ratio is for a company to have at least twice the amount of equity as it has debt. If a company is unwilling or cannot take on additional debt, it must consider equity financing to meet its long-term business needs. Companies aim to achieve an optimal capital structure, which refers to the optimal balance between these two forms of financing.

Businesses have a number of options when it comes to financing their operations and expansions. Although friends and family weren't able to help Ginny McIntyre expand her tailoring business, she was able to get a loan to help her purchase a small shop. In a few years, she plans to expand her business to include more staff and additional shops. She will likely enlist the help of a commercial finance company and possibly even factoring to fund this venture. Ginny, like all business owners, hopes that securing financing for these expenditures will lead to beneficial growth and profits.

▼ You have just read **Objectives 2 & 3**

Want a review? Check out the Study Plan section @
www.my*biz*lab.com.

Accounting Functions <small>pp. 447-452</small>

➤ Accounting is often called the language of business because it provides financial information used for decision making, planning, and reporting. When companies are small, it can seem relatively simple. However, as a company grows and diversifies, accounting becomes increasingly complex. In this section, we'll look at the fundamentals of accounting, the types of accounting, and accounting standards and processes.

Accounting Fundamentals

What is accounting? Remember Cindy Li from the first section? She was asked to make a decision about her company's ability to finance a large project. To make an informed decision, Cindy and her staff relied on financial data that her accounting staff prepared. Similarly, Arnold Sawyer must decide how his niece's catering business will acquire the extra funds it needs to keep the business moving. Arnold will need to review the company's financial information and possibly enlist outside consultants before making a decision. Both situations illustrate how accounting helps business managers make well-informed decisions about the financial needs of a company.

Accounting involves tracking a business's income and expenses through a process of recording financial transactions. The transactions are then summarized into key financial reports that are further used to evaluate the business's current and expected financial status. Accounting is not just for large organizations. In fact, as Arnold Sawyer can attest, it is quite important for businesses of all sizes. Accounting defines the heart and soul of even the smallest business as it helps to

Arnold Sawyer was pretty good at handling figures. When his niece Josephine asked him to oversee finances for her vegan catering business, he figured he could handle it. Arnold's background was in sales, but he assumed he was smart enough to handle accounting. He used QuickBooks to create a basic bookkeeping system. Since the company only had a small but steady stream of clients, the accounting side didn't seem complicated. However, after Josephine appeared on a newscast to talk about the benefits of a vegan diet, sales skyrocketed. With the significant increase in catering contracts, the workload doubled. Josephine needed to increase her staff and supplies, but the company didn't have enough cash to cover the initial costs. Arnold wasn't sure what to do. ➤

Off the Mark How's This for an Accounting Goof?

In August 2007, the assessor's office in Carver County, Minnesota, made an accounting goof that affected 34,000 taxpayers across the county. One of the clerks who was entering property values into the county's database typed the value of a vacant lot as $189 million instead of $18,900. The typing error went unnoticed. Not even the accounting software the county used detected anything out of the ordinary. The county assumed it would be getting $2.5 million in property tax payments and planned accordingly. Jurisdictions in the county created their budgets with the error still in place. Taxpayers received tax estimates from the county and thought they were catching a break because the estimates included the $2.5 million payment. No one was aware of the error until the owner of the vacant lot received a bill for $2.5 million and called officials to complain. Carver County officials had to hustle to adjust budgets properly for the following year. Many taxpayers, who thought they were getting a tax cut, were livid because they actually got a tax hike.[7]

"account for" what the business has done, what it is currently doing, and what it has the potential to do. While accounting involves a great deal of precision, there are also some degrees of interpretation in the process of accounting. This makes accounting both an art and a science.

Types of Accounting

Are there different types of accounting? Accounting is a general term, to say the least. Since different forms of business have varying needs, there are a multitude of specialty areas under the accounting umbrella. Let's discuss each area in detail.

Corporate Accounting

As stated in the beginning of this chapter, financial managers must make many important decisions. Some decisions may involve determining whether the company's financial assets are working most efficiently (that is, earning as much money as possible), evaluating what kind of financing strategy is best, or choosing a way to obtain needed funds. The answers to these decisions and many more, are found in the reports and analysis done by corporate accountants. **Corporate accounting** is the part of an organization's finance department that is responsible for gathering and assembling data required for key financial statements. Corporate accounting has two separate functions: *managerial accounting* and *financial accounting*.

Managerial accounting is necessary to make good business decisions within the company. More specifically, managerial accounting is responsible for tracking sales and the costs of producing the sales (production, marketing, and distribution). By doing so, it helps determine how efficiently a company is run. Moreover, managerial accountants help determine which business activities are most and least profitable. Based on their analysis, management is better equipped to make decisions about whether to continue with, expand, or eliminate certain business activities. Managerial accounting produces budgets so senior management can make informed decisions. For example, a managerial accounting budget can help management decide whether it should increase staff or institute layoffs. In addition, by monitoring the activities involved in planned budgets, managerial accountants help determine and anticipate in what areas the company strays from its budgeted expectations.

While individuals inside a company use managerial accounting to make decisions, interested parties outside a company depend on financial accounting to make financial decisions. **Financial accounting** is an area of accounting that produces financial documents to aid decision makers outside an organization in making decisions regarding investments and credibility. Investors and shareholders rely on financial accounting to help them evaluate a company's performance and profitability. Such information is generally found in key documents like quarterly statements or *annual reports*—documents produced once a year that present the current financial state of a company and future expectations. These documents help investors determine whether it is wise to put funds into the company. Banks and other creditors analyze financial accounting statements to determine the business's financial health and creditworthiness.

Auditing

Auditing is another area of accounting that is responsible for reviewing and evaluating the accuracy of financial reports. Large corporations may have private accountants on staff who work in-house to determine whether the company's financial information is recorded correctly and by using proper procedures. Generally, companies hire independent auditors from outside the company to ensure their financial reports have been prepared accurately and are not biased or manipulated in any way. Companies can avoid devastating budget problems, such as the one experienced by the assessor's office in Carver County, Minnesota (described in the Off the Mark box on the previous page), by performing audits.

Government and Not-for-Profit Accounting

Accounting is not only for organizations that strive to make money; government institutions and not-for-profit companies use accounting as well. **Government and not-for-profit accounting** refers to the accounting required for organizations that are not focused on generating a profit, such as legislative bodies and charities. Governmental and not-for-profit organizations need financial management expertise. Although their goal is not to make a profit, these organizations still must distribute and manage funds, maintain a budget, and plan for future projects. Government and not-for-profit organizations must also report their financial activities so taxpayers and donors can see how funds are spent and used.

Tax Accounting

Paying taxes is an important part of running a business. State and local governments require individuals and organizations to file tax returns annually. **Tax accounting** involves preparing taxes and giving advice on tax strategies. The process for filing taxes can be complicated and is ever changing, so companies often have tax accountants on staff or hire an outside accounting firm such as H&R Block or Jackson Hewitt to prepare their taxes.

Accounting is so important to a business that accountants of all kinds are in high demand. In fact, accounting tops CNNMoney.com's list of most in-demand degrees.[8] ▼ **Table 15.1** explains some of the types of accountants that are currently in high demand.

▼ **Table 15.1**

Types of Accountants	
Certified Management Accountant (CMA)	Provides financial information to managers and other corporate decision makers "inside" the corporation and helps formulate policy and strategic plans.
Certified Public Accountant (CPA)	Provides financial information to stockholders, creditors, and others who are "outside" an organization. CPAs are licensed and have satisfied rigorous requirements.
Independent Auditor	Provides a company with an accountant's opinion that attests to the accuracy and quality of a company's financial report. Independent auditors are not otherwise affiliated with companies for which they offer opinions.
Public Accountant	Provides a broad range of accounting, auditing, tax, and consulting activities for individual and corporate clients. Not all public accountants have the designation of CPA. Many have their own businesses or work for public accounting firms.
Private Accountant	Employed by an organization for the purpose of maintaining financial control and supervising the accounting system.
Tax Accountant	Assists taxpayers in preparation of tax returns. Taxpayers can be individuals or corporations. Corporate tax accountants assist decision makers in strategic plans to minimize tax obligations.

Accounting Standards and Processes

Are there specific standards accountants must adhere to? For any financial information to be useful, it is critical that the information is accurate, fair and objective, and consistent over time. Therefore, accountants in the United States follow a set of *generally acceptable accounting principles (GAAP)* that are standard accounting rules defined by the Financial Accounting Standard Board (FASB), an independent organization. Although GAAP provides accountants with general rules, they are often subject to different interpretations, which can lead to problems. Companies such as WorldCom, Enron, and Tyco made

BizChat

Fraudulent Bigwigs Face Hard Time

Since the implementation of the Sarbanes-Oxley Act of 2002, fraud cases being handled by the FBI have risen 70 percent. One bigwig going to jail is oilman Oscar Wyatt, Jr. In 1996, the United Nations set up a program, Oil-for-Food, that allowed Iraq to trade oil for food, medicine, and other needs. This would allow Iraqi people to have basic necessities while preventing the Iraqi government from getting money to aid the military. Iraqi officials began manipulating the system by demanding monetary bribes in order for companies to gain oil contracts. It is

estimated that the Iraqi government collected $10 billion to $11 billion in illegal bribes.

Before the Oil-for-Food program even started, Oscar Wyatt, Jr., was so close to Iraqi officials that he personally met with Saddam Hussein to discuss the release of American prisoners in Iraq. Wyatt was one of many American oilmen who consented to bribes that led to the buildup of the Iraqi military. Wyatt even worked with the Iraqi government after the U.S. invasion of Iraq in 2003. In November 2007, 83-year-old Wyatt was sentenced to 18 to 24 months in jail.[9]

For more information and discussion questions about this topic, check out the BizChat feature on www.my*biz*lab.com.

headlines and fell into financial ruin in the early 2000s due to very aggressive and fraudulent accounting practices. Hundreds of thousands of investors also lost millions of dollars due to the accounting fraud that occurred in corporate financial disclosures. In 2002, Congress passed the **Sarbanes-Oxley Act**. It was created to protect investors from corporate accounting fraud. The act established the Public Company Accounting Oversight Board, which is responsible for overseeing financial audits of public companies.

Outside the United States, other countries have their own agreed upon accounting standards, which may differ from GAAP. Recently, there has been a movement toward international convergence of accounting standards. Most other countries are beginning to accept a common set of country-neutral accounting standards known as *International Financial Reporting Standards* (*IFRSs*). By doing so, multinational companies that have operations in the United States and other countries, such as Toyota, Nestlé, and Guinness, may avoid the need to convert the financial reports prepared to meet their own country's accounting standards into GAAP specifications.

What is the accounting process? When people think of accounting, most think of the systematic recording of a company's every financial transaction. This precise process is a small but important part of accounting called **bookkeeping**. The process of bookkeeping centers on the fundamental concept that what a company owns (*assets*) must equal what it owes to its creditors (*liabilities*) plus what it owes to its owners (*owners' equity*). This balance is illustrated in ▼ Figure 15.3 and is better described as the **fundamental accounting equation**: assets = liabilities + owners' equity.

Does the accounting equation always stay in balance? To maintain the balance of assets and liabilities plus owner's equity, accountants use a recording system called double entry bookkeeping. **Double entry bookkeeping** recognizes that for every transaction that affects an asset an equal transaction must also affect either a liability or owners' equity. For example, say you were to start a business mowing lawns. Your initial assets are a lawn mower that is worth $500 and $1,500 in cash that you have saved and are willing to use to start the business. Your assets total $2,000. Because the cash and lawn mower were yours to begin with, you do not owe anyone any money, so you have zero liabilities. If you were to close the business tomorrow, the cash and the lawn mower would belong to you; therefore, they are considered owners' equity. The accounting statement for your lawn mowing business would look like the one in ▼ **Figure 15.4**.

Now say the business is growing rapidly. You realize you need to buy another lawn mower and you also want to buy a snow blower so you can expand your business to include snow removal. Together these items cost $2,500. You don't have enough cash to buy either outright, so you have to borrow

▼ **Figure 15.3**
The Fundamental
Accounting Equation

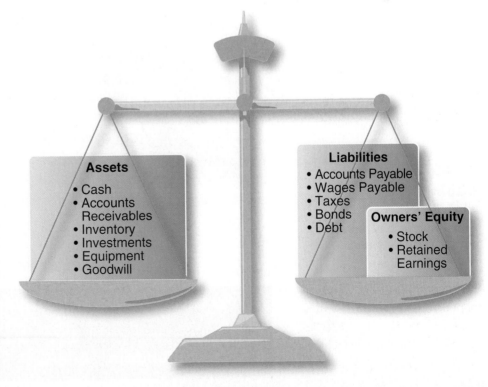

Assets = Liabilities + Owners' Equity

Assets
- Cash
- Accounts Receivables
- Inventory
- Investments
- Equipment
- Goodwill

Liabilities
- Accounts Payable
- Wages Payable
- Taxes
- Bonds
- Debt

Owners' Equity
- Stock
- Retained Earnings

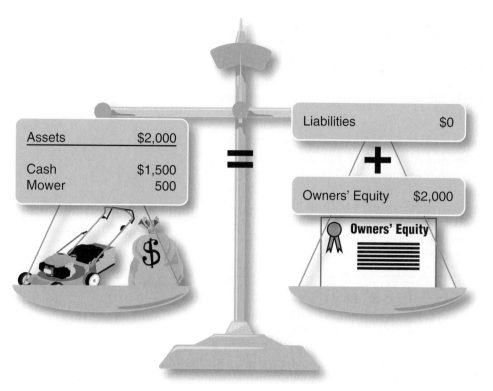

the money. Although you are increasing your assets with a new lawn mower and a new snow blower, you are also adding a liability—the debt you have incurred to buy the new equipment. If the business closed tomorrow, your owners' equity would not change because you could sell the lawn mower and the snow blower to pay off the debt. The accounting statement for your lawn mower business would look like the one in ▼ **Figure 15.5**.

Accounting is necessary for businesses of all sizes to help figure out what they have the potential to do. Arnold Sawyer was able to handle finances for his niece's catering business for a while, but when business boomed he didn't know what to do. He realized he was in over his head and convinced his niece that she needed to hire a full-time accountant to handle these important matters. Having someone on staff who is knowledgeable about accounting is vital to a company's success.

▼ **Figure 15.4**
Business with No Liability
Without any liabilities, assets equal owners equity.

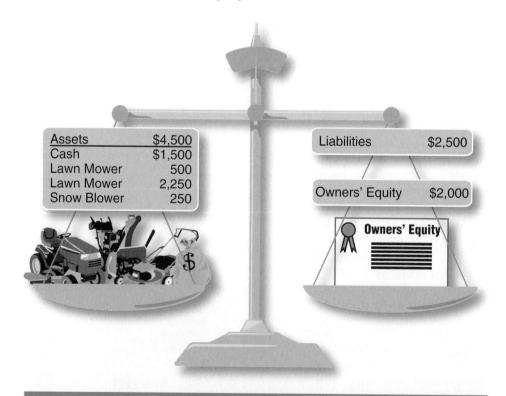

▼ **Figure 15.5**
Business with Liability
Borrowing to buy assets increases assets and liabilities.

▼ You have just read **Objectives 4 & 5**

Want to learn more? Check out the Study Plan section @
www.mybizlab.com.

Financial Statements pp. 453-463

Financial statements are the formal reports of a business's financial transactions that accountants prepare periodically. They represent what has happened in the past and provide management, as well as various outsiders such as creditors and investors, with a perspective of what is going to happen in the future. Publicly owned companies are required to publish three financial statements:

▼ **Figure 15.6** on the next page is a balance sheet for Wal-Mart Stores, Inc. Based on the information given, what can you figure out about the company? For example, Wal-Mart has over $35 billion in inventory. If you weren't familiar with Wal-Mart, what would that number tell you? ➤

- A **balance sheet** shows what the company owns and what it has borrowed (owes) at a fixed point in time and shows the net worth of the business.

- An **income statement** shows how much money is coming into a company and how much money a company is spending over a period. It shows how well a company has done in terms of profit and loss.

- A **statement of cash flows** shows the exchange of money between a company and everyone else it deals with over a period of time. It shows where cash was used.

Let's look more closely at each of these financial statements.

The Balance Sheet

What is the balance sheet used for? A balance sheet is a snapshot of a business's financial condition at a specific moment in time. It reflects what the company owns (assets), what it owes to outside parties (liabilities), and what it owes to the owners (owners' equity). At any point in time, the information in the balance sheet is used to answer questions such as, "Is the business in a good position to expand?" and "Does the business have enough cash to ride out an anticipated lull in sales?" In addition, by analyzing how a balance sheet changes

Wal-Mart Stores, Inc.
Summary of Balance Sheet
as of January 31, 2008
(in thousands)

Assets		Liabilities	
Current Assets		*Current Liabilities*	
Cash and Cash Equivalents	5,569,000	Accounts Payable	44,278,000
Short-Term Investments	0	Other Current Liabilities	14,176,000
Net Receivables	3,654,000	**Total Current Liabilities**	**58,454,000**
Inventory	35,180,000		
Other Current Assets	3,182,000	Long-Term Debt	33,402,000
Total Current Assets	**47,585,000**	Other Liabilities	7,050,000
		Total Long-Term Liabilities	**40,452,000**
Fixed Assets		**Total Liabilities**	**98,906,000**
Property, Plant, and Equipment	97,017,000		
Other Assets	2,841,000	**Owners' Equity**	
Total Fixed Assets	**99,858,000**	Common Stock	397,000
		Retained Earnings	57,319,000
Intangible Assets		Other Owners' Equity	6,892,000
Goodwill	16,071,000	**Total Owners' Equity**	**64,608,000**
Intangible Assets	0		
Total Intangible Assets	**16,071,000**		
Total Assets	**163,514,000**	**Total Liabilities and Owners' Equity**	**163,514,000**

▼ **Figure 15.6**
Wal-Mart Balance Sheet

over time, financial managers can identify trends and then suggest strategies to manage accounts receivable and payable in a way that is most beneficial to the company's bottom line. ▼ **Figure 15.7** is a condensed balance sheet for Google.

What does a balance sheet track? Balance sheets are based on the most fundamental equation in business accounting:

$$\text{assets} = \overbrace{\text{liabilities} + \text{owners' equity}}^{\text{Claims on assets}}$$

It is important to remember that assets (the items on the left side of the balance sheet) must always equal claims on assets, which are liabilities plus owners' equity (the items on the right side of the balance sheet). Let's look at each of these components in a bit more detail, and then see how they all fit together on a balance sheet.

Assets

Assets are the things a company owns, which include cash, investments, buildings, furniture, and equipment. On a balance sheet, assets are organized into three categories: current, fixed, and intangible. These categories are listed on the balance sheet in order of **liquidity**—the speed at which assets can be turned into cash.

- **Current assets** are those assets that can be turned into cash within a year. Examples of current assets include cash, accounts receivable, inventory, and short-term investments such as money market accounts. As you can see in Figure 15.7, as of December 31, 2007, Google had over $17.2 billion in current assets.

- **Fixed assets** are assets that have more long-term use, such as real estate, buildings, machinery, and equipment. Often, the value of a fixed asset, such as machinery or equipment, decreases over time due to usage or obsolescence.

Google Inc.
Summary of Balance Sheet
as of December 31, 2007
(in thousands)

Assets		**Liabilities**	
Current Assets		Current Liabilities	
Cash and Cash Equivalents.........	6,081,593	Accounts Payable/Other......................	2,035,602
Short-Term Investments...............	8,137,020	**Total Current Liabilities**	**2,035,602**
Net Receivables	2,376,312		
Inventory......................................	0	Long-Term Liabilities	
Other Current Assets....................	694,213	Long-Term Debt	0
Total Current Assets	**17,289,138**	Other Liabilities.................................	610,525
		Total Long-Term Liabilities	**610,525**
Fixed Assets			
Property, Plant, and Equipment ...	4,039,261	**Total Liabilities**	**2,646,127**
Other Assets.................................	1,261,443		
Total Fixed Assets	**5,300,704**	**Owners' Equity**	
		Common Stock.....................................	313
		Retained Earnings................................	9,334,772
Intangible Assets		Capital Surplus	13,241,221
Goodwill.......................................	2,299,368	Other Owners' Equity	113,373
Other Assets.................................	446,596	**Total Owners' Equity**............................	**22,689,679**
Total Intangible Assets	**2,745,964**		
Total Assets	**25,335,806**	**Total Liabilities and Owners' Equity**	**25,335,806**

To compensate for such reduction in value over time, accountants use **depreciation** to spread out the cost of the equipment over its useful life. Depreciation helps keep the accounting equation in balance by matching the expense of the asset with the revenue that asset is expected to generate. As of December 31, 2007, Google had approximately $5.3 billion in fixed assets.

▼ **Figure 15.7**
Condensed Balance Sheet for Google Inc.

- **Intangible assets** do not have physical characteristics (you can't touch or see them), but they have value nonetheless. Trademarks, patents, and copyrights are examples of intangible assets, in addition to strong brand recognition and excellent customer or employee relations. Intangible assets are often reflected on financial statements and reports as *goodwill*. Google's goodwill and intangible assets amounted to approximately $2.7 billion.

Liabilities

Liabilities are all debts and obligations owed by the business to outside creditors, suppliers, or other vendors. Liabilities are listed on the balance sheet in the order in which they will come due.

- **Short-term liabilities**, also known as *current liabilities*, are obligations a company is responsible for paying within a year or less and are listed first on the balance sheet. They consist of accounts payable, accrued expenses, and short-term financing. *Accounts payable* are obligations a company owes to vendors and creditors. They are similar to those bills you need to pay every month, such as cable fees, credit card payments, and cell phone charges, and other obligations that are paid less frequently such as taxes and insurance. *Accrued expenses* include payroll, commissions, and benefits that have been earned but not paid to employees. Trade credit and commercial paper make up *short-term financing*. Google had approximately $2 billion in current liabilities.

- **Long-term liabilities** include debts and obligations that are owed by the company that are due more than one year from the current date such as mortgage loans for the purchase of land or buildings, long-term leases on equipment or buildings, and bonds issued for large projects. Google's long-term liabilities are approximately $610 million.

Owners' Equity

The easiest way to think of owners' equity is what is left over after you have accounted for all your assets and taken away all that you owe. For small businesses, **owners' equity** is literally the amount the owners in the business can call their own. Owners' equity increases as the business grows, assuming debt has not increased. It is often referred to as the owners' capital account. For larger publicly owned companies, owners' equity becomes a bit more complicated. Shareholders are the owners of publicly owned companies. Owners' equity, in this case, is the value of the stock issued as part of the owners' (shareholders') investment in the business and **retained earnings**, which are the accumulated profits a business has held onto for reinvestment into the company. The owners' equity (or stockholders' equity because it's a public company) for Google is approximately $22.7 billion.

Analyzing a Balance Sheet

A lot of information about a company can be determined by the balance sheet. For example, just looking at the amount of inventory a company keeps on hand can be an indicator of a company's efficiency. **Inventory** is the merchandise a business owns but has not sold. Inventory on hand is necessary to satisfy customers' needs quickly, which makes for good business. However, there are costs associated with keeping inventory, the most obvious being the money spent to purchase the merchandise. In addition to the initial cost, storing unused inventory incurs warehousing costs and ties up money that could be used elsewhere. An even worse situation can arise if the value of unused inventory decreases over time, causing the company to lose money. This is a big concern for computer companies such as Apple, whose inventory consists of computer parts and other technology-related components that can become obsolete very quickly. For now, understand that it's okay to have a lot of inventory on hand if it's being sold quickly enough to avoid becoming outdated or spoiled. Inventory turnover varies greatly by industry, and companies must always have enough inventory to keep business moving and keep up with competitors.

Ratio Analysis

Although looking at a balance sheet is a good way to determine the overall financial health of a company, the data presented on the sheet can be overwhelming and useless to investors if they are not organized. This is why ratio analysis is crucial when analyzing financial statements. **Ratio analysis** is a comparison of numbers and therefore is used to compare current data to data from previous years, competitors' data, or industry averages. Ratios eliminate the effect of size, so you can reasonably compare a large company's performance to a smaller company's performance. There are three main calculations one can do using information from a balance sheet to determine a company's financial health and liquidity. These measurements are

- **Working capital:** current assets – current liabilities
- **Current ratio:** current assets ÷ current liabilities
- **Debt to equity ratio:** total liabilities ÷ owners' equity

Let's examine these measurements in more detail.

Working Capital

One of the most important reasons one looks at a company's balance sheet is to determine the company's **working capital**. Working capital tells you what is left over if the company pays off its short-term liabilities with its short-term assets.

Working capital is a measure of a company's short-term financial fitness, as well as its efficiency. Working capital ratio is calculated as:

$$\text{current assets} - \text{current liabilities} = \text{working capital}$$

If a company has positive working capital (its current assets are greater than its current liabilities), that means it is able to pay off its short-term liabilities. If a company has negative working capital (its current assets are less than its current liabilities), that means it is currently unable to offset its short-term liabilities with its current assets. In this case, even after adding up all of a company's cash, collecting all funds from accounts receivable, and selling all inventory, the company would still be unable to pay back creditors in the short term. When a company's current liabilities surpass its current assets, many financial difficulties incur, bankruptcy being the most severe. It's important to watch for changes in working capital, as a decline in positive working capital over time can be an indication that a company's financial health is in trouble. For example, a company that is experiencing a decrease in sales will have a decrease in accounts receivable (current assets).

On the other hand, situations like the one faced by Arnold Sawyer and the catering company can arise when a company experiences a sudden spike in sales. It's possible to have positive working capital, but not have enough immediately available to handle a large, unexpected cash need. A good financial manager and accountant must maintain a balance between having enough cash on hand and keeping the available short-term assets from being idle. Because of this, working capital can also be an indicator of a company's underlying operational efficiency.

Current Ratio

Although working capital is an important measurement, it's hard to compare how efficient a company is to the rest of the industry or to its competitors, especially if companies vary significantly in size. The **current ratio** (sometimes called *liquidity ratio*) is a measurement used to determine the extent to which a company can meet its current financial obligations. Current ratio is calculated as

$$\text{current ratio} = \frac{\text{current assets}}{\text{current liabilities}}$$

Google's current ratio (17,289,138/2,035,602) equals 8.5. Current ratio allows for better comparisons, especially when comparing a company to an industry on average. For example, in June 2008, the current ratio for automotive manufacturers was 1.04.[10] During that time, Toyota Motor Corp. had a current ratio of 1.01,[11] putting it slightly below the industry average. Having too high of a current ratio indicates the company may not be very efficient with its cash, but having too low of a current ratio may indicate the company will face potential problems paying back its creditors.

Debt to Equity Ratio

Another way to analyze the activities of a company is to use the debt to equity ratio. Although leverage can be beneficial by freeing up cash for other investments, too much debt can become a problem. Companies with too much long-term debt may end up financially overburdened with interest payments. The **debt to equity ratio** measures how much debt a company has relative to its assets by comparing a company's total liabilities to its total owners' (or shareholders') equity. Debt to equity ratio is calculated as

$$\text{debt to equity ratio} = \frac{\text{total equity}}{\text{owners' equity}}$$

▼ Figure 15.8
Balance Sheet for Google Inc.

This balance sheet shows sources for working capital, current ratio, and debt to equity ratios.

The debt to equity ratio can give a general idea of a company's financial leverage. As you may remember from the beginning of this chapter, *leverage* is the amount of debt use to finance a firm's assets. The debt to equity ratio will tell potential investors how much a company is willing to go into debt with creditors, lenders, and suppliers over debt with shareholders. A lower debt to equity ratio number means that a company is using less leverage and has more equity.

To get a better idea of how ratio analysis is used as a comparison tool, see the information displayed in ▼ Figure 15.8 and ▼ Table 15.2.

Google Inc.
Summary of Balance Sheet
as of December 31, 2007
(in thousands)

Assets		Liabilities	
Current Assets		**Current Liabilities**	
Cash and Cash Equivalents	6,081,593	Accounts Payable/Other	2,035,602
Short-Term Investments	8,137,020	**Total Current Liabilities**	**2,035,602**
Net Receivables	2,376,312		
Inventory	0	**Long-Term Liabilities**	
Other Current Assets	694,213	Long-Term Debt	0
Total Current Assets	**17,289,138**	Other Liabilities	610,525
		Total Long-Term Liabilities	**610,525**
Fixed Assets			
Property, Plant, and Equipment	4,039,261	**Total Liabilities**	**2,646,127**
Other Assets	1,261,443		
Total Fixed Assets	**5,300,704**	**Owners' Equity**	
		Common Stock	313
Intangible Assets		Retained Earnings	9,334,772
Goodwill	2,299,368	Capital Surplus	13,241,221
Other Assets	446,596	Other Owners' Equity	113,373
Total Intangible Assets	**2,745,964**	**Total Owners' Equity**	**22,689,679**
Total Assets	**25,335,806**	**Total Liabilities and Owners' Equity**	**25,335,806**

Working Capital	Current Ratio	Debt to Equity Ratio
Current Assets – Current Liabilities	Current Assets / Current Liabilities	Total Liabilities / Owners' Equity
17,289,138 – 2,035,602 = 15,253,536	17,289,138 / 2,035,602 = 8.49	2,646,127 / 22,689,679 = .11

▼ Table 15.2

Industry Comparison of Balance Sheet Data for Fiscal Year 2007*

Company	Working Capital (Current Assets – Current Liabilities)	Current Ratio (Current Assets/Current Liabilities)	Debt to Equity (Total Liabilities/Owners' Equity)
Google	$15,253,536	8.49	0.72
	($17,289,138 – $2,035,602)	($17,289,138/$2,035,602)	($2,646,127/$22,689,679)
Yahoo!	$937,274	1.4	0.28
	($3,237,722 – $2,300,448)	($3,237,722/$2,300,448)	($2,696,910/$9,532,831)

*Numbers in millions of dollars

Source: Based on Yahoo! Inc. Balance Sheet, December 31, 2007, Yahoo! Finance, at http://finance.yahoo.com/q/bs?s=YHOO&annual.

Income Statements

What does an income statement show? An income statement reflects the profitability of a company by showing how much money the company takes in and how much money it spends. The difference of money in and money out is the profit or loss, sometimes referred to as the *bottom line*. Besides showing overall profitability, income statements also indicate how effectively management is controlling expenses by pinpointing abnormal or excessive expenditures, highlighting unexpected increases in costs of goods sold, or showing a change in returns.

What are the components of an income statement? Recall that the balance sheet relates directly to the fundamental accounting equation: assets = liabilities + owners' equity. Similarly, income statements also work around an equation:

$$\text{revenues} - \text{expenses} = \text{profit (or loss)}$$

The income statement is grouped into four main categories: revenues, costs of goods sold, operating expenses, and net income, which are arranged in the following formula:

$$((\text{revenue} - \text{cost of goods}) - \text{operating expenses}) - \text{taxes} = \text{net income or (loss)}$$

▼ **Figure 15.9** shows an income statement for Google Inc. Let's look at each of these components in more detail, and then see how they all fit together on an income statement.

Revenue

Revenue is the amount of money generated by a business by either selling goods or performing services. If a company has several different product lines or businesses, the income statement shows each product or division in categories to distinguish how much each generated in revenue. For example, Starbucks breaks down its revenue into two sources: retail and specialty. Revenue generated from retail sources is from sales made at all Starbucks stores. Specialty sales include sales made from its Web site and licensing fees from arrangements with Barnes & Nobles, Target, and other locations, which pay for the right to operate Starbucks in their stores.[12]

Cost of Goods Sold

An income statement delineates several categories of expenses. The first category of expenses, **cost of goods sold (COGS)**, is a separate item on an income statement. COGS are the variable expenses a company incurs to manufacture and sell a product, including the price of raw materials used in creating the good along with the labor costs used to produce and sell the items. For Starbucks, obviously, the costs of coffee beans, cups, milk, and sugar are included in COGS. When you subtract cost of goods sold (or cost of sales) from total sales the result is gross profit. **Gross profit** tells you

▼ **Figure 15.9**
Income Statement for Google Inc.

Google Inc. Summary Income Statement as of December 31, 2007 (in thousands)	
Total Revenue	**16,593,986**
Cost of Goods Sold	6,649,085
Gross Profit	**9,944,901**
Operating Expenses	
Research Development	2,119,985
Selling General and Administrative	2,740,516
Total Operating Expenses	**4,860,501**
Operating Income or Loss	**5,084,400**
Income from Continuing Operations	
Total Other Income/Expenses Net	590,783
Earnings Before Interest and Taxes	**5,675,183**
Interest Expense	1,203
Income Before Tax	**5,673,980**
Income Tax Expense	1,470,260
Net Income from Continuing Ops	**4,203,720**
Net Income Applicable to Common Shares	**$4,203,720**

how much money a company makes just from its products and how efficiently management controls costs in the production process. In addition, analysts use gross profit to calculate one of the most fundamental performance ratios used to compare the profitability of companies: *gross profit margin* (which we will discuss later on in this chapter).

Operating Expenses

Although it is certainly important to identify the costs associated with producing the product or service, it is also important to identify **operating expenses**, the overhead costs incurred with running the business. Operating expenses include sales, general, and administrative expenses. These costs may consist of items such as rent, salaries, wages, utilities, depreciation, and insurance. Expenses associated with research and development of new products also are included in operating expenses. Unlike costs of goods sold, operating expenses usually do not vary with the level of sales or production and are constant or "fixed." Outside interested parties (lenders and investors) watch operating expenses closely as an indication of managerial efficiency. Management's goal is to keep operating expenses as low as possible without negatively affecting the underlying business. The amount of profit realized from the business's operations (operating income) is determined when operating expenses are subtracted from gross profit.

Is operating income adjusted further?
Management focuses on operating income as they prepare and monitor budgets. Some feel that operating income is a more reliable and meaningful indicator of profitability than gross profit since it reflects management's ability to control operating expenses. But, it is still not the "bottom line." Adding or subtracting any other income or expense, such as interest payments on outstanding debt obligations or earnings from investments, adjusts operating income further. Lastly, taxes paid to the local and federal governments are subtracted to determine net income (or net income after taxes). **Net income** is the "bottom line" and is usually stated on the very last line of an income statement. For publicly owned companies, however, net income is further adjusted by dividend payments to stockholders, resulting in *adjusted net income*.

Analyzing Income Statements

How do I analyze an income statement?
One of the main purposes of the income statement is to report a company's earnings to its shareholders. However, an income statement reveals much more about a company, such as how effectively management controls expenses or how the company's profits compare to others in its industry. Specifically, the measurements that reveal this information are

- gross profit margin
- operating profit margin
- earnings per share (EPS)

Let's look at each measurement in detail to understand the differences between them and learn how they are used to analyze a company's financial health.

How can I determine a company's overall profitability?
A company's profitability and efficiency can be determined at two levels: profitability of production, and profitability of operations. The **gross profit margin** determines a company's profitability of production. It indicates how efficient management is in using its labor and raw materials to produce goods. A gross profit margin is calculated as

$$\text{gross profit margin} = \frac{(\text{total revenue} - \text{COGS})}{\text{total revenue}}$$

The **operating profit margin** determines a company's profitability of operations. It indicates how efficiently management is in using business operations to generate a profit. An operating profit margin is calculated as

$$\text{operating profit margin} = \frac{(\text{total revenue} - \text{COGS}) - \text{operating expenses}}{\text{total revenue}}$$

Gross profit margin and operating profit margin are equally important to management as well as investors. You may notice they are both ratios, and, as you have learned in this chapter, ratios are best used when comparing two or more companies. Look at ▼ Table 15.3. Google's gross profit (revenues less cost of goods sold) for 2007 is more than $9.9 billion. Yahoo!'s gross profit of $4.1 billion seems to pale in comparison. However, you'll notice that while the two companies' gross profits are quite different, their gross profit margins are very close.

How much of the company's profit belongs to the shareholders?

The portion of a company's profit allocated to the stockholders on a per-share basis is determined by calculating **earnings per share**. The general for earnings per share is calculated as

$$\text{earnings per share} = \frac{\text{net income}}{\text{outstanding shares}}$$

Again, looking at the earning per share number in isolation is not completely meaningful. For example, it might seem reasonable to assume that a company with higher earnings per share will be the better company to invest in than one with lower earnings per share. However, a highly efficient company—and potential good investment—can have a low earnings per share ratio simply because it has a large number of outstanding shares. Still, shareholders and prospective investors monitor earnings per share closely. In some instances, the pressure of maintaining a continued growth record in net income or earnings per share has led management to "cook the books" or misrepresent financial information so that the business's bottom line appears better than it actually is. Such fraudulent behavior was the notable downfall of companies such as Enron, WorldCom, and Tyco, and is the reason why the Sarbanes-Oxley Act of 2002 was passed into law. Therefore, it's best not to rely on any one financial measure and to look at the financial statements and other information as a whole.

▼ **top**

10 Most Profitable Companies of 2007

Company	Profit ($ billions)
1. ExxonMobil	40.61
2. Royal Dutch Shell	31.33
3. Gazprom	23.30
4. General Electric	22.21
5. BP	20.60
6. Total	19.24
7. HSBC Holdings	19.13
8. Chevron	18.69
9. PetroChina	18.21
10. Microsoft	16.96

▼ **Table 15.3**

Benefit of Ratio Analysis

Company	Gross Profit* (Revenue – Cost of Revenue)	Gross Profit Margin (Gross Profit/Revenue × 100)
Based on Annual Income Statement Data for Fiscal Year 2007		
Google	$9,944,901	59.93%
	($16,593,986 – $6,649,085)	($9,944,901/$16,593,986 × 100)
Yahoo!	$4,130,516	59.27%
	($6,969,274 – $2,838,758)	($4,130,516/$6,969,274 × 100)

*Numbers in Millions of Dollars

Source: Based on Yahoo! Inc. Income Statement, December 31, 2007, Yahoo! Finance, at http://finance.yahoo.com/q/is?s=YHOO&annual.

Statement of Cash Flows

What is the statement of cash flows? You have just looked at two important financial statements, the balance sheet and the income statement. The cash flow statement (or statement of cash flows) is the third important financial statement and gives some information that the other two financial statements do not show. The balance sheet is a snapshot of a company's financial position, and the income statement reflects a company's profitability over a specific period. A statement of cash flows is different because it does not reflect the amount of incoming and outgoing transactions that have been recorded on credit. Instead, it only displays cash transactions, similar to a checkbook register. As shown in ▼ Figure 15.10, the cash flow statement organizes and reports cash generated in three business components: operating, investing, and financing activities.

- *Operating activities* measures cash used or provided by the core business of the company.
- *Investing activities* represents the cash involved in the purchase or sale of investments or income-producing assets such as buildings and equipment.
- *Financing activities* shows the cash exchanged between the firm and its owners (or shareholders) and creditors, including dividend payments and debt service.

Why is the statement of cash flows important? The statement of cash flows tells a story that the income statement does not. The income statement reports revenue receipts and expense payments. Because revenue and expenses

▼ **Figure 15.10**

Summary Cash Flow Statement for Google Inc.

Google Inc. Summary Cash Flow Statement as of December 31, 2007 (in thousands)	
Net Income	4,203,720
Operating Activities, Cash Flows Provided By or Used In	
Depreciation	967,658
Adjustments to Net Income	285,487
Changes in Accounts Receivables	(837,247)
Changes in Liabilities	709,679
Changes in Inventories	0
Changes in Other Operating Activities	446,113
Total Cash Flow from Operating Activities	**5,775,410**
Investing Activities, Cash Flows Provided By or Used In	
Capital Expenditures	(2,402,840)
Investments	(372,098)
Other Cash Flows from Investing Activities	(906,651)
Total Cash Flows from Investing Activities	**(3,681,589)**
Financing Activities, Cash Flows Provided By or Used In	
Dividends Paid	0
Sale Purchase of Stock	23,861
Net Borrowings	0
Other Cash Flows from Financing Activities	379,206
Total Cash Flows from Financing Activities	**403,067**
Effect of Exchange Rate Changes	40,034
Change in Cash and Cash Equivalents	**$ 2,536,922**

often are accrued (earned but not paid), the income statement does not tell how efficiently management generates and uses cash. The statement of cash flows, because it focuses specifically on cash, provides this important information. It shows whether all the revenues booked on the income statement have actually been collected. Looking again at Figure 15.10, it is apparent that the bulk of Google's change in cash position came from operations (sale of advertising and search engine technology), rather than its investments. This information is useful to creditors who are interested in determining a company's short-term health, particularly in its ability to pay its bills. In addition, it signals to investors that the business is generating enough money to buy new inventory and to make investments in the business. Accounting personnel, potential employees, or contractors may be interested in cash flow information to determine whether a company will be able to afford salary and other labor obligations.

How is a statement of cash flow analyzed? The bottom number, or change in cash and cash equivalents, reflects the overall change in the company's cash position. If it is positive, it means that the company had an overall positive cash flow. If it's negative, the company paid out more cash than it took in. Recall on the balance sheet in Figure 15.7 that the first line item under current assets is cash and cash equivalents. The difference between cash and cash equivalent figures between periods is the same value that appears at the bottom of the cash flow statement for the same period. The rest of the balance sheet itemizes the broad categories that show what generated that positive cash flow.

Take another look at Wal-Mart's balance sheet at the beginning of this section. Are you able to make sense of it now? Can you explain what each component means, and why it is important? As you've learned, financial statements, including balance sheets, income statements, and statements of cash flow, reveal a great deal about the health and prospects of a company. Although the abundance of numbers and figures might seem overwhelming at first, they can be analyzed and assessed once you know what they all mean and how they are calculated.

▼ You have just read **Objective 6**

Want to test your skills? Check out the Study Plan section @ **www.my*biz*lab.com.**

Chapter Summary

Find your Study Plan and Study Guide @ **www.my*biz*lab.com.**

1. What are the implications of financial management, and how do financial managers fulfill their responsibilities? (pp. 437-441)

- **Financial management** (p. 437) is the strategic planning and budgeting of corporate funds for current and future needs.

- A **financial manager** (p. 438), often the chief financial officer (CFO) of a corporation, assumes the financial management responsibilities. Financial managers generally have some form of accounting background.

- Financial management includes forecasting short- and long-term needs, developing **budgets** (p. 439) and plans to meet the forecasted needs, and establishing controls to ensure the budgets and plans are being followed.

2. How do companies finance their short-term business needs through trade credit, commercial banks, commercial finance companies, and commercial paper? (pp. 442-444)

- It may be necessary to obtain **short-term financing** (p. 442) if cash flow gaps are anticipated.

- Suppliers often offer **trade credit** (p. 443) where payment is deferred for usually 30, 60, or 90 days.

- **Commercial banks** (p. 443) are another source of short-term financing and offer services such as **demand deposit** (p. 443) accounts, credit cards, business **lines of credit** (p. 443), or **secured loans** (p. 443).

- **Commercial finance companies** (p. 444) are financial institutions that make loans to companies, but are not considered banks. **Factoring** (p. 444), selling accounts receivable to a commercial finance company, is an additional way of turning current assets into cash quickly.

- **Commercial paper** (p. 444), an unsecured short-term debt instrument, issued by large, established corporations, is another means of raising funds of $100,000 or more.

3. What is the purpose of each type of long-term financing for companies? (pp. 444-446)

- Large, capital-intensive projects require a different type of financing. Long-term financing is needed when companies take on expansion projects such as securing new facilities, developing new products, or buying other companies.

- Venture capitalists, borrowed funds, or raising owner equity are the primary means of obtaining large amounts of long-term financings.

- **Leverage** (p. 446) is using debt to finance a firm's assets with the intent that the cost of debt will be less than the rate of return on the financed asset. Using leverage can be beneficial unless too much debt is taken on.

4. What are the functions of corporate accounting, tax accounting, auditing, financial accounting, managerial accounting, and government and not-for-profit accounting? (pp. 447-450)

- **Accounting** (p. 447) tracks a business's income and expenses through a process of recording financial transactions.

- **Corporate accounting** (p. 448) is responsible for gathering and assembling data required for the key financial statements.

- **Tax accounting** (p. 449) prepares taxes and advises on tax strategies.

- **Auditing** (p. 449) reviews and evaluates the accuracy of financial reports.

- **Managerial accounting** (p. 448) uses accounting information to help make decisions inside the company.

- **Financial accounting** (p. 449) uses accounting information to guide decision makers outside the company such as investors and lenders.

- **Government and not-for-profit accounting** (p. 449) is required for organizations that are not focused on generating a profit.

5. How is double entry bookkeeping used to maintain the balance of the fundamental accounting equation? (pp. 451-452)

- **Bookkeeping** (p. 451) is a part of the accounting process that is the precise recording of financial transactions.

- Following the concept of the **fundamental accounting equations** (p. 451), where assets equal the sum of liabilities plus owners' equity, bookkeepers use a **double entry bookkeeping system** (p. 451).

- Double entry bookkeeping assures that the accounts are kept in balance. For every transaction that affects an asset, an equal transaction must also affect a liability or owners' equity.

6. What is the function of balance sheets, income statements, and statements of cash flow? (pp. 453-463)

- The **balance sheet** (p. 453) is a snapshot of a business's financial condition at a specific time. It reflects **assets** (p. 440), **liabilities** (p. 455), and **owners' equity** (p. 456).

- The **income statement** (p. 453) reflects the profitability of a company by showing the **revenues** (p. 459) and expenses. The difference between revenue and expense is profit or loss. The income statement can highlight management's efficiency at minimizing expenses while maximizing profits.

- A **statement of cash flow** (p. 453) is like a checkbook register and involves only transactions that have used cash. It reveals important information about a company's ability to meet its cash obligations, such as salary and accounts payable.

For an audio file of the Objectives and Chapter Summary, see the Student Resources section @ www.my*biz*lab.com.

Key Terms

accounting   (p. 447)

assets   (p. 440)

auditing   (p. 449)

balance sheet   (p. 453)

bookkeeping   (p. 451)

budget   (p. 439)

capital budget   (p. 439)

cash flow   (p. 440)

cash flow budget   (p. 440)

commercial banks   (p. 443)

commercial finance companies   (p. 444)

commercial paper   (p. 444)

corporate accounting   (p. 448)

cost of goods sold (COGS)   (p. 459)

current assets   (p. 454)

current ratio (liquidity ratio)   (p. 457)

debt financing   (p. 445)

debt to equity ratio   (p. 457)

demand deposit   (p. 443)

depreciation   (p. 455)

double entry bookkeeping   (p. 451)

earnings per share   (p. 461)

equity financing   (p. 445)

factoring   (p. 444)

financial accounting   (p. 449)

financial manager   (p. 438)

financial management   (p. 437)

financial statements   (p. 453)

fixed assets   (p. 454)

fundamental accounting equation   (p. 451)

government and not-for-profit
        accounting   (p. 449)

gross profit   (p. 459)

gross profit margin   (p. 460)

income statement   (p. 453)

intangible assets   (p. 455)

inventory   (p. 456)

leverage   (p. 446)

liabilities   (p. 455)

line of credit   (p. 443)

liquidity   (p. 454)

long-term financing   (p. 444)

long-term liability   (p. 455)

managerial accounting   (p. 448)

net income   (p. 460)

operating (master) budget   (p. 439)

operating expenses   (p. 460)

operating profit margin   (p. 461)

owners' equity   (p. 456)

ratio analysis   (p. 456)

retained earnings   (p. 456)

revenue   (p. 459)

Sarbanes-Oxley Act   (p. 451)

secured bond   (p. 445)

secured loan   (p. 443)

short-term financing   (p. 442)

short-term liabilities   (p. 455)

statement of cash flows   (p. 453)

tax accounting   (p. 449)

trade credit   (p. 443)

unsecured bond (debenture bond)   (p. 445)

unsecured loan   (p. 444)

venture capital   (p. 446)

working capital   (p. 456)

Self-Test

Multiple Choice Correct answers can be found on page 503.

1. Accounts receivable are considered

   a. a liability.

   b. a fixed asset.

   c. a current asset.

   d. owners' equity.

2. The role of a financial manager can best be described as

   a. outlining the company's short-term and long-term needs.

   b. identifying the sources and uses of funds for company operations.

   c. monitoring cash flow and investing excess funds.

   d. All of the above

3. Ted Hoyt, the owner of an auto-parts store, just placed a large order with his oil filters supplier. The supplier has offered Ted the ability to pay within 60 days before interest is charged on any outstanding balances. Ted is purchasing with

   a. trade credit.

   b. a short-term loan.

   c. a demand deposit.

   d. a business line of credit.

4. As a part of its strategic plan, Gormley Paper Products Inc. is looking to build a new manufacturing facility in another state. It is considering all of its financing options. Which would be a viable possibility for raising the necessary funds for the long-range project?

   a. Issuing bonds

   b. Issuing stock

   c. Seeking venture capital

   d. All of the above

5. Cash flow management is important for which business?

   a. Spring Mountain Ski Shop, which operates between November and March

   b. Lederach Tea Room, which serves breakfast and lunch all year

   c. Tailwinds Airlines, which just had its first stock offering

   d. All of the above

6. Managerial accounting is responsible for

   a. preparing and monitoring budgets.

   b. determining the profitability of business activities.

   c. auditing corporate financial statements.

   d. preparing federal tax returns.

7. Which financial statement shows a snapshot of a company's financial holdings?

   a. Cash flow statement

   b. Profit and loss statement

   c. Balance sheet

   d. Income statement

8. Hunter Wentworth is reviewing last quarter's financial statements and has realized that there has been an increase in working capital. The most likely cause for an increase in working capital is a(n)

   a. decrease in long-term liabilities and an increase in total assets.

   b. increase in current assets and a decrease in current liabilities.

   c. decrease in current assets and an increase in current liabilities.

   d. increase in long-term liabilities and a decrease in total assets.

9. Which ratio tells how much a company makes just from its products and how efficiently management controls costs in the production process?

   a. Gross profit margin

   b. Current ratio

   c. Operating profit margin

   d. Earnings per share

10. The statement that shows how cash is used or generated by the core business of the company is the

    a. income statement.

    b. cash flow statement.

    c. balance sheet.

    d. None of the above

Self-Test

True/False Correct answers can be found on page 503.

1. The cash budget considers the company's long-range plans and outlines the needs for purchases such as real estate, equipment, or expansions.
   ☐ **True** or ☐ **False**

2. Commercial paper can be a means of short-term financing for companies in need of cash, and, for other companies, commercial paper can be a short-term investment.
   ☐ **True** or ☐ **False**

3. Leverage is not a favorable financing strategy since the cost of borrowing will decrease the amount of owners' equity.
   ☐ **True** or ☐ **False**

4. Accounting looks at financial transactions that have happened in the past, and financial management plans for financial transactions in the future.
   ☐ **True** or ☐ **False**

5. Statement of cash flows is analogous to a checkbook register in that it records the cash generated in a business.
   ☐ **True** or ☐ **False**

Critical Thinking Questions

1. Jason worked in a deli for five years before starting his own sandwich delivery store. The business has been quite successful for two years. The quality of the service and the sandwiches has caused an increased demand for his products. Jason now thinks he needs to buy more cars to deliver the sandwiches. He is trying to decide on the most appropriate way of financing the acquisition of two cars.

   a. What methods of financing should Jason consider?

   b. What information will Jason need to have to help make his decision?

   c. How would the financing decisions change if Jason also decided to open another store at a new location?

2. What are the key financial statements, and what is the importance of financial statements? What information do they contain? Which statement do shareholders typically find most useful? Why? What about independent contractors considering working with a firm?

3. Discuss the role of a financial manager in a corporation.

4. Recall Arnold Sawyer from the third section. What advice would you give to him? Why was recording the transactions in QuickBooks not enough?

5. What is the relationship between the balance sheet and the income statement?

Team Time

Industry Analysis

Assemble into groups of four or five.

Process

Step 1. As a group, decide on an industry. Alone or with a partner, pick a company in that industry. The company should be publicly traded so that financial records are easily available.

Step 2. Alone or with a partner, review the annual report and the three key financial statements for the company you chose and prepare a brief analysis of the company's financial situation. Then, calculate the ratios covered in this chapter, and find three other ratios that are meaningful to your analysis.

Step 3. When your report is completed, combine your information with the information from others members of your group into an industry analysis, and determine how each company fits into the industry. Would the conclusions from your independent analysis change once you see the analyses of other companies in the industry?

Step 4. As a group, prepare a presentation summarizing your findings for the industry and each company in the industry and present it to the class.

Ethics and Corporate Social Responsibility

Getting to the Bottom of the Sarbanes-Oxley Act

In 2002, President Bush signed the Sarbanes-Oxley Act into law in the aftermath of some of the largest financial and accounting scandals in recent U.S. history. The intent of the law is to protect investors from accounting fraud.

Reports indicate that complying with the law's requirements has cost U.S. businesses tens of millions of dollars. In addition, critics state that complying with Sarbanes-Oxley has stripped CEOs of their creativity and is making U.S. companies less competitive internationally,[13] although support for the act's provisions is slowly gaining.

Exercise

Research the history behind the Sarbanes-Oxley Act as well as current compliance with the act's provisions. Then, prepare a brief report summarizing your answers to the following questions:

1. What specifically are companies asked to do?

2. How might these requirements affect "CEO creativity" and international competitiveness?

3. What are your thoughts as to the need for and effectiveness of this act? Is it effective, or is it causing more harm than good? Why, and what other measures, if any, do you think should be taken to address these issues?

Web Exercises

1. **Cash Flow Simulation**
   How well would you be able to manage the cash flow of a company? To find out, go to www.bized.co.uk/learn/business/accounting/cashflow/simulation/index.htm and play the Cash Flow simulation. Go through the tutorial and then play the simulation. Even though this is based on a company in the United Kingdom, the principle of cash flow is universal. How did you do?

2. **Balancing a Budget**
   Companies are not the only entities that must create budgets. Cities, states, and other governmental agencies must also prepare budgets, but unlike corporations, they can raise or lower taxes to help balance the budget. However, raising taxes is not always politically favorable, and while lowering taxes helps get the votes, it's not always fiscally prudent. How would you do if you were just hired to close the $3.8 billion budget deficit for New York City? Find out by playing the Budget Game: www.gothamgazette.com/budgetgame.

3. **Exploring Career Possibilities**
   Visit job search sites such as www.monster.com and find postings for financial managers and accountants. What are the job specifications and requirements? What companies are advertising the openings? Are these careers you are interested in pursuing? Why or why not?

4. **Securing Financing**
   Go to the Web site of a local bank and research its options for short-term business financing. What are the terms of its small business loans and lines of credit? Does it offer other commercial financing options, such as factoring? If you were going to open a small business, how would you go about financing it, based on what you learned?

5. **Analyzing Current Ratios**
   Visit www.reuters.com/finance/industries/allIndustries and locate the current ratios for several industries of your choice. How do they compare? What does this number tell you about the industry? What conclusions can you draw based on your findings?

Web Case

To access the Chapter 15 Web case and exercise, see the End of Chapter Assignments section @ www.my*biz*lab.com.

Video Case

To access the Chapter 15 Video case and exercise, see the End of Chapter Assignments section @ www.my*biz*lab.com.

chapter 16

Securities and Investments

▼ Objectives 1–9

1. What are the pros and cons of debt and equity financing? (p. 471)

2. How do companies issue **bonds** and **stocks**? (p. 474)

3. How do **risk return relationships**, risk tolerance, and **asset allocations** relate to the fundamentals of investment? (p. 476)

4. What are the different investment categories of stocks, and how does the stock trade process work? (p. 480)

5. What is stock performance, and what are the factors that lead to changes in stock price? (p. 484)

6. What are the different types and characteristics of bonds, and how is the safety of bonds evaluated? (p. 487)

7. What is the difference among **bond mutual funds**, **money market funds**, and **equity funds**? (p. 490)

8. What are the advantages and disadvantages of **mutual fund** investments? (p. 491)

9. What is an **option** or a **futures contract**? (p. 493)

For more chapter resources, go to www.my*biz*lab.com.

p. 476

Investment Fundamentals
▼ Objective 3
Saving money can be a difficult task for full- or part-time students, but that doesn't mean you're not interested in saving for your long-term goals now. Where do you begin? How do you know what type of investments are best for you?

p. 480

Investing in Stocks
▼ Objectives 4 & 5
When Gina Smith was young, her grandparents invested money for her in Walt Disney, Inc., stock. Now Gina has her first "real" job. She wants to use her earnings to try her hand at the stock market and see what she can make of it. How can she decide in which stocks to invest? How can she buy them?

p. 487

Investing in Bonds
▼ Objective 6
Dennis Sanchez, 55, is starting to think about retirement. He is interested in making some low-risk investments that will also generate income. Dennis believes investing in bonds might be his best option. What type of bonds should he look into?

p. 471

Choosing between Debt and Equity
▼ Objectives 1 & 2
Joseph and Sean were planning large capital growth for their companies. They needed capital and knew they had to go to outside investors for funds. Should they use bonds? Should they use stocks? What factors are involved when they make the decision?

p. 490

Investing in Mutual Funds and Other Opportunities
▼ Objectives 7–9
Keri and Alex Young recently got married and want to start investing in their future immediately. After wedding, honeymoon, and moving expenses, they have only about $2,000 to invest. Why would mutual funds be a good place for them to begin investing?

Choosing between **Debt** and **Equity** pp. 471-475

> As we discussed in Chapter 15, in the process of business expansion, business owners may face the need to raise funds to finance a large capital project. The project may involve building a new factory or corporate office, acquiring another company, expanding into a new product line, buying updated machinery or technology, or just general expansion or added liquidity. For large capital-intensive projects or general expansion, business owners can use **securities**—investment instruments such as *bonds* (debt) or *stock* (equity). The choice between financing large projects with debt or equity is a fundamental decision. Managers can reach the best decision by understanding the financing needs of the project itself and the impact the financing decision has on corporate earnings, cash flow, and taxes. In addition, a company must take into consideration how much debt it already has before issuing bonds or whether it wants to dilute ownership by issuing stock. Lastly, the company must also consider external factors at the time of financing, such as the state of the bond or stock market, the economy, and the anticipated interest of the investors.

Three years ago, Joseph Cortez secured equity investments from a venture capital group to help his company establish a presence in Europe. Since then, his company has continued to expand faster than he expected. Joseph knew that to secure the long-term success of the company, he needed to enter the Asian and Australian markets. Meanwhile, Sean Hendricks, president of an automotive dealership, was looking for capital to finance the acquisition of more dealerships. How should each company meet its financing needs? Should it issue company stock or bonds? Would one option work better for a particular company? What factors would each company need to consider? >

Financing with Bonds (Debt)

Why finance with bonds? In our personal lives, when we want to buy something such as a house or a car that costs more than what we have saved, our best option is to borrow money. We take out a loan (such as a car loan or mortgage) specifically to pay for an item, and that item is used as collateral in case the debt obligations are not satisfied. Similarly, when a company has a project or desired asset that it cannot finance with existing company assets, it can take out a business loan. As we discussed in Chapter 15, common lenders include banks, finance companies, credit card companies, and private corporations. Eventually, a company's financing needs may grow beyond what these common lenders can provide. In these cases, companies may use bonds to acquire the needed funds. **Bonds** are issued by companies or governments with the purpose of raising capital to finance a large project. Investors loan money to a company by purchasing bonds. In return, the investors receive interest on the bonds they purchase.

What are the advantages of financing with bonds? Financing with bonds allows a company to use money from investors to create or obtain business assets. By doing so, companies can finance the project or asset instead of using business profits, thus allowing companies to use their monies more efficiently by retaining profits for other business uses or using them to pay a return to the owners of the company. Although there are costs associated with bond financings, it is worth assuming those costs as long as the project or asset that the company is financing will generate a greater return. In addition, as we'll discuss later, financing with equity by issuing stock dilutes ownership of a company. For many companies, giving up ownership or control of the business is not a feasible or desirable option. Unlike shareholders, bondholders have no voice or control in how the business is managed. Their only requirement is that their loan is paid back on time and with interest.

What must be considered before financing with bonds? As attractive as bond financing sounds, financial managers must consider several factors before deciding to finance with bonds. First and foremost, the cost of the loan—the rate of interest the lender will demand—is an important consideration. If the interest rate is too high, it can force the cost of the project into something that is not affordable or that just doesn't make economic sense. A high interest rate may provoke the company to consider a different line of financing or to scrap the project until interest rates are more attractive. The interest rate is determined by a combination of many factors, including *issuer risk*—whether the lender thinks the company can meet its obligations to pay back the loan. As the risk increases, so does the interest rate. Often, as you'll see later in this chapter, issuers use *bond insurance* to help lower the risk. Although there is a cost to having such insurance, the amount of money saved by having a lower interest rate is greater than the cost of bond insurance.

In addition to issuer risk, the *length of the bond term* affects the rate. Longer-term bonds have a greater chance of default; therefore, they carry additional risk and a higher interest rate. Last, *the general state of the economy* affects the rate. Before making a final decision to issue bonds, a financial manager must also consider how this additional debt obligation affects the overall financial health of the company. From a balance sheet perspective, too much debt may impair the company's credit rating. The statement of cash flows will help determine whether there will be sufficient cash flow to repay the debt. Too much stress on cash flow can quickly launch the company into a disastrous financial tailspin.

How do companies pay back their bond debt? There are two types of payments made to bond investors: interest and principal. Bondholders periodically receive interest payments in amounts and at the specified times arranged in the bond agreement. Most interest payments are semi-annual. The amount of interest is calculated on the amount of principal outstanding and the periodic interest rate associated with the debt. So, if you held a $10,000 bond with a 5 percent interest rate, paid semi-annually, you would receive $250 twice a year. At the end of the loan period, the company is responsible for paying you the entire initial amount you invested (in this case, $10,000). To ensure there is enough money at the end of the loan period to pay off all the bondholders, companies set aside money annually into a **sinking fund**—a type of savings fund in which companies deposit money regularly to help repay a bond issue. ▼ **Figure 16.1** explains the payment cycle of a bond issue.

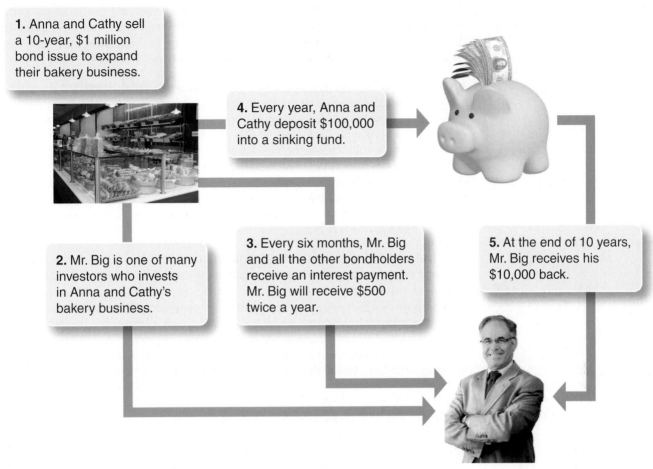

1. Anna and Cathy sell a 10-year, $1 million bond issue to expand their bakery business.

2. Mr. Big is one of many investors who invests in Anna and Cathy's bakery business.

3. Every six months, Mr. Big and all the other bondholders receive an interest payment. Mr. Big will receive $500 twice a year.

4. Every year, Anna and Cathy deposit $100,000 into a sinking fund.

5. At the end of 10 years, Mr. Big receives his $10,000 back.

▼ **Figure 16.1**
Payment Cycle of Bond Issue

Financing with Stock (Equity)

Why finance with stock (equity)? The most common forms of financing for small businesses are personal savings or contributions from family, friends, or business associates. As a business grows, venture capital or funds from angel investors are also possible sources of new capital, but eventually, those options are not sufficient to finance large capital needs. Companies issue stock (often referred to as equity) to finance long-term general funding and ongoing expansion rather than a specific project or need. *Equity* is money that is received in exchange for ownership in a business. **Stock** is a unit of ownership in a company that is sold with the intention of raising capital to finance ongoing or future projects and expansions.

Are there disadvantages to financing with stock? The biggest disadvantage that financing with stock brings is a dilution of ownership. Especially in smaller companies, new stock owners may have a dramatic impact on the way a business operates and is managed. Shareholders do not have direct control over the day-to-day management of a company, but they do have a say in the composition of the board of directors. This means that although shareholders do not directly control how a company is managed, they do directly control who manages the company. As a result, shareholders can have a strong influence on management's decisions. For example, companies are not legally required to pay **dividends**—payments made from a portion of a company's profits—to shareholders. However, when profits are no longer required to fund corporate growth, the board of directors or management may choose to pay dividends in an effort to increase the shareholders' rates of return. These payments are made after taxes and are not tax deductible for the company.

What are the advantages to financing with stock? Unlike bonds and other forms of debt, equity financing does not need to be repaid, even if the company goes bankrupt, and no assets need to be pledged as collateral. In addition, financing with equity enables the company to retain cash and profits in the company rather than using the funds to make interest and principal payments. In many instances, financing with equity can make the balance sheet look stronger, as high levels of debt can be problematic to lenders and investors.

How does a company choose between debt and equity? In reality, companies use both debt and equity to finance projects and business expansion. It is important to note that although debt and equity financing can be used simultaneously, they are very different and should not be considered as substitutes for one another. Instead, they should be viewed as complementary financing, and eventually most large companies will use both types of financing. ▼ **Table 16.1** summarizes the differences between financing with debt and financing with equity. The overall goal is to strike a balance between debt and equity, to take advantage of the positives of each type of financing option, and to minimize the negative consequences that too much of each option might bring.

Are there guidelines for debt and equity levels? The balance between debt and equity varies according to industry and size of the business. For example, capital-intensive manufacturing industries, such as car manufacturers, will have more debt than service industries such as health care providers. Other industries that are expanding rapidly but have large capital reserves, such as computer hardware manufacturers, have a minimal need for debt or equity financing. As we discussed in Chapter 15, one measure of a company's financial leverage is determined by its debt to equity ratio (or total liabilities divided by shareholders' equity).

Primary Security Markets

How do companies issue bonds? Once the decision has been made that bonds are the best financing option, the financial manager contacts a financial advisory firm for expertise. Issuing bonds is a very complex financial and legal process that requires expert advice on the marketplace, timing of the issue, issuing price, structure of the bonds, and other factors. A **financial advisory firm** is a firm that serves as an intermediary between a company issuing the bonds and the investors who purchase the bonds.

Before the sale of the bonds, the financial advisors prepare required documents for filing with the **Securities and Exchange Commission (SEC)**, the federal agency that regulates and governs the securities industry. Financial advisors also help set the price for the bond issue and take the lead in forming and managing a group of financial advisory firms to underwrite, or purchase, the newly issued bonds. In addition to a managing fee, financial advisors make their money by initially purchasing all the bonds at a discounted price and then quickly selling them to investors at a higher price. These transactions take place in the **capital market**, an arena where companies and governments raise long-term funds by selling stocks and bonds and other securities. The

▼ **Table 16.1**

Debt or Equity Financing: What Does Each Mean for the Company?	
Debt	**Equity**
Company profits are used to repay debt, but eventually only shared by company owners.	Company profits retained or shared by shareholders.
Must be repaid or refinanced. Requires regular interest payments.	No required payments to shareholders.
Company must generate cash flow to pay interest and principal.	Company is not required to pay dividends out of cash flow. Dividends, if paid, are out of profits.
Collateral assets are usually required.	No collateral required.
Interest payments are tax deductible.	Dividend payments are not tax deductible.
Debt does not impact control of the company.	Equity requires shared control of the company and may impose restrictions.

primary market is part of the capital market that deals specifically with new bond and stock issues. Since it can take months or years to structure a bond issue successfully, financial advisors have time to generate interest and locate potential buyers for the bonds well ahead of the date of issuance, thus reducing their risk and ensuring the success of the initial issuance.

Do companies issue stocks in the same way as bonds? In essence, yes, stocks are issued in the same manner as bonds, with a few minor differences. The first sale of stock to the public by a company is called an **initial public offering (IPO)**. Similar to the financing of a bond, a financial advisor coordinates the documentation preparation and filing with the SEC. A prospectus is one of the required documents. A **prospectus** is a formal legal document that provides details about an investment. The prospectus helps investors make informed decisions about a new investment. Financial advisors also establish the best timing for the public sale and determine the initial selling price. The advisory firm or bank, along with several other banks, forms a group or syndicate to underwrite the IPO. The syndicate then purchases the stock and sells it back to the public.

The buyers of an IPO are generally large institutional buyers, such as insurance companies and large corporate pension plans, as opposed to individual buyers. The underwriters want to sell the issue as quickly as possible to receive a return on their purchase. Because institutional buyers are more likely to buy large quantities of the IPO, it is ultimately more efficient to sell to them than to sell the IPO in little pieces to individual investors. This is tolerable for the individual investor since buying IPOs is a risky, less desirable venture. As you'll read in the next section of this chapter, investing in stocks requires a lot of analysis to ensure you're making the right decision. Stocks that have been on the market for a while are easier to analyze because you can examine their history. IPOs, by their very nature, have no historical information on which to base any analysis. Unless an investor has specific knowledge of the industry or the company itself, it's best to wait to buy shares of the company in the **secondary market**, the market in which investors purchase securities from other investors rather than directly from the issuing company.

After learning about the pros and cons of financing with debt and equity, have your answers to the questions at the beginning of the section changed? When it comes to deciding how to finance the expansion of a business, there are many factors involved, such as current debt, ownership dilution, the state of the bond and stock markets, and the interests of investors. The decision is not always obvious, as the ever-changing state of the economy determines which choice is more cost effective. Also, business owners must decide if they are willing to compromise the vision they have for their company by allowing stockholders to have a say in company decisions. There is no easy answer to this question, as Joseph Cortez and Sean Hendricks discovered. After weighing the pros and cons of both options, Joseph decided to finance the expansion of his company into the Asian and Australian market with bonds. In contrast, Sean decided that stocks were the best way to finance the ongoing expansion of his automotive company. Joseph and Sean felt confident that their decisions would help their companies achieve growth and maintain a good balance between debt and equity financing.

▼ You have just read **Objectives 1 & 2**

Think you got it? Check out the Study Plan section @
www.my*biz*lab.com.

Investment Fundamentals pp. 476-479

You work hard for your money and most likely, every penny earned has a specific purpose: rent, gas, clothing, food, and entertainment. Ideally, you're also saving by setting aside money on a regular basis. Saving is an important function in your personal financial planning. But often any extra funds are set aside to meet short-term goals like buying a new car or planning a vacation. What about your long-term goals such as buying a house, starting your own company, having children, or retiring? Are you saving for those goals? Although it is tempting to regard saving for long-term goals as a concern for the future, making steps toward meeting your long-term goals now can increase your chances of meeting those goals in the future dramatically.

➤ Saving money by depositing funds into a bank is a way to begin to let your money make money by earning interest. Because most savings accounts are insured by the Federal Deposit Insurance Corporation, you're convinced this is a good strategy since you're guaranteed to receive your money at any time, plus interest earned. However, depending on your long-term needs, the amount your money will earn in a savings account might not be enough. Although saving is important, it isn't the only way to make money. In this section, you'll learn another way of reaching your financial goals: investing.

The Risks and Rewards of Investing

I save my money, isn't that enough? The interest rates for savings accounts and other short-term, low-risk investments are relatively low. In addition, your savings are further compromised by taxes and inflation. To reach your long-term financial goals, you'll most likely need to have your money work harder.

How can I make my money work harder for me? With time on your side, if you continue to save regularly, your savings will accumulate. How much you end up with depends on two things: time and quantity. The sooner you begin to save and the more frequently you put money into savings makes a big difference in the amount accumulated in the end. Keeping your money in a bank and having it build interest will let your savings grow quicker than if you were to just tuck it under your mattress, but there are other options to investigate. To illustrate the power of having your savings work for you, compare the following situations. Imagine if your grandparents began a savings account for you the day you were born. Every month, they deposit $100. On your 16th birthday, the account is worth

I Can't Lose Money by Saving, Right?

It's much safer to simply save your money in a bank account than risk losing it in investments, right? Perhaps. But there are forces beyond your control that you must consider: inflation and taxes. Even after diligent savings, there is still a distinct possibility that you might, over time, lose money due to the effects of inflation and taxes.

Let's say you saved $10 each month for three years in a savings account that earns 4.5 percent annually (although many savings accounts earn less interest than this). If you didn't withdraw any money, at the end of the three-year period, you would have $384.66. That's pretty good considering that if you had just put the money away under your mattress, at the end of three years, you would have only $360. So, just by putting the money in a savings account, you have acquired $24.66. Or have you? Unfortunately, you have to pay taxes on that $24.66. Assuming you're at a 15 percent income tax bracket, you owe $3.70 to Uncle Sam, reducing your earnings to $20.96. Now, consider that inflation is running at a rate of

about 3 percent a year. That means that for every dollar you have, you lose three cents every year in buying power. Therefore, had you just put $360 under your mattress, after three years, because of inflation, it would be worth only $344.69 ($15.31 eroded due to inflation). The money you invested also loses value due to inflation. After deductions for taxes and inflation, your invested money would be worth only $364.29. The entire earnings your savings has generated is almost lost because of two things you have no control over: inflation and taxes. In fact, you're almost where you started, earning only $4.29 after three years of saving!

Although savings accounts help offset the effects of inflation, they do not help you build wealth. Savings accounts are great to keep a "rainy day" account for those unexpected emergencies and short-term cash needs; however, if you are trying to save for a house, college tuition, or retirement, it would be very hard to meet your goals by investing in this type of low-interest account. To achieve big goals, you'll need to make your money work harder.

For more information and discussion questions about this topic, check out the BizChat feature on www.mybizlab.com.

$19,200, and you have the choice to take the money and buy a car or to continue to save the money. Either way, your grandparents will stop contributing to your savings account. As tempting as it is to buy a new car, your father explains that if you keep the money in the bank, earning 4.5 percent interest each year, and if you don't touch it until you are 65, you will have $165,958 to contribute to your retirement. Alternatively, you could put the $19,200 into a conservative investment portfolio that would earn 8.5 percent on average. When you reach 65, you would have over one million dollars—$1,045,582! What would you decide to do?

Investment Risk

Isn't investing too risky? As the above situation illustrates, when you invest the money rather than save it in a bank, your money will have the potential to grow even more. However, investing is using money to buy an asset where there is a chance of losing part or all of your initial investment. Investing and saving are fundamentally different because of the risk involved in each process. Savings has very little, if any, risk, whereas investing has some inherent risk. To determine whether investing is worth the risk, you must know how much risk you can tolerate. The less tolerant you are of risk, the fewer investment chances you can and should take. There are investment strategies that take on less risk than others, though keep in mind that less risky investments will present the least opportunity for return, so you might need to adjust your goals depending on your risk tolerance levels. There is a direct relationship between risk and return for all securities, with the least risky

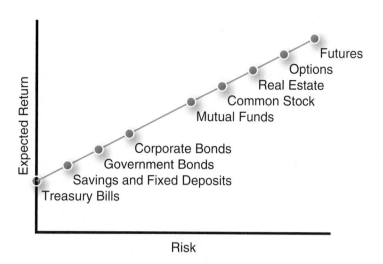

▼ **Figure 16.2**

Risk Return Relationships

investments offering the lowest amount of return and vice-versa. This relationship is knows as a **risk return relationship**. ▼ **Figure 16.2** shows the risk return relationships of various investment vehicles. As you can see, the least risky investments offer the least amount of return. If reducing risk is a necessity, then you need to increase the amount of money you invest, increase the length of time to invest, or lower your expectations.

How do I know my risk tolerance? Most of us have a good idea of how tolerant we are of risk. Your current behavior with money and other situations are indications of whether you are conservative, moderate, aggressive, or somewhere in between. There are also several tests that you can take online to help quantify your tolerance level. The bottom line to risk tolerance is answering this question: "Are my investments going to keep me awake at night with worry?" If the answer is "yes," then you need to reduce the risk level of your investments, and perhaps lower your expectations accordingly. Over time, your tolerance to risk can change depending on your knowledge level and financial situation. As you become more secure financially, you might be willing to risk losing some money for the possibility of earning more. As you begin to learn more about investing, you may be more comfortable with evaluating some of the risks you will take, thus increasing your risk tolerance.

How do I start investing? Depending on how much money you have to invest, you might start investing by purchasing stock in one or two companies or by investing in a mutual fund. We'll discuss both investment options in more detail later in the chapter. As you invest, you should keep in mind two strategies that help to minimize your risk: *diversification* and *asset allocation*. Both strategies center on the notion of not putting all your eggs in one basket to avoid the possibility of losing everything because of one bad investment.

Diversification is having a variety of investments in your portfolio, such as different types of companies in different industries. For example, assume you had $6,000 to invest. You have the option of putting all your money into one company that is growing strong and has great potential for long-term advancements. You also have the option to diversify your holdings and put $1,500 into four different companies that are in four different industries. The first option may be great if the solitary company has indefinite success, but economic factors, consumer demands, competitive advancements, and management performance can combat a company's ability to make money. If you instead invest in several companies that are in different industries, you can insulate yourself from negative influences that affect one company or one industry. You still might

Most Significant U.S. Stock Market Crashes*

	Year	Date Began	Date Ended	Total Loss
1.	1930	April 17, 1930	July 8, 1932	−86.0%
2.	1937	March 10, 1937	March 31, 1938	−49.1%
3.	1906	January 19, 1906	November 15, 1907	−48.5%
4.	1929	September 3, 1929	November 13, 1929	−47.9%
5.	1919	November 3, 1919	August 24, 1921	−46.6%
6.	1901	June 17, 1901	November 9, 1903	−46.1%
7.	1973	January 11, 1973	December 6, 1974	−45.1%
8.	1939	September 12, 1939	April 28, 1942	−40.4%
9.	1916	November 21, 1916	December 19, 1917	−40.1%
10.	2000	January 1, 2000	October 9, 2002	−37.8%

As of November 2008, the market had declined 46.8% since its highest point in October 2007. This would represent the 3rd most significant stock market crash.

experience a loss, but because it's most likely not from all four investments in your portfolio, the loss will not be as significant as it would if it were your only holding. Conventional wisdom, based on these ideas, supports diversification.

Similarly, the concept of **asset allocation** suggests you structure your portfolio with different types of assets (stocks, bonds, mutual funds, real estate, etc.) to reduce the risks associated with these broad types of investments—mostly from inflation and changes in interest rates. Studies have shown that most of an investment portfolio's performance is determined by the allocation of its assets, not by individual investment selection or by market timing.[1] The allocation of assets in a portfolio depends on your risk tolerance and can change as an investor reaches certain milestones such as getting married, paying for college tuition, or retiring. ▼ **Figure 16.3** shows how risk tolerance affects the asset allocation mix in a portfolio.

Building wealth through investments is a process that takes a significant amount of time, so the earlier you begin investing your money the better. Even a small investment of $10 a month starting now can build to nearly $15,000 in 30 years. If you decide you want to start investing your money, you may want to contact a brokerage firm or research a discount broker. You'll learn more about how to invest in the next section.

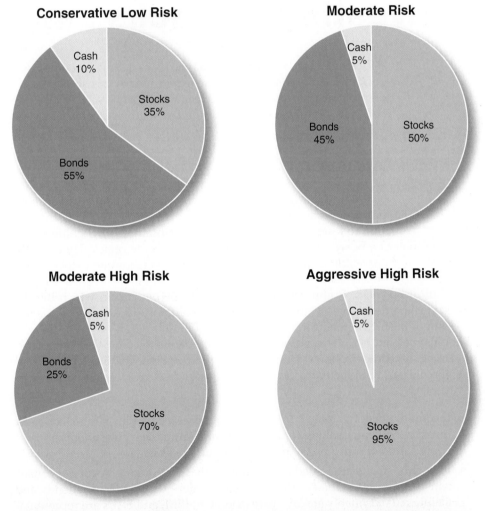

Conservative Low Risk
Cash 10%
Stocks 35%
Bonds 55%

Moderate Risk
Cash 5%
Bonds 45%
Stocks 50%

Moderate High Risk
Cash 5%
Bonds 25%
Stocks 70%

Aggressive High Risk
Cash 5%
Stocks 95%

▼ **Figure 16.3**
Asset Allocation Mix Based on Risk Tolerance

▼ You have just read **Objective 3**

Want a review? Check out the Study Plan section @
www.my*biz*lab.com.

Investing in Stocks pp. 480-486

When she was a baby, Gina Smith's grandparents gave her five shares of Walt Disney, Inc., stock. Every now and then she checks the newspapers to see how her stock is doing and over time has seen the stock price go up and down. That is all the experience Gina has had with investing. Now, having received an unexpected bonus from her first "real" job, Gina wants to do something special with it. She would like to buy more stock, but she doesn't know where to start. What kind of information should she look at to determine what's a good investment for her?

➤ As you read earlier in the chapter, companies sometimes issue stock to raise funds for corporate expansion. In this section, you'll learn about the differences between various types of stocks, how stocks are bought and sold, and the factors that affect stock prices.

Types of Stocks

Are all stocks the same? There are two main types of stocks that companies issue: *common* and *preferred*. You can think of **common stock** as "ordinary" stock. Common stockholders have the right to elect a board of directors and vote on corporate policy. They are also entitled to a share of the company's dividends. However, common stockholders have the least priority as far as ownership and repayment in the event a company goes out of business. **Preferred stock** is a class of ownership in which the preferred stockholders have a claim to assets before common stockholders if the firm goes out of business. In addition, preferred stockholders receive a fixed dividend that must be paid before the payment of any dividends to common stockholders. Preferred shareholders, however, do not have voting privileges. Stocks can also be categorized based on the type of company and expected growth and return of the investment:

- **Income stocks** are issued by utility companies that pay large dividends. Investors who are looking for reliable income from their investments and not appreciation of share value invest in income stocks.

- **Blue chip stocks** are issued by companies that have a long history of consistent growth and stability. Blue chip companies pay regular dividends and maintain a reasonably steady share price. GE, IBM, and Sears are representative of blue chip stocks.

- **Growth stocks** are issued by "young" entrepreneurial companies that are experiencing rapid growth and expansion. These stocks pay little or no dividends. Investment potential is through appreciation in stock value. Growth stocks tend to be riskier than other stocks because entrepreneurial companies do not have a proven track record.

- **Cyclical stocks** are issued by companies that produce goods or services that are affected by economic trends. The prices of these stocks tend to go down when the economy is failing (in a recessionary period) and go up when the economy is healthy. Examples of cyclical stocks include automobiles, home building, and travel.
- **Defensive stocks** are the opposite of cyclical stocks. Defensive stocks are issued by companies producing staples such as food, drugs, and insurance and usually maintain their value regardless of the state of the economy.

No one type of stock is considered to be better than another. Investors have to decide for themselves which type of stock fits best with their financial objectives.

How do I choose which stocks to invest in?
The answer to this question begins with determining your investment goals and objectives, the time in which you have to achieve your goals and objectives, and your risk tolerance level. Once you have a handle on those constraints, you'll be better able to determine what investment strategy best fits your needs.

Many investors begin investing when they form their 401(k) retirement plan at work. This is a good way to start since the 401(k) portfolio manager has narrowed down your investment choices for you. Although there are plenty of professionals to help you, when you start investing on your own, you should research each potential investment for yourself. You can start by evaluating the company's fundamental data, such as earnings, financial statements, and key ratios. Being aware of current events in the news that could influence a stock's price is also important. Often it's helpful to know how a company and its stock have performed in the past. You can study financial charts to compare the historical performances of multiple companies and to observe trends in the data. Additionally, you might want to consider the opinions of industry analysts who independently research and analyze the investment potential of companies. All of this information is available in newspapers, on the Internet, or in your public library. Unfortunately, it takes lots of time and research to determine what the right investments are for you. Keep in mind that if the process were easy and straightforward, we'd all be rich! In reality, there is so much variability and unpredictability in the market, that even with the best analysis, you still might end up with unfavorable results.

Assuming you can select well-run companies that you believe will generate a profit, you also need to determine what kind of company meets your investment goals and objectives. For example, depending on your age and your investment goals, you may want to invest in companies that are in their growth phase—where you'll hopefully make your money through rapid appreciation in stock value. While such companies are more likely to have higher appreciation than are more stable companies, they're also the most risky and are more liable to have their stock lose value quickly, too. Someone who is 22 and just starting his or her career can "afford" to withstand such temporary downfalls. Someone who is 55 may still be saving for retirement and can't endure the possibility of "starting over" if a stock does very poorly. This individual might have a mix of "growth" companies as well as more stable companies that have a strong history of slow but steady growth. These more stable companies generally do not experience wild swings in stock price, and typically offer dividends to their stockholders. Dividends provide another source of income to stockholders beyond appreciation in stock price. Someone who is 70 years old, retired, and reliant on income from his or her investments can't afford to lose much money and is very risk averse. He or she would be wise to invest mostly in companies that offer high dividends and that will experience mild swings in stock price. Regardless of these factors, the world of investing is an ongoing experience, and one that you should not take lightly if you choose to invest. You must be smart about it and continue to do your research—even if you choose to have someone else guide you in the investment process.

How are stocks bought and sold? Before the Internet, people could only buy stocks using a **stockbroker** (or broker), a professional who buys and sells securities on behalf of investors. Brokers also provide advice as to which securities to buy and sell, and receive a fee for their services. Now, individuals have a choice of paying a broker or initiating transactions themselves for a small fee through discount brokers such as E-Trade Financial (www.etrade.com). These discount brokers offer limited advice and guidance and are substantially cheaper than financial services firms like Bank of America that offer full-service brokerage services. Whether you use a discount broker or full-service broker, the process of buying stock is done through a **stock exchange**, an organization that facilitates the exchange of stocks and other securities between brokers and traders. Some of the largest and most dominant stock exchanges in the United States are the **New York Stock Exchange (NYSE)**, in which stocks are bought and sold on a trading floor or via an electronic market, and the **National Association of Securities Dealers Automated Quotations (NASDAQ)**, where stocks are only traded via an electronic market. A typical trade with a broker on the NYSE is similar to the process depicted in ▼ **Figure 16.4**.

▼ **Figure 16.4**

Execution of a Simple Stock Trade on the New York Stock Exchange

Thousands of companies have issued stock and are listed on the NYSE and NASDAQ, as well as many other smaller or international stock exchanges.[2] In fact, the NYSE handles the sales and purchases of over four billion shares

The investor calls her broker to request a transaction.

I want to buy 100 shares of Acme Products Inc.

Broker calls floor clerk and asks for 100 shares of Acme Products Inc.

The floor clerk finds a floor trader who finds another floor trader who is selling Acme Products Inc. stock. The two agree on a price and complete the deal.

The floor trader or clerk notifies the broker that the trade has been placed.

The broker calls you back with the final price. "You bought 100 shares of Acme Products Inc. for $45.50."

every day. Unlike the NYSE, where trades can be made electronically or on the trading floor, the NAS-DAQ stock exchange has always been electronic. Through the NAS-DAQ system, every day over three billion shares of stock trade hands via a large and immensely reliable coordinated network of computer systems. As with the NYSE, you still need a broker, either online or full-service, to initiate your order. The broker will place the order electronically into the NASDAQ system, and when the order is received, the electronic exchange tries to match your buy order with a similar sell order. After the order has been executed, the broker notifies you of the successful completion of the trade. See ▼ **Figure 16.5** to review the steps involved with an electronic stock trade.

The process of selecting a broker can almost be as complicated as the process of selecting a type of investment. Before you decide on a broker, the U.S. Securities and Exchange Commission (SEC) suggests you do the following:

- Think about your financial objectives.
- Speak with potential brokers at several firms. Ask each about their education, investment experience, and professional background.
- Inquire about the history of the brokerage firm. You can find out if any disciplinary action has been taken against a firm or a broker through NASD BrokerCheck at www.nasdbrokercheck.com. Your state securities regulator can also tell you if a broker is licensed to do business in your state.
- Understand how the brokers are paid. The type of commission they receive might affect the advice they offer. Also, ask what fees or charges you will be required to pay on the account.
- Ask if a brokerage firm is a member of the Securities Investor Protection Corporation (SIPC). SIPC gives limited customer protection if a firm goes bankrupt.

▼ **Figure 16.5**
Execution of an Electronic Stock Trade

You log into your online brokerage account and see that Acme is selling for $4.50/share.

You place an electronic order with the broker to buy 100 shares of Acme.

Broker receives the order and transmits it electronically to the stock exchange.

The order goes to the computer dedicated to handling all orders coming from your broker.

The stock exchange tries to match your order electronically with a sell order from someone else.

If a match is made, a notification is sent to your broker who then sends you a confirmation.

You receive and review the transaction confirmation.

◎ Off the Mark The Domestic Diva's Insider Trading Scandal

Insider trading is the buying and selling of securities based on information that has not been disclosed to the public. For example, suppose you own 1,000 shares of XYZ Corp. stock, and you're on friendly terms with the company's chief financial officer (CFO). The CFO tells you the company is going to claim bankruptcy the next day, so you sell all your shares before the information is released so you won't lose your investment. If you do this, you have taken part in illegal insider trading. You can go to jail.

One of the most high-profile insider trading cases of the past decade involved author, TV personality, and domestic diva Martha Stewart. In 2001, Martha Stewart sold almost 4,000 shares of ImClone stock. The next day, the stock price plummeted. She was convicted of insider trading because ImClone's CEO Sam Waksal had informed her that the Food and Drug Administration rejected a cancer drug the company was developing. She received this information one day before it was announced to the public. This gave her an illegal advantage that allowed her to sell her stock and net $229,000, as well as avoid over $45,000 in losses. Stewart claims she had an arrangement with her stockbroker to sell her shares when they dipped below $60 per share. However, Stewart was convicted of insider trading and spent five months in prison and an additional five months under house arrest.[4]

While it is ideal to start investing as early as possible, do not rush into the process. Take the time to do the necessary assessment of your own financial goals and consider the risks you're willing to ta ke to meet those goals.[3]

Changing Stock Prices

What causes stock prices to change? Stock prices can change rapidly. ▼ Figure 16.6 reflects the percent change in closing prices for Apple, Google, General Electric, and Toyota over a three-month period. One thing that is consistent between all the companies is that the stock prices change daily. There are many reasons why stock prices change, but ultimately it all comes down to the forces of supply and demand. If investors like a stock, they will buy more of it, reducing the supply and pushing up the price. On the other hand, if investors don't like a stock, more investors will sell the stock than buy it, creating a greater supply and causing the price to drop. What is harder to determine are the influences that affect investors' attitudes toward individual stocks causing them to favor a stock one day and oppose it another day. The reality is that despite many different theories and prediction strategies, there is not one theory that explains it completely. In general, however, most investors look to see if a stock's price reflects what they think the company is worth. (Stock price times total number of shares outstanding determines a company's capitalization or value.) Often, investors not only look at how the company is currently performing, but also take into consideration expected future growth of the company in anticipation of increased earnings, or profits.

▼ **Figure 16.6**

Percent Change in Stock Price for Apple, General Electric, Google, and Toyota from September to November 2007

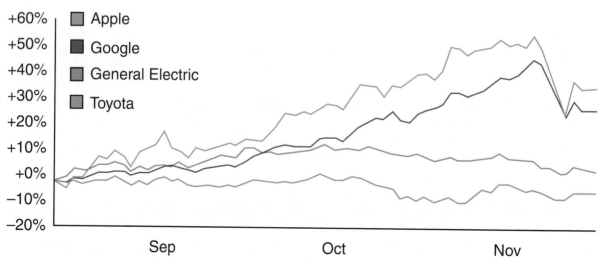

For example, months before June 2007 when consumers could get their hands on the long-awaited iPhone, Apple's stock price began to rise. Investors were buying the stock in anticipation of a positive reaction to Apple's new product. ▼ Figure 16.7 shows the high volume of buyers in January 2007 when Apple announced its intentions of releasing the iPhone and a buildup of the stock price ensued. If investors become concerned that something negative will affect the company's value, they will sell their shares and the stock price will fall. Notice the quick drop in price of Apple's stock in late summer 2007. This was a market reaction to the re-pricing of the iPhone from $599 to $399 that many investors thought was a marketing blunder. However, the phone's price reduction did not affect sales of the iPhone, and the price of Apple stock continued to rise.

How do you know how well a stock is doing relative to other stocks? Stock prices also change in reaction to broader news based on economic forecasts, industry or sector concerns, or global events. In general, financial markets have trends based on investor confidence. A **bull market** indicates increasing investor confidence as the market continues to increase in value. In a bull market, investors are motivated by promises of gains. A **bear market**, however, indicates decreasing investor confidence as the market continues to decline in value.

In addition, industry news can affect the performance of stocks in that industry. Notice in ▼ Figure 16.8 that Apple and Google tend to move similarly, based on news affecting the technology sector, whereas General Electric and Toyota are not affected by technology news, and move more closely with the rest of the market.

The *Standard and Poor's 500 Composite Index (S&P 500)*, the *Dow Jones Industrial Average*, and the *NASDAQ 100* are several benchmarks that indicate the overall health of the U.S. stock market. An **index** represents a collection of related stocks based on certain shared characteristics such as having a similar size, belonging to a common industry, or trading on the same market exchange. The *S&P 500* groups stocks of the 500 largest companies, most of which are American. The *Dow Jones*

▼ **Figure 16.7**
Change in Price and Volume of Apple, Inc., Stock from December 2006 to November 2007

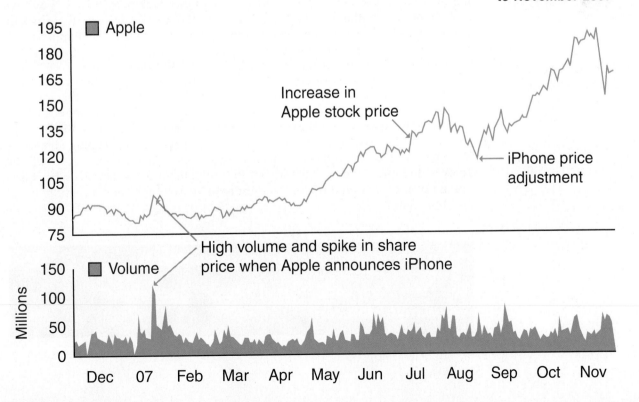

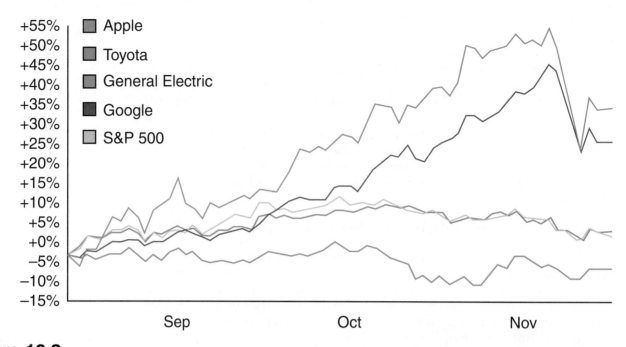

Figure 16.8
Price Movement Compared to
S&P 500 Average

Industrial Average (DJIA) is an index that consists of 30 of the largest capitalized public companies in the United States. Whereas the DJIA composite initially incorporated only those companies that had some connection to heavy industry, today that characteristic is not as prevalent. The *S&P 500* and the *DJIA* are the two most widely watched stock indexes. They are important as they often reflect, and sometimes influence, the state of the U.S. economy. The *NASDAQ 100* includes 100 of the largest domestic and international non-financial companies listed on the NASDAQ stock exchange. The *NASDAQ 100* is distinguished from the *DJIA* and *S&P 500* by not including financial institutions in the group, and including companies incorporated outside the United States.

How do I make money investing in stocks? There are several ways
to earn money investing in stocks. As noted above, one of these ways is by collecting dividends. Another way to make money in the stock market is to "buy low and sell high." In other words, you buy a stock at one price, wait for that stock to appreciate, and then sell the stock at the higher price. When this happens, the investor incurs a **capital gain**. If there is a decrease in value between the purchase price and the selling price, the investor incurs a **capital loss**.

Remember Gina Smith, the young investor from the beginning of this section? When Gina was researching stocks, she reviewed financial documents such as income statements. When she found a few stocks she was interested in buying, she used a discount broker to help finalize her purchase. By keeping abreast of industry news and monitoring stock indexes, she's able to see how well her stock is doing relative to other stocks. Recently, the price of her stock has been going up, and she's waiting for the right time to "sell high" and hopefully incur a capital gain.

▼ You have just read **Objectives 4 & 5**

Want to learn more? Check out the Study Plan section @
www.mybizlab.com.

Investing in Bonds pp. 487-489

➤ We have previously discussed that bonds are like IOUs. As a bond investor, you're lending money to a company for a specific period at a specified interest rate. The main reasons you purchase bonds are to add a stream of fixed income or to diversify your portfolio. Bond performance usually reacts counter to that of stocks. When the stock market is performing well, bonds are generally not; conversely, when the stock market is down, bonds are usually up. Because of this contrary relationship, bonds provide great diversification to a stock portfolio.

Dennis Sanchez just turned 55 years old and is starting to think about retirement. Dennis has been investing money in his company's 401(k) plan for many years and wants to do some investing on his own. Now that he is closer to retirement, he would like to receive a bit of income from his investments. He would also like to take a less risky approach to investing his funds by diversifying his portfolio allocation. Dennis decides investing in bonds would be the best way to meet both of these goals. How does Dennis know what bonds will meet his financial objectives? ➤

Different Types of Bonds

Are there different types of bonds? Governments and corporations issue various types of bonds. These include corporate bonds, government bonds, and municipal bonds.

Corporate Bonds

Corporate bonds are debt securities issued by corporations. There are several types of corporate bonds. **Secured bonds** are backed by collateral, which is generally corporate-owned property that will pass to the bondholders (or be sold to reimburse bondholders) if the issuer does not repay the amount borrowed. *Mortgage backed securities* are special secured bonds that are backed by real property owned by the corporation. **Debenture bonds** are unsecured bonds, backed only by the corporation's promise to pay. Another modification of a traditional bond is a **convertible bond**, which gives the bondholder the right (but not the obligation) to convert the bond into a predetermined number of shares of the company's stock. Convertible bonds generally carry a lower interest rate since the investor will benefit from investing in the underlying stock.

Government Bonds

Government bonds are debt securities issued by national governments. They are the safest investment, because the government backs them. Government bonds are divided into several categories based on their maturity.

- **Treasury bills** (or T-bills) are bonds that mature from 2 weeks to 26 weeks. Treasury bills are sold at a discount, so you are paying less up front. When the bond matures, you receive the full face value of the bond. The difference between the purchase amount and the face value is the interest. For example, to buy a $1,000 T-bill, you might pay $975 up front. When the T-bill matures 26 weeks later, you would receive $1,000. The $25 difference is interest earned.
- **Treasury notes** (or T-notes) are bonds that mature in two, five, or ten years. Interest is paid semiannually. You can hold Treasury notes to maturity or you can sell them prior to their maturity. When a Treasury note matures, you receive the face value.
- **Treasury bonds** are bonds that mature in 30 years and pay interest semiannually. When a Treasury bond matures, you receive the face value.

Municipal Bonds

Municipal bonds (or *munis*) are bonds issued by state or local governments or governmental agencies. There are two varieties of municipal bonds: *general obligation bonds* and *revenue bonds*. **General obligation bonds** are supported by the taxing power of the issuer so they tend to be very safe. **Revenue bonds** are supported by the income generated by the project they finance. For example, the New Jersey Turnpike Authority may issue $1 billion in bonds to finance the construction and renovation of the I-95 corridor that runs through the state. The tolls collected on that portion of I-95 would be used to pay the interest and principal of the bonds. The advantage of buying municipal bonds and government bonds is that incomes generated from many of them are exempt from federal, and in many cases, state, and local income taxes.

A number of municipal bonds, as well as some corporate bonds, are issued as serial bonds. **Serial bonds** have a series of dates on which portions of the total bond mature, unlike traditional bonds that are paid back to the investor all at once on one date (the *maturity date*). Serial bonds are advantageous to the issuer since they reduce the overall interest expense of the bond issue. Additionally, serial bonds allow the issuer to time the maturity dates to the income from the project financed by the bond proceeds. Thus, for the toll road example above, bond series may mature as phases of the toll road are completed. Most corporate and municipal bonds remain outstanding until their maturity date. With **callable bonds**, however, the issuer can either repay the investors their initial investment at the maturity date or the issuer can choose to retire the issue early and repay the investors their investment at the "callable date." Issuers invoke the call option on callable bonds when interest rates have fallen and the bonds can be refinanced at a lower rate. To the investor, callable bonds present a degree of uncertainty, and therefore carry a higher interest rate than similar non-callable bonds.

How can I tell how safe a bond is before investing? Although most bonds are viewed as a conservative investment, they are not entirely risk free. There are different types of risk that affect bonds. *Credit risk* is the risk associated with the bond issuer's ability to meet its financial obligations. As mentioned above, corporate bonds are more risky than government or municipal bonds. Before a bond is issued, it is evaluated by a rating agency, such as Moody's or Standard & Poor's, the two major rating agencies, and later assigned an investment grade. The higher ratings

represent those issues with the least likelihood of default. ▼ **Table 16.2** shows the bond rating scales used by both Moody's and Standard & Poor's. To improve their investment grade, many bonds are backed by insurance policies that guarantee repayment to the bondholders in the event the issuer goes into default. Those bonds with the lowest ratings—and the most risk—are known as **junk bonds**. Because of their high risk, junk bonds offer a high interest rate to attract investors. Investors should be very comfortable with the associated risks before adding junk bonds to their portfolios.

What are the characteristics of a bond?
Several characteristics define a bond: par (face) value, coupon (interest rate), maturity, and issuer.

- **Par (face) value** is the amount of money the bondholder will get back once a bond reaches maturity. Most newly issued bonds sell at par value. As noted earlier, Treasury bills sell for less than par (face) value.

- The **coupon** is the bond's interest rate. Initially, bonds had coupons that the investor would tear off and redeem to receive interest. Coupons are a percent of par, so a coupon of 10 percent on a bond with $1,000 par value would generate $100 in interest a year. While most bonds pay interest twice a year, some bonds offer monthly, quarterly, or annual payments. Today, interest payments are transferred electronically.

- The **maturity date** of a bond is the date on which the bond matures and the investor's principal is repaid. Short-term bonds (generally with a maturity of less than five years) have less variability and therefore a lower interest rate than long-term bonds.

Do I have to hold the bond to maturity?
While you certainly can hold a bond to maturity, many investors sell bonds, especially long-term bonds, prior to maturity. Just like stocks, after they are issued, bonds are bought and sold on the secondary market. What makes buying bonds on the secondary market very complicated is that bonds do not trade at par value but at a price higher than par (at a premium) or lower than par (at a discount). Bond prices move in the opposite direction of interest rates. So, if you are trying to sell a bond that has a coupon of 10 percent and current market interest rates are 8 percent, your bond is worth more to investors, so the price of the bond will go up. Conversely, if current interest rates are 12 percent, demand for your bond is not strong, forcing the price an investor is willing to pay to go down.

When it comes to investing in bonds, there are quite a few things to keep in mind, such as the type of bond, the bond's risk rating, the face value of the bond, and the interest rate. Investors can determine a bond's risk based on the issuer's credit rating. One thing Dennis Sanchez would do before he purchased a bond is review the issuer's credit rating. After doing the necessary research, Dennis is able to establish a diversified, less risky portfolio and receive a bit of income.

▼ **Table 16.2**

Bond Rating Scales Used by Moody's and Standard & Poor's

Risk	Bond Rating	
	Moody's	**Standard & Poor's**
Lowest Risk	Aaa	AAA
Low Risk	Aa and A	AA and A
Medium Risk	Baa	BBB
High Risk	Ba and B	BB and B
Highest Risk	Caa/Ca/C	CCC/CC/C
In Default	C	D

▼ You have just read **Objective 6**

Want to test your skills? Check out the Study Plan section @
www.mybizlab.com.

Investing in **Mutual Funds** and **Other Opportunities** pp. 490-493

Alex and Keri Young recently got married and want to start saving and investing for a family, traveling, and emergencies. Unfortunately, after having a wedding and buying a condo, they have only $2,000 left. Where should they invest their money?

Many investors don't have a large amount of money to invest. One of the possible options for these investors is *mutual funds*. Simply put, a **mutual fund** is a means by which a group of investors pool money together to invest in a diversified set of investments. In this section, you'll read about different types of mutual funds, the pros and cons of investing in them, and other investment opportunities.

Mutual Funds

What is a mutual fund? Let's say you wanted to invest in the stock market but had only $5,000 to invest. After looking at possible investments, you realize that with $5,000, you could buy stock in only one or two companies. In talking to several of your friends who are also trying to invest small amounts of money, you realize that they are experiencing the same problem. Then, as a group, you decide to pool your money and hire an expert to buy a portfolio of stocks. With this arrangement, each of you shares a proportional amount of the investment returns. If you were to do that, you would have created a mutual fund.

What are bond mutual funds? Many firms offer a number of mutual fund options. **Bond mutual funds** consist solely of bonds. Some bond funds are categorized by type of bond to include municipal bond funds, corporate bond funds, and U.S. government bond funds. Alternatively, some bond funds are categorized by maturity to include long-term bond funds, short-term bond funds, and intermediate-term bond funds. ▼ **Table 16.3** summarizes the various types of bond mutual funds.

Money market funds are funds that invest in short-term debt obligations such as Treasury bills and certificates of deposit and are quite safe. Money market funds are popular because the interest rate is often nearly double that of "regular" interest-bearing checking or savings accounts. In addition, money market funds are very liquid so you have quick access to your money, often by simply writing a check. Perhaps the only drawback of a money market fund is that the FDIC does not insure the funds. However, unlike many banks, to date, there has yet to be a money market fund that has failed. Alternatively, you can invest in a *money*

▼ **Table 16.3**

Bond Mutual Funds		
	Fund Type	**Investment Strategy**
By Type	Municipal bond funds	Invest in tax-exempt bonds issued by state and local governments. There are municipal bond funds that are further specialized in bonds issued by a particular state.
	Corporate bond funds	Invest in debt obligations from U.S. corporations.
	U.S. government bond funds	Invest in U.S. Treasury or government securities.
By Term	Short-term bond funds	Invest in bonds with maturities less than two years, including Treasury bills, CDs, and commercial paper.
	Intermediate-term bond funds	Invest in bonds with maturities ranging between two and ten years.
	Long-term bond funds	Invest in bonds with maturities greater than ten years.

market savings account through a savings bank, and as with all bank accounts, the money in that account is insured by the FDIC.

Are there different types of stock mutual funds? Stock mutual funds, sometimes referred to as **equity funds**, are much more popular than bond or money market funds.[5] Similar to bond funds, stock mutual funds are broken down into various categories. Some stock funds invest in stocks with a particular strategy in mind, such as growth funds, value funds, and blend funds. Another popular breakdown of stock funds are those that invest in companies that are defined by their capitalization (cap) or size, such as large-cap funds, mid-cap funds, and small-cap funds. Additionally, there is a wide assortment of funds that center on international investments such as global funds, foreign funds, country-specific funds, or emerging market funds. Lastly, there are sector funds that invest in companies from a particular industry sector such as technology, automotive, banking, and health care. ▼ Table 16.4 summarizes the various types of stock mutual funds.

Why are mutual funds so popular? Mutual funds are the best kind of investment for those who have little to no experience in investing or who might not have a lot of money to invest. There are many reasons why you should consider investing in mutual funds:

- **Diversification:** The notable advantage to investing in mutual funds is diversification. Mutual funds offer small investors a cost-effective means of purchasing a diversified portfolio. Unless you have a lot of money to invest, it's hard to buy a large variety of securities. Remember, having a portfolio of a variety of types of securities helps to reduce risk without significantly affecting returns.

- **Professional Management:** Second to diversification, professional management is another advantage of mutual funds. Someone who has a significant amount of investment experience manages each mutual fund. Additionally, these professionals are spending all their time researching, trading, and watching the investments that make up the fund. This is likely more time than you would be able to spend if you had created a similar portfolio on your own. The fund managers have great incentive to make sure their fund performs at its best.

- **Liquidity:** It is very easy to buy and sell mutual funds, so you can get to your money quickly—usually within a day. Some mutual funds, primarily money market funds, offer check-writing privileges, so accessing your money is even easier.

▼ **Table 16.4**

Stock Mutual Funds		
	Fund Type	**Investment Strategy**
Strategy Types	Growth funds	Invest in stocks of the fastest-growing companies. Often viewed as risky investments. Rarely produce dividend income.
	Value funds	Invest in stocks that are considered to be "undervalued." These stocks are thought to be ready for quick appreciation. Some produce dividends.
	Blend (or balanced) funds	Invest in both growth and value companies.
By Size	Large-cap funds	Invest in companies with large (greater than $9 billion) capitalization (price times outstanding shares).
	Medium-cap funds	Invest in companies of medium capitalization—between $1 billion and $9 billion.
	Small-cap funds	Invest in companies with capitalization less than $1 billion. These companies rarely generate dividends.
International	Global funds	Invest in both U.S. and international stocks.
	Foreign funds	Invest in companies primarily outside the U.S.
	Country- or region-specific funds	Invest in companies from one country or region of the world.
	Emerging market funds	Invest in companies from small developing countries. These funds are considered fairly risky.
Sector		Invest in companies from one particular industrial sector such as technology, pharmaceutical, or automotive.
Index		Funds that try to mimic a particular index such as Standard & Poor's or NASDAQ.

- **Cost:** It takes as little as $1,000 to invest in most mutual funds. Some funds do charge fees with their purchase or sale, though there are quite a few good "no-load" mutual funds that are virtually free of fees and charges.

How do I make money investing in mutual funds? You can make money investing in mutual funds through dividends, interest, capital gains, and fund appreciation. These investment earnings are similar to those generated by individual stock holdings, although they are controlled by the fund manager and distributed to the fund owners periodically. As fund managers adjust the holdings of the fund, they sell some securities and buy others. Capital gains and losses that are incurred through selling securities are passed on to the fund owners. Your mutual fund accumulates any dividends paid by the stocks and interest paid by the bonds held by the mutual fund and periodically distributes the earnings to fund owners. Lastly, mutual funds are measured by the value of the individual holdings. This measure is the **net asset value (NAV)**. The net asset value increases as the securities held by the fund increase in value. If you sell your mutual fund holding at a higher NAV than when you bought it, you will generate a profit.

What do I need to watch out for when investing in mutual funds? While mutual funds are often deemed the "perfect" investment, like any investment, you still need to do your homework before investing. Some mutual funds, referred to as **load funds**, have additional costs (loads) that are rolled into the overall package to cover marketing and other fund expenses. While the ultimate decision to buy a mutual fund is based on its expected performance and the suitability to your investments needs, if given a choice of similar options, try to pick a **no-load fund**, a mutual fund that has little or no additional costs. In addition, it's also important to have a good understanding about who is managing the fund. The same individual or group of managers often runs a fund for years. However, changes happen, so you want to watch out for that. A change in management could quickly make historical fund performance statistics (what you might be using to evaluate a fund's performance before you buy) less significant.

Other Investment Opportunities

Besides stocks and bonds, what else is there? An **option** is a contract that gives a buyer the right (but not obligation) to buy (call) or sell (put) a particular security at a specific price on or before a certain date. Consider this analogy as an example: Your uncle is selling a car that you would love to buy but can't afford. You decide to approach your uncle with a proposal. You would save your money, and at the end of three months, you would have the right to buy the car for $15,000. For accepting this offer, you will give your uncle $1,000 now. Over the course of the next three months, two situations could occur:

1. The car could be ranked one of the best cars, increasing its value from $15,000 to $20,000. You buy the car for the agreed upon $15,000 and then sell the car for $20,000. Taking into consideration the price of the option, you net $4,000.

2. Your uncle gets into an accident and totals the car. Since you have only an option to buy the car, you're not obligated to, but you still lose the $1,000 for the option.

Options work similarly in that you aren't buying the underlying asset (in our example the underlying asset is a car—in reality, it would be a stock). Instead you're paying for the opportunity to buy the asset under certain conditions. If things go wrong, you lose the cost of the option. If things go right, you could profit. Options are complicated, and can be risky. Don't confuse option contracts with stock options your employer may offer as a benefit. The stock option that employers offer gives you the right to buy a specific number of shares of your company's stock at a specific time at a set price. Stock options are used as incentives to retain and motivate employees and will be discussed in Chapter 9.

What are futures? A **futures contract** is an agreement between a buyer and a seller to receive (or deliver) an asset sometime in the future at a specific price agreed upon today. Usually the underlying asset is a commodity such as sugar, coffee, or wheat. For these commodities, a price is agreed on before harvest, when the actual goods are bought and sold. Futures markets also include the buying and selling of government bonds, foreign currencies, or stock market indexes. Most holders of futures contracts rarely hold their contract to expiration. If you hold the futures contract until it expires, you own the commodity. Instead, the contract is traded prior to expiration. If the price of the commodity increases before the contract's expiration date you make a profit. However, if the price decreases, you may lose money. The difference between a futures contract and an options contract is that an option gives you the *right* to purchase the underlying asset while with a futures contract, you have an *obligation* to purchase the underlying asset.

What are ETFs? **Exchange-traded funds (ETFs)** are a pool of stocks like a mutual fund, but they trade like stocks on the exchange. Prices of ETFs change throughout the day as they are bought and sold, whereas mutual funds are traded only at the end of the trading day. ETFs incur a fee from a broker; however, the fee is typically lower than mutual fund fees. This makes ETFs a low-cost way to diversify a portfolio.

▼ You have just read **Objectives 7-9**

Want to quiz yourself? Check out the Study Plan section @
www.mybizlab.com.

1. What are the pros and cons of debt and equity financing? (pp. 471-474)

- An advantage of financing with **bonds** (p. 472) is that it allows a company to finance a project without using other business assets or corporate profits.

- One disadvantage of debt financing is that if the interest rate of the bond is too high, it can force the cost of the project into something that is not affordable or that just doesn't make economic sense.

- Financing with equity allows the company to retain profits and cash in the company rather than using it to pay back debt and make interest payments.

- The biggest disadvantage that equity financing brings is a dilution of ownership.

2. How do companies issue bonds and stocks? (pp. 474-475)

- The steps for issuing bonds are as follows:
  - The company's financial manager contacts a financial advisor for advice.
  - Financial advisors prepare documents with the **Securities and Exchange Commission**, or **SEC** (p. 474). They also help to set the price of the bond issue, and take the lead in forming the group of banks that initially buy the bonds.
  - The financial advisors and bankers generate interest and locate potential buyers for the bonds before issuance.
  - The financial advisory firm initially purchases all the bonds at a discount and then quickly sells them in the **primary market** (p. 475) at a higher price.

- **Stocks** (p. 473) are issued in the same manner as bonds, with a few slight differences:
  - The first issue of stock is an **initial public offering**, or **IPO** (p. 475).
  - A financial advisor coordinates the preparation of a **prospectus** (p. 475) and files it with the SEC.
  - Financial advisors also establish the best timing for the public sale, and determine the initial selling price.
  - Banks form a syndicate to underwrite the IPO. The syndicate then purchases the stock and sells it back to the public.

3. How do risk return relationships, risk tolerance, and asset allocations relate to the fundamentals of investment? (pp. 476-479)

- Various types of investments have different **risk return relationships** (p. 478). On one hand, the least risky investments offer the least amount of return. On the other hand, the most risky investments offer the greatest return.

- Investing is not for everyone, and the level and type of investments is very personal and depends on the investor's risk tolerance level.

- Investment portfolios should be allocated or spread out among different types of investments such as stocks, bonds, and cash to further reduce investment risk. **Asset allocation** (p. 479) changes as investors reach life milestones and portfolios must be adjusted and rebalanced periodically.

4. What are the different investment categories of stocks, and how does the stock trade process work? (pp. 480-484)

- Stocks can be categorized into five categories: **income stocks**, **blue chip stocks**, **growth stocks**, **cyclical stocks**, and **defensive stocks** (pp. 480-481).

- Stocks are purchased through a **stockbroker** (p. 482) who buys and sells stocks on behalf of investors. Brokers also provide advice and receive a fee for their services.

- Stock transactions occur through a **stock exchange** (p. 482) like the **New York Stock Exchange** or **NASDAQ** (p. 482).

5. What is stock performance, and what are the factors that lead to changes in stock price? (pp. 484-486)

- Stock performance is directly related to changes in stock price.

- Stock prices change in reaction to forces of supply and demand. Other factors that can affect stock prices include economic forecasts, industry or sector concerns, or global events. Stocks also tend to move together as a market. If the market is trending positively, it is a **bull market** (p. 485). A declining market is a **bear market** (p. 485).

6. What are the different types and characteristics of bonds, and how is the safety of bonds evaluated? (pp. 487-489)

- There are two issuers of bonds: governments and corporations.
  - **Corporate bonds** (p. 487) are issued by corporations and hold the greatest amount of risk. **Secured bonds** (p. 487) are backed by collateral, and **debenture bonds** (p. 487) are unsecured and backed only by a promise to pay.
  - **Government bonds** (p. 488) are issued by national governments and are the safest investment.
  - **Municipal bonds** (p. 488) are issued by state and local municipalities.

- Bonds are characterized by their **par (face) value** (p. 489), which is the money the bondholder will get back once a bond reaches maturity. Most bonds sell at par value. Bonds are also characterized by the **coupon** (p. 489), or interest rate, and **maturity date** (p. 489).

- Bonds are not risk free. The creditworthiness of the issuer is the main factor affecting a bond's risk.

7. What is the difference among bond mutual funds, money market funds, and equity funds? (pp. 490-491)

- **Bond mutual funds** (p. 490) consist solely of bonds. They can be categorized by type of bond (municipal bond funds, corporate bond funds, or U.S. government bond funds). Alternatively, some bond funds are categorized by maturity (long-term, short-term, or intermediary-term bond funds).

- **Money market funds** (p. 490) invest in short-term debt obligations. The interest rate for these funds is often nearly double that of "regular" interest-bearing checking or savings accounts. In addition, money market accounts provide check-writing privileges so you have quick access to the money.

Continued on next page

Chapter Summary (cont.)

- **Equity funds** (p. 491) are categorized by investment strategy such as growth funds, value funds, and blend (or balanced) funds. These funds are also categorized by size of the companies in which they invest such as large-capitalized (large-cap) funds, medium-cap funds, and small-cap funds.

8. What are the advantages and disadvantages of mutual fund investment? (pp. 491-493)

- **Mutual funds** (p. 490) are popular investments because they provide diversification and professional management. Mutual funds are extremely liquid, and are fairly cost efficient.
- **Load funds** (p. 492), have additional costs to cover marketing and other fund expenses, whereas **no-load funds** (p. 492), have little or no additional costs.

9. What is an option or a futures contract? (p. 493)

- An **option** (p. 493) is a contract that gives a buyer the right (but not obligation) to buy or sell a security at a specific price on or before a certain date. Options are complicated, and therefore quite risky.
- **Futures contracts** (p. 493) are agreements between a buyer and seller to receive (or deliver) an asset sometime in the future, but at a specific price that is agreed upon today.

For an audio file of the Objectives and Chapter Summary, see the Student Resources section @ www.my*biz*lab.com.

Key Terms

asset allocation (p. 479)

bear market (p. 485)

blue chip stocks (p. 480)

bond mutual funds (p. 490)

bond (p. 472)

bull market (p. 485)

callable bond (p. 488)

capital gain (p. 486)

capital loss (p. 486)

capital market (p. 474)

common stock (p. 480)

convertible bonds (p. 488)

corporate bonds (p. 487)

coupon (p. 489)

cyclical stocks (p. 481)

debenture bonds (p. 487)

defensive stocks (p. 481)

diversification (p. 478)

dividends (p. 473)

equity funds (p. 491)

exchange-traded funds (ETFs) (p. 493)

financial advisory firm (p. 474)

futures contract (p. 493)

general obligation bonds (p. 488)

government bonds (p. 488)

growth stocks (p. 480)

income stocks (p. 480)

index (p. 485)

initial public offering (IPO) (p. 475)

junk bonds (p. 489)

load funds (p. 492)

maturity date (p. 489)

money market funds (p. 490)

municipal bonds (p. 488)

mutual fund (p. 490)

National Association of Securities Dealers Automated Quotations (NASDAQ) (p. 482)

net asset value (NAV) (p. 492)

New York Stock Exchange (NYSE) (p. 482)

no-load fund (p. 492)

option (p. 493)

par (face) value (p. 489)

preferred stock (p. 480)

primary market (p. 475)

prospectus (p. 475)

revenue bonds (p. 488)

risk return relationships (p. 478)

secondary market (p. 475)

secured bonds (p. 487)

securities (p. 471)

Securities and Exchange Commission (SEC) (p. 474)

serial bond (p. 488)

sinking fund (p. 472)

stock (p. 473)

stockbroker (p. 482)

stock exchange (p. 482)

stock mutual funds (equity funds) (p. 491)

Treasury bills (p. 488)

Treasury bonds (p. 488)

Treasury notes (p. 488)

Multiple Choice   Correct answers can be found on page 503.

1. Crunchy Chips, Inc., needs to invest in new production equipment to make its potato chip processing more efficient. The managers are considering financing the equipment with bonds. Which of the following is a reason why the company would consider bonds over stocks?

   a. There is no dilution of ownership.

   b. Bond holders do not require interest payments.

   c. Financing with bonds allows the company to retain profits and cash in the company rather than using it to pay back debt.

   d. All of the above

2. Jackson White is looking to raise extra capital to help expand the business operations of his company. Which is *not* a reason to raise the extra capital with stock rather than with bonds?

   a. Company profits are retained by the company.

   b. Cash flow is not used for dividend payments.

   c. Equity does not impact control of the company.

   d. Funds from stock do not need to be paid back.

3. When a company issues stock for the first time, it is creating a(n)

   a. secondary market transaction.

   b. initial public offering.

   c. proprietary underwriting.

   d. individual primary option.

4. Jimmy Schoefeld's portfolio is invested 70 percent in growth stocks, 20 percent in income stocks, 5 percent bonds, and 5 percent cash. Of the growth stocks, Jimmy has invested in three companies in the technology sector and two companies in the biotechnology industry. Jimmy's portfolio is considered to be

   a. divided.

   b. monetized.

   c. amortized.

   d. diversified.

5. Which is *not* a difference between common stock and preferred stock?

   a. Common stockholders have voting rights, and preferred stockholders do not.

   b. Preferred stockholders have first claim to assets over common stockholders in the case of bankruptcy.

   c. Common stockholders receive a fixed dividend, and preferred stockholders may receive a dividend if there is money left over.

   d. Preferred stockholders do not elect a board of directors, and common stockholders do.

6. To determine how well your investments are doing relative to the rest of the market, you might compare your stock's performance to which of the following?

   a. Standard & Poor's 500 Composite Index

   b. New York Stock Exchange

   c. NASDAQ

   d. All of the above

7. Bonds are good investments for those who want

   a. fixed income.

   b. diversification from stocks.

   c. possible tax deductions.

   d. All of the above

8. If you owned a $10,000 bond that had a coupon of 4.5 percent and paid interest semi-annually, how much interest would you receive?

   a. $450 every six months

   b. $225 every six months

   c. $450 once a year

   d. $225 once a year

9. Which is *not* an advantage of investing in mutual funds?

   a. Mutual funds are less risky than investing in stocks or bonds.

   b. Mutual funds provide immediate diversification.

   c. Mutual fund investments are managed by a professional.

   d. Mutual funds are more liquid than stocks and bonds.

10. Income is generated from a stock mutual fund through

   a. dividends.

   b. capital gains.

   c. fund appreciation.

   d. All of the above

Self-Test

True/False   Correct answers can be found on page 503.

1. Companies finance with either stocks or bonds, rarely both.
   ☐ **True** or ☐ **False**

2. Five years ago, Jerome bought 100 shares of Kodak at $40 per share. Last month, he sold the 100 shares at $55 per share. Jerome has a capital gain from the sale.
   ☐ **True** or ☐ **False**

3. People who are risk averse should invest in short-term government bond obligations.
   ☐ **True** or ☐ **False**

4. If you buy a bond as an investment, you cannot sell it before it matures.
   ☐ **True** or ☐ **False**

5. Since mutual funds are professionally managed, you do not need to worry about which mutual fund you invest in.
   ☐ **True** or ☐ **False**

Critical Thinking Questions

1. The balance between debt and equity varies according to industry. Based on Table 16.5, discuss why certain industries have a higher debt/equity ratio than others.

▼ Table 16.5

Average Debt/Equity Ratio by Select Industry	
Industry	**Debt/Equity Ratio**
Automobile Manufacturers	85.0%
Computer Hardware	29.6%
Electric Utilities	108.8%
Health Care Services	66.5%
Major Airlines	249.7%

Source: http://www.iclub.com/investing/stock_watch_list_industry.asp

2. Discuss your life goals and how much time you have to accomplish the goals. What kind of saving and investment strategy might you need to pursue to ensure that you meet your goals?

3. The term "blue chip" applies to stocks issued by a company in excellent financial standing with a record of producing earnings and paying dividends. Stocks in companies such as GE and Chrysler were initially considered blue chip stocks. Today, stocks in companies that were not in existence when the term was coined, such as Intel and Wal-Mart, are considered blue chip stocks. What other companies might you consider blue chip stocks and why?

4. Assume you have $25,000 to invest. Put together a portfolio of five stocks that is well diversified across several industries. What investments did you choose and why?

5. Often mutual funds compare their performance to that of the S&P 500 with the goal of "beating" it. Is this a fair comparison?

Team Time

Take This $50,000 and Invest It!

Assemble in teams of four or five students. Suppose your team is given a theoretical $50,000 that you need to invest. Your team must assemble a portfolio by selecting a minimum of five investments, but no more than ten investments. The portfolios should be well diversified by including different types of assets or including stocks from different industries or sectors.

Process

Step 1. Your team should fill out the following charts as you conduct your research:

Name of Investment	Type of Investment	Industry/Sector

Name of Investment	Purchase Price	# Shares	Initial Value	% of Total Portfolio

Step 2. Your team should then prepare a presentation outlining your investment choices. The presentation should include reasons why you included each investment choice in the portfolio. In addition, the presentation should discuss the diversification strategies you took.

Step 3. **Optional ongoing exercise:** Teams should monitor their portfolios on a weekly basis. At the end of the specified period of time, teams should determine which team portfolio has the highest value.

Ethics and Corporate Social Responsibility

Can Investments Be Socially Responsible *and* Lucrative?

Socially responsible investing describes an investment strategy that invests in companies that offer the potential for maximized gains and that also are involved in businesses that favor practices that are environmentally responsible, support workplace diversity, and increase product safety and quality. Some socially responsible investments also avoid businesses involved in alcohol, tobacco, gambling, weapons, other military industries, and/or abortion.

Process

1. On your own or with a partner, research several individual companies and mutual funds that would qualify as socially responsible investments.

2. In one to two paragraphs, comment on whether this type of investment strategy is historically a sound investment strategy.

Web Exercises

1. Tracking an IPO
Go to the MSN.com Money Web link and find a company that recently created an IPO. Research the method of IPO allocation the company used and track its performance from the day the company went public until now. How have the stock prices changed?

2. Brokering a Good Deal
Compare discount brokers such as Scott Trade (www.scottrade.com) and Schwab (www.schwab.com) with full-service brokers such as Edward Jones (www.edwardjones.com). Do discount brokers offer the same services as full-service brokers? How do fees compare between the brokers? Why might you want to use a full-service broker instead of a discount broker and vice versa?

3. Dogs of the Dow
Several investment strategies help investors select stocks. Dogs of the Dow is one of the most publicized strategies. Research Dogs of the Dow and describe the strategy. Would this be a good investment strategy for you?

4. Virtual Stock Market
Several stock market simulation games enable you to trade in real time using "virtual cash." You create a portfolio of investments by placing orders as you would with a discount broker. Simulations are a great way to test your theories, practice your strategies, and just get your feet wet without the fear of losing your hard-earned cash. Some simulations even offer cash and prizes to portfolio winners. Try these simulation games: http://simulator.investopedia.com, http://vse.marketwatch.com, and www.youngmoney.com/stock_market_game.

5. Municipal Bonds: Paving Roads and Building Schools
Municipal bonds are issued by local and state governments and other municipal organizations such as school districts and toll road authorities. Conduct online research to determine the municipal bonds that the state in which you live has issued. What was the purpose behind the bond issues?

Web Case

To access the Chapter 16 Web case and exercise, see the End of Chapter Assignments section @ www.my*biz*lab.com.

Video Case

To access the Chapter 16 Video case and exercise, see the End of Chapter Assignments section @ www.my*biz*lab.com.

Personal Finance

We often begin planning our personal finances when it's too late—generally when we don't have enough money to cover our expenses when we've lost our job, or when we can no longer work because of illness or injury. We should begin to think seriously of our personal finances when we get our first job, if not earlier. It would be most prudent to begin managing our personal finances from the day we receive our first allowance!

When an individual or a family applies principles of finance to managing the ways in which monies are budgeted, saved, invested, preserved for future life events, and protected against risks, it's called **personal finance**. In its simplest form, personal finance is about setting goals, making choices, and following through. Ultimately, as shown in ▼ **Figure 1**, you need to have a plan for reducing expenses and increasing income and assets so they begin to work for you. This ensures that your money lasts throughout your lifetime. Acquiring appreciating assets, reducing unnecessary expenses, and preparing for unexpected situations are the keys to securing your wealth.

Money management is a key aspect of personal finance and generally includes

- determining what you have;
- setting goals for what you want or need; and
- planning how to achieve your goals.

There are a number of different aspects to effective money management. We'll begin by exploring how to create a financial plan.

▼ **Figure 1**
Basic Personal Finance

Figure contents:

Investment income

BANK

Assets   Liabilities

Interest payments

Income

Pre-tax income   After tax income

Expenses

Taxes & deductions

We want these higher
We want these lower

Need Tools to Help You Manage Your Money?

Many online resources and software tools can help you manage your money. A spreadsheet program like Microsoft Excel can handle simple financial worksheets and budgets, and Intuit's Quicken and Microsoft Money are popular software tools that are more robust in their money-management capabilities. Many Web sites, such as mint.com, wesabe.com, and expensr.com, also offer free tools to help you track and manage your finances. These tools are free, functional, and accessible any time and wherever you have an Internet connection.

Creating a Financial Plan

Let's walk through the steps involved in creating a financial plan.

Step 1: Take a Financial Inventory

The first thing you need to do when beginning a financial plan is *take a financial inventory.* You need to list everything of value that you own (your assets), and then subtract from that total everything that you owe in loans and credit card balances.

to continue   check out **www.my*biz*lab.com**.

➤Answers

CHAPTER 1
Business Basics
Self Test Multiple Choice
   (Answers): 1. a; 2. c; 3. d; 4. d; 5. b; 6. a; 7. b; 8. b; 9. c; 10. a
Self Test True False
   (Answers): 1. True; 2. False; 3. True; 4. True; 5. False

CHAPTER 2
Economics and Banking
Self Test Multiple Choice
   (Answers): 1. d; 2. b; 3. a; 4. c; 5. a; 6. a; 7. b; 8. d; 9. b; 10. c
Self Test True False
   (Answers): 1. False; 2. True; 3. True; 4. False; 5. False

CHAPTER 3
Ethics in Business
Self Test Multiple Choice
   (Answers): 1. d; 2. d; 3. c; 4. b; 5. c; 6. c; 7. a; 8. b; 9. a; 10. c
Self Test True False
   (Answers): 1. False; 2. True; 3. True; 4. False; 5. False

CHAPTER 4
Business in a Global Economy
Self Test Multiple Choice
   (Answers): 1. b; 2. d; 3. a; 4. d; 5. c; 6. a; 7. d; 8. c; 9. d; 10. c
Self Test True False
   (Answers): 1. False; 2. True; 3. False; 4. True; 5. True

CHAPTER 5
Small Business and the Entrepreneur
Self Test Multiple Choice
   (Answers): 1. c; 2. b; 3. a; 4. d; 5. d; 6. d; 7. c; 8. b; 9. c; 10. c
Self Test True False
   (Answers): 1. True; 2. False; 3. True; 4. False; 5. True

CHAPTER 6
Forms of Business Ownership
Self Test Multiple Choice
   (Answers): 1. b; 2. a; 3. d; 4. b; 5. c; 6. b; 7. a; 8. a; 9. c; 10. c
Self Test True False
   (Answers): 1. False; 2. True; 3. False; 4. False; 5. True

CHAPTER 7
Business Management and Organization
Self Test Multiple Choice
   (Answers): 1. d; 2. a; 3. a; 4. b; 5. a; 6. a; 7. c; 8. b; 9. b; 10. c
Self Test True False
   (Answers): 1. False; 2. True; 3. False; 4. False; 5. True

CHAPTER 8
Motivation, Leadership, and Teamwork
Self Test Multiple Choice
   (Answers): 1. d; 2. a; 3. b; 4. c; 5. c; 6. b; 7. a; 8. d; 9. b; 10. c
Self Test True False
   (Answers): 1. False; 2. False; 3. True; 4. True; 5. False

CHAPTER 9
Human Resource Management
Self Test Multiple Choice
   (Answers): 1. b; 2. a; 3. c; 4. d; 5. a; 6. d; 7. b; 8. d; 9. a; 10. d
Self Test True False
   (Answers): 1. False; 2. False; 3. True; 4. True; 5. True

CHAPTER 10
Business Technology
Self Test Multiple Choice
   (Answers): 1. c; 2. b; 3. a; 4. c; 5. b; 6. c; 7. b; 8. b; 9. d; 10. d
Self Test True False
   (Answers): 1. False; 2. True; 3. True; 4. False; 5. False

CHAPTER 11
Production and Operations Management
Self Test Multiple Choice
   (Answers): 1. d; 2. a; 3. a; 4. c; 5. d; 6. d; 7. c; 8. a; 9. d; 10. b
Self Test True False
   (Answers): 1. True; 2. True; 3. False; 4. True; 5. False

CHAPTER 12
Marketing and Consumer Behavior
Self Test Multiple Choice
   (Answers): 1. a; 2. b; 3. d; 4. d; 5. c; 6. c; 7. c; 8. d; 9. d; 10. a
Self Test True False
   (Answers): 1. False; 2. True; 3. False; 4. True; 5. False

CHAPTER 13
Product Development and Pricing Strategies
Self Test Multiple Choice
   (Answers): 1. d; 2. c; 3. b; 4. c; 5. b; 6. a; 7. b; 8. c; 9. d; 10. b
Self Test True False
   (Answers): 1. True; 2. False; 3. False; 4. True; 5. False

CHAPTER 14
Promotion and Distribution
Self Test Multiple Choice
   (Answers): 1. b; 2. d; 3. b; 4. b; 5. c; 6. b; 7. c; 8. a; 9. c; 10. a
Self Test True False
   (Answers): 1. True; 2. True; 3. False; 4. False; 5. True

CHAPTER 15
Financing and Tracking Business Operations
Self Test Multiple Choice
   (Answers): 1. c; 2. d; 3. a; 4. d; 5. d; 6. b; 7. c; 8. b; 9. c; 10. b
Self Test True False
   (Answers): 1. False; 2. True; 3. False; 4. True; 5. True

CHAPTER 16
Securities and Investments
Self Test Multiple Choice
   (Answers): 1. a; 2. c; 3. b; 4. d; 5. c; 6. a; 7. d; 8. b; 9. a; 10. d
Self Test True False
   (Answers): 1. False; 2. True; 3. True; 4. False; 5. False

➤ Glindex

Prospecting identifying qualified potential customers, 412–413

Prospect-to-cash a core business process that outlines the steps from identifying a new business prospect to receiving payment for the product, 309–310

Prospectus formal documentation that describes the details of the corporation that are important to potential investors, 474

Protectionism, 104–106

Protocols the different "languages" used to transfer information across the Internet, 291

Psychographic segmentation market segmentation based on lifestyles, personality traits, motives, and values, 356–357

Psychological influences, 359–360

Psychological pricing the practice of charging a price just below a whole number to give the appearance of a significantly lower price; it is also called *odd* or *fractional pricing*, 391

Psychology
industrial, 230
organizational, 224

Public accountant, 450

Public capital, 101

Public Company Accounting Oversight Board, 451

Publicity information in a news story form about an individual, organization, or product transmitted through mass media at no charge, 408–409

Publicly owned corporations a corporation whose stock is owned by more than 25 stockholders and is regulated by the Securities and Exchange Commission, 173–174

Public relations the management function that establishes and maintains mutually beneficial relationships between an organization and its stakeholders, 400, 407–409, 416

Public service advertising advertising that communicates a message on behalf of a good cause, 404

Purchasing agents, 422

PureEdge Solutions Inc., 184

Purina, 97

"Purple cow" factor, 344

Q

Q-tips, 380

Qualcomm, 256

Quality control the use of techniques, activities, and processes to guarantee that a certain good or service meets a specified level of quality, 324–328

Quality Systems, 18

Quanity discounts, 390

QuickBooks, 289

Quiznos, 6

Quotas quantity limitations on the amount of an export allowed to enter a country, 104

R

Rack jobbers wholesalers that send delivery trucks to retailers, where the delivery people set up displays within stores and bill the retailers only for the goods sold, 421

Radio frequency identification (RFID) tag that allows a computer to keep track of the status and quantity of each item, 321

Radio media, 404–405

RAID (redundant array of independent drives), 286

Rail transport, 315, 426

Rajbhog, Sweets, 140

Random access memory (RAM), 286, 287

Ratings
bond, 488–489
on corporate social responsibility, 74–75

Ratio analysis a comparison of numbers used to compare current data to data from previous years, competitor's data, or industry averages, 456, 461

Raw materials, 374
ethical sourcing and procurement of, 72–73
transportation of, 314

Real capital physical facilities used to produce goods and services, 5

Rebates an amount paid by way of reduction, return, or refund on what has already been paid or contributed, 390, 414

Recession a decline in the gross domestic product for two or more successive quarters of a year, 50

Recovery, in business cycle, 51

Recruitment the process of finding, screening, and selecting people for a job, 253–254

Recruitment consultants, 253–254

Reference pricing the practice of offering an inflated price that is discounted to appear to be a good value, 391

Regional business companies that serve a wider area than local business, but do not server national or international markets, 15–16

Regional free trade agreements, 107–109

Regulatory environment, 350–351

Reich, Robert, 104

Religion, 120–121, 268–269

Remote conferencing a system that allows many people to join a common discussion no matter their physical location, 289

Rensselaer Polytechnic Institute, 153

Repositioning, 384

Research in Motion (RIM), 341

Resellers, 417–418

Reserve requirement the minimum amount of money, as determined by the Federal Reserve Bank, that banks must hold in reserve to cover deposits, 54–55

Reserve stock system an inventory management system in which stock is set aside in reserve, and when the reserve is dipped into, new stock is ordered, 321

Resonance, 232–233

Resource prices, changes in, 38, 39

Resources, natural, 5

Resume, 434–435

Resume posting sites, 255

Retail (or local) advertising advertising that focuses on attracting customers to a fixed location like a department store or grocery store, 404

Retailers intermediaries that buy products for resale to ultimate consumers, 418
types of, 423–424

Retailing, 422–425

Retail organization, 425

Retail sales
e-commerce, 13

Retail stores, 423–424

Retail strategies, 422–423

Retained earnings the accumulated profits a business has held onto for reinvestment into the company, 456

Retirement an event that occurs when employees decide to stop working on a full-time basis or stop working altogether, 266–267

Retirement plans, 263

Revenue the money a business brings in, 3, 386, 459

Revenue bonds municipal bonds supported by the income generated by the project they finance, 488

Reverse logistics, 425

Revlon, 8

Risk return relationship the relationships of risk and return for various types of investments; the least risky investments offer the least amount of return, 478

Risk-taking, by entrepreneurs, 134–135

Risk tolerance, 478

Road transport, 314–315, 426

Robotics, 311

Rolling out the product, 383

Ronald McDonald House Charities, 408–409

Routing the way in which goods are transported, via water, rail, truck, or air, 323

Royal Dutch Shell, 99, 461

Ruby Tuesday, 112

Russia, 34, 46

S

Safety concern, 73

Safety needs a desire to establish safe, stable places to live and work, 225

Safeway, 425

Salary annual pay for a specific job, 262

Sales, maximization of, 387

Sales concept era, 338

Salespeople, 410–411

Sales promotions short-term activities that target consumers and other businesses for the purpose of generating interest in a product—and that have not already been undertaken by advertising, public relations, or personal selling, 400, 413–415, 416

Sales tax, 17

Salvation Army, 81

Samsung, 97

Sanaria, 83

Sarbanes-Oxley Act of 2002 an act passed by the United States Congress that protects investors from possible fraudulent accounting methods used by organizations, 80, 174, 293, 450, 451

SAS Institute, 224–225, 264

Schedules, alternative, 264–265

Scheduling the efficient organization of equipment, facilities, labor, and materials, 323

Schulster, Renate, 65–66

Scientific management, 230

SC Johnson, 371

S corporation organizations that are like C corporations that offer the protection of limited liability, but S corporations allow the shareholders to flow the corporate revenues and expenses through their personal tax returns, 175–176, 177–178

Reference Notes

Chapter 1

1 Jim Hopkins, "Surprise! There's a third YouTube co-founder," *USA Today*, October 11, 2006, http://www.usatoday.com/tech/news/2006-10-11-youtube-karim_x.htm.

2 Nonprofit Corporation, http://www.nolo.com/definition.cfm/term/BAEAC86A-2B5A-4B59-95070F88FB82326E, Accessed June 25, 2008.

3 John Cloud, "The Gurus of YouTube," *Time*, December 16, 2006, http://www.time.com/time/magazine/article/0,9171,1570721-1,00.html.

4 "HDTV sales in the U.S. to grow 71% by 2009," *Parks Associate Press Release*, October 27, 2005, http://www.parksassociates.com/press/press_releases/2005/hdtv-1.html.

5 Yardena Arar, "HDTV Competition Could Bring Deals," *PC World*, August 25, 2004, http://pcworld.about.com/news/Aug252004id117552.htm.

6 Joe Wilcox, "Microsoft, Apple Alliance at Key Juncture," *CNETNew.com* February 22, 2002, http://news.cnet.com/2100-1040-843145.html.

7 "American boomers now a $2 trillion market," *MSNBC*, September 28, 2006, http://www.msnbc.msn.com/id/12288534/.

8 Jeannine Aversa, "Bernanke: Baby Boomers Will Strain U.S.," October 4, 2007, http://www.breitbart.com/article.php?id=D8KHUEE00&show_article=1.

9 "100 Best Companies To Work For 2007: Best employees, most diverse," *Fortune*, http://money.cnn.com/magazines/fortune/bestcompanies/2007/snapshots/90.html, Accessed June 25, 2008.

10 Ryan Z. Cortazar, "Diversity training fails to boost minorities into management," *Harvard University Gazette*, September 16, 2006, http://www.news.harvard.edu/gazette/2006/09.14/25-dobbin.html.

11 Andrea Cooper, "The Influencers," *Entrepreneur.com*, March 11, 2008, http://www.usnews.com/articles/business/small-business-entrepreneurs/2008/03/11/the-influencers_print.htm.

12 Daniel Gross, "Hummer vs. Prius," *Slate*, February 6, 2004, http://www.slate.com/id/2096191/.

13 FedEx, "About Us," http://about.fedex.designcdt.com/our_company/company_information, Accessed June 25, 2008.

14 Mark Kyrnin, "Upgrade or Replace? What to Do With an Older Desktop PC," *About.com*, http://compreviews.about.com/od/general/a/UpgradeReplace.htm, Accessed June 25, 2008.

15 Patty Azzarello, "How to Overcome IT's Credibility Challenges," September 25, 2007, http://cioupdate.com/article.php/3701571.

16 Deloitte Press Release, January 31, 2005, http://www.deloitte.com/dtt/press_release/0,1014,cid%253D72123,00.html.

17 Allan Schweyer, "Managing the virtual global workforce," October 17, 2007, http://www.humanresourcesmagazine.com.au/articles/59/0C045E59.asp?Type=61&Category=1564.

18 "e-commerce," *Encyclopedia Britannica Online* at http://search.eb.com/eb/article-9126084, Accessed June 25, 2008.

19 Sherri Leopard, "B2B vs. B2C marketing — do the differences matter?" *Denver Business Journal*, March 31, 2006, http://www.bizjournals.com/denver/stories/2006/04/03/focus2.html?page=1.

20 Quarterly Retail E-commerce Sales, 4th Quarter 2007, *Retail Indicators Branch*, U.S. Census Bureau February 15, 2008, http://www.census.gov/mrts/www/ecomm.html. Accessed June 25, 2008.

21 Ibid.

22 Steve Schifferes, "How the internet transformed business," *BBC News*, August 3, 2006, http://news.bbc.co.uk/go/pr/fr/-/1/hi/business/5235332.stm.

23 Identity Theft Resource Center Facts and Statistics, April 30, 2007, http://www.idtheftcenter.org/artman2/publish/m_facts/Facts_and_Statistics.shtm.

24 The WaWa Story, http://www.wawa.com/WawaWeb/pdfs/theWawaStory.pdf, Accessed June 25, 2008.

25 "Temporary Disability Insurance," *Rhode Island Department of Labor and Training*, at http://www.dlt.ri.gov/tdi/, Accessed June 25, 2008.

26 "Half of Europe's Citizens Know a Foreign Language," *Associated Press*, September 25, 2005, at http://www.breitbart.com/article.php?id=D8CQJUE02&show_article=1.

27 "Nantucket Nectars from the Beginning," 2006, *Nantucket Allserve, Inc.*, at http://www.nantucketnectars.com/fullstory.php?PHPSESSID=996c6c936ce6351082022525b73e9fce, Accessed June 25, 2008.

28 "Limited Liability Company," *Internal Revenue Service*, United States Department of Treasury, http://www.irs.gov/businesses/small/article/0,,id=98277,00.html, Accessed June 25, 2008.

Chapter 2

1 Tax Foundation—Fiscal Fact No. 89, http://www.taxfoundation.org/publications/show/22469.html, Accessed March 19, 2008.

2 "Universities in Denmark," *International Graduate*, http://www.internationalgraduate.net/denmark_university.htm, Accessed May 9, 2008; "Maternity Leave," *Foreigners in Denmark*, http://www.foreignersindenmark.dk/display.cfm?article=1000403&page=Maternity+leave, Accessed May 9, 2008.

3 Hana Alberts, "Chasing Happiness," *Forbes*, April 23, 2008, http://www.forbes.com/2008/04/23/happiness-world-index-oped-cx_hra_0423happy.html.

4 David O'Connor and Christopher Faille, *Basic Economic Principles* (Westport, CT: Greenwood Press, 2000).

5 Chris Kohler, "Triumph of the Wii: How Fun Won Out in the Console Wars," *Wired*, June 11, 2007, http://www.wired.com/gaming/hardware/news/2007/06/wii.

6 "Microsoft Corporation," *Encyclopædia Britannica*, 2008, http://www.search.eb.com/eb/article-9001522, Accessed May 12, 2008.

7 Darryl Demos, "Productivity Metrics Not Just for Factories," *American Banker Online*, November 5, 2002, http://www.demossolutions.com/pdfs/articles/ProductivityMatrix_1102.pdf.

8 "The U.S. Inflation Rate – 1948-2007," *The U.S. Misery Index*, February 24, 2006, at http://www.miseryindex.us/irbyyear.asp.

9 Michelle Koetters, "Professor: Fed Moves Another Sign of Recession," *Pantagraph.com*, March 17, 2008, http://www.pantagraph.com/articles/2008/03/17/money/doc47def3a003a8c159233270.txt.

Chapter 3

1 "ethics," *The American Heritage® Dictionary of the English Language*, 4th ed. (Boston: Houghton Mifflin Company, 2004), http://dictionary.reference.com/search?q=ethics, Accessed April 24, 2008.

2 The character's name in this story has been changed from the name used in the original article. Ann Pomeroy, "The Ethics Squeeze," *HR Magazine*, March 2006, 53.

3 Authentic Happiness, www.authentichappiness.org, Accessed April 24, 2008.

4 Renae Merle, "Boeing CEO Resigns Over Affair with Subordinate," *Washington Post*, March 8, 2005, http://www.washingtonpost.com/wp-dyn/articles/A13173-2005Mar7.html?nav=rss_topnews, Accessed May 12, 2008.

5 The character's name in this story has been changed from the name used in the original article. Ann Pomeroy, "The Ethics Squeeze," *HR Magazine*, March 2006, 53.

6 Ibid.

7 Kurt Eichenwald, *The Informant: A True Story* (New York: Broadway Books, 2001).

8 "Why We Do What We Do," *Fetzer Vineyards*, http://www.fetzer.com/fetzer/wineries/philosophy.aspx, Accessed April 7, 2008.

9 Miriam Schulman, "Winery with a Mission: Fetzer Vineyards Husbands the Earth's Resources," *Issues in Ethics*, Spring 1996, vol. 7, no. 2, http://www.scu.edu/ethics/publications/iie/v7n2/fetzer.html.

10 "Center for Corporate Citizenship," *The Boston College Center for Corporate Citizenship*, http://www.bcccc.net/, Accessed April 24, 2008.

11 "Women in the Developing World," *Gap Inc.*, http://www.gapinc.com/public/SocialResponsibility/sr_com_target_women.shtml, Accessed April 24, 2008.

12 Brooks Barnes, "Bowing to Pressure, Disney Bans Smoking in Its Branded Movies," *The New York Times*, July 26, 2007, http://www.nytimes.com/2007/07/26/business/media/26disney.html.

13 "Our Approach," *Shell Environment and Society*, http://www.shell.com/home/content/envirosoc-en/environment/air_pollution/our_approach/our_approach_000407.html, Accessed April 24, 2008.

14 Mark Young, "HR as the Guardian of Corporate Values at Cadbury Schweppes," *Strategic HR Review*, Jan/Feb 2006:10.

15 "Changing an Industry," *No Sweat*, http://www.nosweatapparel.com, Accessed April 24, 2008.

16 Jennifer Alsever, "Chiquita Cleans Up Its Act," *Fortune*, November 17, 2006, http://money.cnn.com/magazines/fortune/fortune_archive/2006/11/27/8394414/index.htm.

17 "Citations of Statistics Used in the Film *Wal-Mart: The High Cost of Low Price*," www.Wal-Martmovie.com/facts.php, Accessed April 24, 2008.

18 "Who's Who," *The Corporation*, http://www.thecorporation.com/index.cfm?page_id=3, Accessed April 24, 2008.

19 "Corporate Social Responsibility," *European Business Forum*, London, Summer 2004:10, http://www.johnelkington.com/ebf_CSR_report.pdf.

20 "Corporate Social Responsibility Report," *Time Warner*, May 19, 2006, http://www.timewarner.com/corp/citizenship/index.page/csr_report_060519.pdf.

21 "HIV/AIDS, TB and Malaria," *DATA (debt AIDS trade Africa)*, http://www.data.org/issues/aids.html, Accessed April 24, 2008.

22 John Sparks, "Try Being Nice," *Newsweek*, June 26, 2006, http://www.newsweek.com/id/52247.

23 Ibid.

24 "Consumer Rights and Its Expansion," *CUTS Centre for Consumer Action Research and Training*, http://www.cuts-international.org/Consumer-Rights.htm, Accessed April 24, 2008.

25 "Companies in the News: Enron," *Corporate Social Responsibility News and Resources*, October 2, 2007, http://www.mallenbaker.net/csr/CSRfiles/enron.html.

26 Debby Young, "Repairing a Damaged Reputation: How New CEOS Can Recover from a Corporate Scandal," *Electronic Business*, June 1, 2005, http://www.edn.com/index.asp?layout=article&articleid=CA603493.

27 "Bank of America Announces Pilot Program to Reimburse Associates $3,000 for Purchase of Hybrid Vehicle," *Bank of America*, June 7, 2007, http://newsroom.bankofamerica.com/index.php?s=press_releases&item=7446.

28 "Bank of America Expands Hybrid Vehicle Program," *NAFTC eNews*, April 2007, http://www.naftc.wvu.edu/eNews/April07/boa.html.

29 Georgia Flight, "Whole Fuels," *Business 2.0*, December 1, 2005, http://money.cnn.com/magazines/business2/business2_archive/2005/12/01/8364601/index.htm.

30 Michael Myser, "Hunting a Ruthless Killer," *Business 2.0*, February 7, 2006, http://money.cnn.com/magazines/business2/business2_archive/2006/01/01/8368122/index.htm.

31 Bill Shore, "Bush Recognizes Social Entrepreneurship," *Seattle PI*, January 17, 2007, http://www.sanaria.com/pdf/Press-9-shorehunger17.pdf.

32 Ben Elgin and Bruce Einhorn, "Outrunning China's Web Cops," *Business Week*, February 20, 2006, http://www.businessweek.com/magazine/content/06_08/b3972061.htm?chan=search.

33 "Our Journey," *Interface Sustainability*, http://www.interfacesustainability.com/jour.html, Accessed May 13, 2008.

34 "What is Sustainability?" *Interface Sustainability*, http://www.interfacesustainability.com/whatis.html, Accessed April 24, 2008.

35 "Mission Statement," *Interface Sustainability*, http://www.interfacesustainability.com/visi.html, Accessed May 13, 2008.

36 "Starbucks Statement: Hot Beverage Cups and Recycling," *Starbucks*, September 18, 2007, http://www.starbucks.com/aboutus/pressdesc.asp?id=792.

37 Jocelyn M. Pollock and Ronald F. Becker, "Ethics Training Using Officers' Dilemmas-Police Officers-Focus on Training," *Federal Bureau of Investigation*, November 1996, http://www.fbi.gov/publications/leb/1996/nov964.txt.

38 Mark Young, "HR as the Guardian of Corporate Values at Cadbury Schweppes," *Strategic HR Review*, Jan/Feb 2006, http://www.allbusiness.com/human-resources/1049602-1.html.

Chapter 4

1 "Remarks by the President to Vietnam National University," *Embassy of the United States, Hanoi, Vietnam*, November 17, 2000, http://vietnam.usembassy.gov/pv11172000d.html/.

2 Charles W. L. Hill, *International Business: Competing in the Global Marketplace*, 6th ed (Burr Ridge, IL: Irwin/McGraw-Hill Publishing Co., 2007), pp. 6–8.

3 Ibid.

4 Govindkrishna Seshan, "Fruit Punch," *Business Standard*, February 26, 2008, http://www.business-standard.com/common/news_article.php?leftnm=10&bKeyFlag=BO&autono=314923.

5 Charles W. L. Hill, *International Business: Competing in the Global Marketplace*, 6th ed (Burr Ridge, IL: Irwin/McGraw-Hill Publishing Co., 2007), 10–16.

6 Ibid. Pages 18–24.

7 "North American Free Trade Agreement," *United States Department of Agriculture*, March 3, 2008, http://www.fas.usda.gov/itp/Policy/NAFTA/nafta.asp.

8 "An Interview with Robert Reich," *92nd Street Young Men's and Young Women's Hebrew Association*, September 27, 2005, http://blog.92y.org/index.php/weblog/item/robert_reich/.

9 "The GATT Years: from Havana to Marrakesh," *World Trade Organization*, http://www.wto.org/english/thewto_e/whatis_e/tif_e/fact4_e.htm, Accessed April 24, 2008.

10 "Understanding the WTO," *World Trade Organization*, http://www.wto.org/english/thewto_e/whatis_e/tif_e/tif_e.htm, Accessed April 24, 2008.

11 "Doha Development Agenda: Negotiations, Implementation, and Development," *World Trade Organization*, http://www.wto.org/english/tratop_e/dda_e/dda_e.htm, Accessed April 24, 2008.

12 "Rank Order: Exports," *CIA: The World Factbook*, https://www.cia.gov/library/publications/the-world-factbook/rankorder/2078rank.html, Accessed April 24, 2008; "Rank Order: Imports," *CIA: The World Factbook*, https://www.cia.gov/library/publications/the-world-factbook/rankorder/2087rank.html, Accessed April 24, 2008.

13 "Microsoft Loses Anti-Trust Appeal," *BBC News*, September 17, 2007, http://news.bbc.co.uk/1/hi/business/6998272.stm; "Microsoft Hit by Record EU Fine," *BBC News*, March 24, 2004, http://news.bbc.co.uk/1/hi/business/3563697.stm.

14 "Papa Johns Opens 50th Unit in China," *Franchise International*, Q1 2007, 16, at http://www.franchise-international.net/franchise/Papa-Johns-Pizza/Papa-Johns-opens-50th-unit-in-China/1834.

15 "Ruby Tuesday's Celebrates International Franchises," *Franchise International*, Q4 2006, 14, http://www.franchise-international.net/franchise/Ruby-Tuesday/Ruby-Tuesdays-celebrates-international-franchisees/1485.

16 "Disney Signs India Master," *Franchise International*, Q4 2006, 20, http://www.franchise-international.net/franchise/Walt-Disney-Company/Disney-signs-India-Master/1554.

17 "Domino's Pizza Gunning for 10,000th Store," *Franchise International*, Q3 2006, 33, http://www.franchise-international.net/franchise/Dominos-Pizza-Group/Dominos-Pizza-gunning-for-10000th-store/1270.

18 "Intellectual Property and Licensing," *SRI International*, 2008, http://www.sri.com/rd/hot.html, Accessed April 24, 2008.

19 "International Business," Thomas Gale, a part of the Thompson Corporation, 2006, http://www.referenceforbusiness.com/management/Gr-Int/International-Business.html, Accessed April 24, 2008.

20 "What We're About," *New United Motor Manufacturing, Inc.*, http://www.nummi.com/us_roots.php, Accessed April 25, 2008.

21 "Increasing American Competitiveness Through Strategic Alliances," *The Heritage Foundation*, September 26, 1991, http://www.heritage.org/Research/TradeandForeignAid/BG857.cfm.

22 C.G. Alex and Barbara Bowers, "The American Way to Countertrade," *BarterNews*, 1988 (issue 17), at http://www.barternews.com/american_way.htm.

23 "Cross Cultural Business Blunders," *Kwintessential*, http://www.kwintessential.co.uk/cultural-services/articles/crosscultural-blunders.html, Accessed April 25, 2008.

24 "Results of Poor Cross Cultural Awareness," *Kwintessential*, http://www.kwintessential.co.uk/cultural-services/articles/Results%20of%20Poor%20Cross%20Cultural%20Awareness.html, Accessed April 25, 2008.

25 Chris Taylor, "There's More Vacation Time on Tap for You," *CNN Money*, August 3, 2006, http://money.cnn.com/2006/08/03/technology/fbvacations0803.biz2/index.htm.

26 Ibid.

27 Ibid.

28 "Foreign Corrupt Practices Act," *United States Department of Justice*, http://www.usdoj.gov/criminal/fraud/docs/dojdocb.html, Accessed April 25, 2008.

Mini Chapter 1

[1] Steve Schifferes, "How the internet transformed business," *BBC News*, August 3, 2006, http://news.bbc.co.uk/2/hi/business/5235332.stm.

online content mybizlab.com:

[2] "15 Energy Companies Form Consortium for E-Procurement Exchange," *Duke Energy*, news release, March 29, 2000, http://www.duke-energy.com/news/releases/2000/Mar/2000032901.html.

[3] "What is Infomediary?" *SearchSOA.com*, October 22, 1999, http://searchsoa.techtarget.com/sDefinition/0,,sid26_gci212341,00.html.

[4] The Medica.com, *Global Healthcare Marketplace*, http://www.themedica.com/, Accessed June 19, 2008.

[5] Kent German, "Top 10 dot-com flops," at http://www.cnet.com/4520-11136_1-6278387-1.html, Accessed June 20, 2008.

[6] Robert D. Atkinson, "Revenge of the Disintermediated: How the Middleman is Fighting E-Commerce and Hurting Consumers," *Progressive Policy Institute*, policy report, January 26, 2001, at http://www.ppionline.org/ppi_ci.cfm?contentid=2941&knlgAreaID=140&subsecid=292.

[7] "B2B B2C Web Portals," *Dream Designers*, at http://www.dreamdesigners.co.in/b2c-web-portals.html, Accessed June 20, 2008.

[8] Business Standard main page at http://www.business-standard.com/main.php, Accessed June 20, 2008.

[9] Home page, http://www.netgames.com, Accessed June 20, 2008.

[10] "What Online Sales Are Subject to Sales Tax?" at http://www.allbusiness.com/sales/internet-e-commerce/2652-1.html, Accessed June 20, 2008.

[11] Ibid.

[12] Home page, http://ww21.1800flowers.com/storelocator.do, Accessed June 20, 2008.

[13] Chris Connolly and Peter van Dijk, "What Is E-Commerce Legal Infrastructure?," http://www.galexia.com/public/research/articles/research_articles-pa04.html#Heading296, Accessed June 20, 2008.

[14] "Daily Policy Digest: Legal Jurisdiction Over the Internet," *National Center for Policy Analysis*, April 29, 2003, http://www.ncpa.org/sub/dpd/index.php?Article_ID=5250.

[15] Julia Hanna, "Broadband: Remaking the Advertising Industry," *Harvard Business School Working Knowledge*, September 17, 2007, http://hbswk.hbs.edu/item/5652.html.

[16] Charles C. Mann, "How Click Fraud Could Swallow the Internet," *Wired*, January 2006, http://www.wired.com/wired/archive/14.01/fraud.html.

[17] "Web 2.0," glossary, *Proquest Discovery Guides*, http://www.csa.com/discoveryguides/scholarship/gloss.php. Accessed June 19, 2008.

[18] Ellen Neuborne, "Viral Marketing Alert!," *BusinessWeek Online*, March 19, 2001, http://www.businessweek.com/magazine/content/01_12/b3724628.htm.

[19] Daniel Terdiman, "Marketers Feverish Over Viral Ads," *Wired*, March 22, 2005, http://www.wired.com/techbiz/media/news/2005/03/66960.

[20] "Subservient Chicken," January 3, 2007, http://www.snopes.com/business/viral/chicken.asp.

[21] Frank Rose, "Secret Web Sites, Coded Messages: The New World of Immersive Games," *Wired*, December 20, 2007, http://www.wired.com/entertainment/music/magazine/16-01/ff_args.

[22] Chris Lee, "Teasing Batman," *Los Angeles Times*, March 24, 2008, http://www.latimes.com/entertainment/news/movies/la-et-batmanviral24mar24,0,3414080,full.story.

[23] "42 Entertainment: What We Do," http://www.42entertainment.com/do.html, Accessed June 20, 2008.

[24] "Online Banking: Is It For You," http://www.fool.com/money/banking/banking08.htm, Accessed June 20, 2008.

[25] "Paypal: About Us," https://www.paypal-media.com/aboutus.cfm, Accessed June 20, 2008.

[26] "Safe Internet Banking," *Federal Deposit Insurance Corporation*, July 11, 2007, http://www.fdic.gov/BANK/INDIVIDUAL/ONLINE/SAFE.HTML.

[27] "Adware," January 6, 2007, http://searchcio-midmarket.techtarget.com/sDefinition/0,,sid183_gci521293,00.html.

[28] "Spyware," October 10, 2006, http://searchsecurity.techtarget.com/sDefinition/0,,sid14_gci214518,00.html.

[29] Rebecca Porter, "Who's Watching Your PC?" *Trial*, August 1, 2004, http://goliath.ecnext.com/coms2/gi_0199-107385/Who-s-watching-your-PC.html.

[30] "Phishing," February 2008, http://onguardonline.gov/phishing.html.

Chapter 5

[1] http://www.mcdonalds.com/corp/about/mcd_history_pg1.html, Accessed May 1, 2008.

[2] http://www.corporations.org/wmi/huizenga.html, Accessed May 1, 2008.

[3] http://entrepreneurs.about.com/od/famousentrepreneurs/a/quotations.htm, Accessed May 6, 2008.

[4] "Henry Ford," http://inventors.about.com/library/inventors/blford.htm, Accessed May 1, 2008.

[5] http://www.benjerry.com/our_company/, Accessed May 1, 2008.

[6] Adapted from Jack Kaplan and Anthony Warren, *Patterns of Entrepreneurship*, 2nd ed., John Wiley & Sons, Inc, p. 27, from the U.S. Small Business Administration Report, "The State of Small Business: A Report of the President." (Washington, DC: U.S. Government Printing Office, 1995), p.114.

[7] Roger Fritz, "When Taking Business Risks Is Necessary," *San Francisco Business Times*, August 2, 1996, http://www.bizjournals.com/sanfrancisco/stories/1996/08/05/smallb2.html.

[8] http://www.ceochallenges.com/news/2008/02/29/kennedy-featured-daily-camera-business-plus-chat, Accessed April 16, 2008.

[9] http://www.petes.com/, Accessed May 1, 2008.

10 John Case, "Gazelle Theory," *inc.com*, May 2001, http://www.inc.com/magazine/20010515/22613.html.

11 Creativity Overflowing, http://www.businessweek.com/magazine/content/06_19/b3983061.htm?chan=searchand, Accessed May 1, 2008.

12 How Whirlpool Defines Innovation, http://www.businessweek.com/innovate/content/mar2006/id20060306_287425.htm?chan=search, Accessed May 1, 2008.

13 "Big Bang! UC Davis Business Plan Competition," University of California, Davis, Graduate School of Management, http://bigbang.gsm.ucdavis.edu/, Accessed, May 1, 2008.

14 "Small Business Size Standards," *U.S. Small Business Administration*, http://www.sba.gov/services/contractingopportunities/sizestandardstopics/index.html, Accessed May 1, 2008.

15 "Small Business Contributions to the Economy," *National Federation of Independent Business*, http://www.nfib.com/object/2753115.html, Accessed May 1, 2008.

16 "Statistics & Research," *U.S. Small Business Administration*, http://www.sba.gov/tools/resourcelibrary/smallbusinessstatisticsresearch/index.html, Accessed May 1, 2006.

17 Wells Fargo & Co., *prnewswire.com*, April 28, 2006.

18 "About Omnipod," *myomnipod.com*, http://www.myomnipod.com/, Accessed May 1, 2008.

19 NFIB Small Business Policy Guide quoting from Bo Carlsson, "Small Business, Innovation, and Industrial Dynamics," Are Small Firms Important? Their Role and Impact, (ed.) Zoltan J. Acs, Kluwer Academic Publishers, Boston, MA 1999.

20 Thomas H. Klier and James M. Rubenstein, "The Supplier Industry in Transition—The New Geography of Auto Production," August 2006, *chicagofed.org*, http://www.chicagofed.org/publications/fedletter/cflaugust2006_229b.pdf#search=%22automotive%20supplier%20cutbacks%22.

21 Arlene Weintraub, "Sizzling Hot Growth," *businessweek.com*, May 25, 2006, http://businessweek.com/smallbiz/content/may2006/sb20060525_123647.htm.

22 NFIB Small Business Policy Guide, January 31, 2003, Ch. 3, p. 31, http://www.nfib.com/object/2753115.html, Accessed May 1, 2008.

23 "Small Business Online," *entrepreneur.com*, www.entrepreneur.com/sbe/online/index.html, Accessed May 1, 2008.

24 Dan Tynan, "The 25 Worst Tech Products of All Time," *pcworld.com*, May 26, 2006, http://www.pcworld.com/article/id,125772-page,6/article.html, Accessed May 1, 2008.

25 "About Us," *prolinepr.com*, http://www.prolinepr.com/html/bruce_freeman.html, Accessed May 1, 2008.

26 "What is a franchise business?" *freeadvice.com*, http://business-law.freeadvice.com/franchise_law/franchise_business.htm, Accessed May 1, 2008.

27 Robin Griggs, "Carefully Consider All Aspects of Owning a Franchise," *Crain's Cleveland Business*, December 11, 2006, http://crainscleveland.com/article/20061211/SUB/61208005&SearchID=73285548983914.

28 Yu Lu, "Franchise Popularity Keeps Rising," *chinadaily.com*, March 23, 2006, http://www.chinadaily.com.cn/bizchina/2006-03/23/content_550462.htm.

29 Stacy Perman, Jeffrey Gangemi, and Douglas MacMillan, "Entrepreneurs' Favorite Mistakes," http://images.businessweek.com/ss/06/09/favorite_mistake/index_01.htm, Accessed May 1, 2008.

30 Ibid.

31 National Business Incubation Association, *Business Incubation Works*, Athens, Ohio: 1997.

32 Sarah Pierce, "The Million-Dollar Home Page," *entrepreneur.com*, January 13, 2006, http://www.entrepreneur.com/worklife/successstories/article82936.html, Accessed May 2, 2008.

Chapter 6

1 Nan Mooney, "When Good Friends Make Poor Colleagues," *Inc.com*, September 2006, http://www.inc.com/resources/women/articles/20060901/nmooney.html/.

2 "AOL and TheStreet.com Expand Content Partnership," *TimeWarner*, April 8, 2008, http://www.timewarner.com/corp/newsroom/pr/0,20812,1728738,00.html/.

3 William C. Symonds, "Commentary, Tyco: How Did They Miss a Scam So Big?" *BusinessWeek Online*, September 30, 2002, http://www.businessweek.com/magazine/content/02_39/b3801057.htm/.

4 Maureen Priest, from a personal phone interview conducted by Mary Anne Poatsy.

5 John Waggoner, "Dividends can give your portfolio a lift," *USA Today*, January 16, 2003, http://www.usatoday.com/money/perfi/columnist/waggon/2003-01-16-dividend_x.htm/.

6 "Instructions for Form 2553," *Department of the Treasury, Internal Revenue Service*, December 2007, http://www.irs.gov/pub/irs-pdf/i2553.pdf/, Accessed May 1, 2008.

7 "About Cooperatives," *National Cooperative Business Association*, http://www.ncba.coop/abcoop.cfm, Accessed May 1, 2008.

8 "Noven to Acquire JDS Pharmaceuticals, Expanding Business Model & Broadening Product Pipeline," *Pharmacy Choice*, July 26, 2007, http://www.pharmacychoice.com/News/article.cfm?Article_ID=62984/.

9 Ibid.

10 "Unsolicited Aggression," *BusinessWeek Online*, December 25, 2006, http://www.businessweek.com/magazine/content/06_52/b4015145.htm?chan=search/.

11 G. A. Marken, "Merger & Acquisition Wars Take No Prisoners," *Enterprise Networks & Servers*, May 2005, www.enterprisenetworksandservers.com/monthly/art.php?1457/.

12 Ibid.

13 "Exxon, Mobil in $80B deal," *CNN Money*, December 1, 1998, http://money.cnn.com/1998/12/01/deals/exxon/.

14 IBM Corporate Web site at www-306.ibm.com/software/data/integration/interaction.html/, Accessed May 1, 2008.

15 "Mergers and Acquisitions: Why They Can Fail," *Investopedia ULC*, www.investopedia.com/university/mergers/mergers5.asp/, Accessed May 1, 2008.

Mini Chapter 2

[1] Sarah Bartlett, "Seat of the Pants," *Inc.com*, October 2002, http://www.inc.com/magazine/20021015/24772.html/.

[2] "Pizza Hut Inc.," *Funding Universe*, http://www.fundinguniverse.com/company-histories/Pizza-Hut-Inc-Company-History.html, Accessed June 9, 2008.

[3] "Our History," *Pizza Hut Online*, http://www.pizzahut.co.uk/restaurant/history.html/, Accessed May 21, 2008; David Gumpert, *How to Really Create a Successful Business Plan* (Inc. Publishing, 1990), 17.

online content mybizlab.com:

[4] "The Truth About Cats and Dogs: They're Costly," *Get It Started*, Spring 2003, http://www.wep.wharton.upenn.edu/newsletter/spring03/paws.html, Accessed June 9, 2008.

[5] "Petplan Advantage," http://www.gopetplan.com/WhyPetPlan/PetPlanAdvantage.html, Accessed June 9, 2008.

Chapter 7

[1] Carter McNamara, "Strategic Planning (in nonprofit or for-profit organizations)," *Free Management Library*, http://www.managementhelp.org/plan_dec/str_plan/str_plan.htm, Accessed April 28, 2008.

[2] Domino's Pizza, http://www.dominosbiz.com/Public-EN/Site+Content/Secondary/Inside+Dominos/, Accessed May 8, 2008.

[3] "American Cancer Society Mission Statement," http://www.cancer.org/docroot/AA/content/AA_1_1_ACS_Mission_Statements.asp, Accessed April 29, 2008.

[4] U.S. Department of Labor, Bureau of Labor Statistics, http://www.bls.gov/mls/home.htm, Accessed April 28, 2008.

[5] Business Contingency Planning and Disaster Recovery Programs at Vanguard, 2004, http://www.vanguard.com/pdf/ccri.pdf, Accessed April 28, 2008.

[6] Frank Ostroff, *The Horizontal Organization* (Oxford: Oxford University Press, 1999).

[7] Thomas A. Stewart, "The Search for the Organization of Tomorrow," *Fortune*, May 18, 1992, http://money.cnn.com/magazines/fortune/fortune_archive/1992/05/18/76425/index.htm.

[8] James M. Kouzes and Barry Z. Posner, *The Leadership Challenge*, 3rd ed. (San Francisco: Jossey-Bass, 2003).

[9] Fred Luthans, "Successful vs. Effective Real Managers," *Academy of Management Executive*, 1988, 2(2):127-132.

[10] Ralph Stayer, "How I Learned to Let My Workers Lead," http://www.wku.edu/~hrtm/CFS-452/Readings/stayer.htm, Accessed on April 28, 2008.

[11] William Ouchi, "Markets, Bureaucracies, and Clans." *Administrative Science Quarterly*, 1980, 25:129.

[12] Google corporate philosophy, http://www.google.com/corporate/tenthings.html, Accessed April 30, 2008.

Chapter 8

[1] Mihaly Csikszentmihalyi, *Flow* (New York: HarperCollins, 1990).

[2] "Many Employees Would Fire Their Boss," *Gallup Management Journal*, October 11, 2007, http://gmj.gallup.com/content/28867/Many-Employees-Would-Fire-Their-Boss.aspx.

[3] Jim Goodnight and Richard Florida, "Managing for Creativity," *Harvard Business Review*, July 2005.

[4] "The High Cost of Disengaged Employees," *Gallup Management Journal*, April 15, 2002, http://gmj.gallup.com/content/247/The-High-Cost-of-Disengaged-Employees.aspx.

[5] Stratford Sherman and Anthony Rucci, "Bringing Sears into the New World," *Fortune*, October 13, 1997, http://money.cnn.com/magazines/fortune/fortune_archive/1997/10/13/232506/index.htm.

[6] "What really motivates us?" BBC Educational consultant Nash Popovic video, http://news.bbc.co.uk/nolavconsole/ukfs_news/hi/newsid_4760000/newsid_4764500/nb_rm_4764545.stm, Accessed May 5, 2008.

[7] Strength Based Performance Management, http://www.strengthsmanagement.com, Accessed May 5, 2008.

[8] Marcus Buckingham, *Now, Discover Your Strengths* (New York: Free Press, 2001).

[9] Kristina A. Diekmann, Zoe I. Barsness, and Harris Sondak, "Uncertainty, Fairness Perceptions, and Job Satisfaction: A Field Study," *Social Justice Research*, Vol. 17, No. 3, September 2004.

[10] Sociocracy in Action, http://www.sociocracyinaction.ca/whatis.htm, updated May 3, 2007.

[11] "About us," *Ternary Software*, http://ternarysoftware.com/aboutus.php, Accessed May 5, 2008.

[12] Brian Robertson, "The Sociocratic Method," *Strategy+Business*, Autumn 2006, http://www.strategy-business.com/press/16635507/06314.

[13] Quote Details, http://quotationspage.com/quote/26536.html, Accessed May 5, 2008.

[14] Brian Grow, "Out at Home Depot: Behind the Flameout of Controversial CEO Bob Nardelli," *BusinessWeek*, January 9, 2007, http://www.msnbc.msn.com/id/16469224/.

[15] Jon Huntsman, *Winners Never Cheat: Everyday Values We Learned as Children (But May Have Forgotten)* (Philadelphia: Wharton School Publishing, 2005).

[16] "Great Ideas in Personality." http://www.personalityresearch.org/bigfive/costa.html and the self-test at The Big 5 Personality Test at http://www.outofservice.com/bigfive/, Accessed May 5, 2008.

[17] "16PF Fifth Edition," at http://www.pearsonassessments.com/reports/16pf5couples.pdf, Accessed May 5, 2008.

[18] Del Jones, "Does Height Equal Power? Some CEOs say Yes," *USA Today*, July 17, 2007, http://www.usatoday.com/money/companies/management/2007-07-17-ceo-dominant-behavior_N.htm?POE=click-refer.

[19] Adam Lashinsky, "RAZR's edge: How a Team of Engineers and Designers Defied Motorola's Own Rules to Create the Cellphone that Revived Their Company," *Fortune*, June 1, 2006, http://money.cnn.com/2006/05/31/magazines/fortune/razr_greatteams_fortune/index.htm.

[20] John R. Katzenbach and Douglas K. Smith, *The Wisdom of Teams* (Cambridge, Massachusetts: Harvard University Press, 1993).

21 "Six Teams that Changed the World," *Fortune*, May 31, 2006, http://money.cnn.com/2006/05/31/magazines/fortune/sixteams_greatteams_fortune_061206/index.htm.

22 David C. Smith, "Ford's $3-Billion Mid-Market Plunge: Ford Motor Co. Makes Taurus & Sable Cars," *Ward's Auto World*, February 1985, http://www.highbeam.com/doc/1G1-3628368.html.

23 "Say Goodbye to the Taurus, Ford's '80s Savior," *MSNBC.com*, October 20, 2006, http://www.msnbc.msn.com/id/15338425/.

24 NACS, "Teamwork Concept Questioned," August 11, 2006, http://www.nacs.org/news/081106-teamwork.asp?id=cm.

25 Stephanie Armour, "Generation Y: They've arrived at work with a new attitude," *USA Today*, November 6, 2005, http://www.usatoday.com/money/workplace/2005-11-06-gen-y_x.htm.

26 "What's Ahead for Generation Y?," *The News & Observer*, February 7, 2006, http://www.newsobserver.com/164/story/396500.html.

27 Rhonda Abrams, "You've Got to Play "Small Ball" to be Successful in the Game," *USA Today*, June 2, 2006, http://www.usatoday.com/money/smallbusiness/columnist/abrams/2006-06-02-small-ball_x.htm.

28 2007 National League Baseball Standings, http://www.baseball-reference.com/leagues/NL_2007.shtml, Accessed May 6, 2008.

29 "Six Teams that Changed the World,"*Fortune*, May 31, 2006, http://money.cnn.com/2006/05/31/magazines/fortune/sixteams_greatteams_fortune_061206/index.htm.

30 Lauren Rotman, e-mail message "Students Across the Country To Participate in First-Ever Live Virtual National Constitution Day Event," September 14, 2006, https://mail.internet2.edu/wws/arc/i2-news/2006-09/msg00000.html.

31 J. S. Lurey and M. S. Raisinghani, "An Empirical Study of Best Practices in Virtual Teams," *Information & Management*, 2001.

32 Stephen R. Covey, *The 7 Habits of Highly Effective People* (New York: Free Press, 1989).

Chapter 9

1 LinkedIn.com, http://www.linkedin.com/static?key=company_info&trk=hb_ft_abtli, Accessed May 5, 2008.

2 Lou Adler, "Hiring and Recruiting Challenges Survey 2008 Preliminary Results," http://www.ere.net/articles/db/474AC6F733CF4B6092BC2F47CAC548FD.asp, Accessed May 5, 2008.

3 Michelle V. Rafter, "Unicru breaks through in the science of "smart hiring," *Workforce Management*, May 2005, 84(5):76-78.

4 Stephane Thiffeault, "Poor Reference Check Results in Damages," McMillian Binch Mendelsohn, *Employment & Labour Relations Bulletin*, February 2006.

5 "About the EEOC," http://www.eeoc.gov/abouteeoc/35th/1965-71/index.html, Accessed May 5, 2008.

6 EEOC, "Facts about the Americans with Disabilities Act" at http://www.eeoc.gov/facts/fs-ada.html, Accessed May 5, 2008.

7 EEOC, "Age Discrimination" at http://www.eeoc.gov/types/age.html, Accessed May 5, 2008.

8 http://www.persuasivegames.com/games/game.aspx?game=coldstone, Accessed May 5, 2008; "On the Job Video Gaming," *Business Week*, March 27, 2006, http://www.businessweek.com/magazine/content/06_13/b3977062.htm, Accessed May 5, 2008.

9 Carter McNamara, "Employee Training and Development: Reasons and Benefits," Authenticity Consulting, LLC., http://www.managementhelp.org/ trng_dev/basics/reasons.htm, Accessed May 5, 2008.

10 Karen O'Leonard, "Performance Support Systems," *Bersin & Associates*, February 2005.

11 "Organizational Learning Strategies, Action Learning," http://www.humtech.com/opm/grtl/ols/ols2.cfm, Accessed May 5, 2008.

12 McDonald's Press Release, "McDonald's U.S. Training Curriculum Awarded 46 College Credit Recommendations," http:// mcdonaldsemail.com/usa/news/2005/conpr_11222005.html, Accessed May 5, 2008.

13 http://www.persuasivegames.com/games/game.aspx?game=coldstone, Accessed May 5, 2008; "On the Job Video Gaming," *Business Week*, March 27, 2006, http://www.businessweek.com/magazine/content/06_13/b3977062.htm, Accessed May 5, 2008.

14 Adam Lashinsky, "The Perks of Being a Googler," http://money.cnn.com/magazines/fortune/bestcompanies/2007/index.html, Accessed May 5, 2008.

15 http://www.computerworld.com/html/research/bestplaces/2006/bpchart_05_itturnover.html#region.

16 "Phoenix Enhances Employee Benefits With Paid Paternity Leave, Increased Adoption Assistance," April 17, 2007, http://www.allbusiness.com/services/business-services/4319890-1.html, Accessed May 5, 2008.

17 "Workers on Flexible and Shift Schedules in 2004," http://www.bls.gov/news.release/flex.nr0.htm, Accessed May 5, 2008.

18 "Work Trends Vol 8, No. 1, A Work-Filled Retirement: Workers' Changing Views on Employment and Leisure," *John J. Heldrich Center for Workforce Development, Rutgers University*, http://www.heldrich.rutgers.edu/Publications/RecentPublicationsByPT.aspx?id=Press+Releases, Accessed January 12, 2008.

19 "At Chrysler Unit, Buyouts for Older Workers," *New York Times*, February 24, 2007, http://www.nytimes.com/2007/02/24/automobiles/24auto.html?_r=1&oref=slogin, Accessed May 5, 2008.

20 Carol Hymowitz, "Diversity in a Global Economy—Ways Some Firms Get It Right," *Wall Street Journal Online*, November 16, 2005.

21 Lisa Takeuchi Cullen, "Employee Diversity Training Doesn't Work," *Time*, April 26, 2007, http://www.time.com/time/magazine/article/0,9171,1615183,00.html, Accessed May 5, 2008.

22 Robert Rodriguez, "Diversity finds its place: more organizations are dedicating senior-level executives to drive diversity initiatives for bottom-line effect," *HR Magazine*, August 1, 2006.

23 Andrew Farrell and Joann Muller, "The GM Strike: Seems Like Old Times," September 24, 2007, http://www.forbes.com/markets/2007/09/24/general-motors-updatetwo-markets-equity-cx_af_0924markets20.html, Accessed May 5, 2008.

24 Bureau of Labor and Statistics, January 25, 2007, http://www.bls.gov/news.release/union2.nr0.htm.

25 HR World Editors, "30 Interview Questions You Can't Ask and 30 Sneaky, Legal Alternatives to Get the Same Info," November 15, 2007, http://www.hrworld.com/features/30-interview-questions-111507/, Accessed May 5, 2008.

Chapter 10

1 Karen Gottlieb, "Using Court Record Information for Marketing in the United States: It's Public Information, What's the Problem?", *Privacy Rights Clearinghouse*, January 2004, http://www.privacyrights.org/ar/courtmarketing.htm.

2 "IBM Cognos Supply Chain Analytics," *Cognos ULC*, http://www.cognos.com/products/business_intelligence/applications/supplychain_analytics.html, Accessed May 20, 2008.

3 Galen Gruman, "Managing Mobile Devices," *CIO.com*, January 15, 2007, http://www.cio.com/article/28177/Managing_Mobile_Devices/1.

4 "Applications Showcase Archive," *Internet2*, http://apps.internet2.edu/showcase-archive.html, Accessed May 20, 2008.

5 Susan Heathfield, "Listen with Your Eyes: Tips for Understanding Nonverbal Communication," *About.com*, http://humanresources.about.com/od/interpersonalcommunicatio1/a/nonverbal_com.htm, Accessed May 20, 2008.

6 "Electronic Eavesdropping," *Encyclopedia Britannica*, http://search.eb.com/eb/article-9032334, Accessed May 20, 2008.

7 D. DiTecco, G. Cwitco, A. Arsenault, and M. Andre, "Operator Stress and Monitoring Practices," *Applied Ergonomics* 23(1):29-34.

8 Dan Nakaso, "$1 Tickets Crash Airline's Website," *USA Today*, June 12, 2007, http://www.usatoday.com/travel/flights/2007-06-12-one-dollar-tickets-crash-web_N.htm.

9 Andy McCue, "IT Failure Remains Top Cause of Business Disaster," *silicon.com*, March 11, 2005, http://hardware.silicon.com/storage/0,39024649,39128617,00.htm.

10 Mark Jewell, "T.J. Maxx Theft Believed Largest Hack Ever," *MSNBC.com*, March 30, 2007, http://www.msnbc.msn.com/id/17871485/.

11 Ben Worthen, "Mid-Market: The Big Upgrade to Microsoft Vista," *CIO.com*, November 16, 2006, http://www.cio.com/article/26664/Mid_Market_The_Big_Upgrade_to_Microsoft_Vista.

12 Paul Sloan, "The Quest for the Perfect Online Ad," *CNNMoney.com*, April 3, 2007, http://money.cnn.com/magazines/business2/business2_archive/2007/03/01/8401043/index.htm.

13 Paul Sloan, "The Quest for the Perfect Online Ad," *CNNMoney.com*, April 3, 2007, http://money.cnn.com/magazines/business2/business2_archive/2007/03/01/8401043/index.htm.

14 Jim Jubak, "A 15% Raise? Try China or India," *msnmoney*, January 5, 2007, http://articles.moneycentral.msn.com/Investing/JubaksJournal/A15RaiseTryChinaOrIndia.aspx.

15 "Offshore Outsourcing Basics," *E-business Strategies, Inc.*, http://www.ebstrategy.com/outsourcing/basics/faq.htm, Accessed May 20, 2008.

16 Jim Jubak, "A 15% Raise? Try China or India," *msnmoney*, January 5, 2007, http://articles.moneycentral.msn.com/Investing/JubaksJournal/A15RaiseTryChinaOrIndia.aspx.

17 Justin Fox, "Where Your Job is Going," *Fortune*, November 24, 2003, http://money.cnn.com/magazines/fortune/fortune_archive/2003/11/24/353752/index.htm.

18 "HP Fuels Growth with Print 2.0, Launches $300 Million Global Marketing Campaign," *Hewlett-Packard Development Company, L.P.*, August 28, 2007, http://www.hp.com/hpinfo/newsroom/press/2007/070828xc.html.

19 Jeneanne Rae, "The Keys to High-Impact Innovation," *BusinessWeek.com*, September 27, 2005, http://www.businessweek.com/innovate/content/sep2005/id20050927_002673.htm?chan=search.

20 Fara Warner, "Made in China," *fastcompany.com*, April 2007, http://www.fastcompany.com/magazine/114/open_features-made-in-china.html.

21 U.S. and China Education Fact Sheet, *Internationaled.org*, www.internationaled.org/PressFactSheet-China.doc, Accessed May 20, 2008.

Chapter 11

1 "Ford installs the first moving assembly line 1913," *PBS.org*, 1998 http://www.pbs.org/wgbh/aso/databank/entries/dt13as.html, Accessed June 25, 2008.

2 "Automation," *Encyclopedia Britannica*, http://www.britannica.com/eb/article-24854/automation, Accessed May 13, 2008.

3 Don Tapscott and Anthony D. Williams, "Hack This Product, Please!" *BusinessWeek.com*, February 23, 2007, at http://www.businessweek.com/innovate/content/feb2007/id20070223_399988.htm?chan=innovation_special+report+—+the+power+of+gaming_the+businessweek+wikinomics+series.

4 Russ Storey, "A Customer-driven Manufacturing Approach to Mass Customization," *CVIS*, January 6, 2005, http://www.cvis.cz/eng/hlavni.php?stranka=novinky/clanek.php&id=12.

5 "Robot," *Merriam-Webster Online Dictionary*, http://www.merriam-webster.com/dictionary/robot, Accessed May 13, 2008.

6 David Kucera, "Computer-Aided Design (CAD) and Computer-Aided Manufacturing (CAM)," *Encyclopedia of Business*, 2nd ed., at http://www.referenceforbusiness.com/encyclopedia/Clo-Con/Computer-Aided-Design-CAD-and-Computer-Aided-Manufacturing-CAM.html, Accessed June 11, 2008.

7 Ibid.

8 Tim Mullaney, "An IPO That Might Print You Some Money," *BusinessWeek.com*, November 9, 2005, http://www.businessweek.com/the_thread/dealflow/archives/2005/11/vistaprint.html?chan=search.

9 Tim Feemster, "A Step-by-Step Guide to Choosing the Right Site," *Area Development Online*, November 2007, http://www.areadevelopment.com/Print/siteSelection/nov07/stepByStep.html.

10 "Ford Honors Penske Logistics with Two Q1 Awards," *Investor's Business Daily*, April 22, 2004, http://www.investors.com/breakingnews.asp?journalid=20830645&brk=1.

11 "CNH Global Selects Oracle(r) Transportation Management to Transform Worldwide Logistics Operations," *Oracle* press release, October 16, 2006, http://www.oracle.com/corporate/press/2006_oct/cnh.html.

12 "Our Story," *Karl Strauss Brewing Company*, http://www.karlstrauss.com/PAGES/Our_Company/Our_Story/Start.htm, Accessed April 17, 2008.

13 "Tata Steel ranked world's best steel maker by World Steel Dynamics," *Tata* media release, June 22, 2005, at http://www.tata.com/tata_steel/releases/20050622.htm.

14 Paul Graham, "How to Be Silicon Valley," *paulgraham.com*, May 2006, http://www.paulgraham.com/siliconvalley.html.

15 Paul McDougall, "India, Canada, and China Are Top Outsourcing Destinations: Study," *InformationWeek*, September 21, 2005, http://www.informationweek.com/news/management/trends/showArticle.jhtml;jsessionid=XUMSNKJ40OYTSQSNDLOSKHSCJUNN2JVN?articleID=171000615&_requestid=134064.

16 Karen Breslau, "The Growth in 'Green-Collar' Jobs," *Newsweek.com*, April 8, 2008, http://www.newsweek.com/id/131038/page/2.

17 Mike Musgrove, "Sweatshop Conditions at iPod Factory Reported," *Washington Post*, June 16, 2006, http://www.washingtonpost.com/wp-dyn/content/article/2006/06/15/AR2006061501898.html.

18 "Report on iPod Manufacturing," *Apple Hot News*, August 17, 2006, http://www.apple.com/hotnews/ipodreport/.

19 "Does Your Business Produce Hazardous Waste?" *Local Hazardous Waste Management Program in King County*, http://www.govlink.org/hazwaste/business/does.html, Accessed April 21, 2008.

20 "The IKEA Range," *Inter IKEA Systems B.V.*, http://franchisor.ikea.com/showContent.asp?swfId=range3, Accessed June 24, 2008.

21 Kim Gilmour, "Amazon adventure," *Internet Magazine*, September 2003, http://www.kimgilmour.com/articles/archive/amazon_warehouse.html.

22 Louise Story, "Lead Paint Prompts Mattel to Recall 967,000 Toys," *New York Times*, August 2, 2007, http://www.nytimes.com/2007/08/02/business/02toy.html.

23 "The supplier selection process," *Business Link*, http://www.businesslink.gov.uk/bdotg/action/layer?topicId=1073920782, Accessed June 24, 2008.

24 "Inventory Control," *SCORE (Counselors to America's Small Business)*, Handout 06/02, http://www.ct-clic.com/Newsletters/customer-files/inventory0602.pdf, Accessed June 25, 2008.

25 "What Is ERP?" *techFAQ*, http://www.tech-faq.com/erp.shtml, Accessed May 14, 2008.

26 "Puma Mongolian Shoe BBQ," *Puma AG*, https://www.puma.com/secure/mbbq/pindex.jsp?ip=US, Accessed May 14, 2008.

27 "Inbound Transportation Management and Control: Low Hanging Fruit and How to Grab It," *TransportGistics, Inc.*, http://www.insourceaudit.com/whitepapers/Inbound%20Transportation%20Management.asp, Accessed June 25, 2008.

28 Associated Press, "Bridgestone and Ford Settle Dispute Over Defective Tires," *New York Times*, October 13, 2005, http://www.nytimes.com/2005/10/13/business/13ford.html.

29 "The History of Quality—Overview," *American Society for Quality*, http://www.asq.org/learn-about-quality/history-of-quality/overview/overview.html, Accessed June 25, 2008.

30 "The History of Quality—Total Quality," *American Society for Quality*, http://www.asq.org/learn-about-quality/history-of-quality/overview/total-quality.html, Accessed June 25, 2008.

31 "Quality Quotes," *Society for Technical Communication*, http://www.stcsig.org/quality/q_quotes.htm, Accessed June 25, 2008.

32 "Continuous Improvement," *American Society for Quality*, http://www.asq.org/learn-about-quality/continuous-improvement/overview/overview.html, Accessed June 25, 2008.

33 "Motorola University: Six Sigma in Action," *Motorola, Inc.*, http://www.motorola.com/motorolauniversity.jsp, Accessed June 25, 2008.

34 Roger O. Crocket and Jena McGregor, "Six Sigma Still Pays Off At Motorola," *BusinessWeek.com*, December 4, 2006, http://www.businessweek.com/magazine/content/06_49/b4012069.htm.

35 "ISO's name," *International Organization for Standardization*, at http://www.iso.org/iso/about/discover-iso_isos-name.htm, Accesed June 25, 2008.

Mini Chapter 3

1 Edward G. Wertheim, "The Importance of Effective Communication," http://web.cba.neu.edu/~ewertheim/interper/commun.htm#getting, Accessed May 21, 2008.

online content mybizlab.com:

2 Alan Chapman, "Mehrabian's Communication Research," http://www.businessballs.com/mehrabiancommunications.htm, Accessed May 21, 2008.

3 "Email Privacy," *Nolo*, http://www.nolo.com/article.cfm/objectId/286D456E-73C7-414A-B174343E0225C4C8/catID/96A3E6BC-22BC-43EE-BDE2D470B0972A47/104/284/220/ART/, Accessed May 21, 2008.

4 Alison Overholt, "Intel's Got Too Much Mail," February 2001, http://www.fastcompany.com/magazine/44/intel.html?page=0%2C0.

5 Eric Horng, "No-E-Mail Fridays Transform Office," *ABC News*, April 7, 2007, http://abcnews.go.com/WNT/Story?id=2939232&page=1.

6 Evan Hansen, "Google Blogger: 'I Was Terminated,'" *CNET News.com*, February 11, 2005, http://news.cnet.com/Google-blogger-I-was-terminated/2100-1038_3-5572936.html.

7 Fortune 500 Business Blogging Wiki / Fortune 500 Business Blogging Wiki, http://www.socialtext.net/bizblogs/index.cgi, Accessed May 22, 2008.

Chapter 12

1 "marketing," *American Marketing Association Online Dictionary*, http://www.marketingpower.com/_layouts/Dictionary.aspx?dLetter=M, Accessed May 30, 2008.

2 Advertising Council, http://www.adcouncil.org/, Accessed January 2, 2008.

3 http://www.museummarketingtips.com/quotes/quotes_ac.html, Accessed May 30, 2008.

4 L.L. Bean, http://www.llbean.com/, Accessed January 5, 2008.

5 Michael Malone, "A Dot-Com Pantomime," *www.forbes.com*, November 16, 2000, http://www.forbes.com/2000/11/16/1116malone.html.

6 Low End Macs, http://lowendmac.com/lite/lite07/0913.html, Accessed May 30, 2008.

7 Charles W. Lamb, Jr., Joseph F. Hair, and Carl McDaniel, *Marketing*, 7th edition (Stamford, CT: Thomson Publishing Company, 2004), 33.

8 John Deere, www.deere.com, Accessed January 19, 2008.

9 High Beam Research, http://findarticles.com/p/articles/mi_hb3450/is_200012/ai_n8216539, Accessed May 30, 2008.

10 Fortune, http://www.mutualofamerica.com/articles/Fortune/2002_08_01/fortune.asp, Accessed May 30, 2008.

11 U.S. News and World Report, http://www.usnews.com/sections/rankings, Accessed May 30, 2008.

12 Philip Kotler and Gary Armstrong, *Principles of Marketing*, 12th edition (Upper Saddle River, NJ: Pearson/Prentice Hall, 2008), 131-147.

13 Philip Kotler and Kevin Lane Keller. *Marketing Management*, 12th edition (Upper Saddle River, NJ: Pearson/Prentice Hall, 2006), 211-212; Philip Kotler and Gary Armstrong, *Principles of Marketing*, 12th edition (Upper Saddle River, NJ: Pearson/Prentice Hall, 2008), 161-162.

Chapter 13

1 Theresa Howard, "Coke Finally Scores Another Winner," November 9, 2007, http://www.usatoday.com/money/advertising/adtrack/2007-10-28-coke-zero_N.htm.

2 Oust Frequently Asked Questions, http://www.oust.com/faq.aspx?oust=airSanitizer, Accessed May 14, 2007.

3 Toyota Motor Corp TM Full Description (NYSE), http://stocks.us.reuters.com/stocks/fullDescription.asp?symbol=TM, Accessed April 30, 2008.

4 The Coca-Cola Company: The Beverage Industry Leader, http://www.thecoca-colacompany.com/ourcompany/index.html, Accessed May 14, 2007.

5 Coca-Cola Product List, http://www.thecoca-colacompany.com/brands/brandlist.html, Accessed April 30, 2008.

6 GE Products and Services Overview, http://www.ge.com/, Accessed April 30, 2008.

7 Coca-Cola Products, http://www.thecoca-colacompany.com/brands/index.html, Accessed April 30, 2008.

8 Interbrand and BusinessWeek, "Top 100 Global Brands Scorecard," August 2007, http://bwnt.businessweek.com/interactive_reports/top_brands/, Accessed April 30, 2008.

9 Advertising Council, http://www.adcouncil.org/, Accessed January 2, 2008.

10 "Convenience Packaging Boosts Sales," *DSN Retailing Today*, Oct. 11, 2004, *BNET Business Network*: http://findarticles.com/p/articles/mi_m0FNP/is_19_43/ai_n6245181.

11 The Association for Dressings & Sauces, The Press Room Package of the Year, October 2007, http://www.dressings-sauces.org/pressroom_poty.html.

12 *Consumer Reports*, "Does Hellman's Make for Easy Squeezing?" September 2006, http://www.consumer-reports.org/cro/food/food-shopping/oils-soups-sauces/hellmanns-easy-out/hellmans-easy-out-9-06/overview/0609_hellmans-easy-out_ov.htm.

13 Tiffany & Co. About Tiffany at http://www.tiffany.com/About/Default.aspx?isMenu=1&#p+1-n+6-cg+-c+-s+-r+-t+-ri+-ni+1-x+-pu+linkHistoryTimeline-f, Accessed May 15, 2008.

14 Jennifer Miner, "Green Luxury Packages at Fairmont," February 7, 2008, http://luxuryresorttravel.suite101.com/article.cfm/green_luxury_packages_at_fairmont.

15 Michael E. Ross, "It Seemed Like a Good Idea at the Time," April 22, 2005, http://www.msnbc.msn.com/id/7209828.

16 Robert E. Cannon, "A Tutorial on Product Life Cycle," http://www.mrotoday.com/progressive/online%20exclusives/productlifecycle.htm, Accessed May 15, 2008.

17 Dan Swenson, Shahid Ansari, Jan Bell, and Il-Woon Kim, "Best Practices in Target Costing," *Management Accounting Quarterly*, Winter 2003.

18 Vivian Wai-yin Kwok, "Virgin Blue Set To Challenge Qantas In Trans-Pacific Air Fight," March 31, 2008, http://www.forbes.com/2008/03/31/virgin-australia-qantas-markets-equity-cx_vk_0331markets02_print.html.

19 "U.S. Department of Transportation, What They're Saying: Airline Competition Leads to Lower Fares," http://www.dot.gov/affairs/aviation080516/what_are_they_saying.htm, Accessed June 6, 2008.

Chapter 14

1 Bob Garfield, "The Top 100 Advertising Campaigns of the Century," *The Advertising Century*, Crain Communications, http://adage.com/century/campaigns.html, Accessed May 15, 2008.

2 Theresa Howard, "Dove Ads Enlist All Shapes, Styles, Sizes," *USA Today*, August 28, 2005, http://www.usatoday.com/money/advertising/adtrack/2005-08-28-track-dove_x.htm.

3 "Internet Advertising Revenues Again Reach New Highs, Estimated to Pass $21 Billion in 2007 and Hit Nearly $6 Billion in Q4 2007," *Interactive Advertising Bureau*, February 25, 2008, http://www.iab.net/about_the_iab/recent_press_releases/press_release_archive/press_release/195115?o12499.

4 John Zarwan, "Direct mail delivers.(expenditure of direct mail advertising in America is growing)," *American Printer*, August 2006, http://findarticles.com/p/articles/mi_hb4696/is_200608/ai_n17241174.

5 Paul R. La Monica, "Super Prices for Super Bowl Ads," *cnnmoney.com*, January 3, 2007, http://money.cnn.com/2007/01/03/news/funny/superbowl_ads/index.htm.

6 "'Iron Man' and Audi: R8 Takes Leading Role in New Summer Blockbuster Movie 'Iron Man' from Marvel Studios and Paramount Pictures," April 7, 2008, http://www.audiusa.com/audi/us/en2/Company/News/Iron_Man_and_Audi.html.

7 Davide Dukcevich, "TV's Most Successful Products," *Forbes.com*, November 13, 2002, http://www.forbes.com/home/2002/11/13/cx_dd_1113products.html.

8 ACNielsen, "Has 'Sideways' Put Wine Sales On An Upward Trajectory?" February 1, 2005, http://us.nielsen.com/news/20050221.shtml.

9 Katherine Neer, "How Product Placement Works," *HowStuffWorks.com*, July 4, 2003, http://money.howstuffworks.com/product-placement.htm.

10 Scott M. Cutlip, Allen H. Center, and Glen M. Broom, *Effective Public Relations*, 9th ed. (Upper Saddle River, NJ: Pearson Prentice Hall, 2009), 1, 321.

11 Sandra Moriarty, Nancy Mitchell, and William Wells, *Advertising, Principles and Practices*, 8th ed. (Upper Saddle River, NJ: Pearson Prentice Hall, 2009), 517–526.

12 Sandra Moriarty, Nancy Mitchell, and William Wells, *Advertising, Principles and Practices*, 8th ed. (Upper Saddle River, NJ: Pearson Prentice Hall, 2009), 528.

13 Neal Santelmann, "Companies That Care," *Forbes*, http://www.forbes.com/2004/09/29/cx_ns_0929feat.html. Accessed May 15, 2008.

14 Lisa Z. Eccles, "Point of Purchase Advertising," *Advertising Age Supplement*, September 1994, 1–6.

15 Philip Kotler and Gary Armstrong, *Principles of Marketing*, 12th ed. (Upper Saddle River, NJ: Pearson Prentice Hall, 2008), 386.

16 Ibid.

17 U.S. Bureau of the Census, "Wholesale and Retail Trade—Establishments, Employees, and Payroll by State: 2000 and 2004," *Statistical Abstract of the United States* (Washington DC: Government Printing Office, 2008), Table 10.13.

18 U.S Bureau of the Census, *Statistical Abstract of the United States*, 2006 (Washington DC: Government Printing Office, 2006), 694.

19 Julie M. Donohue, Marisa Cevasco, and Meredith B. Rosenthal, "A Decade of Direct-to-Consumer Advertising of Prescription Drugs," *New England Journal of Medicine*, August 16, 2007, http:// content.nejm.org/cgi/reprint/357/7/673.pdf.

Mini Chapter 4

1 Elaine L. Chao, U.S. Secretary of Labor, Speech at the National Summit on Retirement Savings, March 1, 2006, http://www.dol.gov/_sec/media/speeches/20060301_saver.htm.

2 "Résumé Development," Ball State University Career Center, 2008, http://www.bsu.edu/students/careers/documents/resumes/, Accessed June 25, 2008.

online content mybizlab.com:

3 Allison Doyle, "Cover Letters," http://jobsearch.about.com/od/coverletters/a/aa030401a.htm, Accessed June 25, 2008.

4 Pat Kendall, "Cover Letter Tips," *Advanced Resume Concepts*, 2007, http://www.reslady.com/coverletters.html, Accessed June 25, 2008.

5 Ibid.

6 Allan Hoffman, "Seven Tips for Marketing Yourself," *Monster Career Advice*, 2007, http://career-advice.monster.com/job-search-essentials/technology/Seven-Tips-for-Marketing-Yourself/home.aspx

7 Johanna Schlegel and Brian Braiker, "Inappropriate Questions," *Salary.com*, http://www.salary.com/careers/layouthtmls/crel_display_nocat_Ser16_Par40.html, Accessed June 25, 2008.

8 Christine F. Della Monaca, "Interview Take-Along Checklist," *Monster Career Advice*, 2007, http://career-advice.monster.com/interview-preparation/Interview-Take-Along-Checklist/home.aspx, Accessed June 25, 2008.

Chapter 15

1 Apple, 2007 10-K Annual Report, p. 51 at *United States Securities and Exchange Commission*, http://www.sec.gov/Archives/edgar/data/320193/000104746907009340/a2181030z10-k.htm, Accessed June 5, 2008.

2 U.S. Chamber of Commerce Small Business Center, Cash Flow Budget Worksheet Template, 2008, http://business.uschamber.com/tools/cfbudg_m.asp, Accessed May 7, 2008.

3 Rich Mintzer, "Running a Seasonal Business," March 16, 2007, http://www.entrepreneur.com/management/operations/article175954.html.

4 Jonathan Moreland, *Individual Investor*, August 1995.

5 "6 Sources of Bootstrap Financing," http://www.entrepreneur.com/money/financing/selffinancingandbootstrapping/article80204.html, Accessed June 5, 2008.

6 Cynthia E. Griffin, "Breaking the bank: non-bank lenders are pulling ahead in small-business financing. Here's what the playing field looks like," *Entrepreneur*, March 1998, http://findarticles.com/p/articles/mi_m0DTI/is_n3_v26/ai_20484710.

7 Herón Márquez Estrada, "Carver County contrite about tax goof, but residents fuming," *Minneapolis-St. Paul Star Tribune*, December 12, 2007, http://www.startribune.com/local/west/12448481.html.

8 "Top 10 Degrees in Demand," *CNN/Money*, November 14, 2004, http://money.cnn.com/2004/11/12/pf/college/degrees_jobs/.

9 Associated Press, "Wyatt Pleads Guilty at U.S. Oil-for-Food Trial," October 1, 2007, http://www.foxnews.com/story/0,2933,298744,00.html.

10 "Benchmarks: Auto & Truck Manufacturers," *Reuters*, May 8, 2008, http://www.reuters.com/finance/industries/benchmarks?industryCode=53111.

11 Toyota Motor Corp. Key Statistics, June 5, 2008, *Yahoo Finance*, http://finance.yahoo.com/q/ks?s=TM.

12 Starbucks 2006 Annual Report, http://www.shareholder.com/visitors/dynamicdoc/document.cfm?CompanyID=SBUX&DocumentID=1382&PIN=&Page=60&Zoom=1x&Section=32931#32931, Accessed June 5, 2008.

13 Arney Stone, "SOX: Not So Bad After All?" *Business Week Online*, August 1, 2005, http://www.businessweek.com/bwdaily/dnflash/aug2005/nf2005081_7739_db016.htm?chan=search.

Chapter 16

1 Gary P. Brinson, Brian D. Singer, and Gilbert L. Beebower, "Determinants of Portfolio Performance II: An Update," *Financial Analysts Journal*, May/June, 1991. 47(3):40-48., 40.

2 NYSE Euronext Listings Directory, *NYSE.com*, http://www.nyse.com/about/listed/1170350259411.html, Accessed May 30, 2008.

3 U.S. Securities and Exchange Commission, http://www.sec.gov/investor/pubs/inws.htm, Accessed May 30, 2008.

4 Hannah Rasmussen, "Insider Trading," *About.com*, http://economics.about.com/cs/finance/a/insider_trading.htm; Jake Ulick, "Martha indicted, resigns," *CNNMoney.com*, June 4, 2003 http://money.cnn.com/2003/06/04/news/martha_indict/index.htm?cnn=yes.

5 "Trends in Mutual Fund Investing: August 2007," *ICI.org*, September 27, 2007 http://www.ici.org/stats/mf/trends_08_07.html.

Mini Chapter 5

online content mybizlab.com:

1 Suze Orman, "Buy 'New Used' Instead," http://biz.yahoo.com/pfg/e16buylease/art021.html, Accessed May 2, 2008.

2 "Compound Interest . . . The 8th Wonder!" http://www.greekshares.com/8th.php, Accessed May 2, 2008.

3 "New Tax Brackets for All Taxpayers," December 6, 2007, http://articles.moneycentral.msn.com/Common/Taxes/2007TaxBrackets.aspx.

➤ Sources

Front Matter, *Page P-2*, Based on Colin Rose (1987). Accelerated Learning. Source: http://www.chaminade.org/inspire/learnstl.htm.

Chapter 1, *Page 9*, "Preparing for Baby Boomer Retirement," June 2005, James J. L'Allier, Ph.D. & Kenneth Kolosh, http://www.clomedia.com/content/templates/clo_article.asp?articleid=976&zoneid=25; *Page 13*, Figure 1.2, http://www.census.gov/mrts/www/data/html/07Q4.html; *Page 18*, "The 200 Best Small Companies," October 11, 2007 at http://www.forbes.com/lists/2007/23/biz_07200best_The-200-Best-Small-Companies_Rank.html. Reprinted by Permission of Forbes Magazine © Forbes LLC.

Chapter 2, *Page 34*, Figure 2.1 adapted from *Basic Economic Principles*, David O'Connor, Christopher Faille. Copyright © 2000 by Greenwood Press. Reproduced with permission of Greenwood Publishing Group, Inc., Westport, CT; *Page 46*, Top Ten from https://www.cia.gov/library/publications/the-world-factbook/rankorder/2001rank.html; *Page 47*, Adapted from http:// www.nowandfutures.com/cpi_lie.html; *Page 49*, http://www.msnbc.msn.com/id/20572828/ and http://www.ilo.org/public/english/employment/strat/kilm/download/kilm18.pdf; *Page 52*, The Federal Reserve Board; *Page 53*, NY Federal Reserve Bank; *Page 55*, The Federal Reserve Board.

Chapter 3, *Page 73*, Movie poster image from http://www.imdb.com/title/tt0473107/; *Page 75*, http://www.thirdwayblog.com/category/microsoft/; *Page 83*, http://www.treehugger.com/files/2005/09/biofuel_filling.php; *Page 75*, http://money.cnn.com/magazines/fortune/mostadmired/2008/index.html. Copyright © 2008 Time Inc. All rights reserved; *Page 83*, http://www.independent.co.uk/news/business/analysis-and-features/green-leaders-a-guide-to-the-worlds-greenest-companies-451263.html.

Chapter 4, *Page 97*, Commerce Department data via the Investment Strategies Group Bank of America; *Page 99*, *Fortune* Magazine: Global 500: The Top 25 at http://money.cnn.com/galleries/2007/fortune/0707/gallery.global500_top25.fortune/12.html. Copyright © 2008 Time Inc. All rights reserved; *Page 107*, http://www.wto.org/english/res_e/statis_e/its2005_e/maps_e/m02.pdf; *Page 109*, https://www.cia.gov/library/publications/the-world-factbook/geos/ee.html.

Mini Chapter 1, online content mybizlab.com: *Page MC1-7*, http://google.com/search?hl=en&q=baseball+hats; *Page MC1-10*, http://www.cartoonstock.com/directory/p/phishing.asp.

Chapter 5, *Page 134*, www.fujimed.com, www.flux.utah.edu/~rolke/content/CE-seminar.ppt, www.eiu.edu/scienceed/3290/science/discrepant/polaroid.htm, http://inventorsabout.com, www.computerhope.com/history/198090.htm, http://faculty1.coloradocollege.edu/~djohnson/news/techclass/mp3.pdf; *Page 137*, http://www.facebook.com/press/info.php?factsheet; *Page 139*, http://www.census.gov/epcd/susb/latest/us/US--.HTM#table0; *Page 139*, siteresources.worldbank.org/DATASTATISTICS/Resources/GDP.pdf. World Development Indicators. Copyright 2008 by World Bank. Reproduced with permission of World Bank in the format Textbook via Copyright Clearance Center; *Page 140*, Small Business

Administration: Minorities in Business Report: A Demographic Review of Minority Business Ownership, April 10, 2007; *Page 141*, IDC, "Marketing and Promotion in U.S. SMBs," July 2004; *Page 142*, Frank Magrid Associates; *Page 142*, *Fortune Small Business* at http://money.cnn.com/magazines/fsb/bestplaces/2008/top100/index.html; *Page 145*, Adapted from: http://thebusinessresourcecenter.com/BlueprintForSuccssBrochure.pdf. Created by The Franchise Network (FranNet); *Page 150*, http://usinfo.state.gov/infousa/economy/industry/docs/sb_econ02-03.pdf; *Page 150*, www.businessweek.com/magazine/content/03_34/c3846002_mz003.htm?chan=search.

Chapter 6, *Page 174*, http://www.forbes.com/lists/2008/18/biz_2000global08_The-Global-2000_Rank.html. Reprinted by Permission of Forbes.com © 2008 Forbes.com.

Chapter 7, *Page 209*, *Fortune* at http://money.cnn.com/magazines/fortune/leadership/2007/global/index.html © 2008 Time Inc. All rights reserved.

Chapter 8, *Page 231*, http://money.cnn.com/magazines/fortune/bestcompanies/2008/. © 2008 Time Inc. All rights reserved; *Page 235*, http://www.pearsonassessments.com/reports/16pf5couples.pdf. Copyright © 1995, 2002 by the Institute for Personality and Ability Testing (IPAT), Inc., Champaign, Illinois, USA. All rights reserved. Reproduced by permission from the 16PF5 Couple's Counseling Report. 16PF is a registered trademark of IPAT, Inc.; *Page 241*, http://belbin.com/content/page/731/Belbin_Team_Role_Descriptions.pdf. Reproduced with kind permission of Belbin Associates.

Chapter 9, *Page 256*, http://money.cnn.com/magazines/fortune/bestcompanies/2008/minorities/; *Page 259*, http://img.engadget.com/common/images/3060000000046989.JPG?0.04515998808811916; *Page 260*, http://pdcessentials.com/FormPictures/EmpProEvaluation.jpg.

Chapter 10, *Page 289*, http://www.webex.com/smb/web-meeting-center.html. Reproduced by permission of Cisco Systems, Inc.; *Page 291*, screen shot from Pearson; *Page 293*, http://www.computing.co.uk/vnunet/news/2171556/christmas-roundup-hp-scandal; *Page 294*, http://www1.va.gov/opa/pressrel/pressrelease.cfm?id=1166, http://www.internetnews.com/bus-news/article.php/3608411.

Chapter 11, *Page 308*, http://www.1iverating.com/top/420/; *Page 310*, www.fanucrobotics.com; *Page 327*, http://www.smartdraw.com/tutorials/bpm/tutorial_07.htm; *Page 327*, Adapted from http://www.ganttcharts.com/Evolution.html. Reprinted by permission from Smart Draw, www.SmartDraw.com.

Mini Chapter 3, online content mybizlab.com: *Page MC3-4*, Adapted from "In Search of a Lost Art: How to Write a Business Letter" at http://www.cyberbee.com/science/letpart.html; *Page MC3-5*, Adapted from "Written Communication" at http://www.quamut.com/quamut/business_etiquette/page/written_communication.html.

Chapter 12, *Page 344*, www.geeksquad.com; *Page 344*, Adapted from http://www.netmba.com/marketing/ mix/. Reprinted by permission of NetMBA.com. All rights reserved; *Page 351*, http://www.opensecrets.org/orgs/ list.asp?orderA. Reprinted by permission of Center for Responsive Politics/opensecrets.org; *Page 354*, Based on data released by the FEC on October 29, 2007.

Chapter 13, *Page 371*, http://www.marketingteacher. com/Lessons/lesson_three_levels_of_a_product.htm; *Page 373*, https://secure.lunesta.com/lunestaPromos/ lunesta-coupon.cfm; *Page 378*, http://www.adcouncil.org/ default.aspx?id=325; *Page 385*, Kotler, Philip, Keller, Kevin Lane, *Marketing Management: Analysis, Planning, Implementation and Control*, 12th Edition © 2006. Electronically reproduced by permission of Pearson Education, Inc., Upper Saddle River, NJ, and http://instruct1.cit.cornell.edu/ Courses/cuttingedge/lifeCycle/10.htm.

Chapter 14, *Page 398/402*, 1951 Morton Salt Ad Copyright © Morton International, Inc. Used with permission; *Page 402*, http://adage.com/century/campaigns.html; *Page 405*, TNS Media Intelligence, "TNS Media Intelligence Reports U.S. Advertising Expenditures Increased 4.1 Percent in 2006," March 13, 2007, at http://www.tns-mi.com/news/ 03132007.htm.

Chapter 15, *Page 454*, Wal-Mart Stores Inc. Balance Sheet, January 2008, *Yahoo Finance* at http://finance.yahoo.com/q/ bs?s=WMT; *Page 455*, Google Inc. Balance Sheet, December 2007, *Yahoo Finance* at http://finance.yahoo.com/q/ bs?s=GOOG&annual; *Page 458*, Adapted from Google Inc. Balance Sheet, December 2007, *Yahoo Finance* at http://finance.yahoo.com/q/bs?s=GOOG&annual; *Page 458*, Google Inc. Cash Flow Statement, December 31, 2007, *Yahoo Finance* at http://finance.yahoo.com/q/cf?s=GOOG&annual; *Page 459*, Google Inc. Income Statement, December 31, 2007, *Yahoo Finance* at http://finance.yahoo.com/q/ is?s=GOOG&annual; *Page 461*, http://www.forbes.com/lists/ 2008/18/biz_2000global08_The-Global-2000_Prof.html; *Page 462*, Google Inc. Cash Flow Statement, December 31, 2007, *Yahoo Finance* at http://finance.yahoo.com/q/ cf?s=GOOG&annual.

Chapter 16, *Page 478*, http://sify.com/finance/equity/ fullstory.php?id=13654158; *Page 478*, http://www.mutual-funds-advisor.com/mutual-fund-history/stock-market-crashes. html; *Page 479*, http://www.statefarm.com/mutual/ investors/pricing_perf/life_path/lpwork.asp; *Page 484/485*, BigCharts.com.

Mini Chapter 5, *Page MC5-501*, Basic Personal Finance at http://www.planyourescape.ca/personal-finance-101-an-introduction-11, Peter Milner at http://www. planyourescape.ca.

Credits